D1240500

DELTA'S
Key to the
TOEFL iBT®

Complete Skill Practice

by

Nancy Gallagher

DELTA PUBLISHING COMPANY

© 2016 by NANCY GALLAGHER

Requests for permission to make copies of any part of the work should be sent to:

DELTA PUBLISHING COMPANY
A Divison of DELTA SYSTEMS CO., INC.
P.O. Box 2038
Crystal Lake, IL 60039-2038   USA
(800) 323-8270 or (815) 363-3582
www.deltapublishing.com

Editor:	Patricia Brenner and Linda Ames
Page Layout & Design:	Linda Ames
Cover Design:	Linda Ames
Audio Production:	Jay Kenney and Audio Logic, Inc.

Printed in the United States of America

10 9 8 7 6 5 4

Text & mp3 Audio   9781621677000

ALSO AVAILABLE
Delta's Key to the TOEFL iBT:
Seven Practice Test Book; Revised Edition (2013)
Text & mp3 Audio   9781621670957

Delta's Key to the Next Generation TOEFL Test:
Essential Grammar for the iBT
Text & Audio CD   9781934960165

CONTENTS

DELTA'S KEY TO THE TOEFL IBT®

INTRODUCTION

The TOEFL iBT®

The Test of English as a Foreign Language® (TOEFL®) is a standardized test that measures the English proficiency of students who wish to enter college and university programs where English is the language of instruction. The TOEFL is also a requirement of many employers. The TOEFL is produced and administered by Educational Testing Service, a professional test development organization in Princeton, New Jersey, USA.

The Internet–based TOEFL iBT® was introduced in 2005. The TOEFL iBT replaced the computer–based test (CBT) and the paper–based test (PBT). The TOEFL iBT has four sections to assess reading, listening, speaking, and writing. The test is approximately four hours long, with one ten–minute break following the Listening section.

TOEFL iBT®			
Section	**Content**	**Number of Questions**	**Approximate Time**
Reading	3–4 passages (12–14 questions each)	36–56	60–80 minutes
Listening	2–3 conversations 4–6 lectures (5–6 questions each)	34–51	60–90 minutes
Break			10 minutes
Speaking	2 independent tasks 4 integrated–skills tasks	6	20 minutes
Writing	1 integrated–skills task 1 independent task	2	55 minutes

In the Reading section, test takers read three or four passages and answer questions about them. In the Listening section, they listen to two or three conversations and four to six lectures and then answer questions about them. In the Speaking section, test takers speak in response to two questions about their own experience and four questions about texts that they listen to or read during the test. In the Writing section, test takers complete two writing tasks. One task is about a reading passage and a lecture, and the other is an essay question about a general topic.

The major differences between the TOEFL iBT and previous versions of the test are:

- Note taking is permitted during the test.
- Speaking skills are evaluated.
- Some tasks integrate skills, such as reading, listening, and speaking.
- Knowledge of grammar is not tested separately but is tested indirectly in all sections of the test.

The content of the TOEFL iBT reflects the language used in real college and university settings. Reading passages are similar to those in textbooks and other course materials. Listening content includes conversations, lectures, and discussions about campus situations and academic topics.

The Speaking and Writing sections include some tasks that combine skills. For example, a test taker will read a passage, listen to a lecture, and then write or speak in response. The integrated–skills tasks reflect how people use language in real life. They are a useful measure of how well prospective students will be able to communicate in an English–speaking environment.

The TOEFL iBT does not have a separate grammar section; however, knowledge of English grammar is important in all four sections of the test.

For the most current information about the TOEFL iBT, including information about registration and test dates, go to the official TOEFL Web site: **www.ets.org/toefl**.

THE TEST SCORE

The TOEFL score is a measure of English proficiency for academic study and employment. Educational institutions use TOEFL scores when evaluating prospective students for admission. The admissions officer will look at a student's section scores and total test score to determine if the student's English skills are adequate for enrollment in a specific program of study. There is no single passing score for all institutions; rather, each institution sets its own standards for admission. Generally, graduate programs require a higher score than do undergraduate programs.

In each section of the test, the number of raw points earned is converted to a scaled section score of 0 to 30. The four section scores are combined to obtain the total test score of 0 to 120.

The TOEFL iBT score report will show:

- a section score of 0 to 30 for each of the four language skills;
- a total test score of 0 to 120.

TOEFL IBT® SCORES				
Section	**Number of Questions**	**Raw Points per Correct Answer**	**Raw Points Possible**	**Scaled Section Score**
Reading	36–42	1–4	40–46	0–30
Listening	34	1–2	34–36	0–30
Speaking	6	1–4	24	0–30
Writing	2	1–5	10	0–30
			Total Test Score	0–120

In the Reading section, most correct answers will earn 1 raw point each, but some questions are worth 2, 3, or 4 points. In the Listening section, most correct answers will earn 1 raw point, but some questions may be worth 2 points. In the Speaking section, each of the six responses will earn a raw score of 1 to 4 points. In the Writing section, the two responses will each earn a raw score of 1 to 5 points.

The scoring scale of the TOEFL iBT is different from the scoring scale of the paper–based TOEFL (PBT). The table on the next page shows a general comparison of the total test scores in the two scales.

| TOTAL SCORE COMPARISON ||
TOEFL iBT®	TOEFL® PBT
120	677
100	600
80	550
61	500
46	450

HOW TO USE THIS BOOK

Delta's Key to the TOEFL iBT: Complete Skill Practice is a complete test preparation program for advanced and high–intermediate learners of English. The course has two objectives: (1) to prepare students to take the TOEFL iBT, and (2) to build the language skills necessary for success in college and university.

Complete Skill Practice contains 35 skill units and five full–length practice tests, with 1,300 questions that are similar in form and content to those on the TOEFL iBT. There is ample material for 15 weeks of study. The book and audio can be used in many ways:

- as the primary text in a comprehensive TOEFL preparation course;
- as the primary or secondary text for courses in reading, listening, speaking, or writing skills; or
- as a resource for independent study, laboratory, or tutoring.

Complete Skill Practice is inspired by cognitive learning theory and designed around the five–part unit: *Focus, Study, Practice, Extension*, and *Progress*.

 Pre–Test

The *Pre–Test* is a short version of the TOEFL that can be used to acquaint students with the various question types and to diagnose skill areas requiring special attention and practice. Instructors and students can use Pre–Test results to create individual programs of study based on need.

 Focus

Each unit begins with an exercise to focus attention, activate prior learning, and help students predict the content. *Focus* presents a short text—a reading passage, a conversation, a lecture, or part of an essay—and challenges the learner to identify a relevant principle. *Focus* stimulates inductive thinking. The exercises can be done in class or as homework.

 Study

Study provides instruction in one of the four skill areas: reading, listening, speaking, or writing. *Study* defines relevant terms and concepts, explains how the skill will be tested, provides sample questions, explains answers, and suggests useful strategies. The content can form the basis of classroom instruction, or it can be studied independently.

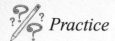 *Practice*

Practice consists of sets of test questions that challenge students to apply their skills. The exercises foster ease with TOEFL form and content and build confidence and skill retention. They can be done in class or assigned as homework.

 *Extension*

People acquire language through social interaction, and *Extension* presents activities that foster cooperation, stimulate discussion, extend skill practice, guide peer review, and link the classroom with the real world. *Extension* activities are student–centered, and many of them engage students in finding or creating their own TOEFL–like texts.

 Progress

Regular assessment is an integral part of skill building. Thirty–four timed quizzes simulate parts of the TOEFL, with each quiz assessing the skills studied in one or more units. Quiz content builds cumulatively, with some quizzes covering material from several units.

 Tests

The five full–length tests contain questions that are similar in form and content to the questions on the TOEFL iBT. The tests can be used to review course material and to assess readiness for taking the real TOEFL iBT. Test sections can be completed in class or as homework.

 *Answer Key*

The *Answer Key* provides the correct answers for all exercises, quizzes and tests. The *Answer Key* includes short explanations and references to relevant units for further study.

 *Audio Scripts*

The *Audio Scripts* are the transcripts for the companion audio. The scripts can be used to check answers. They can also be used in other ways. For example, students can read the conversations aloud in class, or they can study vocabulary and idioms in context.

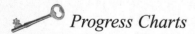 *Progress Charts*

Students can graph their scores for all quizzes and tests on the *Progress Charts* in the back of the book. The charts motivate students and encourage them to set goals for achievement.

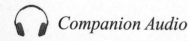 *Companion Audio*

The companion audio is presented in mp3 format on a single disk. The audio files are the listening component for all exercises, quizzes, and tests in the book. In addition to being used for TOEFL preparation, the recordings can be used for practice in note taking and summarizing and for the study of pronunciation, vocabulary, idioms, and English for academic purposes.

SAMPLE COURSE OUTLINES

	15-week Test Preparation Course 75 hours of instruction		
Week	**Units**	**Topics**	**Quiz or Test**
1	— 1.1 – 1.2	**Pre-testing** **Reading:** Facts & Details; Negative Facts	Pre-Test Reading Quiz 1 & 2
2	1.3 2.1 – 2.2	**Reading:** Vocabulary in Context **Listening:** Topic & Main Idea; Details	Reading Quiz 3 & 4 Listening Quiz 1
3	1.4 – 1.5 2.3	**Reading:** Inferences; Purpose **Listening:** Attitude & Purpose	Reading Quiz 5 & 6 Listening Quiz 2 & 3
4	1.6 2.4	**Reading:** Paraphrases **Listening:** Inferences & Predictions	Listening Quiz 4 & 5
5	1.7 2.5 – 2.6	**Reading:** Coherence **Listening:** Function; Organization	Reading Quiz 7 & 8 Listening Quiz 6
6	1.8 – 1.9	**Reading:** Summarizing; Organizing	Reading Quiz 9 Listening Quiz 7 & 8
7	—	**Review and evaluation**	Reading Quiz 10 Test 1
8	3.1 – 3.4	**Speaking:** Independent Tasks	Speaking Quiz 1, 2 & 3
9	3.5 4.1 – 4.3	**Speaking:** Integrated Tasks **Writing:** Integrated Tasks	—
10	3.6 – 3.7 4.4 – 4.5	**Speaking:** Integrated Tasks **Writing:** Sentences; Evaluating Writing	Writing Quiz 1, 2 & 3
11	3.8 – 3.9 4.6 – 4.8	**Speaking:** Integrated Tasks **Writing:** Independent (Essay)	—
12	4.9 – 4.10	**Writing:** Sentences; Evaluating the Essay	Writing Quiz 4, 5 & 6 Test 2
13	3.10	**Speaking:** Evaluating Integrated Tasks	Speaking Quiz 4, 5, 6, 7 & 8 Writing Quiz 7
14	—	**Review and evaluation**	Writing Quiz 8 Test 3
15	—	**Review and evaluation**	Test 4 Test 5

	4-week Intensive Course 24 – 32 hours of instruction	
Week	**Topics**	**Quiz or Test**
1	**Diagnostic pre–testing** **Reading:** selected units as needed	Pre–Test Select from Reading Quiz 1 – 10
2	**Listening:** selected units as needed **Speaking:** selected units as needed	Select from Listening Quiz 1 – 8 Select from Speaking Quiz 1 – 8
3	**Writing:** selected units as needed **Review and evaluation**	Select from Writing Quiz 1 – 8 Test 1 Test 2
4	**Review and evaluation**	Test 3 Test 4 Test 5

Generally, TOEFL preparation should include practice in all four skill areas: reading, listening, speaking, and writing. Depending on student need, some skill areas may require greater attention than do others.

The 15–week Test Preparation Course is suitable for a typical semester of study, in which a class meets for five hours per week. For shorter terms of study, the course outline can be divided into two terms of six to eight weeks each, or it can be condensed to fit a 10–week quarter.

The 4–week Intensive Course is suitable for situations where students have a shorter period to prepare for the TOEFL. In such cases, the Pre–Test may be used to diagnose skill areas requiring attention. Content can be selected based on student need.

Reading Section Directions

The Reading section measures your ability to understand a passage in academic English. You will read a passage and answer questions about it. Answer all questions based on what is stated or implied in the passage.

You have 20 minutes to read the passage and answer the questions.

Most questions are worth one point, but the last question is worth more than one point. The directions indicate how many points you may receive.

The passage may include a word or phrase in **bold** type. For these words and phrases, you will see a definition in a glossary at the end of the passage.

The Work of Cells

1   Living is work, and all forms of life require an ongoing supply of energy to perform the work of life. Energy is the capacity to do work, where work is defined as the ability to move matter or to rearrange a collection of matter. The cell is the basic unit of life. The work of life depends on the ability of cells to use energy to perform their many tasks. Energy enables cells to cause specific changes that are necessary for life. Many cells move or change their shapes. They grow and reproduce. Cells organize small organic molecules into proteins and DNA. Cells pump substances across membranes. They export products that are used in other parts of the organism. Cells must work just to maintain their own complex structure. The changes caused by cellular activities involve the transformation of energy from one type to another. Different kinds of change define the kinds of work performed by cells, which fall into three main categories: mechanical, synthetic, and concentration.

2   Mechanical work involves a physical change in the position of a cell or some part of the cell. One example is the movement of a cell in relation to its environment. Such movement requires the presence of some sort of **appendage**, such as the long, thread–like structure called a flagellum. Many bacteria have such appendages, and they wag these tail–like structures to push themselves through the environment. Sometimes, however, the environment is moved past a cell. This occurs with the beating of cilia, hair–like cellular structures that move rhythmically. The human **trachea** is lined with cilia that beat upward to sweep inhaled particles back to the mouth or nose, thus protecting the lungs. An example of mechanical work that involves not just a single cell but a large number of cells is muscle contraction. Muscle tissue is specialized for mechanical work. It consists of bundles of muscle fibers, each of which is an individual muscle cell containing numerous myofibrils, the contractile elements of the cell. Still another example of mechanical work occurs within a cell, and this is the movement of chromosomes during cell division. Matching pairs of chromosomes move apart and are propelled along the surface of the nucleus by the lengthening spindle fibers between them. The chromosomes eventually travel to opposite poles of the cell.

3   Synthetic work involves changes in chemical bonds. A cell is a miniature chemical industry, where thousands of reactions occur within a microscopic space. Almost every cell is continuously engaged in the important work of biosynthesis, which causes the formation of new bonds and the generation of new molecules. This activity can be observed in a population of growing cells, where the cells increase in size, number, or both, as additional molecules are being synthesized. Most structural components of a cell are in a state of constant turnover. The molecules that compose the structure are continuously being degraded and replaced. Almost all of the energy that cells need for biosynthetic work goes toward making energy–rich organic molecules from simpler starting materials, such as proteins from amino acids, and into activating these molecules for incorporation into larger molecules.

4   Concentration work is the transport of substances across a membrane or boundary when the substances are pumped against the direction of spontaneous movement. The purpose of concentration work is either to accumulate substances within a cell or to remove by–products of cellular activity that are not needed or might be toxic if allowed to remain. The transport of substances enables the cell to maintain internal concentrations of small molecules that differ from concentrations in the environment. For example, compared to its surroundings, an animal cell has a much higher concentration of potassium molecules and a much lower concentration of sodium molecules. The cell's plasma membrane helps maintain these differences by pumping sodium out of the cell and potassium into the cell. A specialized case of concentration work is electrical work, which involves the movement of ions across a membrane against an electrical gradient. Every membrane has some electrical potential that is generated through concentration. Electrical work is important in the mechanism whereby impulses are conducted in nerve and muscle cells.

Glossary:

appendage: a part attached to an organism, such as an arm, leg, or tail

trachea: the tube that carries air from the throat to the lungs; windpipe

1. According to paragraph 1, what is essential to the work of life?

   (A) The discovery that the cell is the unit of life
   (B) The use of energy to cause cellular changes
   (C) The availability of water
   (D) The ability of organisms to adapt to their environment

2. In paragraph 1, the author makes the point that

   (A) cells require energy from outside sources
   (B) a cell's ability to work decreases with age
   (C) all life forms can evolve from simple to complex
   (D) energy changes form during cellular activites

3. Paragraph 1 supports which of the following statements?

   (A) Life is characterized by various kinds of change.
   (B) Energy requirements impose a limit on the size of a cell.
   (C) The work of cells is supported by energy from sunlight.
   (D) Cellular respiration drives the energy use of a cell.

4. The author mentions a flagellum in paragraph 2 in order to

   (A) illustrate how a cell can move through its environment
   (B) compare appendages with other parts of the cell
   (C) identify the most interesting cellular structure of bacteria
   (D) describe the diversity of structures found in cells

5. The word propelled in paragraph 2 is closest in meaning to

   (A) hidden
   (B) pushed
   (C) caught
   (D) absorbed

6. All of the following are given as examples of mechanical work EXCEPT

   (A) the beating of cilia in the human trachea
   (B) the contraction of muscle tissue
   (C) the organization of small molecules into proteins
   (D) the activity of chromosomes during cell division

7. What is the main purpose of paragraph 3?

   (A) To define the concept of work in cell biology
   (B) To compare synthetic work and biosynthesis
   (C) To describe the structural components of a cell
   (D) To explain the function of synthetic work

8. Which sentence below best expresses the essential information in the highlighted sentence in paragraph 3? Incorrect choices change the meaning in important ways or leave out essential information.

   (A) Observation of cell growth is an easy way to learn about the structure of molecules.
   (B) Cell activity during synthetic work involves an increase in the rate of cell growth and reproduction.
   (C) Biosynthesis occurs when new molecules are generated as cells grow in size, number, or both.
   (D) A population of growing cells needs a large input of energy so that new molecules can be synthesized.

9. The word turnover in paragraph 3 is closest in meaning to

   (A) disturbance
   (B) purification
   (C) stress
   (D) replacement

10. By stating in paragraph 4 that substances are pumped against the direction of spontaneous movement, the author implies that

   (A) moving the substances requires the use of force
   (B) this work creates molecules of higher structural complexity
   (C) the substances move in a continuously changing direction
   (D) cell division is necessary to perform concentration work

11. What can be inferred about concentration work from paragraph 4?

   (A) Concentration work is a specialized case of mechanical work.
   (B) Animal cells synthesize new molecules during concentration work.
   (C) Some concentration work generates electrical impulses.
   (D) Concentration work involves a low rate of energy consumption.

12. Look at the four squares, **A**, **B**, **C**, and **D**, which indicate where the following sentence could be added to the passage. Where would the sentence best fit?

The result is not just a change in concentration but also the establishment of an electrical potential across the membrane.

Concentration work is the transport of substances across a membrane or boundary when the substances are pumped against the direction of spontaneous movement. The purpose of concentration work is either to accumulate substances within a cell or to remove by–products of cellular activity that are not needed or might be toxic if allowed to remain. **A** The transport of substances enables the cell to maintain internal concentrations of small molecules that differ from concentrations in the environment. **B** For example, compared to its surroundings, an animal cell has a much higher concentration of potassium molecules and a much lower concentration of sodium molecules. The cell's plasma membrane helps maintain these differences by pumping sodium out of the cell and potassium into the cell. **C** A specialized case of concentration work is electrical work, which involves the movement of ions across a membrane against an electrical gradient. **D** Every membrane has some electrical potential that is generated through concentration. Electrical work is important in the mechanism whereby impulses are conducted in nerve and muscle cells.

13. An introductory sentence for a brief summary of the passage is provided below. Complete the summary by selecting the THREE answer choices that express the most important ideas in the passage. Some sentences do not belong in the summary because they express ideas that are not presented in the passage or are minor ideas in the passage. *This question is worth 2 points.*

Cells use energy to generate the specific changes that define the different kinds of work they do.

- •
- •
- •

Answer Choices

(A) Cells perform mechanical work, which causes the movement of cells in relation to their environment or the movement of components within cells.

(B) Mechanical work can involve a single cell or a large number of cells, such as muscle tissue, which contains bundles of fiber–like cells.

(C) Most cells engage in synthetic work, the formation of new chemical bonds and the generation of new molecules.

(D) Animal cells perform concentration work when they pump potassium and sodium molecules across the plasma membrane.

(E) Cells perform electrical work to maintain the electrical potential across cell membranes, even when the organism is at rest.

(F) Concentration work involves accumulating substances and moving substances across a membrane or against an electrical gradient.

How to Score 2–Point Question	
Answers Correct	**Points Earned**
3	2
2	1
0 – 1	0

Answers to the Reading questions are on page 631.

Use your Pre–Test results to identify the skills and question types that you need to practice.

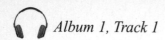 *Album 1, Track 1*

LISTENING SECTION DIRECTIONS

The Listening section measures your ability to understand conversations and lectures in English. You will hear each conversation and lecture only one time. After each conversation or lecture, you will answer some questions about it. Answer the questions based on what the speakers state or imply.

You may take notes while you listen. You may use your notes to help you answer the questions. Your notes will not be scored.

In some questions, you will see this icon: 🎧. This means that you will hear, but not see, part of the question. Some questions have special directions, which appear in a gray box.

You will now begin the Listening section.

 *Album 1, Track 2*

QUESTIONS 1 — 5

Conversation

1. What is the conversation mainly about?

   (A) Arrangements for a guest speaker next week
   (B) Material to review for an upcoming test
   (C) The student's vacation in the mountains
   (D) A report that the student is preparing

2. Listen again to part of the conversation. Then answer the question.

Why does the professor say this:

   (A) To imply that the student does not need advice
   (B) To inform the student that he has only a little time to talk
   (C) To invite the student to come to a meeting
   (D) To suggest that the student's presentation will be too long

3. What types of data does the student plan to use?

   Click on 2 answers.

   [A] A summary of volcanic eruptions
   [B] A photograph of an observatory
   [C] A recorded interview with a geologist
   [D] A series of pictures of a mountain

4. What is the student's opinion of the photographs?

   (A) They are the best photographs she has ever taken.
   (B) They are old and poor in quality, but will have to suffice.
   (C) They show the mountain's changes very clearly.
   (D) They would be more interesting if they were in color.

5. Listen again to part of the conversation. Then answer the question.

What does the professor mean when he says this:

   (A) The audience is very likely to ask about the meaning of the bulge.
   (B) Some questions may require a long time to answer completely.
   (C) The student should prepare a list of questions in advance.
   (D) There will be questions about the volcano on the next test.

 *Album 1, Track 3*

QUESTIONS 6 — 11

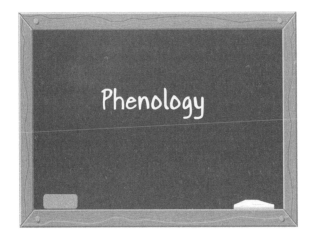

6. What is the lecture mainly about?

(A) How nature's color signals can help us understand climate change

(B) What color pigments in leaves reveal about the health of trees

(C) Technology for collecting data about environmental conditions

(D) The relationship between seasonal changes and animal behavior

7. Why does the professor say this:

(A) To encourage students to observe animals

(B) To predict effects of climate change

(C) To illustrate the concept of phenology

(D) To describe nature in an artistic manner

8. Listen again to part of the discussion. Then answer the question.

Why does the professor say this:

(A) To state that the class will participate in a research study

(B) To signal that he will eventually address the student's question

(C) To introduce a digression to a personal story

(D) To express annoyance at the interruption of his explanation

9. Listen again to part of the discussion. Then answer the question.

What does the professor imply when he says this:

(A) The textbook has many photographs of color pigments.

(B) The students should take notes on what he is about to say.

(C) The textbook contains information that is also available online.

(D) The students should read the explanations in the textbook.

10. What does the professor say about a method of data collection that uses a camera?

(A) The camera obtains better photographs than those in the textbook.

(B) The camera collects color data about the forest for an online database.

(C) The students are required to use a camera to assist in their observations.

(D) The camera does not provide evidence of changes in animal behavior.

11. According to the professor, how will color data about forests be useful to researchers?

(A) The data will enable development of better models for predicting effects of climate change.

(B) The data will either support or disprove the position that phenology is a reliable science.

(C) The data will assist in the creation and manufacture of synthetic color pigments.

(D) The data will answer questions about the relationship of weather patterns and psychology.

 *Album 1, Track 4*

QUESTIONS 12 — 17

Agricultural Management

12. What is the main idea of the talk?

(A) Managers must combine information and resources to produce and market a product.
(B) Farm management is a complex job with responsibility for all of a farm's resources.
(C) Many farm managers hire a farm operator to perform the daily tasks of running the farm.
(D) Farming is a business that involves risk, uncertainty, and constantly changing conditions.

13. Which of the following best describes the organization of the talk?

(A) A comparison of farm managers to other types of managers
(B) A description of a farm's physical, financial, and human resources
(C) A summary of the process for preparing a business plan
(D) A list of the requirements and responsibilities of farm management

14. According to the professor, in which subjects must a farm manager be knowledgeable?

Click on 3 answers.

[A] Engineering
[B] Biological sciences
[C] History of civilization
[D] Communication
[E] Strategic planning

15. Listen again to part of the lecture. Then answer the question.

Why does the professor say this:

(A) To introduce the topic of preparing a business plan
(B) To stress that farm managers must understand ecology
(C) To warn students of the financial risks of farming
(D) To recommend a specific sequence of business courses

16. According to the professor, what should be included in the business plan for a farm?

Click on 2 answers.

[A] A description of the farm and its goals
[B] Photographs of the machinery and workers
[C] Plans for production and marketing
[D] A strategy for public relations

17. What can be inferred about the students in this class?

(A) They have little or no experience in resource management.
(B) They are from families that own farms or other businesses.
(C) They have previously completed courses in general management.
(D) They are interested in farm management as a career.

 Stop

Answers to the Listening questions are on pages 631–632.

Use your Pre–Test results to identify the skills and question types that you need to practice.

DELTA'S KEY TO THE TOEFL IBT®

 *Album 1, Track 5*

SPEAKING SECTION DIRECTIONS

The Speaking section measures your ability to speak in English about a variety of topics. There are six questions. Record your response to each question.

In questions 1 and 2, you will speak about familiar topics.

In questions 3 and 4, you will first read a short text and then listen to a talk on the same topic. You will then be asked a question about what you have read and heard.

In questions 5 and 6, you will listen to part of a conversation or lecture. You will then be asked a question about what you have heard.

You may take notes while you read and while you listen to the conversations and lectures. You may use your notes to help prepare your responses.

Your responses will be scored on your ability to speak clearly and coherently about the topics. For some questions, your responses will be scored on your ability to accurately convey information about what you have read and heard.

 Stop

QUESTION 1

In this question, you will be asked to talk about a familiar topic. After you hear the question, you will have 15 seconds to prepare your response and 45 seconds to speak.

 Album 1, Track 6

> What city would you like to visit? Explain why you would like to go there. Include details and examples in your explanation.

 Stop

Preparation Time – 15 seconds
Response Time – 45 seconds

QUESTION 2

In this question, you will be asked to give your opinion about a familiar topic. After you hear the question, you will have 15 seconds to prepare your response and 45 seconds to speak.

 Album 1, Track 7

> Some people enjoy having a pet animal. Other people do not want a pet. What is your opinion about having a pet? Include details and examples in your explanation.

 Stop

Preparation Time – 15 seconds
Response Time – 45 seconds

QUESTION 3

In this question, you will read a short passage about a campus situation, listen to a conversation, and then speak in response to a question about what you have read and heard. After you hear the question, you have 30 seconds to prepare your response and 60 seconds to speak.

Read the following information from a university website.

Reading Time – 45 seconds

NEW BLOCK SCHEDULE

Starting in the fall quarter, students will be able to take classes in an entirely new way. Now they will have the option to take English composition classes linked with subject–area courses in "blocks" as an integrated learning experience. There will be three interest tracks: Society and the Individual, the Natural World, and Business and Leadership. Each track will be offered in multiple blocks of time, giving students more flexibility around their busy schedules. Students can concentrate their classes in mornings or afternoons on four or five days a week, or in mornings and afternoons twice a week.

Now cover the passage and listen to the recording. When you hear the question, begin preparing your response.

 Album 1, Track 8

> The man expresses his opinion about the block schedule. State his opinion and explain the reasons he gives for holding that opinion.

 Stop

Preparation Time – 30 seconds
Response Time – 60 seconds

QUESTION 4

In this question, you will read a short passage, then listen to a lecture on the same topic, and then speak in response to a question about what you have read and heard. After you hear the question, you have 30 seconds to prepare your response and 60 seconds to speak.

Read the following information from a textbook.

Reading Time – 45 seconds

PROVERBS

A proverb is an expression that conveys a bit of traditional wisdom that has been passed down from previous generations. The language of a proverb is simple and direct, offering advice on how to live. In most cases, the origin of a proverb is unknown. The images in proverbs usually refer to everyday objects and experiences. A proverb's effectiveness lies mainly in its simplicity and its memorability. Several linguistic techniques aid our ability to remember proverbs, such as rhythm, rhyme, and parallelism. Another common technique is alliteration, the repetition of the same consonant sound at the beginning of two or more words.

Now cover the passage and listen to the recording. When you hear the question, begin preparing your response.

 Album 1, Track 9

> Define what a proverb is, and use the examples from the talk to explain the effectiveness of proverbs.

 Stop

Preparation Time – 30 seconds
Response Time – 60 seconds

QUESTION 5

In this question, you will listen to a conversation. You will then be asked to talk about the information in the conversation and to give your opinion about the ideas presented. After you hear the question, you have 20 seconds to prepare your response and 60 seconds to speak.

 Album 1, Track 10

> The students discuss two possible solutions to the woman's problem. Briefly describe the problem. Then state which solution you prefer and explain why.

 Stop

Preparation Time – 20 seconds
Response Time – 60 seconds

QUESTION 6

In this question, you will listen to a short lecture. You will then be asked to summarize important information from the lecture. After you hear the question, you have 20 seconds to prepare your response and 60 seconds to speak.

 Album 1, Track 11

> Using points and examples from the lecture, explain how the future is portrayed in advertising.

 Stop

Preparation Time – 20 seconds
Response Time – 60 seconds

Key points for the Speaking questions are on pages 632–633.

Each response earns a score of 1, 2, 3, or 4, with 4 being the highest score.

Use your Pre–Test results to identify the skills and question types that you need to practice.

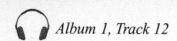 Album 1, Track 12

WRITING SECTION DIRECTIONS

The Writing section measures your ability to use writing to communicate in an academic environment. There are two questions.

Question 1 is a writing task based on reading and listening. You will read a passage, listen to a lecture, and then write a response to a question about the relationship between the lecture and the reading. You have 20 minutes to plan and write your response.

Question 2 is writing based on knowledge and experience. You will write an essay in response to a question that asks you to state, explain, and support an opinion on an issue. You have 30 minutes to plan and write your essay.

 Stop

QUESTION 1

For this task, you will write a response to a question about a reading passage and a lecture. You may take notes, and you may use your notes to help you write your response. Your response will be scored on the quality of your writing and on how well you connect the points in the lecture with points in the reading. Typically, an effective response will have 150 to 225 words.

Reading Time – 3 minutes

Freshwater ecosystems are classified according to water flow. Lotic ecosystems are characterized by water that is moving continually from the earth or over its surface. Springs, brooks, streams, and rivers are lotic ecosystems, and their most important physical factor is water flow. Water flow, or current, is influenced by the amount of water in the stream or river, and this varies with rainfall patterns, snow melt, and other seasonal changes. When the water level of a stream or river increases, its current becomes faster and stronger.

Another characteristic is the ecosystem's oxygen and nutrient content. Lotic ecosystems typically have high oxygen levels because water flowing over rocks, logs, and other objects causes turbulence that oxygenates the water. The more rapid and turbulent the flow, the more oxygen the water carries through the system.

A third characteristic is the production of organic matter. In lotic ecosystems, most of the production comes from surrounding land habitats and is carried into the stream in runoff from rainfall. Fallen leaves from dense, overhanging vegetation can add substantial amounts of organic matter. This matter enters the stream, where it becomes a food source for other organisms. The nutrient content of a lotic ecosystem is largely determined by the terrain and vegetation through which the stream or river flows. Because most lotic ecosystems are relatively shallow and have long shorelines, terrestrial production can usually supply the energy needs of the ecosystem. Fast-flowing streams and rivers do not support large communities of plankton because these microscopic organisms are washed away by the flow of water.

Now listen to the recording. When you hear the question, begin your response. You may look at the reading passage during the writing time.

 Album 1, Track 13

The lecture discusses lentic ecosystems. Summarize the points made in the lecture, and explain how they contrast with specific points made in the reading passage.

 Stop

Writing Time – 20 minutes

QUESTION 2

For this task, you will write an essay in response to a question that asks you to state and support your opinion on a topic. Your essay will be scored on the quality of your writing, including how well you organize and develop your ideas and how well you use language to express your ideas. Typically, an effective essay will have a minimum of 300 words.

Read the question below and make any notes that will help you plan your response. Then begin typing your essay.

Do you agree or disagree with the following statement?

The world will be a better place 100 years from now.

Use specific reasons and details to support your opinion.

Writing Time – 30 minutes

Key points for Writing Question 1 are on page 633.

Responses to Writing Question 2 will vary.

Each response earns a score of 1, 2, 3, 4 or 5, with 5 being the highest score.

Use your Pre–Test results to identify the skills and question types that you need to practice.

PART 1 – READING

The Reading section of the TOEFL measures your ability to read and understand passages in English. You will be tested on your comprehension of major ideas, important information, vocabulary, and relationships among ideas in the passages. You will be required to:

- identify major ideas and distinguish them from minor ideas;
- verify what information is true and what information is not true or not included in the passage;
- define words and phrases as they are used the passage;
- make inferences about information that is not directly stated;
- identify the author's purpose;
- connect ideas within sentences and among sentences; and
- summarize and organize important ideas from across the passage.

All of the passages have 650 to 750 words. The passages are about subjects that students usually study in their first two years of university: natural sciences, social sciences, business, and the arts. The language is generally formal and academic rather than informal or conversational. The rhetorical purpose of the passages may be expository, argumentative, historical, or biographical. All of the questions are based on the information in the passages. You do not need special knowledge of the topics to answer the questions.

In some forms of the TOEFL iBT, the Reading section will have three passages. In other forms, the Reading section will have four passages.* You will not know which form of the test you have until the day of the test.

READING SECTION					
Form	**Reading Texts**	**Time per Passage**	**Questions per Passage**	**Total Time**	**Total Questions**
Short	3 passages	20 minutes	12 – 14	60 minutes	36 – 42
Long	4 passages	20 minutes	12 – 14	80 minutes	48 – 56

In the short form of the Reading section, there are three passages and a total of 60 minutes for the entire section. In the long form of the Reading section, there are four passages and a total section time of 80 minutes. In both short and long forms, the time allowed includes the time that you spend reading the passages and answering the questions.

A few words in the passages, especially technical terms, may be defined in a glossary that is available to you during the test. If a word is highlighted in the text, click on the word to read a glossary definition of it.

*The information about the Reading section reflects changes to the TOEFL iBT as of November 2011.

READING

The computer will present one question at a time. You will be able to see the passage while you are answering the questions. You may skip a question without answering by clicking the **Next** button at the top of the screen. You may return to the question later by clicking the **Back** button or the **Review** button. The **Back** button will take you to the previous question. The **Review** button will take you to a list of all questions in the Reading section. From the review list, you may return to any previous question to review or change your answer.

There are three types of reading questions. For each question type, you will use the mouse to click on an answer or to move text. Some questions are worth more than one point. These questions have special directions that indicate how many points you can receive.

Strong reading skills are necessary for success in North American colleges and universities. Students are required to read large amounts of course material. In your program of study, you will be expected to read extensively, understand major and minor ideas in the material, and discuss the material in class. You will also be required to paraphrase and summarize ideas from your reading when you write reports and term papers.

Delta's Key to the TOEFL iBT: Complete Skill Practice provides ample practice in reading short and long passages on a variety of academic topics. Each reading unit allows you to focus on a particular reading skill.

Unit	Reading Skill	Number of Questions on 3–Passage TOEFL iBT
1.1	Understanding Facts and Details	10 – 12
1.2	Identifying Negative Facts	2 – 3
1.3	Understanding Vocabulary in Context	10 – 12
1.4	Making Inferences	3 – 4
1.5	Determing Purpose	3 – 4
1.6	Recognizing Paraphrases	3
1.7	Recognizing Coherence	3
1.8	Summarizing Important Ideas	2 – 3
1.9	Organizing Information	0 – 1
	Total Number of Questions	36 – 42

READING PASSAGES AND QUESTIONS

The Reading section contains three or four passages. Each passage is followed by a set of comprehension questions. Here is part of a sample passage.

ACIDS AND BASES

1   Acids and bases are substances that form compounds and solutions with an electrical charge. When acids dissolve in water, they donate additional hydrogen ions to the solution. An acid, therefore, is a substance that increases the hydrogen ion concentration of a solution. A base, on the other hand, reduces the hydrogen ion concentration of a solution.

2   The strength of acids and bases is measured by using a numeric scale known as pH, a measurement that represents the number of hydrogen ions in a solution. pH is measured with a pH meter or with paper strips that have color indicators. The pH scale runs from 0 to 14, with the midpoint at 7. A neutral solution, such as pure water, has a pH of 7.0. A pH value of less than 7.0 denotes an acidic solution, and a value above 7.0 denotes a basic, or alkaline, solution. The pH of a solution declines as the concentration of hydrogen ions increases: the lower the number, the more acidic the solution. For example, a solution with a pH of 4.5 is far more acidic than one with a pH of 6.0. The pH for bases, or alkalis, is above 7.0: the higher the number, the greater the basicity or alkalinity. A pH of 8.5 is more alkaline than a pH of 7.5.

3   The internal pH of most living cells is close to 7.0. Most biological fluids measure within the pH range of 6.0 to 8.0. There are a few exceptions, however, including the strongly acidic digestive juice of the human stomach, which has a pH of about 2.0. The chemical processes of living cells are very sensitive to the concentrations of hydrogen ions. Biological fluids resist changes to their pH when acids or bases are introduced because of the presence of buffers, substances that minimize changes in the concentrations of these ions. Buffers in human blood, for example, normally maintain the blood pH very close to 7.4 because a person cannot survive very long if the blood pH drops to 7.0 or rises to 7.8.

4   Acids and bases are used in food preparation and in industrial processes. They can be very dangerous, causing burns and other injuries to people and animals, as well as damage to the environment, so they must be used properly and handled with care. Acids are very important substances. They cause lemons to taste sour, they digest food in the stomach, and they dissolve rock to make fertilizer. They also dissolve tooth enamel to form cavities. Vinegar is a weak acid, a dilute solution of acetic acid used in food preservation. Lemon juice (citric acid) is added to foods and beverages to give them a sour flavor. Other acids have agricultural uses, such as hydrochloric acid—also known as muriatic acid—which is used as a fertilizer for acid–loving plants. Bases, or alkalis, have a bitter taste and a slippery feel. Most hand soaps and commercial products for unclogging drains are highly basic. Household ammonia and lye are bases. Slaked lime (calcium hydroxide) is a base that is used in cements and paints.

5   Most plants and animals have preferred pH ranges, where they attain their best growth and health. Acid materials can be made less acidic by adding basic materials to them. In the pH management of soil, compounds that are basic—like slaked lime or crushed limestone—are added to the soil to raise its pH. Limestone has a pH of about 8.2, which will lower the acidity of acid soil.

Question Type 1 – Click on One Answer

For this multiple–choice type of question, you will choose the best of four possible answers. You will see:

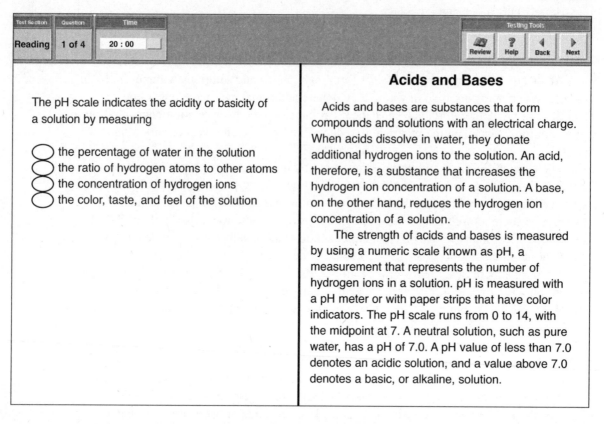

The pH scale indicates the strength of acids and bases by measuring *the concentration of hydrogen ions* in a solution. Therefore, you should click on the oval next to the third answer.

When you click on an oval, the oval will darken. To change your answer, click on a different oval. When you are satisfied that you have chosen the right answer, click on **Next**. The computer will move to the next question.

Question Type 2 – Add a Sentence

For this type of question, you will click on a square to add a sentence to the passage. You will see:

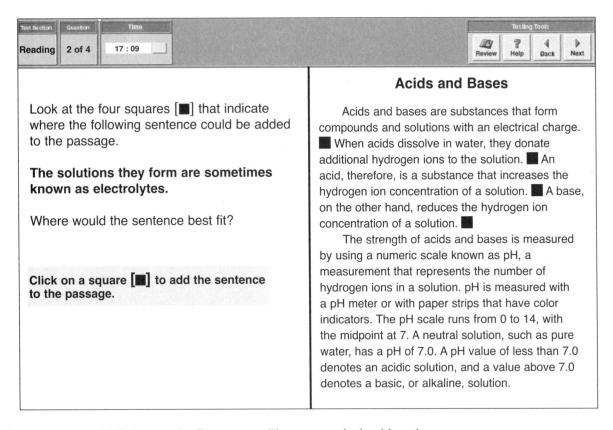

The sentence would fit best at the first square. The paragraph should read:

> Acids and bases are substances that form compounds and solutions with an electrical charge. **The solutions they form are sometimes known as electrolytes.** When acids dissolve in water, they donate additional hydrogen ions to the solution. An acid, therefore, is a substance that increases the hydrogen ion concentration of a solution. A base, on the other hand, reduces the hydrogen ion concentration of a solution.

When you click on a square, the sentence will appear there. To change your answer, click on a different square. The sentence will then appear at this new location. When you are ready to proceed, click on **Next**. The computer will move to the next question.

Question Type 3 – Drag Answer Choices

For this type of question, you will use the mouse to drag text to complete a summary or table. You will see:

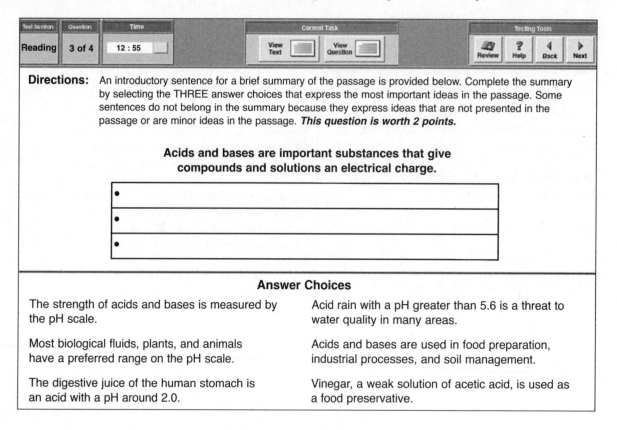

The three most important ideas in the passage are:

> The strength of acids and bases is measured by the pH scale.
> Most biological fluids, plants, and animals have a preferred range on the pH scale.
> Acids and bases are used in food preparation, industrial processes, and soil management.

To complete the summary, move the cursor to the answer choice that you want to move. Click and hold to drag the sentence to the space where it belongs. The sentence will appear in that space. To change an answer, click on it. Then drag your new choice to the correct space.

If you choose all three correct answers, you will receive two points. If you choose two correct answers, you will receive one point. If you choose only one correct answer, or no correct answers, you will receive no points.

Here is another example of a question in which you will use the mouse to drag text. You will see:

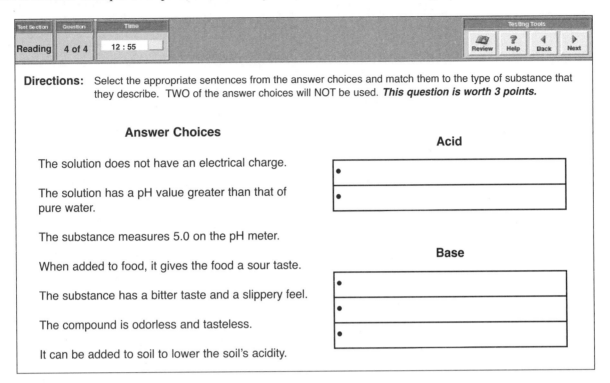

The correct answers are:

Acid	Base
• The substance measures 5.0 on the pH meter.	• The solution has a pH value greater than that of pure water.
• When added to food, it gives the food a sour taste.	• The substance has a bitter taste and a slippery feel.
	• It can be added to soil to lower the soil's acidity.

To answer, move the cursor to the answer choice that you want to move. Click and hold to drag the answer to the space where it belongs. This question is worth 3 points. Five correct answers will earn 3 points; four correct answers, 2 points; and three correct answers, 1 point.

STRATEGIES FOR THE READING SECTION

Before the Test

- Read on a variety of topics to build your English vocabulary. Most of the TOEFL reading passages are about topics in the natural sciences, the social sciences, business, and the arts. Read as much as you can in these subject areas, particularly from textbooks, journals, magazines, and newspapers.

- Practice trying to guess the meaning of unfamiliar words from how they are used in context. Use other words in the sentence, your understanding of the passage, and your general knowledge as clues to the meaning of unfamiliar words.

⚬ Become familiar with the various types of questions and how to answer them. Become familiar with the testing tools, such as **Next**, **Back**, and **Review**. Practice using the mouse to click on and drag text.

⚬ Your own best strategy: _____

_____

During the Test

⚬ Begin each passage by skimming it. *Skimming* is reading quickly for a general understanding of the topic and organization. Read the first few sentences of the first paragraph, and the first sentence of each paragraph after that. Notice key words and phrases that are repeated throughout the passage.

⚬ Identify exactly what each question wants to know. Does it ask you about…

  ⚬ rinformation that is stated in the passage?
  ⚬ rinformation that is NOT stated directly in the passage?
  ⚬ rthe meaning of a word?
  ⚬ rthe author's purpose for making a particular statement?
  ⚬ rthe major and minor ideas in the passage?

⚬ When a question asks about specific information, scan the passage to find this information. *Scanning* is looking for specific information: key words and phrases. Sometimes the computer will highlight text to help you scan a specific place in the text.

⚬ In questions about vocabulary, look for context clues in the passage. Use your knowledge of sentence structure, punctuation, word parts, and other ideas in the passage.

⚬ Think carefully about questions that ask you to make an inference. Eliminate answer choices that you cannot reasonably infer from the information in the passage.

⚬ Do not leave any questions unanswered. It is best to answer all questions about one passage before you move on to the next passage.

⚬ Work as quickly as you can. Pay attention to the number of questions and the amount of time you have left. You can review previous questions and change previous answers as long as you have time left.

⚬ If you cannot find the correct answer, use the *process of elimination*. This means you should omit the choices you know are incorrect. If you can eliminate one or two choices, you will improve your chance of selecting the correct answer. Your score is based on the number of questions you answer correctly, and incorrect answers are not subtracted.

⚬ Your own best strategy: _____

_____

1.1 Understanding Facts and Details

FOCUS

Read the following passage and answer the question:

> In one study, 83 percent of 140 male and female executives in a variety of businesses report having a mentor when they were younger. Generally, they view the mentor–protégé relationship as an important aspect of the initial phase of their careers. Mentors are given credit for teaching protégés the key elements of the job, and for providing a key relationship in the young adult's shift from dependence on parents to complete independence.
>
> Within organizations, protégés are more likely to be promoted, get larger raises, and have more opportunities within a company, law firm, or other group than are young workers who have no mentor. But it is difficult to know whether these advantages arise from the mentoring process itself, since those who are selected as protégés are usually the most strongly motivated or best skilled among the younger workers.
>
> According to the passage, one way in which mentors help protégés is by
>
> ◯ giving them credit for excellent work
> ◯ encouraging them to aim for executive positions
> ◯ teaching them important aspects of the job
> ◯ arranging for them to receive a larger salary

The question asks about a ***detail*** in the passage: one way in which mentors help protégés. The correct answer is *teaching them important aspects of the job*. A key idea in the first paragraph is *Mentors are given credit for teaching protégés the key elements of the job*.

Now answer another question:

> Why is it difficult to know whether certain advantages for a protégé are the result of having a mentor?
>
> ◯ Most people chosen as protégés are already highly motivated and skilled.
> ◯ Mentors do not have direct control over workers' promotions and salaries.
> ◯ Having a mentor is a fairly common experience for junior executives.
> ◯ Little research has been done concerning why protégés are successful.

The question asks about a ***fact*** in the passage. The answer to a *Why*–question will be a reason. The correct answer is both a reason and a fact: *Most people chosen as protégés are already highly motivated and skilled.* What key words provide clues to help you find the answer?

 STUDY

1. Facts and Details

A *fact* is a real occurrence, event, or phenomenon—something that happens or has happened. Facts are information that is presented as real and true. Sometimes a fact functions as a supporting detail in a passage.

A *detail* is a specific bit of information, such as an example, a reason, a statistic, a description, or an illustration. In written English, both facts and details are used to support the thesis or main idea of the work. Facts and details are evidence that make main ideas stronger and more convincing.

Fact and detail questions on the TOEFL test your ability to answer questions about information that is stated directly in the passage. Questions about facts and details look like this:

According to the passage,   what _____?
which _____?
why _____?
how _____?
who _____?
where _____?
when _____?

According to the passage, which of the following statements is true?

In paragraph __, what does the author say about _____?

What point does the author make about _____?

What reason is given for _____?

The author argues that _____.

The author mentions _____ as an example of _____.

Which of the following statements applies to _____?

Which statement best describes _____?

2. Useful Skills

Three skills that will help you answer fact questions are skimming, scanning, and scrolling.

Skimming is reading quickly to understand the general message of a passage. Skimming involves looking at key sentences that give you an idea of the major ideas and overall organization. When you skim, your eyes move quickly through the passage, and you do not read every word.

Scanning is looking through a passage to find specific information. The test question usually tells you what kind of information to scan for, such as reasons, examples, causes, effects, or characteristics. Scanning is searching for the facts and details that will help you answer the question.

Scrolling is moving quickly through text on the computer by using the scroll bar. You must scroll through a passage when it is too long for you to see all of it on the screen at the same time. Scrolling is a useful skill when you skim for overall meaning and when you scan for specific details.

3. Transitions

Certain expressions are clues that can help you understand the relationships between ideas within sentences and paragraphs. These words and phrases are called *transitions*.

Illustrate	for example for instance	one example is to illustrate	such such as
Explain	at this point because	furthermore how	in fact in this case
Give Reasons	as a result of because	because of due to	one reason is since
Show Result	accordingly as a result	consequently otherwise	therefore thus
Compare	both equally important	like the same	similarly similar to
Contrast	although conversely however in contrast	instead nevertheless on the contrary on the other hand	rather unlike whereas while
Add	also another as well as	finally first, second, third… furthermore	moreover not only…but also too
Limit	although but	except for even though	however yet
Emphasize	certainly clearly	indeed in fact	most importantly surely

4. Answer Choices

In questions about facts and details, the correct answer may paraphrase information from the passage. To *paraphrase* means to restate the same information by using different words.

The incorrect answer choices may be incorrect because they:

- repeat information from the passage but do not answer the question;
- incorrectly state information or ideas from the passage;
- are inaccurate or untrue according to the passage; or
- are irrelevant or not mentioned in the passage.

5. Sample Questions

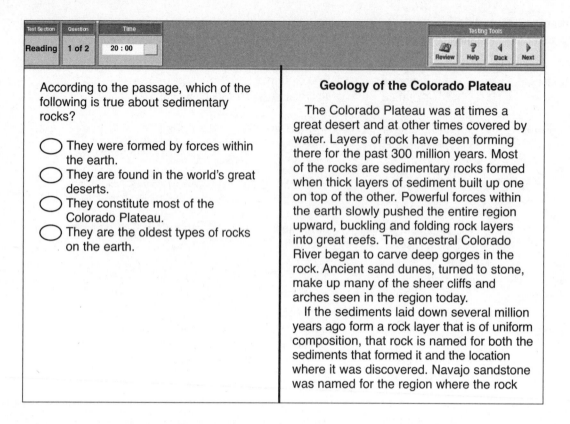

The question asks you to identify a fact from the passage. The key phrase *sedimentary rocks* enables you to scan the passage for the needed information. The correct answer is *They constitute most of the Colorado Plateau.* The first paragraph introduces the topic of the Colorado Plateau and also states that *Most of the rocks are sedimentary rocks*—a statement that is paraphrased in the correct answer.

Why are the other three answers incorrect? *They were formed by forces within the earth* repeats information from the passage but does not describe sedimentary rocks. *They are found in the world's great deserts* and *They are the oldest types of rocks on earth* are not mentioned in the passage, so you do not know whether these statements are true or not.

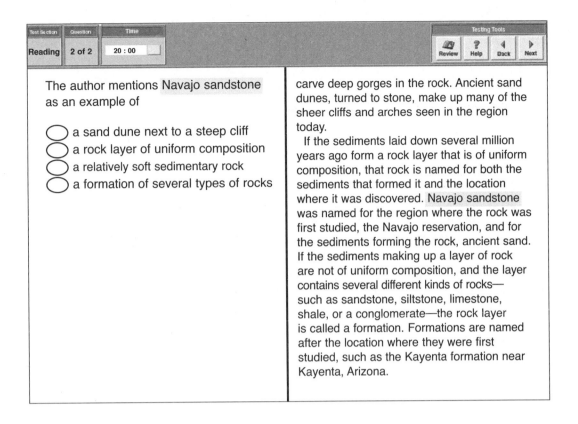

The question is about a detail, *Navajo sandstone*. If you scan the passage, you can find where *Navajo sandstone* is mentioned. Sometimes the computer highlights text to help you scan quickly. If you read the previous sentence, you will see that Navajo sandstone is an example of *a rock layer that is of uniform composition, ... named for both the sediments that formed it and the location where it was discovered*. Therefore, the correct answer is *a rock layer of uniform composition*.

Why are the other three answers incorrect? *A sand dune next to a steep cliff* is inaccurate because the author says nothing about Navajo sandstone being next to a steep cliff. *A relatively soft sedimentary rock* is not mentioned in the passage. *A formation of several types of rocks* is untrue because it describes a rock layer that is not of uniform composition.

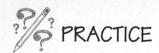 PRACTICE

Exercise 1.1.A

Read the passages and choose the best answer to each question.

QUESTIONS 1–3

1   The cells of a plant are organized into three tissue systems: dermal, vascular, and ground tissue. Each tissue system is continuous throughout the plant's body. The specific characteristics of each tissue, however, are different in the different organs of the plant.

2   The dermal tissue system is the "skin" of the plant. The dermal system, or epidermis, is a single layer of cells covering the entire body of the plant. The main function of the epidermis is to protect the plant. The epidermis also has specialized characteristics for the particular organs it covers. For example, the epidermis of leaves and stems has a waxy coating that helps the plant conserve water, and the epidermal cells near the tips of the plant's roots help the plant absorb water and nutrients from the soil.

3   The second tissue system—the vascular system—is the transportation system for water and nutrients. Vascular tissue also helps to support the plant's structure. The third system— the ground tissue—makes up the bulk of a plant, filling all of the spaces between the dermal and vascular tissue systems. Ground tissue functions in photosynthesis, storage, and support.

1. How are the three tissue systems of a plant similar to each other?

   (A) They all continue throughout the plant's body.
   (B) They all have a protective waxy coating.
   (C) They all consist of a single layer of cells.
   (D) They all perform the same bodily functions.

2. Which of the following statements best describes the plant's epidermis?

   (A) It helps the plant to stand upright.
   (B) It transports water and nutrients.
   (C) It covers the plant's entire body.
   (D) It is found only in young plants.

3. Which type of tissue does a plant's body mainly consist of?

   (A) Dermal
   (B) Vascular
   (C) Epidermis
   (D) Ground

QUESTIONS 4–6

1   By the decades just before the Civil War of the 1860s, the Southern states had developed an economic culture distinct from that of the North. The economy of the South depended largely on two things: cotton and slave labor. Because of the rising demand for cotton from the mills of England, and the invention of the cotton gin in 1793, the cotton production of the South increased tremendously. In 1790, cotton output had been 9,000 bales a year, but by the 1850s, output had soared to five million bales. In the South, cotton was "king." The most readily available source of labor was the institution of slavery. Thus, cotton and slavery became interdependent, and the South grew more reliant on both.

2   This was in sharp contrast to the North, where farming was becoming more mechanized and diversified. Northern farmers would boast of improvements in the form of new roads, railways, and machinery, and of the production of a variety of crops. In the South, however, farmers bought laborers instead of equipment, and a man's social status depended on the number of slaves he owned. The economic differences between the two regions would ultimately lead to armed conflict and the social restructuring of the South.

4. Why did the Southern output of cotton greatly increase between 1790 and 1850?

   (A) Southern farmers invested in transportation.
   (B) Mills in England demanded more cotton.
   (C) The South was trying to dominate the North.
   (D) Southern cotton was superior to Northern cotton.

5. What was associated more with the North in the period discussed?

   (A) Farm machinery
   (B) Slave labor
   (C) Military service
   (D) Reliance on one crop

6. The author argues that the Civil War between the North and the South

   (A) was a conflict over control of the cotton trade
   (B) began in 1790 and lasted almost seventy years
   (C) was largely the result of economic differences
   (D) forced the South to produce different crops

READING

QUESTIONS 7–10

1   Play is common to the young of most mammals. Some birds play, but it is rare in cold–blooded animals such as fish and reptiles. Why some animals play, and others do not, is not entirely understood, but the most playful—such as dolphins and monkeys—are also the most intelligent and sociable. Play may seem something of a puzzle. Not only is it apparently unproductive, but it also places the participant at risk of being surprised by predators. However, there must be a good reason for play. The most widely held scientific explanation is that play allows the social behaviors of the species to be explored and learned. Other benefits include physical exercise and the learning of survival skills such as hunting. A kitten that grows up separated from other kittens becomes both a social misfit and a poor hunter, largely because it is deprived of play.

2   Kittens start playing when they are about three weeks old. Early play consists of mock attacks with the mother and littermates, clearly previewing the territorial behavior of adult life. As the kittens grow older, more elaborate play patterns develop. At four weeks they can wrestle. The sideways leap and the pounce may be learned by the fifth week. By six weeks they can chase and leap on each other with reasonable accuracy. Kittens stalk, chase, and fall over each other. They recognize these patterns as being playful, even though the same signals in adult life may have a more serious meaning.

7. The author makes the point that the most playful animals are

   (A) cold–blooded animals
   (B) highly intelligent and sociable
   (C) easily surprised by predators
   (D) not a subject of scientific study

8. The author mentions dolphins and monkeys as examples of

   (A) rare species
   (B) fish and reptiles
   (C) playful animals
   (D) predators

9. According to paragraph 1, a kitten that has no contact with other kittens will

   (A) have to play with toys
   (B) be afraid of people
   (C) exercise more than other kittens
   (D) not learn social and hunting skills

10. According to paragraph 2, which of the following statements is true?

   (A) The mock attacks of young kittens disappear by the age of six weeks.
   (B) Actions that are playful in kittens convey a different meaning in adult cats.
   (C) Territorial behavior in kittens is a sign of developmental problems.
   (D) Kittens and human children share many of the same play patterns.

Exercise 1.1.B

Read the passages and choose the best answer to each question.

QUESTIONS 1–3

1   Erik Erikson believed that personality development is a series of turning points, which he described in terms of the tension between desirable qualities and dangers. He emphasized that only when the positive qualities outweigh the dangers does healthy psychosocial development take place.

2   An important turning point occurs around age six. A child entering school is at a point in development when behavior is dominated by intellectual curiosity and performance. He or she now learns to win recognition by producing things. The child develops a sense of industry. The danger at this stage is that the child may experience feelings of inadequacy or inferiority. If the child is encouraged to make and do things, allowed to finish tasks, and praised for trying, a sense of industry is the result. On the other hand, if the child's efforts are unsuccessful, or if they are criticized or treated as bothersome, a sense of inferiority is the result. For these reasons, Erikson called the period from age six to eleven *Industry vs. Inferiority*.

1. According to Erikson's theory, what desirable quality should develop in a child who is six to eleven years old?

   (A) A liking for school
   (B) A feeling of inadequacy
   (C) An ability to finish tasks
   (D) A sense of industry

2. According to Erikson's theory, what will happen if a child's efforts are criticized?

   (A) The child will dislike his teacher.
   (B) The child will avoid other children.
   (C) The child will try harder to win recognition.
   (D) The child will feel inferior.

3. *Industry vs. Inferiority* is an example of

   (A) the tension between a positive quality and a danger
   (B) a personality disorder in children
   (C) the difference between a child of six and a child of eleven
   (D) an educational strategy

QUESTIONS 4–6

1   In the storytelling traditions of West Africa, the tiny rabbit appears frequently as a rascal who teases or plays jokes on bigger animals. In one story, Mr. Rabbit tricks Mr. Elephant and Mrs. Whale into a tug of war with each other. Such tales about Mr. Rabbit continue to be part of the oral traditions of the Wollof people of Senegal.

2   The African–American folktales of the U.S. South also feature a trickster rabbit in the character of Brer Rabbit. In his American incarnation, Brer Rabbit uses his wits to overcome circumstances and even to enact playful revenge on his larger, stronger adversaries, Brer Fox, Brer Wolf, and Brer Bear. Although he is not always successful, Brer Rabbit's efforts make him both a folk hero and a friendly comic figure. Joel Chandler Harris, a journalist in Georgia, had heard old men tell Brer Rabbit tales by the fireside when he was a young boy. Harris wrote down and published many of the stories, popularizing them for the general public.

3   A folklorist named Alcée Fortier recorded very similar versions of the same stories in southern Louisiana, where the rabbit character was known as Compair Lapin in Creole French. More recently, the rabbit has enjoyed another incarnation as the cartoon character Bugs Bunny—a rascally rabbit who causes trouble, tricks the hunter, and always gets the final word.

4. What trait belongs to the rabbit character in tales of West African origin?

(A) Storytelling ability
(B) Very keen eyesight
(C) Ability to fool others
(D) Strong, athletic body

5. How did a wide audience of people know about the Brer Rabbit stories?

(A) They studied the oral traditions of West Africa.
(B) They heard old men tell the stories by the fireside.
(C) They read the stories published by a journalist.
(D) They listened to recordings from southern Louisiana.

6. What do Brer Rabbit, Compair Lapin, and Bugs Bunny have in common?

(A) All are cartoon characters.
(B) All play tricks on others.
(C) All save others from trouble.
(D) All speak Creole French.

QUESTIONS 7–10

1   A hot spot is a giant underground caldron of molten rock in one of the world's many volcanically active areas. The steamy geysers, thermal pools, and mud pots of Yellowstone National Park owe their origins to hot spots.

2   Annually, more than 200 geysers erupt in Yellowstone, making this one of the most interesting places in the world for geologists. Over 100 geysers lie within the Upper Geyser Basin, a one–square–mile area near Old Faithful, the most famous geyser in the world. The Yellowstone hot spot was created around ten million years ago, and the center of the park is still volcanically active, with molten rock only a mile or two beneath the Earth's surface.

3   When rain and melted snow seep down through tiny cracks in the Earth, the water eventually reaches underground chambers of lava–heated rock. The rock heats the water, and the boiling water and steam often make their way back up to the surface in the form of a geyser, a thermal pool, or a mud pot.

4   In a geyser, water trapped in an underground chamber heats up beyond the boiling point and forms steam. Since steam takes up 1,500 times more space than water, pressure builds up, eventually forcing the superheated water to burst to the surface as a geyser. A thermal pool is formed when the water from the hot spot reaches the surface before cooling off. If the water does not make it all the way to the surface, steam and gases may dissolve rocks and form a bubbling mud pot instead.

7. Where do hot spots occur?

   (A) In rocky regions near the equator
   (B) Below the ground near active volcanoes
   (C) About a mile above a volcano's crater
   (D) In the center of ancient volcanoes

8. According to the passage, why is Yellowstone National Park an interesting place for geologists?

   (A) There are 100 square miles of hot spots.
   (B) Over 200 geysers erupt there each year.
   (C) There are more than 100 different kinds of geysers.
   (D) More than 200 types of rock are found there.

9. How do hot spots contribute to the formation of geysers?

   (A) Hot spots melt all of the snow falling into a volcano's crater.
   (B) Water is trapped in an underground chamber and cannot escape.
   (C) Hot rocks create boiling water, steam, and pressure underground.
   (D) Water from hot spots rises to the surface before it cools off.

10. When do mud pots form?

   (A) When steam and gases dissolve rocks near the surface
   (B) When underground water exceeds the boiling point
   (C) When snow melts in Yellowstone's geyser basins
   (D) When superheated water bursts to the surface

Exercise 1.1.C

Read the passages and choose the best answer to each question.

QUESTIONS 1–3

1   Most matter exists as compounds—combinations of atoms or oppositely charged ions of two or more different elements held together in fixed proportions by chemical bonds. Compounds are classified as organic or inorganic. Organic compounds contain atoms of the element carbon, usually combined with itself and with atoms of one or more other elements such as hydrogen, oxygen, nitrogen, sulfur, phosphorus, and chlorine. Many materials important to us—food, vitamins, blood, skin, cotton, wool, paper, oil, plastics—are organic compounds.

2   Larger and more complex organic compounds, called polymers, consist of a number of basic structural units linked together by chemical bonds. Important organic polymers include carbohydrates, proteins, and nucleic acids. Carbohydrates, such as the complex starches in rice and potato plants, are composed of a number of simple sugar molecules. Proteins are produced in plant and animal cells by the linking of different numbers and sequences of about twenty different structural units known as amino acids. Most animals, including humans, can manufacture about ten of these amino acids in their cells, but the other ten, called essential amino acids, must be obtained from food in order to prevent protein deficiency. Nucleic acids are composed of hundreds to thousands of four different units called nucleotides linked together in different numbers and sequences. DNA and RNA in plant and animal cells are nucleic acids.

1. Which of the following statements applies to all organic compounds?

   (A) They are composed of carbon and one or more other elements.
   (B) They contain atoms of the seven most abundant elements.
   (C) They have stronger chemical bonds than inorganic compounds do.
   (D) They are produced by linking several simple sugar molecules.

2. Carbohydrates, proteins, and nucleic acids are types of

   (A) elements
   (B) inorganic compounds
   (C) polymers
   (D) amino acids

3. Why is it important for humans to obtain some amino acids from food?

   (A) Without certain amino acids, humans store too much fat.
   (B) Organically grown food is the only source of amino acids.
   (C) Sufficient amino acids are necessary for DNA production.
   (D) Humans cells cannot make the ten essential amino acids.

QUESTIONS 4–6

1   By the 1840s, British North America had developed a vibrant commercial economy based on its abundant natural resources and a growing international trade. Fish, furs, timber, and grains represented over 90 percent of all economic activity. The oldest of the resource commodities, fish, was traditionally associated with Newfoundland and continued to dominate that colony's economy throughout the nineteenth century. The other traditional resource, fur, had a much smaller economic value compared to other resources. However, the fur trade was of tremendous value politically because it provided the means for Great Britain to retain its claim over much of Canada, and also formed the basis of the relationship between the British and the aboriginal peoples.

2   Timber and grain eventually replaced fish and fur in economic importance. Every province of British North America except Newfoundland was involved in the timber trade. In New Brunswick, the timber industry controlled every aspect of life, and settlement was closely connected to the opening of new timber territory. In the extensive agricultural lands of the St. Lawrence Valley and Upper Canada, wheat quickly became the dominant crop. Wheat met a growing demand abroad and it transported well as either grain or flour.

4. Which resource was the earliest to contribute to the economy of British North America?

   (A) Timber from New Brunswick
   (B) Fur from across Canada
   (C) Fish from Newfoundland
   (D) Wheat from Upper Canada

5. According to the passage, what is the main reason for the importance of the fur trade?

   (A) Fur had more economic value than any other natural resource.
   (B) Fur formed the basis of the local economy everywhere in Canada.
   (C) The fur trade supplied all of the fur needed in Great Britain.
   (D) The fur trade allowed Great Britain to control a large part of Canada.

6. Which statement best describes the British North American economy around 1840?

   (A) Four important resources supported most of the commercial activity.
   (B) The economy was based mainly on the exportation of timber and wheat.
   (C) Economic activity varied greatly from one province to another.
   (D) Great Britain maintained strict control over all aspects of the economy.

Questions 7–10

1   The youngest child of a prosperous Midwestern manufacturing family, Dorothy Reed was born in 1874 and educated at home by her grandmother. She graduated from Smith College and in 1896 entered Johns Hopkins Medical School. After receiving her M.D. degree, she worked at Johns Hopkins in the laboratories of two noted medical scientists. Reed's research in pathology established conclusively that Hodgkin's disease, until then thought to be a form of tuberculosis, was a distinct disorder characterized by a specific blood cell, which was named the Reed cell after her.

2   In 1906, her marriage to Charles Mendenhall took Reed away from the research laboratory. For ten years, she remained at home as the mother of young children before returning to professional life. She became a lecturer in Home Economics at the University of Wisconsin, where her principal concerns were collecting data about maternal and child health and preparing courses for new mothers.

3   Dorothy Reed Mendenhall's career interests were reshaped by the requirements of marriage. Her passion for research was redirected to public health rather than laboratory science. Late in life, she concluded that she could not imagine life without her husband and sons, but she hoped for a future when marriage would not have to end a career of laboratory research.

7. What was Dorothy Reed's area of research at Johns Hopkins?

   (A) Manufacturing
   (B) Pathology
   (C) Tuberculosis
   (D) Maternal health

8. Why did Reed stop working in the research laboratory?

   (A) Marriage required that she remain at home.
   (B) She became more interested in public health.
   (C) Johns Hopkins did not like women doing research.
   (D) Her work on Hodgkin's disease was completed.

9. What did Dorothy Reed Mendenhall conclude about marriage?

   (A) Marriage inspired her passion for laboratory research.
   (B) It was a mistake for her to give up her career for marriage.
   (C) Marriage need not keep women from careers in laboratory science.
   (D) Women cannot have both a happy marriage and a successful career.

10. Which fact should be included in a biography of Dorothy Reed Mendenhall?

   (A) She was the first woman in her family to earn a degree in medicine.
   (B) Marriage and motherhood prevented her from resuming her career.
   (C) She proved that Hodgkin's disease was characterized by a certain blood cell.
   (D) Her career was devoted to finding a cure for tuberculosis in children.

Answers to Exercises 1.1.A through 1.1.C are on pages 633–634.

 EXTENSION

1. Outside of class, look in a newspaper, a magazine, or a university textbook. Select a short passage of one to three paragraphs. Make a photocopy and bring it to class. In class, work with a partner. Read the passage and underline the most important ideas. Circle the important facts, details, and examples. With your partner, practice asking each other questions and giving answers about the facts.

2. Outside of class, work with a partner. Look in a magazine or a university textbook. Select a short passage of around 100 words. Write two questions about facts and details in the passage. You do not have to write the answers. For examples of how to write the questions, see the list of questions on page 36. Write the passage and questions on an overhead projector transparency, or make enough copies of the passage and questions for everyone in your class. Your class now has a reading test made entirely by students! As a class, take the test by either writing or discussing answers to the questions. Can you answer all of the questions about each passage by using only the information provided in the passage?

1.2 Identifying Negative Facts

FOCUS

Read the following passage and answer the question:

> Like air and water, soil is also vulnerable to pollution from several sources. One source is the atmosphere, as many harmful air pollutants leach through the soil into groundwater supplies. Another source is hazardous waste, the deadly byproducts of industrial processes, buried in landfills or dumped in fields. One of the most critical soil–quality problems is the increase in concentration of dissolved salts, commonly referred to as salinization. Natural processes or human activities can salinize lands. Irrigation water contains large quantities of salt, and as this water evaporates, it leaves the salt behind.
>
> All of the following are given as causes of soil pollution EXCEPT
>
> ◯ the leaching of air pollutants
> ◯ the decomposition of organic matter
> ◯ the increasing amount of dissolved salts
> ◯ the dumping of hazardous waste

The question asks you to identify which *three* causes of soil pollution are mentioned in the passage and which *one* is not mentioned. The correct answer is the one choice that is NOT mentioned in the passage: *the decomposition of organic matter.* All of the other choices are given as causes of soil pollution.

Some TOEFL questions ask about **negative facts**: information that is not given in the passage.

STUDY

1. Negative Facts

A *fact* is a real occurrence, event, phenomenon, or other type of information that is presented as true. A *negative fact* is information that is not presented as true. A negative fact may be presented as false, or it may be omitted from the passage.

Negative fact questions test your ability to verify what information is true and what information is not true, or not included, in the passage. Questions about negative facts look like this:

> The passage discusses all of the following EXCEPT _____.
> All of the following are mentioned in the passage EXCEPT _____.
> All of the following are examples of _____ EXCEPT _____.
> _____ are characterized by all of the following EXCEPT _____.
> According to the passage, all of the following statements are true EXCEPT:
> Which of the following is NOT mentioned as _____?
> Which of the following is NOT given as a reason for _____?

2. Answer Choices

In questions with the word EXCEPT or NOT, *three* answer choices will be true, and one will be either false or not mentioned. Look for the *one* answer choice containing information that is:

- not mentioned in the passage
  or
- not true according to the passage.

Scanning is a skill that will help you answer negative fact questions. The question and answer choices tell you what information to scan for: examples, reasons, causes, effects, or characteristics. Scanning is searching for specific information that will help you answer the question.

3. Sample Question

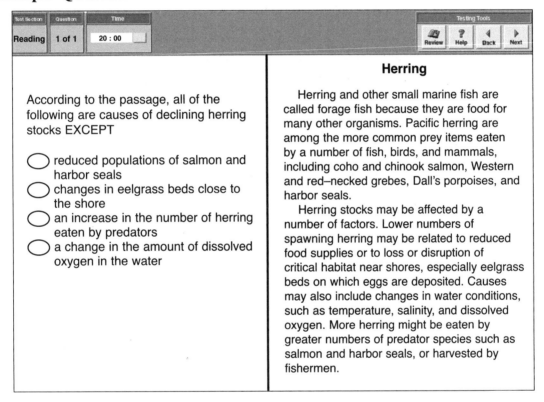

An important word in the question is *EXCEPT*. It tells you to look for the one answer that is *not* given as a cause of declining herring stocks. Begin by scanning the passage for key words from each answer choice. Which answer is *not* a cause of declining herring stocks?

The correct answer is *reduced populations of salmon and harbor seals* because it is not true according to the passage. The passage states: *More herring might be eaten by greater numbers of predator species such as salmon and harbor seals....*

The other three answers are given as causes of declining herring stocks:

Lower numbers of spawning herring may be related to...loss or disruption
of critical habitat near shores, especially eelgrass beds on which eggs are deposited.
More herring might be eaten by greater numbers of predator species....
Causes may also include changes in water conditions, such as...dissolved oxygen.

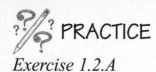 PRACTICE

Exercise 1.2.A

Read the passages and choose the best answer to each question.

QUESTION 1

An important element of drama is that it is a presentation by performers in front of an audience—for example, a ceremony conducted by civic leaders before members of a community. Another aspect is costumes, such as those worn by tribal chiefs who impersonate animals or gods. Moreover, drama involves storytelling—recitation of myths or legends, teaching lessons through stories—to a group of listeners. Sometimes the storyteller imitates the characters in the story by changing his or her voice for different characters.

1. The passage mentions all of the following as aspects of drama EXCEPT

(A) wearing costumes
(B) performing before an audience
(C) writing dialogue for characters
(D) narrating a story

QUESTION 2

Skin cancer is the most prevalent of all cancers. The principal cause of skin cancer is overexposure to sunlight, according to most medical experts. Chronic sun exposure—especially when it causes sunburn or blistering—results in more skin cancer than does any other risk factor, including exposure to x–rays and a family history of the disease. The most effective preventative measure is sun avoidance.

2. All of the following are factors that can cause skin cancer EXCEPT

(A) exposure to x–rays
(B) sun blistering
(C) family history of skin cancer
(D) sun avoidance

QUESTIONS 3–4

1   Laughter is a key to a good life and good health: it can diminish feelings of tension, anger, and sadness. Just as exercise conditions our bodies, frequent laughter can train our bodies to be healthier. When laughter is a regular experience, it lowers blood pressure and boosts brain chemicals that fight pain. It can also reduce stress hormones that increase vulnerability to illness, as well as increase hormones that have been shown to help produce restful sleep. Laughter is like an instant vacation in the way it changes our psychobiology.

2   To make laughter a regular part of your life, try keeping a humor journal in which you record some of the amusing things that happen to you. Another technique is to create a weekly fun time to look forward to, such as watching a comedy video or having a dinner with friends that features joke telling. Another sure source of laughter is spending time with children and animals.

3. According to the passage, laughter provides all of the following benefits EXCEPT

 (A) elevating brain chemicals that prevent pain
 (B) increasing the body's vulnerability to illness
 (C) promoting a more restful kind of sleep
 (D) reducing feelings of stress and anger

4. The author recommends all of the following EXCEPT

 (A) playing tricks on family and friends
 (B) planning a special fun time every week
 (C) enjoying time with pets and children
 (D) writing down humorous experiences

QUESTIONS 5–6

Nearly all animals have a good sense of their own bodies, the trait of physical self–awareness. For this reason, animals do not generally bump into things. Horses know how much room they have around them when they move through narrow spaces. A horse can run between two trees or around large rocks in a way that clearly shows the horse's knowledge of its own body size. Animals show self–awareness in how they respond to discomfort. A dog, for example, has no trouble knowing where to scratch itself to kill a flea. Many animals show self–awareness when they recognize their own reflection. While looking at itself in a mirror, an elephant may move its trunk over different parts of its body. A chimpanzee will make faces, look inside its mouth, or stick out its tongue in front of a mirror.

5. The passage describes all of the following animals as self–aware EXCEPT

 (A) horses
 (B) dogs
 (C) fleas
 (D) elephants

6. Which of the following is NOT given as an example of self–awareness?

 (A) Running between trees without touching them
 (B) Using sign language to communicate
 (C) Scratching to relieve discomfort
 (D) Making faces in front of a mirror

QUESTIONS 7–8

1 Indian filmmaker Satyajit Ray is still regarded by many film critics as one of the world's great directors. Ray's films are known for their compassion, honesty, and quiet dignity. His Apu Trilogy, three films about Bengali life, was hailed as a national epic in the 1950s. The first film, *Pather Panchali*, is the story of a Bengali family's noble struggle against poverty and the heartbreaks of life. It was followed by *Aparajito*, in which the son of the family, Apu, grows to manhood. In the final film, *The World of Apu*, the young man marries, but fails at his life's ambitions, and then, after losing his wife, he wanders across the country for several years before returning home to claim his son.

2 Satyajit Ray's movies have never been very popular in India itself, but those who appreciate his unobtrusive technique and his compassion for his characters view his films as a poetic record of Indian life.

7. According to the passage, the films of Satyajit Ray are characterized by all of the following EXCEPT

 (A) adventure
 (B) honesty
 (C) compassion
 (D) dignity

8. The third film of the Apu Trilogy deals with all of the following themes EXCEPT

 (A) failure at a major goal
 (B) loss of a spouse
 (C) struggle against poverty
 (D) going home after a long absence

QUESTIONS 9–10

1 Archaeology is the study of prehistoric and historic cultures through the analysis of material remains. Archaeologists interpret the past from the objects made by past peoples. Often these objects lie buried in the ground, so our image of the archaeologist is of a scientist who is always digging. Archaeological digs include ruins of buildings and monuments, and also objects made by people who often had no written language and therefore no other record of their way of life. Tools, weapons, body ornaments, household furnishings, and items used in religious ceremonies are all examples of artifacts that typically turn up in digs.

2 Like historians, archaeologists establish the sequence of events that occurred in a given place and time period. But unlike historians, they take on a time span of roughly half a million years. Archaeologists try not only to piece together what happened in a particular setting but also to fit these small pieces into a much bigger picture. They aim to document how big changes occurred in the way peoples exploited their environment and one another.

9. The passage mentions all of the following as studied by archaeologists EXCEPT

 (A) weapons
 (B) religious objects
 (C) diaries
 (D) remains of buildings

10. Archaeologists do all of the following EXCEPT

 (A) plan and design more efficient uses for objects and materials
 (B) determine what took place in a specific place and time period
 (C) dig up the remains of objects that are buried in the ground
 (D) explain how past humans related to others and their environment

Exercise 1.2.B

Read the passages and choose the best answer to each question.

QUESTION 1

In the 1930s, the Great Plains of North America came to be called the Dust Bowl after several large dust storms destroyed the region. The Dust Bowl was the result of human activity and bad weather that led to soil erosion. In the previous decade, farmers had plowed millions of acres of grassland to make room for growing wheat. Consequently, when a period of dry weather struck the region, there were no native grasses to hold the soil in place. The wind lifted the dry soil and carried it away in great clouds. The Dust Bowl was an ecological and economic disaster, resulting in severe soil loss, crop failures, and economic hardship.

1. Which of the following is NOT given as a cause of the Dust Bowl?

   (A) Cold weather
   (B) Soil erosion
   (C) Loss of native grasses
   (D) Lack of rain

QUESTIONS 2–3

Political parties are necessary in the exercise of democracy in nation states. The enlargement of the electorate—the body of qualified voters—has increased the importance of parties to the point where it is practically impossible for a candidate to get elected without the support of a party organization. This is because the variety of issues facing nation states has complicated the problem of creating an informed electorate that can use its vote responsibly. The job of influencing popular opinion through newspapers, television, the Internet, and other mass media is too complicated and costly for an individual candidate to undertake. Although individual candidates continue to appear at public meetings—to answer questions and shake hands with voters—the influencing of public opinion on a mass scale has become a specialized technique. Building political support on a nation–wide scale carries a high cost, and it requires nationally organized and well–financed parties. Party organizations thus have come to occupy a prominent place in the functioning of democracies.

2. According to the passage, what is one effect of the enlargement of the electorate?

   (A) There are more political parties than ever before.
   (B) Candidates need political parties to get elected.
   (C) Political parties control all forms of mass media.
   (D) It is impossible to have a perfect democracy.

3. All of the following are given as reasons for the necessity of political parties EXCEPT:

   (A) Influencing popular opinion through the media is a large and complex job.
   (B) It is difficult to inform voters about the variety of important issues.
   (C) Building nation–wide support is too expensive for individual candidates.
   (D) Voters prefer candidates that express the values of an established party.

QUESTION 4

The music called "blues" has deep roots in African–American history. In the Mississippi Delta, men working in the cotton fields and on construction crews chanted and sang as they worked. These work songs and "field hollers" expressed the pain and sorrow of the workers and helped to pass the time. During the evenings, the workers sang these songs, accompanied by guitar and banjo. Live dance bands started playing blues songs, and female singers further developed the style. The blues spread from its birthplace in the Mississippi Delta to other rural areas of the South. Eventually, the music traveled northward with African Americans who moved from the South to cities in the North. The blues contributed to the development of other types of music, such as the big–band jazz of the 1930s.

4. According to the passage, all of the following statements are true EXCEPT:

(A) Field hollers and songs helped workers to pass the time.
(B) Blues music originated in the Mississippi Delta.
(C) Dance bands in northern cities invented the blues.
(D) The blues had an influence on big–band jazz music.

QUESTIONS 5–6

1   Coral reefs are one of the earth's most ancient ecosystems and also the richest, most diverse, and most beautiful ecosystems in any ocean. The huge cities built by corals provide shelter and food for billions of other marine animals. A quarter of all sea creatures depend on coral reefs during some part of their life cycles.

2   In the past century, the ocean's surface temperature has risen an average of 1.8 degrees Fahrenheit. It has taken only this slight increase in sea–surface temperature to sicken the world's coral reefs. The brilliant blue, purple, green, gold, and pink have begun to disappear as a disease called bleaching drains the color and the life from the reefs. Scientists have reported mass bleaching on reefs in the Caribbean, in southern Japan, in Indonesia, and on the world's largest coral reef, the Great Barrier Reef, where the corals have bleached to a dirty white.

3   Bleaching has killed more corals than all other causes combined. More than 16 percent of the world's corals have sickened and died from bleaching. Millions of aquatic animals that depend directly or indirectly on corals have died as well—anemones, sponges, mollusks, shrimp, crabs, fish, turtles, and seabirds—making the loss of corals a catastrophe for the natural world.

5. Which of the following is NOT stated about coral reefs?

(A) They are among the oldest ecosystems in the world.
(B) They have caused sea–surface temperatures to rise.
(C) They are brilliantly colored when they are healthy.
(D) They supply shelter for a diversity of marine life.

6. All of the following are effects of the bleaching of coral reefs EXCEPT

(A) fading colors
(B) loss of dependent animals
(C) death of corals
(D) rising water level

QUESTIONS 7–8

1   What made Native American and European subsistence cycles so different from one another in colonial America had less to do with their use of plants than with their use of animals. Domesticated grazing animals and the plow were the most distinguishing characteristics of European agricultural practices. The Native Americans' relationship to the deer, moose, and beaver they hunted was far different from that of the Europeans to the pigs, cows, sheep, and horses they owned.

2   Where Natives had contented themselves with burning the woods and concentrating their hunting in the fall and winter months, the English sought a much more total and year–round control over their animals' lives. The effects of that control could be seen in most aspects of New England's rural economy. By the end of the colonial period, the Europeans were responsible for a host of changes in the New England landscape: endless miles of fences, a system of country roads, and new fields covered with grass, clover, and buttercups.

7. What point does the author make about Native Americans and Europeans?

   (A) They competed over the same plants and animals.
   (B) They both tried to control New England's animals.
   (C) They taught each other techniques for hunting animals.
   (D) They differed in their attitudes toward animals.

8. All of the following were agricultural practices of Europeans in New England EXCEPT

   (A) constructing fences
   (B) burning the woods
   (C) plowing fields
   (D) planting grass and clover

QUESTIONS 9–10

1   Landscape architects design landscapes in residential areas, public parks, and commercial zones. They are hired by many types of organizations, from real estate firms starting new developments to municipalities constructing airports or parks. They usually plan the arrangement of vegetation, walkways, and other natural features of open spaces.

2   In planning a site, landscape architects first consider the nature and purpose of the project, the funds available, and the proposed elements. Next, they study the site and map such features as the slope of the land, the positions of existing buildings, existing utilities, roads, fences, walkways, and trees. Then, working either as the leader of a design team or in consultation with the project architect or engineer, they draw up plans to develop the site. If the plans are approved, they prepare working drawings to show all existing and proposed features. They outline the methods of constructing features and draw up lists of building materials.

3   Newcomers to the field usually start as junior drafters, tracing drawings and doing other simple drafting work for architectural, landscape architectural, or engineering firms. After two or three years, they can carry a design through all stages of development. Highly qualified landscape architects may become associates in private firms, but usually those who progress this far open their own offices.

9. Landscape architects do all of the following EXCEPT

   (A) design landscapes in residential and commercial zones
   (B) decide where to build walkways in public parks
   (C) draw or paint scenes from the natural environment
   (D) plan the arrangement of vegetation and other natural features

10. All of the following are listed as stages in the landscape design process EXCEPT

   (A) thinking about the project's purpose and the funding
   (B) building a fence around the construction site
   (C) making drawings that include old and new features
   (D) preparing lists of building materials and methods

Answers to Exercises 1.2.A through 1.2.B are on pages 634–635.

 EXTENSION

1.   Fact or Opinion? Select a passage from each of the following sources:

      a science textbook   the international page of a newspaper
      a book of essays   the editorial page of a newspaper

Make enough copies of each passage for everyone in your class. In class, identify statements in the passages that are facts and statements that are opinions. Discuss the following questions:

    a. What is a fact?
    b. Is a fact always true for every person?
    c. What is an opinion?
    d. How do writers use facts and opinions?
    e. How can you distinguish a fact from an opinion?

PROGRESS – 1.1 through 1.2

QUIZ 1

Time – 15 minutes

Read the passages and choose the best answer to each question. Answer all questions about a passage on the basis of what is stated or implied in that passage.

EFFECTS OF IONIZING RADIATION

1   Everyone on Earth is continually exposed to small, relatively harmless amounts of ionizing radiation, known as background radiation, from natural sources such as soil and rock. However, other types of ionizing radiation—x–rays, ultraviolet radiation from the sun, and alpha, beta, and gamma radiation emitted by radioactive isotopes—have the potential to harm the human body. Ionizing radiation has enough energy to remove one or more electrons from the atoms it hits to form positively charged ions that can react with and damage living tissue. Most damage occurs in tissues with rapidly dividing cells, such as the bone marrow, where blood cells are made, and the digestive tract, whose lining must be constantly renewed.

2   Exposure to ionizing radiation can damage cells in two ways. The first is genetic damage, which alters genes and chromosomes. This can show up as a genetic defect in children or in later generations. The second type of damage is somatic, which causes victims direct harm in the form of burns, miscarriages, eye cataracts, some types of leukemia, or cancers of the bone, thyroid, breast, skin, and lung. Small doses of ionizing radiation over a long period of time cause less damage than the same total dosage given all at once. Exposure to a large dose of ionizing radiation over a short time can be fatal within a few minutes to a few months later.

1. According to the passage, what is one difference between background radiation and other types of ionizing radiation?

   (A) Background radiation is rare in nature, while other types are not.
   (B) Background radiation is less likely to harm the human body.
   (C) Background radiation cannot form positively charged ions.
   (D) Background radiation causes more damage to the environment.

2. What types of tissues are harmed most by ionizing radiation?

   (A) Tissues with cells that divide quickly
   (B) Tissues on the outside surface of the body
   (C) Tissues exposed to background radiation
   (D) Tissues with a large number of chromosomes

3. All of the following are examples of somatic damage EXCEPT

   (A) genetic defects
   (B) eye cataracts
   (C) radiation burns
   (D) lung cancer

4. Which exposure to ionizing radiation causes the most serious damage to humans?

   (A) Continuous exposure to background radiation in the environment
   (B) Small doses of ionizing radiation over a long period of time
   (C) A single dose of a moderate amount of ionizing radiation
   (D) Exposure to a large amount of ionizing radiation in a short period

THE COYOTE

1   All North American canids have a doglike appearance characterized by a graceful body, long muzzle, erect ears, slender legs, and bushy tail. Most are social animals that travel and hunt in groups or pairs. After years of persecution by humans, the populations of most North American canids, especially wolves and foxes, have decreased greatly. The coyote, however, has thrived alongside humans, increasing in both numbers and range.

2   Its common name comes from *coyotl*, the term used by Mexico's Nahuatl Indians, and its scientific name, *canis latrans*, means "barking dog." The coyote's vocalizations are varied, but the most distinctive are given at dusk, dawn, or during the night and consist of a series of barks followed by a prolonged howl and ending with short, sharp yaps. This call keeps the band alert to the locations of its members. One voice usually prompts others to join in, resulting in the familiar chorus heard at night throughout the West.

3   The best runner among the canids, the coyote is able to leap fourteen feet and cruise normally at 25–30 miles per hour. It is a strong swimmer and does not hesitate to enter water after prey. In feeding, the coyote is an opportunist, eating rabbits, mice, ground squirrels, birds, snakes, insects, many kinds of fruit, and carrion—whatever is available. To catch larger prey, such as deer or antelope, the coyote may team up with one or two others, running in relays to tire prey or waiting in ambush while others chase prey toward it. Often a badger serves as involuntary supplier of smaller prey: while it digs for rodents at one end of their burrow, the coyote waits for any that may emerge from an escape hole at the other end.

4   Predators of the coyote once included the grizzly and black bears, the mountain lion, and the wolf, but their declining populations make them no longer a threat. Man is the major enemy, especially since coyote pelts have become increasingly valuable, yet the coyote population continues to grow, despite efforts at trapping, shooting, and poisoning the animals.

5. According to the passage, the coyote is unlike other North American canids in what way?

   (A) The coyote's body is not graceful.
   (B) The coyote is not hunted by humans.
   (C) The coyote population has not decreased.
   (D) The coyote does not know how to swim.

6. All of the following statements describe the coyote's vocalizations EXCEPT:

   (A) Vocalizations communicate the locations of other coyotes.
   (B) The coyote uses its distinctive call to trick and catch prey.
   (C) A group of coyotes will often bark and howl together.
   (D) The coyote's scientific name reflects its manner of vocalizing.

7. According to the passage, the coyote is an opportunist because it

   (A) knows how to avoid being captured
   (B) likes to team up with other coyotes
   (C) has better luck than other predators
   (D) takes advantage of circumstances

8. Which animal sometimes unknowingly helps the coyote catch food?

   (A) Wolf
   (B) Rodent
   (C) Deer
   (D) Badger

9. According to the passage, the chief predator of the coyote is

    (A) the wolf
    (B) the mountain lion
    (C) the human
    (D) the grizzly bear

10. According to the passage, all of the following statements are true EXCEPT:

    (A) The coyote is a serious threat to human activities.
    (B) The coyote is a skillful and athletic predator.
    (C) The coyote hunts cooperatively with other coyotes.
    (D) The coyote survives despite persecution by humans.

Answers to Reading Quiz 1 are on page 635.

Record your score on the Progress Chart on page 790.

READING

PROGRESS – 1.1 through 1.2

QUIZ 2

Time – 35 minutes

Read the passages and choose the best answer to each question. Answer all questions about a passage on the basis of what is stated or implied in that passage.

RURAL CANADA

1   In the 1880s, over three–fourths of Canada's population lived outside urban centers. One view of rural Canada at that time portrays it as a vast wasteland of isolated farm communities. However, a more accurate view shows that rural Canadians had access to considerable information. The postal service was efficient and inexpensive and connected rural Canadians with the outside world. Many farm families received at least one newspaper through the mail, usually within a day of publication. The daily newspapers of the period were more substantial than those of today, and many reproduced precise accounts of court trials and public events. Rural Canadians read magazines and books and held discussions about them at club meetings.

2   Rural Canadians were also able to get together socially. The local school served other functions besides providing formal education, and school districts were often the only sign of political organization in vast regions of the country. Every community valued its one–room schoolhouse as a meeting place, especially during the winter, when work on the farm was much lighter and people had more time for a variety of social and cultural events. People of all ages got together to sing and play musical instruments, perform skits, and play parlor games.

3   Between 1880 and 1920, there was a growing exodus from farms to the city, mainly because smaller farms could not afford to modernize their technology and were no longer able to support the entire family. However, most Canadians continued to hold rural values, and artists and writers romanticized the family farm. In the novel *Anne of Green Gables* (1908), Lucy Maud Montgomery wrote about a young woman who strove to reconcile the beauty and peace of the rural landscape with the need to leave it in order to fulfill her ambitions. For large numbers of young Canadians, growing up meant leaving the farm to find work in the city.

1. According to the passage, rural Canada in the 1880s was not an isolated wasteland because

   (A) most farms were close to the city
   (B) education was inexpensive
   (C) the rural population was growing
   (D) information was available to farmers

2. The author makes the point that the postal service

   (A) did not reach rural areas until the 1880s
   (B) served an important function in rural Canada
   (C) provided jobs for many rural Canadians
   (D) was expensive to operate in rural areas

3. Many social gatherings took place during the winter because

   (A) there was less work to do on the farm
   (B) there were fewer court trials or political activities
   (C) social gatherings were forbidden at other times
   (D) many holidays occurred in the winter

4. According to the passage, the rural school provided all of the following services EXCEPT

(A) formal education
(B) public health clinics
(C) political organization
(D) social and cultural events

5. What reason is given for large numbers of people leaving the family farm?

(A) There was not enough work on the farm during the winter.
(B) People grew tired of the social isolation of rural life.
(C) Small farms could no longer support the whole family.
(D) Modern farm technology was not available in many areas.

6. Which statement best describes the period from 1880 to 1920?

(A) Literature portrayed a romanticized view of life on the farm.
(B) More Canadians lived in urban areas than in rural areas.
(C) Rural communities began to acquire characteristics of the city.
(D) People gave up their rural values when they moved to the city.

7. The novel *Anne of Green Gables* serves to illustrate

(A) the need for farmers to modernize their technology
(B) the view of rural Canada as an isolated wasteland
(C) the importance of social connections in rural Canada
(D) the experience of many young Canadians of the period

READING

ICE

1   Two conditions are necessary for the formation of ice: the presence of water and temperatures below freezing. Ice in the atmosphere and on the ground can assume various forms, depending on the conditions under which water is converted to its solid state. Ice that forms in the atmosphere can fall to the ground as snow, sleet, or hail. Snow is an assemblage of ice crystals in the form of flakes; sleet is a collection of frozen raindrops, which are actually ice pellets. Hail consists of rounded or jagged lumps of ice, often in layers like the internal structure of an onion. Ice also forms directly on the ground or on bodies of water. In North America, ice forms in late autumn, winter, and early spring. On very large bodies of water, it may not form until late winter because there must be several months of low temperatures to chill such large amounts of water.

2   On puddles and small ponds, ice first freezes in a thin layer with definite crystal structure that becomes less apparent as the ice thickens. On lakes large enough to have waves, such as the Great Lakes, the first ice to form is a thin surface layer of slush, sometimes called grease ice, which eventually grows into small floes of pancake ice. If the lake is small enough or the weather cold enough, the floes may freeze together into a fairly solid sheet of pack ice. Pack ice may cover the entire lake or be restricted to areas near the shore.

3   Because water expands when it freezes, ice is less dense than liquid water and therefore floats rather than sinks in water. As ice floats on the surface of a lake, ocean, or river, it acts as an insulator and is thus important in maintaining the balance of the ecosystem. Without the insulating effect of floating ice sheets, surface water would lose heat more rapidly, and large bodies of water such as the Arctic Ocean and Hudson Bay might freeze up completely.

8. What condition is necessary for water in the atmosphere to change to its solid state?

   (A) A solid cloud cover that absorbs the sun's heat
   (B) A weather forecast for snow, sleet, or hail
   (C) A position directly above a large body of water
   (D) A temperature below water's freezing point

9. In paragraph 1, the author makes the point that

   (A) ice can take a variety of forms
   (B) sleet and snow differ from ice
   (C) in some years ice never forms at all
   (D) ice rarely forms on the ground in cities

10. Ice that forms in the atmosphere in the form of layered lumps is known as

   (A) snow
   (B) pack ice
   (C) hail
   (D) grease ice

11. All of the following are forms of ice that form on bodies of water EXCEPT

   (A) sleet
   (B) slush
   (C) pancake ice
   (D) pack ice

12. Why does ice form later on very large bodies of water?

   (A) Most large bodies of water are located at low elevations or low latitudes.
   (B) It takes several months of cold temperatures to cool a large body of water.
   (C) Large bodies of water are fed by underground springs of warmer water.
   (D) The waves on large bodies of water prevent the water from freezing quickly.

13. When ice starts to form on small bodies of water,

 (A) it takes the shape of small floes
 (B) it freezes more quickly in the center
 (C) its surface feels greasy to the touch
 (D) its crystal structure can be seen

14. Which statement is true about pancake ice?

 (A) It forms on puddles and small ponds.
 (B) It falls from the atmosphere to the ground.
 (C) It may become a sheet of pack ice.
 (D) It is the least dense form of ice.

15. Which of the following is an effect of the density of ice?

 (A) Ice that forms on large lakes has a greasy consistency.
 (B) Each ice crystal is unique, but all are six–sided structures.
 (C) Pack ice is restricted to areas near the shore of a lake.
 (D) Floating ice sheets prevent bodies of water from losing heat.

16. The passage mentions all of the following characteristics of ice EXCEPT

 (A) its appearance
 (B) where it forms
 (C) the rate at which it melts
 (D) its effect on the ecosystem

READING

THE ROLE OF GOVERNMENT IN THE ECONOMY

1   Because most people do not volunteer to pay taxes or police their own financial affairs, governments cannot influence economic activity simply by asking people to pollute less, to give money to the poor, or to be innovative. To accomplish these things, governments have to pass laws. Since the early twentieth century, governments of countries with advanced industrial or service economies have been playing an increasing role in economics. This can be seen in the growth of government taxation and spending, in the growing share of national income devoted to income–support payments, and by the enormous increase in the control of economic activity.

2   The large–scale organization of business, as seen in mass production and distribution, has led to the formation of large–scale organizations—corporations, labor unions, and government structures—that have grown in importance in the past several decades. Their presence and growing dominance have shifted capitalist economies away from traditional market forces and toward government administration of markets.

3   In the United States, government provides a framework of laws for the conduct of economic activity that attempt to make it serve the public interest. For instance, the individual states and the federal government have passed laws to shield investors against fraud. These laws specify what information has to be disclosed to prospective investors when shares of stocks or bonds are offered for sale. Another important area of law concerns the labor force, such as regulation of work hours, minimum wages, health and safety conditions, child labor, and the rights of workers to form unions, to strike, to demonstrate peacefully, and to bargain collectively through representatives of their own choosing.

4   In other nations, the ways in which governments intervene in their economies have varied; however, governments everywhere deal with essentially the same issues and participate in economic activity. Even governments that are reluctant to regulate commerce directly have undertaken large–scale projects such as hydroelectric and nuclear energy developments, transportation networks, or expansion of health, education, and other public services.

17. According to the passage, why do governments intervene in economic activity?

    (A) People do not willingly regulate their own business affairs.
    (B) Governments understand the economy better than anyone else does.
    (C) Businesses pay governments to participate in economic activity.
    (D) The economy would fail without the help of government.

18. According to the passage, governments intervene in economic activity mainly by

    (A) asking people not to pollute
    (B) requiring innovation
    (C) passing laws
    (D) producing goods and services

19. According to the passage, how has the growth of large–scale organizations such as corporations and labor unions affected capitalist economies?

    (A) It has forced governments to pass laws protecting traditional markets.
    (B) It has destroyed capitalism and replaced it with government ownership.
    (C) It has led to the increasing role of government in economic activity.
    (D) It has caused unfair competition between large and small businesses.

20. In paragraph 3, the author mentions two areas of law that aim to

    (A) serve borrowing and lending institutions
    (B) restrict the size of corporations and labor unions
    (C) regulate domestic and international trade
    (D) protect the rights of investors and workers

21. In paragraph 3, the author mentions laws to shield investors against fraud as an example of

    (A) laws that organize business
    (B) laws that serve the public interest
    (C) laws that protect the labor force
    (D) laws that set the price of stocks

22. All of the following are given as issues concerning the labor force EXCEPT

    (A) stock ownership
    (B) health and safety
    (C) hours of work
    (D) the right to strike

23. In paragraph 4, the author states that all governments

    (A) use the same economic strategies
    (B) confront similar economic issues
    (C) have laws regulating labor unions
    (D) dislike intervening in markets

24. What point does the author make about governments that do not want to regulate business directly?

    (A) They cannot compete effectively with government–controlled economies.
    (B) They have capitalist economies based on traditional market forces.
    (C) They have no laws for protecting the environment and public health.
    (D) They participate in the economy through public projects and services.

25. According to the passage, all of the following are examples of government participation in economic activity EXCEPT

    (A) taxation and spending
    (B) small business ownership
    (C) income–support payments
    (D) transportation networks

READING

Answers to Reading Quiz 2 are on pages 635–636.

Record your score on the Progress Chart on page 790.

1.3 Understanding Vocabulary in Context

FOCUS

Read the following passage and answer the question:

> A 1625 map of North America drawn by Henry Briggs is one of the most notorious
> maps in the history of North American cartography. It was the first printed map to show
> California as an island. Briggs based his map on information from the 1602 Spanish
> expedition to the West Coast in search of a safe haven for the Spanish colonial fleets.
> Briggs also wrote a treatise based on the Spanish account, in which he described
> California as a "goodly islande." The map and treatise initiated one of the most famous
> and persistent of all cartographical misconceptions, and California was still being depicted
> as an island in atlases issued in Amsterdam as late as the 1790s.
>
> What is cartography ?
>
> ◯ geography
> ◯ exploration
> ◯ printing
> ◯ mapmaking

Look at the word cartography in the passage. What other words in the passage help you understand the
meaning of this word? Some possible clues are *map*, *drawn*, *history of*, and *printed map*. These clues will
help you see that the correct answer is *mapmaking*.

Now answer another question:

> The word depicted in the passage is closest in meaning to
>
> ◯ promised
> ◯ drawn
> ◯ developed
> ◯ sought

Some clues to the meaning of depicted are:

> …the first printed map to show California as an island.
> …California was still being depicted as an island in atlases….

In the passage, *depicted* means shown or drawn. Therefore, the correct answer is *drawn*.

 STUDY

1. Vocabulary in Context

The *context* is the setting—the sentence and paragraph—in which a word or phrase appears. The meaning of a word or phrase *in context* is its meaning in the sentence and paragraph in which it is used. A single English word can have many different meanings. Its precise meaning always depends on the context.

TOEFL questions about vocabulary in context look like this:

> The word/phrase _____ in the passage is closest in meaning to _____.
> The word/phrase _____ in the passage means _____.
> What is _____?
> In stating that _____ in paragraph _____, the author means that _____.

2. Context Clues

To understand the meaning of a word in context, you can use different types of *context clues*: your knowledge of structure, punctuation, and the meaning of other words in the same sentence or paragraph. In the reading that you do in the real world, there may not be context clues to help you. However, sometimes you can guess the meaning of an unfamiliar word by using your overall understanding of the ideas in a passage as well as your common sense.

Structural clues are one type of context clue. Structural clues are words, phrases, or sentence structures that point to the relationships among the parts of a sentence. These clues help you understand the meaning of an unfamiliar word by showing how the word relates to other parts of the sentence.

3. Clue: *Be*

Example

A supernova *is* a massive star that undergoes a gravitational collapse, then a gigantic explosion, blasting away the outer layers into space.

Explanation

The meaning of *supernova* is given by the information after the verb *is*. A *supernova* is a massive star that collapses and then explodes.

Example

Sometimes one goal or another has to come first; deciding which goals are most important *is* setting priorities.

Explanation

The meaning of *priorities* is given by the information before the verb *is*. *Priorities* are the most important goals.

4. Clue: *Or*

Example

The inclination *or* tilt of the earth's axis with respect to the sun determines the seasons.

Explanation

The meaning of *inclination* is given by the information after the conjunction *or*. *Inclination* means tilt.

Example

A skyscraper, *or* building more than twenty stories high, is built on a foundation of concrete supported by piles driven into the ground.

Explanation

The meaning of *skyscraper* is given by the information after the conjunction *or*. A *skyscraper* is a building more than twenty stories high.

5. Clue: Appositive

Example

Thermal power stations are designed to pass as much energy as possible from the fuel to the turbines, *machines whose blades are turned by the movement of the steam.*

Explanation

The meaning of *turbines* is given by the appositive, the noun phrase after the comma. *Turbines* are machines with blades that are turned by the movement of the steam.

6. Clue: Adjective Clause or Phrase

Example

The sun crosses the equator twice a year at the equinoxes, *when day and night are nearly equal in length.*

Explanation

The meaning of *equinoxes* is given in the adjective clause beginning with *when*. *Equinoxes* are times when day and night are nearly equal in length.

Prescribed fire, *ignited by forest rangers under controlled conditions to restore balance in the forest,* is a safe way to mimic natural fire conditions.

The meaning of *prescribed* is given in the adjective phrase beginning with *ignited*. *Prescribed* describes something done under controlled conditions to restore balance.

The radiating surface of the sun is called the photosphere, and just above it is the chromosphere, *which is visible to the naked eye only during total solar eclipses, appearing then to be a pinkish–violet layer.*

The meaning of *chromosphere* is given in the adjective clause beginning with *which* and in the adjective phrase beginning with *appearing*. The *chromosphere* is a pinkish–violet layer that is visible to the naked eye only during total solar eclipses.

7. Clue: List or Series

Example

Because of their similar teeth, seals and walruses are believed to have evolved from the same ancestral groups as the *weasels, badgers, and other* mustelids.

Explanation

Items in a list or series are related in some way. The meaning of *mustelids* is suggested by the other words in the list: *weasels, badgers, and other*. *Mustelids* are animals like weasels and badgers.

If someone is said to have "a chip on his shoulder," he is angry, pugnacious, sullen, and looking for trouble.

The meaning of *pugnacious* is suggested by the other words and phrases in the list: *angry, sullen, and looking for trouble*. *Pugnacious* means inclined to fight.

READING

8. Clue: Example

for example	for instance	like	such as

Example

Several personnel managers complain about the lag of business colleges in eliminating obsolete skills. *For instance*, shorthand is still taught in many secretarial programs although it is rarely used.

Explanation

The meaning of *obsolete* is given by the information after *for instance*. Shorthand is an example of an obsolete skill. *Obsolete* describes something that is no longer useful.

Intangible assets, *such as* a company's recognized name and its goodwill, are neither physical nor financial in nature.

The meaning of *intangible assets* is given by the information after *such as*. A company's name and goodwill are examples of intangible assets. More information is provided after the verb *are*. *Intangible assets* are not physical and not financial.

9. Clue: Contrast

alternatively	different	instead	rather
but	however	nevertheless	unlike
conversely	in contrast	on the contrary	whereas
despite	in spite of	on the other hand	while

Example

Twilight rays are nearly parallel, *but* because of the observer's perspective, they appear to diverge.

Explanation

The meaning of *diverge* is given by *but* and *parallel*. From this, you know that *diverge* is different from *parallel*.

Songbirds are early risers and remain active throughout the day, except during the warmest hours in summer. Owls, *on the other hand*, are primarily nocturnal.

The meaning of *nocturnal* is given by *on the other hand* and *active throughout the day*. From this, you know that *nocturnal* is different from active throughout the day. *Nocturnal* means active at night.

Unlike sun pillars, which are caused by reflection of light, arcs and haloes are caused by refraction of light through ice crystals.

The meaning of *refraction* is given by *unlike* and *reflection*. From this, you know that *refraction* is different from *reflection*.

10. Punctuation Clues

Punctuation clues are another type of context clue that can help you understand the meaning of unfamiliar words. Punctuation marks often show that one word identifies, renames, or defines another word.

comma	,	parentheses	( )
dash	—	quotation marks	" "
colon	:	brackets	[ ]

Example

Crepuscular rays—alternating bright and dark rays in the sky—appear to radiate from the sun.

Virtually every community college now offers contract education: short–term programs, ranging from a few hours to several days, for employees of specific companies, which pay a share of the cost.

Folate supplementation before and during pregnancy can prevent certain defects of the brain and spine, such as anacephaly (absence of a major part of the brain).

Explanation

The meaning of *crepuscular rays* is given by the information between the dashes. *Crepuscular rays* are alternating bright and dark rays in the sky.

The meaning of *contract education* is given by the information after the colon. *Contract education* is short–term programs for employees of specific companies.

The meaning of *anacephaly* is given by the information inside the parentheses. *Anacephaly* is absence of a major part of the brain.

11. Key Words

Key words in a sentence or passage can be context clues. Use the meanings of key words and your understanding of the sentence or paragraph as a whole to help you guess the meaning of an unfamiliar word.

Example

Accessories add interest to a room. They can accent or highlight an area and give a room beauty and personality.

Light output, measured in lumens, depends on the amount of electricity used by a bulb.

Explanation

The meaning of *accessories* is suggested by other words in the sentence: *interest, accent, highlight, beauty,* and *personality.* From these key words, you know that *accessories* are things that improve a room.

The meaning of *lumens* is suggested by other words in the sentence: *light output, measured,* and *electricity.* From these key words, you know that a *lumen* is a unit of measurement of light output.

12. Word Parts

Word parts can help you understand the meaning of unfamiliar words. Many English words are made up of parts of older English, Greek, and Latin words. If you know the meanings of word parts, you will have a general understanding of some unfamiliar words, especially in context.

There are three types of word parts: *prefixes*, *stems*, and *suffixes*. A **prefix** is a word beginning. A prefix affects the meaning of a word. A **stem** is the basic, underlying form of a word. Groups of words that have the same stem are related in meaning. A **suffix** is a word ending. A suffix affects the function of a word, for example, making it a noun or a verb.

Prefix	Stem	Suffix	Word
con	feder	ate	confederate
intro	duc	tion	introduction
syn	chron	ize	synchronize

Study the following lists of common prefixes and stems. Can you add any more examples?

Prefix	Meaning	Examples
ab–	away, from	abolish, abnormal, abstract
ad–	to, toward	advance, admire, adhere
anti–	against	antiwar, antipathy, antibiotic
auto–	self, same	autobiography, autoimmune
bene–, bon–	good	benefit, benevolence, bonus
bi–	two	bilingual, binary, bilateral
co–, com–, con–	with, together	cooperate, compose, convene
contra–, counter–	against	contrary, contradict, counteract
de–	down, from, away	descend, derive, dehydration
dia–	through, across	dialogue, diagram, diagonal
dis–	not, take away	disease, disability, disappear
e–, ec–, ex–	out	emigrate, ecstasy, export
fore–	front, before	forehead, forecast, foreshadow
in–, im–	in, into, on	invade, immigrate, impose
in–, im–, il–, ir–	not	inequality, illegal, irrational
inter–	between	international, intersect
intro–, intra–	within, inside	introspection, intravenous
micro–	small	microchip, microscope
mis–	bad, wrong	misprint, misunderstand
mono–	one	monopoly, monotonous
multi–	many	multiply, multinational
ob–, op–, of–	against, facing	object, opposite, offend
out–	beyond	outlive, outnumber, outspend
over–	too much	overbearing, overcompensate
para–	beside, alongside	parallel, paraphrase, paragraph
post–	after	postwar, posterior, postpone
pre–	before	prepare, prevent, preview
pro–	forward	process, promote, produce
re–	back, again	return, replay, reunite
se–	apart, aside	separate, secede, segregate

Prefix	Meaning	Examples
sub–, sup–, sus–	below, under, after	subsidize, support, suspend
syn–, sym–, syl–	with, together	synthesis, symbol, syllabus
tele–	far, distant	telephone, telepathy
trans–	across	translate, transmit, transaction
un–	not	unable, unreal, unreasonable
uni–	one	unit, uniform, universe

Stem	Meaning	Examples
–bio–	life	biology, biodiversity, antibiotic
–cap–, –capit–	head, chief	captain, capital, decapitate
–cede–, –ceed–, –cess–	go, move	concede, proceed, success
–chron–	time	chronicle, anachronism
–cred–	believe	credit, incredible, creed
–dic–, –dict–	say, speak	dictator, predict, jurisdiction
–dorm–	sleep	dormant, dormitory
–duc–, –duct–	lead	duct, introduce, reduction
–fact–, –fect–	make, do	factory, manufacture, effect
–fid–, –feder–	trust, faith	confidence, federation
–flect–, –flex–	bend	deflect, reflect, flexible
–geo–	earth	geology, geothermal
–graph–, –gram–	write, draw	graphic, photography, grammar
–hydro–	water	hydroelectric, dehydrate
–log–, –ology–	word, study	logic, catalog, psychology
–luc–, –lum–, –lus–	light	translucent, illuminate, luster
–man–, –manu–	hand	manual, manager, manuscript
–mit–, –miss–	send	transmit, omit, mission
–mob–, –mot–, –mov–	move	automobile, emotion, remove
–mort–	death	mortality, immortal, mortify
–nov–	new	novice, innovation, renovate
–phon–, –son–	sound	microphone, supersonic
–polis–, –polit–	city	metropolis, politics, police
–pon–, –pos–	put, place	postpone, position, deposit
–port–	carry	portable, reporter, import
–rect–	right, straight	correct, rectangle, rectify
–scrib–, –script–	write	describe, script, inscription
–secut–, –sequ–	follow	consecutive, sequence
–spec–, –spect–	look at, see, observe	spectator, spectacle, inspector
–struct–	build	structure, instruct, destructive
–therm–	heat	thermometer, hypothermia
–ven–, –vene–	come	convention, intervene
–ver–	true	verify, conversation, universal
–vid–, –vis–	see	video, visit, invisible
–viv–, –vita–	alive, life	vivid, revive, vitamin
–voc–, –vok–	call, voice	vocal, vocabulary, revoke

13. Sample Questions

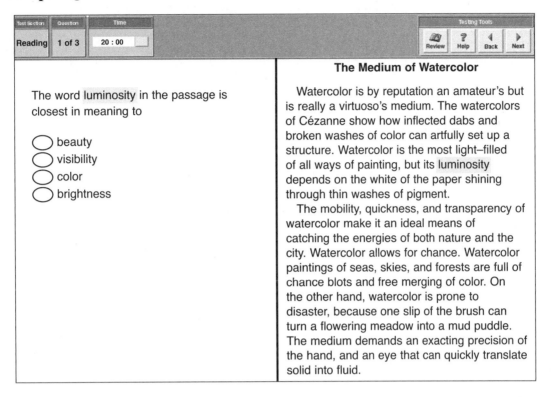

The correct answer is *brightness*. Some context clues in the sentence are *light–filled* and *shining*. Also, *luminosity* contains the stem *–lum–*, which means *light*.

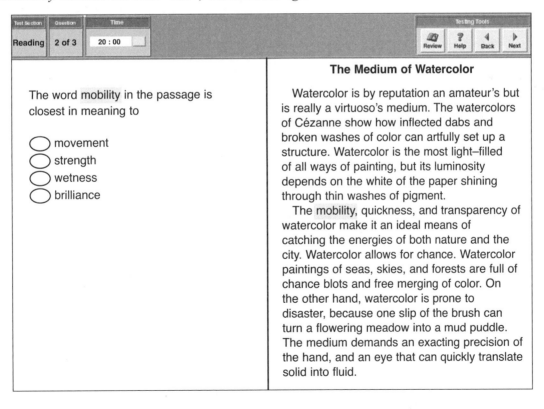

The correct answer is *movement*. Some context clues in the sentence are *quickness* and *energies of both nature and the city*. Also, *mobility* contains the stem *–mob–*, which means *move*.

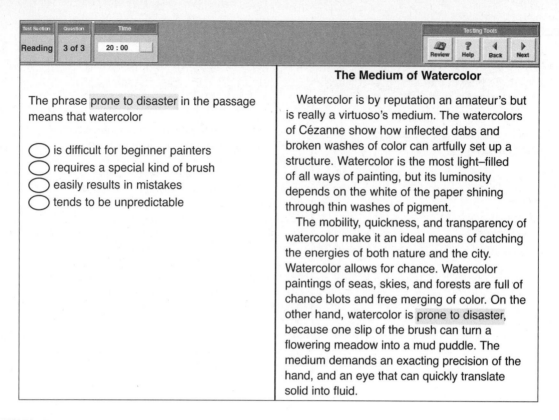

	The Medium of Watercolor
The phrase prone to disaster in the passage means that watercolor ◯ is difficult for beginner painters ◯ requires a special kind of brush ◯ easily results in mistakes ◯ tends to be unpredictable	Watercolor is by reputation an amateur's but is really a virtuoso's medium. The watercolors of Cézanne show how inflected dabs and broken washes of color can artfully set up a structure. Watercolor is the most light–filled of all ways of painting, but its luminosity depends on the white of the paper shining through thin washes of pigment. The mobility, quickness, and transparency of watercolor make it an ideal means of catching the energies of both nature and the city. Watercolor allows for chance. Watercolor paintings of seas, skies, and forests are full of chance blots and free merging of color. On the other hand, watercolor is prone to disaster, because one slip of the brush can turn a flowering meadow into a mud puddle. The medium demands an exacting precision of the hand, and an eye that can quickly translate solid into fluid.

The correct answer is *easily results in mistakes*. Some context clues in the passage are *chance blots; on the other hand*; and *one slip of the brush can turn a flowering meadow into a mud puddle*.

 PRACTICE

Exercise 1.3.A

Read the passages and choose the best answer to each question.

QUESTION 1

   Although the sensory receptors and brain pathways for taste and smell are independent, the two senses do interact. A great deal of what we consider taste is actually smell. If the sense of smell is obstructed, as by a head cold, the perception of taste is sharply reduced.

1. The word obstructed in the passage is closest in meaning to

   Ⓐ involved
   Ⓑ increased
   Ⓒ developed
   Ⓓ blocked

QUESTION 2

A water molecule consists of two hydrogen atoms attached to a single, larger oxygen atom. The angle between the two hydrogen atoms is 120 degrees—the same angle as the angles of a hexagon—which accounts for the characteristic six–sided structure of ice crystals.

2. The phrase accounts for in the passage means

   (A) explains
   (B) decreases
   (C) connects
   (D) summarizes

QUESTION 3

Reports on an organization's projects may fill several major functions at the same time. A report can be used to educate and gain support from key people and groups, to facilitate and inform decision–making about current and future projects, and to provide documentation for the organization's records. The employees who are responsible for preparing the report must have a clear understanding of how the report will be used before they compile it.

3. The word compile in the passage is closest in meaning to

   (A) agree with
   (B) put together
   (C) ask about
   (D) look forward to

QUESTION 4

The evolutionary origins of music are wrapped in mystery. There is ample concrete evidence of musical instruments dating back to the Stone Age and much presumptive evidence about the role of music in organizing work groups, hunting parties, and religious rites. Many scholars suspect that musical and linguistic expression had common origins but then split off from one another several hundred thousand years ago.

4. The phrase split off in the passage is closest in meaning to

   (A) separated
   (B) borrowed
   (C) evolved
   (D) learned

READING

QUESTIONS 5–6

Modern tourism began with the transition from a rural to an industrial society, the rise of the automobile, and the expansion of road and highway systems. Before the Second World War, travel for pleasure was limited to the wealthy, but since then, improved standards of living and the availability of transportation have allowed more people to indulge. In the 1960s, improvements in aircraft technology and the development of commercial jet airlines enabled fast international travel. The tourism industry exploded. Today, airports in nearly every country can accommodate jumbo jets full of tourists seeking exotic destinations.

5. The word indulge in the passage is closest in meaning to

    Ⓐ participate
    Ⓑ migrate
    Ⓒ survive
    Ⓓ change

6. The word exploded in the passage is closest in meaning to

    Ⓐ was competitive
    Ⓑ expanded rapidly
    Ⓒ was expensive
    Ⓓ became dangerous

QUESTIONS 7–8

At the college level, the best preparation for management is a liberal arts education. Individuals who will guide the future of their companies must broaden and deepen their understanding of the world. This means covering the whole range of the liberal arts, from science to literature to mathematics to history. Today's executives must have some grasp of economic realities and the political process, as well as some comprehension of the basic framework within which scientific and technological changes take place. They must gain an understanding of human nature, including its negative aspects, such as the sources of human conflict and the pitfalls of power.

7. The word grasp in the passage is closest in meaning to

    Ⓐ understanding
    Ⓑ communication
    Ⓒ criticism
    Ⓓ prediction

8. The word pitfalls in the passage is closest in meaning to

    Ⓐ benefits
    Ⓑ stages
    Ⓒ causes
    Ⓓ hazards

QUESTIONS 9–10

It is a popular notion that autumn leaves are tinted by freezing temperatures. In truth, the foliage is dulled, not colored, by frost. Red leaves such as maples are brightest when sunny days are followed by cool—but not freezing—nights. Under such conditions, sun–made sugars are trapped in the leaves, where they form the red pigment anthocyanin. Leaves that appear yellow in autumn are no less yellow in spring and summer. However, in spring and summer the yellow pigments—carotenoid and xanthophyll—are masked by the green pigment chlorophyll, which breaks down with the diminishing sunlight of fall.

9. The word foliage in the passage means

   Ⓐ season of year
   Ⓑ type of chemical
   Ⓒ mass of leaves
   Ⓓ species of tree

10. The word masked in the passage is closest in meaning to

   Ⓐ created
   Ⓑ colored
   Ⓒ captured
   Ⓓ concealed

Exercise 1.3.B

Read the passages and choose the best answer to each question.

QUESTIONS 1–2

1   Earthshine—the faint light that allows us to see the dark side of the moon when the moon is a thin crescent—is sunlight reflected from the earth to the moon, then back again. Earthshine is variable because the earth's reflectivity changes as large cloud masses come and go. The moon with its earthshine acts as a crude weather satellite by reporting, in a very simple way, the general state of terrestrial cloudiness. Because the amount of light reflected from the earth depends on the amount of cloud cover, the brightness of the dark side of the moon varies.

2   As the phase of the moon progresses beyond a thin crescent, earthshine fades in a day or two. This is because the amount of sunlit earth available to make earthshine diminishes as the moon orbits the earth. Also, there is the increasing glare of the moon's growing crescent, which causes a loss of visibility by irradiation.

1. The word crude in paragraph 1 is closest in meaning to

   Ⓐ false
   Ⓑ stormy
   Ⓒ random
   Ⓓ simple

2. The word glare in paragraph 2 is closest in meaning to

   Ⓐ cloud cover
   Ⓑ bright light
   Ⓒ wave frequency
   Ⓓ dark sphere

QUESTIONS 3–4

1   *Cool* has withstood the fleeting nature of most slang. As a modifier, as a noun, and as a verb, *cool* has been around a long time. Shakespeare used *cool* as a verb, and the word later evolved into other parts of speech. It has been used as an adjective since 1728 to describe large sums of money, as in "worth a cool ten million."

2   *Cool*, meaning "excellent" or "first-rate," was popularized in jazz circles, and jazz musicians and jazz lovers still refer to great works as "cool." As long as Miles Davis's classic 1957 album, *Birth of the Cool*, remains one of the best-selling jazz recordings of all time, *cool* will stay cool—it will carry the same weight as it did more than 50 years ago. One reason for the endurance of *cool* is that its meaning continues to evolve. While it meant "wow!" two decades ago, today it is more often used to mean, "That's OK with me," as in "I'm cool with that."

3. The word fleeting in paragraph 1 is closest in meaning to

    (A) temporary
    (B) youthful
    (C) emotional
    (D) popular

4. The phrase carry the same weight in paragraph 2 means

    (A) refer to great music
    (B) refer to a large sum of money
    (C) have the same importance
    (D) have the same meaning

QUESTIONS 5–6

1   The dominant feature on the map of Canada is the two-million-square-mile mass of ancient rock known as the Canadian Shield. The shield sweeps in a great arc around Hudson Bay from far northwest to far northeast, touching the Great Lakes on the south and extending eastward deep into Quebec. The rock of the shield consists mainly of granite and gneiss formed nearly four billion years ago. During the ice ages, huge glaciers advanced and retreated over the region, scouring the surface, removing most of the existing soil, and hollowing out countless lakes.

2   Clay soils exist in a few areas on the shield's southern edge, but attempts to bring them into agricultural use have been largely unsuccessful. However, the region's mineral wealth has sustained both temporary and permanent settlements during the past century, and more recently, some of its vast potential for hydroelectric power has been tapped.

5. The word scouring in paragraph 1 is closest in meaning to

    (A) freezing
    (B) uplifting
    (C) improving
    (D) scraping

6. The word sustained in paragraph 2 is closest in meaning to

    (A) prevented
    (B) protected
    (C) supported
    (D) ruined

Questions 7–10

1   A growing number of companies are finding that small–group discussions allow them to develop healthier ways to think about work. People at all levels of the corporate structure are starting groups that meet weekly or monthly to talk over ways to make workplaces more ethical and just.

2   Several factors must be present for small–group discussions to be successful. First, it is important to put together the right group. Groups work best when they consist of people who have similar duties, responsibilities, and missions. This does not mean, however, that everyone in the group must think in lockstep.

3   All participants should agree on the group's purpose. Finding the right subject matter is essential. There are several ways to fuel the discussion: by using the company's mission statement, by finding readings on work and ethics by experts in the topic, or by analyzing specific workplace incidents that have affected the company or others like it.

4   Finally, the dynamics of the group should be balanced, and the discussion leader must not be allowed to overwhelm the conversation or the agenda. Groups work best when the same person is not always in charge. It is better to rotate the leadership for each meeting and let that leader choose the material for discussion.

7. The phrase talk over in paragraph 1 is closest in meaning to

    Ⓐ demand
    Ⓑ overlook
    Ⓒ explore
    Ⓓ remove

8. The phrase in lockstep in paragraph 2 is closest in meaning to

    Ⓐ alike
    Ⓑ critically
    Ⓒ aloud
    Ⓓ quickly

9. The word fuel in paragraph 3 is closest in meaning to

    Ⓐ categorize
    Ⓑ stimulate
    Ⓒ sequence
    Ⓓ conclude

10. The word overwhelm in paragraph 4 is closest in meaning to

    Ⓐ dominate
    Ⓑ plan
    Ⓒ summarize
    Ⓓ contradict

Exercise 1.3.C

Read the passages and choose the best answer to each question.

QUESTIONS 1–4

1 There is growing evidence that urbanization has a sharp impact on climate, causing changes that can wreak havoc on precipitation patterns that supply the precious resource of water. The heavy amounts of heat and pollution rising from cities both delay and stimulate the fall of precipitation, depriving some areas of rain while drenching others.

2 Cities are on average one to ten degrees warmer than surrounding undeveloped areas. Cities also produce large amounts of pollutants called aerosols, gaseous suspensions of dust particles or byproducts from the burning of fossil fuels. Both heat and aerosols change the dynamics of clouds. When hoisted up in the sky, the microscopic particles act as multiple surfaces on which the moisture in clouds can condense as tiny droplets. This can prevent or delay the formation of larger raindrops that fall more easily from the sky, or it can cause the rain to fall in another location.

3 In California, pollution blows eastward and causes a precipitation shortage of around one trillion gallons a year across the Sierra Nevada mountain range. By contrast, in very humid cities, such as Houston, heat and pollutants seem to invigorate summer storm activity by allowing clouds to build higher and fuller before releasing torrential rains.

1. The phrase wreak havoc on in paragraph 1 means

   (A) disrupt
   (B) omit
   (C) strengthen
   (D) separate

2. The word drenching in paragraph 1 is closest in meaning to

   (A) almost missing
   (B) severely damaging
   (C) thoroughly wetting
   (D) entirely avoiding

3. The word hoisted in paragraph 2 is closest in meaning to

   (A) lifted
   (B) grouped
   (C) returned
   (D) pointed

4. The word torrential in paragraph 3 is closest in meaning to

   (A) unexpected
   (B) warm
   (C) infrequent
   (D) heavy

QUESTIONS 5–10

1 So much sentimentality is attached to the rose in popular culture that it is difficult to separate the original mythological and folkloric beliefs from the emotional excess that surrounds the flower. Yet if we look into the beliefs, we find that the rose is much more than the mere symbol of romantic love invoked by every minor poet and painter.

2 One of the rose's most common associations in folklore is with death. The Romans often decked the tombs of the dead with roses; in fact, Roman wills frequently specified that roses were to be planted on the grave. To this day, in Switzerland, cemeteries are known as rose gardens. The Saxons equated the rose with life, and they believed that when a child died, the figure of death could be seen plucking a rose outside the house.

3 The rose has a long association with female beauty. Shakespeare mentions the rose more frequently than any other flower, often using it as a token of all that is lovely and good. For the Arabs, on the other hand, the rose was a symbol not of feminine but of masculine beauty.

4 Later the rose became a sign of secrecy and silence. The expression sub rosa, "under the rose," is traced to a Roman belief. During the sixteenth and seventeenth centuries, it was common practice to carve or paint roses on the ceilings of council chambers to emphasize the intention of secrecy.

READING

5. The word sentimentality in paragraph 1 is closest in meaning to

   (A) confusion
   (B) beauty
   (C) feeling
   (D) popularity

6. The word invoked in paragraph 1 is closest in meaning to

   (A) avoided
   (B) called on
   (C) criticized
   (D) taken away

7. The word decked in paragraph 2 is closest in meaning to

   (A) painted
   (B) separated
   (C) decorated
   (D) disguised

8. The word plucking in paragraph 2 is closest in meaning to

   (A) growing
   (B) smelling
   (C) wearing
   (D) picking

9. The word token in paragraph 3 is closest in meaning to

   (A) symbol
   (B) proof
   (C) justification
   (D) contradiction

10. The phrase sub rosa in paragraph 4 means

   (A) romantically
   (B) intentionally
   (C) secretly
   (D) commonly

Exercise 1.3.D

Read the passages and choose the best answer to each question.

QUESTIONS 1–5

1   In the nineteenth century, Americans were becoming more familiar with European homes and luxuries. When "period" furniture became popular, American furniture factories attempted to duplicate various styles of French and English furniture of the seventeenth and eighteenth centuries. At the same time, designers in England were attempting a return to handicrafts as a means of self–expression. William Morris and other leaders of the English Arts and Crafts movement created home furnishings that celebrated the individuality of the designer.

2   In the United States, a similar movement soon followed. The American Arts and Crafts—or Craftsman—movement was based not only on individualism but also on a return to simplicity and practicality. Like the Arts and Crafts furniture in England, the Craftsman furniture in America represented a revolt from mass–produced furniture. Makers of Craftsman furniture sought inspiration in human necessity, basing their furniture on a respect for the sturdy and primitive forms that were meant for usefulness alone.

3   Gustav Stickley, pioneer of the Craftsman movement, believed that average working people wanted furniture that was comfortable to live with and would also be a good investment of money. Stickley felt that any American style in furniture would have to possess the essential qualities of durability, comfort, and convenience. Craftsman furniture was plain and unornamented—made to look as if the common man could build it himself in his own workshop. Locally obtained hardwoods and simple, straight lines were the hallmarks of its construction. The severity of the style departed greatly from the ornate and pretentious factory–made "period" furniture that had dominated in homes up till then.

1. What is "period" furniture?

   (A) Reproductions of earlier styles
   (B) Furniture that is made by hand
   (C) The last pieces made in any style
   (D) Nineteenth–century designer furniture

2. The word revolt in paragraph 2 is closest in meaning to

   (A) style
   (B) benefit
   (C) break
   (D) inspiration

3. The word primitive in paragraph 2 is closest in meaning to

   (A) special
   (B) beautiful
   (C) innovative
   (D) simple

4. The word hallmarks in paragraph 3 is closest in meaning to

   (A) features
   (B) limits
   (C) commands
   (D) plans

5. The word ornate in paragraph 3 is closest in meaning to

   (A) ugly
   (B) complex
   (C) practical
   (D) expensive

QUESTIONS 6–10

1   Zora Neale Hurston devoted five years to the collection of rural black folklore in Haiti, the West Indies, and the American South. Her ear for the rhythms of speech and her daring in seeking initiation into many voodoo cults resulted in ethnographic studies such as *Mules and Men*, which conveyed the vitality, movement, and color of rural black culture.

2   Hurston continued her fieldwork in the Caribbean but eventually followed her most cherished calling, that of fiction writer. *Their Eyes Were Watching God* (1937), a novel about a black woman finding happiness in simple farm life, is now her most famous book, although for thirty years after publication, it was largely unknown, unread, and dismissed by the male literary establishment. In this novel, Hurston gives us a heroic female character, Janie Crawford, who portrays freedom, autonomy, and self–realization, while also being a romantic figure attached to a man. This novel reveals an African American writer struggling with the problem of the hero as woman and the difficulties of giving a woman character such courage and power in 1937.

3   From the beginning of her career, Hurston was criticized for not writing fiction in the protest tradition. Her conservative views on race relations put her out of touch with the temper of the times. She argued that integration would undermine the strength and values of African American culture. Hurston died in poverty and obscurity in 1960, and it was only afterward that later generations of black and white Americans were to rediscover and revere her celebrations of black culture.

6. The word vitality in paragraph 1 is closest in meaning to

   (A) politics
   (B) energy
   (C) disadvantages
   (D) humor

7. The word calling in paragraph 2 is closest in meaning to

   (A) profession
   (B) example
   (C) character
   (D) description

8. The word autonomy in paragraph 2 is closest in meaning to

   (A) independence
   (B) selfishness
   (C) evil
   (D) romance

9. The phrase out of touch in paragraph 3 means that

   (A) other writers were not interested in race relations
   (B) Hurston ignored the topic of race relations
   (C) Hurston's opinions differed from those of most other people
   (D) there was no contact between Hurston and other writers

10. The word revere in paragraph 3 is closest in meaning to

   (A) imitate
   (B) be amused by
   (C) disagree with
   (D) honor

Answers to Exercises 1.3.A through 1.3.D are on pages 636–638.

EXTENSION

1. With your teacher and classmates, discuss ways to improve your English vocabulary. Answer these questions:

     a. What is the best way to acquire new English vocabulary?
     b. How did you learn in the past?
     c. What method or methods work best for you now?

    (Possible answers: listen to lectures; watch television and movies; have an English–speaking roommate; write down three new words every day; memorize word lists; translate words into your native language; read an English newspaper; read various types of materials; read textbooks in your major field of study.)

    On the board, make a list of the various ways to learn new words. Then, decide which three ways work best for you. Practice these ways to improve your vocabulary!

2. Every week, learn five prefixes and five stems from the charts on pages 73–74. In reading done outside of class, look for examples of words with these prefixes and stems. Bring examples to share in class.

3. Outside of class, look in a magazine, a newspaper, or a university textbook. Find a paragraph in which you have learned a new word. Underline the word. Make four copies of the paragraph to bring to class.

    In class, form groups of four students. In your group, give each classmate a copy of your paragraph. Read each paragraph from your classmates. Work as a team. Look for context clues and word parts that help you understand the meaning of each underlined word. Is the word a noun, a verb, an adjective, or some other part of speech? Write a short definition of each underlined word. Then, look up the word in an English–only dictionary. How close is your group's definition to the dictionary definition?

4. In reading done outside of class, find three sentences, each of which contains a word that is new for you. Bring the sentences to class. Choose one sentence to write on the board, but omit the new word, leaving a blank space where the word should be. Your classmates must think of words that would fit the context of the sentence. How many words would be correct in the sentence? Compare these words with the real missing word.

5. Start a vocabulary notebook to help you prepare for the TOEFL. In the notebook, write new words that you have learned through reading. Include examples of the words used in context. Organize the notebook into word categories. (Possible categories: words by subject area, such as science, business, and the arts; important terms from your major field of study; words with the same prefix or stem; words that are difficult to remember; words that have an interesting sound.)

PROGRESS – 1.3

QUIZ 3   *Time – 15 minutes*

Read the passages and choose the best answer to each question. Answer all questions about a passage on the basis of what is stated or implied in that passage.

JOHNNY APPLESEED

1   In 1801, a 26–year–old man named John Chapman wandered the sparsely populated "western country" that was still two years away from becoming the state of Ohio. Chapman had a simple purpose: wherever he found suitable soil, he planted apple seeds. To the settlers of the Ohio frontier, Chapman became known as Johnny Appleseed, a strange man who wore odd clothes and went barefoot. He was a pacifist in a time of warfare and brutality against the Indians, treating Indians and settlers alike with respect. He killed no animals and was a vegetarian. He even opposed pruning his apple trees because he did not want to cause them pain.

2   Chapman spent forty years wandering as Johnny Appleseed. Journeying by foot and canoe through Ohio and Indiana, he planted seeds, sold and gave away apple saplings, and exchanged knowledge of medicinal plants with Indians and settlers. He prepared the way for farms and towns by planting apple seeds in clearings along rivers and constructing simple wooden fences to keep animals out of his primitive orchards.

3   The agricultural development that Chapman anticipated was in fact marching across the eastern half of the continent at an ever–increasing pace. When Chapman started his "apple seeding" in 1801, the population of Ohio was 45,000, and ninety percent of the land was still covered with elm, ash, maple, oak, and hickory trees. By the time of Chapman's death in 1845, the state's population had reached two million, and more than forty percent of the land had been cleared of trees and converted to farms. Not until 1880 did the cutting of trees subside. By then, three–quarters of Ohio had been cleared, and people were becoming aware of the limits of expansion. Only then did they begin to take seriously the tree–loving ideas of Johnny Appleseed, who had become the subject of folk tales.

1. The phrase sparsely populated in paragraph 1 means that

   (A) the area had many resources
   (B) most of the people were young
   (C) few people lived in the region
   (D) the land was undeveloped

2. The word pacifist in paragraph 1 is closest in meaning to

   (A) citizen soldier
   (B) peace advocate
   (C) social scientist
   (D) respected speaker

3. The word marching in paragraph 3 is closest in meaning to

   (A) crawling
   (B) advancing
   (C) attacking
   (D) declining

4. The word subside in paragraph 3 is closest in meaning to

   (A) matter
   (B) succeed
   (C) resume
   (D) decrease

THE ORIGIN OF THE UNIVERSE

1   Astronomers believe that the universe began with a large, dense mass of gas consisting mainly of hydrogen, the simplest of all the naturally occurring chemical elements. The mass of hydrogen was very hot and caused intense light and much expanding motion. As the universe expanded, its light became dimmer, yet even now some of the primeval light may be present.

2   The original universe underwent a physical transition that gradually differentiated it into galaxies, stars, and planets. As the original mass of gas expanded and cooled, large clouds separated themselves from the parent mass. Gravity played an important role in this mechanism. Matter is subject to gravity, yet matter is also the cause of gravity since it is matter's mass that determines the strength of the gravitational force.

3   Scientists believe that the original mass of gas in the universe was not completely uniform, and there were some regions that were slightly denser and capable of generating stronger gravitational fields than others. Since gravity tends to pull matter together, the denser regions tended to become even more compact. Thus, small variations in the original mass evolved into denser clouds that gradually separated from the expanding parent mass. From these clouds, the galaxies were formed.

4   At the end of the first phase of the universe, a great number of huge clouds had become separate entities that could start their own independent evolution. These turbulent clouds—ancient galaxies—contained variations that grew in importance over time. The clouds divided into smaller and smaller "cloudlets" that gravity caused to contract. The increase in pressure from this contraction caused the temperature to rise until the cloudlets began to glow as individual, luminous stars.

5   Astronomers believe that the earliest galaxies were small when they formed most of their stars, but accumulated most of their mass later through collisions. Large galaxies formed in stages as smaller galaxies were attracted to one another by gravity. As the smaller galaxies were pulled together over time, they merged into larger and larger structures, eventually forming massive galaxies. As many as half of all galaxies are thought to have been involved in some sort of collision.

5. The word primeval in paragraph 1 is closest in meaning to

   (A) original
   (B) important
   (C) expanding
   (D) beautiful

6. The word transition in paragraph 2 is closest in meaning to

   (A) transaction
   (B) struggle
   (C) combination
   (D) change

7. The word uniform in paragraph 3 is closest in meaning to

   (A) suitable
   (B) unusual
   (C) consistent
   (D) filled

8. The word compact in paragraph 3 is closest in meaning to

   (A) distinct
   (B) dense
   (C) disconnected
   (D) distant

9. The word luminous in paragraph 4 is closest in meaning to

- (A) light–emitting
- (B) densely packed
- (C) high–pressure
- (D) very beautiful

10. The word merged in paragraph 5 is closest in meaning to

- (A) bent
- (B) froze
- (C) blended
- (D) eroded

Answers to Reading Quiz 3 are on page 638.

Record your score on the Progress Chart on page 790.

READING

PROGRESS – 1.1 through 1.3

QUIZ 4

Time – 35 minutes

Read the passages and choose the best answer to each question. Answer all questions about a passage on the basis of what is stated or implied in that passage.

ROAD BUILDING AND THE AUTOMOBILE

1   Car registrations in the United States rose from one million in 1913 to ten million in 1923. By 1927, Americans were driving some twenty–six million automobiles, one car for every five people in the country. Automobile sales in the state of Michigan outnumbered those in Great Britain and Ireland combined. For the first time in history, more people lived in cities than on farms, and they were migrating to the city by automobile.

2   The automobile was every American's idea of freedom, and the construction of hard–surface roads was one of the largest items of government expenditure, often at great cost to everything else. The growth of roads and the automobile industry made cars the lifeblood of the petroleum industry and a major consumer of steel. The automobile caused expansions in outdoor recreation, tourism, and related industries—service stations, roadside restaurants, and motels. After 1945, the automobile industry reached new heights, and new roads led out of the city to the suburbs, where two–car families transported children to new schools and shopping malls.

3   In 1956 Congress passed the Interstate Highway Act, the peak of a half–century of frenzied road building at government expense and the largest public works program in history. The result was a network of federally subsidized highways connecting major urban centers. The interstate highways stretched American mobility to new distances, and two–hour commutes, traffic jams, polluted cities, and Disneyland became standard features of life. Like almost everything else in the 1950s, the construction of interstate highways was justified as a national defense measure.

4   The federal government guaranteed the predominance of private transportation. Since the 1950s, 75 percent of federal funds for transportation has been spent on highways, while a scant one percent has gone to buses, trains, or subways. Even before the interstate highway system was built, the American bias was clear, which is why the United States has the world's best road system and nearly its worst public transit system.

1. The author makes the point that in the early twentieth century

    (A) automobiles were very expensive
    (B) there were more cars than people in the United States
    (C) automobile use increased rapidly
    (D) there were few good roads for automobiles

2. The phrase the lifeblood in paragraph 2 is closest in meaning to

    (A) a supervisor
    (B) an important part
    (C) an opponent
    (D) a serious threat

3. The word frenzied in paragraph 3 is closest in meaning to

(A) intense
(B) scientific
(C) disorganized
(D) wasteful

4. Which sentence best describes road building in the 1940s and 1950s?

(A) It was the last public works project funded by the federal government.
(B) It cost more money than the government spent on national defense.
(C) It produced a network of highways that favored large cities and suburbs.
(D) It led to an increase in the demand for better public transit systems.

5. The word scant in paragraph 4 is closest in meaning to

(A) more important
(B) barely sufficient
(C) very generous
(D) privately funded

6. According to the passage, the growth in the number of cars had a positive impact on all of the following EXCEPT

(A) tourism
(B) service stations
(C) subway systems
(D) shopping malls

7. According to the passage, the American attitude toward the automobile has resulted in

(A) a preference for private cars over public transportation
(B) loss of farmland and destruction of traditional farm life
(C) an increase in the number of deaths due to car accidents
(D) criticism of the amount of money spent on roads

BIRD SONG

1   One instance in the animal kingdom with parallels to human music is bird song. Much
has recently been discovered about the development of song in birds. Some species are
restricted to a single song learned by all individuals, while other species have a range of
songs and dialects, depending on environmental stimulation. The most important auditory
stimuli for birds are the sounds of other birds, including family or flock members and
territorial rivals. For all bird species, there is a prescribed path to development of the final
song, beginning with the subsong, passing through plastic song, until the bird achieves the
species song or songs. This process is similar to the steps through which young children pass
as they first babble and then mimic pieces of the songs they hear around them, although the
ultimate output of human singers is much vaster and more varied than even the most
impressive bird **repertoire**.

2   Underlying all **avian** vocal activity is the syrinx, an organ unique to birds that is located
at the first major branching of the **windpipe** and is linked to the brain. There are general
parallels between the syrinx in birds and the larynx in humans. Both produce sound when
air is forced through the windpipe, causing thin membranes to vibrate. However, compared
to the human larynx, which uses only about two percent of exhaled air, the syrinx is a far
more efficient sound–producing mechanism that can create sound from nearly all the air
passing through it.

3   Possibly the most interesting aspect of bird song from the perspective of human
intelligence is its foundation in the central nervous system. Like humans, birds have large
brains relative to their body size. Song is a complex activity that young birds must learn, and
learning implies that higher–brain activity must be complex in the control of song. This control
is associated with two song–control centers in the avian brain. If the links between these
centers and the syrinx are interrupted, a bird is unable to produce normal song. Moreover, bird
song is one of the few instances in the animal kingdom of a skill that is lateralized; the song–
control centers are located in the left side of the avian brain. A lesion there will destroy bird
song, while a similar lesion in the right half of the brain will result in much less damage.

Glossary:
  repertoire: stock of songs
  avian: relating to birds
  windpipe: main airway to the lungs; trachea

8. The word range in paragraph 1 is closest in
   meaning to

   (A) region
   (B) memory
   (C) variety
   (D) system

9. How does the development of song in birds
   parallel its development in humans?

   (A) Bird song and human music evolved
       during the same period in history.
   (B) All birds and humans are capable of
       learning a large number of songs.
   (C) The song repertoire of both birds and
       humans changes over their lifetime.
   (D) Song development progresses through
       stages in both birds and humans.

10. The word mimic in paragraph 1 is closest in meaning to

   (A) imitate
   (B) enjoy
   (C) compose
   (D) memorize

11. The word underlying in paragraph 2 is closest in meaning to

   (A) restricting
   (B) surrounding
   (C) recording
   (D) supporting

12. In what way are the avian syrinx and the human larynx different?

   (A) The syrinx is located near the windpipe, but the larynx is not.
   (B) The syrinx is larger than the larynx relative to body size.
   (C) The syrinx produces a wider variety of sounds than the larynx.
   (D) The syrinx uses much more of the passing air to produce sound.

13. What aspect of bird song suggests the involvement of the brain in the control of song?

   (A) The purpose of song is similar in birds and humans.
   (B) Song is a complex activity that must be learned.
   (C) Birds can produce two separate sounds at the same time.
   (D) Song consists of a wide variety of musical notes.

14. The word lateralized in paragraph 3 is closest in meaning to

   (A) linked to a specific area of the brain
   (B) highly evolved
   (C) shared by all species
   (D) easily damaged or destroyed

15. All of the following statements characterize bird song EXCEPT:

   (A) Birds learn song mainly by listening to the sounds of other birds.
   (B) Birds are born with the full ability to sing their species song.
   (C) Song is produced in the syrinx, which is linked to the avian brain.
   (D) The central nervous system has the lead role in the control of song.

READING

MACHIAVELLI

1   Niccolo Machiavelli, an Italian statesman and political philosopher of the early sixteenth century, is considered the founder of modern political thinking. Machiavelli was a product of Renaissance Florence, a city–state that was struggling for expansion and survival among a competing group of similar states. As a public servant and diplomat, Machiavelli came to understand power politics by observing the spectacle around him without any illusions. In 1512, he was briefly imprisoned and then forced to leave public life. He retired to his country estate, where he recorded his reflections on politics. Two of his books would become classics in political theory: *Discourses on the First Ten Books of Livy*, a set of essays on ancient and modern politics, and *The Prince*, a potent little book that would shock readers for centuries.

2   Machiavelli saw politics as an affair separate from religion and ethics, an activity to be practiced and studied for its own sake. Politics was simply the battle of men in search of power, and since all men were brutal, selfish, and cowardly, politics must follow certain rules. In his most famous work, *The Prince* (1532), Machiavelli described the means by which a leader may gain and maintain power. The ideal prince was the man who had studied his fellow men, both by reading history and by observing the present, and was willing to exploit their weaknesses. Machiavelli thought that his own time was too corrupt to permit any alternative to the Renaissance despots that he saw all around him.

3   Machiavelli's philosophy arose more from a deeply pessimistic view of human nature than from a lack of moral sense, which many readers criticized in him. He was, and still is, misunderstood to have promoted atheism over religion and criminality over other means of governing. Despite the ruthless connotation of the term "Machiavellian," many of his works, such as the *History of Florence* (1532), express republican principles. Machiavelli's supporters saw him not as a cynic who gloried in evil but as a scientist of politics who saw the world more clearly than others and reported what he saw with lucidity and honesty.

4   The cultural impact of Machiavelli's philosophy was far–reaching, and negative interpretations have persisted. The dramatic literature of the late sixteenth century, notably the plays of Shakespeare, often featured a villainous but humorous character type known as the Machiavel. The Machiavel character loved evil for its own sake, and this delight in evil made all other motivation unnecessary. The Machiavel had a habit of using humorous monologues to comment on his own wickedness and contempt for goodness. Shakespeare's principal Machiavel characters are the treacherous Iago in *Othello*, the ruthlessly ambitious Edmund in *King Lear*, and the murderous title character in *Richard III*.

16. According to the passage, what was a major influence on Machiavelli's political philosophy?

   (A) The power struggles within and among city–states
   (B) The desire to express his anger for being imprisoned
   (C) The rejection of ancient theories about politics
   (D) The shock and disgust he felt toward political leaders

17. The word illusions in paragraph 1 is closest in meaning to

   (A) conclusions
   (B) false beliefs
   (C) limits
   (D) good intentions

18. The word potent in paragraph 1 is closest in meaning to

   (A) influential
   (B) dishonest
   (C) poetic
   (D) humorous

19. What is the subject of *The Prince*?

   (A) The trial and imprisonment of Machiavelli
   (B) The relationship between politics and religion
   (C) The ways that a ruler gains and maintains power
   (D) The history of the political leadership of Florence

20. The word pessimistic in paragraph 3 is closest in meaning to

   (A) negative
   (B) cautious
   (C) religious
   (D) emotional

21. Machiavelli's political philosophy included all of the following beliefs EXCEPT:

   (A) Politics is the power struggle among men who are all brutal and selfish.
   (B) The ideal ruler understands and exploits the weaknesses of others.
   (C) People must organize to fight against evil and corruption in politics.
   (D) Politics should be studied and practiced separately from religion and ethics.

22. According to the author, how has Machiavelli been misunderstood?

   (A) Some people think he was cowardly for retiring from public life.
   (B) Some of his writings seem to support religion, while others oppose it.
   (C) Some of his principles of republican government have been misused.
   (D) Some people interpret his writings as promoting evil in government.

23. The word lucidity in paragraph 3 is closest in meaning to

   (A) distaste
   (B) clarity
   (C) respect
   (D) concern

24. The word monologues in paragraph 4 is closest in meaning to

   (A) speeches
   (B) actions
   (C) noises
   (D) costumes

25. The Machiavel character in drama has all of the following characteristics EXCEPT

   (A) dislike for goodness
   (B) humorous commentary
   (C) enjoyment of evil
   (D) complex motivation

Answers to Reading Quiz 4 are on pages 638–639.

Record your score on the Progress Chart on page 790.

1.4 Making Inferences

FOCUS

Read the following passage and answer the question:

---

1   When Thomas Lincoln took his family across the Ohio River into Indiana in 1816, he was searching for a permanent homestead site. He found it near Little Pigeon Creek on a plot of land he had laid claim to earlier. The family settled down and remained here for fourteen years, and it was here that Thomas's wife, Nancy Hanks, died from "milksick," an illness caused by milk from cattle that had eaten snakeroot leaves.

2   Today, bronze castings of sill logs and a stone hearth mark the site of the Lincoln cabin. Just beyond this, a reconstruction of the little house contains the clutter of Abraham Lincoln's boyhood home: log table and benches, spinning wheels, and a fireplace with iron pots. A few horses, sheep, and chickens complete the scene, and interpreters in period dress are at hand to answer questions. A walkway leads to the small hill where the president's mother is buried, and another path has stones marking important events in Lincoln's early life.

It can be inferred from paragraph 1 that "milksick"

○ was a common illness on farms
○ did not affect children
○ was caused by a poisonous plant
○ killed both people and cattle

What do you know about "milksick" from the passage? You know that it killed a woman and that it was *caused by milk from cattle that had eaten snakeroot leaves.* You can infer that "milksick" *was caused by a poisonous plant*—the correct answer. The other answer choices cannot be inferred from the passage.

Now answer another question:

Which of the following can be inferred from the passage?

○ The Lincoln family was originally from Indiana.
○ Tobacco was raised on the Lincoln farm.
○ The Lincoln cabin was constructed of bronze and stone.
○ The site of the Lincoln homestead is now a museum.

You can infer that *The site of the Lincoln homestead is now a museum.* Some clues are:

Today…mark the site of the Lincoln cabin.   …interpreters in period dress…
…a reconstruction of the little house…   …stones marking important events…

The other answer choices cannot reasonably be inferred from the passage.

 STUDY

1. Inferences

An *inference* is a conclusion you can make from the information given in a passage. An inference is an idea that you can reasonably take to be true, based on what the author says. Some inferences can be made from a single sentence. Some inferences are based on a whole paragraph or on the entire passage.

An inference is a "hidden" idea. To make an inference, you must understand an idea that the author does not state directly. To do this, you must interpret the information that is stated directly. What the author does not state directly and openly, he or she may *imply* or *suggest* by mentioning certain facts and details. When an author implies something, you must *infer* or *conclude* the meaning based on what the author does say.

When you make inferences, use key words and ideas in the passage and your overall understanding of the author's message, as well as reason, logic, and common sense.

TOEFL questions about inferences look like this:

> What can be inferred about _____?
> It can be inferred from paragraph __ that _____.
> Which of the following can be inferred from paragraph __?
> Which of the following statements is most likely true about _____?
> What probably occurred after _____?
> It can be inferred from the passage that the author most likely believes which of the following about _____?
> Which of the following statements most accurately reflects the author's opinion about _____?
> Paragraph __ supports which of the following statements about _____?

2. Answer Choices

In inference questions, an answer choice may be incorrect because it:

- is not supported by the information stated or implied in the passage;
- is too general or too vague;
- is inaccurate or untrue according to the passage; or
- is irrelevant or not mentioned in the passage.

READING

3. Sample Questions

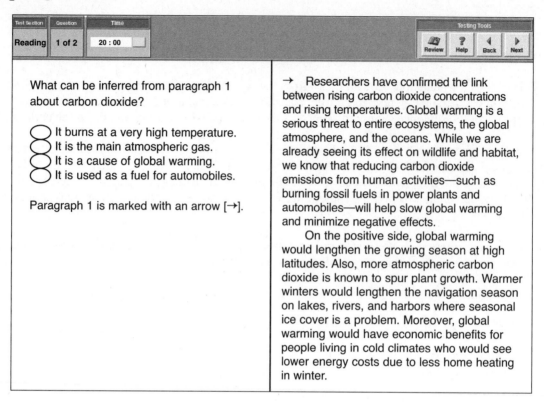

The question asks you to make an inference about carbon dioxide. The correct answer is *It is a cause of global warming*. Some clues in paragraph 1 are:

> …confirmed the link between rising carbon dioxide concentrations and rising temperatures…
> …reducing carbon dioxide emissions…will help slow global warming….

The other answer choices are not supported by the information in the passage. *It burns at a very high temperature* is not mentioned. *It is the main atmospheric gas* is too vague and is not supported by the information given. *It is used as a fuel for automobiles* is inaccurate because carbon dioxide is a product or effect of burning fossil fuels—not a fuel itself.

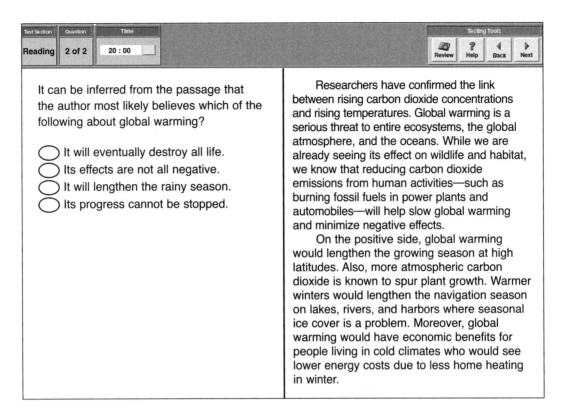

It can be inferred from the passage that the author most likely believes which of the following about global warming?

○ It will eventually destroy all life.
○ Its effects are not all negative.
○ It will lengthen the rainy season.
○ Its progress cannot be stopped.

Researchers have confirmed the link between rising carbon dioxide concentrations and rising temperatures. Global warming is a serious threat to entire ecosystems, the global atmosphere, and the oceans. While we are already seeing its effect on wildlife and habitat, we know that reducing carbon dioxide emissions from human activities—such as burning fossil fuels in power plants and automobiles—will help slow global warming and minimize negative effects.

On the positive side, global warming would lengthen the growing season at high latitudes. Also, more atmospheric carbon dioxide is known to spur plant growth. Warmer winters would lengthen the navigation season on lakes, rivers, and harbors where seasonal ice cover is a problem. Moreover, global warming would have economic benefits for people living in cold climates who would see lower energy costs due to less home heating in winter.

The question requires you to infer what the author probably believes about global warming. You must make this inference based on what the author says. Look at each answer choice and determine if it can reasonably be inferred from the information in the passage. Are there words or ideas in the passage that support the answer?

The author most likely believes *Its effects are not all negative*, and this is the correct answer. Some clues are:

> On the positive side, global warming would….
> Warmer winters would lengthen the navigation season on lakes, rivers, and harbors….
> Moreover, global warming would have economic benefits….

It will eventually destroy all life is not supported by the information in the passage. *It will lengthen the rainy season* is inaccurate; according to the passage, global warming will *lengthen the navigation season*, not the rainy season. *Its progress cannot be stopped* is inaccurate; the author says that *reducing carbon dioxide emissions from human activities…will help slow global warming and minimize negative effects*.

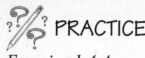 PRACTICE

Exercise 1.4.A

Read the passages and choose the best answer to each question.

QUESTION 1

In classical and medieval times, the study of music shared many features with the discipline of mathematics, such as an interest in proportions, special ratios, and recurring patterns. In the twentieth century, the introduction of twelve–tone music and the widespread use of computers inspired further study into the relationship between musical and mathematical abilities. Musical performances require sensitivity to ratios that are often complex, and to appreciate the operation of rhythms, a performer must have some basic numerical competence.

1. Which of the following can be inferred from the passage?

   Ⓐ The disciplines of music and mathematics originated in classical times.
   Ⓑ People have long been aware of links between music and mathematics.
   Ⓒ Both music and mathematics require an understanding of computers.
   Ⓓ Professional musicians must study mathematics at the university level.

QUESTION 2

Corvids are sociable and tend to form social groups. This is particularly true of rooks, which stay in their flocks all year round. The raven, largest of the corvids, joins a social group as a juvenile, pairing off at around the age of three and mating for life. Courtship can involve such games as pair snow sliding and the synchronized flight test. Corvids can be found all over the world. The adaptability and intelligence of this family have made them extremely successful. For centuries, the raven and the crow have held a special place in the mythology of various cultures.

2. It can be inferred from the passage that corvids are

   Ⓐ a family of birds
   Ⓑ games for children
   Ⓒ members of a sports club
   Ⓓ imaginary beings

QUESTION 3

The input of solar energy supplies 99 percent of the energy needed to heat the earth and all buildings on it. How is this possible? Most people think of solar energy in terms of direct heat from the sun. However, broadly defined, solar energy includes direct energy from the sun as well as a number of indirect forms of energy produced by this direct input. Major indirect forms of solar energy include wind, hydropower, and biomass—solar energy converted to chemical energy in trees, plants, and other organic matter.

3. It can be inferred from the passage that the author most likely believes which of the following about solar energy?

    (A) Solar energy is not used as much as it could be used.
    (B) It is not possible to develop direct forms of solar energy.
    (C) Trees, plants, and organic matter can store solar energy.
    (D) The definition of solar energy will continue to change.

QUESTION 4

The reasons for the migration from rural to urban life were exploitation and lack of economic opportunity. The family members who would not inherit a share in the property were exploited by the laws of inheritance. The system was particularly hard on women, who usually did not share in the ownership of the farm and who rarely were paid for their labor. The workday for women was even more demanding than it was for men. Women were responsible for the kitchen garden and the small livestock as well as the care of the family. Unmarried women increasingly left the farm in search of economic opportunity in the factories that processed fish or farm products.

4. It can be inferred from the passage that women under this system

    (A) moved from farm to farm in search of work
    (B) were paid less than men for the same work
    (C) did not acquire property through inheritance
    (D) had to get married in order to stay on the farm

QUESTIONS 5–6

One of the most significant elements of age stratification in all cultures is the pattern of experiences connected to marriage and parenting—a pattern that sociologists call the family life cycle. In North America, about 90 percent of adults marry, and the great majority of them have children and thus a family life cycle related to family experiences. When the family's first child is born, the parents embark on a sequence of experiences linked to the child's development—from infancy and toddlerhood, through school age and adolescence, and eventually, to departure from the nest. Each of these periods in the child's life makes a different set of demands on the parents.

5. The phrase embark on in the passage is closest in meaning to

   (A) attempt
   (B) begin
   (C) discuss
   (D) avoid

6. It can be inferred from the passage that the family life cycle

   (A) takes place whether or not people have children
   (B) does not occur in cultures outside of North America
   (C) must be redefined from one generation to the next
   (D) shapes several years in the lives of most adults

QUESTIONS 7–8

1   Some people believe that odors and fragrances affect the body and mind and are capable of healing anxiety, stress, and other sources of disease. Interest in aromatherapy—and the use of aromatherapy products such as lotions and inhalants—continues to boom. Some popular essential oils and their uses in aromatherapy include lavender and chamomile, which are reputed to ease stress and promote sleep. The scent of jasmine will uplift the mood and reduce depression. Orange eases anxiety and depression and promotes creativity. Peppermint has antibacterial and analgesic qualities, eases mental fatigue, and relieves headaches.

2   However, aromatherapy is not for everyone. For people who suffer from fragrance sensitivity, asthma, or allergies, aromas like perfumes can prompt disabling health problems, including headaches, dizziness, nausea and vomiting, fatigue, difficulty breathing, difficulty concentrating, flu–like symptoms, and anaphylaxis.

7. It can be inferred that aromatherapy is

   (A) the main use of essential oils from plants
   (B) the use of certain scents to promote health
   (C) not recommended for treating headaches
   (D) not an effective method of curing disease

8. All of the following fragrances are believed to reduce stress EXCEPT

   (A) lavender
   (B) jasmine
   (C) chamomile
   (D) orange

QUESTIONS 9–10

1   Animal behaviorists believe the orangutan is a cultured ape, able to learn new living habits and to pass them along to the next generation. Some orangutan parents teach their young to use leaves as napkins, while others demonstrate the technique of getting water from a hole by dipping a branch in and then licking the leaves. Orangutans have been observed saying goodnight with the gift of a juicy raspberry. Such social interactions lead researchers to conclude that if orangutans have culture, then the capacity to learn culture is very ancient.

2   In the evolutionary timeline, orangutans separated from the ancestors of humans many millions of years ago, and they may have had culture before they separated. The discovery of orangutan culture suggests that early primates—including ancestors of humans—might have developed the ability to invent new behaviors, such as tool use, as early as 14 million years ago, approximately 6 million years earlier than once believed.

9. What can be inferred from paragraph 1 about social interactions related to teaching and learning?

(A) They are behaviors that only orangutans have displayed.
(B) They are misunderstood by animal behaviorists.
(C) They indicate similarities between orangutans and other apes.
(D) They provide evidence that orangutans have culture.

10. Which of the following can be inferred from paragraph 2?

(A) The ancestors of humans learned culture from orangutans.
(B) Orangutans were more advanced than most other early primates.
(C) Primate culture may be older than scientists used to believe.
(D) Scientists have found orangutan tools that are 6 million years old.

Exercise 1.4.B

Read the passages and choose the best answer to each question.

QUESTIONS 1–2

1   In the early nineteenth century, most of the Europeans who immigrated to the United States were from northern and western European countries such as England, Germany, France, and Sweden. However, most of the fifteen million Europeans arriving between 1890 and 1914 came from southern and eastern Europe, with the largest numbers coming from Russia, Italy, Greece, Austria–Hungary, and Armenia.

2   A similar pattern occurred in Canada, where most immigrants were traditionally from England and the United States. After 1890, an increasing number came from eastern Europe, particularly Russia and Ukraine. Many of these headed for the Prairie Provinces. The Doukhobors, a pacifist sect from southern Russia, established communal settlements in Saskatchewan. Together with other immigrants, they arrived in such numbers that in the two decades between the completion of the main railroad network and the outbreak of war in 1914, the population of the prairies had increased from about 150,000 to 1.5 million.

1. Which of the following can be inferred from paragraph 1 about European immigration to the United States in the nineteenth century?

   (A) The sources of immigrants shifted to different parts of Europe.
   (B) Most of the European immigrants could not speak English.
   (C) More immigrants came from Europe than from other continents.
   (D) Northern and western Europeans did not immigrate after 1890.

2. It can be inferred from paragraph 2 that the Doukhobors

   (A) were the largest immigrant group in North America
   (B) also immigrated to the United States
   (C) mainly settled in the Canadian prairies
   (D) helped to build Canada's railroad network

QUESTIONS 3–6

1   David Smith worked primarily in iron, exploring its possibilities more fully than any other sculptor before or since. To Smith, iron spoke of the power, mobility, and vigor of the industrial age. Smith was born in Indiana in 1906, the descendant of a nineteenth–century blacksmith. His iron sculptures flowed naturally out of the mechanized heart of America, a landscape of railroads and factories. As a child, Smith played on trains and around factories, as well as in nature on hills and near creeks. He originally wanted to be a painter, but after seeing photographs of the metal sculpture of Picasso in an art magazine, he began to realize that iron could be handled as directly as paint.

2   Many of Smith's sculptures are "totems" that suggest variations on the human figure. They are not large iron dolls, although several have "heads" or "legs." Still, they forcefully convey posture and gesture. Their message flows from the internal relations of the forms and from the impression of tension, spring, and alertness set up by their position in space.

3   Later in his career, Smith produced two series of sculptures in stainless steel: the *Sentinels* in the 1950s and the *Cubis* in the 1960s. He also began placing his sculptures outdoors, in natural light, where the highly reflective stainless steel could bring sunlight and color into the work. In the late afternoon sun, the steel planes of the *Cubis* reflect a golden color; at other times, they have a blue cast. The mirror–like steel creates an illusion of depth, which responds better to sunshine than it would to the static lighting of a museum.

3. The word vigor in paragraph 1 is closest in meaning to

   (A) history
   (B) poverty
   (C) lifestyle
   (D) strength

4. Which of the following can be inferred from paragraph 1 about David Smith's background?

   (A) He gained experience while working in a blacksmith factory.
   (B) His childhood exposed him to the uses and possibilities of iron.
   (C) His early sculptures revealed his desire to be a landscape painter.
   (D) He first learned about metals by seeing pictures in a magazine.

5. What can be inferred about the *Sentinels* and the *Cubis*?

   (A) They are the best–known examples of Smith's "totem" sculptures.
   (B) Smith originally intended to use iron instead of stainless steel.
   (C) The *Sentinels* are made of blue steel, and the *Cubis* are of gold steel.
   (D) They each consist of a number of pieces placed in outdoor settings.

6. It can be inferred from the passage that the author most likely believes which of the following about David Smith's works?

   (A) His metal sculptures are more interesting than are those of Picasso.
   (B) His sculptures attempt to portray the proportions of the human body.
   (C) His pieces capture the power of industry and the beauty of natural light.
   (D) His works are best appreciated when viewed all at once in a museum.

QUESTIONS 7–10

1   Long ago, people looked up in the sky and noticed groups of stars that looked like pictures. These patterns of stars, constellations, have been part of human culture for thousands of years. Ancient Syrians and Babylonians named many constellations and created stories about them. The Greeks and Romans later adopted these constellations and translated their names and stories into their own language. After the decline of these ancient cultures, most knowledge of constellations remained hidden in private libraries. Beginning in the eighth century, scholars rediscovered this knowledge. The study of astronomy spread quickly throughout the Mediterranean world, becoming part of university study. Astronomers identified many constellations only a few centuries ago. When Western astronomers started traveling to South Africa in the seventeenth century, they found numerous brilliant stars in the Southern sky. They named some of these Southern constellations after the scientific inventions of the time, such as the Microscope and the Air Pump.

2   Today's astronomers view constellations simply as areas of the sky where interesting objects await observation and study. The entire sky is divided into 88 such regions. In the 1920s, the International Astronomical Union established the boundaries of these regions. In each region, astronomers give Greek letters to a constellation's brighter stars, usually in order of brightness. Hence, the "alpha star" is the brightest star of that constellation. Scientists and ordinary people still refer to many constellations by their popular names, for example, the Lion, the Hunter, and the Great Bear.

7. Which of the following can be inferred from paragraph 1?

   (A) Constellations have interested people for a very long time.
   (B) People once believed incorrect stories about constellations.
   (C) Ancient cultures disagreed about the shapes of constellations.
   (D) Most knowledge of constellations has been lost forever.

8. It can be inferred from paragraph 1 that the ancient Greeks and Romans

   (A) were the first people to notice patterns of stars in the sky
   (B) built universities all over the Mediterranean region
   (C) hid knowledge of constellations in private libraries
   (D) acquired knowledge of constellations from earlier cultures

9. It can be inferred from paragraph 2 that

   (A) there are no constellations in some areas of the sky
   (B) scientists today continue to study constellations
   (C) the boundaries of the constellations change every year
   (D) the International Astronomical Union no longer exists

10. According to paragraph 2, which of the following statements is most likely true?

   (A) Future scientists will divide the sky into fewer regions.
   (B) There are no more constellations for scientists to discover.
   (C) A constellation's alpha star is the one that is easiest to see.
   (D) Few people know the traditional names of constellations.

Exercise 1.4.C

Read the passages and choose the best answer to each question.

QUESTIONS 1–4

1   The human ear contains the organ for hearing and the organ for balance. Both organs involve fluid–filled channels containing hair cells that produce electrochemical impulses when the hairs are stimulated by moving fluid.

2   The ear can be divided into three regions: outer, middle, and inner. The outer ear collects sound waves and directs them to the eardrum separating the outer ear from the middle ear. The middle ear conducts sound vibrations through three small bones to the inner ear. The inner ear is a network of channels containing fluid that moves in response to sound or movement.

3   To perform the function of hearing, the ear converts the energy of pressure waves moving through the air into nerve impulses that the brain perceives as sound. Vibrating objects, such as the vocal cords of a speaking person, create waves in the surrounding air. These waves cause the eardrum to vibrate with the same frequency. The three bones of the middle ear amplify and transmit the vibrations to the oval window, a membrane on the surface of the cochlea, the organ of hearing. Vibrations of the oval window produce pressure waves in the fluid inside the cochlea. Hair cells in the cochlea convert the energy of the vibrating fluid into impulses that travel along the auditory nerve to the brain.

4   The organ for balance is also located in the inner ear. Sensations related to body position are generated much like sensations of sound. Hair cells in the inner ear respond to changes in head position with respect to gravity and movement. Gravity is always pulling down on the hairs, sending a constant series of impulses to the brain. When the position of the head changes—as when the head bends forward—the force on the hair cells changes its output of nerve impulses. The brain then interprets these changes to determine the head's new position.

1. What can be inferred about the organs for hearing and balance?

   (A) Both organs evolved in humans at the same time.
   (B) Both organs send nerve impulses to the brain.
   (C) Both organs contain the same amount of fluid.
   (D) Both organs are located in the ear's middle region.

2. Hearing involves all of the following EXCEPT

   (A) motion of the vocal cords so that they vibrate
   (B) stimulation of hair cells in fluid–filled channels
   (C) amplification of sound vibrations
   (D) conversion of wave energy into nerve impulses

3. It can be inferred from paragraphs 2 and 3 that the cochlea is a part of

   (A) the outer ear
   (B) the eardrum
   (C) the middle ear
   (D) the inner ear

4. What can be inferred from paragraph 4 about gravity?

   (A) Gravity has an essential role in the sense of balance.
   (B) The ear converts gravity into sound waves in the air.
   (C) Gravity is a force that originates in the human ear.
   (D) The organ for hearing is not subject to gravity.

QUESTIONS 5–10

1   The Pacific Northwest coast of North America is a temperate rain forest, where trees like the red cedar grow straight trunks more than two meters thick at the base and sixty meters high. Western red cedar is often called the canoe cedar because it supplied the native people of the region with the raw material for their seagoing dugout canoes. These extraordinary crafts, as large as twenty meters in length, were fashioned from a single tree trunk and carried as many as forty people on fishing and whaling expeditions into the open ocean.

2   The Haida people from the Queen Charlotte Islands off British Columbia were noted for their skill in canoe building. After felling a giant tree with controlled burning, the canoe makers split the log into lengthwise sections with stone wedges. They burned away some of the heartwood, leaving a rough but strong cedar shell. They then carved away wood from the inside, keeping the sections below the waterline thickest and heaviest to help keep the canoe upright in stormy seas. To further enhance the canoe's stability, they filled the hull with water and heated it to boiling by dropping in hot stones. This rendered the wood temporarily flexible, so the sides of the hull could be forced apart and held with sturdy wooden thwarts, which served as both cross braces and seats. The canoes were often painted with elaborate designs of cultural significance to the tribe.

3   The Haida raised canoe building to a high art, designing boats of such beauty and utility that neighboring tribes were willing to exchange quantities of hides, meats, and oils for a Haida canoe. These graceful vessels became the tribe's chief item of export. In their swift and staunch canoes, the first people of the Northwest were able to take full advantage of the riches provided by the sea. With harpoons of yew wood, baited hooks of red cedar, and lines of twisted and braided bark fibers, they fished for cod, sturgeon, and halibut, and hunted whales, seals, and sea otters.

5. The word fashioned in paragraph 1 is closest in meaning to

 A thrown
 B lowered
 C made
 D decorated

6. Why did the canoe makers keep the sections of the canoe below the waterline thickest and heaviest?

 A To prevent the canoe from overturning in rough water
 B To shorten the work of carving wood from the inside
 C To avoid having to paint the bottom of the canoe
 D To make the canoe strong enough to hold forty people

7. Which of the following can be inferred from paragraph 2?

 A Carving changed the texture and strength of the wood.
 B It took the canoe makers several months to build a canoe.
 C The wood was beaten with stone tools to make it flexible.
 D Canoes were important cultural artifacts of the Haida.

8. The word staunch in paragraph 3 is closest in meaning to

 A silent
 B strong
 C scented
 D severe

9. It can be inferred from paragraph 3 that

    (A) canoes were the Haida's only known art form

    (B) the Haida dominated trade among local tribes

    (C) the people used up all of the natural resources

    (D) trees provided essential tools for obtaining food

10. Which of the following statements can be inferred from the passage?

    (A) The western red cedar thrives in a variety of climates.

    (B) The skill of the Haida canoe makers has never been copied.

    (C) Haida canoes were of great value in the regional economy.

    (D) People no longer use cedar canoes for fishing and whaling.

Answers to Exercises 1.4.A through 1.4.C are on pages 639–640.

 EXTENSION

1. Work in a group of three or four students. Read the passage below, and write a list of statements that can be inferred from the information in the passage. Work for ten minutes. Then, share your inferences with the whole class. Your classmates must determine which information in the passage supports each inference made by your group.

> A distinction between two kinds of intelligence—crystallized and fluid intelligence—has been widely studied by researchers studying adult learning. Crystallized intelligence is heavily dependent on education and experience. It consists of the set of skills and knowledge that we each learn as part of growing up in any culture. It includes such skills as vocabulary, the ability to reason clearly about real–life problems, and the technical skills we learn for our jobs. Crystallized abilities are "exercised" abilities.
>
> Fluid intelligence, in contrast, is thought to be a more "basic" set of abilities, not so dependent on specific education. These are the "unexercised" abilities. Most tests of memory tap fluid intelligence.
>
> Crystallized abilities generally continue to rise over our lifetime, while fluid abilities begin to decline much earlier, beginning perhaps at age 35 or 40.

2. With your teacher and classmates, discuss the difference between facts and inferences. When someone you know makes a statement, how can you tell if it is a fact or an inference? Are facts and inferences ever the same?

3. Select a passage from a newspaper, a magazine or a university textbook. In class, work in a group of three or four students. Read the passage, and write a list of facts in the passage. Then write a list of statements that can be inferred or concluded from the information in the passage. In your classroom, post the passage, your facts, and your inferences where your classmates can read them.

1.5 Determining Purpose

FOCUS

Read the following passage and answer the question:

> As with most economic issues, economists disagree over the exact causes of inflation. But they do generally agree that a sharp increase in the cost of one essential item is likely to be a contributing factor. When oil prices rose sharply in the mid–1970s, consumers were suddenly hit with higher prices for oil and for many other things. All the companies that used oil—to heat their buildings or run their machines—suddenly had to raise their prices to cover the increased cost of the oil. Anything transported by truck cost more. At the same time, all the consumers who bought oil in the form of gasoline for their cars had to spend a much larger portion of their paychecks on oil. These higher prices were a form of inflation.
>
> Why does the author mention oil prices?
>
> ○ To track the increases and decreases in oil prices in a certain period
> ○ To explain how companies determine the price of an item
> ○ To show how a price increase for one item contributes to inflation
> ○ To compare prices paid by consumers with prices paid by companies

The question asks about the author's purpose in mentioning a specific detail, *oil prices*. The correct answer is *To show how a price increase for one item contributes to inflation*. What key words and phrases help you determine this? There are several clues in the passage, especially:

...the exact causes of inflation.
...a sharp increase in the cost of one essential item is likely to be a contributing factor.
...higher prices for oil and for many other things.
These higher prices were a form of inflation.

 STUDY

1. Purpose

The *purpose* of a passage is the reason the author wrote it. The author wants you to understand the topic in a certain way. Every good piece of writing has a purpose. The purpose may be to inform, define, explain, illustrate, compare, criticize, or do something else. The author's purpose is closely related to the main points made about the topic.

Each part of a passage may have a different purpose. For example, one paragraph may define a concept, another paragraph may give examples to illustrate the concept, and yet another paragraph may compare the concept to other ideas.

Many questions on the TOEFL ask about the purpose of a specific detail. Some ask about why the author used a certain word or phrase. Questions about purpose look like this:

> Why does the author discuss _____?
> Why does the author mention _____ in paragraph __?
> Why does the author compare _____ to _____?
> The author mentions _____ in order to _____.
> The author discusses _____ in paragraph __ in order to _____.
> Why does the author order the information by _____?
> Why does the author use the word _____ in discussing _____?
> What is the main purpose of paragraph __?

2. Answer Choices

Some purpose words you may see in the answer choices are:

argue	define	illustrate	prove
caution	describe	introduce	show
classify	emphasize	persuade	summarize
compare	explain	point out	support
contrast	give examples	praise	trace
criticize	identify	predict	warn

In questions about purpose, an answer choice may be incorrect because it is:

- too general: a purpose that is beyond the focus of the question;
- inaccurate: not true or only partly true according to the passage; or
- irrelevant: not mentioned in the passage or not related to the question.

3. Sample Questions

Questions about purpose require you to scan the passage for specific information. Here are some examples:

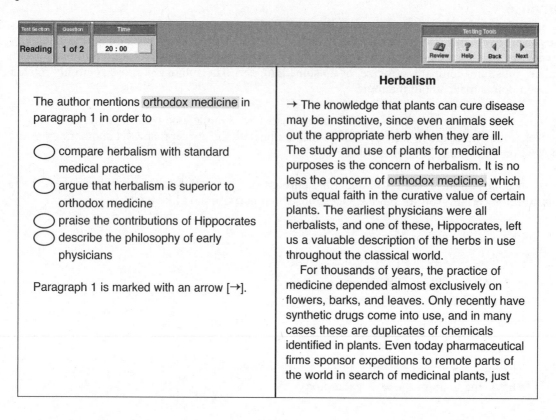

The question asks about the author's purpose in mentioning a specific detail, *orthodox medicine*. The correct answer is to *compare herbalism with standard medical practice*. Some clues in paragraph 1 are:

> …use of plants for medicinal purposes is the concern of herbalism.
> …no less the concern of orthodox medicine, which puts equal faith in…
> The earliest physicians were all herbalists….

Why are the other three answers incorrect? *Argue that herbalism is superior to orthodox medicine* is inaccurate; *praise the contributions of Hippocrates* and *describe the philosophy of early physicians* are too general.

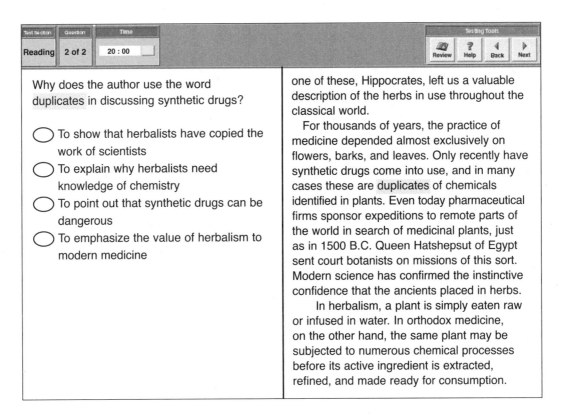

The question asks about the author's purpose in using a specific word, *duplicates*, in discussing synthetic drugs. *Duplicates* means to copy exactly. The correct answer is *To emphasize the value of herbalism to modern medicine*. Some clues in the passage are:

...the practice of medicine depended almost exclusively on...
...these are duplicates of chemicals identified in plants.
Modern science has confirmed the instinctive confidence that the ancients placed in herbs.

Why are the other three answers incorrect? *To show that herbalists have copied the work of scientists* and *To explain why herbalists need knowledge of chemistry* are inaccurate. *To point out that synthetic drugs can be dangerous* is not mentioned in the passage.

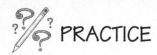 PRACTICE

Exercise 1.5.A

Read the passages and choose the best answer to each question.

QUESTIONS 1–2

1   In economics and finance, nothing can be measured with the precision possible in the physical sciences. However, approximate measurement is often sufficient as long as the method of measurement remains the same over time. It is important for anyone who is considering buying stock in a company to know that the usual methods of accounting have been followed.

2   Unfortunately, even when auditors certify that a company has prepared its financial reports properly, they cannot always be certain that all figures are 100 percent accurate. Because a company's books are not open to public scrutiny, it is possible for a company to distort its financial status. Accounting scandals occur because of dishonesty, questionable accounting practices, or outright criminal behavior. Although the accounting profession and government agencies have attempted to reform some of these abuses, the principle of *caveat emptor*—let the buyer beware—must still guide one's financial transactions.

1. Why does the author mention the physical sciences in paragraph 1?

   (A) To point out that financial measurements are not always precise
   (B) To compare the physical sciences unfavorably with other sciences
   (C) To explain why methods of measurement are important in different fields
   (D) To argue that economics and finance should be considered physical sciences

2. Why does the author mention the principle of *caveat emptor* in paragraph 2?

   (A) To recommend that the government review all stock purchases
   (B) To criticize inadequate efforts to stop bad accounting practices
   (C) To argue that buying stock is the best way to make money fast
   (D) To warn potential buyers of the possibility of accounting abuses

QUESTIONS 3–4

1 Lake Wissanotti, just outside the town of Mariposa, is one of Canada's most popular and enduring fictional places. The lake and town are the setting of Stephen Leacock's masterpiece, *Sunshine Sketches of a Little Town*, a collection of comic sketches and witty observations originally published in 1912. Leacock, one of the founders of Canadian literature, worked for most of his life as a professor of economics. His reputation as a political economist was worldwide, but it is Lake Wissanotti and Mariposa for which he is most remembered today.

2 *Sunshine Sketches* is a portrait of small–town Canadian life in the early twentieth century. Mariposa represents a past to be cherished, a pastoral and idyllic town that allows for human folly. If there is any satire, it is immediately bathed in warm sunshine. Although *Sunshine Sketches* has the complexity of a novel, it is more properly defined as a short–story cycle. A vital force is the book's narrator, who is at times intimately close to the comings and goings of Mariposa life, but distant enough to sustain the focus on human folly.

3. Why does the author discuss Stephen Leacock in paragraph 1?

   (A) To give the name of the main character in a book
   (B) To provide biographical information about the author
   (C) To point out a relationship between literature and economics
   (D) To identify the narrator of a book of stories about a town

4. Why does the author use the phrase bathed in warm sunshine in the passage?

   (A) To describe the tone of the book
   (B) To explain the meaning of satire
   (C) To compare a novel and a short story
   (D) To illustrate the theme of human folly

QUESTIONS 5–7

1   Everyone in a particular society recognizes social roles: father, mother, child, teacher, student, police officer, store clerk, doctor, judge, political leader, and so on. Every culture expects certain types of behavior from people who play certain social roles. Anyone occupying a given position is expected to adopt a specific attitude. A store clerk is expected to take care of customers patiently and politely, and a judge is expected to make wise and fair decisions about laws.

2   Informal social roles are not always easy to recognize, but can be identified with careful research. They are key indicators of a group's health and happiness. Within the family, one informal role is the family hero, the person who defines integrity and upholds family morality. Others are the family arbitrator, the person who keeps the peace, and the family historian, often a grandparent, who relays valuable cultural information that maintains both the family and the larger society. And finally, there is the family friend, the person who provides comfort and companionship to the family members with emotional needs.

5. Why does the author mention a store clerk and a judge in paragraph 1?

- (A) To give examples of people who hold positions of respect
- (B) To explain why social roles are important to a society
- (C) To illustrate the behavior required of certain social roles
- (D) To compare the responsibilities of two different occupations

6. Why does the author use the term key indicators in discussing informal social roles?

- (A) To identify the most important type of social role
- (B) To explain how to identify informal social roles
- (C) To point out that informal roles are unique to families
- (D) To emphasize the value of informal roles to a group

7. Which informal social role supports the family by preserving the family's culture?

- (A) Friend
- (B) Hero
- (C) Historian
- (D) Arbitrator

QUESTIONS 8–10

1   The many parts of the earth's atmosphere are linked with the various parts of the
earth's surface to produce a whole—the climate system. Different parts of the earth's
surface react to the energy of the sun in different ways. For example, ice and snow reflect
much of it. Land surfaces absorb solar energy and heat up rapidly. Oceans store the energy
without experiencing a significant temperature rise. Thus, the different types of surfaces
transfer heat into the atmosphere at different rates.

2   We can view climate as existing in three domains: space, time, and human perception.
In the domain of space, we can study local, regional, and global climates. In time, we can
look at the climate for a year, a decade, a millennium, and so forth. Finally, we depend on
our perceptions of the data, so we must include our own human perception into our model.
Human perception ranges from our personal observations to our public predictions about
climate. Human perception must be included if our understanding of climatic processes is
to be translated into societal actions. As a society, we make informed choices about how
to use the beneficial effects of climate, such as deciding when and where to plant crops.
We also make choices about how to minimize the harmful effects of climate—storms,
blizzards, and droughts.

8. Why does the author discuss different parts of
the earth's surface in paragraph 1?

(A) To explain why humans live in some parts
but not in others
(B) To show that the entire earth is made of
the same materials
(C) To compare how various surfaces transfer
heat into the atmosphere
(D) To describe changes in the earth's
appearance throughout the year

9. According to the author, why must we include
human perception in our study of climate?

(A) We must interpret data and take actions
related to climate.
(B) We must create an interesting model of the
climate system.
(C) We must develop an understanding of our
environment.
(D) We must change our traditional ways of
studying climate.

10. Why does the professor mention storms,
blizzards, and droughts in paragraph 2?

(A) To explain why humans are afraid of the
unknown
(B) To show how the atmosphere and the earth
are linked
(C) To give examples of dangerous effects of
climate
(D) To illustrate the effects of human activity
on climate

READING

Exercise 1.5.B

Read the passages and choose the best answer to each question.

QUESTIONS 1–3

1   Several men have been responsible for promoting forestry as a profession. Foremost was Gifford Pinchot, the father of professional forestry in America. He was chief of the Forest Service from 1898 until 1910, working with President Theodore Roosevelt to instigate sound conservation practices in forests. Later he was professor of forestry and founder of the Pinchot School of Forestry at Yale University. Another great forester was Dr. Bernard E. Fernow, the first head of the U.S. Forest Service. He organized the first American school of professional forestry at Cornell University.

2   The foresters of today, like Pinchot and Fernow in the past, plan and supervise the growth, protection, and utilization of trees. They make maps of forest areas, estimate the amount of standing timber and future growth, and manage timber sales. They also protect the trees from fire, harmful insects, and disease. Some foresters may be responsible for other duties, ranging from wildlife protection and watershed management to the development and supervision of camps, parks, and grazing lands. Others do research, provide information to forest owners and to the general public, and teach in colleges and universities.

1. Why does the author call Gifford Pinchot the father of professional forestry in America?

   (A) To emphasize his contributions to the field
   (B) To describe his family background
   (C) To praise his management skills
   (D) To illustrate his influence on the president

2. Why does the author compare Pinchot and Fernow to the foresters of today?

   (A) To describe different philosophies of forestry management
   (B) To show how the field of forestry has changed in 100 years
   (C) To argue for the expansion of university forestry programs
   (D) To introduce the types of work done by professional foresters

3. All of the following are mentioned in the passage EXCEPT

   (A) what foresters do besides protecting trees
   (B) how to select a good school of forestry
   (C) people who promoted forestry as a career
   (D) management of timber and timber sales

QUESTIONS 4–6

1   One's style of dress reveals the human obsession with both novelty and tradition. People use clothing to declare their membership in a particular social group; however, the rules for what is acceptable dress for that group may change. In affluent societies, this changing of the rules is the driving force behind fashions. By keeping up with fashions, that is, by changing their clothing style frequently but simultaneously, members of a group both satisfy their desire for novelty and obey the rules, thus demonstrating their membership in the group.

2   There are some interesting variations regarding individual status. Some people, particularly in the West, consider themselves of such high status that they do not need to display it with their clothing. For example, many wealthy people in the entertainment industry appear in very casual clothes, such as the worn jeans and work boots of a manual laborer. However, it is likely that a subtle but important signal, such as an expensive wristwatch, will prevail over the message of the casual dress. Such an inverted status display is most likely to occur where the person's high status is conveyed in ways other than with clothing, such as having a famous face.

4. According to the author, fashions serve all of the following purposes EXCEPT

   (A) satisfying an interest in novelty
   (B) signaling a change in personal beliefs
   (C) displaying membership in a social group
   (D) following traditional rules

5. Why does the author discuss individual status in paragraph 2?

   (A) To state that individual status is not important in the West
   (B) To argue that individuals need not obey every fashion rule
   (C) To contrast the status of entertainers with that of manual laborers
   (D) To explain how high status may involve an inverted status display

6. Why does the author mention a wristwatch in paragraph 2?

   (A) To give an example of an item that conveys one's actual status
   (B) To recommend wearing an expensive wristwatch with casual clothes
   (C) To explain why it is not necessary to dress entirely in one style
   (D) To show that a wristwatch is an important fashion accessory

QUESTIONS 7–10

1   The war for independence from Britain was a long and economically costly conflict. The New England fishing industry was temporarily destroyed, and the tobacco colonies in the South were also hard hit. The trade in imports was severely affected, since the war was fought against the country that had previously monopolized the colonies' supply of manufactured goods. The most serious consequences were felt in the cities, whose existence depended on commercial activity. Boston, New York, Philadelphia, and Charleston were all occupied for a time by British troops. Even when the troops had left, British ships lurked in the harbors and continued to disrupt trade.

2   American income from shipbuilding and commerce declined abruptly, undermining the entire economy of the urban areas. The decline in trade brought a fall in the American standard of living. Unemployed shipwrights, dock laborers, and coopers drifted off to find work on farms and in small villages. Some of them joined the Continental army, or if they were loyal to Britain, they departed with the British forces. The population of New York City declined from 21,000 in 1774 to less than half that number only nine years later in 1783.

3   The disruptions produced by the fighting of the war, by the loss of established markets for manufactured goods, by the loss of sources of credit, and by the lack of new investment all created a period of economic stagnation that lasted for the next twenty years.

7. Why does the author mention the fishing industry and the tobacco colonies?

   (A) To show how the war for independence affected the economy
   (B) To compare the economic power of two different regions
   (C) To identify the two largest commercial enterprises in America
   (D) To give examples of industries controlled by British forces

8. Why were the effects of the war felt most in the cities?

   (A) Most of the fighting occurred in the cities.
   (B) The British army destroyed most of the cities.
   (C) The cities depended on manufacturing and trade.
   (D) The urban population did not support the war.

9. Why does the author mention the population of New York City in paragraph 2?

   (A) To show that half of New York remained loyal to Britain
   (B) To compare New York with other cities occupied during the war
   (C) To emphasize the great short–term cost of the war for New York
   (D) To illustrate the percentage of homeless people in New York

10. What probably occurred during the years right after the war for independence?

   (A) Development of new shipbuilding technology
   (B) A return to traditional methods of manufacturing
   (C) A shift to an agricultural economy in New York
   (D) Shortages of money and manufactured goods

Answers to Exercises 1.5.A through 1.5.B are on pages 640–641.

 EXTENSION

1. Outside of class, look in a magazine or a university textbook. Select a short passage of two to three paragraphs. Type or photocopy the paragraphs. Make three copies to bring to class. In class, form groups of three students each. In your group, give each classmate a copy of your passage. Individually, read all of your group's passages. For each one, write an answer to these questions:

    a. Why did the author write this?
    b. What is the author's attitude toward the topic?
    c. What is the purpose of each paragraph?
    d. What details in the passage support the author's purpose?
    e. What words does the author use to emphasize points?

When everyone in your group has finished reading and answering the questions for all passages, compare your answers with your classmates' answers. Are the answers similar or different? Work as a team to agree on the best answer to each question.

PROGRESS – 1.4 through 1.5

QUIZ 5

Time – 15 minutes

Read the passages and choose the best answer to each question. Answer all questions about a passage on the basis of what is stated or implied in that passage.

FREEZING FOOD

1   The discovery of freezing has changed our eating habits more than any other related invention. Because many foods contain large amounts of water, they freeze solidly at or just below 32 degrees Fahrenheit. When we lower the temperature to well below the freezing point and prevent air from penetrating the food, we retard the natural process of decay that causes food to spoil. Freezing preserves the flavor and nutrients of food better than any other preservation method. When properly prepared and packed, foods and vegetables can be stored in the freezer for one year.

2   Most vegetables and some fruits need blanching before they are frozen, and to avoid this step would be an expensive mistake. The result would be a product largely devoid of vitamins and minerals. Proper blanching curtails the enzyme action, which vegetables require during their growth and ripening but which continues after maturation and will lead to decay unless it is almost entirely stopped by blanching. This process is done in two ways, either by plunging vegetables in a large amount of rapidly boiling water for a few minutes or by steaming them. For steam blanching, it is important that timing begin when the water at the bottom of the pot is boiling. Different vegetables require different blanching times, and specified times for each vegetable must be observed. Underblanching is like no blanching at all, and overblanching, while stopping the enzyme action, will produce soggy, discolored vegetables.

1. Why does the author mention 32 degrees Fahrenheit?

   (A) To suggest the storage temperature for most foods
   (B) To identify the freezing point of water
   (C) To state the correct setting for a freezer
   (D) To give the temperature for blanching

2. Why does the author use the term expensive mistake in discussing blanching?

   (A) To state that blanching is expensive but very effective
   (B) To warn that not blanching will harm the food's nutritional value
   (C) To emphasize the importance of blanching only a few items at a time
   (D) To show that many people waste food by blanching improperly

3. What can be inferred about enzyme action in vegetables?

   (A) It eventually causes vegetables to spoil.
   (B) It is a necessary step in the blanching process.
   (C) It stops after the vegetables have ripened.
   (D) It preserves the flavor of frozen vegetables.

4. It can be inferred that underblanched vegetables would

   (A) spoil quickly
   (B) taste like canned vegetables
   (C) lack vitamins and minerals
   (D) be soggy and discolored

EUROPEAN SETTLEMENT OF NORTH AMERICA

1   The large–scale settlement of North America by Europeans began in the seventeenth century. France took the early lead in the contest for the temperate regions of North America. In 1608, the first permanent French colony was established at Quebec. In 1682, La Salle explored the Mississippi River and claimed the entire river system for France. But despite these early successes, there were never enough French settlers to make French North America a large center of population.

2   The Dutch under Henry Hudson explored the eastern coast of the continent and claimed a large area, including the river that was named after him. The Dutch colony of New Netherlands started with a few trading posts on the Hudson River, where New York City is now located, and expanded into enterprises in New Jersey, Delaware and Connecticut. The Dutch settlements suffered a lot of competition from the English, and eventually the Dutch governor was forced to surrender all Dutch lands to the English.

3   England's commercial and political growth at home soon gave it the lead in the colonial race, but this success came only after some early losses, such as the failed colony on Roanoke Island. The first success for England was in 1607 at Jamestown. There were also permanent colonies farther north, in the area known as New England.

4   The colonies of North America grew dramatically beyond the first settlements at Quebec and Jamestown. Population figures for the seventeenth century show that in 1625 there were around 500 settlers in French Canada and 200 in Dutch settlements, but there were 2,000 in the English colonies. Fifty years later, the English had absorbed the Dutch colonies. By 1700, New France had around 20,000 people, but the English colonies had a quarter of a million.

5   The European conquest of North America contributed to international conflict. In the seventeenth and eighteenth centuries, the European powers fought several wars in North America. Most of these conflicts were extensions of wars taking place in Europe at the same time, but some were started by the colonists themselves. The conflicts—especially those between England and France—were mostly over commercial interests and signaled the intense rivalry for control of North American land and resources.

5. What can be inferred from paragraph 1 about the French settlement of North America in the seventeenth century?

(A) The French were more successful than any other European nation at the time.

(B) French settlement never extended beyond the original colony at Quebec.

(C) The French settled North America in order to control international trade.

(D) The French colonies had fewer people than did other North American colonies.

6. Why does the author use the word race in paragraph 3?

(A) To emphasize the competition among European groups

(B) To trace the origin of a popular sport in North America

(C) To show that failure comes more quickly than success

(D) To describe the ethnic differences among Europeans

7. What can be inferred about England in the seventeenth century?

(A) England had colonies on every continent.

(B) England was a leading European power.

(C) England had a democratic political system.

(D) England won every war in which it fought.

8. The author discusses population numbers in paragraph 4 in order to

(A) compare the populations of North America and Europe

(B) show how humans influenced the natural environment

(C) explain why Europeans migrated to North America

(D) illustrate England's growing power in North America

9. What can be inferred about the relationship between the Dutch and English colonies?

(A) The Dutch and the English were each other's largest trading partners.

(B) The Dutch settled in areas where the English had failed earlier.

(C) The Dutch and the English competed for land, and the English prevailed.

(D) The Dutch joined forces with the French to fight against the English.

10. According to the passage, why did the European powers fight wars in North America?

(A) The European powers wanted to conquer the native population.

(B) There was great competition for control of land and resources.

(C) The French and English armies wanted to test their new weapons.

(D) The European nations were trying to spread their political systems.

Answers to Reading Quiz 5 are on page 641.

Record your score on the Progress Chart on page 790.

PROGRESS – 1.1 through 1.5

QUIZ 6

Time – 35 minutes

Read the passages and choose the best answer to each question. Answer all questions about a passage on the basis of what is stated or implied in that passage.

THE QUEEN ANNE HOUSE

1   The house style that dominated American housing during the 1880s and 1890s was known as Queen Anne, a curious name for an American style. The name was, in fact, a historical accident, originating with fashionable architects in Victorian England who coined it with apparently no reason other than its pleasing sound. The Queen Anne style was loosely based on medieval structures built long before 1702, the beginning year of Queen Anne's reign.

2   A distinctive characteristic found in most Queen Anne houses is the unusual roof shape—a steeply pitched, hipped central portion with protruding lower front and side extensions that end in gables. It is often possible to spot these distinctive roof forms from several blocks away. Another feature of this style is the detailing, shown in the wood shingle siding cut into fanciful decorative patterns of scallops, curves, diamonds, or triangles. Queen Anne houses are almost always asymmetrical. If you draw an imaginary line down the middle of one, you will see how drastically different the right and left sides are, all the way from ground level to roof peak. A final characteristic is the inviting wraparound porch that includes the front door area and then extends around to either the right or left side of the house.

3   Queen Anne houses faded from fashion early in the twentieth century as the public's taste shifted toward the more modern Prairie and Craftsman style houses. Today, however, Queen Anne houses are favorite symbols of the past, painstakingly and lovingly restored by old-house buffs and reproduced by builders who give faithful attention to the distinctive shapes and detailing that were first popularized more than one hundred years ago.

1. Why does the author use the word curious in describing the name of an American style?

   (A) The style was invented before Queen Anne's reign.
   (B) The name was accidentally misspelled.
   (C) The style was more popular in Victorian England.
   (D) The name did not originate in America.

2. The word asymmetrical in paragraph 2 is closest in meaning to

   (A) inefficient
   (B) bold
   (C) strange
   (D) unbalanced

3. Which of the following is NOT mentioned as a characteristic feature of Queen Anne houses?

   (A) Decorative windows
   (B) Wood shingle exterior walls
   (C) Large porch
   (D) Steeply pitched roof

4. Which of the following can be inferred from paragraph 2?

   (A) The Queen Anne style combined several other styles.
   (B) The Queen Anne style had to be built in the city.
   (C) The Queen Anne style was elaborate and ornate.
   (D) The Queen Anne style was not popular.

5. According to the passage, why did Queen Anne houses go out of style?

   (A) People came to see them as a symbol of the past.
   (B) People started moving to the suburbs and the prairies.
   (C) People were more interested in newer house styles.
   (D) People could no longer afford to build such large houses.

6. The word buffs in paragraph 3 is closest in meaning to

   (A) experts
   (B) sellers
   (C) critics
   (D) painters

SPORTS COMMENTARY

1   One of the most interesting and distinctive of all uses of language is commentary. An oral reporting of ongoing activity, commentary is used in such public arenas as political ceremonies, parades, funerals, fashion shows, and cooking demonstrations. The most frequently occurring type of commentary may be that connected with sports and games. In sports there are two kinds of commentary, and both are often used for the same sporting event. "Play–by–play" commentary narrates the sports event, while "color–adding" or "color" commentary provides the audience with pre–event background, during–event interpretation, and post–event evaluation. Color commentary is usually conversational in style and can be a dialogue with two or more commentators.

2   Play–by–play commentary is of interest to linguists because it is unlike other kinds of narrative, which are typically reported in past tense. Play–by–play commentary is reported in present tense. Some examples are "he takes the lead by four" and "she's in position." One linguist characterizes radio play–by–play commentary as "a monologue directed at an unknown, unseen mass audience who voluntarily choose to listen…and provide no feedback to the speaker." It is these characteristics that make this kind of commentary unlike any other type of speech situation.

3   The chief feature of play–by–play commentary is a highly formulaic style of presentation. There is distinctive grammar not only in the use of the present tense but also in the omission of certain elements of sentence structure. For example, "Smith in close" eliminates the verb, as some newspaper headlines do. Another example is inverted word order, as in "over at third is Johnson." Play–by–play commentary is very fluent, keeping up with the pace of the action. The rate is steady and there is little silence. The structure of the commentary is cyclical, reflecting the way most games consist of recurring sequences of short activities—as in tennis and baseball—or a limited number of activity options—as in the various kinds of football. In racing, the structure is even simpler, with the commentator informing the listener of the varying order of the competitors in a "state of play" summary, which is crucial for listeners or viewers who have just tuned in.

7. The word arenas in paragraph 1 is closest in meaning to

   (A) settings
   (B) holidays
   (C) properties
   (D) journals

8. The word background in paragraph 1 is closest in meaning to

   (A) artwork
   (B) amusement
   (C) knowledge
   (D) criticism

9. Which of the following statements is true of color commentary?

   (A) It narrates the action of the event in real time, using the present tense.
   (B) It is a monologue given to an audience that does not respond to the speaker.
   (C) It is steady and fluent because it must keep up with the action of the event.
   (D) It gives background on the event, and interprets and evaluates the event.

10. How is play–by–play commentary distinct from other types of narrative?

   (A) It is not published in magazines.
   (B) It is not spoken in past tense.
   (C) It involves only one reporter.
   (D) It takes place after the event.

11. Why does the author quote a linguist in paragraph 2?

   (A) To describe the uniqueness of radio play–by–play
   (B) To show how technical sports commentary is
   (C) To give examples of play–by–play commentary
   (D) To criticize past trends in sports commentary

12. All of the following are examples of play–by–play commentary EXCEPT:

   (A) "He pitched for Chicago."
   (B) "Junior out of bounds."
   (C) "Straight away it's Owens."
   (D) "He can't make the shot."

13. The word pace in paragraph 3 is closest in meaning to

   (A) plan
   (B) score
   (C) cause
   (D) speed

14. The word crucial in paragraph 3 is closest in meaning to

   (A) fascinating
   (B) important
   (C) confusing
   (D) generous

15. It can be inferred from the passage that the author most likely agrees with which of the following statements about sports commentary?

   (A) Color commentary is more important than play–by–play commentary.
   (B) Sports commentators do not need special knowledge of the sport.
   (C) Commentary enhances the excitement and enjoyment of sports.
   (D) Sports commentators should study to improve their grammar.

THE CIRCULATORY SYSTEM OF TREES

1   Inside the tree's protective outer bark is the circulatory system, consisting of two cellular pipelines that transport water, mineral nutrients, and other organic substances to all living tissues of the tree. One pipeline, called the xylem—or sapwood—transports water and nutrients up from the roots to the leaves. The other, the phloem—or inner bark—carries the downward flow of foodstuffs from the leaves to the branches, trunk, and roots. Between these two pipelines is the vascular cambium, a single–cell layer too thin to be seen by the naked eye. This is the tree's major growth organ, responsible for the outward widening of the trunk, branches, twigs, and roots. During each growing season, the vascular cambium produces new phloem cells on its outer surface and new xylem cells on its inner surface.

2   Xylem cells in the roots draw water molecules into the tree, taking in hydrogen and oxygen and also carrying chemical nutrients from the soil. The xylem pipeline transports this life–sustaining mixture upward as xylem sap, all the way from the roots to the leaves. Xylem sap flows upward at rates of 15 meters per hour or faster. Xylem veins branch throughout each leaf, bringing xylem sap to thirsty cells. Leaves depend on this delivery system for their water supply because trees lose a tremendous amount of water through transpiration, evaporation of water from air spaces in the leaves. Unless the transpired water is replaced by water transported up from the roots, the leaves will wilt and eventually die.

3   How a tree manages to lift several liters of water so high into the air against the pull of gravity is an amazing feat of **hydraulics**. Water moves through the tree because it is driven by negative pressure—tension—in the leaves due to the physical properties of water. Transpiration, the evaporation of water from leaves, creates the tension that drives long–distance transport up through the xylem pipeline. Transpiration provides the pull, and the cohesion of water due to hydrogen bonding transmits the pull along the entire length of xylem. Within the xylem cells, water molecules adhere to each other and are pulled upward through the trunk, into the branches, and toward the cells and air spaces of the leaves.

4   Late in the growing season, xylem cells diminish in size and develop thicker skins, but they retain their capacity to carry water. Over time the innermost xylem cells become clogged with hard or gummy waste products and can no longer transport fluids. A similar situation occurs in the clogging of arteries in the aging human body. However, since the vascular cambium manufactures healthy new xylem cells each year, the death of the old cells does not mean the death of the tree. When they cease to function as living sapwood, the dead xylem cells become part of the central column of heartwood, the supportive structure of the tree.

Glossary:
    hydraulics: the science of the movement of water and other fluids

16. What are the primary components of the tree's circulatory system?

    (A) Water, minerals, and organic substances
    (B) Xylem and phloem
    (C) Leaves, branches, and trunk
    (D) Roots and heartwood

17. The function of the vascular cambium is to

    (A) lift water from the roots to the leaves
    (B) deliver food to the whole tree
    (C) manufacture the tree's food supply
    (D) produce new cells for the tree to grow

18. It can be inferred from paragraph 1 that the xylem is located

(A) on the surface of the outer bark
(B) inside the phloem and the vascular cambium
(C) next to the inner bark
(D) between the vascular cambium and the phloem

19. What can be inferred from paragraph 2 about xylem sap?

(A) It is composed mainly of water.
(B) It causes water loss by transpiration.
(C) It gives leaves their green color.
(D) It is manufactured in the leaves.

20. The word wilt in paragraph 2 is closest in meaning to

(A) melt
(B) grow
(C) swell
(D) sag

21. Why is the process of transpiration essential to the tree's circulatory system?

(A) It supplies the hydrogen and oxygen that trees need to live and grow.
(B) It produces new phloem and xylem in the trunk, branches, and roots.
(C) It causes the negative pressure that moves water through the xylem.
(D) It replaces the water vapor that is lost through the leaves' air spaces.

22. The phrase adhere to in paragraph 3 is closest in meaning to

(A) depend on
(B) stick to
(C) warm up
(D) respond to

23. The word gummy in paragraph 4 is closest in meaning to

(A) sticky
(B) liquid
(C) smelly
(D) fluffy

24. Why does the author mention arteries in the aging human body in paragraph 4?

(A) To show that trees and people get the same diseases
(B) To imply that trees might provide a solution to human problems
(C) To compare what happens in two aging circulatory systems
(D) To explain the cause of death in most trees

25. All of the following are functions of the xylem EXCEPT

(A) transporting food from the leaves to the trunk
(B) taking in chemical nutrients from the soil
(C) forming part of the tree's structural support
(D) moving water upward through the trunk

Answers to Reading Quiz 6 are on page 642.

Record your score on the Progress Chart on page 790.

1.6 Recognizing Paraphrases

FOCUS

Read the following passage and answer the question:

> Global warming has already left its fingerprint on the natural world. Teams of researchers have been tracking changes in the range and behavior of plant and animal species in Europe and North America. They have found ample evidence of plants blooming and birds nesting earlier in the spring, leading them to conclude that rising global temperatures are shifting the ranges of hundreds of species northward. These studies are hard evidence that the natural world is already responding dramatically to climate change, even though the change has just begun. If global warming trends continue, changes in the environment will have an enormous impact on world biology. Birds especially play a critical role in the environment by pollinating plants, dispersing seeds, and controlling insect populations, and changes in their populations will reverberate throughout the ecosystems they inhabit.
>
> Which sentence below best expresses the essential information in the highlighted sentence?
>
> ◯ It is difficult for researchers to find reliable evidence of climate change.
> ◯ The natural world has always responded to sudden changes in climate.
> ◯ Scientists do not understand why environmental changes are so dramatic.
> ◯ Climate change is recent, but there is strong proof that species are reacting.

The question asks you to identify the answer that best conveys the meaning of this sentence:

These studies are hard evidence that the natural world is already responding dramatically to climate change, even though the change has just begun.

Look at the ideas in each part of the sentence:

These studies are hard evidence...
...the natural world is already responding dramatically to climate change...
...even though the change has just begun.

The correct answer is *Climate change is recent, but there is strong proof that species are reacting.* Compare the ideas in both sentences:

These studies are hard evidence...   ...there is strong proof...
...the natural world is already responding
 dramatically to climate change...   ...species are reacting.
...even though the change has just begun.   Climate change is recent...

The correct answer is a **paraphrase** of the original sentence. It expresses the same ideas in different words.

 STUDY

1. Paraphrases

A *paraphrase* is a restatement of another sentence that gives the same information as the original sentence but in a different way. Paraphrases may have different sentence structure or use different words. They often use **synonyms**, words that have the same meaning, or nearly the same meaning, as the words in the original sentence.

You can identify the paraphrase of a sentence by focusing on the essential information in the original sentence. **Essential information** is the most important information in the sentence. It includes the ideas that are basic to understanding the author's message and purpose.

Paraphrase questions look like this:

> Which sentence below best expresses the essential information in the highlighted sentence in the passage? Incorrect choices change the meaning in important ways or leave out essential information.

2. Sentence Structure

A paraphrase may have different sentence structure, or it may put the clauses in a different order.

Original Sentence
Despite the social, technical, and functional aspects of buildings—those that link architecture most closely to history—architecture exists in the realm of the visual arts.

Paraphrase
Architecture is one of the visual arts, even though the social, technical, and functional aspects of buildings link architecture to history.

Original Sentence
Most birds have body temperatures between 40 and 42 degrees Celsius, while most mammals have body temperatures between 36 and 38 degrees.

Paraphrase
The body temperatures of most mammals are between 36 and 38 degrees Celsius, and those of birds are between 40 and 42 degrees.

3. Synonym Clues

A paraphrase may contain synonyms. A **synonym** is a word or phrase with the same meaning as another word or phrase. Here are some examples, with synonyms shown in *italics*.

Original Sentence
Generally, most adult human stomachs hold *slightly more than* four cups of food, but the stomach can *expand to accommodate* as many as 16 cups.

Paraphrase
The stomach of an adult person is usually full when it contains *just over* four cups of food, but it can *stretch to hold* up to 16 cups.

Original Sentence
The supply of natural ice was an *industry unto itself* in the late nineteenth century, and refrigeration with ice became *more inexpensive and accessible.*

Paraphrase
Natural ice supply was a *separate business* in the late nineteenth century, and refrigeration with ice became *cheaper and more available.*

READING

4. Pronoun Clues

A pronoun in the highlighted sentence may refer to something in a previous sentence. The correct paraphrase may use the referent instead of the pronoun. Here are some examples, with pronouns and their referents shown in *italics*:

Original Sentence
Culture consists of the *language, values, norms, and artifacts* that define and unite a society. *These* can be spread from one society to another through culture contact.

Paraphrase
Contact with other cultures is a way of spreading language, values, norms, and artifacts.

In 1889, an Austrian physicist named *Ernst Mach created a system of numbers for measuring "supersonic" speeds.* *This* is why when a plane travels at a speed faster than the speed of sound, its speed is referred to as Mach 1.

A plane moving faster than the speed of sound has a speed of Mach 1, after the inventor of the numbering system.

5. Answer Choices

In paraphrase questions, the incorrect answer choices may be incorrect because they:

- have a different meaning from that of the original sentence;
- omit information or ideas that are necessary to the meaning of the original sentence; or
- include information or ideas that are not in the original sentence.

6. Sample Questions

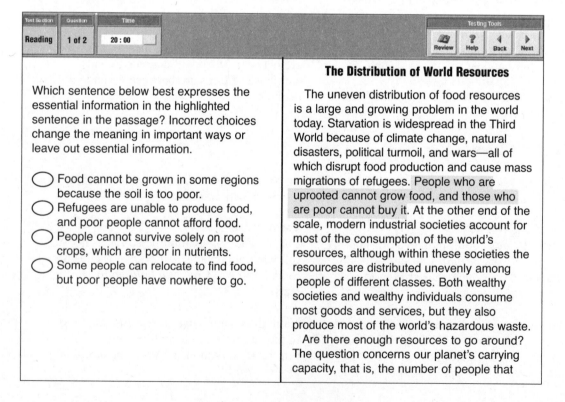

Test Section	Question	Time		Testing Tools
Reading	1 of 2	20 : 00		Review Help Back Next

Which sentence below best expresses the essential information in the highlighted sentence in the passage? Incorrect choices change the meaning in important ways or leave out essential information.

○ Food cannot be grown in some regions because the soil is too poor.
○ Refugees are unable to produce food, and poor people cannot afford food.
○ People cannot survive solely on root crops, which are poor in nutrients.
○ Some people can relocate to find food, but poor people have nowhere to go.

The Distribution of World Resources

The uneven distribution of food resources is a large and growing problem in the world today. Starvation is widespread in the Third World because of climate change, natural disasters, political turmoil, and wars—all of which disrupt food production and cause mass migrations of refugees. People who are uprooted cannot grow food, and those who are poor cannot buy it. At the other end of the scale, modern industrial societies account for most of the consumption of the world's resources, although within these societies the resources are distributed unevenly among people of different classes. Both wealthy societies and wealthy individuals consume most goods and services, but they also produce most of the world's hazardous waste.

Are there enough resources to go around? The question concerns our planet's carrying capacity, that is, the number of people that

DELTA'S KEY TO THE TOEFL iBT®

The question asks you to identify the paraphrase of the highlighted sentence. The correct answer is *Refugees are unable to produce food, and poor people cannot afford food*. Look at the information in the original sentence and how it is paraphrased in the correct answer:

Original Sentence	**Paraphrase**
People who are uprooted cannot grow food	Refugees are unable to produce food
those who are poor cannot buy it	poor people cannot afford food

Why are the other three answers incorrect? *Food cannot be grown in some regions because the soil is too poor* and *People cannot survive solely on root crops, which are poor in nutrients* both have a different meaning from that of the original sentence. *Some people can relocate to find food, but poor people have nowhere to go* has a new idea, *poor people have nowhere to go*, which is not in the original sentence.

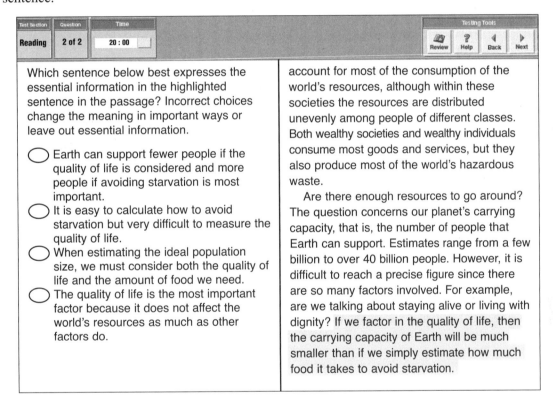

The correct answer is *Earth can support fewer people if the quality of life is considered and more people if avoiding starvation is most important*. Look at the information in the original sentence and how it is paraphrased in the correct answer:

Original Sentence	**Paraphrase**
If we factor in the quality of life	if the quality of life is considered
then the carrying capacity of Earth will be much smaller than	Earth can support fewer people
if we simply estimate how much food it takes to avoid starvation	if avoiding starvation is most important

The other three answers do not accurately express the essential information in the original sentence.

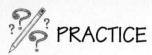 PRACTICE

Exercise 1.6.A

Read the passages and choose the best answer to each question.

QUESTION 1

   In a typical business conference, associates meet to discuss policy or to solve problems. The average participants do not do much specific preparing; their background and thinking usually formulate their contribution. But it is best if all participants know in advance the purpose of the conference. Some general preparation may be in order, and participants may want to take into the conference materials or data that might be useful if a matter comes up.

1. Which sentence below best expresses the essential information in the highlighted sentence in the passage?

(A) Although participants cannot be expected to do too much, they should do some general preparation.
(B) The conference leader should prepare all of the materials and data that will be used in the conference.
(C) There is a general order to most conferences, with participants contributing ideas and information.
(D) As general preparation, participants can bring materials or data that might be a part of the discussion.

QUESTION 2

   Because they absorb heat from the environment rather than generate much of their own, reptiles are said to be ectotherms, a term identifying their major source of body heat as being external. Ectotherms heat directly with solar energy by basking in the sun, rather than through the metabolic breakdown of food, as in mammals and birds. This means that a reptile can survive on less than 10 percent of the calories required by a mammal of equivalent size.

2. Which sentence below best expresses the essential information in the highlighted sentence in the passage?

(A) Because a reptile heats with solar energy, it requires less than 10 percent of the calories that a mammal of the same size needs.
(B) A reptile obtains only 10 percent of its calories from the metabolic breakdown of food; it obtains the rest by basking in the sun.
(C) Some reptiles and mammals are equal in size, but they require vastly different quantities of calories for survival.
(D) Reptiles need to spend only 10 percent of their time eating because they do not need as many calories as mammals of equal size.

QUESTION 3

Architecture is concerned with the large–scale manipulation of elements in the dimensions of length, width, and height. These dimensions may apply to a solid, such as the Egyptian pyramids, or to hollow interior spaces, ranging in size and complexity from a domestic room to a vast cathedral. They may also apply to the spaces around and between buildings. Moreover, every building has a physical context in relation to other buildings. Sometimes the designer disregards the context on the assumption that surrounding structures will later be replaced. However, it is more often posterity that destroys the once appropriate original context.

3. Which sentence below best expresses the essential information in the highlighted sentence in the passage?

   (A) Some architects do not like other buildings to be too close to the building they are designing.

   (B) Most buildings eventually have to be replaced, so the physical context is not very important.

   (C) Architects often believe that nearby structures will not always be there, so they ignore them.

   (D) Designers should ignore the assumptions of people who plan to destroy the original context.

QUESTION 4

The first great collector of Canadian folk traditions was Marius Barbeau, who oversaw the preservation of thousands of texts in what is now the National Museum of Canada. Fearing that these traditions would disappear unless gathered and catalogued, Barbeau preserved the folklore and folk songs of cultures ranging from rural Quebec to the Tsimshian Indians of British Columbia. These folkways—songs, dialects, legends, tall tales, riddles, and children's rhymes—were all part of Canada's traditional rural experience. They provided evidence of the everyday life of the people that was far richer than that in most other historical texts.

4. Which sentence below best expresses the essential information in the highlighted sentence in the passage?

   (A) There is a lot of information in historical texts, but most of it does not deal with real life.

   (B) Canada's folkways give us a much better description of daily life than most histories do.

   (C) The texts collected by Barbeau reveal that some rural Canadians were richer than others.

   (D) The Canadian people provided a lot of materials that illustrate their traditional values.

QUESTION 5

Ruminants—cattle, bison, sheep, goats, deer, antelopes, and giraffes—have a large four–chambered stomach that enables them to digest fibrous plant matter. When a ruminant first swallows a mouthful of grass or leaves, the food enters the stomach's first chamber, the rumen, where bacteria start to break down the cellulose–rich matter and form it into small balls of cud. The ruminant periodically returns the cud to its mouth where it is chewed at length to crush the fibers, making them more accessible to further bacterial action. The ruminant then reswallows the cud, which passes through the other three chambers of the stomach for further digestion.

5. Which sentence below best expresses the essential information in the highlighted sentence in the passage?

(A) Ruminants eat continuously, spending long periods eating grass and chewing their cud in order to access the nutrients.
(B) The bacterial action begins when the ruminant puts the cud in its mouth and starts the long process of chewing.
(C) The ruminant's strong teeth must crush the plant fibers in the cud in order to neutralize the cud's harmful bacteria.
(D) The cud is sent back to the ruminant's mouth and chewed extensively so that the fibers can be digested more easily.

QUESTION 6

Cities differ from towns in the size, density, and diversity of their population. The city offers a wider variety of goods and services, as well as more extensive employment and cultural opportunities. City life is characterized by impersonal and formal social relationships, greater privacy, and more lifestyle choices—a way of life referred to as urbanism. The urban spirit is sophisticated and dynamic, stimulating the mind through contrasts and encouraging tolerance of differences. However, urbanism is not restricted to city dwellers; it can be considered a trait of all modern societies at a high level of technological development. The urban spirit spreads beyond the city via the mass media: television, movies, music, and the Internet.

6. Which sentence below best expresses the essential information in the highlighted sentence in the passage?

(A) City dwellers do not let urbanism restrict their ability to develop new technology.
(B) Urbanism characterizes all highly developed societies, not just people who live in cities.
(C) All modern societies have a sophisticated level of technology; this is the primary goal of urbanism.
(D) Living in the city limits one's knowledge to only the most advanced technology.

QUESTIONS 7–8

1   Alligators have no natural predators except humans. In fact, humans drove alligators to near extinction in many of their marsh and swamp habitats in North America. Hunters once killed large numbers of these animals for their meat and soft belly skin, which was used to make shoes, belts, and wallets. Between 1950 and 1960, hunters wiped out 90 percent of the alligators in Louisiana and greatly reduced the alligator population in the Florida Everglades.

2   In 1967 the federal government placed the American alligator on the endangered species list. In the next decade, protected by hunters and averaging about 40 eggs per nest, the alligator made a strong comeback. It was reclassified from endangered to threatened in Florida, Louisiana, and Texas, where the vast majority of the animals live. As a threatened species, it is still protected from excessive harvesting by hunters; however, limited hunting is allowed in some areas to keep the population from growing too large.

7. Which sentence below best expresses the essential information in the highlighted sentence in paragraph 1?

(A) It is a fact that humans forced alligators to live in North America's marshes and swamps.

(B) Many alligators were killed when people built roads and drove cars through their habitats.

(C) People almost destroyed the native alligator population in many North American environments.

(D) In North America, humans and alligators rarely choose to live together in the same area.

8. Which sentence below best expresses the essential information in the highlighted sentence in paragraph 2?

(A) Alligators are still protected, but hunters are allowed to kill a certain number to control their population in some places.

(B) In order to prevent alligators from growing too large, hunters can harvest adult alligators that exceed a specified size.

(C) Hunting is restricted to areas where alligators are no longer a threatened species and therefore do not need protection.

(D) Alligators are more threatened than ever by excessive hunting, and hunters should not be allowed to destroy all of them.

QUESTIONS 9–10

1   Current archaeological theory holds that the first humans in the Americas were bands of advanced Stone Age people who crossed over from what is now Siberia in Asia sometime between 12 and 30 thousand years ago. Some scientists think that these early humans crossed what is now the Bering Sea on a land bridge, a stretch of glacial ice connecting Asia and North America. Others speculate that they may have crossed that 55–mile–wide channel by boat.

2   These early humans probably migrated southward along an ice–free corridor. After several thousand years, perhaps at a pace of only ten miles every year, the migrants spread over this new land from Alaska to the tip of South America, a trail over ten thousand miles long. In South America, where the glaciers from the ice age melted first, the migrants took strong root in the fertile soil and warming climate of Patagonia. As the ice receded farther north, civilization in what is now Central America and Mexico began to take shape and flourish.

9. Which sentence below best expresses the essential information in the highlighted sentence in paragraph 1?

(A) Theories vary widely over how the first humans arrived in the Americas, but most state that it occurred around 30 thousand years ago.

(B) The best current theory states that between 12 and 30 thousand early humans crossed over from Siberia to North America.

(C) Human beings originated in Siberia in Asia and later formed into bands that migrated to the Americas during the Stone Age.

(D) Archaeologists believe that groups of Stone Age humans first came to the Americas from Asia about 12 to 30 thousand years ago.

10. Which sentence below best expresses the essential information in the highlighted sentence in paragraph 2?

(A) When the glaciers in South America melted, the climate became warmer in Patagonia, helping the people grow strong.

(B) The favorable conditions in Patagonia attracted migrants from other parts of South America, where there were still glaciers.

(C) The ice age glaciers melted earliest in South America, where the migrants settled in the warm, fertile region of Patagonia.

(D) The migrants in Patagonia in South America survived on the root crops that grew well in the fertile soil and warm climate.

Exercise 1.6.B

Read the passages and choose the best answer to each question.

QUESTIONS 1–3

1   A subculture is a cultural group within the larger society that provides social support to people who differ from the majority in terms of status, race, ethnic background, religion, or other factors. Whenever these differences lead to exclusion or discrimination, subcultures develop as a shield to protect members from the negative attitudes of others. Subcultures unify the group and provide it with values, norms, and a history.

2   Some subcultures do not experience discrimination yet differ from the mainstream enough to generate a "we" feeling among members and a sense of separateness. Examples include military officers, college students, information technology specialists, social workers, jazz musicians, or any subgroup with its own special language and customs. Subcultures usually have values that are variations on those of the dominant culture. These variations are close enough for the subgroup to remain under the societal umbrella but different enough to reflect the unique experience of subgroup members. In North America today, teenagers are a distinct subculture with a special way of talking and dressing so that insiders can recognize one another while keeping outsiders out.

1. Which sentence below best expresses the essential information in the highlighted sentence in paragraph 1?

   (A) People are excluded from subcultures for various reasons, but especially if they have a negative attitude.
   (B) When some people discriminate against others, it is the responsibility of the majority culture to do something.
   (C) When people are different from others, they may experience negative effects, including discrimination.
   (D) Subcultures form to protect people who differ from the majority when these people face discrimination.

2. All of the following are given as characteristics of subcultures EXCEPT

   (A) a desire to join the dominant culture
   (B) experiences outside those of the mainstream
   (C) special customs and way of talking
   (D) a "we" feeling among members

3. Which sentence below best expresses the essential information in the highlighted sentence in paragraph 2?

   (A) The different experiences of subgroups cause their members to seek protection in the values and customs of their own group.
   (B) Every society is like a large umbrella that covers people from a wide variety of backgrounds and cultures, protecting everyone equally.
   (C) A subculture's values show its separateness yet resemble the majority's values enough to keep the subgroup within the larger society.
   (D) Each group member has experiences that differ from those of all other members and are completely outside those of the mainstream.

QUESTIONS 4–6

1   The cerebral cortex of the human brain is divided into two hemispheres that are linked by a thick band of fibers called the corpus callosum. Each hemisphere has four discrete lobes, and researchers have identified a number of functional areas within each lobe. The left hemisphere has areas for controlling speech, language, and calculation, while the right hemisphere controls creative ability and spatial perception. This centering of functions in specific areas of the brain is known as lateralization.

2   Much of our knowledge about brain lateralization comes from studies of "split–brain" patients, people with a damaged corpus callosum. In one experiment, a subject holding a key in his left hand, with both eyes open, was able to name it as a key. However, when the subject's eyes were covered, he could use the key to open a lock, but was unable to name it as a key. The center for speech is in the left hemisphere, but sensory information from the left hand crosses over and enters the right side of the brain. Without the corpus callosum to function as a switchboard between the two sides of the brain, the subject's knowledge of the size, texture, and function of the key could not be transferred from the right to the left hemisphere. The link between sensory input and spoken response was disconnected.

4. Which sentence below best expresses the essential information in the highlighted sentence in paragraph 1?

   (A) Each half of the brain consists of four types of tissues that are identified by their size and location.

   (B) The brain's two hemispheres each have four separate parts, and each part controls several functions.

   (C) There are a number of functional centers in the brain, and these can be divided into four main groups.

   (D) Research has shown that the brain controls four basic functions, each with a number of variations.

5. According to the passage, what is one effect of a damaged corpus callosum?

   (A) Functions from one side of the brain are transferred to the other side.

   (B) People with their eyes open cannot see an object held in the left hand.

   (C) The connection between sensory input and spoken response is broken.

   (D) Creative ability and spatial perception are greatly diminished.

6. Which sentence below best expresses the essential information in the highlighted sentence in paragraph 2?

   (A) Information about the key could not travel from one side of the brain to the other because the corpus callosum did not provide the link.

   (B) Some people are born without a corpus callosum, so they cannot exchange knowledge between the two hemispheres of the brain.

   (C) Both sides of the brain control knowledge of familiar objects, and the corpus callosum functions as a key to that knowledge.

   (D) The corpus callosum acts like a computer keyboard in the way that it takes information from the hands and enters it into the brain.

QUESTIONS 7–10

1   Organic compost (partially decomposed organic matter) requires four basic elements: carbon, nitrogen, air, and water. The carbon comes from dead organic matter, such as dried leaves, straw, and wood chips. The nitrogen comes from fresh or green materials, such as vegetative kitchen waste, untreated grass clippings, and animal manure. Fungi, bacteria, and other microorganisms use the carbon for energy and the nitrogen to grow and reproduce. The microorganisms secrete enzymes that break down the cells of the dead vegetation and animal matter. These enzymes are the glue that cements the soil particles into larger, coarser grains. Coarse soil crumbles easily, which aerates the soil and allows it to absorb moisture efficiently. This partially digested mixture is compost.

2   Compost is a stage of decay in which most of the organic matter has been broken down, but it may still be possible to identify individual parts such as leaves and twigs. The final phase of decay is called humus—a dark, sticky, nutrient–rich substance in which the original materials can no longer be distinguished. Although the terms "compost" and "humus" are often used interchangeably, they are not synonymous.

7. Which sentence below best expresses the essential information in the highlighted sentence in paragraph 1?

   (A) Enzymes from the microorganisms break apart when they come into contact with organic matter.
   (B) Nonliving plant and animal matter is digested when microorganisms produce certain enzymes.
   (C) Vegetation and animal matter contain enzymes that hinder the growth of dangerous microorganisms.
   (D) Microorganisms invade the cells of plants and animals, eventually causing the death of the host.

8. The word cements in paragraph 1 is closest in meaning to

   (A) lifts
   (B) freezes
   (C) sorts
   (D) combines

9. It can be inferred from paragraph 1 that organic compost

   (A) is less expensive than other types of compost
   (B) relies on the digestive processes of microorganisms
   (C) is based on the belief that everything in nature changes
   (D) requires about a year before it can be used in the soil

10. Which sentence below best expresses the essential information in the highlighted sentence in paragraph 2?

   (A) Compost and humus are different substances, but people sometimes confuse the two words.
   (B) It is often possible to change compost into humus, but you cannot change humus into compost.
   (C) "Compost" used to be a synonym for "humus," but the meaning of both words has changed over time.
   (D) Some people think that compost eventually becomes humus, but actually the reverse is true.

Answers to Exercises 1.6.A through 1.6.B are on page 643.

 EXTENSION

1. Outside of class, look in a magazine or a university textbook. Select a short passage of one to three paragraphs. In class, work with a partner. Identify the nouns and verbs in each selected passage. Then, use a dictionary, synonym finder, or thesaurus to find as many synonyms as possible for the nouns and verbs you have identified. Names and other proper nouns will not have synonyms. Also, be aware that not every synonym will be appropriate for the context of your passage, and some synonyms will be more appropriate than others. If you are not sure whether a synonym is correct in the context, ask your teacher.

2. In reading done outside class, select a short passage of no more than 100 words. Write a paraphrase of the passage by restating each sentence in a different way, using different words. You may also combine ideas from more than one sentence into one sentence. To extend this activity further, bring the original passage and your paraphrase to class. Exchange your original passage with a partner's. Next, write a paraphrase of this new passage while your partner paraphrases the original passage from you. When you are both finished writing, compare the two paraphrases. Do both paraphrases contain the same essential information as the original?

3. Outside of class, select a short passage of no more than 100 words. Make a copy of the passage for each student in your class, or write the passage on an overhead projector transparency. Choose one sentence from the passage and restate it in a different way, using different words. In class, write the paraphrased sentence on the board or the overhead projector. Your class must read the passage and the paraphrased sentence and determine which sentence in the original passage is being paraphrased. Does your paraphrase include all of the essential information from the original sentence?

1.7 Recognizing Coherence

🔍 FOCUS

Read the sentences below. Put them in order. Which sentence should come first? Beside each sentence, write 1, 2, or 3 to show the correct order:

___ The trunk's inner core consists of vertically oriented cells that are closely packed together in parallel rows.

___ Millions upon millions of such cells form the heartwood—the nonliving central pillar on which the living tree hoists itself skyward.

___ The most distinguishing characteristic of a mature tree is its self–supporting woody spine, or trunk.

The most logical order, from top to bottom, is: 2, 3, 1. Now look at the sentences in a paragraph:

> ■ The most distinguishing characteristic of a mature tree is its self–supporting woody spine, or trunk. ■ The trunk's inner core consists of vertically oriented cells that are closely packed together in parallel rows. ■ Millions upon millions of such cells form the heartwood—the nonliving central pillar on which the living tree hoists itself skyward. ■

Now read the following sentence, which can be added to the above paragraph.

All trees share certain growth characteristics that distinguish them from other members of the plant kingdom.

Where would the sentence best fit? Choose the square [■] where the sentence could be added.

The sentence would best fit at the first square. Now read the paragraph with the sentence added in the correct place. Notice how each sentence leads into the next sentence, helping the paragraph flow smoothly.

> **All trees share certain growth characteristics that distinguish them from other members of the plant kingdom.** The most distinguishing characteristic of a mature tree is its self–supporting woody spine, or trunk. The trunk's inner core consists of vertically oriented cells that are closely packed together in parallel rows. Millions upon millions of such cells form the heartwood—the nonliving central pillar on which the living tree hoists itself skyward.

All of the sentences in the paragraph flow smoothly and logically. This logical order gives the paragraph *coherence*.

 STUDY

1. Coherence

Coherence is the quality of unity and order among the parts of a written passage. If a passage is ***coherent***, there are logical and orderly connections among the ideas within sentences and among the sentences within paragraphs. There are also orderly connections among the various paragraphs. Coherent writing makes sense. It is easy to understand because all of its parts fit together and flow logically one after another.

Coherence questions on the TOEFL test your ability to identify where a sentence can be added to a passage. Questions about coherence look like this:

> Look at the four squares [■] that indicate where the following sentence could be added to the passage.
>
> **(Sentence)**
>
> Where would the sentence best fit?
>
> Click on a square [■] to add the sentence to the passage.

Squares in the passage will indicate the answer choices. When you click on a square, the sentence will appear in that place. You can try putting the sentence at any square until you are satisfied that the passage reads logically and coherently.

Your understanding of the organization and purpose of the passage, and your knowledge of pronouns and transitions, will help you determine where to add the sentence. You can also determine where *not* to add the sentence by identifying places where adding it would interrupt the logical connection between ideas in consecutive sentences.

2. Purpose Clues

Coherence and purpose are related. A passage is coherent if the author's purpose is clear and logically presented. Look at this example:

> *Two reasons* for government regulation of industry stand out. *First*, economists have traditionally stressed the importance of containing market power. A *second reason*, deriving from public–choice theories, is that the regulators are captured by the regulated.

Two reasons, *first*, and *second reason* tell you that the author's purpose is to list reasons for government regulation. The sentence order is coherent. Adding a sentence between any of the sentences might interrupt the logical flow of ideas.

Look at another example:

> Good managers adjust plans when necessary. Flexible plans allow for several contingencies. *Contingencies are* events that might affect what you plan to do, but rarely are out of your control. *For example*, rain is a contingency that might affect the success of an outdoor event, so plans for an outdoor event should include a "rain plan."

The author's purpose is to define the term *contingency* and give an example to illustrate. The sentence order is coherent. Adding a sentence between any of the sentences might interrupt the logical flow of ideas supporting the purpose: to introduce a term, define it, and illustrate it with an example.

3. Pronoun Clues

Pronouns and their referents are clues to coherence. A ***pronoun*** is a word that substitutes for a noun or refers to a noun. A ***referent*** is the noun to which a pronoun refers. Usually the noun referent is mentioned before the pronoun, but sometimes it comes later. The referent may be in the same sentence as the pronoun, or it may be in another sentence.

You may see the following pronouns in coherence questions on the TOEFL:

Subject Pronouns	he	she	it	they
Object Pronouns	him	her	it	them
Possessive Adjectives	his	her	its	their
Demonstratives	this	that	these	those
Relative Pronouns	who	whom	which	whose
Other Pronouns	all	either	none	the first
	another	a few	one	the last
	any	many	others	the former
	both	most	several	the latter
	each	neither	some	the other

In the following examples, pronouns and their referents are shown in *italics*. The use of pronouns and referents is a clue to the coherent order of sentences. Adding a sentence between any of the sentences below might interrupt the connection between the noun and the pronoun used in its place.

Every society has *a favorite imagined figure* that is seen in the surface markings of the full moon. In Asia and Europe, *it* is commonly a hare, while North Americans see the "man in the moon."

Because *she* was essentially a realist, *Willa Cather* made human nature the subject of *her* novels. Many of *her* characters were based on real people that *she* knew and loved.

The brain of a computer is its *central processing unit*. In the case of a microcomputer, *this* is a chip called the *microprocessor*, *which* is connected to the other units by groups of wires.

Driving while intoxicated is illegal. However, *this* is not the only reason to avoid drinking and driving.

Like the gray and fox squirrels, *the Eastern chipmunk* often feeds on acorns and hickory nuts. Essentially a ground species, *this pert rodent* does not hesitate to climb large oak trees when the acorns are ripe.

Three common herbs are effective remedies for a sore throat: *angelica*, *sage*, and *vervain*. *All* are available in health food stores.

Only two *elements* are liquids at normal temperatures. *One* is mercury and *the other* is bromine.

The bassoon and the oboe are members of the woodwind family. *The former* is a low–pitched double–reed instrument that can produce high and delicate legato sounds, as well as low and loud staccato notes.

4. Transition Clues

Certain words and phrases called *transitions* are clues to coherence because they connect ideas and control the order of sentences. Transitions identify relationships of ideas among sentences and among paragraphs. Some commonly used transitions are:

Addition	Contrast	Example	Cause/Result
also	although	for example	as a result
another	however	for instance	because
other	in contrast	including	consequently
first, second...	instead	one example is	hence
moreover	rather than	such as	therefore
too	while	to illustrate	thus

Transitions show the relationship between consecutive sentences. Look at this example:

> Akira Kurosawa's masterful works burst on the international film scene in the 1950s with the sound of fireworks and epic battles. *In contrast*, the quiet dignity and unobtrusive techniques of Satyajit Ray's films also placed him among the world's great directors.

In contrast is a transition that shows contrast and determines the sentence order. *In contrast* indicates that the information in the second sentence should come after the information in the first sentence.

Look at another example:

> At least one central quality of music—rhythmic organization—can exist apart from the ability of people to hear it. Music's rhythms can be translated into a visual series of colored forms or performed by a dance troupe. *Hence*, certain aspects of the musical experience are accessible even to deaf individuals who cannot appreciate its auditory qualities.

Hence is a transition that introduces result. *Hence* shows that the idea *certain aspects of the musical experience are accessible even to deaf individuals* is a result of the ideas about music's rhythmic organization mentioned in the previous sentences.

5. Answer Choices

In questions about coherence, an answer choice may be incorrect because adding the sentence there would:

- interrupt the logical flow of ideas in consecutive sentences;
- interrupt the logical connection between a pronoun and its referent; or
- interfere with the correct use of transitions.

6. Sample Questions

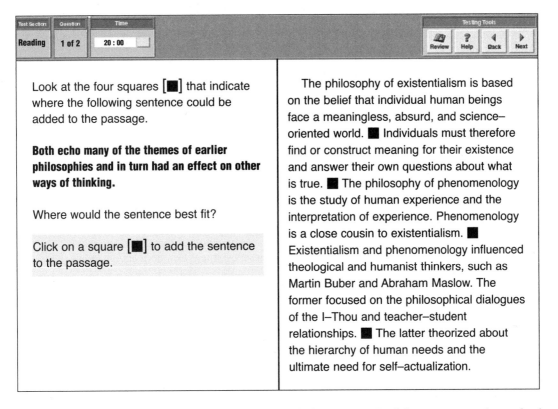

The sentence best fits at the third square. In the added sentence, *Both* is a pronoun clue referring to *phenomenology* and *existentialism* in the previous sentence. Also, the added sentence introduces the idea of *an effect on other ways of thinking*, which the next sentence develops with examples of theological and humanist thinkers. With the added sentence in the correct place, the passage reads:

> The philosophy of existentialism is based on the belief that individual human beings face a meaningless, absurd, and science–oriented world. ■ Individuals must therefore find or construct meaning for their existence and answer their own questions about what is true. ■ The philosophy of phenomenology is the study of human experience and the interpretation of experience. Phenomenology is a close cousin to existentialism. **Both echo many of the themes of earlier philosophies and in turn had an effect on other ways of thinking.** Existentialism and phenomenology influenced theological and humanist thinkers, such as Martin Buber and Abraham Maslow. The former focused on the philosophical dialogues of the I–Thou and teacher–student relationships. ■ The latter theorized about the hierarchy of human needs and the ultimate need for self–actualization.

Adding the sentence anywhere else would interrupt the connection between the pronoun and its referents. It would also interrupt the logical flow of ideas.

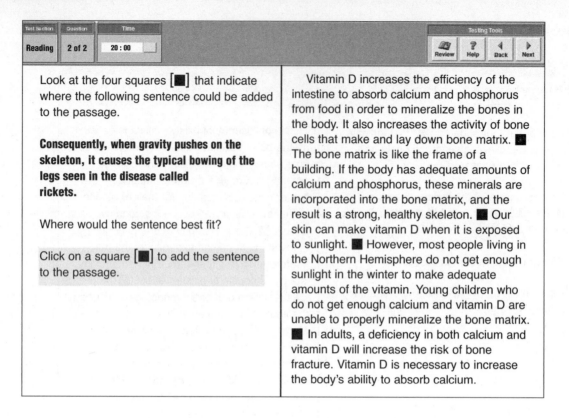

The sentence best fits at the fourth square. In the added sentence, *Consequently* is a transition that introduces result. It shows that *the typical bowing of the legs seen in the disease called rickets* is a result of the idea in the previous sentence that children lacking calcium and vitamin D are *unable to properly mineralize the bone matrix*. With the added sentence in the correct place, the passage reads:

Vitamin D increases the efficiency of the intestine to absorb calcium and phosphorus from food in order to mineralize the bones in the body. It also increases the activity of bone cells that make and lay down bone matrix. ■ The bone matrix is like the frame of a building. If the body has adequate amounts of calcium and phosphorus, these minerals are incorporated into the bone matrix, and the result is a strong, healthy skeleton. ■ Our skin can make vitamin D when it is exposed to sunlight. ■ However, most people living in the Northern Hemisphere do not get enough sunlight in the winter to make adequate amounts of the vitamin. Young children who do not get enough calcium and vitamin D are unable to properly mineralize the bone matrix. **Consequently, when gravity pushes on the skeleton, it causes the typical bowing of the legs seen in the disease called rickets.** In adults, a deficiency in both calcium and vitamin D will increase the risk of bone fracture. Vitamin D is necessary to increase the body's ability to absorb calcium.

Adding the sentence anywhere else would interfere with the correct use of transitions and interrupt the logical flow of ideas.

 PRACTICE

Exercise 1.7.A

Read the passages and choose the best answer to each question.

1. Look at the four squares, **A**, **B**, **C**, and **D**, which indicate where the following sentence could be added to the passage. Where would the sentence best fit?

   Most of them like to talk, especially in front of a group.

   Kindergartners are quite skillful with language. **A** Providing a "sharing time" gives children a natural opportunity for talking. However, many will need help in becoming good listeners. **B** Some sort of rotation scheme is usually necessary to divide talking opportunities between the talkative and silent extremes. **C** Teachers can provide activities or experinces for less confident children to talk about, such as a field trip, a book, or a film. **D**

2. Look at the four squares, **A**, **B**, **C**, and **D**, which indicate where the following sentence could be added to the passage. Where would the sentence best fit?

   However, the ground surface is spongy and wet to the touch.

   Bogs are a distinctive type of wetland. **A** They appear relatively dry, with only small amounts of shallow water visible. **B** The surface material is largely sphagnum moss or other organic matter rather than mineral soil. **C** Bogs are usually characterized by evergreen trees and shrubs and are underlain by deep peat deposits. **D** Bogs will develop in former glacial lakes by the gradual accumulation of organic matter falling from beneath a floating mat of vegetation advancing out over the water.

3. Look at the four squares, **A**, **B**, **C**, and **D**, which indicate where the following sentence could be added to the passage. Where would the sentence best fit?

   The narrower leaves of trees like willows and mimosa provide a dappled shade, which may be more beneficial to lawns and garden plants.

   While all living things need sunlight, too much of it can be oppressive, even damaging. **A** Any overheated dog or cat can appreciate the relief provided by a mature shade tree on a sunny day. **B** The densest foliage, and so the densest shade, is found under the broad leaves of deciduous trees like oaks and maples. **C** By cooling the surrounding air, the shade from trees reduces the demand for air conditioning in nearby homes. **D** This translates into reduced emissions of carbon dioxide from oil– or coal–fired electrical generators.

4. Look at the four squares, **A**, **B**, **C**, and **D**, which indicate where the following sentence could be added to the passage. Where would the sentence best fit?

This is due to the beating of the double reed through which the air travels as it leaves the player's mouth.

The highest of the standard orchestral instruments, the flute is unlike the other woodwinds because it is held across the player's mouth. **A** The air inside is set in vibration by the action of the airstream against the edge of the hole. **B** The flute has no reed, so its tone is pure and creamy. **C** In contrast, the oboe has a rasping, "sawtooth" configuration to its sound when played loud. **D** However, the oboe can produce a quiet and gentle sound when called for, and it can even approximate the human voice.

5. Look at the four squares, **A**, **B**, **C**, and **D**, which indicate where the following sentence could be added to the passage. Where would the sentence best fit?

It is the only method available for obtaining a variety of colors in bamboo.

For centuries, bamboo has provided building materials for Eastern cultures. Now it is becoming more popular and available in the West, particularly as a substitute for expensive hardwood flooring. **A** As a flooring material, natural honey–colored bamboo is more stable than carbonized bamboo. **B** Carbonizing is a technique of steaming and pressurizing the bamboo to introduce carbon fibers that darken the original material. **C** However, it lowers the hardness factor, making the darker bamboo more susceptible to damage. **D**

6. Look at the four squares, **A**, **B**, **C**, and **D**, which indicate where the following sentence could be added to the passage. Where would the sentence best fit?

No one can be made better off without making someone else worse off.

An economy is efficient if there is no way of reorganizing production and distribution to improve everyone's satisfaction. Economists call such a state *allocative efficiency*. **A** When people come to a market with goods they have produced, they trade their goods for those of others. **B** Every completed trade raises the satisfaction of both sides. **C** When all of the beneficial trades have been completed, no one can find another trade to improve his situation. **D** Under such conditions, the economy has attained allocative efficiency.

7. Look at the four squares, **A**, **B**, **C**, and **D**, which indicate where the following sentence could be added to the passage. Where would the sentence best fit?

Researchers found that high–pitched tones made people think of bright colors, while low tones brought dark colors to mind.

For people with a condition called *synesthesia*, sound is directly linked to the sense of sight, and they experience sounds by seeing them as colors. **A** However, different sounds sometimes remind everyone of different colors. **B** In one study, students were asked to relate colors to different tones of music. **C** White, yellow, and pink were associated with tones in the 4,000–Hz range; blue and green were associated with tones in the 1,000–Hz range; and brown, gray, and black were associated with tones in the 200–Hz range. **D**

8. Look at the four squares, **A**, **B**, **C**, and **D**, which indicate where the following sentence could be added to the passage. Where would the sentence best fit?

This irritation is caused by viruses or bacteria, exposure to tobacco smoke, or air pollution.

Bronchitis is an inflammation of the bronchial tubes in the lungs. **A** It often appears after a cold or an upper respiratory infection that does not heal completely. It also may accompany childhood infections such as measles, whooping cough, and typhoid fever. **B** The inflamed bronchial tubes secrete a sticky mucus called sputum. It is difficult for the tiny hairs on the bronchi to clear out this sputum. **C** The cough that comes with bronchitis is the body's attempt to eliminate it. **D** Other symptoms include discomfort or tightness in the chest, low fever, sore throat, and sometimes wheezing. Severe cases of bronchitis may lead to pneumonia.

9. Look at the four squares, **A**, **B**, **C**, and **D**, which indicate where the following sentence could be added to the passage. Where would the sentence best fit?

Courses included Far Eastern, Spanish, and Native American dances as well as basic ballet.

Among the modern dance innovators of the early twentieth century was Ruth St. Denis, whose dances were lush and graceful, tinged with exoticism and mysticism. **A** St. Denis was particularly expert in the manipulation of draperies and veils so that the moving fabrics seemed like magical extensions of her own body. **B** St. Denis's 1914 marriage to dancer–choreographer Ted Shawn resulted in a wedding of names, Denishawn, which first became a school and then a dance company. **C** Denishawn drew its inspiration and derived its curriculum from a variety of ethnic sources. **D** The touring Denishawn company might offer on a single program a Hindu dance, a rhythmic interpretation of concert music, a romantic duet, a hula, and a demonstration of the latest ballroom craze.

10. Look at the four squares, **A**, **B**, **C**, and **D**, which indicate where the following sentence could be added to the passage. Where would the sentence best fit?

Both biological and chemical oceanographers are trying to make ocean life and industrial progress compatible so marine ecosystems will not be endangered.

A Within the field of oceanography, the major areas stressed are physical, biological, chemical, geological, engineering, and technological. However, each of these areas is interdependent of the others. Both physical oceanographers and ocean engineers are involved in harnessing the energies of the ocean to fill the demand for electrical power. **B** Even if oceanographers have an area of major interest, they are consistently forced to take a more interdisciplinary view of their work because the various sciences overlap. **C** Oceanographers of different backgrounds depend on each other to further their own research. **D** A conference of marine scientists might include discussions of plate tectonics, effects of offshore mining on fisheries, effects of climate change on marine life, technology for deep–sea exploration, and other related topics.

Exercise 1.7.B

Read the passages and choose the best answer to each question.

QUESTIONS 1–3

1   The 2,000–year–old complex of mounds occupying thirteen acres on the banks of the Scioto River in southwestern Ohio is one of the most important sites of the Hopewell Indian culture. Their mound construction was especially intensive in this area. It offers evidence that this society flourished in the Ohio Valley for five hundred years.

2   The 23 mounds are spaciously placed but with no overall pattern. Archaeologists have determined that the complex—called Mound City—was apparently both a village and a burial site. Numerous artifacts have been found in excavations of the burial mounds. They include shell beads, bear and shark teeth, pottery, and ear spools of copper and silver. A number of pipes found in one mound—probably belonging to a chief or priest—are remarkable for their exquisite workmanship and·stylized realism in the likenesses of animals and birds: wildcat, beaver, great blue heron, and raven.

1. The word flourished in paragraph 1 is closest in meaning to

(A) suffered
(B) fished
(C) lived
(D) competed

2. The word likenesses in paragraph 2 is closest in meaning to

(A) forms
(B) bones
(C) behavior
(D) habitats

3. Look at the four squares, **A**, **B**, **C**, and **D**, which indicate where the following sentence could be added to the passage. Where would the sentence best fit?

The quantity and type of burial objects in particular mounds indicates the status and occupation of the deceased.

The 23 mounds are spaciously placed but with no overall pattern. Archaeologists have determined that the complex—called Mound City—was apparently both a village and a burial site. **A** Numerous artifacts have been found in excavations of the burial mounds. **B** They include shell beads, bear and shark teeth, pottery, and ear spools of copper and silver. **C** A number of pipes found in one mound—probably belonging to a chief or priest—are remarkable for their exquisite workmanship and stylized realism in the likenesses of animals and birds: wildcat, beaver, great blue heron, and raven. **D**

QUESTIONS 4–6

1   Although some fish appear capable of swimming at extremely high speeds, most fish, such as trout and minnows, can actually swim only about ten body lengths per second. Translated into kilometers per hour, it means that a 30–centimeter trout can swim only about 10.4 kilometers per hour. Generally speaking, the larger the fish the faster it can swim.

2   We can understand how fish swim by studying the motion of a very flexible fish such as an eel. The movement is **serpentine**, with **undulations** moving backward along the body by alternate contraction of the muscles on either side of the eel's body. While the undulations move backward, the bending of the body pushes sideways against the water, producing a reactive force that is directed forward at an angle. The movement has two components: thrust and lateral force. Thrust is used to propel the fish forward, and lateral force tends to make the fish's head deviate from the course in the same direction as the tail. This side–to–side head movement is very obvious in a swimming eel, but fish with large, rigid heads have enough surface resistance to minimize the lateral movement.

Glossary:
   serpentine: like a snake
   undulation: wavelike motion

4. It can be inferred from paragraph 1 that a 60–centimeter fish can swim

  (A) at extremely high speeds
  (B) faster than a 30–centimeter fish
  (C) only about 10.4 kilometers per hour
  (D) fast enough to catch an eel

5. Which sentence below best expresses the essential information in the highlighted sentence in the passage?

  (A) The fish uses thrust when moving forward, and lateral force when moving backward or sideways.
  (B) Both force and lateral thrust are needed for the fish to maintain its intended course.
  (C) Thrust can be seen in the fish's head, while lateral force is seen in both its head and its tail.
  (D) Thrust pushes the fish forward, and lateral force pushes both its head and its tail to the same side.

6. Look at the four squares, **A**, **B**, **C**, and **D**, which indicate where the following sentence could be added to the passage. Where would the sentence best fit?

The front end of the body bends less than the back end, so each undulation increases in size as it travels along the body.

We can understand how fish swim by studying the motion of a very flexible fish such as an eel. **A** The movement is serpentine, with undulations moving backward along the body by alternate contraction of the muscles on either side of the eel's body. **B** While the undulations move backward, the bending of the body pushes sideways against the water, producing a reactive force that is directed forward at an angle. **C** The movement has two components: thrust and lateral force. **D** Thrust is used to propel the fish forward, and lateral force tends to make the fish's head deviate from the course in the same direction as the tail. This side–to–side head movement is very obvious in a swimming eel, but fish with large, rigid heads have enough surface resistance to minimize the lateral movement.

QUESTIONS 7–10

1   Both the Greeks and the Romans minted coins. The Romans called the place where coins were made and stored by the Latin word *moneta*, the ancestor of the English word *money*. Even after coins were developed, however, the world was still a long way away from our current system of money. Each city made its own coins, with no common way of exchanging one type for another. Gradually, traders worked out different rates of exchange.

2   Another complication lay in the fact that for thousands of years, most people did not use money for important purchases. Although the wealthier classes used money for major transactions, ordinary people continued to barter for most things in their daily lives. For example, workers would be paid in food, clothing, and shelter, rather than in money. Farmers would grow food and make items for themselves, trading the tiny surplus for whatever they could not make or grow.

3   Paper money had a lot of advantages: it was lighter and easier to carry. It was also a lot cheaper to make. The development of paper money meant that people had grasped the difference between money as a symbol and money as something that was worth only the actual cost of the paper and ink in making a bill. The first known use of paper money was in China, around the year 1300. The first use of paper money in Europe was in Sweden in the 1600s, a time of extensive international trade and exploration. Because paper money made trade easier and more efficient, its use quickly caught on throughout the world.

7. Which sentence below best expresses the essential information in the highlighted sentence in the passage?

(A) Because the majority of people did not have much money, they had to use other methods of exchange.
(B) Rich people used money for important purchases, but common people traded goods and services directly.
(C) The daily life of the rich and the poor differed mainly in the amount of money that was available to them.
(D) The wealthier classes had more control over how they used their money than did members of the lower classes

8. The word grasped in paragraph 3 is closest in
   meaning to

   (A) reduced
   (B) challenged
   (C) understood
   (D) hidden

9. Look at the four squares, **A**, **B**, **C**, and **D**, which indicate where the following sentence could
   be added to the passage. Where would the sentence best fit?

   **However, this was a long, slow process that often developed differently, depending on
   the individual trader.**

   Both the Greeks and the Romans minted coins. The Romans called the place where
   coins were made and stored by the Latin word *moneta*, the ancestor of the English word
   money. **A** Even after coins were developed, however, the world was still a long way away
   from our current system of money. **B** Each city made its own coins, with no common way
   of exchanging one type for another. **C** Gradually, traders worked out different rates of
   exchange. **D**

10. Look at the four squares, **A**, **B**, **C**, and **D**, which indicate where the following sentence could
    be added to the passage. Where would the sentence best fit?

    **As trade became an ever more important part of the world economy, people began to use
    paper money as well as coins.**

    A Paper money had a lot of advantages: it was lighter and easier to carry. **B** It was
    also a lot cheaper to make. **C** The development of paper money meant that people had
    grasped the difference between money as a symbol and money as something that was
    worth only the actual cost of the paper and ink in making a bill. The first known use of
    paper money was in China, around the year 1300. **D** The first use of paper money in
    Europe was in Sweden in the 1600s, a time of extensive international trade and
    exploration. Because paper money made trade easier and more efficient, its use quickly
    caught on throughout the world.

    Answers to Exercises 1.7.A through 1.7.B are on page 644.

 EXTENSION

1. Outside of class, look in a newspaper, a magazine, or a university textbook. Select a short passage of one to three paragraphs. Make a photocopy and bring it to class. In class, work with a partner. Read the passage and underline the transitions, pronouns, and other key words and phrases that help make the passage coherent.

2. Outside of class, select a paragraph of four to six sentences from a magazine or a university textbook. Copy out the sentences in the form of a list. Now, *mix up the order of the sentences*. In class, write the list of sentences in the mixed–up, incorrect order on the board or an overhead projector transparency. As a class, put the sentences into a coherent order as a paragraph. What words and phrases are clues to coherence? What makes the order of sentences logical? Is there more than one possible order for the sentences? Does changing the order of sentences change the meaning of the paragraph?

3. Outside of class, select a paragraph of four to six sentences from a magazine or university textbook. Copy out the paragraph on an overhead projector transparency, *but omit one sentence*. Write the omitted sentence in a separate box above or below the paragraph. In class, work in pairs or small groups to determine where the omitted sentence would best fit in the paragraph. Compare your answer with the answers of other students and with the original passage.

PROGRESS – 1.6 through 1.7

QUIZ 7

Time – 20 minutes

Read the passages and choose the best answer to each question. Answer all questions about a passage on the basis of what is stated or implied in that passage.

HISTORY OF LANGUAGE

1   In evolutionary history, the development of language set humans apart from the rest of the animal kingdom. Spoken language originated when early humans began to string grunts and squeals together to form a sound–meaning system. Language provided humans with the tools to create ideas and then to communicate these ideas to other people.

2   As human knowledge and civilization expanded, a system that stored information became necessary. The first writing systems used pictures to represent objects. These early systems were successful in recording concrete details concerning trade and taxes, but they could not convey abstract ideas and emotions. Between 800 and 500 B.C., the ancient Greeks began to use a phonetic alphabet that used symbols to represent sounds, with each sound making up part of a word. Thus, written language became a means of mass communication.

3   The expansion of humanity from an oral society to one that also used the written word for communication was a defining point in human civilization. Early oral cultures required a tribal mentality with histories defined by family or clan perspectives, but writing allowed a broader, global perspective to emerge.

1. Which sentence below best expresses the essential information in the highlighted sentence in paragraph 1? Incorrect choices change the meaning in important ways or leave out essential information.

 (A) Humans evolved as the most powerful species after they developed language.
 (B) The creation of human language has its origins in the language of animals.
 (C) The emergence of language distinguished early humans from other animals.
 (D) Humans and animals developed completely different systems of communication.

2. Which sentence below best expresses the essential information in the highlighted sentence in paragraph 3? Incorrect choices change the meaning in important ways or leave out essential information.

 (A) Civilization changed a great deal when humans rejected oral communication in favor of more complex systems of communication.
 (B) Human societies were not able to define themselves until they developed written language.
 (C) The power of language is humanity's most basic characteristic because language provides new tools of communication.
 (D) An important development in human history occurred when writing was added to speaking as a form of communication.

3. Look at the four squares, ■A■, ■B■, ■C■, and ■D■, which indicate where the following sentence could be added to the passage. Where would the sentence best fit?

Before written language evolved, there was no way of permanently recording language.

■A■ As human knowledge and civilization expanded, a system that stored information became necessary. The first writing systems used pictures to represent objects. ■B■ These early systems were successful in recording concrete details concerning trade and taxes, but they could not convey abstract ideas and emotions. ■C■ Between 800 and 500 B.C., the ancient Greeks began to use a phonetic alphabet that used symbols to represent sounds, with each sound making up part of a word. ■D■ Thus, written language became a means of mass communication.

PAIN

1   Virtually all animals experience pain. Pain is a distress call from the body signaling some damaging stimulus or internal disorder. It is one of the most important sensations because it is translated into a negative reaction, such as withdrawal from danger. Rare individuals who are born without the ability to feel pain may die from such conditions as a ruptured appendix because they are unaware of the danger.

2   Pain receptors are unspecialized nerve fiber endings that respond to a variety of stimuli signaling real or possible damage to tissues. Some groups of pain receptors respond to specific classes of chemicals released from damaged or inflamed tissue. When pain fibers respond to peptides released by injured cells, this is called slow pain. Fast pain responses—for example, a pinprick or hot or cold stimuli—are a more direct response of the nerve endings to mechanical or thermal stimuli.

3   There is no pain center in the **cerebral cortex**. However, discrete areas have been located in the brain stem where pain messages from various parts of the body terminate. These areas contain two kinds of small peptides, endorphins and enkephalins, which have activity similar to morphine or opium. When these peptides are released, they bind with specific opiate receptors in the midbrain, decreasing the perception of pain.

Glossary:
    cerebral cortex: part of the brain that controls high–level functions such as thought and sensation

4. Which sentence below best expresses the essential information in the highlighted sentence in paragraph 1? Incorrect choices change the meaning in important ways or leave out essential information.

  Ⓐ Escaping from danger is a negative reaction, but it is the most important thing an individual learns.
  Ⓑ The ability to sense pain is extremely important because pain signals the body to respond to a threat.
  Ⓒ Experiencing pain is one type of reaction to a negative stimulus; another type is avoiding danger.
  Ⓓ We experience a lot of sensations, and the most important ones are translated into appropriate actions.

5. Look at the four squares, **A**, **B**, **C**, and **D**, which indicate where the following sentence could be added to the passage. Where would the sentence best fit?

They respond to stimuli such as changes in temperature and pressure, and movement of the tissue.

Pain receptors are unspecialized nerve fiber endings that respond to a variety of stimuli signaling real or possible damage to tissues. **A** Some groups of pain receptors respond to specific classes of chemicals released from damaged or inflamed tissue. **B** When pain fibers respond to peptides released by injured cells, this is called slow pain. **C** Fast pain responses—for example, a pinprick or hot or cold stimuli—are a more direct response of the nerve endings to mechanical or thermal stimuli. **D**

6. Look at the four squares, **A**, **B**, **C**, and **D**, which indicate where the following sentence could be added to the passage. Where would the sentence best fit?

Thus, they are considered the body's own natural painkillers.

There is no pain center in the brain's cerebral cortex. **A** However, discrete areas have been located in the brain stem where pain messages from various parts of the body terminate. **B** These areas contain two kinds of small peptides, endorphins and enkephalins, which have activity similar to morphine or opium. **C** When these peptides are released, they bind with specific opiate receptors in the midbrain, decreasing the perception of pain. **D**

PRESTIGE

1   Prestige refers to a person's social standing—the level of respect that other people are willing to show. A person with high prestige is honored or esteemed by other people, while a person with low prestige is disrespected or marginalized. Prestige is a valued resource for people at all levels of a society, and this can be seen among inner–city youth, where to disrespect or "diss" someone has negative consequences. Exactly what qualities are respected will vary from one society to another.

2   In the United States, the top–status occupations are the professions—physicians, lawyers, professors, and clergy—requiring many years of education and training. At the other end of the hierarchy, the lowest prestige is associated with occupations requiring little formal education—for example, bus drivers, sanitation workers, and janitors. Prestige is linked to income, but there are exceptions, such as college professors, who have high prestige but relatively low salaries compared to physicians and lawyers. Conversely, some low–prestige workers receive high union wages and benefits. Criminals are often well rewarded with income and respect in their communities, while politicians—many of whom are wealthy—are frequently less respected than occupations such as secretary and bank teller.

7. Which sentence below best expresses the essential information in the highlighted sentence in paragraph 1? Incorrect choices change the meaning in important ways or leave out essential information.

    (A) The most valuable resource in any society is prestige, but young people who disrespect others reject this.
    (B) People at all social levels value prestige, and to disrespect another is punished, for example, among urban youth.
    (C) The disrespectful behavior of some young people shows that prestige is not valued equally throughout a society.
    (D) There are serious consequences when teenagers from the inner city do not show respect for other groups.

8. Look at the four squares, **A**, **B**, **C**, and **D**, which indicate where the following sentence could be added to the passage. Where would the sentence best fit?

Some societies honor wisdom and old age; others value warriors or youth.

    Prestige refers to a person's social standing—the level of respect that other people are willing to show. **A** A person with high prestige is honored or esteemed by other people, while a person with low prestige is disrespected or marginalized. **B** Prestige is a valued resource for people at all levels of a society, and this can be seen among inner–city youth, where to disrespect or "diss" someone has negative consequences. **C** Exactly what qualities are respected will vary from one society to another. **D**

9. Which sentence below best expresses the essential information in the highlighted sentence in paragraph 2? Incorrect choices change the meaning in important ways or leave out essential information.

   (A) If an occupation has high prestige, then it usually has a high income; college professors, physicians, and lawyers are good examples.

   (B) Occupational status depends on income, although there is a wide range of income levels in occupations such as college professor.

   (C) The fact that college professors have high prestige but relatively low incomes is an exception to the rule that prestige and income are related.

   (D) It is unfair for college professors to have low salaries compared to other high–prestige professions that have high salaries.

10. Look at the four squares, **A**, **B**, **C**, and **D**, which indicate where the following sentence could be added to the passage. Where would the sentence best fit?

   In postindustrial societies, prestige is linked to occupational status, although income is also important.

   A In the United States, the top–status occupations are the professions—physicians, lawyers, professors, and clergy—requiring many years of education and training. **B** At the other end of the hierarchy, the lowest prestige is associated with occupations requiring little formal education—for example, bus drivers, sanitation workers, and janitors. Prestige is linked to income, but there are exceptions, such as college professors, who have high prestige but relatively low salaries compared to physicians and lawyers. **C** Conversely, some low–prestige workers receive high union wages and benefits. **D** Criminals are often well rewarded with income and respect in their communities, while politicians—many of whom are wealthy—are frequently less respected than occupations such as secretary and bank teller.

Answers to Reading Quiz 7 are on pages 644–645.

Record your score on the Progress Chart on page 790.

PROGRESS – 1.1 through 1.7

QUIZ 8

Time – 35 minutes

Read the passages and choose the best answer to each question. Answer all questions about a passage on the basis of what is stated or implied in that passage.

THE LONGHOUSE

1   The people of the longhouse lived in fortified villages in elevated areas that were easy to defend and were located near a water supply. Twenty–foot palisades surrounded a group of longhouses and acted as a defensive wall that also kept forest animals from foraging within the village. The longhouse was the typical housing unit within the stockade. A number of families were housed within each longhouse, which varied in size from 20 by 16 feet to huge multiple family structures of 60 by 18 feet. In the more populous villages, longhouses could be more than 300 feet long. The longhouse was more than just a shelter; it was the basic unit upon which the entire society was constructed.

2   In building the longhouse, a row of forked poles was placed in the ground, between four and five feet apart. Cross poles were lashed to the forked uprights to form an arched roof. Slender poles or rafters were then secured to the roof frame, and traverse poles were added to further strengthen the overhead structure. Large pieces of bark were then tied to the frame. An outer set of poles kept the bark in place on the sides and roof. Smoke holes were built into the roof at about twenty–foot intervals. Two families shared the stone–lined hearth beneath each smoke hole.

3   At each end of the longhouse was a door with a covering of animal hide or hinged bark that could be lifted up for entering and exiting. Along each inside wall were bunks that served as beds at night and benches in the day. Corn, dried fish, and other foods hung from overhead. The dwelling was compartmentalized to accommodate each family. At the front of the longhouse, over the door, carved images of clan symbols represented the families living there.

1. The word palisades in paragraph 1 is closest in meaning to

  (A) roads
  (B) fences
  (C) bridges
  (D) ponds

2. The author discusses the dimensions of longhouses in paragraph 1 in order to

  (A) describe the village's strong defenses
  (B) illustrate the importance of certain families
  (C) explain why rivalry occurred among families
  (D) show that villages varied in population

3. Which sentence below best expresses the essential information in the highlighted sentence in paragraph 1?

  (A) The largest longhouses could provide shelter to everyone who was a member of the society.
  (B) The longhouse was basically a shelter that also served important functions related to the defense of the village.
  (C) Everyone in the society had a role in building the longhouse because a variety of construction skills were needed.
  (D) The longhouse not only provided housing for families but also formed the foundation of the whole society.

4. The frame of a longhouse was constructed of

- (A) tree bark
- (B) animal hide
- (C) wooden poles
- (D) flat stones

5. The word secured in paragraph 2 is closest in meaning to

- (A) attached
- (B) forced
- (C) sent
- (D) frozen

6. According to the passage, all of the following statements are true EXCEPT:

- (A) Each longhouse was a separate village.
- (B) People cooked and stored food in a longhouse.
- (C) The longhouse was like an apartment building.
- (D) The people of the longhouse belonged to clans.

7. Look at the four squares, **A**, **B**, **C**, and **D**, which indicate where the following sentence could be added to the passage. Where would the sentence best fit?

Elm, ash, cedar, fir, or spruce trees were the usual sources of bark.

In building the longhouse, a row of forked poles was placed in the ground, between four and five feet apart. Cross poles were lashed to the forked uprights to form an arched roof. **A** Slender poles or rafters were then secured to the roof frame, and traverse poles were added to further strengthen the overhead structure. **B** Large pieces of bark were then tied to the frame. **C** An outer set of poles kept the bark in place on the sides and roof. Smoke holes were built into the roof at about twenty–foot intervals. **D** Two families shared the stone–lined hearth beneath each smoke hole.

LANGSTON HUGHES

1   Among the many talented African American writers connected with the Harlem Renaissance of the 1920s and 1930s, Langston Hughes was the most popular in his time. His two most important achievements were the incorporation of the rhythms of black music into his poetry and the creation of an authentic black folk speaker in the character of Jesse B. Semple. Through both poetry and storytelling, Hughes captured in written form the dominant oral and improvisatory traditions of black culture.

2   Langston Hughes was born in Missouri in 1902. He began to write poetry in high school and later attended Columbia University in New York. After one year at university, Hughes commenced a nomadic life in the United States and Europe. He shipped out as a merchant marine and worked in a Paris nightclub, all the while writing and publishing poetry. His prolific literary career was launched in 1926 with the publication of his first book, *The Weary Blues*, a collection of poems on African American themes set to rhythms from jazz and blues. His first novel appeared in 1930, and from that point on Hughes was known as "the bard of Harlem."

3   In the activist 1930s, Hughes was a public figure. He worked as a journalist, published works in several media, and founded African American theaters in New York, Chicago, and Los Angeles. Hughes's concern with race, mainly in an urban setting, is evident in his poetry, plays, screenplays, novels, and short stories. His poetry includes lyrics about black life and black pride as well as poems of racial protest. His major prose writings are those concerned with the character Jesse B. Semple, a shrewd but supposedly ignorant Harlem resident nicknamed Simple. Simple was a wise fool, an honest man who saw through sham and spoke plainly. The Simple stories were originally published as newspaper sketches and later collected in five book volumes.

4   By the 1960s, readers preferred themes that reflected the struggles of the times, and Hughes's writings were overshadowed by those of a younger generation of black poets. However, in more recent decades, scholars and readers have rediscovered Hughes and regard him as a major literary and social influence. His poetry and stories remain an enduring legacy of the Harlem Renaissance, and for this reason his position in the American canon is secure.

8. It can be inferred from paragraph 1 that the Harlem Renaissance is the name of

   (A) a university
   (B) a literary movement
   (C) a newspaper
   (D) a book of poems

9. The word prolific in paragraph 2 is closest in meaning to

   (A) surprising
   (B) transitory
   (C) mature
   (D) productive

10. What is significant about *The Weary Blues*?

   (A) It expressed themes of protest and unrest.
   (B) Hughes wrote it when he was in high school.
   (C) It put the rhythms of black music into poetry.
   (D) Hughes performed it in a Paris nightclub.

11. According to the passage, Langston Hughes did all of the following EXCEPT

   (A) teach university courses
   (B) write novels and screenplays
   (C) start theater companies
   (D) set poetry to jazz and blues

12. The word sham in paragraph 3 is closest in meaning to

(A) falsehood
(B) the media
(C) blindness
(D) literature

13. The word overshadowed in paragraph 4 is closest in meaning to

(A) copied
(B) respected
(C) performed
(D) dominated

14. Which sentence below best expresses the essential information in the highlighted sentence in paragraph 4?

(A) The writings of Hughes, although still well known, are not as relevant today as they were at the time of the Harlem Renaissance.
(B) Hughes attained prominence in American literature because his writings represent the accomplishments of the Harlem Renaissance.
(C) Today Hughes is most remembered for the humorous poetry and stories that made Americans feel secure in the 1930s.
(D) Americans like the old–style rhythms of Hughes's poems and stories, and this is why a musical composition was dedicated to him.

15. Look at the four squares, **A**, **B**, **C**, and **D**, which indicate where the following sentence could be added to the passage. Where would the sentence best fit?

The success of this book helped finance Hughes's further education at Lincoln University in Pennsylvania.

  Langston Hughes was born in Missouri in 1902. He began to write poetry in high school and later attended Columbia University in New York. **A** After one year at university, Hughes commenced a nomadic life in the United States and Europe. **B** He shipped out as a merchant marine and worked in a Paris nightclub, all the while writing and publishing poetry. **C** His prolific literary career was launched in 1926 with the publication of his first book, *The Weary Blues*, a collection of poems on African American themes set to rhythms from jazz and blues. **D** His first novel appeared in 1930, and from that point on Hughes was known as "the bard of Harlem."

COASTS AND SHORES

1   The terms "coast" and "shore" are often used interchangeably, but there are actually differences between them. One difference is that "coast" applies only to oceans, but "shore" can apply to other bodies of water as well. A shore is the zone at the edge of an ocean, lake, or river that is subject to the regular action of tides, waves, and currents. The shore is the area between the high–water mark and the low–water mark, and thus every part of it is sometimes underwater. The shifting line where the shore meets the water is called the shoreline. An ocean shore extends seaward to the edge of the continental shelf—the submerged edge of the continental block—or to the beginning of the continental slope, which extends down into deep water.

2   A coast is the land just inland from the shore, beyond the usual reach of high water. On the shore side, the boundary of the coast—the coastline—may be either a cliff face or a line marking the inland limit of tidewater. On the landward side, the boundary is usually the edge of a highland or some other kind of terrain distinct from the shore; however, some coastal boundaries have no clear distinction. Many coasts are sea bottoms uplifted by earthquakes to become dry land, so they may show some features of shores, even though the sea never reaches them.

3   In areas where river valleys meet the sea along a rocky coast, bays are likely to occur. The direction of the structural "grain" of the coastal rock affects the shape of the coastline. If the grain is mostly parallel to the coast, as along the Oregon coast, the mouths of few rivers will indent the coastline because river valleys tend to follow the grain. Such coastlines—called Pacific type—are likely to be smooth, straight, or gently curving. On the other hand, if the grain of the rock is at an angle to the coast, as in Maine and Norway, many more valleys will reach the coastline, forming closely spaced bays. Such coastlines are of the Atlantic type.

4   Coasts and shores are areas of continuous change. Like all other terrain, coasts and shores are subject to the processes of weathering, erosion, deposition, and tectonic activity. Unlike other terrain, shores are also subject to the daily action of tides, waves, and currents. These forces erode rocky shores and transport sand and debris from place to place, depleting some beaches and building up others. During storms, waves crash against sea cliffs, weakening them and creating rockfalls and landslides. Storm waves batter beaches and—especially at high tide—rush beyond them, sweeping away docks, roads, and buildings. Over time, coastal processes change as tectonic activity raises, lowers, and disrupts the terrain and the sea bottoms near shores. Coastal processes are also affected by changes in sea level due to melting glaciers and changes in the density and temperature of ocean water.

16. Why does the author discuss the terms "coast" and "shore" in paragraph 1?

    (A) To show how each term has changed over time
    (B) To describe how a coast can change into a shore
    (C) To clarify the distinctions between the two terms
    (D) To explain why more people use the term "coast"

17. The word submerged in paragraph 1 is closest in meaning to

    (A) moveable
    (B) irregular
    (C) steep
    (D) underwater

18. All of the following statements accurately describe coasts and shores EXCEPT:

    (A) A shore is the area at the water's edge, and a coast is the land next to the shore.
    (B) A coast extends to the continental shelf; a shore extends inland to a highland.
    (C) Only oceans have coasts, but lakes, rivers, and oceans all have shores.
    (D) A coast is beyond the high–water mark, but a shore is at times underwater.

19. According to the passage, why do many coasts have characteristics of shores?

    (A) "Coast" and "shore" are the same thing.
    (B) Both coasts and shores are shaped by tides.
    (C) Many coasts are former sea bottoms.
    (D) Shorelines move inland because of erosion.

20. It can be inferred from paragraph 3 that the Oregon coast is

    (A) relatively straight
    (B) lined with cliffs
    (C) very rainy
    (D) indented with bays

21. Which of the following is given as a cause of the different shapes of Pacific and Atlantic type coastlines?

    (A) A difference in direction of the structural "grain" of coastal rock
    (B) Different rates of erosion caused by tides, waves, and currents
    (C) A difference in the frequency of offshore tectonic activity
    (D) Differences in population and the amount of developed land

22. Which sentence below best expresses the essential information in the highlighted sentence in paragraph 4?

    (A) The forces of erosion improve the appearance and comfort of some beaches, while completely destroying others.
    (B) Some shores are very rocky, and others have beautiful sandy beaches that encourage people to move there.
    (C) Tides, waves, and currents wear away shores in some places and deposit sand and rock elsewhere along the shore.
    (D) Because of powerful natural forces that erode shores, it is impossible to predict which beaches are safe to build on.

23. The word batter in paragraph 4 is closest in meaning to

    (A) create
    (B) strike
    (C) improve
    (D) avoid

24. According to paragraph 4, tectonic activity affects coasts and shores by

    (A) wearing away rocks on beaches
    (B) causing abnormally high tides
    (C) raising the temperature of sea water
    (D) changing the terrain and sea bottom

25. Look at the four squares, **A**, **B**, **C**, and **D**, which indicate where the following sentence could be added to the passage. Where would the sentence best fit?

The straightness or irregularity of a coastline depends on the processes that have shaped it.

    A In areas where river valleys meet the sea along a rocky coast, bays are likely to occur. The direction of the structural "grain" of the coastal rock affects the shape of the coastline. **B** If the grain is mostly parallel to the coast, as along the Oregon coast, the mouths of few rivers will indent the coastline because river valleys tend to follow the grain. **C** Such coastlines—called Pacific type—are likely to be smooth, straight, or gently curving. **D** On the other hand, if the grain of the rock is at an angle to the coast, as in Maine and Norway, many more valleys will reach the coastline, forming closely spaced bays. Such coastlines are of the Atlantic type.

Answers to Reading Quiz 8 are on pages 645–646.

Record your score on the Progress Chart on page 790.

1.8 Summarizing Ideas

FOCUS

Read the following passage:

> Several companies are classified as small businesses, including gift shops, cafés, clothing boutiques, self–service laundries, and shoe repair shops. Franchise operations such as fast food restaurants and gas stations may also be small businesses. Real estate is often a small business, and consultants in various fields run their own small businesses from an office in their home.
>
> The three most common types of small businesses are sole proprietorships, partnerships, and corporations. In a sole proprietorship, one person—the proprietor—owns the business. In a partnership, two or more people own the business together. In both sole proprietorships and partnerships, the owners keep the company's profits, but they are also liable for the company's debts. In the third type of business, the corporation, the owners are usually the officers, and they cannot be held personally responsible for the firm's debts.

Which sentences below are important ideas in the passage? Check all of the sentences that are major ideas.

___ A variety of businesses are considered to be small businesses.

___ Clothing boutiques and fast food franchises are expanding elements in the service economy.

___ Sole proprietorships, partnerships, and corporations are the three main types of small businesses.

___ A sole proprietorship has one owner.

___ A corporation's owners are not responsible for the company's debts.

The two most important ideas in the passage are:

A variety of businesses are considered to be small businesses.
Sole proprietorships, partnerships, and corporations are the three main types of small businesses.

The other sentences either are about something that is not mentioned or are minor ideas in the passage.

 STUDY

1. Summarizing

To **summarize** is to state the major ideas in a shorter form. A **summary** is a brief report of the most important ideas in the passage. A summary does not include minor ideas or supporting details.

TOEFL questions about summarizing ideas have special directions:

> An introductory sentence for a brief summary of the passage is provided below. Complete the summary by selecting the THREE answer choices that express the most important ideas in the passage. Some sentences do not belong in the summary because they express ideas that are not presented in the passage or are minor ideas in the passage. ***This question is worth 2 points.***

2. Answer Choices

In summary questions, the incorrect answer choices may be incorrect because they:

- are minor ideas or supporting details rather than major ideas;
- are inaccurate or untrue according to the passage; or
- are not mentioned in the passage.

3. Sample Question

THE HISTORY OF THE PIANO

In the twelfth century, there was an instrument called the dulcimer, consisting of a flat, wooden box of strings that players struck with sticks. In the late seventeenth century, a harpsichord maker in Florence was seeking ways to vary the volume of plucked harpsichord strings. He remembered the dulcimer's ability to vary its volume according to the force of the strike, so he experimented on his harpsichords. He eventually built an instrument that could indeed play both softly and loudly ("piano" and "forte"), giving it the name "pianoforte," later shortened to "piano."

Over the next century, piano construction was constantly improving. To preserve the strings, the piano's hammers were covered in a soft material—usually leather—which imparted a dull sound in the low and middle registers. Improvements accelerated as concert halls grew in size and composers became more demanding. By 1800, it was clear that composers preferred the piano to the harpsichord for its greater power and wider range of expression. Beethoven's sonatas, written between 1783 and 1822, illustrate not only his compositional development but also the ever–greater refinements available on the piano.

In domestic settings, the piano was proving popular, but smaller rooms required instruments that took up less space. The so–called "square piano" needed less room, while the "giraffe piano" needed even less floor space but much height because it resembled a grand piano stood on end. The first upright "parlor piano" was made in Germany around 1770, and this became the chief means of providing home musical entertainment up till the early decades of the twentieth century, when the gramophone replaced it.

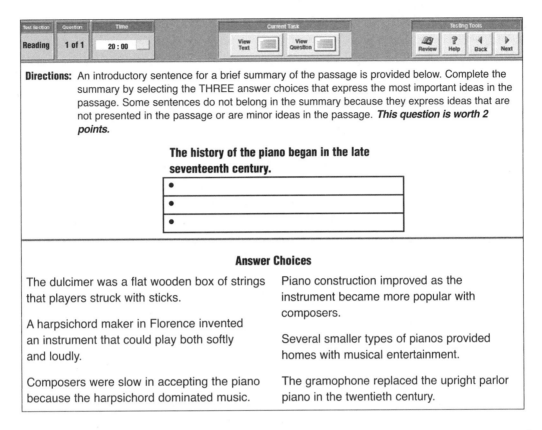

A summary includes only the major ideas and most important information in a passage. Therefore, the correct answers are:

> A harpsichord maker in Florence invented an instrument that could play both softly and loudly.
> Piano construction improved as the instrument became more popular with composers.
> Several smaller types of pianos provided homes with musical entertainment.

Some key information in the passage is:

> …a harpsichord maker in Florence…built an instrument that could indeed play both softly and loudly….
> Improvements accelerated as…composers became more demanding. By 1800, it was clear that composers preferred the piano….
> In domestic settings, the piano was proving popular, but smaller rooms required instruments that took up less space. …"square piano"…"giraffe piano"… "parlor piano"….

Why are the other three answers incorrect? *The dulcimer was a flat wooden box of strings that players struck with sticks* is a minor idea. *Composers were slow in accepting the piano because the harpsichord dominated music* is not mentioned in the passage. *The gramophone replaced the upright parlor piano in the twentieth century* is a minor idea.

How to Score 2–Point Question	
Answers Correct	**Points Earned**
3	2
2	1
0 – 1	0

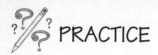 PRACTICE

Exercise 1.8.A

Read the passages and answer each question based on what is stated or implied in that passage.

WINSLOW HOMER

1   Winslow Homer, one of the most prominent nineteenth–century painters, was responsible for raising watercolor to its position as an important medium in American art. Homer was a master of watercolor, and his best watercolor paintings equal his larger oil paintings in both structure and intensity. Through long practice, Homer understood and exploited the requirements of watercolor, which he applied where most appropriate—to the recording of immediate experience. He had great powers of visual analysis and never looked at a scene without seeing its underlying structure.

2   Some of Homer's watercolors of the Adirondack woods, with their complicated weaving of vertical tree trunks against a background of deep autumnal tones, are demonstrations of masterful completeness. In one particular Adirondack painting, *The Blue Boat* (1892), all elements come together with perfect unity: the deep blue of the boat's hull, the green and gold landscape, the alertness of the fishermen, the brilliant clouds and their reflections on the water. Furthermore, its design unites the structural elements with the artist's enjoyment of marking and coloring the paper—all are blended as though in a single moment of vision and action.

1. An introductory sentence for a brief summary of the passage is provided below. Complete the summary by selecting the THREE answer choices that express the most important ideas in the passage. Some sentences do not belong in the summary because they express ideas that are not presented in the passage or are minor ideas in the passage. *This question is worth 2 points.*

The painter Winslow Homer made watercolor an important medium in American art.

•
•
•

Answer Choices

(A) Homer was a master of watercolor and used it to record immediate experience.

(B) Homer is best known for his dramatic oil paintings of seascapes.

(C) His understanding of structure is shown in watercolors of masterful completeness.

(D) Winslow Homer was born in Massachusetts in 1836.

(E) *The Blue Boat* is a watercolor painting of fishermen in a boat on the water.

(F) Homer's Adirondack watercolors combine structural elements and color in perfect unity.

MORAINES

1   The term *moraine* refers to the rock debris carried or deposited by a glacier. The term applies to the debris moved along within the glacier or on its surface, the debris left behind after the glacier melts, and the landforms made up of these debris deposits. The debris transported by a glacier is produced either by erosion of the rock beneath the glacier or by erosion on the slopes rising above the surface of the glacier. Material eroded by the glacier is carried primarily at the base of the glacier and along the outer margins of the glacier.

2   While rivers sort transported rock according to size, a glacier transports its material like a factory conveyer belt, moving the largest blocks and the finest dust next to each other at the same rate of movement over the same distance. Thus, moraine debris remains unsorted both during its transport and after it has been deposited. This unsorted glacial material is called drift. Some moraines are composed only of coarse material and large boulders, while others contain large quantities of finer–grained material such as silt and clay.

3   Once the glacial ice has retreated, the moraine deposits are left exposed on the land surface. The various landforms—moraines—indicate the position of the debris within or on the glacier during the glacier's movement. Their shape and composition also provide information about the shape, mass, and ice flow of the glacier.

2. An introductory sentence for a brief summary of the passage is provided below. Complete the summary by selecting the THREE answer choices that express the most important ideas in the passage. Some sentences do not belong in the summary because they express ideas that are not presented in the passage or are minor ideas in the passage. ***This question is worth 2 points.***

A moraine is the rock debris carried or deposited by a glacier.

•
•
•

Answer Choices

(A) The mapping of moraines is an important part of fieldwork in the study of glaciers.

(B) Glaciers transport debris from the erosion of rock below the glacier or from the slopes above the glacier.

(C) Rivers sort rocks according to size while the rocks are being transported.

(D) We can compare the movement of a glacier to that of a factory conveyer belt.

(E) Moraine debris may include large and small rocks that remain unsorted both during and after transport.

(F) After a glacier melts, the moraine deposits remain as various landforms that are also called moraines.

How to Score 2–Point Question	
Answers Correct	**Points Earned**
3	2
2	1
0 – 1	0

CULTURAL EVOLUTION

1   The history of life is the story of biological evolution on a changing planet, and at no time has change ever been as rapid as in the age of humans. The evolution of humans and their culture has had enormous consequences, making humans a new force in the history of life.

2   Cultural evolution has occurred in stages, beginning with the nomads who hunted and gathered food on the African grasslands two million years ago. These hunter–gatherers made tools, organized communal activities, and divided labor. Next came the development of agriculture in several parts of the world 10 to 15 thousand years ago. Agriculture led to permanent settlements, the first cities, and trade among societies. An important cultural leap was the Industrial Revolution, which began in the eighteenth century. Since then, new technology has escalated exponentially, and so has the human impact on the planet.

3   Throughout this cultural evolution, from simple hunter–gatherers to high–tech societies, humans have not changed much biologically. Our knowledge is stored not in our genes but in the product of thousands of years of human experience. Cultural evolution has enabled us to defy our physical limitations and shortcut biological evolution. We no longer have to wait to adapt to our environment through natural selection; we simply change the environment to meet our needs. We are the dominant species of life and bring environmental change wherever we go.

3. An introductory sentence for a brief summary of the passage is provided below. Complete the summary by selecting the THREE answer choices that express the most important ideas in the passage. Some sentences do not belong in the summary because they express ideas that are not presented in the passage or are minor ideas in the passage. *This question is worth 2 points.*

Cultural evolution has made humans a new force in the history of life.

•
•
•

Answer Choices

(A) Biological evolution is the most important force in the history of life.

(B) There have been several stages in the evolution of human culture.

(C) The development of agriculture 10 to 15 thousand years ago resulted in permanent settlements, the first cities, and trade.

(D) Human technology has advanced rapidly, increasing the human role in environmental change.

(E) Cultural evolution has allowed humans to change their environment, thus avoiding the need for biological evolution.

(F) Humans are changing the world faster than many other species can adapt.

SHAKESPEARE'S ROMANCES

1   Shakespeare's late comedies—including *Cymbeline, The Tempest* and *The Winter's Tale*—are classified as romances. They are based on a tradition of romantic literature going back at least to ancient Greece, in which the central theme of love serves as the trigger for extraordinary adventures. Love is subjected to abnormal strains, often involving separation, jealousy, and other elements of tragedy. There are also fantastic journeys to exotic lands, and absurd coincidences and mistaken identities that complicate the plot, but everything is resolved in the traditional happy ending of comedy.

2   All of Shakespeare's romances share a number of these classical themes, such as the theme of separation and reunion of loved ones, particularly family members. Daughters are separated from parents, and wives from husbands, in *Cymbeline* and *The Winter's Tale*. Sons are separated from fathers in *The Winter's Tale* and *The Tempest*. The related idea of exile also occurs, with the banished characters—usually rulers or future rulers—restored to their rightful position at the end of the play. The theme of jealousy is prominent, with the conclusion that love requires patience in times of adversity. The characters are frequently subjected to long journeys, many involving shipwrecks. Magical developments arise and supernatural beings appear, most notably in *The Tempest*, in which the leading character is a sorcerer.

4. An introductory sentence for a brief summary of the passage is provided below. Complete the summary by selecting the THREE answer choices that express the most important ideas in the passage. Some sentences do not belong in the summary because they express ideas that are not presented in the passage or are minor ideas in the passage. ***This question is worth 2 points.***

> **Shakespeare's late comedies are considered romances because they are based on an older romantic tradition.**

•
•
•

Answer Choices

(A) The main theme of love provides the characters with remarkable adventures in strange lands.

(B) The romances involve many elements of tragedy but have the traditional happy ending of comedy.

(C) Shakespeare's romances are less well known than his comedies, tragedies, and history plays.

(D) *Cymbeline, The Tempest* and *The Winter's Tale* are examples of Shakespeare's romances.

(E) In many of the plays, love is subjected to jealousy and separation but ultimately to resolution and reunion.

(F) The romances often feature shipwrecks that separate characters.

How to Score 2–Point Question	
Answers Correct	**Points Earned**
3	2
2	1
0 – 1	0

WATER LOSS

1   Metabolic activities require a constant supply of certain materials such as water, oxygen, and salts, and cells must replace these materials by withdrawing them from the environment. Humans lose water by evaporation from respiratory and body surfaces and must replenish such losses by drinking water, by obtaining water from food, and by retaining metabolic water formed in cells by oxidation of foods, especially carbohydrates.

2   Humans obtain half of their total water requirement by drinking. With enough water to drink, the human body can withstand extremely high temperatures while preventing a rise in body temperature. When the surrounding air temperature rises, the body's internal environment responds to this change by the evaporative cooling method of sweating. The ability to keep cool in this way was impressively demonstrated in the eighteenth century by a British scientist who stayed for 45 minutes in a room heated to 260 degrees Fahrenheit (126 degrees Celsius). He survived uninjured and his body temperature did not rise because he continuously drank water and sweated. A steak he had brought into the room with him, however, was thoroughly cooked.

3   Sweating rates may exceed three liters of water per hour under such conditions and cannot be tolerated unless the lost water is replaced. Without water to drink, the body will continue to sweat and lose water. When the water deficit exceeds 10 percent of the body weight, collapse occurs, and when the water deficit reaches about 15 to 20 percent, death occurs.

5. An introductory sentence for a brief summary of the passage is provided below. Complete the summary by selecting the THREE answer choices that express the most important ideas in the passage. Some sentences do not belong in the summary because they express ideas that are not presented in the passage or are minor ideas in the passage. *This question is worth 2 points.*

> **The human body needs a constant supply of water for metabolism.**
>
> | |
> | --- |
> | • |
> | • |
> | • |

Answer Choices

(A) Water lost through evaporation from respiratory and body surfaces must be replaced.

(B) Water is an important product of the oxidation of carbohydrates.

(C) Given water to drink, humans can tolerate high temperatures by using the cooling method of sweating.

(D) A scientist remained in a 260–degree room for 45 minutes, which was long enough to cook a steak.

(E) Unless water is replaced by drinking, continuous sweating will eventually lead to collapse and death.

(F) No human has ever survived more than two days in a desert without water.

How to Score 2–Point Question	
Answers Correct	**Points Earned**
3	2
2	1
0 – 1	0

Exercise 1.8.B

Read the passages and answer each question based on what is stated or implied in that passage.

MATHEMATICIANS

1   Like a painter or a poet, a mathematician is a creator of patterns, but mathematical patterns are made with ideas rather than paint or words. Mathematicians are motivated by the belief that they may be able to create a pattern that is entirely new, one that changes forever the way that others think about the mathematical order. Mathematics allows great speculative freedom, and mathematicians can create any kind of system they want. However, in the end, every mathematical theory must be relevant to physical reality, either directly or by importance to the body of mathematics.

2   Mathematicians have an exceptional ability to manage long chains of reasoning. They routinely develop theories from very simple contexts and then apply them to very complex ones. For example, they may develop a formula for the movement of an ameba and then try to apply it to successive levels of the animal kingdom, concluding with a theory of human walking.

3   An extended chain of reasoning may be intuitive, and many mathematicians report that they sense a solution long before they have worked out each step in detail. However, even when guided by intuition, they must eventually work out the solution in exact detail if they are to convince others of its validity. They must demonstrate the solution without any errors or omissions in definition or in line of reasoning. In fact, errors of omission (forgetting a step) or of commission (making some assumption that is untrue) can destroy the value of a mathematical contribution. The mathematician must be rigorous: no fact can be accepted unless it has been proved by steps conforming to universally accepted principles.

4   At the center of mathematical talent lies the ability to recognize significant problems and then to solve them. One source of delight for mathematicians is finding the solution to a problem that has long been considered insoluble. Other accomplishments are inventing a new field of mathematics and discovering links between otherwise separate fields of mathematics.

1. Which sentence below best expresses the essential information in the highlighted sentence in paragraph 1?

   (A) Mathematicians are more creative than ordinary people in the ways that they think about patterns and order.
   (B) Motivation is less important to mathematicians than the belief in their own ability to change other people.
   (C) Mathematicians use their creative talent to motivate other people to look for new ways to solve important problems.
   (D) The idea of establishing a completely new way of understanding mathematics is what motivates mathematicians.

2. According to the passage, why must mathematicians be able to manage long chains of reasoning?

   (A) A solution must be demonstrated in detail to convince others of its validity.
   (B) Mathematicians enjoy creating complex solutions to simple problems.
   (C) There are often no computer programs that are able to solve the problem.
   (D) Mathematical problems involve abstract ideas that are difficult to explain.

3. The word insoluble in paragraph 4 is closest in meaning to

   (A) irrelevant to reality
   (B) not mathematical
   (C) impossible to solve
   (D) not interesting to others

4. An introductory sentence for a brief summary of the passage is provided below. Complete the summary by selecting the THREE answer choices that express the most important ideas in the passage. Some sentences do not belong in the summary because they express ideas that are not presented in the passage or are minor ideas in the passage. This question is worth 2 points.

The work of mathematicians involves several skills and abilities.

•
•
•

Answer Choices

(A) Mathematicians share many characteristics with painters and poets.

(B) Mathematicians must be able to recognize significant problems and find relevant solutions to them.

(C) The ability to handle long chains of reasoning is essential in developing complex theories.

(D) Mathematicians often have to explain mathematical concepts in simple terms to people from other fields.

(E) Mathematicians must be rigorous in demonstrating solutions in precise detail with no errors in definition or reasoning.

(F) The ability to find links between separate fields of mathematics is a test of mathematical talent.

How to Score 2–Point Question	
Answers Correct	**Points Earned**
3	2
2	1
0 – 1	0

WHITE–COLLAR CRIME

1   A variety of illegal acts committed by people in the course of their employment, for their own personal gain, are collectively known as white–collar crime. Embezzlement, theft, and trading securities on the basis of insider information are common forms of white–collar crime. The majority of cases involve low–level employees who steal because they are under temporary financial stress. Many plan to put the money back as soon as possible but may never do so. Their crimes are usually never discovered because the amounts of money are small, no one notices the loss, and law enforcement agencies have few resources for investigating this type of crime.

2   However, there are some very large cases of white–collar crime, such as multimillion–dollar stock market or banking scams that take years to discover and are extremely difficult and expensive to prosecute. In the 1980s, hundreds of executives of American savings and loan associations took advantage of a change in the law that allowed them to make unsecured loans to friends and relatives—which they then did, in the amount of $500 billion in unpaid debt. Only a few of those executives were prosecuted, and little of the money was recovered. American taxpayers ultimately covered the amount at a cost of about $4,000 per person.

3   White–collar crime is not confined to the business sector. Government employment, especially at the city level, also provides opportunities to line one's pockets. For example, building inspectors accept bribes and kickbacks, auctioneers rig sales of seized property, and full–time employees receive welfare payments.

4   Although white–collar crime is less violent than street crime, it involves far more money and harm to the public than crimes committed by street criminals. It is likely that there are more criminals in the office suites than in the streets, yet the nature of white–collar crime makes it difficult to uncover the offenses and pursue the offenders. As the economy shifts from manufacturing to services and electronic commerce, opportunities for white–collar crime will multiply, while the technology needed to stop such crimes will lag behind.

5. Why does the author mention savings and loan associations in paragraph 2?

   (A) To compare stock market scams with savings and loan scams
   (B) To give an example of a very large case of white–collar crime
   (C) To argue in favor of changing the law to restrict unsecured loans
   (D) To explain why American taxpayers do not trust the government

6. The phrase line one's pockets in paragraph 3 means

   (A) bribe officials
   (B) advance one's career
   (C) take money illegally
   (D) hide one's crimes

7. Which sentence below best expresses the essential information in the highlighted sentence in paragraph 4?

   (A) White–collar criminals may be more numerous than street criminals but are difficult to catch because the crimes often go unnoticed.
   (B) It is easier to solve crimes that take place in the office than to solve crimes that occur in the streets, but street crimes are more serious.
   (C) White–collar crime is very similar to street crime, although street crime gets more attention because it is more offensive.
   (D) It takes a very long time to discover white–collar crime and identify the criminals, but street crimes are solved relatively quickly.

8. An introductory sentence for a brief summary of the passage is provided below. Complete the summary by selecting the THREE answer choices that express the most important ideas in the passage. Some sentences do not belong in the summary because they express ideas that are not presented in the passage or are minor ideas in the passage. *This question is worth 2 points.*

> **White–collar crime refers to illegal acts committed by people in the course of their employment.**

- •
- •
- •

Answer Choices

(A) Most white–collar crime involves low–level employees who take small amounts of money and are never found out.

(B) Examples of white–collar crime are embezzlement and trading securities on the basis of insider information.

(C) White–collar crime occurs in both business and government, causing great harm to the public.

(D) Some employees commit white–collar crime by destroying documents and making false statements.

(E) In the 1980s, a change in the law allowed executives to make unsecured loans to friends and relatives.

(F) The nature of white–collar crime makes it difficult to discover and expensive to prosecute.

| How to Score 2–Point Question ||
Answers Correct	Points Earned
3	2
2	1
0 – 1	0

Exercise 1.8.C

Read the passages and answer each question based on what is stated or implied in that passage.

SOCIAL BEHAVIOR IN ANIMALS

1   Social behavior is communication that permits a group of animals of the same species to become organized cooperatively. Social behavior includes any interaction that is a consequence of one animal's response to another of its own species, such as an individual fighting to defend a territory. However, not all **aggregations** of animals are social. Clusters of moths attracted to a light at night or trout gathering in the coolest pool of a stream are groupings of animals responding to environmental signals. Social aggregations, on the other hand, depend on signals from the animals themselves, which stay together and do things together by influencing one another.

2   Social animals are not all social to the same degree. Some species cooperate only long enough to achieve reproduction, while others—such as geese and beavers—form strong pair bonds that last a lifetime. The most persistent social bonds usually form between mothers and their young. For birds and mammals, these bonds usually end when the young can fly, swim, or run and find enough food to support themselves.

3   One obvious benefit of social organization is defense—both passive and active—from predators. Musk oxen that form a passive defensive circle when threatened by a pack of wolves are much less vulnerable than an individual facing the wolves alone. A breeding colony of gulls practices active defense when they, alerted by the alarm calls of a few, attack a predator as a group. Such a collective attack will discourage a predator more effectively than individual attacks. Members of a town of prairie dogs cooperate by warning each other with a special bark when a predator is nearby. Thus, every individual in a social organization benefits from the eyes, ears, and noses of all other members of the group. Other advantages of social organization include cooperation in hunting for food, huddling for protection from severe weather, and the potential for transmitting information that is useful to the society.

Glossary:
   aggregation: gathering; group

1. Why does the author mention moths and trout in paragraph 1?

   (A) To show how social behavior benefits each individual in a group
   (B) To point out the role of the environment in social organization
   (C) To give examples of groupings that do not represent social behavior
   (D) To explain how not all social behavior has the same purpose

2. All of the following are examples of social behavior EXCEPT

   (A) a bird fighting to defend its territory
   (B) a group of turtles sunning on a log
   (C) musk oxen forming a defensive circle
   (D) a pack of wolves hunting together

3. The word huddling in paragraph 3 is closest in meaning to

   (A) gathering
   (B) hiding
   (C) escaping
   (D) searching

4. An introductory sentence for a brief summary of the passage is provided below. Complete the summary by selecting the THREE answer choices that express the most important ideas in the passage. Some sentences do not belong in the summary because they express ideas that are not presented in the passage or are minor ideas in the passage. *This question is worth 2 points.*

Social behavior allows animals of the same species to organize cooperatively.

•
•
•

Answer Choices

Ⓐ Social behavior is defined as any beneficial grouping of animals of the same species.

Ⓑ Any exchange resulting from the response of one animal to another of the same species is social behavior.

Ⓒ The most important social bond occurs between mother animals and their young.

Ⓓ Members of a group influence one another in different degrees and for various reasons.

Ⓔ Living together provides many benefits including the defense of the group from danger.

Ⓕ Prairie dogs are organized into social units that alert each other when danger threatens.

THE PRODUCTION OF COFFEE

1   All great coffee comes from the same tree, *Coffea arabica*. The distinguishing taste of coffee is a product of the climate, air, and soil in which it is grown. The perfect climate for coffee production exists between the latitudes of 25 degrees north and 25 degrees south of the equator. The coffee plant is particular about temperature, and changes of more than 20 degrees in twenty–four hours, or temperatures of over 70 degrees Fahrenheit, tend to have harmful effects on production. In general, coffee trees are comfortable where people are. If people feel too cold or hot, especially during flowering and fruit development, the trees are not likely to do well.

2   Altitude is an important factor, and most coffee–producing countries grade their coffees according to the altitude at which they were grown. The best–tasting coffees are grown at between five and eight thousand feet in elevation, in the thin air and rocky soil of places such as the mountain ridges of Central America and Africa.

3   Coffee trees require certain nutrients to produce beans in economically viable quantities; thus, soil chemistry is carefully watched in commercial operations. A soil rich in nitrogen, phosphorus, and potassium will yield a coffee more complex in character. Nitrogen in soil gives rise to coffee's sparkling acidity; potassium produces fuller–bodied coffees; and phosphorus, while having no bearing on coffee in the final cup, helps the tree to develop a healthy root system. Generally, the more balanced the soil, the better the coffee.

4   Caring for the coffee tree is critical to the character of the final product. Stock for new coffee trees is usually grown from seeds produced by trees already growing on the farm. After the seeds germinate, the seedlings are transferred to nursery beds, which are typically kept under mesh netting that filters out direct sunlight. Young seedlings grow slowly, are very delicate, and require careful replanting. The transfer from nursery to plantation is a critical part of the process, and a seedling that is mishandled at this stage may die after it is replanted. Most varieties take at least three years before they begin producing fruit.

5. It can be inferred that the best coffee would come from which region?

   (A) A mountainous region close to the equator
   (B) A region with a large coffee–drinking population
   (C) A coastal region with a moderate amount of rainfall
   (D) A region with an average temperature of 70 degrees F

6. The word bearing in paragraph 3 is closest in meaning to

   (A) opinion
   (B) influence
   (C) stress
   (D) dependence

7. Which sentence below best expresses the essential information in the highlighted sentence in paragraph 4?

   (A) Coffee trees require a large amount of care because they are delicate.
   (B) The most important step in coffee production is selecting the stock.
   (C) People care more about the taste of coffee than the appearance of the tree.
   (D) The quality of the finished coffee depends on the care given to the tree.

8. An introductory sentence for a brief summary of the passage is provided below. Complete the summary by selecting the THREE answer choices that express the most important ideas in the passage. Some sentences do not belong in the summary because they express ideas that are not presented in the passage or are minor ideas in the passage. This question is worth 2 points.

   Several factors are important in the production of high–quality coffee.

•
•
•

   Answer Choices

   (A) Coffee is best grown in climates within specific latitudes and at certain altitudes.
   (B) Coffee is graded according to the altitude at which it is grown.
   (C) Some people prefer rich, full–bodied coffees, while others like coffees that taste clean and crisp.

   (D) The best commercial coffee is grown in soil containing a balance of essential chemical nutrients.
   (E) A special kind of mesh netting filters out direct sunlight over nursery beds.
   (F) Coffee growers must carefully cultivate the coffee plant through all stages of its life.

How to Score 2–Point Question	
Answers Correct	**Points Earned**
3	2
2	1
0 – 1	0

Answers to Exercises 1.8.A through 1.8.C are on pages 646–647.

 EXTENSION

1. With your teacher and classmates, discuss situations in which writing summaries is important. On the board, write a list of as many situations as you can think of. (Possible situations: college research papers; letters to parents; monthly reports for the company where you work; personal diary.)

    Make another list of situations in which reading summaries is important. What types of summaries have you read recently? Find examples of different kinds of summaries to bring to class, such as a summary in a research paper, a summary at the end of a chapter in a textbook, and the executive summary of a business report.

2. In reading done outside class, select a short passage of one to three paragraphs. Make three photocopies and bring them to class. In class, work in a group of three students. Work as a team to identify key words and sentences that provide clues to the major ideas in each passage. Write a brief summary of each passage. Include only the ideas and information that are essential for a general understanding of each passage. Each summary should have no more than four sentences.

1.9 Organizing Information

FOCUS

Read the following passage:

> Human diseases can be classified according to their effect and duration. An acute disease is an illness such as measles, influenza, or typhoid fever, from which the victim either recovers or dies in a relatively short time. Many acute diseases are also transmissible, which means they are caused by living organisms such as bacteria and viruses and can be spread from one person to another by air, water, or food.
>
> Chronic diseases, on the other hand, develop slowly and last for a long time, sometimes for a lifetime. Examples include cardiovascular disorders, most cancers, diabetes, emphysema, alcoholism, and malnutrition. Although a chronic disease may go into remission, it may flare up periodically (malaria), become progressively worse (cancers and cardiovascular disorders), or disappear with age (childhood asthma).
>
> One hundred years ago, two of the major causes of death in North America were epidemics of influenza and intestinal infections—short-term acute diseases that struck young and old alike and ran quickly through the population. In contrast, the leading causes of death today are chronic illnesses, the types of heart disease and cancer that take a long time to develop and get progressively worse.

The passage compares two types of diseases. Put the following sentences in the correct column below.

They take a long time to develop.
The victim recovers or dies quickly.
They are major causes of death today.
Measles and influenza are examples.
They run quickly through a population.
The victim gets progressively worse.

Acute diseases	Chronic diseases

The question asks you to organize information from the passage. The correct organization is:

Acute diseases	Chronic diseases
The victim recovers or dies quickly.	*They take a long time to develop.*
Measles and influenza are examples.	*They are major causes of death today.*
They run quickly through a population.	*The victim gets progressively worse.*

 STUDY

1. Organization

The organization of a passage is closely linked with its function. The *organization* of a passage is how the author presents ideas and information to meet a specific purpose. Recognizing the organization of a text is an important reading skill because it deepens your understanding of the material and increases your ability to remember it.

Some reading passages on the TOEFL are organized according to these functions:

- to compare or contrast things or ideas;
- to describe different parts of something; or
- to present alternative arguments.

On the TOEFL, you must demonstrate your reading comprehension by organizing information from across the entire passage. You will be asked to organize information into categories, classes, divisions, or types.

Questions about organizing information have special directions:

> Select the appropriate sentences from the answer choices and match them to the type of _____ that they describe. TWO of the answer choices will NOT be used. *This question is worth 3 points.*

Question of this type are worth either 3 or 4 points, depending on the number of answer choices given. It is possible to receive partial credit. You must put at least some of the answer choices in the correct place to earn credit. Here is how the points are earned:

How to Score 3–Point Question	
Answers Correct	**Points Earned**
5	3
4	2
3	1
0 – 2	0

How to Score 4–Point Question	
Answers Correct	**Points Earned**
7	4
6	3
5	2
4	1
0 – 3	0

2. Answer Choices

The reading skill of scanning will help you answer questions about organizing information. *Scanning* is searching the passage for specific information. If your answers are correct, they should be easy to confirm by scanning the passage to locate relevant information.

The correct answers will summarize information from across the whole passage. The correct answers represent major ideas and important supporting information in the passage.

Two of the answer choices will be incorrect for either category in the table. An answer choice may be incorrect because it is:

- inaccurate or untrue according to the passage; or
- irrelevant or not mentioned in the passage.

3. Sample Question

> ### ENERGY QUALITY
>
> Energy is the power to do work or to cause a heat transfer between two objects. Energy varies in its quality, that is, its ability to perform useful work. High–quality energy is organized or concentrated and has great ability to do useful work. Some high–quality forms of energy are electricity, coal, gasoline, concentrated sunlight, high–temperature heat, and nuclei of uranium–235. Conversely, low–quality energy is disorganized or dilute and has little ability to do useful work. An example is the low–temperature heat in the air around us or in a river, lake, or ocean. Heat is so widely dispersed in the ocean that we cannot use it to move objects or to heat objects to high temperatures.
>
> Scientists have repeatedly demonstrated that in any conversion of energy from one form to another, there is always a decrease in energy quality or the amount of useful energy. This law of energy quality degradation is known as the second law of thermodynamics. It is a fundamental scientific law that in any conversion of energy from one form to another, some of the initial energy input is always degraded to lower–quality, less useful energy, usually low–temperature heat that flows into the environment. This low–quality energy is so disordered and dispersed that it is unable to perform useful work.

Select the appropriate phrases from the answer choices and match them to the type of energy that they illustrate. TWO of the answer choices will NOT be used. *This question is worth 3 points.*

Drag your answer choices to the spaces where they belong. To remove an answer, click on it.

Answer Choices

Concentrated sunlight

Heat stored in the ocean

Psychological energy

Energy with great ability to do work

High–temperature heat

Energy that is disorganized

Conversion of energy

High–quality
-
-
-

Low–quality
-
-

The passage contrasts high–quality and low–quality energy. The correct answers are:

Answer Choices	**High–quality**
	• Concentrated sunlight
	• Energy with great ability to do work
Psychological energy	• High–temperature heat
	Low–quality
	• Heat stored in the ocean
Conversion of energy	• Energy that is disorganized

Some key information about high–quality energy is:

> High–quality energy is organized or concentrated and has great ability to do useful work.
> Some high–quality forms of energy are…concentrated sunlight, high–temperature heat….

Some key information about low–quality energy is:

> Heat is so widely dispersed in the ocean….
> This low–quality energy is so disordered and dispersed that it is unable to perform useful work.

Psychological energy is incorrect because it is not mentioned in the passage. *Conversion of energy* is incorrect because it is neither high–quality nor low–quality energy but rather the changing of energy from one form to another.

 PRACTICE

Exercise 1.9.A

Read the passages and answer each question based on what is stated or implied in that passage.

THE ENLIGHTENMENT AND ROMANTICISM

The Romantic Movement in music and literature was a reaction against the Enlightenment philosophy that had dominated much of the eighteenth century. Enlightenment ideals held that human society could reach perfection through rational thought, while Romantic philosophy reveled in the beauty and unpredictable power of Nature. The Enlightenment gloried in civilization and believed in princely rule of a benevolent kind. Romanticism believed in democracy and the common people, reviving folk traditions, ballads, and medieval sagas that made heroes of rural characters. Artistically, the Enlightenment condemned excess and dictated that the discipline of formal structure was beneficial to artistic expression. Romanticism, on the other hand, celebrated emotions and the senses, believing that the emotional demands of a particular work should dictate its form. While the Enlightenment believed in a generally positive approach to life and the abandonment of superstition, Romanticism found inspiration in death as an "other kingdom" and in the supernatural; hence, literature developed a "Gothic" streak that eventually found its way into music.

1. Select the appropriate sentences from the answer choices and match them to the philosophy that they illustrate. TWO of the answer choices will NOT be used. *This question is worth 3 points.*

Answer Choices

(A) There is value in emotions, the senses, and the power of Nature.

(B) The discipline of formal structure benefits artistic expression.

(C) Death and the supernatural are sources of inspiration.

(D) Artistic values are more important than social themes.

(E) Human society can reach perfection through rational thought.

(F) Folk traditions are important because common people are heroes.

(G) Symbols and patterns of images convey artistic meaning.

Enlightenment

-
-

Romanticism

-
-
-

How to Score 3–Point Question	
Answers Correct	**Points Earned**
5	3
4	2
3	1
0 – 2	0

VALLEY FLOORS

1   The floor of a river valley develops in one of two ways: as a rock–floored valley bottom or as an accumulation valley floor. A rock–floored valley is formed by a stream that no longer incises by cutting downward but rather erodes laterally in a course that winds from side to side across the valley floor. In a rock–floored valley, the valley slopes are undercut and steepened by the sideways erosion. The floor of the river channel lies in the bedrock, and on either side of the channel it is covered by only a thin layer of gravel and sand. As the stream swings across the valley floor, it deposits material on the insides of the bends in the channel.

2   The second type of valley bottom, the accumulation floor, cannot easily be distinguished from a rock–floored valley on its surface. An accumulation valley floor is created by the continuous deposition of gravel and sand in an existing incised valley where the accumulation of material has replaced the cutting action. Both the channel floor and the floodplain—the part of the valley floor flooded frequently at high water—are composed entirely of these gravel and sand deposits. An accumulation floor is much less resistant to erosion than a rock floor since the gravel and sand of its channel bed have already been transported and may easily be removed during the next flood.

2. Select the appropriate sentences from the answer choices and match them to the type of valley floor that they describe. TWO of the answer choices will NOT be used. ***This question is worth 3 points.***

Answer Choices

(A) The river channel flows directly over the bedrock.

(B) The top layer of rock is more resistant to erosion than the underlying rock.

(C) Deposits of gravel and sand accumulate on the valley floor.

(D) The river swings from side to side, leaving material on the insides of bends in the channel.

(E) Sand and rock accumulate parallel to the coast but separated from it by a channel.

(F) The sideways erosion of the river undercuts and steepens the valley slopes.

(G) The channel floor and the floodplain are made entirely of gravel and sand deposits.

Rock Floor

•
•
•

Accumulation Floor

•
•

How to Score 3–Point Question	
Answers Correct	**Points Earned**
5	3
4	2
3	1
0 – 2	0

ANIMALS AND PLANTS

1   We can distinguish animals from plants by looking at their contrasting modes of nutrition. Unlike plants, animals cannot manufacture their own food. Animals cannot construct organic molecules from inorganic chemicals as plants can during photosynthesis. Animals must take pre–formed organic molecules into their bodies. Most animals do this by ingestion—that is, by eating other organisms or organic material. Animals store their food reserves as glycogen, whereas plants store their food as starch.

2   Animal cells lack the cell walls that characterize plant cells, and animal cells have unique types of junctions between them. In most animals, cells are successively organized into tissues, organs, and organ systems. Animals have two types of tissues that plants do not have. The first is nervous tissue, for the conduction of electrical impulses, and the other is muscle tissue, for movement. Nerves and muscles, which control active behavior, are unique to animals.

3   Animal life began in the Precambrian seas with the evolution of multi–cellular forms that lived by eating other organisms. This new way of life led to an evolutionary explosion of diverse forms. Early animals populated the seas, fresh water, and eventually the land. The diversity of animal life on Earth today is the result of over half a billion years of evolution from those first ancestors that consumed other life forms.

3. Select the appropriate sentences from the answer choices and match them to the form of life that they describe. TWO of the answer choices will NOT be used. ***This question is worth 4 points.***

Answer Choices

Plants

•
•
•

(A) They are not able to manufacture their own food.

(B) They construct organic molecules from inorganic chemicals.

(C) They have the ability to survive on another planet.

(D) Nerves and muscles control their active behavior.

Animals

•
•
•
•

(E) They evolved from multi–cellular forms that ate other organisms.

(F) They store their food reserves as starch.

(G) They have evolved very little over one billion years.

(H) They have neither nervous tissue nor muscle tissue.

(I) Their cells do not have walls.

How to Score 4–Point Question	
Answers Correct	**Points Earned**
7	4
6	3
5	2
4	1
0 – 3	0

Exercise 1.9.B

Read the passages and answer each question based on what is stated or implied in that passage.

COMMERCIAL ARCHITECTURE OF THE NINETEENTH CENTURY

1   Arcades were built in Paris as early as 1799 and in London in 1816, but these were primarily arched passages through buildings to connect institutions. American arcades, by contrast, were not just passages to some other destination but the entire focus of large commercial blocks, and were, in effect, prototypical shopping malls. The Providence Arcade (1829) in Rhode Island's capital illustrates the American transformation of the arcade into a temple of shopping. The Arcade's pitched glass roof sheltered a large open space surrounded by tiered shops. The Arcade was set at the edge of Providence's business district, making it a focal point for future growth. On the two street sides, six huge granite columns modeled on a Greek temple dominated the building's facades.

2   Nineteenth–century urban Americans flocked to another ancestor of the contemporary shopping mall, the department store, a controlled indoor world where an array of goods were organized under a single management. The origins of the department store were in Cincinnati, where in 1829, a new kind of building was dedicated to trade, business, and culture. This building, called the Bazaar, featured a four–story rotunda beneath a huge dome that meant to unite multiple functions under one symbolic roof. Unfortunately, however, the Bazaar was short–lived. A more successful commercial and architectural prototype was the department store known as the Marble Palace, which opened in New York in 1846. Monumental in style, the building's impressive facade of Corinthian columns, with large plate glass display windows between them, easily lured in the city's wealthy customers.

1. Select the appropriate sentences from the answer choices and match them to the type of building that they describe. TWO of the answer choices will NOT be used. ***This question is worth 3 points.***

Answer Choices

(A) It is a passage under or through a building to connect streets.

(B) A glass roof encloses an area lined with vertical rows of shops.

(C) A wide variety of goods are organized under one management.

(D) It is designed to be the entire focus of a large commercial block.

(E) The earliest example had a four–story rotunda under a large dome.

(F) It specializes in selling a single category of high–quality good.

(G) Its large display windows are designed to attract customers.

Arcade

•
•

Department Store

•
•
•

RESEARCH DESIGNS

1   In the fields of psychology and sociology, a crucial decision for researchers is which research design to use. When the subject of the study is how people change or develop over time, two designs are frequently used: the cross–sectional design and the longitudinal design.

2   Cross–sectional studies look at a cross–section of subjects and compare their responses. The essential characteristics of the design are that it includes groups of subjects at different age levels, and that each subject is tested or interviewed only once. For example, researchers may give a memory test to adults in their twenties through seventies, select the youngest group as a standard, and then compare each older group to that norm. Cross–sectional studies are relatively quick to do and can provide information about possible age differences. However, they do not reveal anything about individual change over time, since each subject is tested only once.

3   Longitudinal studies differ from cross–sectional studies because they test or interview the same subjects over time and therefore allow us to look at consistency or change within the same individual. The typical procedure is to select a relatively small group of subjects who are all about the same age at the beginning of the study and then look at them repeatedly over a period of time. Short–term longitudinal studies cover several years and are common in research on both children and adults. Long–term longitudinal studies follow subjects from childhood into adulthood, from early to middle adulthood, or from middle adulthood to old age. One advantage of longitudinal studies is that any changes found are real changes, not just age–group differences.

2. Select the appropriate sentences from the answer choices and match them to the research design that they describe. TWO of the answer choices will NOT be used. ***This question is worth 3 points.***

Answer Choices

(A) A group of subjects of the same age is tested repeatedly over a long period.

(B) Researchers examine an existing relationship between two groups of subjects.

(C) This design allows researchers to study human behavior indirectly.

(D) Researchers test or interview each subject only one time.

(E) This type of study may reveal differences that are not just age–group differences.

(F) Researchers can study consistency or change within the same individual.

(G) This design can tell us about possible differences among various age groups.

Cross–sectional

-
-

Longitudinal

-
-
-

How to Score 3–Point Question	
Answers Correct	**Points Earned**
5	3
4	2
3	1
0 – 2	0

PROXIMATE AND ULTIMATE CAUSATION

1   Behavioral biologists ask two basic types of questions about animal behavior: how animals behave and why they behave as they do. The "how" questions seek to understand the proximate or immediate causes underlying a behavior at a particular time and place. For example, a biologist might want to explain the singing of a male white–throated sparrow in the spring in terms of hormonal or neural mechanisms. Such physiological causes of behavior are proximate factors. Alternatively, another biologist might ask what purpose singing serves the sparrow, and then attempt to understand events in the evolution of birds that led to springtime singing. These are "why" questions that focus on ultimate causation, the evolutionary origin and purpose of behavior. These two types of questions are very independent approaches to behavior.

2   Questions about proximate causation examine how animals perform their various functions at the molecular, cellular, organismal, and population levels. The biological sciences that address proximate causes are known as experimental sciences because they use the experimental method of: (1) predicting how a system will respond to a disturbance, (2) making the disturbance, and (3) comparing the observed results with the predictions. Researchers repeat the experimental conditions many times to eliminate chance results that might lead to false conclusions.

3   Questions about ultimate causation ask what produced biological systems and their distinctive properties through evolutionary time. The sciences dealing with ultimate causes are known as evolutionary sciences, and they mainly use the comparative method rather than experimentation. Researchers compare characteristics of molecular biology, cell biology, anatomy, development, and ecology among related species to identify patterns of variation.

3. Which sentence below best expresses the essential information in the highlighted sentence in paragraph 1?

(A) All questions asked by behavioral biologists fall into two basic categories.

(B) Proximate and ultimate causation are distinct ways of thinking about behavior.

(C) "Why" questions and questions about ultimate causes require very different methods.

(D) Behavioral biologists must think very independently about important questions.

4. Select the appropriate sentences from the answer choices and match them to the type of cause that they describe. TWO of the answer choices will NOT be used. ***This question is worth 3 points.***

Answer Choices

(A) Researchers want to know about the evolutionary origin and purpose of behavior.

(B) Behavioral biologists use the experimental method to answer a question.

(C) A scientist wants to know how a male sparrow produces its springtime song.

(D) Some animal behaviors are random and serve no beneficial function.

(E) Scientists compare characteristics of related species to identify similarities and differences.

(F) Researchers disagree over the reason for a particular behavior.

(G) A behavior at a specific time and place has an immediate, underlying cause.

Proximate

•
•
•

Ultimate

•
•

How to Score 3–Point Question	
Answers Correct	**Points Earned**
5	3
4	2
3	1
0 – 2	0

Answers to Exercises 1.9.A through 1.9.B are on pages 647–648.

 EXTENSION

1. Outside of class, select an article from a magazine or journal or part of a chapter from a university textbook. Do the following activity as an individual or small–group exercise, making as many photocopies of the article as necessary.

   Read the article and think about its organization and purpose. Answer the following questions:

   a. What is the function of the article? Why did the author write it?
   b. How are the ideas and information organized?
   c. What is the purpose of each paragraph or division?
   d. What are the major ideas and most important information in the article?

   Make a table or chart of the article. Show the article's major divisions and the most important ideas and information in each division.

PROGRESS – 1.8 through 1.9

QUIZ 9   *Time – 20 minutes*

Read the passages and choose the best answer to each question. Answer all questions about a passage on the basis of what is stated or implied in that passage.

LIFE EXPECTANCY

1   The greatest demographic story of the twentieth century was the enormous increase in life expectancy, the average number of years a person can expect to live. In most modern societies, life expectancy rose dramatically, from about 47 years in 1900 to about 76 years in 2000. This does not mean, however, that people suddenly died on their forty–seventh birthday in 1900. It means that if half of the people born in 1900 died in childhood and the rest lived 95 years, the average age at death was around 47. The data for 1900 reflect high infant and childhood mortality rates. At that time, surviving the first fifteen years of life was the key to living to old age. Over the century, several factors increased life expectancy, most notably improvements in public health, such as pasteurized milk, sewers, and indoor plumbing. Advances in medical practice, including the use of antibiotics and vaccinations for childhood illnesses, made it increasingly likely that infants would reach adulthood.

2   On the one hand, increased life expectancy is a sign of societal well being; on the other hand, an aging population poses its own set of problems. Large numbers of elderly, many with chronic diseases, become a burden on the health care system and on their families. In societies where care of the elderly is a family responsibility, adult children caring for aging parents experience great personal and financial stress.

1. An introductory sentence for a brief summary of the passage is provided below. Complete the summary by selecting the THREE answer choices that express the most important ideas in the passage. Some sentences do not belong in the summary because they express ideas that are not presented in the passage or are minor ideas in the passage. *This question is worth 2 points.*

Life expectancy in modern societies has increased dramatically.

•
•
•

Answer Choices

(A) Around half of the population died on their forty–seventh birthday in 1900.

(B) The average number of years a person could expect to live rose from 47 to 76 in only a century.

(C) The leading causes of death in 1900 were epidemic diseases.

(D) Mortality rate is the number of deaths in a period as a proportion of the entire population.

(E) Improvements in public health and medical practices significantly raised life expectancy.

(F) An aging population increases the stress on a society's health care system and on families.

ARTISTS' USE OF OIL AND ACRYLIC PAINTS

1   The oil technique for painting on canvas is superior to other methods mainly because of its great flexibility and ease of manipulation, as well as the wide range of effects that can be produced. Colors do not change to any great extent on drying, which means that the color the artist puts down is, with only slight variation, the color desired in the finished work. The artist is free to combine transparent and opaque effects in the same painting. However, the principal defect of oil painting is the darkening of the oil over time, but this may be reduced by using the highest quality materials.

2   The most widely used artists' colors based on the synthetic resins are made by dispersing pigment in acrylic emulsion. Acrylic paints are thinned with water, but when they dry, the resin particles coalesce to form a tough film that is impervious to water. Acrylic colors may be made mat or glossy and can imitate most of the effects of other water–based colors. They are a boon to painters with a high rate of production because a painting can be completed in one session that might have taken days in oil because of the drying time required between layers of paint.

3   Acrylic colors are not a complete substitute for oil paints, and artists whose styles require the special manipulative properties of oil colors—including delicacy in handling or smoothly blended tones—find that these possibilities are the exclusive properties of oils. Although painting in acrylics has certain advantages over painting in oils, the latter remains the standard because the majority of painters find that its advantages outweigh its defects and that in optical quality oil paints surpass all others.

2. Select the appropriate sentences from the answer choices and match them to the type of paint that they describe. TWO of the answer choices will NOT be used. *This question is worth 3 points.*

Answer Choices

(A) They appear transparent on paper.
(B) The colors can be thinned with water.
(C) They allow for smoothly blended tones.
(D) The paints are applied to wet plaster.
(E) They are the preferred paints among artists.
(F) They have a relatively fast drying time.
(G) The colors will eventually darken.

Oil Paints

•
•
•

Acrylic Paints

•
•

How to Score 2–Point Question	
Answers Correct	**Points Earned**
3	2
2	1
0 – 1	0

How to Score 3–Point Question	
Answers Correct	**Points Earned**
5	3
4	2
3	1
0 – 2	0

WORLD CLIMATIC PATTERNS

1   Climate is the general pattern of atmospheric conditions, seasonal variations, and weather extremes in a region over a period of decades. One major factor determining the uneven patterns of world climates is the variation in the amount of solar energy striking different parts of the earth. The amount of incoming solar energy reaching the earth's surface varies with latitude, the distance north or south from the equator. Air in the **troposphere** is heated more at the equator (zero latitude), where the sun is almost directly overhead, than at the high–latitude poles, where the sun is lower in the sky and strikes the earth at a low angle.

2   The large input of heat at and near the equator warms large masses of air. These warm masses rise and spread northward and southward, carrying heat from the equator toward the poles. At the poles, the warm air becomes cool and falls to the earth. These cool air masses then flow back toward the equator near ground level to fill the space left by rising warm air masses. This general air circulation pattern in the troposphere results in warm average temperatures near the equator, cold average temperatures near the poles, and moderate average temperatures at the middle latitudes.

3   The larger input of solar energy near the equator evaporates huge amounts of water from the earth's surface into the troposphere. As the warm, humid air rises, it cools rapidly and loses most of its moisture as rain near the equator. The abundant rainfall and the constant warm temperatures near the equator create the world's tropical rain forests.

4   Two major factors cause seasonal changes in climate. One is the earth's annual orbit around the sun; the other is the earth's daily rotation around its tilted axis, the imaginary line connecting the two poles. When the North Pole leans toward the sun, the sun's rays strike the Northern Hemisphere more directly per unit of area, bringing summer to the northern half of the earth. At the same time, the South Pole is tilted away from the sun; thus, winter conditions prevail throughout the Southern Hemisphere. As the earth makes its annual rotation around the sun, these conditions shift and cause a change of seasons.

5   As the earth spins around its axis, the general air circulation pattern between the equator and each pole breaks into three separate belts of moving air, or prevailing surface winds, which affect the distribution of precipitation over the earth.

Glossary:
   troposphere: the lowest region of the earth's atmosphere

3. Select the appropriate sentences from the answer choices and match them to the location that they describe. TWO of the answer choices will NOT be used. ***This question is worth 3 points.***

Answer Choices

(A) Solar energy strikes the earth at a low angle.
(B) Average annual temperatures are moderate.
(C) The large input of solar energy heats great masses of air.
(D) A large quantity of water evaporates into the atmosphere.
(E) Warm air cools and sinks to the earth's surface.
(F) The sun is almost directly overhead.
(G) There are three belts of prevailing surface winds.

At the Equator

•
•
•

At the Poles

•
•

4. An introductory sentence for a brief summary of the passage is provided below. Complete the summary by selecting the THREE answer choices that express the most important ideas in the passage. Some sentences do not belong in the summary because they express ideas that are not presented in the passage or are minor ideas in the passage. *This question is worth 2 points.*

Several factors influence the earth's climatic patterns.

> •
>
> •
>
> •

Answer Choices

(A) The variation in the amount of solar energy reaching different parts of the earth has a great influence on global climate.

(B) Warm air flows from the equator toward both poles, where it cools and then flows back toward the equator, creating a general air circulation.

(C) The moisture–holding capacity of air, humidity, increases when air is warmed and decreases when it is cooled.

(D) The consistently warm temperatures and heavy rainfall near the equator result in tropical rain forests.

(E) The earth's annual circling of the sun and its daily spinning around its axis cause its seasonal changes in climate.

(F) The chemical content of the troposphere is another factor determining the earth's average temperatures and thus its climates.

How to Score 2–Point Question	
Answers Correct	**Points Earned**
3	2
2	1
0 – 1	0

How to Score 3–Point Question	
Answers Correct	**Points Earned**
5	3
4	2
3	1
0 – 2	0

Answers to Reading Quiz 9 are on page 648.

Record your score on the Progress Chart on page 790.

PROGRESS – 1.1 through 1.9

QUIZ 10

Time – 35 minutes

Read the passages and choose the best answer to each question. Answer all questions about a passage on the basis of what is stated or implied in that passage.

NORTH AMERICAN GRASSLANDS

1   Grasslands occur around the world, mostly in dry temperate or subtropical regions with relatively little rainfall, and generally as intermediate zones between drier desert and moister forest habitats. In North America, native grasslands occur primarily in the prairies of the Great Plains in the middle of the continent. The North American prairie **biome** is one of the most extensive grasslands in the world, extending from the edge of the Rocky Mountains in the west to the deciduous forest in the east, and from northern Mexico in the south to Canada in the north. Average annual rainfall ranges from 16 inches (40 cm) in the west to 31 inches (80 cm) in the east. Average annual temperatures range from 50 to 68 degrees Fahrenheit (10 to 20 Celsius). In the moist regions of the North American grasslands, especially in the northern Great Plains, rainfall is distinctly seasonal, and temperatures can vary widely from very hot in summer to bitter cold in winter.

2   The prairie soil is rich in nutrients derived mainly from the decomposition of the deep, many–branched grass roots. Native grasses have very long roots, with up to two–thirds of the plant growing underground. The soil beneath the prairie is a dense mat of roots. The above ground grass stems die back every winter, but the underground root system keeps the plants alive until the next growing season. Even after the roots die, their tangled mass holds the soil together, while the decaying matter provides nutrients for living plants. Animals also contribute to soil quality. Herds of grazing deer and elk add nitrogen from their droppings. Colonies of prairie dogs, large burrowing rodents, dig extensive underground tunnel systems that aerate the soil and allow water to reach below the surface.

3   One hundred fifty years ago, the Great Plains grasslands were one vast, unbroken prairie. Starting in the late nineteenth century, large numbers of people have immigrated to the region, altering the landscape significantly. Much of the prairie is now farmland, the most productive agricultural region in the world. The landscape is now dominated by monocultures, the cultivation of a single variety of plant covering a large area. Monocultures of wheat, barley, soybeans, corn, and sunflowers occupy the land that was once prairie. In areas given over to grazing lands for cattle and sheep, virtually all of the major native grasses have been replaced by nonnative species.

4   An important feature of the northern Great Plains grasslands is the presence of millions of glacial depressions that are now small ponds known as prairie potholes. The potholes were formed during the most recent Ice Age, when streams flowed in tunnels beneath glacially formed sandy ridges. When the Ice Age ended around 12,000 years ago, the retreating glaciers created about 25 million depressions across a 300,000–square–mile landscape, with a distribution of about 83 potholes per square mile. As the ice blocks melted, much of the water was left behind, forming wetlands ranging in size from a tenth of an acre to several acres. The wetlands were soon surrounded by waves of grasses: shortgrass, mixed grass, and tallgrass.

5   Today these small wetlands still cover the prairies, although much of the landscape, including both native grasses and potholes, has been transformed to cropland and grassland for grazing. What does remain of the wetlands, however, serves as an important breeding

area for more than 300 bird species, including large numbers of migrating shorebirds and waterfowl. The potholes fill up with water during spring rains and usually dry out by late summer. Every spring, birds arrive in great numbers, including northern pintails, mallards, coots, and pied–billed grebes. Four to six million birds come to breed and feed in the seasonal wetlands that dot portions of Minnesota, Iowa, North and South Dakota, Montana, Alberta, Saskatchewan, and Manitoba. Prairie pothole country produces half of North America's 35 to 40 million ducks and is renowned worldwide as a "duck factory." The potholes also have an important role in flood control. Although small, the potholes can hold significant amounts of water. During periods of heavy rain and snow melt, they absorb surges of water, slowing runoff across the prairies and thereby reducing the severity of flooding in rivers.

Glossary:
biome: one of the world's major natural communities, classified by predominant vegetation

1. Paragraph 1 supports which of the following statements about the North American prairie biome?

   (A) The biome covers a large area with varying weather conditions.
   (B) The biome contains a diversity of grasses, shrubs, and trees.
   (C) The biome is the only native grassland in the Western Hemisphere.
   (D) The biome exists because of seasonal drought and occasional floods.

2. The word tangled in paragraph 2 is closest in meaning to

   (A) shallow
   (B) wet
   (C) dense
   (D) smooth

3. According to paragraph 2, which function is performed by a prairie animal?

   (A) Keeping plants from growing too tall
   (B) Holding the soil in place
   (C) Spreading grass seed across the prairie
   (D) Enabling air and water to enter the soil

4. What has taken place in the Great Plains grasslands during the last century and a half?

   (A) The average annual rainfall has risen and fallen several times.
   (B) Large parts of the prairie have been converted to agricultural use.
   (C) Melting glaciers have formed numerous depressions in the soil.
   (D) Human activity has transformed the region into one large wetland.

5. The prairie potholes owe their origins mainly to

   (A) the variation in temperature throughout the year
   (B) the heavy rains that fall in the spring and summer
   (C) the glaciers that melted at the end of the last Ice Age
   (D) the increase in greenhouse gases in the atmosphere

6. All of the following statements are true about the northern Great Plains EXCEPT:

   (A) Summer temperatures are very hot, while winter temperatures are very cold.
   (B) An unbroken prairie now extends from the western mountains to the eastern forest.
   (C) The original vegetation consisted of short-grass, mixed grass, and tallgrass.
   (D) A large number of small wetlands are found throughout the region.

7. Which sentence below best expresses the essential information in the highlighted sentence in paragraph 5? Incorrect choices change the meaning in important ways or leave out essential information.

(A) The wetlands completely cover the landscape, making it difficult to grow crops and grass for grazing.

(B) The native grasses that grew in the potholes have been replaced with crops that are more beneficial.

(C) Except for the potholes region, the entire prairie has been converted to cropland and grazing land.

(D) Even though a large portion of the prairies is used for crops and grazing, the small ponds remain.

8. The word dot in paragraph 5 is closest in meaning to

(A) cover
(B) drain
(C) warm
(D) damage

9. Why does the author use the term "duck factory" in paragraph 5?

(A) To point out that ducks are the region's main product for export

(B) To show that the potholes are important to the region's economy

(C) To illustrate the tremendous growth of the poultry industry

(D) To emphasize the region's value as a breeding ground for ducks

10. Look at the four squares, **A**, **B**, **C**, and **D**, which indicate where the following sentence could be added to the passage. Where would the sentence best fit?

The original grassland associations of plants and animals have been almost completely destroyed.

   A One hundred fifty years ago, the Great Plains grasslands were one vast, unbroken prairie. **B** Starting in the late nineteenth century, large numbers of people have immigrated to the region, altering the landscape significantly. **C** Much of the prairie is now farmland, the most productive agricultural region in the world. **D** The landscape is now dominated by monocultures, the cultivation of a single variety of plant covering a large area. Monocultures of wheat, barley, soybeans, corn, and sunflowers occupy the land that was once prairie. In areas given over to grazing lands for cattle and sheep, virtually all of the major native grasses have been replaced by nonnative species.

11. An introductory sentence for a brief summary of the passage is provided below. Complete the summary by selecting the THREE answer choices that express the most important ideas in the passage. Some sentences do not belong in the summary because they express ideas that are not presented in the passage or are minor ideas in the passage. *This question is worth 2 points.*

The grasslands of North America occur mainly in the prairies of the Great Plains.

•
•
•

Answer Choices

(A) The rich prairie soil is largely a result of the growth and decay of the roots of native grasses.

(B) Most of the native prairie grasses have been replaced with cereal crops and nonnative grasses for grazing.

(C) Grass that is not grazed accumulates a layer of mulch that can inhibit growth.

(D) In the northern prairies, every square mile contains 83 million glacial potholes.

(E) Millions of small seasonal wetlands serve as breeding sites for birds and as resources for flood control.

(F) Northern pintails, mallards, coots, and pied-billed grebes migrate to the northern region.

How to Score 2–Point Question	
Answers Correct	**Points Earned**
3	2
2	1
0 – 1	0

THEORIES OF EXPERIENCE AND EDUCATION

1   In the late nineteenth century, American educators began to develop new theories about how people think and learn. Informed by the modern science of experimental psychology, these theories examined the nature of truth and emphasized the relationships among thinking, learning, knowledge, and experience. Two philosophers, William James and John Dewey, were particularly influential in developing new philosophies of education for the modern world. Both James and Dewey believed that the truth of any idea is a function of its usefulness and that experience is central to learning.

2   William James (1842–1910) was a philosopher and psychologist who believed that truth is not absolute and unchangeable; rather, it is made in actual, real–life events. In a person's life, there are experiences that have meaning and truth for that person. Truth cannot be separated from experience, and in order to understand truth, we have to study experience itself. Thus, for James, human experience should be the primary subject of study, and he called upon thinkers to concentrate on experience instead of essences, abstractions, or universal laws.

3   James focused on what he called the "stream" of experience, the sequential course of events in our lives. He believed that human consciousness is a stream of thoughts and feelings, and that this stream of consciousness is always going on, whether we are awake or asleep. The stream consists of very complex waves of bodily sensations, desires and aversions, memories of past experiences, and determinations of the will. One wave dissolves into another gradually, like the ripples of water in a river.

4   In James's theory, thought and experience are connected. Incoming waves of thought flow in next to outgoing waves of previous experience and thus become associated with each other. An incoming thought is "workable" only if it is meaningful and can be associated with something already in the person's mind. James's theory supports later theories of associative learning, which assert that new learning involves activating previous learning to find "hooks" on which to hang new information.

5   The theories of John Dewey (1859–1952), philosopher and educator, have had a tremendous impact on generations of thinkers. Dewey viewed life as a continuously reconstructive process, with experience and knowledge building on each other. He believed that learning is more than the amassing and retention of information; learning is learning how to think. Thinking is not something abstract; it is a living process that starts when old habits meet new situations.

6   For Dewey, experience cannot be separated from nature because all experience is rooted in nature. Nature is what we experience: air, stones, plants, diseases, pleasure, and suffering. Dewey believed that experience is an interaction between what a person already knows and the person's present situation. Previous knowledge of nature interacts with the present environment, and together they lead to new knowledge that in turn will influence future experience.

7   Dewey asserted that experience is central to education; however, experience cannot be equated with education because all experiences are not necessarily educative. Experience is educative only when it contributes to the growth of the individual. It can be miseducative if it distorts the growth of further experience. It is the quality of experience that matters. Thus, productive experience is both the means and the goal of education. Dewey felt that education should be problem–centered and interdisciplinary rather than subject–centered and fragmented. The methods and curricula of education must make the child's growth the central concern. Furthermore, truly progressive education must involve the participation of the learner in directing the learning experience.

12. Which sentence below best expresses the essential information in the highlighted sentence in paragraph 2?

(A) We can comprehend what truth is only if we separate truth from experience and study each individually.

(B) The truth of any experience cannot be understood unless it is compared with past experiences.

(C) It is more important to learn from personal experience than to study philosophy to understand truth.

(D) We must study experience to know the meaning of truth because the two are necessarily connected.

13. The word sequential in paragraph 3 is closest in meaning to

(A) continuous
(B) apparent
(C) conscious
(D) interesting

14. Why does the author mention a river in paragraph 3?

(A) To describe how thoughts and feelings flow into each other

(B) To compare the processes of falling asleep and waking up

(C) To emphasize the complexity of bodily sensations

(D) To show that truth is not absolute and unchangeable

15. The word "workable" in paragraph 4 is closest in meaning to

(A) difficult to understand
(B) large enough to measure
(C) capable of being learned
(D) likely to be rejected

16. The word reconstructive in paragraph 5 is closest in meaning to

(A) exciting
(B) creative
(C) unifying
(D) aimless

17. According to John Dewey, the interplay between a person's previous knowledge and present situation is

(A) truth
(B) consciousness
(C) education
(D) experience

18. All of the following ideas are part of Dewey's theory of experience and education EXCEPT:

(A) Knowledge and experience interact.
(B) Present experience affects future experience.
(C) Every experience is educative.
(D) Experience should develop the individual.

19. According to Dewey, progressive education should include

(A) both positive and negative experiences
(B) an emphasis on specific core subjects
(C) complete rejection of traditional methods
(D) the active participation of the student

20. It can be inferred from the passage that William James and John Dewey would probably agree on which of the following statements?

(A) The truth of an idea is something that all people can agree upon.

(B) Our life experiences are a very important part of our education.

(C) To be truly educated, we must have our own theory of experience.

(D) The quantity of experience is more important than the quality.

21. Look at the four squares, **A**, **B**, **C**, and **D**, which indicate where the following sentence could be added to the passage. Where would the sentence best fit?

The incoming thoughts will come to resemble the outgoing thoughts, even though the two have never been experienced together before.

    In James's theory, thought and experience are connected. **A** Incoming waves of thought flow in next to outgoing waves of previous experience and thus become associated with each other. **B** An incoming thought is "workable" only if it is meaningful and can be associated with something already in the person's mind. **C** James's theory supports later theories of associative learning, which assert that new learning involves activating previous learning to find "hooks" on which to hang new information. **D**

22. Select the appropriate sentences from the answer choices and match them to the correct philosopher. TWO of the answer choices will NOT be used. *This question is worth 3 points.*

Answer Choices

(A) Learning is not merely the storing of information; it is learning how to think.

(B) Truth is absolute and unchangeable because it is based on universal laws of nature.

(C) Human consciousness is a stream of experiences, sensations, thoughts, and feelings.

(D) Education should be problem–centered and interdisciplinary, and it should provide productive experience.

(E) A new thought is workable when it is associated with previous experience or learning.

(F) Experience and knowledge grow upon and influence each other in an ongoing process.

(G) The goal of education should be the development of the child's ability to think abstractly.

William James

•
•

John Dewey

•
•
•

How to Score 3–Point Question	
Answers Correct	**Points Earned**
5	3
4	2
3	1
0 – 2	0

Answers to Reading Quiz 10 are on pages 648–649.

Record your score on the Progress Chart on page 790.

PART 2 – LISTENING

The Listening section of the TOEFL measures your ability to understand conversations and lectures in English. You will listen to several conversations, discussions, and lectures and answer questions about them. You will be tested on your comprehension of the general ideas and supporting details of the conversations and lectures. You will also be asked to identify a speaker's purpose in making a particular statement or to identify a speaker's attitude toward a particular topic.

The conversations reflect typical experiences of university students in North America. The lecture topics are academic and come from various fields of study in the natural sciences, the social sciences, business, and the arts. All of the questions are based on what the speakers state or imply. You do not need special knowledge of the topics to answer the questions.

In some forms of the TOEFL iBT, the Listening section will have two conversations and four lectures. In other forms, the Listening section will have three conversations and six lectures. You will not know which form of the test you have until the day of the test.

LISTENING SECTION

Form	Part	Audio Texts	Length of Each Text	Questions per Text	Total Time	Total Questions
Short	1	1 conversation	2–3 minutes	5	60 minutes	34
		2 lectures	3–5 minutes	6		
	2	1 conversation	2–3 minutes	5		
		2 lectures	3–5 minutes	6		
Long	1	1 conversation	2–3 minutes	5	90 minutes	51
		2 lectures	3–5 minutes	6		
	2	1 conversation	2–3 minutes	5		
		2 lectures	3–5 minutes	6		
	3	1 conversation	2–3 minutes	5		
		2 lectures	3–5 minutes	6		

In the short form of the Listening section, there are two separately timed parts. Each part includes one conversation and two lectures, with a response time of 10 minutes to answer the questions. In the short form, the entire Listening section takes approximately 60 minutes. The long form of the Listening section has three parts and a total time of approximately 90 minutes.

In both short and long forms of the Listening section, the total time includes the time that you spend listening to the directions, conversations, lectures, and questions, as well as the response time for answering the questions. A clock at the top of the screen shows you how much response time you have for that part. Each part allows 10 minutes of response time. The clock counts down only during the response time; it does not count down while you are listening to the conversations, lectures, and questions.

The test supervisor will give you paper for taking notes. You may take notes on paper while you are listening. You may use your notes to help you answer the questions. However, at the end of the test you must give all of your notes to the test supervisor. Your notes will not be scored.

You will use headphones to listen to the conversations and lectures. You can change the volume of the sound at any time during the test. You will hear each conversation and lecture only one time. You will both *hear* and *see* each question. You must answer each question before you can go on to the next question. You can change your answer as many times as you like—until you click on **OK**. When you click on **OK**, the computer will go to the next question. Once you have finished a question, you cannot return to that question or to any other previous question.

There are four types of listening questions. For each type of question, you will use the mouse to click on one or more answers or to move text. Some questions have special directions, which will appear in a gray box. Most correct answers will earn one point, but some questions may be worth two points.

Delta's Key to the TOEFL iBT provides ample practice in listening. Each listening unit allows you to focus on a particular listening skill.

Unit	Listening Skill	Number of Questions in Short Form of Test
2.1	Identifying the Topic and Main Idea	4 – 6
2.2	Listening for Details	10 – 12
2.3	Determining Attitude and Purpose	8 – 10
2.4	Making Inferences and Predictions	4 – 8
2.5	Understanding Function	1 – 2
2.6	Listening for Organization	1 – 2
	Total Number of Questions	34

CONVERSATIONS AND QUESTIONS

The Listening section contains two or three conversations. Some conversations involve a student and a professor talking about a course–related issue. Other conversations are service encounters, in which a student talks with an adviser, a librarian, a coach, a secretary, or some other university officer. Each conversation is two to three minutes long and is followed by a set of five questions.

Here is an example. While you are listening, you will see a picture of the speakers:

(Narrator)   Listen to a conversation between a student and a professor.

(Woman)   Excuse me, Dr. Gupta. May I speak with you?
(Professor)   Sure. What can I do for you?
(Woman)   I'm… uh… I'd like to change the topic of my paper. I was planning to write about trade, but I thought of something more interesting.
(Professor)   Oh…?
(Woman)   I was thinking… my friend introduced me to her grandparents, who came from Japan around seventy years ago. They're really interesting people, and we talked for a long time. So I got the idea it might be good to write about them… I mean, about Japanese immigration and the stories of people who came here from Japan. I could interview my friend's grandparents and their friends. Is that OK?
(Professor)   Yes, I'd say that's a good research topic. But, in addition to the interview data, you'll want to be sure you have some historical facts. Focus on the history, and use the interviews to illustrate the history.
(Woman)   I… um… I found some books on the *Issei* and the *Nisei*. Is that what you mean?
(Professor)   That's a good place to start. You should also check out cultural organizations, like the Japanese American Historical Society. I'm sure many of these organizations have Web pages. You may find links to other useful information.
(Woman)   Sure, sure, of course I'll do that. So… uh… it's all right to change my topic?
(Professor)   Certainly. And let me know how it's going.
(Woman)   I sure will. Thanks, Dr. Gupta.

Then you will hear the first question. You will see the question and four possible answers:

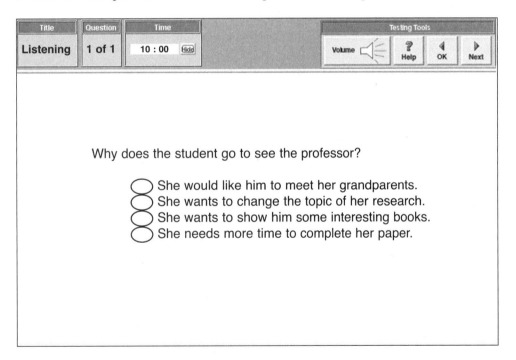

The best answer to the question *Why does the student go to see the professor?* is *She wants to change the topic of her research.* Therefore, you should click on the oval next to that answer.

When you click on an oval, the oval will darken. To change your answer, click on a different oval. When you are satisfied that you have chosen the correct answer, click on **Next**. Then click on **OK**. The computer will move to the next question.

LECTURES AND QUESTIONS

The Listening section contains four to six academic lectures or discussions. Each lecture or discussion is approximately three to five minutes long and is followed by a set of comprehension questions.

Here is an example.

Geology

(Narrator)   Listen to part of a lecture in a geology class.

While you are listening, you will see a picture of the professor and the class:

(Professor)   After the water drains from a cave, a new kind of growth may begin. Delicate straws grow from the ceiling. Twisted fingers protrude from the walls and floor. Smooth mounds appear in pools. All of these amazing formations are called speleothems. They sometimes grow in sandstone and lava–tube caves, but most commonly we see them in limestone caves.

Among the most interesting speleothems are stalactites and stalagmites. People always want to know: how do you keep straight… which is a stalactite and which is a stalagmite? There's an easy way to remember. "Stalactite" is spelled with a "c" and it hangs from the ceiling. "Stalagmite" is spelled with a "g" and it grows up from the ground.

You may see a blackboard with key terms from the lecture:

stalactite
stalagmite

You may also see other pictures:

(Professor) Both stalactites and stalagmites begin with a drop of water on a cave ceiling. The ground–water seeping into the cave contains carbon dioxide from the atmosphere or the soil, as well as dissolved limestone that it picked up from the layers of rock above the cave.

As a drop of water hangs from the ceiling, a tiny amount of carbon dioxide escapes—just like bubbles from a can of soda pop. Now the water drop can't carry much dissolved limestone, and a tiny ring of stone called dripstone forms around its outside edges. The drop of water hangs for a moment, then it falls.

Each drop of water adds another layer as it trickles down through the growing ring of dripstone. Eventually, the dripstone forms a slender tube. These slender, hollow tubes are called tubular stalactites, or—because they look like straws—soda–straw stalactites. They're very fragile. As they grow, their own weight may cause them to break off and fall to the floor. Soda straws can grow into conical stalactites as dripstone builds up on the outside. Stalactites don't grow very quickly… on average, only about a half–inch in a hundred years.

The dripping water that hits the floor still contains some dissolved limestone. The impact of the water hitting the floor causes it to break into droplets, releasing the excess carbon dioxide. Then limestone crystals start to grow upward, forming stalagmites… starting with tiny finger–like structures, and eventually forming large, rounded domes up to ten meters tall and ten meters in diameter.

At the end of the lecture, you will see:

> Now get ready to answer the questions.
>
> You may use your notes to help you answer.

There are four types of questions. However, you may not see all of the types when you take the test.

Question Type 1 – Click on One Answer

For this multiple–choice type of question, you will choose the best of four possible answers. You will see:

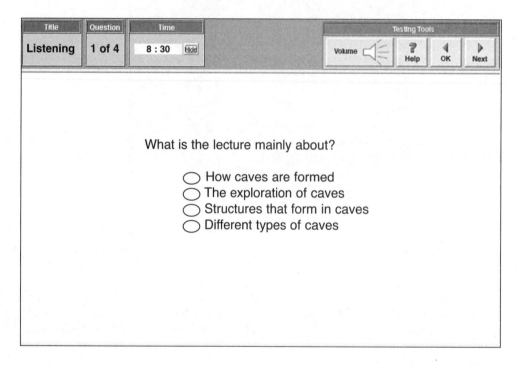

Title	Question	Time				Testing Tools			
Listening	1 of 4	8 : 30 Hide				Volume	? Help	◄ OK	► Next

What is the lecture mainly about?

○ How caves are formed
○ The exploration of caves
○ Structures that form in caves
○ Different types of caves

The topic of the lecture is *Structures that form in caves*. Therefore, you should click on the oval next to the third answer.

When you click on an oval, the oval will darken. To change your answer, click on a different oval. When you are satisfied that you have chosen the correct answer, click on **Next**. Then click on **OK**. The computer will move to the next question.

Question Type 2 – Click on More than One Answer

For this type of question, you will click on two or three answers. You will click on boxes instead of ovals. You will see:

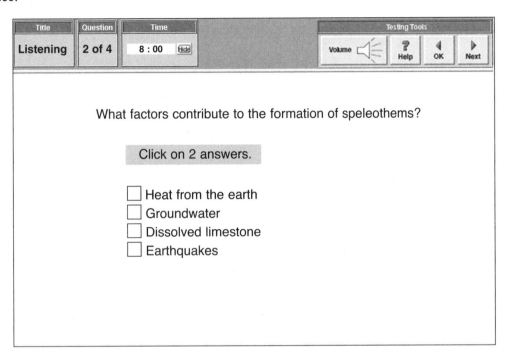

The professor says:

> Both stalactites and stalagmites begin with a drop of water on a cave ceiling. The groundwater seeping into the cave contains carbon dioxide from the atmosphere or the soil, as well as dissolved limestone that it picked up from the layers of rock above the cave.

Therefore, you should click on the boxes next to *Groundwater* and *Dissolved limestone*.

When you click on a box, an X will appear in it. To change an answer, click on a different box.

You must choose both correct answers to receive credit for answering the question correctly. In some questions of this type, you must choose three correct answers to receive credit.

Question Type 3 – Listen Again to Part of the Text

For this type of question, you will hear part of the audio again. You will hear and see:

Listen again to part of the lecture.

Then answer the question.

Then you will hear:

(Professor) People always want to know: how do you keep straight... which is a stalactite and which is a stalagmite? There's an easy way to remember. "Stalactite" is spelled with a "c" and it hangs from the ceiling. "Stalagmite" is spelled with a "g" and it grows up from the ground.

(Narrator) Why does the professor say this:

(Professor) "Stalactite" is spelled with a "c" and it hangs from the ceiling. "Stalagmite" is spelled with a "g" and it grows up from the ground.

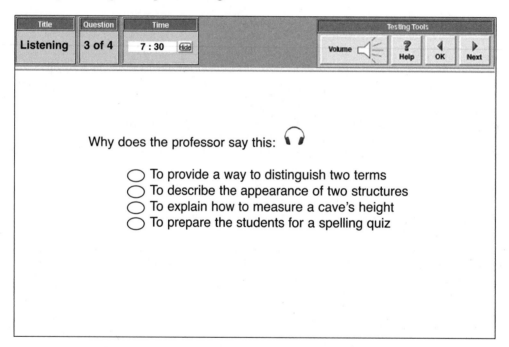

When you see the symbol 🎧 next to a question, it means that part of the question will not appear on the screen. However, you will hear part of the lecture again, so you must listen carefully.

The professor says:

> People always want to know: how do you keep straight... which is a stalactite and which is a stalagmite? There's an easy way to remember.

Then the professor discusses the spelling of stalactite and stalagmite. The correct answer is *To provide a way to distinguish two terms*. Therefore, you should click on the oval next to the first answer.

Question Type 4 – Click on a Table

For this type of question, you will click on boxes in a table. You will see:

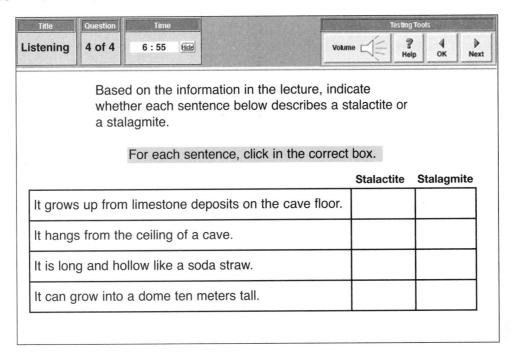

The professor says:

"Stalactite"… hangs from the ceiling. "Stalagmite"… grows up from the ground.

These slender, hollow tubes are called… because they look like straws—soda–straw stalactites.

Then limestone crystals start to grow upward, forming stalagmites… eventually forming large, rounded domes up to ten meters tall….

Therefore, the correct answers are:

	Stalactite	Stalagmite
It grows up from limestone deposits on the cave floor.		✔
It hangs from the ceiling of a cave.	✔	
It is long and hollow like a soda straw.	✔	
It can grow into a dome ten meters tall.		✔

When you click on a box, a ✔ will appear in it. You must click on one box in each row. To change an answer, click on a different box in the same row. You must put all of the ✔s in the correct space to receive credit for answering the question correctly.

STRATEGIES FOR THE LISTENING SECTION

Before the Test

- Work on building your vocabulary. Use the conversations and lectures in this book to become familiar with the level of vocabulary on the TOEFL.

- Listen to a variety of academic talks, such as recordings of real college lectures, documentaries, and educational television programs. Most of the lectures on the TOEFL deal with topics in the natural sciences, the social sciences, the arts, and business. Listen to material in these subject areas to build comprehension.

- Work on developing efficient note–taking skills. Develop a system of using abbreviations and symbols for common words.

- Become familiar with the four types of questions and how to answer them.

- Become familiar with the TOEFL testing tools, such as **Next** and **OK**. Practice using the mouse to click on and drag text.

- Your own best strategy: _____

_____

During the Test

- While you are listening to the conversations and lectures, focus on overall meaning and purpose. Listen for key words and concepts that are repeated throughout the piece.

- When you take notes, write down only essential terms and concepts. Do not allow your writing to detract from your listening.

- Work as quickly as possible. Although you can control the amount of time you spend answering each question, there is a time limit for answering the total number of questions in the Listening section.

- For multiple choice questions, use the ***process of elimination***. This means that if you do not find the correct answer right away, omit the choices you know are incorrect. If you can eliminate one or two choices, you will improve your chance of selecting the correct answer.

- Click on **OK** only when you are certain you are ready to go on to the next question. After you click on **OK**, you cannot return to the previous question.

- Your own best strategy: _____

_____

2.1 Identifying the Topic and Main Idea

 FOCUS

 Album 2, Track 1

> What is the subject of the conversation?
>
> ○ A political organization
> ○ A course reading list
> ○ A physical science class
> ○ A summer school program

 *Stop*

The subject of the conversation is the most general answer to the question *What are the people talking about?*

The speakers use several key words and phrases:

Dr. Perry's class	check the computer	substantial amount of reading
Political Science	summer session	print out a copy
book list	Here…found	few minutes

The man asks about the book list for Dr. Perry's Introduction to Political Science class, and the woman offers to print out a copy for him. Therefore, the correct answer is *A course reading list.*

 **STUDY**

1. The Topic

The *topic* is the general subject of the conversation or lecture. The topic is the most general answer to the question *What are the speakers talking about?*

TOEFL questions about the topic sound like this:

> What are the speakers mainly discussing?
> What is the man's problem?
> What is the lecture mainly about?
> What is the main topic of the talk?
> What aspect of _____ does the professor mainly discuss?

2. Content Words

Key words and phrases can help you identify the topic of the conversation or lecture. Sometimes speakers emphasize key words and phrases. Sometimes speakers use the same key words more than once. Listen for words and phrases that are stressed or repeated by the speakers.

Key words are usually ***content words***: nouns, verbs, adjectives, and adverbs. Content words can help you identify the topic and general message.

Listen again to the recording for the Focus exercise. Listen for key words and phrases that the speakers emphasize and repeat. Listen for content words: nouns, verbs, adjectives, and adverbs.

 Album 2, Track 1

W:	Good afternoon. May I help you?
M:	Hello. I'm thinking of taking <u>Dr. Perry's class</u> this summer—<u>Intro to Political Science</u>. And I was wondering… uh… is there a… do you happen to have a <u>book list for that class</u>?
W:	I can <u>check the computer</u> to see if she submitted it yet.
M:	Thanks. I'd appreciate it.
W:	Did you say Introduction to Political Science?
M:	Yes. For <u>summer session</u>.
W:	<u>Here</u> it is, I <u>found</u> it. Oh… and it sure looks like a <u>substantial</u> amount of <u>reading</u>!
M:	Really? Is it <u>long</u>?
W:	Would you like me to <u>print</u> out a <u>copy</u> for you?
M:	Yeah, that would be great!
W:	All right. This will only take a <u>few minutes</u>.
M:	Thank you. I really appreciate it.

 Stop

3. The Main Idea

The ***main idea*** is the general message of the conversation or lecture. The main idea is what is important about the topic, according to the speakers. Key words and phrases can help you identify what the speakers think is important about the topic. In a longer piece, there may be two or more major ideas that together form the general message.

TOEFL questions about the main idea sound like this:

> What is the speaker's main point?
> What is the main idea of the lecture?
> How does the man help the woman?

4. Answer Choices

In questions about the topic and main idea, an answer choice may be incorrect because it is:

- too general: an idea that is beyond the focus of the conversation or lecture;
- too specific: a supporting detail instead of a main idea;
- inaccurate: not true, or only partly true, according to the speakers; or
- irrelevant: about something that the speakers do not mention.

When you answer questions about the topic and main idea, think about the overall message of the conversation or lecture. Try not to *overthink* this type of question; it is often best to trust your first impression.

 PRACTICE

Exercise 2.1.A

Listen to the recording and choose the best answer to each question. To make this practice more like the real test, cover the questions and answers during each conversation.

 Album 2, Track 2

1. What is the woman's problem?

   (A) She does not have enough time to finish writing her paper.
   (B) She is concerned about receiving a poor grade in history.
   (C) She is confused by her professor's response to her paper.
   (D) She does not think her professor graded her paper fairly.

2. What is the conversation mainly about?

   (A) A place that is special
   (B) Problems with families
   (C) Plans for a school vacation
   (D) A popular beach resort

3. What is the woman mainly discussing?

   (A) Her courses in child development
   (B) Her internship at a children's agency
   (C) How to look for a job after graduation
   (D) How to organize a political campaign

4. What problem does the man have?

   (A) He has difficulty remembering some terms.
   (B) He is not skilled at climbing trees.
   (C) He will not be able to take the botany quiz.
   (D) He can't decide which botany course to take.

5. How does the woman help the man?

   (A) She shows him how to put words in alphabetical order.
   (B) She tells him that memorization is not a good way to study.
   (C) She gives him a list of names beginning with "P" and "X".
   (D) She suggests that he imagine a tree with key letters on it.

 Stop

Exercise 2.1.B

Listen to the recording and choose the best answer to each question. To make this practice more like the real test, cover the questions and answers during each lecture.

 Album 2, Track 3

1. What is the talk mainly about?

   (A) The best places to park on campus
   (B) Services of the Safety and Security Office
   (C) The increasing need for campus security
   (D) Reporting criminal incidents on campus

2. What does the professor mainly discuss?

   (A) The origins of bread
   (B) The culture of the Nile Valley
   (C) Agricultural development
   (D) Early trade in the Middle East

3. What is the lecture mainly about?

   (A) Traditional agricultural practices
   (B) The shortage of clean water
   (C) The high use of water by irrigation
   (D) Why water evaporates from fields

4. What is the lecture mainly about?

   (A) How ancient rivers created deserts
   (B) How scientists work in the desert
   (C) How to walk on sand dunes
   (D) How sand dunes shift position

5. What is the lecture mainly about?

   (A) Research in pain management
   (B) The benefits of exercise
   (C) Why people have faith in doctors
   (D) The chemistry of the human brain

 Stop

Exercise 2.1.C

Listen to the recording and choose the best answer to each question. To make this practice more like the real test, cover the questions and answers during each lecture.

 Album 2, Track 4

1. What is the speaker's main point?

   (A) Attitudes toward aging can affect how long a person lives.
   (B) People have difficulty learning new skills as they get older.
   (C) Young adults generally have a negative view of older adults.
   (D) People live longer than they did in the past.

2. What is the topic of the talk?

   (A) Worker productivity
   (B) An increase in lawsuits
   (C) Management training
   (D) Diversity in the workplace

3. What is the speaker's main point?

   (A) The American population is more diverse than ever before.
   (B) Responding to a diverse workforce is an economic decision.
   (C) Workers are demanding more rights.
   (D) Management training should focus on decision–making.

4. What is the lecture mainly about?

   (A) Different types of wetlands
   (B) Animal life in marshes
   (C) Characteristics of marshes
   (D) How marshes cause disease

5. What is the professor's main point?

   (A) Marshes are energy–rich, ecologically important areas.
   (B) A variety of insects, amphibians, reptiles, and birds live in marshes.
   (C) There are several reasons to convert wetlands to agricultural use.
   (D) Marshes are habitat for a large number of endangered species.

6. What is the main topic of the discussion?

   (A) The beans of the cocoa tree
   (B) Native trees of the tropical forest
   (C) Workers on a plantation
   (D) The flavor of chocolate

7. What aspect of the cocoa tree does the professor mainly discuss?

   (A) Ideal growing conditions
   (B) Biological classification
   (C) The tree's physical structure
   (D) Steps in processing the beans

8. What main point does the professor make?

   (A) A cocoa pod is 10 to 30 centimeters long and contains several beans.
   (B) There are important factors in the production of top quality cocoa.
   (C) Fermentation prevents cocoa beans from sprouting during transit.
   (D) The best grades of chocolate are made with a secret ingredient.

 Stop

Answers to Exercises 2.1.A through 2.1.C are on page 650.

 EXTENSION

1. Listen again to the conversations and lectures in Exercises 2.1.A through 2.1.C (Album 2, Tracks 2 through 4). While you are listening, write down key content words: nouns, verbs, adjectives, and adverbs. Don't try to write down everything. Write down only the words and phrases that are keys to understanding the overall message. Compare the words that you wrote down with those that your classmates wrote down. Which words and phrases are the most important for understanding the message?

2. With a classmate, discuss why the incorrect answer choices in Exercises 2.1.A through 2.1.C are incorrect. Are the answers wrong because they are:

   - too general: beyond the focus of the conversation or lecture?
   - too specific: supporting detail instead of main idea?
   - inaccurate: not true, or only partly true, according to the speakers?
   - irrelevant: about something that the speakers do not mention?

3. Listen again to the conversations in Exercise 2.1.A (Album 2, Track 2). With your classmates, discuss the meaning of the underlined expressions in the script below. In what other situations might these expressions be used?

How's it going?	Hi, Kelsey! <u>How's it going</u>?
get (something) back	I just <u>got my history paper back</u>….
You'd better	<u>You'd better</u> go talk to him.
find out	You need to <u>find out</u> what he's thinking.
hang out	I'm going to Mexico to <u>hang out</u> on the beach!
How about you?	Four of us will be staying at a resort…. <u>How about you?</u>
not mind	But, I <u>don't mind</u>. It's my turn.
(one's) turn.	It's <u>my turn</u>. He's done so much for me in the past.
do an internship	I'll be <u>doing an internship</u> instead.
sounds like	That <u>sounds like</u> a great experience because….
if only I could	I guess so, <u>if only I could</u> remember the difference between….
get it straight	I can't seem to <u>get it straight</u> on which one….

4. Make a short audio recording from the radio or television. Record two or three minutes of a speech, documentary, or educational program. Bring your recording to class. Play the recording for your classmates. Then, discuss the recording. Identify the topic and important ideas. What key words and phrases help you to identify the topic and what is important about it?

2.2 Listening for Details

FOCUS

 Album 2, Track 5

---

1. At what decibel level does the risk of hearing loss begin?

   ◯ 60 decibels
   ◯ 90 decibels
   ◯ 125 decibels
   ◯ 140 decibels

2. Which sounds could contribute to hearing loss?

   Click on 2 answers.

   ☐ A conversation at close range
   ☐ A rock band at close range
   ☐ A jet engine at close range
   ☐ A vacuum cleaner at close range

Stop

Question 1 asks you to identify the decibel level at which the risk of hearing loss begins. The professor says:

> The danger zone—the risk of injury—begins at around 90. Continual exposure to sounds above 90 decibels can damage your hearing.

Therefore, the correct answer is *90 decibels*.

Question 2 asks you to identify the sounds that could contribute to hearing loss. For this question, there are two correct answers. The professor says:

> Lots of everyday noises are bad for us in the long run. For example…. A rock band at close range is 125 decibels. A jet engine at close range is one of the worst culprits at an ear–busting 140 decibels.

The correct answers are *A rock band at close range* and *A jet engine at close range*.

These two questions ask about some important details in the talk. The details support the main idea that long–term exposure to noise can cause hearing loss. What other details can you recall from the talk?

 STUDY

1. Details

Details are specific bits of information, such as facts, descriptions, definitions, reasons, and examples. Detail questions on the TOEFL involve facts that are stated by the speakers. Detail questions ask you to recall specific information from the conversation or lecture, but do not require you to make inferences.

TOEFL questions about details sound like this:

What does the woman want to know?

What does the man suggest the woman do?

What reason is given for _____?

What does the professor say about _____?

How does the speaker describe _____?

What point does the professor make about _____?

What _____?

Who _____?

Where _____?

When _____?

Which _____?

How _____?

Why _____?

2. Taking Notes

During the test, you will hear each conversation and lecture only one time. You may take notes while you listen. Taking notes will help you remember important details, so it is a useful skill to develop.

In lectures, the speaker will often define and explain key terms. Sometimes you will see a blackboard with key words or phrases. Whenever you see a blackboard, listen carefully and take notes about that information because there is likely to be a question about it.

3. Content Words

Listen again to the recording for the Focus exercise. Listen for important details and content words.

 Album 2, Track 5

Long–term <u>exposure to noise</u> can lead to <u>loss of hearing</u>. The relative loudness of sounds is <u>measured</u> in <u>decibels</u>. Just to give you an idea of what this means, the sound of a <u>whisper</u> is <u>30 decibels</u>, while a <u>normal conversation is 60</u> decibels. The noise a <u>vacuum cleaner</u> makes is around 85 decibels.

The <u>danger zone</u>—the risk of injury—begins at around <u>90</u>. Continual exposure to sounds above 90 decibels can <u>damage</u> your hearing. <u>Loud noises</u>—especially when they come at you <u>every day</u>—all this noise can <u>damage</u> the delicate hair cells in your inner ear. Lots of everyday noises are <u>bad</u> for us in the long run. For example, a <u>car horn</u> sounds at around <u>100 decibels</u>. A <u>rock band</u> at close range is <u>125</u> decibels. A <u>jet engine</u> at close range is one of the <u>worst</u> culprits at an ear–busting <u>140</u> decibels.

The <u>first thing to go</u> is your <u>high–frequency hearing</u>, where you detect the consonant sounds in words. That's why a person with hearing loss can hear voices, but has <u>trouble understanding</u> what's being said.

 Stop

4. Answer Choices

In questions about details, an answer choice may be incorrect because it:

- repeats some of the speakers' words but has a different message;
- uses words that sound similar to the speakers' words;
- is incorrect or inaccurate, according to the speakers; or
- is about something that the speakers do not mention.

Remember, you can answer all of the questions based on the information you hear in the conversations and lectures. You do not need special knowledge of the topics to answer the questions correctly.

PRACTICE

Exercise 2.2.A

Listen to the recording and choose the best answer to each question. To make this practice more like the real test, cover the questions and answers during each conversation.

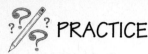 *Album 2, Track 6*

1. What does the woman suggest the man do?

    (A) Look at the posted job openings
    (B) Call for information about a job
    (C) Make an appointment with a counselor
    (D) Apply for a job in the student center

2. What type of job does the man want?

    (A) A job that pays well
    (B) A job that will let him study
    (C) A job in his field of interest
    (D) A job as a counselor

3. What does the woman agree to do?

    (A) Donate some books to the library
    (B) Meet the man outside the library
    (C) Volunteer to work as a cashier
    (D) Buy books at the annual book sale

4. How are book sale workers compensated?

    (A) They take any ten books that they want.
    (B) They are paid ten dollars an hour in cash.
    (C) They receive a set of encyclopedias.
    (D) They get credit to buy books at the sale.

5. When will the woman arrive at the book sale?

    (A) 10:00
    (B) 12:00
    (C) 3:00
    (D) 6:00

6. Why does the woman like her class with Professor Hahn?

    (A) Professor Hahn is a well–known scientist.
    (B) The assignments and lectures are valuable.
    (C) The students solve practical problems in class.
    (D) Political science is the woman's favorite subject.

7. What does the man say about Professor Hahn?

    (A) She is the best teacher at the college.
    (B) She tries to amuse her students.
    (C) She cares a lot about her students.
    (D) She expects her students to work hard.

8. What does the professor want the woman to do?

    (A) Help him write a paper
    (B) Arrange some articles
    (C) Look up information
    (D) Organize a research study

9. What is the subject of the professor's research?

    (A) Animal behavior
    (B) Journal writing
    (C) Time management
    (D) Child psychology

10. When will the woman do the work?

    (A) That afternoon
    (B) The next day
    (C) The day after tomorrow
    (D) The following week

 Stop

DELTA'S KEY TO THE TOEFL IBT®

Exercise 2.2.B

Listen to the recording and choose the best answer to each question. To make this practice more like the real test, cover the questions and answers during each conversation and lecture.

 Album 2, Track 7

1. When did the hunting season take place?

   (A) In spring and summer
   (B) In summer and early fall
   (C) From fall until midwinter
   (D) From midwinter until spring

2. What animals did the northwoods tribes hunt?

   Click on 2 answers.

   [A] Lion
   [B] Eagle
   [C] Deer
   [D] Moose

3. According to the man, how did women participate in hunting?

   (A) Managing the camps
   (B) Snaring small animals
   (C) Searching for game
   (D) Making the bows and arrows

4. Which activities did women control?

   Click on 2 answers.

   [A] Fishing
   [B] Clan leadership
   [C] Education
   [D] Agriculture

5. According to the professor, what factors are important in choosing a career in the arts?

   Click on 2 answers.

   [A] Wealth
   [B] Talent
   [C] Luck
   [D] Experience

6. According to the professor, why does a career in the arts require a special calling?

   (A) Public tastes in art change frequently.
   (B) Employment in the arts can be uncertain.
   (C) Art schools are expensive and difficult.
   (D) Artistic talent cannot be measured fairly.

7. How does the professor suggest one get started in a career in the arts?

   (A) Ask a famous artist for a letter of recommendation.
   (B) Look at the job advertisements in the newspaper.
   (C) Do part–time or volunteer work in one's chosen art.
   (D) Apply for a scholarship to a prestigious art school.

8. According to the instructor, what is the first step in preparing a speech?

   (A) Choose a topic that your teacher will like.
   (B) Realize the speech's importance to you.
   (C) Develop your ideas with examples.
   (D) Read a book about preparing a speech.

9. What examples of purpose are mentioned in the discussion?

   Click on 2 answers.

   [A] To inform others about your subject
   [B] To describe an interesting experience
   [C] To make your audience laugh
   [D] To explain how to do something

10. What does the instructor want the students to do next?

    (A) Practice their speeches in small groups
    (B) Write down ideas that they think of
    (C) Choose from a list of possible topics
    (D) Brainstorm ways to entertain the class

 Stop

Exercise 2.2.C

Listen to the recording and choose the best answer to each question. To make this practice more like the real test, cover the questions and answers during each lecture.

 Album 2, Track 8

1. What is a pigment?

   (A) A chemical used for cleaning painting equipment
   (B) A cover to protect paintings from the effects of sunlight
   (C) A substance that gives its color to another material
   (D) A synthetic fabric that is suitable for painting on

2. According to the instructor, what characteristic should a pigment have?

   (A) Ability to be applied at any temperature
   (B) Ability to dry quickly after application
   (C) No loss of strength when dissolved
   (D) No harmful reaction with other pigments

3. How are pigments generally classified?

   (A) By origin
   (B) By texture
   (C) By color
   (D) By quality

4. Which natural pigment did the Romans obtain from a shellfish?

   (A) Raw umber
   (B) Indigo
   (C) Tyrian purple
   (D) Ochre

5. According to the instructor, why are synthetic pigments superior to natural pigments?

   Click on 2 answers.

   [A] They last for a longer time.
   [B] They have a smoother surface.
   [C] They are less expensive.
   [D] They provide stronger, brighter colors.

6. What is the lecture mainly about?

   (A) What parents should consider when buying toys for young children
   (B) Differences between children and monkeys in their choice of toys
   (C) The importance of play in the socialization of preschool children
   (D) The relationship of gender and toy preferences in young children

7. According to the professor, what does research reveal about toy choices in the youngest children?

   (A) Very young children prefer brightly colored toys.
   (B) There are few differences between boys and girls.
   (C) Children do not always like the toys they are given.
   (D) The research on this topic has been controversial.

8. According to research mentioned by the professor, what types of toys do male monkeys prefer?

   (A) Cars and balls
   (B) Paper and crayons
   (C) Dolls and pots
   (D) Blocks and sticks

9. At what age do children start showing gender differences in their choice of toys?

   (A) Two
   (B) Five
   (C) Eight
   (D) Twelve

10. What is the main point made in the lecture?

   (A) It is a sexist plot to have different toys for boys and girls.
   (B) Girls like playing with dolls because of social conditioning.
   (C) Most children do not care if their toys are for boys or girls.
   (D) Boys and girls naturally prefer different types of toys.

 Stop

Exercise 2.2.D

Listen to the recording and choose the best answer to each question. To make this practice more like the real test, cover the questions and answers during each conversation and lecture.

 Album 2, Track 9

1. What are the students discussing?

   (A) Terms from a lecture
   (B) Questions on a test
   (C) Property rights
   (D) Topics for a term paper

2. What does "primogeniture" mean?

   (A) A state in which the ruler owns all property
   (B) Dividing property among several children
   (C) A system of inheritance by the firstborn son
   (D) Paying property taxes to the state

3. According to the professor, why do many small businesses fail?

   (A) They do not demand hard work from their employees.
   (B) They do not expand into large businesses.
   (C) They have poor–quality products and services.
   (D) They lack the financial reserves to absorb losses.

4. According to the professor, what is essential for success as a small business owner?

   (A) A master's degree in business
   (B) Friends in positions of power
   (C) A large amount of credit
   (D) Good management skills

5. What are two responsibilities of a store owner?

   Click on 2 answers.

   [A] Buying the store building
   [B] Keeping track of inventory
   [C] Promoting the store's products
   [D] Inventing new products

6. What does the woman want to discuss with the teaching assistant?

   (A) Trouble that happened in class last week
   (B) A friend she met on a field trip
   (C) Something she saw when she was hiking
   (D) A problem with one of her classmates

7. Where did the woman meet the young man who had a problem?

   (A) In high school
   (B) In biology class
   (C) On a mountain road
   (D) On a desert trail

8. What help did the young man receive?

   Click on 2 answers.

   [A] The woman gave him water.
   [B] A doctor repaired his leg.
   [C] The ranger showed him a map.
   [D] His teacher brought him food.

9. Why did the young man experience muscle cramps?

   (A) His muscles were weak from too little exercise.
   (B) The cells in his muscles did not have enough oxygen.
   (C) He injured his leg when he fell on a rock.
   (D) An excessive amount of salt collected in the muscles.

10. What point does the teaching assistant make about what the woman saw?

    (A) The woman recognized biology in real life.
    (B) The woman saw two foolish young men.
    (C) The woman should try to forget what she saw.
    (D) The woman will see more interesting things.

 Stop

Answers to Exercises 2.2.A through 2.2.D are on pages 650–652.

 EXTENSION

1. Listen again to the conversations in Exercise 2.2.A (Album 2, Track 6). With your classmates, discuss the meaning of the underlined expressions in the script below. In what other situations might these expressions be used?

check out	You should <u>check out</u> the job board in the student center.
spare time	…I need the money but I don't have a lot of <u>spare time</u>.
free	If you're <u>free</u> in the afternoon…
help out	…why not volunteer to <u>help</u> us <u>out</u>?
I guess I could	<u>I guess I could</u> spare a few hours.
put (one's) name down	I can <u>put your name down</u> then?
make (someone do something)	She really <u>makes us think</u>.
	And she really <u>makes you work</u> in her class!
figure out	I'm starting to <u>figure</u> things <u>out</u> as a result of this class.
go through	These are all journal articles that I need to <u>go through</u> for my research.
deal with	Most are about primate behavior, but a few <u>deal with</u> other mammals or birds….

2. Listen again to the first lecture in Exercise 2.2.C. As you listen, write the correct words on the blank lines in the script below. Check your answers with the audio script on page 703.

Album 2, Track 8

Listen to a talk in an _____ class. The instructor is talking about _____.

Whether you're working with oil, tempera, or _____, it's the pigment that gives

the paint its _____. A pigment can either be _____ with another material or

applied over its _____ in a thin layer. When a pigment is _____ or ground

in a liquid vehicle to form _____, it does not dissolve but remains _____ in

the liquid.

A paint pigment should be a _____, finely divided powder. It should withstand

the action of _____ without changing color. A pigment should not exert a harmful

_____ reaction upon the medium, or upon other color _____ it is mixed

with.

LISTENING

Generally, _____ are classified according to their _____, either natural or _____. Natural inorganic pigments, also known as _____ pigments, include the native "earths" such as ochre—_____ iron oxide—and raw umber—_____ iron oxide. Natural organic pigments come from _____ and animal sources. Some examples are indigo, from the indigo _____, and Tyrian purple, the imperial _____ the Romans prepared from a _____ native to the Mediterranean.

Today, many pigments are _____ varieties of traditional inorganic and _____ pigments. Synthetic organic pigments provide _____ of unmatched intensity and tinting _____. The synthetic counterparts of the _____ and red earths are more _____ and, if well prepared, are _____ in all other respects to the _____ products. Inorganic synthetic colors made with the aid of strong _____ are generally the most _____ for all uses. In contrast, pigments from _____ sources are less permanent than the average synthetic _____.

Stop

3. Listen again to each lecture in Exercise 2.2.C (Album 2, Track 8). Imagine that you are in class, listening to the professor speak. While you are listening, take notes about the important ideas and details. Do not try to write down every word or memorize the lecture. After each lecture, use your notes and your own words to (1) write a short summary, or (2) present an oral summary of the main ideas.

4. Look in a newspaper, a magazine, or a textbook. Find a short passage of two or three paragraphs and bring it to class. In class, form groups of four students. Read your passage to the students in your group. When you are finished, your classmates must report the details that they heard. One student writes the details as a list. Then, working together, write questions about the details.

Use these question words:

What _____?	Where _____?	Why _____?
Who _____?	When _____?	How _____?

PROGRESS – 2.1 through 2.2

QUIZ 1

Time – approximately 10 minutes

Listen to the recordings and choose the best answer to each question. To make this quiz more like the real test, cover the questions and answers during each conversation and lecture. When you hear the first question for each set, uncover the questions and answers.

 Album 2, Track 10

1. What is the discussion mainly about?

   (A) The computerized workplace
   (B) Health dangers in the workplace
   (C) How to arrange office furniture
   (D) Disorders of the neck and back

2. What does the instructor recommend for relieving eyestrain?

   (A) Turn off the computer for 30 minutes.
   (B) Look at objects that are far away.
   (C) Adjust the level of the room lights.
   (D) Wash the eyes with warm water.

3. According to the discussion, why is it important to have the right chair?

   (A) Your chair is the best place to take a nap.
   (B) The right chair will impress your boss.
   (C) The chair's color affects your level of stress.
   (D) The right chair can help you avoid back pain.

4. According to the instructor, what health problem is associated with copy machines?

   (A) Eyestrain
   (B) Neck pain
   (C) Skin rash
   (D) Back pain

5. Where in the workplace might ozone be a problem?

   (A) At a computer terminal
   (B) On the elevator
   (C) Near the copy machines
   (D) In the parking lot

DELTA'S KEY TO THE TOEFL IBT®

Album 2, Track 11

6. What is the main topic of the lecture?

(A) How trade led to the growth of tourism
(B) Past and present reasons for traveling
(C) The changing concept of personal enrichment
(D) New developments in the travel industry

7. According to the professor, what is the main reason that people traveled many centuries ago?

(A) The search for resources
(B) The advancement of science
(C) The desire for adventure
(D) The interest in preserving nature

8. According to the professor, which of the following originated in the past two centuries?

Click on 2 answers.

[A] Traveling in search of food
[B] Traveling for scientific purposes
[C] Traveling to establish colonies
[D] Traveling for recreation

9. What does the professor say about ethnic tourism?

(A) It began in the seventeenth century.
(B) Its goal is conquest and colonization.
(C) Its primary activity is big game hunting.
(D) It helps preserve traditional cultures.

10. What is the main point made in the lecture?

(A) The growth of trade stimulated the growth of tourism.
(B) Traveling for personal enrichment is a modern idea.
(C) The reasons for traveling have changed over the centuries.
(D) People today would rather photograph wildlife than kill it.

 Stop

Answers to Listening Quiz 1 are on page 652.

Record your score on the Progress Chart on page 791.

2.3 Determining Attitude and Purpose

 FOCUS

 Album 3, Track 1

---

1. Why does the student go to see her adviser?

   ○ She needs a tutor for her psychology course.
   ○ She has decided to change her field of study.
   ○ She wants to talk about a terrible accident.
   ○ She needs advice about running a business.

2. What is the student's attitude toward the school counselors that she observed?

   ○ She is shocked by their terrible work.
   ○ She is surprised that they work so hard.
   ○ She does not think they are necessary.
   ○ She is inspired by their good work.

 Stop

Question 1 asks you to identify the student's purpose for starting the conversation. The student says:

> I wanted to talk about the school psychology program. I've been thinking about this for a while, and I've decided to change my major to counseling.

The student plans to change her major field of study to counseling. The correct answer is *She has decided to change her field of study*.

Question 2 asks you to identify the student's attitude about the counselors at the school where she is a tutor. The student says:

> …I'm just so impressed with what the counselors are doing there.

> I had a chance to observe some of the counselors talking to the kids, helping them deal with the tragedy. They—the counselors, that is—they were so, so… they were really amazing. It really got me thinking about… how to help people heal. I started thinking, "This is something I'd like to do."

The student is impressed by the work of the counselors in helping the children. The experience of observing the counselors has contributed to the student's decision to change her major to counseling. The correct answer is *She is inspired by their good work*.

 STUDY

1. Purpose

The **purpose** of a conversation or lecture is its function, the main reason why the conversation or lecture takes place. In conversations, a speaker's purpose is related to the topic of the conversation, the relationship between the speakers, and the context in which the speakers meet.

In TOEFL conversations, questions about purpose sound like this:

> Why does the student go to see the professor?
> What is the man's problem?
> What is the purpose of the conversation?

The purpose of a talk or lecture is related to the main idea. Questions about purpose sound like this:

> What is the purpose of the talk?
> What is the main purpose of the lecture?
> What is the speaker's main purpose?

Some purpose questions focus on only part of the conversation or lecture:

> Why does the student say _____?
> Why does the professor mention _____?
> Why does the instructor talk about _____?
> Why does the speaker tell a story about _____?

In some questions you will listen again to part of the conversation or lecture. Then you will hear a question about the speaker's purpose. Here is an example:

> Listen again to part of the lecture. Then answer the question. 🎧
> (You hear, but not see, part of the lecture again.)
> Why does the professor say this: 🎧

Some examples of purpose are:

> To ask for advice   To give reasons
> To define a term   To illustrate with examples
> To emphasize importance   To introduce a new concept
> To explain causes or effects   To recommend a course of action

Sometimes a speaker states his or her purpose directly:

> "I need advice about my paper."
> "I'm concerned about my grade for this class."
> "I'm applying to graduate school, and I was wondering if you'd write me a letter of recommendation."

However, often speakers do not state their purpose directly; rather, they communicate purpose indirectly. Intonation can often help you understand the meaning behind the words.

2. Attitude

The *attitude* of a speaker is his or her thoughts or feelings about something that is being discussed. For example, the speaker's attitude may be one of like, dislike, interest, boredom, surprise, or anxiety.

TOEFL questions about attitude sound like this:

> What is the student's attitude toward _____?
> What is the speaker's opinion of _____?
> What is the professor's point of view concerning _____?

3. Key Words

Listen again to the recording for the Focus exercise. Listen for key words, phrases, and intonation that help you determine purpose and attitude.

 Album 3, Track 1

W: Hi, Greg. Um…do you <u>have a minute</u>?

M: Nicole. Hello. I have… uh… about twenty minutes. Come in and sit down.

W: Thanks. I <u>wanted to talk</u> about the <u>school psychology program</u>. I've been thinking about this for a while, and I've decided to <u>change my major</u> to counseling.

M: Really? It's quite a <u>change</u> from being an accountant to being a counselor!

W: I know. It's funny, isn't it? All my life I thought I wanted to run my own business someday. But this year I've been working as a volunteer tutor—at Garfield Elementary—and I'm just so <u>impressed</u> with what the <u>counselors</u> are doing there.

M: Did you say Garfield?

W: Yes, where those kids in the <u>accident</u> went to school. That was <u>terrible</u>, that accident. It was such a <u>shock</u> to the whole <u>school</u>. But it was <u>eye opening</u> for me. I had a <u>chance to observe</u> some of the <u>counselors talking to the kids</u>, <u>helping them</u> deal with the <u>tragedy</u>. They—the counselors, that is—they were so, so… they were <u>really amazing</u>. It really <u>got me thinking</u> about… about how to make… how to <u>help people heal</u>. I started thinking, "This is <u>something I'd like to do</u>."

 Stop

4. Answer Choices

In questions about attitude and purpose, an answer choice may be incorrect because it:

- repeats some of the speaker's words but has a different message;
- uses words that sound similar to the speaker's words;
- is incorrect or inaccurate, according to the speakers; or
- is about something that the speakers do not mention.

 **PRACTICE**

Exercise 2.3.A

Listen to the recording and choose the best answer to each question. To make this practice more like the real test, cover the questions and answers during each conversation.

 Album 3, Track 2

1. Why does the student go to see his professor?

   (A) He is transferring to a school in Oklahoma.
   (B) He must leave school for a family emergency.
   (C) He wants to discuss his term paper.
   (D) He needs to have surgery.

2. What is required for an Incomplete?

   (A) Completing the work within a certain time
   (B) Writing an additional term paper
   (C) Paying a fee of sixty dollars
   (D) Enrolling in a special make–up course

3. What is the purpose of the conversation?

   (A) The man wants permission to bring food to class.
   (B) The man is applying for a job as cafeteria cashier.
   (C) The man was overcharged and is requesting a refund.
   (D) The man would like a different meal arrangement.

4. Why does the woman say this:

   (A) To complain about the cafeteria breakfast
   (B) To criticize the man's choice of food
   (C) To emphasize the importance of breakfast
   (D) To show that she is a morning person

5. Why does the woman tell the man about Plan C?

   (A) To list the special diets that are available
   (B) To give him another choice of meal plan
   (C) To recommend a different place to eat
   (D) To explain the benefits of each meal plan

6. Why does the student speak to the professor?

   (A) She wants to take a quiz that she missed.
   (B) She would like to discuss her grade.
   (C) She is having difficulty in the class.
   (D) She must miss class the following day.

7. What does the professor suggest the student do?

   (A) Read the chapter over again
   (B) Study harder for the next quiz
   (C) Write about what she learned
   (D) Try not to be absent from class

8. What are the speakers mainly discussing?

   (A) A field trip
   (B) A reading assignment
   (C) A guest speaker
   (D) A term paper

9. Why does the man say this:

   (A) To emphasize the professor's qualifications
   (B) To state a desire to read the professor's books
   (C) To predict that the seminar attendance will be high
   (D) To imply that the seminar needs improvement

10. What is the man's opinion of the assignment?

   (A) The assignment will improve their public speaking skills.
   (B) The assignment will help them meet people in their field.
   (C) The assignment is more difficult than he had expected.
   (D) The assignment has taken too much of their time.

 Stop

Exercise 2.3.B

Listen to the recording and choose the best answer to each question. To make this practice more like the real test, cover the questions and answers during each conversation and lecture.

 Album 3, Track 3

1. What is the main purpose of the discussion?

   (A) The professor is giving a writing assignment.
   (B) The class is evaluating last week's assignment.
   (C) The professor is changing the reading assignment.
   (D) The class is summarizing the assigned readings.

2. What is the woman's attitude toward the assignment?

   (A) She is confused by it.
   (B) She likes it very much.
   (C) She thinks it is too difficult.
   (D) She finds it boring.

3. What is the main purpose of the talk?

   (A) To contrast Native American and European concepts of resources
   (B) To explain why Native Americans valued personal alliances
   (C) To list the commodities found in the New England environment
   (D) To show that the European economic system originated in New England

4. What does the professor say about the Native Americans' use of resources?

   (A) They traded resources with the European colonists.
   (B) They used resources to show wealth and social status.
   (C) They used resources mainly for economic subsistence.
   (D) They viewed resources as commodities to buy and sell.

5. Listen again to part of the discussion. Then answer the question.

   Why does the professor say this:

   (A) To state that the Native Americans were very poor
   (B) To show similarities between economic systems
   (C) To explain differences in wealth among people
   (D) To define the Native American concept of wealth

6. Why does the professor say this: 🎧

   (A) To illustrate the colonists' view of commodities
   (B) To emphasize the scarcity of resources in New England
   (C) To suggest that the colonists did not use many resources
   (D) To describe the growth of the New England economy

7. What is the purpose of the talk?

   (A) To imagine life without culture
   (B) To compare various cultures
   (C) To explain cultural differences
   (D) To define what culture is

8. Why does the professor mention student culture?

   (A) To illustrate how culture involves shared ideas and behaviors
   (B) To encourage students to think critically about their culture
   (C) To compare the student culture of the past and the present
   (D) To give students ideas for conducting their own research

9. What is the woman's attitude toward student culture?

 Ⓐ She enjoys being a part of it.
 Ⓑ She is frustrated by all the work.
 Ⓒ She thinks it is similar to a club.
 Ⓓ She doesn't understand its rules.

10. What does the professor think of comparing a culture to a club?

 Ⓐ A culture is exactly the same as a club.
 Ⓑ The comparison is imperfect.
 Ⓒ It is easier to define a culture than a club.
 Ⓓ Clubs are important in most cultures.

 Stop

Exercise 2.3.C

Listen to the recording and choose the best answer to each question. To make this practice more like the real test, cover the questions and answers during each lecture.

 Album 3, Track 4

1. What is the main purpose of the talk?

 Ⓐ To list qualities of effective managers
 Ⓑ To explain why workers criticize management
 Ⓒ To describe negative effects of stress
 Ⓓ To discuss ways of dealing with stress

2. What is the professor's opinion of rest?

 Ⓐ Too much rest can have negative results.
 Ⓑ Activity and exercise are forms of rest.
 Ⓒ Managers should allow rest time for workers.
 Ⓓ Few people know the real meaning of rest.

3. What is the purpose of the lecture?

 Ⓐ To compare clinical diagnosis and treatment
 Ⓑ To describe how psychologists diagnose problems
 Ⓒ To support the use of psychological testing
 Ⓓ To diagnose the problems of students

4. How do clinical psychologists diagnose a client's problems?

 Click on 2 answers.

 ☐A Psychic readings
 ☐B Psychological tests
 ☐C Interviews
 ☐D Personal letters

5. Why does the professor discuss taking a client's case history?

 Ⓐ To show that a client's past behavior assists in diagnosis
 Ⓑ To compare the case histories of various clients
 Ⓒ To explain why some clients lie and some tell the truth
 Ⓓ To entertain the students with stories of unusual clients

6. According to the professor, why are personality tests useful?

 Ⓐ They are short and easy to administer.
 Ⓑ They allow clients to diagnose their own problems.
 Ⓒ They give the psychologist data for publication.
 Ⓓ They reveal feelings the client cannot talk about.

7. What is the main purpose of the talk?

   (A) To describe the migration of bats
   (B) To promote an appreciation of bats
   (C) To give advice about contact with bats
   (D) To explain how to care for young bats

8. Why does the speaker say this:

   (A) To describe the reproductive behavior of bats
   (B) To show similarities between bats and mosquitoes
   (C) To give an example of how bats benefit us
   (D) To warn students about dangerous insects

9. How can you prevent bats from entering your house?

   (A) By blocking every opening
   (B) By planting bushes near the doors
   (C) By training your dog to hunt bats
   (D) By using poison to kill the bats

10. Why does the speaker recommend getting medical advice if you come in physical contact with a bat?

   (A) Bats are needed for medical research.
   (B) Contact with humans is unhealthy for bats.
   (C) Bats' sharp teeth can cause a painful bite.
   (D) The bat might be carrying a fatal disease.

 Stop

Exercise 2.3.D

Listen to the recording and choose the best answer to each question. To make this practice more like the real test, cover the questions and answers during the lecture.

 Album 3, Track 5

1. According to the professor, why do most people welcome laughter?

   (A) People like to learn new ways to communicate.
   (B) Laughter releases stress and gives pleasure.
   (C) Humans enjoy several kinds of entertainment.
   (D) Laughter can express every human emotion.

2. Why does the professor say this:

   (A) To give examples of stress that is carefully controlled
   (B) To show that children like to pretend they are flying
   (C) To describe how children respond when they are afraid
   (D) To give parents advice about child development

3. Which of the following is a universal characteristic of situations where people laugh?

   (A) Confusion about what is happening
   (B) Injury to someone who is a stranger
   (C) Ability to remember a funny name
   (D) Shock or stress in a safe situation

4. Why does the professor talk about social rules and conventions?

   (A) To suggest that many rules for comedians are not effective
   (B) To find out what students think about rules and conventions
   (C) To show that humor is a safe way to bring about social change
   (D) To explain why people enjoy telling stories that are not true

5. Listen again to part of the lecture. Then answer the question.

   Why does the professor say this:

   (A) To show how humor can be understood across cultures
   (B) To emphasize the importance of humor in managing anxiety
   (C) To explain why humans are the only animals that laugh
   (D) To warn students that the world is dangerous

 Stop

Exercise 2.3.E

Listen to the recording and choose the best answer to each question. To make this practice more like the real test, cover the questions and answers during the lecture.

 Album 3, Track 6

1. What is the main purpose of the talk?

   (A) To show similarities in rocks from different places
   (B) To trace the early exploration of the local area
   (C) To explain how erosion shaped certain landforms
   (D) To describe the beauty of the desert landscape

2. Why does the professor say this:

   (A) To give examples of different kinds of tables
   (B) To suggest possible ideas for student projects
   (C) To list the chemical components of a mesa
   (D) To preview what students will see on a field trip

3. What reasons are given for the erosion of a mesa?

   Click on 2 answers.

   [A] The rock on the sides is softer than that on the top.
   [B] Strong earthquakes frequently shake the region.
   [C] Plants dissolve the cements in the surface rock.
   [D] The force of water cuts away the softer rock.

4. Listen again to part of the talk. Then answer the question.

   Why does the professor say this:

   (A) To show similarities between spires and sand
   (B) To describe the appearance of spires
   (C) To identify the material on the classroom floor
   (D) To warn students not to step on rocks

5. Listen again to part of the talk. Then answer the question.

   Why does the professor say this:

   (A) To compare the mineral composition of two types of rock
   (B) To show that erosion continually changes the shape of rock
   (C) To emphasize that erosion requires the presence of water
   (D) To suggest that erosion is a topic of scientific debate

 Stop

Answers to Exercises 2.3.A through 2.3.E are on pages 652–654.

 EXTENSION

1. Listen again to the conversations in Exercise 2.3.A (Album 3, Track 2). With your classmates, discuss the meaning of the underlined expressions in the script below. In what other situations might these expressions be used?

take an Incomplete	I was wondering if I could <u>take an Incomplete</u> for your class.
make up	…you would have six weeks to <u>make up</u> the term paper….
take care of	…why don't we <u>take care of</u> it right now?
take turns	We <u>take turns</u> bringing doughnuts or bagels to have at the break.
sounds like	Oh, really? Hmm. That <u>sounds like</u> a good deal.
have to	My daughter was sick yesterday, and I <u>had to</u> stay home with her.
get out of	…the most important thing you <u>got out of</u> the chapter.
turn out	This assignment…has <u>turned out</u> to be harder than I thought.

2. The conversations in Exercise 2.3.A (Album 3, Track 2) mention the following aspects of North American university life:

a grade of Incomplete	a meal plan	a sabbatical
a term paper	a make–up test	a seminar
a final exam	a one–page report	a guest speaker

   With your classmates, discuss whether these are part of university life in your country. Which of the items are present at the school where you are currently studying?

3. Listen again to the three discussions in Exercise 2.3.B (Album 3, Track 3). Imagine that you are one of the students in each discussion. In your own words, write a brief summary of each discussion. The following expressions may be useful:

Today my professor talked about…	I asked…
We discussed…	What I wanted to know was…
Then she asked…	I made a comment about…
My professor explained how…	I described…

4. Listen again to the first lecture in Exercise 2.3.C. As you listen, write the correct words on the blank lines in the script below. Check your answers with the audio script on page 708.

🎧 *Album 3, Track 4*

Listen to part of a talk in a business management class.

Management _____ a great deal of energy and _____—more than most _____ care to make. One _____ that affects managers and _____ their capacity to provide leadership is _____. Stress has lots of causes—work _____, criticism from workers—and can have _____ health effects, including loss of _____.

It's a fact: _____ have to deal with stress. Some _____ it by making time to be by themselves. Most have some _____ place or pastime—a beach to _____ on, maybe a stream to _____ in, or a game to play with the _____. It's important to have some form of _____ and relaxation—creating art, working with your _____, gardening, playing _____—the list goes on. Rest doesn't _____ mean inactivity. For some people, _____ is rest.

🎧 *Stop*

5. Listen again to the lecture in Exercise 2.3.D. As you listen, write the correct words on the blank lines in the script below. Check your answers with the audio script on pages 708–709.

🎧 *Album 3, Track 5*

Listen to part of a lecture in an anthropology class. The professor is discussing _____ and laughter.

Being amused is a _____ we're all familiar with, but what exactly is a _____ of humor? Well, it's something very _____, and yet we communicate it to others by _____. Laughter is a universal human _____. All normal human beings can _____. Children as young as one _____ old will laugh. People often laugh _____, and people laugh _____ and more frequently when other _____ around them are also laughing. Every _____ knows this, and research has confirmed it.

_____, laughter is an involuntary tensing of the _____ muscles, followed by a rapid inhalation and exhalation of _____—a mechanism that _____ tension. For most people, a good laugh is _____—and worth looking for—because it brings _____ and relief.

_____ adults everywhere in the world _____ making their children laugh. Adults make playful _____ on their children, tickling, _____, and even pretending to _____ them. Adults will throw small children up in the air and _____ them again. This causes the child to experience mild _____, but in a secure setting because the stress is carefully _____ by the parent. And when the child laughs, it's a _____ that he or she has successfully dealt with mild _____ of insecurity. This teaches the child about the _____ and fears that are part of human _____, and which every human eventually has to _____ with. This element of shock in an otherwise _____ situation is a universal characteristic of situations where people _____.

Our sense of humor allows us to tell _____ about situations we haven't _____ firsthand. We call these little stories "_____." We tell jokes to show our _____ with the society we live in, especially its… well, its _____. Social rules and conventions provide us with a _____ of situations that we can turn into _____. And the things we joke about—the _____ and rules we live by—are sort of _____ areas in our society, they're _____ where we can see the _____ for change. Humor gives us the _____ to think about changing the rules. Making _____ and laughing are safe ways to _____ our social rules and conventions. Therefore, comedians—whether they _____ it or not—are agents of _____ change.

The ability to laugh is a _____ part of being human. People who _____ together—or laugh at each other's jokes—feel _____ to each other. Laughter creates a sense of _____. Humor can also help us _____ with anxieties that we can't _____. Failure, fear, pain, and _____—they're all real to us, as they are to no other _____ on Earth. And without a _____ of humor, it would be difficult for us to _____ with everything we that know about the _____.

 Stop

Delta's Key to the TOEFL iBT®

6. Listen again to the lectures in Exercise 2.3.D (Album 3, Track 5) and Exercise 2.3.E (Album 3, Track 6). Imagine that you are in class, listening to the professor speak. While you are listening, take notes about the important ideas and details. Do not try to write down every word or memorize the lecture. After each lecture, use your notes and your own words to (1) write a short summary, or (2) present an oral summary of the main ideas.

7. Think about the last time you spoke to one of the following people:

adviser	mechanic	roommate
best friend	neighbor	school staff person
co–worker	parent	supervisor
librarian	professor	tutor

Why did you speak to that person? What was the purpose of your conversation? Write down two or three things that you and the other person said. With a classmate, write a dialogue. Then act out the conversation for the rest of the class. Your classmates must determine the purpose of the conversation.

8. With a classmate, discuss what you would say to your professor if you wanted to do the following things. What words and expressions would you use?

Make an appointment	Request more time to complete an assignment
Get help with an assignment	Discuss a grade that you think is unfair
Make up work that you missed	Ask for a letter of recommendation

PROGRESS – 2.1 through 2.3

QUIZ 2

Time – approximately 10 minutes

Listen to the recordings and choose the best answer to each question. To make this quiz more like the real test, cover the questions and answers during each conversation and lecture. When you hear the first question for each set, uncover the questions and answers.

 Album 3, Track 7

1. Why does the student speak to the professor?

   (A) He wants to discuss the details of a project he is working on.
   (B) He is concerned about material that will be on a test.
   (C) He would like to tell her about his favorite buildings.
   (D) He wants to know why every lecture is about the same thing.

2. What is the main topic of the conversation?

   (A) The history of art in the 1930s
   (B) Popular designs for theaters and hotels
   (C) How new buildings are constructed
   (D) Differences between two architectural styles

3. According to the professor, which of the following are characteristics of Art Deco?

   Click on 2 answers.

   [A] Geometric designs
   [B] Rounded corners
   [C] Sleek lines and slender forms
   [D] Flat roofs and smooth walls

4. According to the professor, how is Art Moderne different from Art Deco?

   (A) Art Moderne is seen in homes, but Art Deco is not.
   (B) Art Moderne is simpler and more streamlined.
   (C) Art Moderne is modernistic, but Art Deco is not.
   (D) Art Moderne contains more decorative details.

5. Listen again to part of the conversation. Then answer the question.

   Why does the professor say this:

   (A) To confirm that the building's style is Art Deco
   (B) To describe the history of the Maritime Building
   (C) To argue that Art Deco is superior to Art Moderne
   (D) To point out a small problem with the building

Album 3, Track 8

6. What is the main purpose of the talk?

   (A) To describe some of the functions of banks
   (B) To explain why banks charge interest on loans
   (C) To compare banks with other financial institutions
   (D) To outline the history of bank failures

7. For what reasons do individuals take out bank loans?

   Click on 2 answers.

   [A] To build a housing complex
   [B] To do medical research
   [C] To pay for education
   [D] To purchase a home

8. How do banks make a profit?

   (A) Banks pay fewer taxes than other businesses.
   (B) Banks sell ideas and products to the government.
   (C) Banks collect more interest than they pay out.
   (D) Banks lend money only to large corporations.

9. Why does the professor say this:

   (A) To encourage students to close their bank accounts
   (B) To show that banks are the safest place to store money
   (C) To recommend more government regulation of banks
   (D) To explain how bank failures have occurred

10. Why were banks closed during the Great Depression of the 1930s?

   (A) The government encouraged people to spend more money.
   (B) Banks could not afford to let people withdraw all their money.
   (C) The president was experimenting with a new system of banking.
   (D) Bank managers needed time to hire and train more employees.

 Stop

Answers to Listening Quiz 2 are on page 654.

Record your score on the Progress Chart on page 791.

PROGRESS – 2.1 through 2.3

QUIZ 3

Time – approximately 10 minutes

Listen to the recordings and choose the best answer to each question. To make this quiz more like the real test, cover the questions and answers during each conversation and lecture. When you hear the first question for each set, uncover the questions and answers.

 Album 3, Track 9

1. What is the lecture mainly about?

   (A) Past and present uses of coal
   (B) The formation of coal
   (C) Different grades of coal
   (D) The impact of coal as a fuel

2. According to the professor, when did coal begin to form on Earth?

   (A) At the time that Earth was formed
   (B) Three hundred billion years ago
   (C) After the evolution of land plants
   (D) In the nineteenth century

3. According to the lecture, which of the following are stages in coal formation?

   Click on 3 answers.

   [A] Plant matter collects and decays under water.
   [B] New plant species evolve in the ocean.
   [C] Sediments accumulate upon beds of peat.
   [D] Peat undergoes pressure and heat.
   [E] Peat is burned as a source of heat.

4. Why does the professor say this:

   (A) To explain why the Mississippi River is changing course
   (B) To describe a major cause of water pollution
   (C) To show the relationship between plants and global warming
   (D) To give an example of where coal is forming today

5. Why does the professor say this:

   (A) To argue that coal is linked to air pollution and global warming
   (B) To point out that coal is the most efficient source of energy
   (C) To explain why scientists disagree over the value of coal
   (D) To emphasize the consequences of diminishing supplies of coal

Album 3, Track 10

6. What is the main idea of the lecture?

   (A) Television research is an interesting field.
   (B) Advertising is effective in selling products.
   (C) Television promotes a culture of consumerism.
   (D) The television industry should be regulated.

7. According to the professor, why do researchers study television?

   (A) To learn about the types of programs
   (B) To understand the culture of the society
   (C) To decide which programs to export
   (D) To measure how well it sells products

8. According to the professor, why do advertisers have control over television programming?

   (A) Advertisers have the best ideas about what viewers want.
   (B) The television industry depends on money from advertisers.
   (C) The government permits advertisers to vote for programs.
   (D) Most television stations are owned by large corporations.

9. Listen again to part of the lecture. Then answer the question.

   Why does the professor say this: 🎧

   (A) To argue that television images of life lack depth and meaning
   (B) To warn students not to spend more money than they can afford
   (C) To show that television programs can contribute to personal growth
   (D) To recommend that students watch only high–quality programs

10. What is the professor's opinion of television?

   (A) Television is the best way to advertise products and services.
   (B) Television has had a mostly negative effect on society.
   (C) Television has been unfairly criticized by intellectuals.
   (D) Television deserves credit for creating an affluent society.

 Stop

Answers to Listening Quiz 3 are on pages 654–655.

Record your score on the Progress Chart on page 791.

2.4 Making Inferences and Predictions

 FOCUS

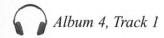 *Album 4, Track 1*

---

1. What does the professor imply about the student's paper?

   ○ It contains grammatical errors.
   ○ It does not meet the assignment.
   ○ It deals with a strange topic.
   ○ It needs a stronger ending.

2. What will the student probably do?

   ○ Write about a different topic
   ○ Rewrite the conclusion
   ○ Correct the sentence errors
   ○ Make the introduction longer

 Stop

Question 1 asks you to determine the professor's message to the student about her paper. The professor says:

> …I can't tell where you're going with it.

> You start out strong… The middle part, too…that's very engaging… But after that… well, I'm lost. What does it all mean? It just gets a little vague.

> Well, it's a little too open. You need to tie it all together… leave your reader with one clear thought….

The professor does not directly state what he means. Rather, he implies his meaning. The professor implies that the student's paper lacks a strong ending. Therefore, the correct answer is *It needs a stronger ending*.

Question 2 asks you to predict what the student will do. The student says:

> Do you mean my conclusion's not clear?

> Oh well, I see. Um… maybe I'd better work on that part some more.

The professor implies that the student's paper needs a stronger ending, so the student will probably rewrite that part. The correct answer is *Rewrite the conclusion*.

In each question, you can infer the correct answer from what the speakers say. The other answers are incorrect because you cannot reasonably infer them from the conversation.

 STUDY

1. Inferences

An *inference* is a conclusion that you make when something is not directly stated. An inference is a "hidden" idea. To make an inference, you must interpret a message that is not stated directly. When a speaker *implies* or *suggests* something, you must *infer* the meaning. You infer the meaning from the information that the speaker gives. You infer the message behind the speaker's words.

TOEFL questions about inferences sound like this:

> What can be inferred about _____?
> What does the speaker imply about _____?
> What is probably true about _____?
> What can be concluded about _____?
> What can be inferred from the talk?
> How does the student probably feel?
> What can be inferred about the professor when he says this: 🎧

2. Predictions

A *prediction* is a type of inference in which you determine what will probably happen in the future. You make a prediction when you know what a speaker will probably do in the future, based on what he or she says.

For example, when someone says…

> "I'd better see a dentist about my toothache"

…you can reasonably predict that he or she will make an appointment with a dentist.

When a student says…

> "I have a lot of material to review for my chemistry test tomorrow"

…you can predict that the student will probably study for the test.

TOEFL questions about predictions sound like this:

> What will the woman probably do?
> What will the student probably do next?
> What will probably happen next?
> What will the professor probably discuss next?
> What will the next lecture probably be about?

To make inferences and predictions, use key ideas and your overall understanding of the topic and context, as well as logic and common sense.

3. Key Words and Phrases

Listen again to the recording for the Focus exercise. Look at the script below. Listen for key words and phrases that help you infer the professor's meaning and predict what the student will do.

 Album 4, Track 1

W: Professor Elliott, did you <u>read the draft of my paper</u> yet?

M: Well hello, Amy. Uh, yes, I did read it. As a matter of fact, I wanted to talk to you about it. I'm glad you stopped by. I think I have your paper… here we go, I have it right here.

W: Is there <u>something wrong with it</u>?

M: No, not terribly, but… <u>I can't tell where you're going</u> with it.

W: Oh. I'm not sure I understand.

M: <u>Let me put it like this</u>. You <u>start out strong</u>. In fact, your introduction is done quite well. You really get your teacher interested in technology and society and how they're related and all. <u>The middle part</u>, too—where you interview the engineer—that, that's <u>very engaging</u>. Lots of good and original ideas. <u>But after that</u>… well, <u>I'm lost</u>. What does it all mean? It just <u>gets a little vague</u>.

W: Oh, I think I see what you mean. Do you mean my <u>conclusion's not clear</u>?

M: Well, it's <u>a little too open</u>. You need to <u>tie it all together</u>… leave your reader with <u>one clear thought</u>, one new way of thinking about technology.

W: Oh well, I see. Um… maybe <u>I'd better work on that part some more</u>. I really appreciate your comments. This helps me a lot. Thanks, Professor Elliott.

M: My pleasure. Any time.

 Stop

4. Paraphrases

Some questions ask you to identify a paraphrase of something that a speaker says. A ***paraphrase*** is the restatement of a message in different words. To ***paraphrase*** is to say the same thing in another way. A paraphrase has the same general meaning as the original message.

TOEFL questions about paraphrases sound like this:

What does the professor mean by this statement:

What does the student mean when she says this:

What does the professor imply when he says this:

When you see the icon , this means you will hear, but not see, part of the question.

5. Generalizations

Some questions ask you to make a generalization based on what a speaker says. A *generalization* is a type of inference in which you make a general statement about the information that you hear. To *generalize* is to state a general principle or to draw a general conclusion about information.

TOEFL questions involving generalization sound like this:

> With which statement would the professor most likely agree?
>
> Based on the information in the talk, indicate which statement below describes _____.
>
> Based on the information in the lecture, indicate whether each statement below reflects the ideas of _____.

6. Answer Choices

In questions about inferences and predictions, an answer choice may be incorrect because it:

- is not supported by what the speakers state or imply;
- cannot reasonably be concluded from what the speakers say;
- repeats some of the speakers' words but has a different message;
- is incorrect or inaccurate, according to the speakers; or
- is about something that the speakers do not mention.

Remember, you can answer all of the questions based on the information you hear in the conversations and lectures. You can infer the correct answer from what the speakers say.

7. Sample Question

> Listen again to part of the lecture. Then answer the question. 🎧
>
> "The philosophy of pragmatism has had a tremendous influence on education. Pragmatists believe that the meaning and truth of any idea is a function of its practical outcome and worth to society. Knowledge that is useful has value."
>
> What does the professor mean when she says this: 🎧
>
> "Knowledge that is useful has value."
>
> ◯ Ideas with a practical use are important to society.
> ◯ Pragmatism has too much influence on education.
> ◯ Education should prepare students for jobs.
> ◯ Life experience is more important than education.

The question requires you to recognize a paraphrase of the professor's statement *Knowledge that is useful has value*. The correct answer is *Ideas with a practical use are important to society*. The other answers cannot be inferred from what the professor says.

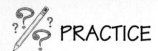 PRACTICE

Exercise 2.4.A

Listen to the recording and choose the best answer to each question. To make this practice more like the real test, cover the questions and answers during each conversation.

🎧 *Album 4, Track 2*

1. Why does the student go to see his adviser?

   Ⓐ To enroll in her geometry class next quarter
   Ⓑ To discuss an assignment for his history class
   Ⓒ To get extra help with a difficult problem
   Ⓓ To obtain advice about dropping a class

2. What will the student probably do?

   Ⓐ Make up a geometry test
   Ⓑ Transfer to another school
   Ⓒ Not continue in his history class
   Ⓓ Not enroll in classes next quarter

3. What is the man's problem?

   Ⓐ He can't afford to be a full–time student.
   Ⓑ There is an unpaid charge on his account.
   Ⓒ His charge account is no longer valid.
   Ⓓ All of the courses he needs are closed.

4. What will the man probably do?

   Ⓐ Pay his roommate to fix the shower door
   Ⓑ Have an argument with his roommate
   Ⓒ Speak to someone in the accounting office
   Ⓓ Try to register for next quarter in person

5. Why does the student go to see her professor?

   Ⓐ There was a problem with her registration.
   Ⓑ She will miss the beginning of the summer term.
   Ⓒ She wants advice about joining a study group.
   Ⓓ She would like to discuss her research project.

6. What does the professor imply?

   Ⓐ It is not acceptable to miss class time.
   Ⓑ The first day of class has been changed.
   Ⓒ Students are required to take the course.
   Ⓓ The summer course has been canceled.

7. What will the student probably do?

   Ⓐ Take the course during the fall
   Ⓑ Make up the work she misses
   Ⓒ Join an available study group
   Ⓓ Cancel her trip to Vancouver

8. What are the students mainly discussing?

   Ⓐ Problems with parking on campus
   Ⓑ Off–campus apartments for students
   Ⓒ Free bus transportation to campus
   Ⓓ Ways for students to manage money

9. What can be inferred about the woman?

   Ⓐ She does not own a car.
   Ⓑ She has a roommate.
   Ⓒ She is not married.
   Ⓓ She has a job off campus.

10. What will the man probably do?

   Ⓐ Transfer to a different university
   Ⓑ Look for a less expensive car
   Ⓒ Move to a building for married students
   Ⓓ Find out more about the apartments

 Stop

Exercise 2.4.B

Listen to the recording and choose the best answer to each question. To make this practice more like the real test, cover the questions and answers during each lecture.

 Album 4, Track 3

1. What does the instructor imply about composition?

   (A) Composition in painting is similar to composition in writing.
   (B) Composition is less important than shape, tone, and color.
   (C) Composition must be complex in order to be interesting.
   (D) Composition is the only concept that artists must understand.

2. With which statement would the instructor most likely agree?

   (A) To be interesting, a composition should be complex.
   (B) Composition can mean various things to different artists.
   (C) A successful composition conveys a single message.
   (D) If a picture contains many elements, it will possess unity.

3. What is the main purpose of the talk?

   (A) To explain why people become scientists
   (B) To describe different scientific disciplines
   (C) To persuade students to become biologists
   (D) To introduce students to the course

4. According to the professor, why is biology the most demanding of all sciences?

 > Click on 2 answers.

   [A] Biology studies complex living systems.
   [B] Biology deals with controversial issues.
   [C] Biology requires knowledge of other sciences.
   [D] Biology cannot answer every question about life.

5. What does the professor imply about scientists?

   (A) Scientists are motivated to save the environment.
   (B) Scientists are more intelligent than artists.
   (C) Scientists are fascinated by scientific technology.
   (D) Scientists are enthusiastic in their study of nature.

6. What is probably true about the students in this course?

   (A) They are students at a community college.
   (B) They plan to apply to medical school.
   (C) They are pursuing various fields of study.
   (D) They have never taken a science course before.

7. What do plant hormones do?

   (A) Regulate the plant's temperature
   (B) Transport water through the plant
   (C) Stimulate responses in cells and tissues
   (D) Make the plant unattractive to animals

8. What can be inferred about phototropism in plants?

   (A) It is similar to phototropism in animals.
   (B) It relies on hormones produced by the plant.
   (C) It functions only in the absence of sunlight.
   (D) It stimulates the production of seeds

9. Which grass seedlings would probably NOT bend toward light?

   Click on 2 answers.

   [A] Seedling in a moist ecosystem
   [B] Seedling with the tip cut off
   [C] Seedling wearing a black cap
   [D] Seedling with multiple shoots

10. What can be inferred about the tip of a plant's stem?

   (A) It stops growing once the plant produces real leaves.
   (B) It plays an important role in temperature control.
   (C) It can be removed with no influence on the plant.
   (D) It produces a hormone that affects the stem's growth.

 Stop

Exercise 2.4.C

Listen to the recording and choose the best answer to each question. To make this practice more like the real test, cover the questions and answers during each conversation.

 Album 4, Track 4

1. What is the man's problem?

   (A) He will not have time to finish his paper.
   (B) He is confused by cultural differences.
   (C) He cannot think of a topic for his paper.
   (D) He thinks the assignment is too artificial.

2. What will the man probably do?

   (A) Describe his hometown culture
   (B) Move to a different community
   (C) Ask his professor for more time
   (D) Write about culture shock

3. Why does the professor say this:

   (A) She will not be in class the next day.
   (B) The student has to drop out of school.
   (C) There was a death in the student's family.
   (D) The coursework is very difficult.

4. What will the student probably do next?

   (A) Arrange to take the test next week
   (B) Apply for a job in the office
   (C) Look for a tutor to help him study
   (D) Change the time of his appointment

5. What is the man's problem?

(A) The university bookstore does not have a book he needs.
(B) He just bought more books than he is able to read.
(C) The books that he needs are a strain on his finances.
(D) The third edition of the chemistry book is not available.

6. What can be inferred about the man?

(A) He finds science courses very difficult.
(B) He lives in the Pioneer District.
(C) He enjoys studying with the woman.
(D) He is taking a chemistry course.

7. What will the man probably do?

(A) Look for a cheaper copy of the chemistry book
(B) Return all of the books to the university bookstore
(C) Buy a different edition of the chemistry book
(D) Complain to the university about the cost of books

8. What does the man imply about the medication?

(A) It may be dangerous if taken incorrectly.
(B) It is the least expensive allergy medication.
(C) It should be available only by prescription.
(D) It is an effective remedy for many illnesses.

9. Listen again to part of the conversation. Then answer the question.

What can be inferred about the woman?

(A) She has never taken allergy medicine before.
(B) She is concerned about taking the drug before her test.
(C) She does not think the medicine will make her sleepy.
(D) She does not understand the man's instructions.

10. What will the woman probably do?

(A) Complain to the manager of the pharmacy
(B) Go back to the nurse for additional advice
(C) Buy a different medicine and hope it works
(D) Take the medicine a few hours before the test

 Stop

Exercise 2.4.D

Listen to the recording and choose the best answer to each question. To make this practice more like the real test, cover the questions and answers during the lecture.

 Album 4, Track 5

1. What topics does the speaker discuss?

   Click on 2 answers.

   A Causes and effects of the agricultural revolution
   B A change in the design of human settlements
   C The significance of trees in urban spaces
   D Why people prefer living in romantic villages

2. How did early rural villages differ from the cities of today?

   A Villages grew organically around features of the land.
   B Villages were more likely to inspire landscape painters.
   C Villages were designed as perfect rectangular grids.
   D Villages provided better economic opportunities.

3. What is the urban forest?

   A The forest surrounding a city
   B A park designed by an architect
   C The trees cultivated on farms
   D All of the trees in an urban area

4. Why does the speaker talk about New York City?

   A To give an example of an urban park project
   B To recommend places to visit in New York
   C To describe urban architecture and culture
   D To compare New York to other large cities

5. Listen again to part of the lecture. Then answer the question.

   What does the speaker imply about New York's Central Park?

   A It is the largest urban forest in the world.
   B It was the first park to be designed by architects.
   C It contains beautiful buildings of steel and stone.
   D It contributes to the quality of life in the city.

6. What is the speaker's opinion of the city?

   A The city is better than a traditional village.
   B The city is a symbol of human achievement.
   C The city is too hard, straight, and unnatural.
   D The city is a like an organic machine.

   Stop

Exercise 2.4.E

Listen to the recording and choose the best answer to each question. To make this practice more like the real test, cover the questions and answers during the discussion.

 Album 4, Track 6

1. What is the discussion mainly about?

    (A) The food web in the Pacific Ocean
    (B) The life cycle of the Pacific salmon
    (C) The consequences of overfishing
    (D) The importance of preserving salmon habitat

2. What does the professor mean when she says this:

    (A) Reproduction is the goal of the salmon's run.
    (B) Salmon can swim very fast to escape predators.
    (C) Future generations of salmon will face habitat loss.
    (D) Salmon migrate great distances in search of food.

3. According to the discussion, how do salmon find their way to their home stream?

    Click on 2 answers.

    [A] By following other fish
    [B] By seeing the sun's position
    [C] By listening for waterfalls
    [D] By smelling the water

4. Listen again to part of the discussion. Then answer the question.

    Why does the student say this:

    (A) She saw one large fish eat many smaller fish.
    (B) She felt sick after seeing dead fish in the river.
    (C) The sight of leaping salmon amazed her.
    (D) There were more salmon than she could count.

5. According to the discussion, why are salmon an important link in the food chain?

    (A) They eat small fish that make other animals sick.
    (B) They move vegetation downstream to the sea.
    (C) They produce more eggs than they need.
    (D) They carry nutrients from the ocean to streams.

6. What can be concluded from this statement:

    (A) Baby salmon eat the bodies of dead salmon.
    (B) Several natural food sources are endangered.
    (C) Salmon eat a variety of other life forms.
    (D) An adult salmon reproduces several times.

 Stop

Answers to Exercises 2.4.A through 2.4.E are on pages 655–656.

 EXTENSION

1. Listen again to the conversations in Exercise 2.4.A (Album 4, Track 2). With your classmates, discuss the meaning of the underlined expressions in the script below. In what other situations might these expressions be used?

a hard time	…I'm having <u>a hard time</u> keeping up in geometry.
keep up	…I'm having a hard time <u>keeping up</u> in geometry.
drop a class	…why not <u>drop</u> your <u>history class</u>?
catch up	If I drop history, maybe then I'll be able to <u>catch up</u> in geometry.
run into	I <u>ran into</u> a problem when I tried to register by telephone.
clear it up	You'd better go to the accounting office and try to <u>clear it up</u>.
make sure	I'd better <u>make sure</u> my roommate pays for the damage.
make up	Could I… um… <u>make up</u> the work when I get back?
can't afford	Summer session is only six weeks, and you <u>can't afford</u> to get a late start.
see (someone) around	I haven't <u>seen you around</u> lately.
look into	Maybe I'll <u>look into</u> that.
Why not?	<u>Why not?</u> The apartments are nice and spacious….

2. Listen again to the conversations in Exercise 2.4.C (Album 4, Track 4). With your classmates, discuss the meaning of the underlined expressions in the script below. In what other situations might these expressions be used?

come up with	I'm having trouble <u>coming up with</u> a good idea.
What about	<u>What about</u> the culture of your family?
grow up	I <u>grew up</u> in a small town….
Bingo!	<u>Bingo!</u> Write about the culture of the orchard community.
pass away	My great aunt <u>passed away</u> and her funeral is tomorrow.
make–ups	Eric handles all <u>make–ups</u>. He's the instructional aide….
stop by	Can you <u>stop by</u> the office today…?
out of sight	Science books are always <u>out of sight</u>.
not a bad idea	That's <u>not a bad idea</u>. Where did you say that was again?
drive (someone) crazy	I've been having sneezing fits, and it's <u>driving me crazy</u>.
It doesn't matter	<u>It doesn't matter</u>. Hmm… capsules, I guess.
knock (someone) out	Do you have anything else that's effective but won't <u>knock me out</u>?

3. Listen again to the first lecture in Exercise 2.4.B. As you listen, write the correct words on the blank lines in the script below. Check your answers with the audio script on page 713.

🎧 *Album 4, Track 3*

Listen to an art instructor talk about composition.

       Composition is the _____ of shapes and forms into a _____—

an expressive whole. The elements of composition—_____, shape, tone, and

_____—need to be well–arranged, need to be _____. They need to be

coherent… just like the _____ and phrases and sentences in a piece of

_____.

       All paintings have a compositional _____. Successful paintings sort of suggest

the _____ dimension, the sense that the _____ goes beyond the picture

frame. A picture's _____—which includes the shapes, _____ and colors—

is linked to what the _____ has to say. The artist's message is strongest when it's

_____. A composition is better if it says one thing _____ than if it tries

to say too many things. A _____ composition is sort of fussy and splintered and

_____ unity. Even a painting of a _____ object needs thoughtful

composition so the _____ of the object is present in every _____.

🎧 *Stop*

4. Listen again to the lecture in Exercise 2.4.D (Album 4, Track 5). Imagine that you are in class, listening to the professor speak. While you are listening, take notes about the important ideas and details. Do not try to write down every word or memorize the lecture. After the lecture, use your notes and your own words to (1) write a short summary, or (2) present an oral summary of the main ideas.

5. Obtain an audio recording of a real university lecture. In class, listen to a four–minute section of the recording. While you are listening, take notes about the information that you hear. Take notes about (1) topics and main ideas, and (2) details and facts. Form groups of three or four students. Compare your notes with those of the students in your group. Then, with your group, write a list of statements that you can infer, conclude, or generalize from the information. What is the probable purpose of the lecture? Who is the probable audience? Is it easy or difficult to make inferences? Why?

PROGRESS – 2.1 through 2.4

QUIZ 4

Time – approximately 10 minutes

Listen to the recordings and choose the best answer to each question. To make this quiz more like the real test, cover the questions and answers during each conversation and lecture. When you hear the first question for each set, uncover the questions and answers.

 Album 4, Track 7

1. What is the conversation mainly about?

   (A) A job opening in the computer lab
   (B) An interesting television program
   (C) An application for a scholarship
   (D) An opportunity at a television station

2. Why does the man want to get the internship?

   Click on 2 answers.

   [A] He will earn a high internship wage.
   [B] He would like television work in the future.
   [C] He likes the other people who work there.
   [D] He will gain production experience.

3. What does the man imply when he says this:

   (A) He is certain that he will meet many interesting people.
   (B) He will apply for several different internships.
   (C) He is not confident that he will get the internship.
   (D) He thinks he is the most qualified person for the job.

4. Why does the woman tell a story about her friend?

   (A) To reassure the man about his chance of getting the position
   (B) To find out if the man would like to meet her friend
   (C) To encourage the man to apply for a different internship
   (D) To impress the man with her political connections

5. What does the man want the woman to do?

   (A) Give him an internship application
   (B) Help him with an assignment
   (C) Watch a television program
   (D) Write a letter of recommendation

Album 4, Track 8

6. What is the discussion mainly about?

   Ⓐ Hiking safely in bear habitat
   Ⓑ Why bears are aggressive
   Ⓒ Training bears to trust humans
   Ⓓ Ways to predict bear behavior

7. What does the naturalist think of bear bells?

   Ⓐ They are not effective in keeping away bears.
   Ⓑ They destroy the peace and quiet of the woods.
   Ⓒ They sound like the language of bears.
   Ⓓ They trick bears into thinking you are a bear.

8. Listen again to part of the discussion. Then answer the question.

   Why does the naturalist say this:

   Ⓐ To explain why certain trails have become overused
   Ⓑ To list the resources that bears need to survive
   Ⓒ To warn that bears may not notice you in certain conditions
   Ⓓ To recommend the most interesting places to observe bears

9. What can be inferred about the behavior of bears?

   Ⓐ Bears may respond to people suddenly.
   Ⓑ Bears growl fiercely before they attack.
   Ⓒ Bears like to socialize in large groups.
   Ⓓ Bear behavior is very predictable.

10. Which situations should hikers avoid?

      Click on 2 answers.

   Ⓐ Carrying bear bells
   Ⓑ Approaching a bear
   Ⓒ Shouting at a bear
   Ⓓ Hiking when it is dark

 Stop

Answers to Listening Quiz 4 are on pages 656–657.

Record your score on the Progress Chart on page 791.

PROGRESS – 2.1 through 2.4

QUIZ 5

Time – approximately 12 minutes

Listen to the recordings and choose the best answer to each question. To make this quiz more like the real test, cover the questions and answers during each conversation and lecture. When you hear the first question for each set, uncover the questions and answers.

 Album 4, Track 9

1. What is the talk mainly about?

   - (A) The changing concept of leadership
   - (B) Leaders of the restaurant industry
   - (C) How leadership and power are related
   - (D) Why too much power can lead to evil

2. Why does the professor talk about the headwaiter in a restaurant?

   - (A) To show that having power does not imply leadership
   - (B) To compare the quality of service in two restaurants
   - (C) To explain how leaders influence other people
   - (D) To give an example of leadership in everyday life

3. Why does the professor say this:

   - (A) To explain why dictators have so much power
   - (B) To distinguish between leaders and power holders
   - (C) To compare qualities of dictators and robbers
   - (D) To warn students about the presence of danger

4. According to the professor, how are leadership and power similar?

   - (A) Both require the ability to exercise physical force.
   - (B) Both are benefits one gets from a university education.
   - (C) Both are necessary for people who commit crimes.
   - (D) Both involve the ability to bring about wanted results.

5. Listen again to part of the talk. Then answer the question.

   What does the professor imply about successful managers?

   - (A) They know how and when to use their power.
   - (B) Their leadership skills are present from birth.
   - (C) They are the only ones who can increase spending.
   - (D) Their power comes from the use of physical force.

Album 4, Track 10

6. What is the talk mainly about?

   Click on 2 answers.

   A Forestry as a profession
   B Different forest ecosystems
   C Where foresters work
   D Job openings in forestry

7. What can be inferred about the profession of forestry?

   (A) It is a broad field requiring diverse skills.
   (B) It has donated land to the government.
   (C) It hires over 700 new employees each year.
   (D) It requires a master's degree in biology.

LISTENING

8. Why does the student say this:

   (A) He would like the forester to recommend places to camp and hike.
   (B) He wants to understand how national parks and forests are different.
   (C) He wants to share his personal experiences with the class.
   (D) He doesn't think camping should be allowed in national forests.

9. Listen again to part of the talk. Then answer the question.

   What can be inferred about national parks?

   (A) National parks administer their own schools of forestry.
   (B) National parks have more employees than national forests do.
   (C) National parks do not allow hiking and recreation.
   (D) National parks do not supply commercial wood products.

10. Listen again to part of the talk. Then answer the question.

    Why does the forester say this:

    (A) To encourage students to major in forestry management
    (B) To impress students with his knowledge of biology
    (C) To show that foresters and biologists have shared interests
    (D) To discuss controversial policies of the national parks

 Stop

Answers to Listening Quiz 5 are on page 657.

Record your score on the Progress Chart on page 791.

2.5 Understanding Function

 FOCUS

 Album 5, Track 1

Why does the professor say this: 🎧

- ◯ To invite the student to a meeting
- ◯ To suggest where the student can find more information
- ◯ To tell the student that his research is incomplete
- ◯ To signal an end to the conversation

 *Stop*

The student is asking the professor for advice about a project. The professor makes some suggestions, but then she says:

> Is that all? I have a faculty meeting in five minutes.

The professor does not directly state her true meaning. She says that she has a faculty meeting in five minutes, but her full meaning is that she must end the conversation in order to attend the meeting. Therefore, the correct answer is *To signal an end to the conversation*. You must use your understanding of the context to infer the function of her statement.

STUDY

1. Language Function

Language has a ***function***, a communication purpose in a particular setting. Words, phrases, and sentences convey meaning by serving a specific function in a social context.

Speakers use language for various functions. They use language to express feelings such as likes, dislikes, agreement, disagreement, interest, surprise, disbelief, confusion, and anxiety. They also use language to manage conversations, for example, to indicate a change of topic or to end a conversation.

TOEFL questions about function sound like this:

> Why does the speaker say this: 🎧
>
> What can be inferred about the professor?
>
> What can be inferred about the student when he says this: 🎧
>
> What does the professor imply when she says this: 🎧
>
> What does the man mean when he says this: 🎧
>
> How does the woman feel about _____?
>
> Select the sentence that best expresses how the man probably feels.

Speakers may use language to perform the following functions in conversations and lectures:

Signal a change of topic	Introduce a new concept
Point out a mistake	Give an example
Express surprise or disbelief	Emphasize importance
Express disagreement	Start a digression
Ask for clarification	Tell a personal story
Signal the end of a conversation	Draw a conclusion

2. Indirect Meaning and Purpose

A speaker's true meaning and purpose may be different from what the actual words denote. A speaker may convey meaning indirectly, for example, by emphasizing key words. A speaker may use pauses and intonation to communicate his or her level of certainty. Listening carefully to a speaker's voice can help you understand the true meaning behind the words.

Understanding function sometimes requires you to make an ***inference***, a conclusion based on what a speaker implies. For example, when one student says to another student:

> "What? I don't know…are you sure that's right? I thought the TA said first we need to calculate the present value of an asset."

You can infer that the student probably means:

> "I disagree with your solution to the problem."

When a professor tells a personal story or digresses from the main topic, he or she will sometimes indicate this. For example, the professor may say:

> "Speaking of strange occurrences, that reminds me of something that happened when I was in college."
> > or
> "In the news today—you don't have to take notes about this—but did anyone notice the story about squirrels?"

You can infer that what the professor says after that will be a personal story or a digression from the main idea or purpose.

3. Context Clues

When a speaker's meaning is not directly stated, you must infer the true meaning by considering the context in which the statement is made. Listen again to the recording for the Focus exercise. Listen for clues to the context and for key sentences that express function.

 Album 5, Track 1

M:	Professor Engel, <u>I need to ask you something about my project</u>.
W:	All right.
M:	Could I ... uh ... <u>I'm having trouble finding enough information</u> to support my thesis. I mean, I found a couple of articles, but they're kind of old. There don't seem to be any studies more recent than five years ago.
W:	Did you check the list of abstracts in the database I talked about in class?
M:	Yes, but I still couldn't find much.
W:	Maybe you need to refine your search.
M:	Maybe ... uh ... all right. <u>I guess I can keep trying</u>. I'll also go through the articles I found more carefully. There's probably something in there I can use.
W:	<u>Is that all? I have a faculty meeting in five minutes.</u>
M:	Uh... <u>There is something else I wanted to talk about</u>, another idea I have. <u>I'll come back tomorrow</u> during your office hours.
W:	All right, Dylan. See you then.

 Stop

The context of the conversation is an encounter between a student and a professor in which the student asks for advice about his project. After making a few suggestions, the professor signals that she does not have time to continue the conversation now. She says *Is that all? I have a faculty meeting in five minutes.* The student signals that he understands when he says *I'll come back tomorrow during your office hours.*

4. Answer Choices

In questions about function, an answer choice may be incorrect because it:

- is not supported by what the speakers state or imply; or
- cannot reasonably be concluded from the context.

 PRACTICE

Exercise 2.5.A

Listen to the recording and choose the best answer to each question. To make this practice more like the real test, cover the questions and answers during each conversation.

 Album 5, Track 2

1. Listen again to part of the conversation. Then answer the question.

   What can be inferred about the woman?

   (A) She thinks the requirements are unfair.
   (B) She does not mind filling out forms.
   (C) She is confused by what the man said.
   (D) She does not enjoy writing essays.

2. Listen again to part of the conversation. Then answer the question.

   What does the woman mean?

   (A) She is asking for clarification.
   (B) She is suggesting that he made a mistake.
   (C) She is expressing doubt in her writing ability.
   (D) She is protesting the requirements.

3. Listen again to part of the conversation. Then answer the question.

   What does the man imply?

   (A) She has little chance of winning a scholarship.
   (B) An essay will strengthen her application.
   (C) It will not matter if her application is late.
   (D) The requirements are unnecessarily complex.

4. Why does the student speak to his professor?

   (A) He needs clarification about an assignment.
   (B) He wants advice about organizing his paper.
   (C) He is concerned about his grade for the course.
   (D) He wants permission for his brother to visit class.

5. Listen again to part of the conversation. Then answer the question.

   What does the professor imply when she says this:

   (A) He does not have to drive his brother all the time.
   (B) Riding the bus is less expensive than driving a car.
   (C) The bus system is confusing to some people.
   (D) She looks forward to meeting his brother.

6. Why does the student say this:

   (A) To help the professor better understand his problem
   (B) To convince the professor that he will complete the work
   (C) To show the professor that he is not worried about his grade
   (D) To state that he will turn in his assignments the next day

Stop

LISTENING

Exercise 2.5.B

Listen to the recording and choose the best answer to each question. To make this practice more like the real test, cover the questions and answers during each discussion.

 Album 5, Track 3

1. Listen again to part of the discussion. Then answer the question.

   Why does the student say this:

   - (A) To find out if what the professor said will be on the test
   - (B) To suggest that the professor said something incorrect
   - (C) To ask the professor to give another example
   - (D) To express amazement at the structure of flowers

2. Why does the professor say this:

   - (A) To ask if the students have questions
   - (B) To tell a personal story
   - (C) To review material for a test
   - (D) To shift attention to her next point

3. Listen again to part of the discussion. Then answer the question.

   What does the professor imply when she says this:

   - (A) The students' lab reports are due today.
   - (B) The time of the lab session has been delayed.
   - (C) The information she gave was incorrect.
   - (D) The students will learn more in the lab.

4. Why does the professor say this:

   - (A) To illustrate a point with a personal story
   - (B) To tell students about a good place to work
   - (C) To give advice for a successful job interview
   - (D) To contrast different styles of clothing

5. Listen again to part of the discussion. Then answer the question.

   Why does the woman say this:

   - (A) She does not like the colors blue and gold.
   - (B) She does not understand the man's point.
   - (C) She finds the man's example amusing.
   - (D) She knows someone else who works there.

6. Listen again to part of the discussion. Then answer the question.

   Why does the professor say this:

   - (A) To show his preference for a traditional workplace
   - (B) To draw a conclusion about what the student said
   - (C) To challenge a point made by the student
   - (D) To encourage the student to clarify her point

 Stop

Answers to Exercises 2.5.A through 2.5.B are on pages 657–658.

 EXTENSION

1. Listen again to the conversations in Exercise 2.5.A (Album 5, Track 2). With your classmates, discuss the meaning of the underlined expressions in the script below. In what other situations might these expressions be used?

fill out	For every one, there's a form to <u>fill out</u>.
Let me	Okay. <u>Let me</u> get you those packets.
go crazy	You'll <u>go crazy</u> if you wait until the last minute.
can't hurt	It <u>can't hurt</u>.
pull up	Okay, I've <u>pulled up</u> your record.
show (someone) around	...I have to <u>show him around</u> and help him find a place to live.
get settled	My parents want me to help him <u>get settled</u>.
get it together	Don't worry. I'll <u>get it together</u>.

2. With your teacher and classmates, discuss various ways that people use English to serve the functions in the list below. What expressions do speakers use? Are these expressions formal or informal? Are there contexts in which any of the expressions would not be appropriate?

Signal a change of topic	Express surprise
Signal the end of a conversation	Express disbelief
Point out a mistake	Express disagreement

LISTENING

2.6 Listening for Organization

 FOCUS

 Album 5, Track 4

> Which of the following best describes the organization of the lecture?
>
> ○ A list of causes and effects
> ○ A comparison of two objects
> ○ A definition with examples
> ○ A description of a process

 *Stop*

The question requires you to recognize how the information in the lecture is organized. The professor says:

> The chemical reactions of photosynthesis take place in two stages: the light–dependent reactions and the light–independent reactions. First, when sunlight shines on a leaf during the light–dependent stage.... Then, during the light–independent stage....

The professor also says:

> In the process, excess oxygen is released to the outside air through the leaf's pores. Finally, the plant transports the products of photosynthesis.

The professor is describing the process of photosynthesis in plants. Therefore, the correct answer is *A description of a process*.

 **STUDY**

1. Organization

The *organization* of a talk or lecture is the order in which the speaker presents information. The organization is usually related to the speaker's main point and purpose. A good speaker organizes the information so that it best supports the main idea of the talk or lecture.

TOEFL questions about organization sound like this:

> How does the professor develop the topic?
> Which of the following best describes the organization of the talk?
> How does the speaker organize the information that he presents?
> In what order does the professor talk about _____?
> What aspect of _____ does the professor mainly discuss?

Some patterns of organization that may occur are:

Classification of information	Explanation of differences
Comparison of objects or ideas	Explanation of effects
Definition with examples	History of an event
Description of how something is used	List of instructions
Description of properties	List of reasons
Explanation of causes	Summary of a process

2. Key Words

Listen again to the recording for the Focus exercise. Listen for key words and phrases that reveal the organization of the lecture.

 Album 5, Track 4

Listen to part of a lecture in a botany class.

All leaves carry out <u>photosynthesis</u> in basically the same way. When carbon dioxide and water are present, <u>photosynthesis can begin</u>. Water enters the leaf through the stem. The <u>chemical reactions</u> of photosynthesis take place in <u>two stages</u>: the <u>light–dependent reactions</u> and the <u>light–independent reactions</u>. <u>First,</u> when sunlight shines on a leaf during the <u>light–dependent stage</u>, light energy is absorbed by the leaf's chlorophyll molecules. This energy is used to split the hydrogen and oxygen in the water in the leaf. <u>Then,</u> during the <u>light–independent stage</u>, hydrogen from the water combines with carbon dioxide, forming carbohydrates, including the sugar glucose and other molecules that are rich in food energy for the plant. <u>In the process,</u> excess oxygen is released to the outside air through the leaf's pores. <u>Finally,</u> the plant transports the products of photosynthesis. Microscopic veins in the leaf carry the food out through the stem and into the cells of the plant. Photosynthesis continues all throughout the growing season, that is, as long as the leaves remain green.

 Stop

When you see questions about organization on the TOEFL, think about the speaker's purpose. The answer choices may contain words that match the speaker's purpose: *classify, compare, describe, explain, illustrate, outline,* or *summarize.*

PRACTICE

Exercise 2.6.A

Listen to the recording and choose the best answer to each question. To make this practice more like the real test, cover the questions and answers during each talk.

 *Album 5, Track 5*

1. Which of the following best describes the organization of the talk?

   (A) Reasons to buy property–liability insurance
   (B) Instructions for buying life insurance
   (C) A classification of insurance
   (D) A history of insurance

2. What is the speaker mainly discussing?

   (A) Popular bachelor's degree programs
   (B) The art and science of engineering
   (C) Educational programs for engineers
   (D) How engineers contribute to society

3. How does the speaker organize the information that he presents?

   (A) By comparing the benefits of various engineering specialties
   (B) By outlining the steps for applying to engineering school
   (C) By tracing the development of the engineering profession
   (D) By giving examples of undergraduate and graduate programs

4. What aspect of RSI does the instructor mainly discuss?

   (A) Similarities to other illnesses
   (B) Causes and effects
   (C) Reasons for its rapid growth
   (D) Available treatments

5. How does the instructor develop the topic of RSI?

   (A) She compares treatments for RSI.
   (B) She explains how to avoid RSI.
   (C) She discusses recent research on RSI.
   (D) She describes symptoms of RSI.

6. What is the lecture mainly about?

   (A) The dangers of driving in the mountains
   (B) Avalanche control on a mountain highway
   (C) Military training in the mountains
   (D) Predicting the size of an avalanche

7. Which of the following best describes the organization of the lecture?

   (A) A summary of a procedure
   (B) A classification of avalanches
   (C) A comparison of two approaches
   (D) An explanation of consequences

8. According to the lecture, which of the following statements describe steps in achieving a controlled avalanche?

   Click on 2 answers.

   [A] Technicians determine when the snow is ready to slide.
   [B] Traffic is directed onto the road below the slide path.
   [C] A large gun fires shells into the snow slopes.
   [D] Fresh snow falls on top of layers of existing snow.

 Stop

Exercise 2.6.B

Listen to the recording and choose the best answer to each question. To make this practice more like the real test, cover the questions and answers during each talk.

 Album 5, Track 6

1. Which of the following best describes the organization of the talk?

   (A) A definition and examples
   (B) An explanation of causes
   (C) A set of instructions
   (D) A comparison of methods

2. How does the speaker develop the topic of drums?

   (A) She traces the history of drums.
   (B) She explains how to play a drum.
   (C) She compares drums to other instruments.
   (D) She classifies drums by shape.

3. What is the talk mainly about?

   (A) The process of making a film
   (B) The job of film producer
   (C) Parts of a film script
   (D) Techniques for editing film

4. How does the professor organize the information that he presents?

   (A) He gives reasons for choosing a film career.
   (B) He classifies different types of films.
   (C) He describes the major steps in filmmaking.
   (D) He contrasts the jobs of producer and editor.

5. How does the instructor organize the information that she presents?

   (A) She explains the scientific method of classifying leaves.
   (B) She discusses the annual growth of a wildflower's leaves.
   (C) She compares leaf arrangements of flowers, shrubs, and trees.
   (D) She describes each leaf arrangement and gives an example.

6. Based on the information in the talk, indicate whether each sentence below describes the alternate, opposite, or basal leaf arrangement.

   For each sentence, click in the correct box. This question is worth 2 points.

	Alternate	Opposite	Basal
The plant's leaves are paired on the opposite sides of the stem.			
All of the plant's leaves are at ground level.			
Each leaf is attached at a different level on the stem.			
The leaves are attached at the same level on the stem, but on different sides.			

7. What will the students probably do next?

   (A) Bring flowers to class
   (B) Look at flower samples
   (C) Count a flower's leaves
   (D) Draw pictures of flowers

 Stop

How to Score 2–Point Question	
Answers Correct	**Points Earned**
4	2
3	1
0 – 2	0

Answers to Exercises 2.6.A through 2.6.B are on page 658.

 EXTENSION

1. Listen again to the first lecture in Exercise 2.6.B. As you listen, write the correct words on the blank lines in the script below. Check your answers with the audio script on page 722.

 *Album 5, Track 6*

Listen to part of a talk in an art class.

If you are unsure of _____ directly in pen and _____, start off with a light _____ sketch. This will allow you to make sure that your proportions are _____ and that you are happy with the _____. Take a few minutes to _____ your subject—this chair and _____. Notice how the straight _____ of the chair differ from the _____ of the violin. Once you are _____ to begin drawing, define the _____ of the chair with clean straight lines. Then add _____ by drawing the _____ of the violin with gently curved lines. You may have to _____ more pressure to the nib when _____ curved lines to allow the ink to _____ easily. When you have drawn the outlines of _____ objects, add in the finer _____, such as the _____ of the chair and the violin _____. Suggest the texture of the _____ seat by using light and dark _____ of the pen.

Stop

2. In professional journals, textbooks and other course materials, look for examples of the organizational patterns listed below. Bring examples to share in class.

Classification	Explanation of effects
Comparison	History of an event
Definition with examples	List of instructions
Explanation of causes	Summary of a process

PROGRESS – 2.1 through 2.6

QUIZ 6

Time – approximately 12 minutes

Listen to the recordings and choose the best answer to each question. To make this quiz more like the real test, cover the questions and answers during each conversation and lecture. When you hear the first question for each set, uncover the questions and answers.

 Album 5, Track 7

1. What topics do the speakers mainly discuss?

> Click on 2 answers.

- A A course in food service
- B A missing article of clothing
- C The menu in the cafeteria
- D The university budget

2. Why does the man say this:

- A To ask for advice about food nutrition
- B To lead into a complaint about the cafeteria food
- C To state that the menu changes too frequently
- D To imply that the food choices are boring

3. What is the man's opinion of the food in the cafeteria?

- A There is too much fried food and not enough nutritious options.
- B There is not much variety and the prices are too expensive.
- C The pizza is delicious even though it is not a healthy choice.
- D The cafeteria offers all of the foods that most students want.

4. How does the woman respond to the man's comments?

- A She explains why she cannot change the cafeteria menu.
- B She suggests that the man talk to the manager of the organic farm.
- C She agrees that sushi would be a nice addition to the menu.
- D She promises to add more fresh vegetables and vegetarian pizza.

5. What does the woman imply when she says this: 🎧

- A She cannot make changes without permission from her supervisor.
- B A small number of changes would greatly improve food service.
- C Her actions are limited by the amount of money she has to spend.
- D She will try to do a better job of responding to student feedback.

LISTENING

Album 5, Track 8

6. What is the talk mainly about?

- (A) Epidemics around the world
- (B) Why diseases change over time
- (C) How epidemiologists gather data
- (D) Experimental studies of diseases

7. How does the speaker develop the topic?

- (A) By describing the history of epidemics
- (B) By explaining different research methods
- (C) By comparing two treatment groups
- (D) By presenting statistical evidence

8. According to the talk, why do some epidemiologists observe two groups of people?

- (A) To learn why some people get a disease and others do not
- (B) To compare different people's attitudes toward work
- (C) To explain why some people take better care of themselves
- (D) To understand cultural differences in approaches to disease

9. Which of the following statements describes experimental epidemiology?

- (A) Researchers use statistics to describe the trend of a disease over time.
- (B) Researchers examine the eating habits of sick and well people.
- (C) Researchers observe subjects without interfering in the process.
- (D) Researchers intervene to test a hypothesis about cause and effect.

10. Listen again to part of the talk. Then answer the question.

Why does the speaker talk about her own work?

- (A) To show how one organization uses various approaches to epidemiology
- (B) To describe her organization's efforts to develop a way to quit smoking
- (C) To inform the students that she prefers doing research to giving lectures
- (D) To encourage students to work at her organization after they graduate

🎧 *Stop*

Answers to Listening Quiz 6 are on page 659.

Record your score on the Progress Chart on page 791.

PROGRESS – 2.1 through 2.6

QUIZ 7

Time – approximately 20 minutes

Listen to the recordings and choose the best answer to each question. To make this quiz more like the real test, cover the questions and answers during each conversation and lecture. When you hear the first question for each set, uncover the questions and answers.

 Album 5, Track 9

1. Why does the student speak to the professor?

   (A) She is concerned about the assigned group project.
   (B) She has a question about a suitable topic for research.
   (C) She is not interested in being the leader of a group.
   (D) She wants to improve her grade for the course.

2. What does the student mean when she says this:

   (A) She does not understand the requirements of the assignment.
   (B) Her project will require additional time to complete.
   (C) She does not want to work on her project with other students.
   (D) Her ideas are more interesting than those of her classmates.

3. What reason does the professor give for doing the project as assigned?

   (A) The student will make professional contacts that will help her find a job.
   (B) The student will gain teamwork experience that will be useful in the workplace.
   (C) The student will learn important methods of performing field research.
   (D) The student will change her opinion about what defines a good system.

4. What does the professor suggest the student do?

   (A) Observe in a workplace before choosing a research topic
   (B) Meet with classmates to learn about their ideas
   (C) Ask questions during the lecture on the following day
   (D) Revise the information in her project plan

5. Listen again to part of the conversation. Then answer the question.

   Why does the student say this:

   (A) To ask for clarification
   (B) To imply that her classmates are lazy
   (C) To show surprise at the professor's suggestion
   (D) To express doubt about what the professor said

Album 5, Track 10

6. What is the main idea of the lecture?

   A) Children do not care much about the feelings of other people.
   B) Children need guidance in developing their social skills.
   C) Children become more egocentric when they are teenagers.
   D) Children go through stages of mental and social development.

7. At what age is a child least able to recognize the thoughts of other people?

   A) Four
   B) Eight
   C) Twelve
   D) Fifteen

8. Listen again to part of the lecture. Then answer the question.

   Why does the professor say this:

   A) To explain why children are sometimes rude to other people
   B) To illustrate how children must experience directly to understand
   C) To give examples of enjoyable classroom activities for children
   D) To challenge a conventional theory about abstract thinking

9. What can be inferred about children in the multiple role–taking stage?

   A) They know that different social roles require certain behavior.
   B) They prefer taking roles that younger children will admire.
   C) They understand that every person has only one social role.
   D) They know how to amuse their classmates by role playing.

10. According to the professor, which of the following statements describe stages in the social development of children?

   Click on 2 answers.

   A) The child understands actions as others see them.
   B) The child prefers large crayons and paint brushes.
   C) The child is interested in learning about nature.
   D) The child can judge actions as they affect all people.

11. With which statement would the professor most likely agree?

   A) Children of all ages should learn how to solve problems using abstract thinking.
   B) There is no proven connection between the physical and social development of children.
   C) Children progress from being self–centered to being able to understand how others feel.
   D) Younger children cannot learn from older children because they are at different stages of development.

Album 5, Track 11

12. What is the discussion mainly about?

- (A) The early history of American jazz
- (B) How musicians learn improvisation
- (C) Improvisation in ancient Greece
- (D) The meaning of improvisation

13. According to the discussion, why is improvisation difficult to define?

   Click on 2 answers.

- [A] There are several kinds of improvisation.
- [B] People disagree about what improvisation is.
- [C] No musicians have recorded improvisation.
- [D] The dictionary does not define improvisation.

14. How does the professor develop the topic of improvisation?

- (A) By analyzing improvisation in classical music
- (B) By giving the correct definition of improvisation
- (C) By discussing the history of improvisation
- (D) By demonstrating improvisation on the organ

15. Why does the professor say this:

- (A) To state that the Greeks invented improvisation
- (B) To provide historical examples of improvisation
- (C) To compare improvisation with other musical methods
- (D) To argue that one form of improvisation is superior to others

16. Based on the information in the discussion, indicate whether each phrase below describes prehistoric people or jazz musicians.

   For each phrase, click in the correct box.

	Prehistoric people	Jazz musicians
Improvised music for work, play, and war		
Combined their own music with stock melodies		
Used music as a force to show relationships		
Improvised on the music of other bands		

17. What point does the professor make about early jazz improvisation?

- (A) Jazz musicians copied the music of ancient people.
- (B) Jazz was an entirely new way to compose music.
- (C) Improvisation changed the nature of popular music.
- (D) Trained musicians brought improvisation to jazz.

 Stop

Answers to Listening Quiz 7 are on pages 659–660.

Record your score on the Progress Chart on page 791.

PROGRESS – 2.1 through 2.6

QUIZ 8

Time – approximately 20 minutes

Listen to the recordings and choose the best answer to each question. To make this quiz more like the real test, cover the questions and answers during each conversation and lecture. When you hear the first question for each set, uncover the questions and answers.

 Album 5, Track 12

1. Why does the woman go see her professor?

   (A) To find out how her project will be graded
   (B) To discuss a problem she has with her boss
   (C) To talk about ideas for her project
   (D) To ask for more time to finish her project

2. When is the project plan due?

   (A) The following day
   (B) The next week
   (C) At the end of the month
   (D) On the first of next month

3. Listen again to part of the conversation. Then answer the question.

   Select the sentence that best expresses how the woman probably feels.

   (A) She regrets disagreeing with the professor.
   (B) She does not understand the assignment.
   (C) She enjoys what she is learning in the class.
   (D) She is concerned about her grade.

4. What topics will the woman write about?

   Click on 2 answers.

   A An economic development organization
   B Why all women should have an education
   C How an organization promotes social change
   D A group of women company presidents

5. What information will the woman include in her project?

   Click on 2 answers.

   A Photographs of art
   B Comparison of two markets
   C An interview with her boss
   D Description of a product catalog

Album 5, Track 13

6. How does the professor mainly organize the information that she presents?

- (A) She explains why anthropologists use the methods of physiology and genetics.
- (B) She traces the development of anthropology as a physical science.
- (C) She summarizes the process of conducting field work in anthropology.
- (D) She compares the two main divisions of the science of anthropology.

7. Listen again to part of the discussion. Then answer the question.

Why does the professor say this:

- (A) To request that the student be patient
- (B) To ask the student for clarification
- (C) To state that she will speak in a louder voice
- (D) To correct the student's mistake

8. What does the professor say about the Leakey family?

- (A) Their research is less influential today than it was in the past.
- (B) They found physical evidence of early humans in East Africa.
- (C) They developed new technologies for gathering data in the field.
- (D) Their field work documented cultural practices in Samoa.

9. According to the professor, which of the following would most likely be done by a physical anthropologist?

- (A) Writing an ethnography of a community being studied
- (B) Analyzing fossils and tools for clues to human evolution
- (C) Making predictions about the future of cultural change
- (D) Comparing child–rearing practices of modern societies

10. Listen again to part of the discussion. Then answer the question.

What can be inferred about cultural anthropology?

- (A) It is concerned with all human cultures of the past and present.
- (B) It attracts researchers from a variety of cultural backgrounds.
- (C) It conducts more research than physical anthropology does.
- (D) It focuses on the similarities between humans and other primates.

11. Why does the professor say this:

- (A) To inform students of an upcoming field trip
- (B) To begin instructions for a writing assignment
- (C) To encourage student interest in the course
- (D) To recommend that students start the reading early

Album 5, Track 14

12. What is the lecture mainly about?

 (A) The geology of the Cascade Range
 (B) Properties of dormant volcanoes
 (C) A specific period of volcanic activity
 (D) How geologists measure volcanic strength

13. According to the professor, how did the cycle of volcanic eruptions begin?

 (A) Several earthquakes and avalanches occurred.
 (B) A cloud of ash traveled around the world.
 (C) The volcano erupted suddenly without warning.
 (D) Magma poured out of the top of the mountain.

14. Why does the professor say this:

 (A) To tell of his own experience of watching the mountain
 (B) To explain why the events were a surprise to geologists
 (C) To show that the eruptions interested a lot of people
 (D) To criticize the media for interfering with the scientists

15. Listen again to part of the lecture. Then answer the question.

 What does the professor mean when he says this:

 (A) It had been a long time since the previous eruption of St. Helens.
 (B) The public suddenly lost interest in watching the eruptions.
 (C) Scientists took a few days off before continuing their work.
 (D) The small eruptions paused briefly just before the major eruption.

16. What were some effects of the eruption?

 Click on 2 answers.

 [A] Geologists were criticized for failing to predict it.
 [B] Large numbers of animals and people were killed.
 [C] The ash cloud affected weather around the world.
 [D] Tourists were afraid to visit the Cascade Range.

17. What can be concluded about Mount St. Helens?

 (A) It is a harmless inactive volcano.
 (B) It is no longer of interest to geologists.
 (C) It is the largest volcano in the world.
 (D) It is likely to erupt in the future.

 Stop

Answers to Listening Quiz 8 are on pages 660–661.

Record your score on the Progress Chart on page 791.

PART 3 – SPEAKING

The Speaking section measures your ability to speak in English about a variety of topics. There are six questions in this section. All of the questions are about topics that are appropriate for international students. You do not need special knowledge of any subject to respond to the questions.

The first two questions are independent speaking tasks in which you will speak from your own personal knowledge and experience. The next two questions are integrated–skills tasks in which you will read a passage, listen to a conversation or lecture, and then speak in response to a question about what you have read and heard. The last two questions are integrated–skills tasks in which you will listen to a conversation or lecture, and then speak in response to a question about it.

SPEAKING SECTION				
Question	**Reading Time**	**Listening Time**	**Preparation Time**	**Speaking Time**
1 Independent Task	—	—	15 seconds	45 seconds
2 Independent Task	—	—	15 seconds	45 seconds
3 Integrated Task	45–50 seconds	1 – 2 minutes	30 seconds	60 seconds
4 Integrated Task	45–50 seconds	1 – 2 minutes	30 seconds	60 seconds
5 Integrated Task	—	1 – 2 minutes	20 seconds	60 seconds
6 Integrated Task	—	2 minutes	20 seconds	60 seconds

The entire Speaking section takes approximately 20 minutes to complete. This includes the time that you spend reading the directions, reading the passages, listening to the conversations and lectures, preparing your responses, and recording your responses. For the integrated–skills tasks, you will use headphones to listen to the conversations and lectures. You will be able to change the volume of the sound.

The test supervisor will give you paper for taking notes. You may take notes on paper while you listen to the conversations and lectures. You may use your notes to help you respond to the tasks. However, at the end of the test you must give all of your notes to the test supervisor. Your notes will not be scored; only what you say during the recording time will be scored.

For each speaking task, you will both *hear* and *see* the question. You will have time to prepare your response before you begin speaking. A clock shows how much preparation time you have left. When the preparation time is up, you will hear a beep. The beep is your signal that the recording time will begin immediately.

You will answer the questions by speaking into a microphone. You have 45 or 60 seconds to record each response. A clock shows how much recording time you have left. When the response time is up, the computer will begin the next question. There is no pause between questions.

Two qualified evaluators will listen to each of your responses. They will assign to each a score on a scale of 1 to 4, with 4 being the highest score possible. You will receive a score of 0 if you do not respond to the given question. Your scores on the independent speaking tasks will be combined with your scores on the integrated speaking tasks. The total number of points you earn for all six speaking questions will be converted to a Speaking section score of 0 to 30.

INDEPENDENT SPEAKING TASKS

There are two independent speaking tasks on the test. Each task measures your ability to speak in response to a question about a familiar topic. You must use your own knowledge and experience to develop your ideas.

In your responses, you must demonstrate your ability to:

- state and support an opinion;
- develop points with appropriate details and explanation;
- express ideas coherently; and
- make yourself understood by speaking clearly and fluently.

Here is an example of an independent speaking task:

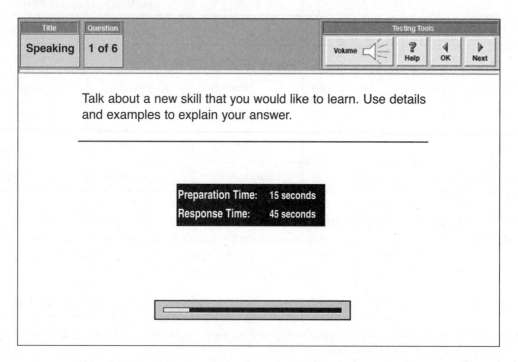

During the preparation time, the clock will count down the seconds remaining. When the preparation time is up, the response time will begin, and the clock will count down the seconds remaining. When the response time is up, the computer will begin the next question.

INTEGRATED SPEAKING TASKS

There are four integrated–skills speaking tasks on the test. Each task measures your ability to understand key information from one or more sources and to speak in response to a question about this information. The sources include reading passages, conversations, and lectures. The reading passages will be timed, and you will hear each conversation and lecture only one time. You may take notes and you may use them to help you answer the questions. You must determine what information in the sources is relevant to the question.

In your responses, you must demonstrate your ability to:

- convey relevant information from one or two sources;
- develop points with appropriate details and explanation;
- express ideas coherently; and
- make yourself understood by speaking clearly and fluently.

There are two different types of integrated–skills speaking tasks: reading–listening–speaking and listening–speaking.

Task Type 1 – Read–Listen–Speak

For this type of task, you will read a short passage, listen to a conversation or lecture, and then speak in response to a question about what you have read and heard. After the question appears, you will have 30 seconds to prepare your response and 60 seconds (1 minute) to speak.

First, you have either 45 or 50 seconds to read a passage. Here is an example:

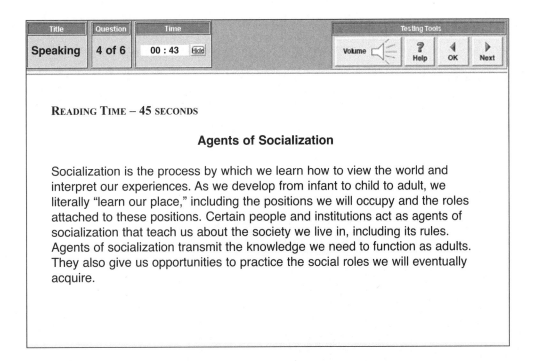

When the reading time is up, the passage will disappear, and you will not see it again. You will then listen to a conversation or lecture about the same topic. You will see a picture of the speaker or speakers.

(Narrator)   Now listen to part of a lecture in a sociology class.

(Professor) Your first agents of socialization are your parents or the other adults who take care of you when you're a baby. Your parents give you the first important lessons in how to behave in society. They teach you a world of meaning—what to believe, how to look at the world, and how to relate to others around you, especially your family. Your parents teach you what is and isn't proper behavior. Your parents serve as role models for adulthood—a social role you will eventually occupy. As you get older, they may prepare you for adulthood by giving you more responsibility or more freedom to make your own choices.

When you're a teenager, your peers—your friends and classmates—are important agents of socialization. Your peers support you and help you grow up and out of your family's nest. Through interactions with your peers, you learn the social role of friend.

Your parents and your peers are important agents of socialization, but in different ways. Your parents give you guidance on long–term goals, like career choice, but your peers are more likely to influence your immediate lifestyle choices, like how you dress and what you do for fun.

Then you will both *hear* and *see* the speaking task:

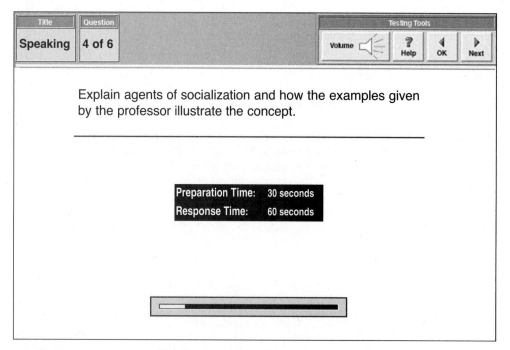

During the preparation time and the response time, the clock will count down the seconds remaining. When the time is up, the computer will begin the next question.

Task Type 2 – Listen–Speak

For this type of task, you will listen to a conversation or lecture and then speak in response to a question about it. The listening part is one to two minutes long. After the question appears, you will have 20 seconds to prepare your response and 60 seconds (1 minute) to speak.

Here is an example. While you are listening, you will see a picture of the speaker or speakers.

(Narrator)   Listen to a conversation between two students.

(Man)   How do you like your apartment?

(Woman)   Well … it's okay. I mean, I like the apartment, and I don't mind living off campus, but it's kind of far away. There's a bus, but the schedule doesn't work out very well for my early morning class.

(Man)   How so?

(Woman)   I have a seven o'clock class, three days a week, but the bus I need to catch leaves at six—there's only one bus an hour—and that's just way too early for me. Then I get to campus forty minutes earlier than I need to.

(Man)   Well, you could always use that extra time to eat breakfast on campus. The food's pretty good in the Corner Café. I eat there sometimes. It's never busy before seven o'clock.

(Woman)   Yeah, maybe.

(Man)   Do you have a bicycle?

(Woman)   No, but I'm seriously thinking about getting one. If I had a bicycle, I could leave home whenever I wanted to. I wouldn't have to leave so early. There's a bike path along the river, so I wouldn't have to ride on the streets, except for the few blocks near my apartment.

(Man)   You wouldn't even have to buy a bike because you can rent one at the bike shop.

(Woman)   Hmm. I didn't know that.

Then you will both *hear* and *see* the speaking task:

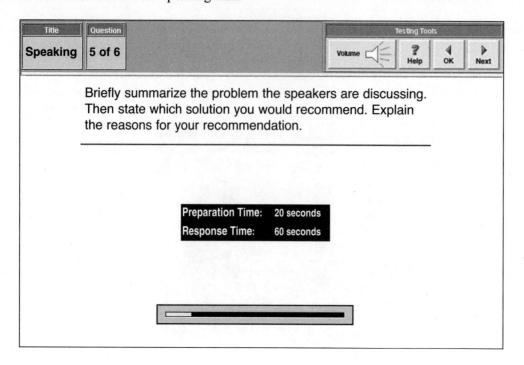

During the preparation time and the response time, the clock will count down the seconds remaining. When the time is up, the computer will begin the next question.

STRATEGIES FOR THE SPEAKING SECTION

Before the Test

- Work on building your spoken vocabulary. Practice using transitions—connecting words and expressions—to make your speech more fluent and coherent.

- Work to improve your pronunciation. Pay special attention to stress and intonation.

- Record your voice, and listen to the recording. Ask yourself this question: *Will other people understand what I am saying?*

- Listen to a variety of recorded materials that use academic English, such as university lectures, documentaries, and in–depth radio news programs. Practice taking notes as you listen. Practice summarizing in your own words the information that you hear.

- Record your responses to the Practice exercises in this section of the book. Use a timer. Become familiar with how much you can say in 45 seconds and in 60 seconds. Learn to pace yourself so you can say everything you want to say in the time allowed for each task.

- Your own best strategy: _____

_____

During the Test – Independent Tasks

⚬ Use the preparation time wisely. Read the question carefully and note everything that it asks you to do. Think about what you want to convey in a simple, organized way. Make mental notes about two points that you want to make, with one or two supporting details for each point.

⚬ During the recording time, speak clearly into the microphone. Pronounce words carefully, especially important content words. Speak at a normal speed—not too fast and not too slow. Keep the structure of your sentences fairly simple. Use appropriate transitions, such as *first*, *second*, *next*, *also*, *finally*, and *most importantly*.

⚬ Watch how much time you have left. Pace yourself so you are able to say everything you want to say. If you finish answering but still have recording time left, restate your main idea.

⚬ Your own best strategy: _____

_____

During the Test – Integrated Tasks

⚬ While you are reading the short passages, focus on the topic and general message. Do not try to memorize every detail. Take only very short notes on the main points. If the reading includes the definition of an unfamiliar term, write notes that will help you recall the definition.

⚬ While you are listening to the conversations and lectures, focus on major ideas. Listen for key words and concepts that the speakers emphasize or repeat. Listen for verbal signposts that indicate key points.

⚬ Take notes only about the information that will be important to remember: key points, examples, and reasons. Do not try to write down everything you hear. Do not allow your writing to detract from your listening.

⚬ Use the preparation time wisely. Read the question carefully and note everything that it asks you to do. Do not try to write a response. Review your notes, and concentrate on what you will say. Plan to state and support two or three points.

⚬ During the recording time, respond to each part of the question. Use key ideas and relevant details from the conversation or lecture to support your points.

⚬ Speak clearly into the microphone. Pronounce words carefully, especially important content words. Speak at a normal speed—not too fast and not too slow. Keep the structure of your sentences fairly simple. Use appropriate transitions to make your speech more fluent and coherent. Use the vocabulary that you are familiar with. Avoid saying "uh" or "um" to fill space while you are thinking. It is better to leave blank space.

⚬ Pace yourself so you have enough time to cover all of your points. Watch how much time you have left. If you finish answering but still have recording time left, you may add a brief conclusion or a summary of your points.

⚬ Your own best strategy: _____

_____

3.1 Independent Speaking: Developing a Topic

 FOCUS

Imagine you are having a conversation with an older friend who advises you about many important things. Your friend asks you the following question:

> What new skill would you like to learn? Why do you want to learn it?

How would you respond? Check all of the things that you would do:

____ Take a few seconds to think about what to say.

____ Change the subject and talk about something else.

____ Describe all of the skills that you already have.

____ Choose one new skill that you would like to have.

____ Think of two or three ways that this skill would help you.

When faced with a serious question like this, it is wise to take a few seconds to think. Thinking will allow you to make a choice and to organize your thoughts.

It is not a good idea to change the subject and talk about something else, nor to describe all of the skills you already have. Neither of these actions would satisfy your friend.

Your friend has asked you to (1) name a skill that you would like to learn, and (2) explain why you want to learn this skill. The best way to respond is to answer directly. Choose one new skill you would like to have. Think of two or three reasons for learning this skill—these reasons will support your choice.

 STUDY

1. The Independent Speaking Tasks

The first two speaking questions on the TOEFL are independent speaking tasks in which you will talk about familiar topics. You must use your own personal knowledge and experience to develop the topics.

In the first of these tasks, you will be asked to choose a relevant person, place, object, idea, quality, or event to talk about. You must provide details and examples to support your choice. After the question is presented, you will have 15 seconds to prepare your response and 45 seconds to speak. Your response will be evaluated on how well you speak and on how well you develop the topic.

Use the preparation time to choose the information that you want to convey about the topic. For example, if the question asks you to describe a person that you admire, the first thing to do is choose a person to talk about. Then, plan at least two points to make about that person. Think of examples, reasons, and other details that will develop your points. Make mental notes to help remember your points.

2. Sample Task and Plan

> Describe a person that you admire. Explain why you admire this person. Include details and examples to support your explanation.

Task	Describe a person that you admire.
Topic	grandfather
Supporting Points and Details (why you admire your grandfather)	• 2 jobs • railroad, hotel • stories • fam. hist., work

You have 45 seconds to speak. This is enough time to answer the question by stating your topic and then developing it with examples or reasons. You have time to make at least two points about your topic. You have time to make a total of six or seven statements.

Here is a general plan for the independent speaking tasks:

Introductory Statement	State your topic.
Point 1	State point. Develop with examples or reasons.
Point 2	State point. Develop with examples or reasons.
Concluding Statement	If time allows, restate your main idea.

3. Sample Response

> "One person I admire is my grandfather. In his long life, my grandfather has done many things to admire. When he was a young man, he worked at two jobs to support his family. He was a railroad worker during the day, and he was a hotel clerk at night. Now my grandfather is old, and he tells many interesting stories about our family history. Some stories are about people he met at the railroad. For these reasons, my grandfather is a person I admire very much."

The sample response is successful because it clearly presents the topic in an introductory statement.

> "One person I admire is my grandfather."

The response gives appropriate reasons for this choice:

> "...he worked at two jobs to support his family."
> "...he tells many interesting stories...."

Each reason is developed with details:

> "He was a railroad worker during the day, and he was a hotel clerk at night."
> "...stories about our family history. ...about people he met at the railroad."

The response restates the main idea in a concluding statement:

> "For these reasons, my grandfather is a person I admire very much."

PRACTICE

Exercise 3.1.A

For each independent speaking question below, allow 15 seconds to prepare your response and 45 seconds to speak. Record your response.

Preparation Time – 15 seconds
Response Time – 45 seconds

1. What was your favorite toy when you were a child? Describe this toy and explain why it was important to you. Include details and examples to support your explanation.

2. What famous person would you like to visit for one hour? Explain why you would like to meet this person and what you would talk about. Include details and examples in your explanation.

3. Describe a place where you go for rest and relaxation. Explain why it is a good place for you to relax. Include details and examples in your explanation.

4. Talk about an event in your life that made you very happy. Explain what happened and why you felt so happy. Include details and examples in your explanation.

5. Describe an object that is very special in your life. Explain why this object is important to you. Include details and examples in your explanation.

6. Talk about an important lesson you have learned from a family member. Explain the significance of this lesson in your life. Include details and examples in your explanation.

Answers to Exercise 3.1.A will vary.

EXTENSION

1. With your teacher and classmates, discuss the characteristics of a good speaker. On the board, write the names of good speakers that you know. They can be famous people or people that you know personally. Next to each name, list the qualities that make that person a good speaker. Which qualities on your list are important when you take the TOEFL?

2. Listen to your recorded response to one of the speaking questions in Exercise 3.1.A. Analyze and evaluate your response by answering the following questions:

   a. Does my response present a topic that answers the question?
   b. Does my response provide relevant information about my topic?
   c. What specific details, examples, or reasons develop my topic?
   d. Does my response answer the question effectively? Why or why not?
   e. How can I improve my responses for this type of question in the future?

3.2 Independent Speaking: Stating and Supporting a Position

 FOCUS

Imagine you are having a discussion with some of your friends. You are all students, and you are discussing the following question:

> Sometimes students have to write papers. Sometimes they have to give oral presentations. Which activity do you think is better for students, and why? Include details and examples in your explanation.

How would you respond to this question? How would you expect other students to respond? If one of your friends had an opinion that differed from yours, would you want to know your friend's reasons for holding that opinion?

We all have opinions about things that affect us. We have reasons for holding our opinions. We express our opinions at times, and we explain why we hold these opinions.

Sometimes we face choices in life. Sometimes we must decide which of two activities is better. Making such choices involves evaluating the two activities and having reasons for choosing one over the other.

One speaking question on the TOEFL will require you to choose between two possible options. In this question, you must state your choice and support that choice with examples and explanation.

 STUDY

1. Supporting a Position

In the second independent speaking task, you will be presented with two possible actions or situations. You must choose which position you prefer and explain the reasons for your choice. You must state your opinion clearly and support it with appropriate details.

You have 15 seconds to prepare your response. You must quickly choose one of the positions offered. Plan at least two supporting points. What examples from your own personal experience will support your position? Think about what you will say, and in what order. Make mental notes.

You have 45 seconds to speak. This is enough time to answer the question effectively. It is enough time to state your position and support it with examples or reasons. It is enough time to make five to seven statements.

Your response will be evaluated on how well you speak and on how well you support your position. The evaluators who listen to your response are not interested in *which* position you choose but rather in *how* you support your choice. Do not be concerned about whether the evaluators will agree with your position. Be concerned about whether you state your position clearly and support it with appropriate reasons and examples.

2. Sample Task and Responses

> Sometimes students have to write papers. Sometimes they have to give oral presentations. Which activity do you think is better for students, and why? Include details and examples in your explanation.

Here is mental preparation for one position on the topic:

Task	Choose which is better: writing papers or giving oral presentations.
Opinion	Writing papers is better.

Supporting Points and Details (why writing papers is better)	• need strong writing skills
	   • reading and writing
	   • prepare for exams
	• show understanding
	   • more time to explain
	   • think deeply

SAMPLE RESPONSE

"I think writing papers is better for students. First, we need to develop strong writing skills. We go to school mainly to learn reading and writing, so we need a lot of practice. Examinations require a lot of writing, so writing papers is good preparation. Also, I think writing is a better way to show that I understand. When I write a paper, I can think deeply because I have more time to explain my ideas."

Here is mental preparation for a different position on the same topic:

Task	Choose which is better: writing papers or giving oral presentations.
Opinion	Giving oral presentations is better.

Supporting Points and Details (why giving oral presentations is better)	1 easier
	   • less time to prepare
	2 interesting for other students
	3 important job skill
	   • confidence

SAMPLE RESPONSE

"Students have to write papers and give oral presentations. I think oral presentations are better because they are easier and take less time to prepare. Another reason is oral presentations are interesting for other students who are listening. Finally, many jobs require oral presentations, so students can learn an important skill and develop confidence in speaking to a group. This is why I prefer oral presentations."

Both students have responded to the question effectively. Both state their position clearly and support their position with appropriate examples and reasons.

 PRACTICE

Exercise 3.2.A

For each independent speaking question below, allow 15 seconds to prepare your response and 45 seconds to speak. Record your response.

Preparation Time – 15 seconds
Response Time – 45 seconds

1. Some people eat their main meal of the day around noon. Others have their main meal in the evening. What time of day do you think is better, and why? Include details and examples in your explanation.

2. Some people take one long vacation each year. Others take several short vacations. Which do you prefer and why? Include details and examples in your explanation.

3. Some people like going to large parties where there are many people they don't know. Other people prefer small parties with a few close friends. Which type of party do you prefer and why? Include details and examples in your explanation.

4. Some high schools require students to wear uniforms. Others allow students to wear clothing of their own choice. Which situation do you think is better and why? Include details and examples in your explanation.

5. Some people like going to concerts to hear music played live. Others prefer listening to recorded music. Which musical experience do you think is better, and why? Include details and examples in your explanation.

6. Some people get up early in the morning and go to bed early at night. Others get up late in the morning and stay up until late at night. Which do you think is better and why? Include details and examples in your explanation.

Answers to Exercise 3.2.A will vary.

 EXTENSION

1. Listen to your recorded response to one of the speaking questions in Exercise 3.2.A. Analyze and evaluate your response by answering the following questions:

    a. Does my response clearly state an opinion about the given topic?
    b. What points support my opinion?
    c. What specific details, examples, or reasons develop my explanation?
    d. Does my response answer the question effectively? Why or why not?
    e. How can I improve my responses for this type of question in the future?

3.3 Independent Speaking: Clarity and Coherence

 FOCUS

Look at the following independent speaking task and sample response:

> Describe a person that you admire. Explain why you admire this person. Include details and examples to support your explanation.

"I admire Nelson Mandela for several reasons. First, he is an excellent speaker, and his ideas inspire many people. Second, he spent over twenty years in jail as a political prisoner. However, that experience didn't stop his dream. Third, he became the president of South Africa when he was seventy years old. I admire Nelson Mandela because he was a strong leader for his country at a time of change."

Which of the following statements apply to the response? Check all of the statements that are true:

____ The speaker's opinion is difficult to understand.
____ Each sentence conveys a complete thought.
____ The speaker uses some words incorrectly.
____ Each point is developed with appropriate details.
____ The speaker expresses ideas coherently.

Without taking pronunciation into account, most people would think the speaker has provided a clear and coherent response. The speaker's opinion is clearly stated at the beginning:

"I admire Nelson Mandela for several reasons."

The speaker then clearly states three reasons:

"First, he is an excellent speaker, and his ideas inspire many people."
"Second, he spent over twenty years in jail as a political prisoner. However, that experience didn't stop his dream."
"Third, he became the president of South Africa when he was seventy years old."

Each sentence conveys a complete thought. Each point is developed with appropriate details. The speaker expresses ideas coherently. The transitions *first*, *second*, and *third* help to make the points clear and coherent.

 STUDY

1. Making Yourself Understood

To convey your opinion, you must speak clearly and coherently. Think of your listeners and try to make your response easy for them to understand. Your speech will be easier to understand if:

- each sentence conveys a complete thought;
- your sentence structure is fairly simple;
- you use vocabulary correctly;
- you pronounce words clearly and correctly; and
- you speak at a natural speed.

Your response will be easier to understand if you speak in phrases. This means grouping words into idea units—according to their meaning and connection to each other. For example, look at this sentence:

"I admire Nelson Mandela because he was a strong leader for his country at a time of change."

This sentence is easier to understand if it is spoken in phrases, like this:

"I admire / Nelson Mandela / because he was / a strong leader / for his country / at a time / of change."

2. Speaking Coherently

Your response will be easier to understand if your speech is coherent. **Coherence** is the quality of order in speech. When speech is coherent, it is more likely that listeners will understand the message. The following **transitions** will help you convey examples and reasons coherently.

Give Examples		
for example	one example	also
such as	another example	in addition

Give Reasons		
because	one reason	first, second, third…
so (that)	another reason	finally

3. Pronunciation

Your response will be easier to understand if you pronounce words clearly and correctly, especially key transitions and **content words**: nouns, verbs, and adjectives that convey important information. Use voice stress to emphasize key words.

"I admire **Nelson Mandela** for **several reasons**. **First**, he is an **excellent speaker**, and his ideas **inspire** many people. **Second**, he spent over **twenty years** in **jail** as a **political prisoner**. However, that experience **didn't stop** his **dream**. **Third**, he became the **president** of **South Africa** when he was **seventy** years old. I **admire** Nelson Mandela because he was a **strong leader** for his country at a **time** of **change**."

SPEAKING

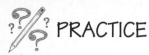 PRACTICE

Exercise 3.3.A

For each independent speaking question below, allow 15 seconds to prepare your response and 45 seconds to speak. Record your response.

Preparation Time – 15 seconds
Response Time – 45 seconds

1. How do you like to spend your leisure time? Choose a leisure activity and explain why you like to do it. Include details and examples in your explanation.

2. Some students like to take classes early in the morning. Others prefer having classes later in the day. Which time of day is better for you and why? Include details and examples in your explanation.

3. What type of animal would you like to have, either as a pet or for some other reason? Choose an animal and explain why you would like to own this type of animal.

4. Some people plan every detail of their vacation in advance. Others prefer to leave most details flexible or open to chance. Which do you think is better and why? Include details and examples in your explanation.

5. What place or landmark in your country do you recommend that other people visit? Explain why you think people should go there.

6. Some people like to eat most of their meals with other people. Others prefer eating most of their meals alone. Which do you prefer and why? Include details and examples in your explanation.

7. Describe a place that you consider to be beautiful. Explain why certain qualities of this place make it beautiful. Include details and examples to support your explanation.

8. Some people relax by staying home. Others relax by going out. Which type of relaxation is better for you and why? Include details and examples in your explanation.

9. Describe an occasion when you were surprised. What happened to you, and why did you feel surprised? Include details and examples in your explanation.

10. Some students prepare for tests by studying alone. Others prepare for tests by studying with other students or a tutor. Which study method do you think is better? Explain why.

11. What type of home would you like to live in? Describe the characteristics of such a home, and explain why you would like to live there.

12. Some people exercise early in the morning. Others exercise in the afternoon or evening. Which time of day do you think is better for exercising and why? Include details and examples to support your explanation.

13. What is your favorite color? Explain why this color is special or important to you.

14. Some people like to eat two or three full meals in a day. Others prefer having four or more small meals per day. Which do you think is better? Explain why.

15. What sport or game do you NOT enjoy playing? Explain why you do not like to play it.

16. Some people like to shop and buy things in stores. Others prefer shopping online. Which do you prefer, and why? Include details and examples in your explanation.

17. What is your favorite season or time of the year? Explain why you like this time of the year.

18. Some people like having a job that has rules for how employees should dress. Others prefer a job where they are free to wear whatever clothing they choose. Which kind of job do you prefer? Explain your reasons.

Answers to Exercise 3.3.A will vary.

 EXTENSION

1. With your teacher and classmates, write a list of possible independent speaking topics. Select one of the topics. Think about the topic for 15 seconds, and then begin speaking.

2. Practice how much you can say in 45 seconds, speaking at a natural speed. For the independent speaking tasks, you have 45 seconds to state an opinion and support it with at least two examples or reasons. Listen to your recorded responses to the speaking tasks in Exercise 3.3.A. Did you say everything you wanted to say in 45 seconds? Did you have time left over? Did you use notes to help remember your points?

3. Listen to your recorded responses to the speaking questions in Exercise 3.3.A. Analyze and evaluate each response by answering the following questions:

   a. Does my response clearly present my topic? Does it state an opinion?
   b. What examples, explanation, or details are given? Do they develop my topic?
   c. Would my response be easily understood by other listeners? Why or why not?
   d. Is my response coherent? Did I use transitions?
   e. Does my response answer the question effectively? Why or why not?

4. Share and discuss your recorded response to one of the speaking questions in Exercise 3.3.A. Work in a group of three or four students. Listen to each student's recorded response. Discuss each response by answering the following questions:

   a. Does the speaker clearly state an opinion about the topic? What is the speaker's opinion? Is the opinion supported?
   b. What examples, explanation, or other details are included? Do they successfully develop the topic?
   c. Can the response be easily understood? Why or why not?
   d. Is the response coherent? Why or why not?
   e. Does the response answer the question effectively? Why or why not?

Make suggestions that will help each student improve in the future.

3.4 Evaluating Independent Speaking

 FOCUS

If you ask someone for information, what do you want to hear? What does a speaker do to make you understand? What makes a speaker a good communicator?

Circle **T** if the statement is true. Circle **F** if the statement is false.

T	**F**	A good communicator listens and responds to what I am asking.
T	**F**	I understand better if the speaker uses a strong, clear voice.
T	**F**	It's better if the speaker uses big words and complex sentences.
T	**F**	Good speakers pronounce words distinctly and correctly.
T	**F**	It's easier to understand if the speaker gives numerous details.
T	**F**	A good communicator conveys more information by talking fast.
T	**F**	A good speaker avoids saying "um" or "ah" too many times.

Which statements are true? If you circled **T** for these sentences…

> A good communicator listens and responds to what I am asking.
> I understand better if the speaker uses a strong, clear voice.
> Good speakers pronounce words distinctly and correctly.
> A good speaker avoids saying "um" or "ah" too many times.

…you would find that most people agree with you.

Good speakers make themselves understood to their listeners. They provide all of the information that is requested. They speak in a clear voice, and they pronounce important words distinctly. They avoid saying "um" and "ah." Good speakers do not force their listeners to work hard to understand them.

 STUDY

1. How Your Responses Will Be Evaluated

When you take the TOEFL, two trained evaluators will listen to your response to each independent speaking task. They will judge each response on how well you answer the question by stating and supporting your points. They will also consider the clarity and coherence of your speech.

Among other things, your responses will be evaluated on how well you:

- state and support an opinion;
- develop points with appropriate examples and details;
- express ideas coherently; and
- make yourself understood by speaking clearly.

The evaluators will assign a score of 1 to 4, with 4 the highest score possible. They will use criteria similar to those in the table below. A few small mistakes in vocabulary or pronunciation will not necessarily lower your score.

	INDEPENDENT SPEAKING TASK **Description of Score Levels**

4	**A response at this level**
	  ⌐ effectively addresses the task and is generally well developed and coherent; and
	  ⌐ demonstrates effective use of grammar and vocabulary, but may contain minor language errors that do not interfere with meaning; and
	  ⌐ demonstrates clear, fluid speech with high overall intelligibility, but may contain minor problems with pronunciation or intonation.

3	**A response at this level**
	  ⌐ conveys ideas and information relevant to the task, but overall development is somewhat limited, and connections among ideas are sometimes unclear; and
	  ⌐ demonstrates somewhat effective use of grammar and vocabulary, but may contain language errors that do not seriously interfere with meaning; and
	  ⌐ demonstrates generally clear, somewhat fluid speech, but may contain minor problems with pronunciation, intonation, or pacing and may occasionally require some listener effort.

2	**A response at this level**
	  ⌐ is related to the task, although the development of ideas is limited, and connections among ideas are unclear; or
	  ⌐ demonstrates a limited range and control of grammar and vocabulary; or
	  ⌐ demonstrates some clear speech, but contains problems with pronunciation, intonation, or pacing and may require significant listener effort.

1	**A response at this level**
	  ⌐ fails to provide much relevant content because ideas that are expressed are inaccurate, limited, or vague; or
	  ⌐ demonstrates a limited control of grammar and vocabulary that severely limits expression of ideas and connections among ideas; or
	  ⌐ demonstrates fragmented speech with frequent pauses and consistent problems with pronunciation and intonation that obscure meaning and require great listener effort.

0	**A response at this level**
	  ⌐ is not related to the topic; or
	  ⌐ is absent.

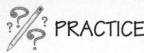 PRACTICE

Exercise 3.4.A

Listen to the independent speaking task. Then listen to and read the sample response.

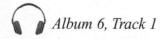 *Album 6, Track 1*

> Talk about a new skill that you would like to learn. Use details and examples to explain your answer.

SAMPLE RESPONSE   *Score:* _____

> "I would like to learn how to play the guitar. Right now I can't play any musical instruments, so that would be a new skill for me. It would be a good skill to have because I could take my guitar to parties and play music for my friends. Also, I could join a band and play songs with other musicians. Maybe I could make money, but I don't care about that. The most important reason is because I enjoy music, and I would like to understand it better."

 Stop

1. What opinion is stated in the response? What details and examples support this opinion?

2. Evaluate the sample response according to the descriptions of the four levels on page 303. What score do you think the response should receive? Why?

Answers to Exercise 3.4.A are on page 661.

 EXTENSION

1. Study the descriptions of the four score levels on page 303. Make sure you understand the description for each level. Check your understanding of the meaning of these words and phrases:

addresses the task	fluid speech	pacing
coherent	intelligibility	listener effort
minor	intonation	vague
interfere	limited	fragmented speech

2. Review your recorded responses to the integrated speaking questions in units 3.1 through 3.3. Evaluate each response according to the descriptions of the four levels on page 303. What score would your responses receive? What are the areas of strength in your speaking? What are your most serious problems? What can you do to improve your speaking and earn a high score on the TOEFL?

PROGRESS – 3.1 through 3.4

QUIZ 1

Time – approximately 5 minutes

There are two questions in this quiz. Use your own personal knowledge and experience to answer each question. After you hear the question, you have 15 seconds to prepare your response and 45 seconds to speak. Record your response to each question. Each response will earn a score of 1, 2, 3, or 4, with 4 the highest score. Add the two scores to obtain your total score.

QUESTION 1

 Album 6, Track 2

> What is the most interesting class you have ever taken? Explain the aspects of the class that made it interesting. Include details and examples in your explanation.

 Stop

Preparation Time – 15 seconds
Response Time – 45 seconds

QUESTION 2

 Album 6, Track 3

> Some people like to read classic works of literature. Others prefer watching film versions of the same stories. Which do you prefer and why? Include details and examples in your explanation.

 Stop

Preparation Time – 15 seconds
Response Time – 45 seconds

Responses will vary.

Record your total score on the Progress Chart on page 792.

SPEAKING

PROGRESS – 3.1 through 3.4

QUIZ 2

Time – approximately 5 minutes

There are two questions in this quiz. Use your own personal knowledge and experience to answer each question. After you hear the question, you have 15 seconds to prepare your response and 45 seconds to speak. Record your response to each question. Each response will earn a score of 1, 2, 3, or 4, with 4 the highest score. Add the two scores to obtain your total score.

QUESTION 1

 Album 6, Track 4

> Describe a city or town where you have lived. Explain why this place is either a good place or not a good place to live. Include details and examples in your explanation.

 Stop

Preparation Time – 15 seconds
Response Time – 45 seconds

QUESTION 2

 Album 6, Track 5

> Some students take one long examination at the end of a course. Others have several shorter tests throughout the course. Which situation do you think is better for students, and why? Include details and examples in your explanation.

 Stop

Preparation Time – 15 seconds
Response Time – 45 seconds

Responses will vary.

Record your score on the Progress Chart on page 792.

PROGRESS – 3.1 through 3.4

QUIZ 3

Time – approximately 5 minutes

There are two questions in this quiz. Use your own personal knowledge and experience to answer each question. After you hear the question, you have 15 seconds to prepare your response and 45 seconds to speak. Record your response to each question. Each response will earn a score of 1, 2, 3, or 4, with 4 the highest score. Add the two scores to obtain your total score.

QUESTION 1

 Album 6, Track 6

> Describe your idea of the perfect job. Explain why this job would be appealing to you. Include details and examples in your explanation.

 Stop

Preparation Time – 15 seconds
Response Time – 45 seconds

QUESTION 2

 Album 6, Track 7

> Some people like taking their vacation in a city. Others prefer spending their vacation in the countryside. Which do you prefer and why? Include details and examples in your explanation.

 Stop

Preparation Time – 15 seconds
Response Time – 45 seconds

Responses will vary.

Record your score on the Progress Chart on page 792.

3.5 Integrated Speaking: Connecting Information

 FOCUS

Imagine you are attending a university, and you see the following notice posted on a campus bulletin board:

NOTICE OF VOTE ON CAMPUS FOOD SERVICE

Students are encouraged to vote on the university's proposal to change the food service on campus. Students should vote for which of two options they prefer. Option 1 would expand the main cafeteria in the Student Center, including the addition of more food choices and more dining space; this option would also close the two snack bars on campus. Option 2 would close the cafeteria in the Student Center but would maintain the two snack bars, and would add five food service areas across campus, including two cafes, a deli, a barbecue grill, and a fine dining room.

How would you respond to the notice? Check all of the things that you would do.

____ Ignore the notice.
____ Discuss the two food service options with your friends.
____ Write to the university president about the food service.
____ Listen to various opinions about the options.
____ Vote for the option you prefer.

Some students would ignore the notice. However, students who regularly eat on campus might discuss the two options with their friends. They might listen to various opinions before deciding which option is better. They might express their opinion and give their reasons. Then they would vote.

 STUDY

1. Integrated Reading–Listening–Speaking

On the TOEFL, the first two integrated speaking tasks involve reading, listening, and speaking.

In one of these tasks, you will read a short passage about a campus situation. You have 45 seconds to read the passage. Then the passage will disappear, and you will not see it again. Next, you will listen to a conversation about the same topic. One of the speakers will express an opinion. After the conversation, the speaking task will appear. The task will require you to state the speaker's opinion and explain the speaker's reasons for that opinion.

This type of task looks like this:

> The man/woman expresses his opinion about _____. State his/her opinion and explain the reasons he/she gives for holding that opinion.

You have 30 seconds to prepare your response and 60 seconds to speak. Your response will be evaluated on how well you speak and how well you convey relevant information from the passage and the conversation.

2. Connecting Information from Two Sources

The reading passage provides general or background information on a topic of campus interest. The conversation will not merely repeat information from the passage; rather, it will expand on the topic. The task requires you to connect information from the two sources. It asks you to restate the opinion of one of the speakers, but it does not ask for your opinion.

While you are listening to the conversation, focus on the general message of each speaker. Listen for their opinions. Limit your note taking to the reasons a speaker gives for his or her opinion.

3. Sample Task and Response

Read the following notice from a campus bulletin board.

Reading Time – 45 seconds

NOTICE OF VOTE ON CAMPUS FOOD SERVICE

Students are encouraged to vote on the university's proposal to change the food service on campus. Students should vote for which of two options they prefer. Option 1 would expand the main cafeteria in the Student Center, including the addition of more food choices and more dining space; this option would also close the two snack bars on campus. Option 2 would close the cafeteria in the Student Center but would maintain the two snack bars, and would add five food service areas across campus, including two cafes, a deli, a barbecue grill, and a fine dining room.

The key points in the reading are:

- There will be a change in the food service. Students can vote for the option they prefer.
- Option 1 would expand the main cafeteria and close the snack bars.
- Option 2 would close the main cafeteria and add several food service areas across campus.

SPEAKING

Listening and Speaking

Album 6, Track 8

(Narrator)

Now listen to two students as they discuss the campus food service.

W: Have you voted on the food service yet?

M: No, but I intend to. I'm going to vote for the second option.

W: That's the one that closes the main cafeteria, isn't it?

M: Right.

W: But the main cafeteria is in the Student Center. That's where everyone goes at lunchtime. Doesn't it make sense to have food there?

M: But it's always so crowded in there at lunchtime. You have to wait a long time in the food line. And there are never enough places to sit.

W: That's true, but they say they'll add more tables.

M: There aren't enough bike racks outside either. I have no place to put my bike. Most of the time I eat at one of the snack bars. Besides, I like the idea of having several smaller eating places all over campus. That seems a lot more convenient, since we have classes all over campus anyway. It also means less crowding, and you don't have to wait as long to get your food. More food choices, too—I kind of like the idea of barbecue on campus.

W: Yeah, that does sound good, doesn't it?

(Narrator)

The man expresses his opinion about the campus food service. State his opinion and explain the reasons he gives for holding that opinion.

Stop

Preparation Time – 30 seconds
Response Time – 60 seconds

The task requires you to do two things: (1) state the man's opinion about the campus food service, and (2) explain the reasons he gives for holding that opinion. To respond to the question effectively, you must connect information from the conversation with information in the reading.

The key points that the man makes are:

- He is going to vote for Option 2.
- He thinks the main cafeteria is crowded and there are not enough bike racks outside.
- He likes the idea of several smaller eating places all over campus (Option 2) because it will be more convenient and less crowded, and there will be more food choices.

DELTA'S KEY TO THE TOEFL IBT®

SAMPLE RESPONSE

"The man's opinion about the campus food service is that Option 2 is better. The man likes this option because it adds several more places to get food. He will not vote for Option 1 because he doesn't like the cafeteria. The cafeteria is too crowded and there is no place to put his bike. He prefers having many places to eat on campus because this will be less crowded and more convenient. Also, there will be more food choices, such as barbecue."

The sample response effectively addresses the task. It states the man's opinion and gives the man's reasons for holding that opinion.

 PRACTICE

For each exercise, record your spoken response.

Exercise 3.5.A

For this task, you will read a short passage about a campus situation, listen to a conversation, and then speak in response to a question about what you have read and heard. Do not look at the question until the conversation has ended. Do not look at the reading passage while you are speaking.

Read the following information from a university bulletin.

Reading Time – 45 seconds

TRAINING COURSE FOR TUTORS

Western University announces a new course in the practice of professional tutoring. The course combines a discussion class with practical experience in either the Math Center or the Writing Center. In the discussion class, students will explore tutoring theories, examine the role of the peer tutor, and develop effective tutoring practices. In their practical experience, students will observe peer tutoring and advance to supervised tutoring. Students who are considering graduate school in related fields will benefit from this course.

Now cover the passage and listen to the conversation. You may take notes, and you may use your notes to help you answer the question. After you hear the question, begin preparing your response. You may look at the question, but NOT at the passage. You have 30 seconds to prepare your response and 60 seconds to speak.

 Album 6, Track 9

> The woman expresses her opinion about the training course for tutors. State her opinion and explain the reasons she gives for holding that opinion.

 Stop

Preparation Time – 30 seconds
Response Time – 60 seconds

Exercise 3.5.B

For this task, you will read a short passage about a campus situation, listen to a conversation, and then speak in response to a question about what you have read and heard. Do not look at the question until the conversation has ended. Do not look at the reading passage while you are speaking.

Read the following announcement about a proposal from the dean's office.

Reading Time – 45 seconds

PROPOSAL TO CHANGE THE PHYSICAL EDUCATION REQUIREMENT

The college is considering a proposal from the dean's office that would increase the physical education requirement of the core curriculum from one course to two courses. If approved by a vote of the administration, the new requirement will become effective in the fall semester. At the same time, the college will offer several new physical education courses, including martial arts, dance, and team sports. Students are invited to express their views on the proposed change at a meeting in Room 100 of the Administration Building at 2:00 this Friday.

Now cover the passage and listen to the conversation. You may take notes, and you may use your notes to help you answer the question. After you hear the question, begin preparing your response. You may look at the question, but NOT at the passage. You have 30 seconds to prepare your response and 60 seconds to speak.

 Album 6, Track 10

> The man expresses his opinion about the physical education requirement. State his opinion and explain the reasons he gives for holding that opinion.

 Stop

Preparation Time – 30 seconds
Response Time – 60 seconds

Exercise 3.5.C

For this task, you will read a short passage about a campus situation, listen to a talk, and then speak in response to a question about what you have read and heard. Do not look at the question until the conversation has ended. Do not look at the reading passage while you are speaking.

Read the following information from a campus bulletin.

Reading Time – 45 seconds

CHILDCARE ON CAMPUS

Students can use an on–campus childcare center for children from 12 months to 6 years. Hours of operation are 6:45 a.m. to 9:00 p.m., Monday through Thursday, and 6:45 a.m. to 6:00 p.m., Friday. The Child Care Center is conveniently located near the main classroom buildings and the library. The Center offers safe playrooms, an outdoor playground, trained staff, and a safe and caring environment. Full–time students have priority to enroll their children at the center. Space is limited, so we recommend that you enroll your children early.

Now cover the passage and listen to the talk. You may take notes, and you may use your notes to help you answer the question. After you hear the question, begin preparing your response. You may look at the question, but NOT at the passage. You have 30 seconds to prepare your response and 60 seconds to speak.

 Album 6, Track 11

> The woman expresses her opinion on the on–campus childcare. State her opinion and explain the reasons she gives for holding that opinion.

 Stop

Preparation Time – 30 seconds
Response Time – 60 seconds

Key points for Exercises 3.5.A through 3.5.C are on page 661.

 EXTENSION

1. Listen to your recorded response to one of the speaking tasks in Exercise 3.5.A through 3.5.C. Analyze and evaluate your response by answering the following questions:

    a. What information from the conversation does my response include?
    b. Does my response accurately explain the opinion stated in the conversation?
    c. Does my response answer the question effectively? Why or why not?
    d. How can I improve my responses for this type of question in the future?

3.6 Integrated Speaking: Taking Notes

 FOCUS

Read the following passage:

THE EFFECTS OF COLOR

Color is one of the most powerful qualities in the environment. Color is a communication tool that can influence mood or signal action. Certain colors cause physiological reactions, such as elevated blood pressure, increased metabolism, or eyestrain. Interior designers must understand how people perceive and react to different colors around them. Perceptions of color are somewhat subjective, but some effects of color have universal meaning. For example, colors in the red area of the spectrum are considered warm because they evoke "warm" emotions. In contrast, colors on the blue side of the spectrum are associated with "cool" emotions.

Now cover the passage and listen to part of a lecture. While you are listening, write down words and phrases that will help you remember the important points.

 Album 6, Track 12

_____

_____

_____

_____

 Stop

During a talk or lecture, you must listen carefully for important information. When you take notes, concentrate on terms, definitions, examples, and other details that will help you recall the information.

 STUDY

1. Integrated Reading–Listening–Speaking

On the TOEFL, two of the integrated speaking tasks involve reading, listening, and speaking.

In one of these tasks, you will read a short passage about an academic topic. You have 45 or 50 seconds to read the passage. Then the passage will disappear, and you will not see it again. Next, you will listen to a short lecture in which a professor expands on the topic from the reading. After the lecture, the speaking task will appear. The task will require you to explain how the information given by the professor supports or illustrates a major idea from the reading. This type of task looks like this:

> Explain _____ and how the examples given by the professor illustrate the concept.
>
> The professor describes _____. Explain how _____ is an example of _____.
>
> Use the examples from the lecture to explain the concept of _____.

You have 30 seconds to prepare your response and 60 seconds to speak. Your response will be evaluated on how well you speak and how well you convey relevant information from the passage and the lecture.

2. Taking Notes

Taking notes, or **note taking**, is writing down important information. Taking notes is an essential academic skill. During your university experience, you must take notes to help you remember important ideas and details from lectures and class discussions.

Just before the TOEFL begins, the test supervisor will give you paper to write on. You may use the paper to take notes, and you may use your notes to help you answer the integrated speaking question. Your notes will not be scored. Only what you speak into the microphone will be scored.

When you take notes, do not allow your writing to detract from your listening. Do not try to write down everything the speaker says. Develop shortcuts for common words and phrases. Use symbols and abbreviations to help you write more quickly. Here are some examples:

op	opinion
mi–R	main idea of the reading
mi–L	main idea of the lecture
ex	example
r	reason
1, 2, 3	first point, second point, third point
+	positive effect, add, more
neg	negative effect, consequence
=	equal, same
~	around, approximately, almost
→	causes, leads to
↑	up, increase, raise, improve
↓	down, decrease, lower, harm

SPEAKING

wo	without
sb	should be
sim	similar
pt	part, part–time
sm	small
lg	large
av	average

3. Listening for Key Information

In the lecture, the professor will explain a concept or idea from the reading. The professor may illustrate a general point with a specific example. While you are listening, focus on the professor's main points and supporting examples. Limit your note taking to the important examples and details.

Sometimes the professor emphasizes certain words or repeats certain ideas. Listen for information that the professor emphasizes or repeats. He or she may use certain *signpost* expressions to point to important ideas. For example, the speaker may state that something is important to know or necessary to keep in mind. Listen for what follows, and take notes about this information.

The speaker may use the following words or phrases as signposts to signal important information:

associated with	key	one, another	cause
characteristic	main	first, second, third	consequence
essential	necessary	for example	effect
feature	primary	for instance	produce
function	quality	for one thing	reason
generally	role	in other words	result
important	significant	this means	this is why

4. Sample Task

Read the following information from a textbook.

Reading Time – 45 seconds

THE EFFECTS OF COLOR

Color is one of the most powerful qualities in the environment. Color is a communication tool that can influence mood or signal action. Certain colors cause physiological reactions, such as elevated blood pressure, increased metabolism, or eyestrain. Interior designers must understand how people perceive and react to different colors around them. Perceptions of color are somewhat subjective, but some effects of color have universal meaning. For example, colors in the red area of the spectrum are considered warm because they evoke "warm" emotions. In contrast, colors on the blue side of the spectrum are associated with "cool" emotions.

Listening and Speaking

 Album 6, Track 12

(Narrator)

Now listen to part of a lecture in a design class.

(Professor)

    The warm colors cause feelings ranging from comfort and love to anger and hostility. Red is the color that we pay the most attention to. It is the warmest and most energetic color. Red can raise the blood pressure and make the heart beat faster. Red can add excitement to a room, but it would not be the color of choice for a hospital or a prison. Orange is a warm color, with an effect like red, but to a lesser extent. Orange expresses energy and enthusiasm, which is why we see a lot of orange in shopping malls and restaurants.

    And then we have the cool colors. These generally have a calming effect. Blue represents peace, harmony, unity, and security. Blue is the color of water and the sky. Blue causes the body to produce calming chemicals, so it's often used in bedrooms and in the doctor's waiting room. Another cool color, green, is one of the most–cited favorite colors and currently the most popular decorating color. Green refreshes the body and mind. Green symbolizes nature. It evokes a sense of health, youth, and renewal. Green is the easiest color on the eye and can actually improve vision, so it's a good choice for the office or workroom.

(Narrator)

Use the examples from the lecture to explain the effects of color.

 Stop

Preparation Time – 30 seconds
Response Time – 60 seconds

5. Sample Notes

Here are some notes taken during the sample lecture:

warm col → comfort, love, anger
    red – warmest   blood press, heart beat ↑
                        <u>not</u> – hosp, prison
    orange – energy   shopping mall, rest.
cool → calm
    blue – peace, security, water, sky   bedrm, doc
    green – fresh, nature, health
        imprv vision – office

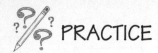 PRACTICE

For each exercise, record your spoken response.

Exercise 3.6.A

For this task, you will read a short passage, listen to a lecture on the same topic, and then speak in response to a question about what you have read and heard. Do not look at the question until the lecture has ended. Do not look at the reading passage while you are speaking.

Read the following information from a textbook.

Reading Time – 50 seconds

EMOTIONAL INTELLIGENCE

Emotional intelligence consists of self–awareness, self–control, self–motivation, enthusiasm, and social ability. People with emotional intelligence understand their feelings and manage them in ways that are positive and helpful. They make decisions about life— what job to pursue, what direction to take, and whom to marry—with greater confidence and skill than people with low or no emotional intelligence. Their people skills make them more likely to succeed at relationships, cooperation, and leadership, and less likely to engage in risky or criminal behavior.

Now cover the passage and listen to the lecture. You may take notes, and you may use your notes to help you answer the question. After you hear the question, begin preparing your response. You may look at the question, but NOT at the passage. You have 30 seconds to prepare your response and 60 seconds to speak.

 Album 6, Track 13

> Explain emotional intelligence and how the examples given by the professor illustrate the concept.

 Stop

Preparation Time – 30 seconds
Response Time – 60 seconds

Exercise 3.6.B

For this task, you will read a short passage, listen to a lecture on the same topic, and then speak in response to a question about what you have read and heard. Do not look at the question until the lecture has ended. Do not look at the reading passage while you are speaking.

Read the following information from a textbook.

Reading Time – 50 seconds

ROLE CONFLICT

Everyone has a role in a social system. One person may have a number of roles because he or she belongs to various social systems, such as home, school, workplace, and community. A person in a particular social role will follow the rules of behavior for that role. Each role in a social system is related to other roles in the system. Relationships such as parent and child, student and teacher, and supervisor and staff are known as role partners. When there is competition or conflict between the expectations of different role partners, we have something called role conflict.

Now cover the passage and listen to the lecture. You may take notes, and you may use your notes to help you answer the question. After you hear the question, begin preparing your response. You may look at the question, but NOT at the passage. You have 30 seconds to prepare your response and 60 seconds to speak.

 Album 6, Track 14

> Explain role conflict and how the examples given by the professor illustrate the concept.

 Stop

Preparation Time – 30 seconds
Response Time – 60 seconds

Exercise 3.6.C

For this task, you will read a short passage, listen to a lecture on the same topic, and then speak in response to a question about what you have read and heard. Do not look at the question until the lecture has ended. Do not look at the reading passage while you are speaking.

Read the following information from a textbook.

Reading Time – 50 seconds

SPATIAL MEMORY

     An important survival skill of animals is their spatial memory, the ability to remember objects based on their relationship to other things in the environment. Animals use their spatial memory to make a list of paths leading to various goals. Navigating by landmarks, such as rocks or trees, is a simple but effective procedure. An animal learns from experience that turning right at one landmark and then left at another will lead to its destination. Some animals can recognize a landmark from different directions, making it possible to find their way to a familiar goal even when approaching from an unfamiliar direction.

Now cover the passage and listen to the lecture. You may take notes, and you may use your notes to help you answer the question. After you hear the question, begin preparing your response. You may look at the question, but NOT at the passage. You have 30 seconds to prepare your response and 60 seconds to speak.

 Album 6, Track 15

> The professor describes the behavior of a species of bird. Explain how the birds' behavior illustrates the concept of spatial memory.

 Stop

Preparation Time – 30 seconds
Response Time – 60 seconds

Key points for Exercises 3.6.A through 3.6.C are on pages 661–662.

EXTENSION

1. Listen to your recorded response to one of the speaking tasks in Exercise 3.6.A through 3.6.C. Analyze and evaluate your response by answering the following questions:

    a. What key points from the lecture does my response convey?
    b. What examples, explanation, or details does my response include?
    c. Does my response answer the question effectively? Why or why not?
    d. How can I improve my responses for this type of question in the future?

2   Share and discuss your recorded response to one of the speaking questions in Exercises 3.6.A through 3.6.C. Work in a group of three or four students. Listen to each student's recorded response. Discuss each student's response by answering the following questions:

    a. What key points from the lecture does the response convey?
    b. What examples, explanation, or other details does the response include? Do these details accurately convey information from the lecture?
    c. Can the response be easily understood? Why or why not?
    d. Does the response answer the question effectively? Why or why not?

    Make suggestions that will help each student improve in the future.

3. As you listen to the conversations and lectures for units 3.7 through 3.10, take notes about the main idea, key points, and important details. Use the format shown below. Do not try to write down every word that you hear. Train your listening to focus on the essential information.

    Main idea/problem: _____

    Key points: _____ Details: _____

    _____ _____

    _____ _____

    _____ _____

4. Obtain a recording of a real college or university lecture. Topics in history, anthropology, sociology, and psychology are good choices. Bring the recording to class. With the whole class, listen to two minutes of the recording. While you are listening, takes notes about important information in the lecture. Do not try to write down everything. Write only the key words and phrases that you think are important to remember.

    Then break into groups of three or four students. Compare your notes with the notes taken by the others in your group. Listen again to the same two–minute recording. In your group, discuss the key points made in the lecture. Choose one person to read your group's list of key points to the whole class.

3.7 Integrated Speaking: Delivering Your Response

 FOCUS

Listen to the lecture. What points does the professor make?

 *Album 6, Track 16*

 Stop

The professor discusses effects of warm and cool colors on human emotions and the human body. She makes these points:

- Warm colors cause warm, energetic emotions.
- Cool colors have a calming effect.

She develops these points with examples and explanation. She gives examples of warm colors: red and orange. She gives examples of cool colors: blue and green. She gives examples of emotions associated with warm and cool colors. She gives examples of how specific colors affect the human body. She explains why certain colors are used in specific types of buildings or rooms.

The speaking task requires you to talk about the examples given by the professor. A well–developed response will include appropriate examples and explanation from the lecture.

 STUDY

1. Addressing the Task

The first two integrated speaking tasks involve reading, listening, and speaking. For these tasks you will:

- read a short passage about a campus situation or an academic topic;
- listen to a short conversation or lecture about the same topic; and
- speak in response to a question about information in the two sources.

These tasks do not ask for your opinion. Your opinion is irrelevant and should not be included in your responses. Your responses should be based only on what you have just read and heard. To be effective in addressing the task, your response should:

- convey information relevant to the task;
- make two or three points;
- develop points with appropriate examples and explanation; and
- express ideas clearly and coherently.

2. Preparing Your Response

After the speaking task appears, you have 30 seconds to prepare your response. Review the notes you took during the conversation or lecture. Select only information that is relevant to the task. Underline this information. Think about what you will say.

Plan to make two or three points, and choose relevant details to develop these points. On your note paper, make a quick plan. Your plan may be as simple as numbering the information you have underlined. Here is a general plan for the reading–listening–speaking tasks:

Introductory Statement	State the speaker's opinion or the main idea.
Point 1	State point. Give supporting information.
Point 2	State point. Give supporting information.
Point 3	State point. Give supporting information.
Concluding Statement	If time allows, summarize the points.

3. Making Yourself Understood

Your response will be more effective if you speak clearly and make yourself understood to your listeners. Your response will be better understood if:

- each sentence conveys a complete thought;
- your sentence structure is fairly simple;
- you use vocabulary correctly;
- you pronounce words clearly; and
- you speak at a natural speed.

You have 60 seconds to speak. This is enough time to state and develop two or three points. Speak at a natural speed—as if you were talking to your teacher. Do not rush, but watch the countdown clock. If you make three points, you have approximately 20 seconds to state and develop each point.

4. Speaking Coherently

An effective response is coherent. **Coherence** is the quality of unity and order. Speech is coherent when statements flow naturally, one after the other, following a logical order. Coherent speech is generally easy for listeners to understand.

The following *transitions* and other expressions will help you express yourself coherently.

Introduce Key Points from the Two Sources

The man's opinion is that _____.

The woman believes that _____.

According to the lecture, _____.

The professor made the point that _____.

The reading stated that _____.

Give Examples

for example	one example is	also
such as	another example is	in addition

Give Reasons

because	one reason is	first, second, third...
since	another reason is	next
so that	most importantly	finally

---

5. Sample Task and Response

Read the following information from a textbook.

Reading Time – 45 seconds

THE EFFECTS OF COLOR

Color is one of the most powerful qualities in the environment. Color is a communication tool that can influence mood or signal action. Certain colors cause physiological reactions, such as elevated blood pressure, increased metabolism, or eyestrain. Interior designers must understand how people perceive and react to different colors around them. Perceptions of color are somewhat subjective, but some effects of color have universal meaning. For example, colors in the red area of the spectrum are considered warm because they evoke "warm" emotions. In contrast, colors on the blue side of the spectrum are associated with "cool" emotions.

Listening and Speaking

 Album 6, Track 16

Use the examples from the lecture to explain the effects of color.

 Stop

The task requires you to do two things: (1) explain a concept from the reading and lecture (the effects of color), and (2) use examples from the lecture to illustrate the concept. To respond to the question effectively, you must connect information from the lecture and the reading.

The key points in the lecture are:

- Warm and cool colors have different effects on people.

- Warm colors cause warm, energetic emotions, such as comfort, love, and anger. Red and orange are warm colors. Red can raise the blood pressure and heart rate, so it is not a good choice for a hospital or prison. Orange expresses energy and enthusiasm; orange is used in shopping malls and restaurants.

- Cool colors have a calming effect. Blue and green are cool colors. Blue represents peace and security. Blue is used in bedrooms and in the doctor's waiting room. Green refreshes the body and mind; it symbolizes nature and evokes health and youth. Green can improve vision, so it is a good choice for the office or workroom.

SAMPLE RESPONSE

"Warm colors and cool colors have different effects. Warm colors cause feelings such as love and anger. Red is the warmest color. Red can increase blood pressure and heart beat, so it's not a good color for a hospital. Another warm color is orange. Orange expresses energy. The professor gives examples of cool colors, which have a calm effect. Blue is a peaceful color, so it's used in bedrooms and the doctor's office. Another cool color is green. Green is fresh, like nature. Green improves vision, so it's a good color for the office."

The sample response effectively addresses the task. It explains the different effects of warm and cool colors and gives examples from the lecture.

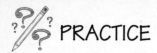 PRACTICE

For each exercise, record your spoken response.

Exercise 3.7.A

For this task, you will read a short passage about a campus situation, listen to a conversation, and then speak in response to a question about what you have read and heard. Do not look at the question until the conversation has ended. Do not look at the reading passage while you are speaking.

Read the following information from a university catalog.

Reading Time – 45 seconds

ON–CAMPUS HOUSING

Most first–year students live on campus, and virtually all of them have one or more roommates. Living on campus has many advantages, with varying accommodations available through the Housing Office. On–campus housing includes four apartment buildings and eight dormitories. With living units ranging from one–, two–, and four–bedroom apartments, to single and double dormitory rooms, students are close to classrooms and other campus facilities. The university also offers "specialty dorms" designated by academic major; these are good ways to meet people with interests similar to yours.

Now cover the passage and listen to the conversation. You may take notes, and you may use your notes to help you answer the question. After you hear the question, begin preparing your response. You may look at the question, but NOT at the passage. You have 30 seconds to prepare your response and 60 seconds to speak.

 Album 6, Track 17

> The man expresses his opinion about the woman's desire to live on campus. State his opinion and explain the reasons he gives for holding that opinion.

 Stop

Preparation Time – 30 seconds
Response Time – 60 seconds

Exercise 3.7.B

For this task, you will read a short passage, listen to a lecture on the same topic, and then speak in response to a question about what you have read and heard. Do not look at the question until the lecture has ended. Do not look at the reading passage while you are speaking.

Read the following information from a textbook.

Reading Time – 50 seconds

DEPRESSION

Depression is a psychological disorder in which a person is overwhelmed by an emotional crisis. Symptoms of depression include feelings of hopelessness, sadness, and despair; loss of interest and pleasure in things; weight loss or weight gain; difficulty falling asleep or sleeping more than usual; lack of motivation; and loss of energy. A growing body of evidence suggests that several types of depression are linked to biological and environmental factors. In cases of mild or situational depression, the symptoms usually decline with a change of scenery or routine, or when the problem that caused the depression disappears.

Now cover the passage and listen to the lecture. You may take notes, and you may use your notes to help you answer the question. After you hear the question, begin preparing your response. You may look at the question, but NOT at the passage. You have 30 seconds to prepare your response and 60 seconds to speak.

 Album 6, Track 18

> The professor describes seasonal affective disorder—SAD. Explain how SAD is an example of depression.

 Stop

Preparation Time – 30 seconds
Response Time – 60 seconds

Exercise 3.7.C

For this task, you will read a short passage about a campus situation, listen to a conversation, and then speak in response to a question about what you have read and heard. Do not look at the question until the conversation has ended. Do not look at the reading passage while you are speaking.

Read the following information from a college catalog.

Reading Time – 45 seconds

THE PROGRAM SEMINAR

The program seminar is the primary mode of instruction for students at Central College. A program of study might involve 80 students and four faculty members, but most of class time is spent in small group discussions—the seminar. Seminar content centers on a theme or issue relevant to the program. For students, the close interaction with faculty and fellow students provides perspective through differing viewpoints, and depth through concentrated group effort. Students learn to express themselves and to work cooperatively—two traits that our graduates have found particularly helpful in their lives and careers.

Now cover the passage and listen to the conversation. You may take notes, and you may use your notes to help you answer the question. After you hear the question, begin preparing your response. You may look at the question, but NOT at the passage. You have 30 seconds to prepare your response and 60 seconds to speak.

 Album 6, Track 19

> The woman expresses her opinion about seminars. State her opinion and explain the reasons she gives for holding that opinion.

 Stop

Preparation Time – 30 seconds
Response Time – 60 seconds

Exercise 3.7.D

For this task, you will read a short passage, listen to a lecture on the same topic, and then speak in response to a question about what you have read and heard. Do not look at the question until the lecture has ended. Do not look at the reading passage while you are speaking.

Read the following information from a textbook.

Reading Time – 50 seconds

BOYCOTTS

Boycotts are a form of nonviolent protest, the practice of applying power to achieve sociopolitical goals, without the use of physical force. People who participate in a boycott refuse to buy, sell, or otherwise trade with an individual or business that they believe to be doing something morally wrong. The purpose of a boycott is to call attention to a wrong and to punish those responsible for the wrong. Usually, the punishment is economic, but sometimes it brings shame to the offenders. When a boycott is long–term and widespread, it can be a factor in causing social change.

Now cover the passage and listen to the lecture. You may take notes, and you may use your notes to help you answer the question. After you hear the question, begin preparing your response. You may look at the question, but NOT at the passage. You have 30 seconds to prepare your response and 60 seconds to speak.

 Album 6, Track 20

Explain boycotts and how the examples given by the professor illustrate the concept.

 Stop

Preparation Time – 30 seconds
Response Time – 60 seconds

Exercise 3.7.E

For this task, you will read a short passage about a campus situation, listen to a conversation, and then speak in response to a question about what you have read and heard. Do not look at the question until the conversation has ended. Do not look at the reading passage while you are speaking.

Read the following announcement from a college bulletin.

Reading Time – 45 seconds

COMMUNITY COURSE IN THEATER

Members of the community are invited to join students in the Baxter College Theater Arts program in a fully staged college theater production. In this course, you will learn theory, methods, and an analysis of theater production in acting or technical theater. You will assist with scenery construction and costumes, box office procedures, and lighting and sound systems during the production of a play. The instructor has extensive experience in the performing arts and is director of the college's Theater Arts program. This course is not open to full–time or part–time students of Baxter College.

Now cover the passage and listen to the conversation. You may take notes, and you may use your notes to help you answer the question. After you hear the question, begin preparing your response. You may look at the question, but NOT at the passage. You have 30 seconds to prepare your response and 60 seconds to speak.

 Album 6, Track 21

> The man expresses his opinion about the theater course. State his opinion and explain the reasons he gives for holding that opinion.

 Stop

Preparation Time – 30 seconds
Response Time – 60 seconds

Exercise 3.7.F

For this task, you will read a short passage, listen to a lecture on the same topic, and then speak in response to a question about what you have read and heard. Do not look at the question until the lecture has ended. Do not look at the reading passage while you are speaking.

Read the following information from a textbook.

Reading Time – 50 seconds

THE IMPACT OF SLEEP ON LEARNING

People learn better if they learn smaller bits of information over a period of days than if they learn a large amount all at once. This is because periods of sleep between sessions of learning will help people retain what they learn. Sleep has at least two separate effects on learning. First, sleep unifies memories, which protects the memories against later interference or loss. Second, sleep helps to recover lost memories. Brain activity during sleep promotes higher–level learning, such as the ability to learn language.

Now cover the passage and listen to the lecture. You may take notes, and you may use your notes to help you answer the question. After you hear the question, begin preparing your response. You may look at the question, but NOT at the passage. You have 30 seconds to prepare your response and 60 seconds to speak.

 Album 6, Track 22

> Explain the impact of sleep on learning and how the example given by the professor supports this idea.

 Stop

Preparation Time – 30 seconds
Response Time – 60 seconds

Key points for Exercises 3.7.A through 3.7.F are on page 662.

 EXTENSION

1. Listen to your recorded response to one of the speaking tasks in Exercise 3.7.A through 3.7.F. Analyze and evaluate your response by answering the following questions:

    a. What key points does my response make? Do these points accurately convey information from the conversation/lecture and reading?
    b. What examples, explanation, or details does my response include? Does this information successfully develop the key points?
    c. Is my response coherent? Would it be easily understood by other listeners?
    d. Does my response answer the question effectively? Why or why not?
    e. How can I improve my responses for this type of question in the future?

2. Share and discuss your recorded response to one of the speaking questions in Exercises 3.7.A through 3.7.F. Work in a group of three or four students. Listen to each student's recorded response. Discuss each student's response by answering the following questions:

    a. What key points does the speaker make in the response? Do these points accurately convey information from the conversation/lecture and reading?
    b. What examples, explanation, or other details from the conversation/lecture are included? Do they successfully develop the speaker's points?
    c. Can the response be easily understood? Why or why not?
    d. Is the response coherent? Why or why not?
    e. Does the response answer the question effectively? Why or why not?

Make suggestions that will help each student improve in the future.

3.8 Integrated Speaking: Summarizing a Problem

 FOCUS

 Album 6, Track 23

 Stop

What is the topic of the conversation? _____

What problem does the woman have? _____

What solutions do the speakers discuss? _____

_____

What do you think the woman should do? _____

Why do you think she should do that? _____

One of the integrated speaking tasks on the TOEFL will have a conversation about a problem and solutions. You will listen to a conversation and then speak about what you have heard. You will describe the problem and talk about a possible solution to the problem.

 STUDY

1. Integrated Listening–Speaking

On the TOEFL, two of the integrated speaking tasks involve the language skills of listening and speaking. In the first of these tasks you will:

- listen to a short conversation in which the speakers discuss a problem and possible solutions;
- summarize the problem in your own words; and
- state and support the solution you prefer.

This type of task looks like this:

> Briefly summarize the problem the speakers are discussing. Then state which solution you would recommend. Explain the reasons for your recommendation.
>
> The speakers discuss two possible solutions to the man's problem. Briefly describe the problem. Then state which solution you prefer and explain why.
>
> The students discuss a problem that the woman has. Briefly summarize the problem. Then state what you think the woman should do, and explain why.

2. Listening for Key Information

In the conversation, one of the speakers will describe a problem that he or she is facing. The problem may involve a decision that the speaker must make. Take notes about the problem and the solutions offered by the speakers. Generally, there will be two solutions given, but sometimes there will be three. In some cases, only one of the speakers mentions possible solutions. In other cases, each speaker offers a different possible solution. The speakers do not decide on the correct solution during the conversation. You must do that in your response.

The speakers may use certain expressions to identify the problem and suggest solutions.

Identify Problem	
I need help with _____.	I can't figure out _____.
I'm having trouble _____.	I'd like to _____ but _____.
I just don't see how _____.	If I _____, then I _____.

Suggest Solutions	
You need to _____.	Here's what you could do.
You should _____.	One thing you can do is _____.
You'd better _____.	Try _____.
Couldn't you _____?	If you _____, it might _____.
Why don't you _____?	If I were you, I'd _____.

3. Summarizing a Problem and Recommending a Solution

A *summary* is a brief report of the important ideas. To *summarize* is to state the major ideas of a text in a shorter form. In this task, the major ideas will concern a problem and suggestions for how to solve it.

After the conversation, the speaking task will appear. The task will require you to briefly describe the problem and to recommend a solution. You do *not* have to summarize every solution that the speakers mention. You only have to state which *one* of the solutions you prefer. There is no single correct solution to the problem. You must choose one solution and then explain why you prefer that solution.

You have 20 seconds to prepare your response and 60 seconds to speak. Your response will be evaluated on how accurately you describe the problem and how well you express and support the solution that you prefer. Here is a general plan for this task:

Summarize	Briefly describe the problem.
Recommend	Recommend one of the given solutions.
Support	Give one reason why you prefer this solution.
	Give another reason for this solution.

4. Making Yourself Understood

Your response will be easier to understand if each sentence conveys a complete thought. Keep your sentence structure fairly simple. Use transitions to make your speech coherent. The following expressions will help you describe the problem, recommend a solution, and explain why.

Describe Problem

The man's problem is that _____.

The woman wants to _____, but _____.

Recommend Solution and Explain Why

I think the man should _____. One reason is _____. Another reason is _____.

I recommend that the woman _____. If she _____, then _____.

The solution I prefer is _____. This would be better because _____.

In my opinion, the better choice is _____. First, _____. Also, _____.

If the woman _____, she can/will _____.

There are two reasons for _____. First, _____. Second, _____.

Your response will be easier to understand if you speak in phrases. This means grouping words together into idea units. For example, look at this sentence:

"I think the woman should quit the newspaper because then she would have more time for swimming practice."

This sentence is easier to understand if it is spoken in phrases, like this:

"I think / the woman should quit the newspaper / because then / she would have more time / for swimming practice."

5. Sample Task and Responses

 Album 6, Track 23

(Narrator)

Listen to part of a conversation between two students.

M: The college newspaper is so much better now that you're the editor.
W: Thanks!
M: And you want to go to graduate school for journalism, so being editor is valuable experience.
W: Yes, I know. But, unfortunately, I might have to quit soon.
M: Quit? Why?
W: The paper takes a lot of time. There are so many meetings, and so much to do. I stay up late every night, and I have swimming practice early in the morning.
M: You can't quit the paper! You need to stay on as editor. The experience will help you get into graduate school.
W: I know. I'd like to stay at the paper, but if I quit, I'll have more time for swimming practice. My coach just recommended me for the sport scholarship, and he thinks I have a really good chance at winning this scholarship, if I just train a little harder. I'd have to get up earlier, but with my late nights at the newspaper ... well ... it's a conflict. I just don't see how I can do both.
M: Well, in that case, maybe you should leave the newspaper. Maybe the sports scholarship is more important.
W: The newspaper is important to me too, but it leaves me less time for swimming.

(Narrator)

The students discuss possible solutions to the woman's problem. Briefly describe the problem. Then state which solution you prefer and explain why.

 Stop

Preparation Time – 20 seconds
Response Time – 60 seconds

The task requires you to do three things: (1) describe the woman's problem, (2) state your opinion about what the woman should do, and (3) explain why you think the woman should do that.

The key points in the conversation are:

- The woman has a conflict between her work as editor of the college newspaper and her chance at winning a sport scholarship. She stays up late for her newspaper work, but she has to get up early for swimming practice. She cannot continue to do both.

- One solution is to quit as editor of the newspaper so she has more time for swimming practice.

- Another solution is to stay as editor of the paper, which gives her experience that may help her get into graduate school.

The response should begin by describing the problem. Then it should state and support an opinion about which solution is better. Opinions about the solution will vary. There is no single correct response.

SAMPLE RESPONSE 1

"The woman's problem is a conflict between her work as editor of the newspaper and her time for swimming practice. The newspaper takes a lot of time, and she has to stay up late. However, she must get up early for swimming practice. Her coach recommended her for a sport scholarship, so she wants to quit the newspaper. I think the woman should quit the newspaper because then she would have more time for swimming practice. If she practices more, she can win a scholarship, so I prefer this solution."

SAMPLE RESPONSE 2

"The woman is the editor of the college newspaper. It takes a lot of time. She has many meetings and stays up late every night. She also has a chance to win a scholarship for swimming, but she needs more time to practice. Her problem is that she must choose either to quit the newspaper or to stay. The solution I prefer is staying at the newspaper. The main reason is she wants to go to graduate school, and her experience will help her with that goal. This is a better solution because she wants to study journalism."

Both responses effectively address the task. They describe the problem clearly, state which solution is better, and support this opinion with one or more reasons.

 PRACTICE

To make this practice more like the TOEFL, cover each question while you are listening to the audio. You may take notes, and you may use your notes to help you answer the question. When you hear the question, you may look at it and begin preparing your response. Record your response for each exercise.

Exercise 3.8.A

For this task, you will listen to a conversation. You will then be asked to talk about the information in the conversation and to give your opinion about the ideas presented. After you hear the question, you have 20 seconds to prepare your response and 60 seconds to speak.

 Album 6, Track 24

> Briefly summarize the problem the speakers are discussing. Then state which solution you would recommend. Explain the reasons for your recommendation.

 Stop

Preparation Time – 20 seconds
Response Time – 60 seconds

Exercise 3.8.B

For this task, you will listen to a conversation. You will then be asked to talk about the information in the conversation and to give your opinion about the ideas presented. After you hear the question, you have 20 seconds to prepare your response and 60 seconds to speak.

 Album 6, Track 25

> Briefly summarize the problem the speakers are discussing. Then state which solution you would recommend. Explain the reasons for your recommendation.

 Stop

Preparation Time – 20 seconds
Response Time – 60 seconds

Exercise 3.8.C

For this task, you will listen to a conversation. You will then be asked to talk about the information in the conversation and to give your opinion about the ideas presented. After you hear the question, you have 20 seconds to prepare your response and 60 seconds to speak.

 Album 6, Track 26

> The students discuss a problem that the man has. Briefly summarize the problem. Then state what you think the man should do, and explain why.

 Stop

Preparation Time – 20 seconds
Response Time – 60 seconds

Exercise 3.8.D

For this task, you will listen to a conversation. You will then be asked to talk about the information in the conversation and to give your opinion about the ideas presented. After you hear the question, you have 20 seconds to prepare your response and 60 seconds to speak.

 Album 6, Track 27

> The students discuss possible solutions to the woman's problem. Briefly describe the problem. Then state which solution you prefer and explain why.

 Stop

Preparation Time – 20 seconds
Response Time – 60 seconds

Exercise 3.8.E

For this task, you will listen to a conversation. You will then be asked to talk about the information in the conversation and to give your opinion about the ideas presented. After you hear the question, you have 20 seconds to prepare your response and 60 seconds to speak.

 Album 6, Track 28

> The speakers discuss a problem that the man has. Briefly summarize the problem. Then state what you think the man should do, and explain why.

 Stop

Preparation Time – 20 seconds
Response Time – 60 seconds

Key points for Exercises 3.8.A through 3.8.E are on pages 662–663.

EXTENSION

1. Listen again to the conversations in Exercises 3.8.A through 3.8.E. As you listen, fill in the missing information on the blank lines in the scripts. Do not try to write down every word. Take brief notes about only the key information. Check your notes with the audio scripts on pages 732–733.

CONVERSATION 3.8.A

Album 6, Track 24

W: Is something wrong with _____?

M: Not really, it's just that _____. It's been
      _____ lately. I think _____.

W: That's too bad. Why don't you _____?

M: Oh, it's not that bad. It's just _____.

W: But you're _____ in a funny way. You should
      _____. You could _____.
      We're heading toward the _____ right now.

M: I don't have the time to _____. I have
      _____.

W: Baseball practice! You shouldn't _____!

M: I can't afford to _____. I've missed too much already,
      and _____. He said _____
      _____. I don't want that to
      happen. Baseball is important to me. I can't let the team down.

W: Then you'd better _____, but be sure to
      _____. Tell him you _____.
      You need to _____. You could make it a lot worse if
      _____.

Stop

CONVERSATION 3.8.B

Album 6, Track 25

W: I need help with _____.

M: Okay. What kind of help?

W: I still need to _____, so I need

_____, but it doesn't look like anything will

_____.

M: Hmm. I see what you mean. You've already got a full schedule. But I'm sure we can

_____. Aaaah... well ... you could

_____. There are lots of

_____ for Winter Quarter.

W: An evening course. I _____. It makes the day so long.

M: Well, with your schedule, this may be your best choice for Winter Quarter. Another

possibility, of course, is to _____ and

_____. Can you do that—

_____?

W: I'm doing _____ in the spring. That will

be full–time, and I'm not sure I can handle another course on top of that. I expect

_____. And then I hope to

_____. So this is kind of a problem for me.

Stop

CONVERSATION 3.8.C

Album 6, Track 26

W: How are your classes going?

M: All right mostly, well, that is, except for _____. The

class is fine, but _____

_____.

W: That's not good. You need to _____. You can't

_____. You need to _____

_____. He has to take responsibility

for his part of the project.

SPEAKING

M: That's for sure. He's hard to get a hold of, too. I've left several messages on his answering machine.

W: You'd better _____. Maybe

_____.

M: It's kind of late for that. Besides, _____

_____.

W: You never know. Maybe you could _____. But I would

_____.

🎧 *Stop*

CONVERSATION 3.8.D

🎧 *Album 6, Track 27*

M: Hi, Nicole. How's it going?

W: My classes are going well. _____.

M: What's wrong with your _____?

W: I'm not sure, exactly. It just _____. It gave me a lot of

trouble this morning. It _____

_____. I need to have it checked out, but

_____.

M: You could _____. They have

_____

_____.

W: But I'm not _____.

M: Check it out anyway. Maybe you don't have to be _____

_____. Just tell them you're a student.

W: Well, maybe.

M: Another place you could try is _____. People

sometimes advertise services like this. Maybe you can _____

_____.

W: Hmm. Maybe. Thanks for the tips.

M: No problem. Good luck.

🎧 *Stop*

CONVERSATION 3.8.E

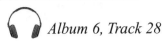 *Album 6, Track 28*

M: Professor Fisher, I'm _____, so I'll

_____. I was wondering if _____.

W: Well, you know my policy is not to _____. If you

_____, then you can try to _____

_____. But … haven't you already _____?

M: Um … yeah, I _____ a few weeks ago.

W: Then try not to _____, and try to do well on it too. Your test scores

so far have not been strong. You could be _____

_____.

M: Do you mean I might _____?

W: At this point, you need to _____. Why

don't you _____, or _____

_____?

M: Well, I guess I could. But, to tell the truth, I don't have _____

_____.

W: Then, in that case, you need to _____

_____. If you're too busy to _____,

you should _____.

 Stop

2. Listen to your recorded response to one of the speaking tasks in Exercise 3.8.A through 3.8.E.
   Analyze and evaluate your response by answering the following questions:

   a. Does my response accurately convey information about the problem?
   b. Does my response clearly recommend a solution to the problem? What reasons are given
      in my response to support the recommended solution?
   c. Is my response coherent? Would it be easily understood by other listeners?
   d. Does my response answer the question effectively? Why or why not?
   e. How can I improve my responses for this type of question in the future?

3.9 Integrated Speaking: Summarizing Information

FOCUS

Imagine you have just listened to a lecture in a world history class. The professor spoke about human migration in the nineteenth century. While you were listening, you took notes. Now a teaching assistant writes the following question on the board and calls on you to respond orally.

> Describe the mass migrations of people in the nineteenth century, and explain why these migrations occurred.

The teaching assistant gives you 20 seconds to prepare your response. How would you use this time?

_____ Close your eyes and relax for 20 seconds.

_____ Panic and forget everything that you heard in the lecture.

_____ Write a statement that you will read aloud.

_____ Plan to talk about a different topic that you know more about.

_____ Review your notes and think about what you will say.

Is it a good idea to close your eyes and relax? It's good to relax, but taking a break during your preparation time is probably not a good choice. If you have enough practice with this type of activity, you will not panic and forget everything that you just heard.

Should you write a statement and then read it aloud? You do not have enough time to do that. No one can write that fast. Should you plan to talk about a different topic? Definitely not—doing so would not address the question.

The best way to use your preparation time is to review your notes and think about what you will say. Think about the professor's major points. Scan your notes for ideas and examples that will help you explain mass migrations in the nineteenth century. Collect your thoughts and get ready to speak.

For one of the integrated speaking tasks on the TOEFL, you will listen to a lecture and then speak about information in the lecture. You will summarize the points made by the professor.

 STUDY

1. Integrated Listening–Speaking

On the TOEFL, two of the integrated speaking tasks involve the language skills of listening and speaking. In the second of these tasks you will:

- listen to a short lecture about an academic topic; and
- summarize the important information in the lecture.

This type of task looks like this:

> Using points and examples from the lecture, explain _____.
> Using points and details from the talk, describe _____, explaining _____.

2. Summarizing Information

A *summary* is a brief report of the most important points. The second listening–speaking task will require you to *summarize* the major ideas from a lecture. Your opinion is irrelevant and should not be included in your response. Your response should be based only on the information in the lecture.

You will not see the question until after you hear the lecture. However, you can expect the question to ask about key ideas in the lecture. While you are listening to the lecture, focus on the ideas that are most important, and take notes about them. Do not try to write down everything. Limit your notes to key ideas and examples.

3. Preparing Your Response

After the speaking task appears, you have 20 seconds to prepare your response. Read the question carefully. Review your notes and select information that will help you answer the question. Plan to make two or three points. Choose relevant details to develop these points.

Introductory Statement	State the main idea of the lecture.
Point 1	State point. Support with details and explanation.
Point 2	State point. Support with details and explanation.
Point 3	State point. Support with details and explanation.
Concluding Statement	If time allows, summarize the points.

You have 60 seconds to speak. Speak at a natural speed. Do not rush, but watch the countdown clock. If you make three points, you have approximately 20 seconds to state and develop each point.

An effective response will:

- convey relevant information from the lecture;
- develop points with appropriate details and explanation;
- express ideas coherently; and
- be easy for listeners to understand.

4. Making Yourself Understood

Your response will be easier to understand if you pronounce words clearly and correctly, especially key content words from the lecture. Use voice stress to emphasize the key content words—nouns, verbs, and adjectives—that supply relevant information.

> "There were ***several reasons*** for the ***mass migrations***. ***One*** reason was the new types of ***transportation***, such as the ***railroad*** and ***steamship***. ***Another*** reason was the people could get ***free land***, for example, in the ***United States*** and ***Canada***."

5. Sample Task and Response

 Album 6, Track 29

(Narrator)

Listen to part of a lecture in a world history class. The professor is talking about mass migrations of people.

(Professor)

In the nineteenth century, there were several periods when large numbers of people moved from one place to another around the world. In many cases, people moved to another continent. These mass migrations were on a much larger scale than any previous migrations in history. One major movement was from Europe to the Americas, Australia, and Africa. This migration of Europeans involved around 60 million people over one hundred years. Another mass migration was from Russia to Siberia and Central Asia. Another was from China, India, and Japan to Southeast Asia.

These large movements of people were made possible by the new cheap and fast means of transportation, specifically railroads and steamships. Another important factor was the rapid growth in banking and capital, by which large investors financed a lot of the settlement. In some places, immigrants were given free land and other benefits if they settled there. This is what encouraged a lot of people—both immigrant and native–born—to move westward in the United States and Canada. Thus, most regions of the U.S. and Canada were populated by the end of the nineteenth century.

The majority of the people in these mass migrations came from the lower social and economic classes of society. The immigrants were motivated mainly by the hope of a better life for themselves and their children. Since most of the immigrants were unskilled workers, their main contribution to their new countries was the labor they supplied. It was the hard work and high hopes of the immigrants that contributed to the economic growth of their new countries.

(Narrator)

Using points and examples from the lecture, describe the mass migrations of people in the nineteenth century, and explain why these migrations occurred.

 Stop

Preparation Time – 20 seconds
Response Time – 60 seconds

The above task requires you to do two things: (1) describe the mass migrations of people in the nineteenth century, and (2) explain why these migrations occurred.

The key points in the lecture are:

- People moved from one part of the world to another on a much larger scale than they had during any previous migrations.
- The mass migrations occurred because of new cheap and fast means of transportation.
- The migrations occurred because large investors financed a lot of the settlement and gave immigrants free land.
- Most immigrants were motivated mainly by the hope of a better life for themselves and their children.

SAMPLE RESPONSE

"Mass migrations of people occurred in the nineteenth century. Many people moved from Europe to other countries, also from China and Japan to other countries. There were several reasons for the mass migrations. One reason was the new types of transportation, such as the railroad and steamship. Another reason was the people could get free land, for example, in the United States and Canada. Also, the people wanted a better life for their children, so they moved to another country. They worked hard to have a better life and build their new country."

The sample response effectively addresses the task. It describes mass migrations and explains why they occurred.

 PRACTICE

To make this practice more like the TOEFL, cover each question while you are listening to the audio. You may take notes, and you may use your notes to help you answer the questions. When you hear the question, you may look at it and begin preparing your response. Record your response for each exercise.

Exercise 3.9.A

For this task, you will listen to part of a lecture. You will then be asked to summarize important information from the lecture. After you hear the question, you have 20 seconds to prepare your response and 60 seconds to speak.

 Album 6, Track 30

> Using points and examples from the talk, describe the duties of different types of managers in large hotels.

 Stop

Preparation Time – 20 seconds
Response Time – 60 seconds

Exercise 3.9.B

For this task, you will listen to part of a lecture. You will then be asked to summarize important information from the lecture. After you hear the question, you have 20 seconds to prepare your response and 60 seconds to speak.

 Album 6, Track 31

> Using points and examples from the lecture, explain how two features of the earth's surface influence climate.

 Stop

Preparation Time – 20 seconds
Response Time – 60 seconds

Exercise 3.9.C

For this task, you will listen to part of a lecture. You will then be asked to summarize important information from the lecture. After you hear the question, you have 20 seconds to prepare your response and 60 seconds to speak.

 Album 6, Track 32

> Using points and examples from the lecture, explain how crowd behavior can be unpredictable.

 Stop

Preparation Time – 20 seconds
Response Time – 60 seconds

Exercise 3.9.D

For this task, you will listen to part of a lecture. You will then be asked to summarize important information from the lecture. After you hear the question, you have 20 seconds to prepare your response and 60 seconds to speak.

 Album 6, Track 33

> Using points and details from the lecture, describe the Flatiron Building and explain how it got its name.

 Stop

Preparation Time – 20 seconds
Response Time – 60 seconds

Exercise 3.9.E

For this task, you will listen to part of a lecture. You will then be asked to summarize important information from the lecture. After you hear the question, you have 20 seconds to prepare your response and 60 seconds to speak.

 Album 6, Track 34

> Using points and details from the talk, describe the physical differences that animals had to adapt to when they moved from water to land.

 Stop

Preparation Time – 20 seconds
Response Time – 60 seconds

Key points for Exercises 3.9.A through 3.9.E are on page 663.

 EXTENSION

1. Listen again to the sample lecture. As you listen, fill in the missing information on the blank lines in the script. Do not try to write down every word. Take brief notes about only the key information. Check your notes with the audio script on page 734.

🎧 *Album 6, Track 29*

Listen to part of a talk in a world history class. The professor is talking about _____ _____.

In the nineteenth century, there were several periods when large numbers of people _____ _____ _____. These mass migrations were _____. One major movement was _____. This migration of Europeans involved around _____. Another mass migration was _____. Another was _____.

These large movements of people were made possible by _____ _____. Another important factor was _____ _____. In some places, immigrants were _____. This is what encouraged a lot of people—both immigrant and native–born—_____ _____ _____.

The majority of the people in these mass migrations came from _____ _____. The immigrants were motivated mainly by _____ _____.

Since most of the immigrants were unskilled workers, _____ _____ _____.

 Stop

2. Listen to your recorded response to one of the speaking tasks in Exercise 3.9.A through 3.9.E. Analyze and evaluate your response by answering the following questions:

   a. Does my response accurately summarize the main idea and major points from the lecture?
   b. Does my response include relevant supporting details and explanation from the lecture?
   c. Is my response coherent? Would it be easily understood by other listeners?
   d. Does my response answer the question effectively? Why or why not?
   e. How can I improve my responses for this type of question in the future?

3. Share and discuss your recorded response to one of the speaking questions in Exercise 3.9.A through 3.9.E. Work in a group of three or four students. Listen to each student's recorded response. Discuss each response by answering the following questions:

   a. Does the response accurately summarize the major ideas from the lecture?
   b. Does the response include relevant supporting details and explanation from the lecture?
   c. Is the response coherent? Why or why not?
   d. Can the response be easily understood? Why or why not?
   e. Does the response answer the question effectively? Why or why not?

   Make suggestions that will help each student improve in the future.

4. Obtain a recording of a real college or university lecture. Topics in history, anthropology, sociology, and psychology are good choices. Bring the recording to class. With the whole class, listen to two minutes of the recording. While you are listening, takes notes about important information in the lecture. Do not try to write down everything. Write only the key words and phrases that you think are important to remember.

   Then break into groups of three or four students. Compare your notes with the notes taken by the others in your group. Listen again to the same two–minute recording. In your group, discuss the key points made in the lecture. Choose one person to read your group's list of key points to the whole class.

3.10 Evaluating Integrated Speaking

FOCUS

What are the characteristics of good speakers in classroom discussions? Check all of the things that successful students do.

____ Listen to the points made by others.

____ Think before speaking.

____ Summarize ideas from assigned readings.

____ Talk only about topics relevant to the discussion.

____ Express ideas in complete sentences.

____ Speak so that others may understand.

____ Use appropriate vocabulary.

In fact, all of these qualities are important in classroom discussions. All are characteristics of successful students. Moreover, all are important in the integrated speaking tasks on the TOEFL.

STUDY

1. How Your Responses Will Be Evaluated

When you take the TOEFL, two trained evaluators will listen to your response to each integrated speaking task. They will judge each response on how well you answer the question by presenting relevant information from the reading and listening texts. They will also consider the clarity and coherence of your speech.

Among other things, your responses will be evaluated on how well you:

- convey relevant information from the reading and listening;
- develop points with appropriate examples and explanation;
- express ideas coherently; and
- make yourself understood by speaking clearly.

The evaluators will assign a score of 1 to 4, with 4 the highest score possible. They will use criteria similar to those in the table on the next page. A few small mistakes in vocabulary or pronunciation will not necessarily lower your score.

	INTEGRATED SPEAKING TASK **Description of Score Levels**
4	**A response at this level** ➤ effectively addresses the task by conveying relevant information and appropriate details from the listening and reading texts; and ➤ demonstrates a coherent expression of ideas, with appropriate grammar and vocabulary, but may contain some minor language errors; and ➤ demonstrates clear, fluid speech with high overall intelligibility, but may contain minor problems with pronunciation or intonation.
3	**A response at this level** ➤ conveys information relevant to the task, but shows some incompleteness, inaccuracy, or lack of detail; and ➤ demonstrates a fairly coherent expression of ideas, but may contain some errors in grammar or vocabulary that do not seriously interfere with meaning; and ➤ demonstrates generally clear, somewhat fluid speech, but may contain minor problems with pronunciation, intonation, or pacing and may occasionally require some listener effort.
2	**A response at this level** ➤ conveys some relevant information but omits key ideas, shows limited development, or shows misunderstanding of key ideas; or ➤ demonstrates a limited expression of ideas, inaccurate or unclear connections among ideas, or limited or inaccurate grammar and vocabulary; or ➤ demonstrates some clear speech, but contains problems with pronunciation, intonation, or pacing and may require significant listener effort.
1	**A response at this level** ➤ fails to provide much relevant content because ideas that are expressed are inaccurate, limited, or vague; or ➤ demonstrates a limited control of grammar and vocabulary that severely limits expression of ideas and connections among ideas; or ➤ demonstrates fragmented speech with frequent pauses and consistent problems with pronunciation and intonation that obscure meaning and require great listener effort.
0	**A response at this level** ➤ is not related to the topic; or ➤ is absent.

SPEAKING

 PRACTICE

Exercise 3.10.A

Read the following information from a textbook. Then listen to the lecture and question. Then listen to and read the sample response.

Reading Time – 45 seconds

AGENTS OF SOCIALIZATION

Socialization is the process by which we learn how to view the world and interpret our experiences. As we develop from infant to child to adult, we literally "learn our place," including the positions we will occupy and the roles attached to these positions. Certain people and institutions act as agents of socialization that teach us about the society we live in, including its rules. Agents of socialization transmit the knowledge we need to function as adults. They also give us opportunities to practice the social roles we will eventually acquire.

 Album 6, Track 35

> Explain agents of socialization and how the examples given by the professor illustrate the concept.

SAMPLE RESPONSE   Score: _____

> "Agents of socialization are the people who teach us important lessons about life. They teach us about our social roles. For example, the professor talks about parents. Parents are the first agents of socialization because they teach us how to behave. They teach us how to see the world and how to treat our family. Parents are role models for how to be an adult. Another example is peers. They are friends and classmates. They teach us the social role of friend. Also, they teach us how to have fun. Parents and peers are different, but both influence our goals. Both parents and peers are important agents of socialization."

 Stop

Now evaluate the sample response according to the descriptions of the four levels on page 353. What score do you think the response should receive? Why?

Exercise 3.10.B

Listen to the conversation and question. Then listen to and read the sample response.

 Album 6, Track 36

> Briefly summarize the problem the speakers are discussing. Then state which solution you would recommend. Explain the reasons for your recommendation.

SAMPLE RESPONSE   Score: _____

"The woman has a problem. She lives in an apartment off campus. She rides the bus to school, but the bus schedule doesn't work well for her. Her class starts at seven o'clock, but the bus leaves at six o'clock. She arrives at campus too early for her class. The speakers discuss possible solutions to the problem. One solution is a bicycle. If the woman had a bicycle, she could leave her apartment later because she would not have to get up early to take the bus. I recommend that she gets a bicycle. I prefer this solution because she could arrive at campus at a better time. Also, she could ride her bicycle on a path by the river, which would be safe and pleasant."

 Stop

1. Does the response accurately summarize the problem? What details from the conversation are included?

2. What opinion is stated in the response? What reason is given to support this opinion?

3. Evaluate the sample response according to the descriptions of the four levels on page 353. What score do you think the response should receive? Why?

Exercise 3.10.C

For this task, you will read a short passage about a campus situation, listen to a conversation, and then speak in response to a question about what you have read and heard. Do not look at the question until the conversation has ended. Do not look at the reading passage while you are speaking. Record your response.

Read the following announcement from a university president.

Reading Time – 45 seconds

A NEW BUILDING ON CAMPUS

To address our growing student population and the consequent need for facilities, the president of Walker University is proud to announce the approval of plans for construction of a new classroom building on the east side of campus. The two–story structure will contain three lecture halls, eight seminar rooms, a study lounge, and twenty offices for faculty and staff. The project also includes a paved courtyard that will function as a multipurpose outdoor space. An adjoining parking lot will accommodate 200 vehicles. Construction is scheduled to begin in the spring, and the new building will be ready for use in the fall term.

Now cover the passage and listen to the conversation. You may take notes, and you may use your notes to help you answer the question. After you hear the question, begin preparing your response. You may look at the question, but NOT at the passage. You have 30 seconds to prepare your response and 60 seconds to speak. Record your response.

 Album 6, Track 37

> The woman expresses her opinion about the plan for a new building. State her opinion and explain the reasons she gives for holding that opinion.

 Stop

Preparation Time – 30 seconds
Response Time – 60 seconds

Listen to your recorded response. Analyze and evaluate your response by answering the following questions:

1. Does my response include accurate and relevant information from the conversation and the reading?

2. Does my response accurately describe the woman's opinion? Does it explain the reasons for her opinion?

3. Evaluate your response according to the descriptions of the four levels on page 353. What score do you think your response should receive? Why?

Exercise 3.10.D

For this task, you will listen to part of a lecture. You will then be asked to summarize important information from the lecture. After you hear the question, you have 20 seconds to prepare your response and 60 seconds to speak. Record your response.

 Album 6, Track 38

> Using points and examples from the lecture, explain some of the properties and functions of spider webs.

 Stop

Preparation Time – 20 seconds
Response Time – 60 seconds

Listen to your recorded response. Analyze and evaluate your response by answering the following questions:

1. Does my response accurately summarize the main idea and major points from the lecture? Does it include relevant examples and explanation from the lecture?

2. Is my response coherent? Would it be easily understood by other listeners?

3. Evaluate your response according to the descriptions of the four levels on page 353. What score do you think your response should receive? Why?

Answers to Exercise 3.10.A through 3.10.D are on page 664.

 **EXTENSION**

1. Study the descriptions of the four score levels on page 353. Make sure you understand the description for each level. Check your understanding of the meaning of these words and phrases:

addresses the task	incompleteness	listener effort
coherent	inaccuracy	key ideas
fluid speech	lack of detail	vague
intelligibility	pacing	fragmented speech

2. Review your recorded responses to the integrated speaking tasks in units 3.5 through 3.9. Evaluate each response according to the descriptions of the four levels on page 353. What score would your response receive? What are the areas of strength in your speaking? What are your most serious problems? What can you do to improve your speaking and earn a high score on the TOEFL?

PROGRESS – 3.5 through 3.10

QUIZ 4

Time – approximately 15 minutes

There are four questions in this quiz. You may take notes, and you may use your notes to help prepare your responses. Record your responses. Each response will earn a score of 1, 2, 3, or 4, with 4 the highest score. Add the four scores to obtain your total score.

QUESTION 1

In this question, you will read a short passage about a campus situation, listen to a conversation, and then speak in response to a question about what you have read and heard. After you hear the question, you have 30 seconds to prepare your response and 60 seconds to speak.

Read the following announcement from a university newspaper.

Reading Time – 45 seconds

NOTICE OF FREE CAREER WORKSHOP

Taylor University invites all students and prospective students to take part in a free career workshop and resource fair, on Saturday, February 10. The purpose of the daylong event is to provide resources to students who want to pursue careers in business, health services, or community development. Dr. Janis Morris, past president of the university, will give the opening address. The resource fair will provide information on employment in the region and educational programs at the university. Employers and career counselors will answer questions.

Now cover the passage and listen to the recording. When you hear the question, begin preparing your response.

 Album 7, Track 1

> The man expresses his opinion about the career workshop. State his opinion and explain the reasons he gives for holding that opinion.

 Stop

Preparation Time – 30 seconds
Response Time – 60 seconds

QUESTION 2

In this question, you will read a short passage, then listen to a lecture on the same topic, and then speak in response to a question about what you have read and heard. After you hear the question, you have 30 seconds to prepare your response and 60 seconds to speak.

Read the following information from a textbook.

Reading Time – 50 seconds

RECIPROCITY

Reciprocity is an interchange between parties in which both sides benefit equally. Reciprocity is based on sharing and balance. To share is to bond. Sharing establishes a reciprocal relationship that is not easily denied. People give in order to receive. When both parties expect reciprocity, each is more likely to be satisfied than if one side felt entitled to receive without giving. We enter into reciprocal relationships almost every time we interact with others. When we buy something, we expect it to be a balanced exchange, in which we give and receive equal value. Reciprocity contributes to our sense of fairness.

Now cover the passage and listen to the recording. When you hear the question, begin preparing your response.

 Album 7, Track 2

Use the examples from the lecture to explain the concept of reciprocity.

 Stop

Preparation Time – 30 seconds
Response Time – 60 seconds

QUESTION 3

In this question, you will listen to a conversation. You will then be asked to talk about the information in the conversation and to give your opinion about the ideas presented. After you hear the question, you have 20 seconds to prepare your response and 60 seconds to speak.

 Album 7, Track 3

> Briefly summarize the problem the students are discussing. Then state which solution you would recommend. Explain the reasons for your recommendation.

 Stop

Preparation Time – 20 seconds
Response Time – 60 seconds

QUESTION 4

In this question, you will listen to part of a lecture. You will then be asked to summarize important information from the lecture. After you hear the question, you have 20 seconds to prepare your response and 60 seconds to speak.

 Album 7, Track 4

> Using points and examples from the talk, describe the uses of gestures and facial expressions in human communication.

 Stop

Preparation Time – 20 seconds
Response Time – 60 seconds

Key points for Speaking Quiz 4 are on page 664.

Record your score on the Progress Chart on page 792.

PROGRESS – 3.5 through 3.10

QUIZ 5

Time – approximately 15 minutes

There are four questions in this quiz. You may take notes, and you may use your notes to help prepare your responses. Record your responses. Each response will earn a score of 1, 2, 3, or 4, with 4 the highest score. Add the four scores to obtain your total score.

QUESTION 1

In this question, you will read a short passage about a campus situation, listen to a conversation, and then speak in response to a question about what you have read and heard. After you hear the question, you have 30 seconds to prepare your response and 60 seconds to speak.

Read the following information from a college course catalog.

Reading Time – 45 seconds

BASIC COLLEGE WRITING

The objective of this course is to write effective college essays that integrate assigned readings, class discussions, and the writer's knowledge and experience. Students will produce a total of six essays. Each week, students will have two hours of lecture and discussion, two hours in a writing workshop, and one hour in a peer feedback group. In the feedback group, students will read and respond to each other's writing. The course will help students prepare for future study and/or careers in writing, humanities, literature, and teaching.

Now cover the passage and listen to the recording. When you hear the question, begin preparing your response.

 Album 7, Track 5

> The man expresses his opinion about the peer feedback group. State his opinion and explain the reasons he gives for holding that opinion.

 Stop

Preparation Time – 30 seconds
Response Time – 60 seconds

QUESTION 2

In this question, you will read a short passage, then listen to a lecture on the same topic, and then speak in response to a question about what you have read and heard. After you hear the question, you have 30 seconds to prepare your response and 60 seconds to speak.

Read the following information from a textbook.

Reading Time – 50 seconds

COHORTS

Social scientists use the term "cohort" to describe a group of individuals who were born around the same time, usually within a span of five to ten years. Members of the same cohort move through history together. They share certain historical and cultural influences because they experience major events at the same age. The life experiences of one cohort will be different from those of another, even a cohort that is just a few years older or younger. This is because the timing of historical events interacts with developmental issues, producing unique patterns of influence for each cohort.

Now cover the passage and listen to the recording. When you hear the question, begin preparing your response.

 Album 7, Track 6

> Explain the concept of cohort and how the examples given by the professor illustrate the concept.

 Stop

Preparation Time – 30 seconds
Response Time – 60 seconds

QUESTION 3

In this question, you will listen to a conversation. You will then be asked to talk about the information in the conversation and to give your opinion about the ideas presented. After you hear the question, you have 20 seconds to prepare your response and 60 seconds to speak.

 Album 7, Track 7

> The speakers discuss two possible solutions to the woman's problem. Briefly describe the problem. Then state which solution you prefer and explain why.

 Stop

Preparation Time – 20 seconds
Response Time – 60 seconds

QUESTION 4

In this question, you will listen to part of a lecture. You will then be asked to summarize important information from the lecture. After you hear the question, you have 20 seconds to prepare your response and 60 seconds to speak.

 Album 7, Track 8

> Using points and details from the lecture, explain what the pyramid chart and the wheel chart reveal about a company.

 Stop

Preparation Time – 20 seconds
Response Time – 60 seconds

Key points for Speaking Quiz 5 are on page 665.

Record your score on the Progress Chart on page 792.

PROGRESS – 3.5 through 3.10

QUIZ 6

Time – approximately 15 minutes

There are four questions in this quiz. You may take notes, and you may use your notes to help prepare your responses. Record your responses. Each response will earn a score of 1, 2, 3, or 4, with 4 the highest score. Add the four scores to obtain your total score.

QUESTION 1

In this question, you will read a short passage about a campus situation, listen to a conversation, and then speak in response to a question about what you have read and heard. After you hear the question, you have 30 seconds to prepare your response and 60 seconds to speak.

Read the following announcement from a university bulletin board.

Reading Time – 45 seconds

VOLUNTEERS NEEDED FOR CONFERENCE

Students are needed to work as volunteers during the university's 2–day conference on global warming, April 6–7. Volunteer positions are available to set up conference rooms, assist guest speakers, and work at the information booth. Volunteers are asked to work a 2–hour shift on the day before the conference or on either day during the conference. In return, volunteers receive a free conference T–shirt and admission to the reception for guest speakers on April 7. To volunteer, go to the planning meeting on March 15 or talk to Steve in the Environmental Studies office.

Now cover the passage and listen to the recording. When you hear the question, begin preparing your response.

 Album 7, Track 9

> The woman expresses her opinion about volunteering for the conference. State her opinion and explain the reasons she gives for holding that opinion.

 Stop

Preparation Time – 30 seconds
Response Time – 60 seconds

QUESTION 2

In this question, you will read a short passage, then listen to a lecture on the same topic, and then speak in response to a question about what you have read and heard. After you hear the question, you have 30 seconds to prepare your response and 60 seconds to speak.

Read the following information from a textbook.

Reading Time – 45 seconds

THE CHASE FILM

The chase film was a popular form of comedy during the silent film era of the early twentieth century. In a chase film, the story was simple to tell and simple for the audience to follow. All that filmmakers needed to do was to establish some offense—a theft, an insult, or a boy's naughty behavior—and then start a humorous chase after the offender. The chase could be extended for several minutes, through any number of scenes and situations. The fast movement of the chase provided visual excitement, often with the person being chased and the chasers all running forward, past the camera.

Now cover the passage and listen to the recording. When you hear the question, begin preparing your response.

 Album 7, Track 10

> Define the chase film, and explain how the examples given in the lecture illustrate the definition.

 Stop

Preparation Time – 30 seconds
Response Time – 60 seconds

QUESTION 3

In this question, you will listen to a conversation. You will then be asked to talk about the information in the conversation and to give your opinion about the ideas presented. After you hear the question, you have 20 seconds to prepare your response and 60 seconds to speak.

 Album 7, Track 11

> Briefly summarize the problem the students are discussing. Then state which solution you would recommend. Explain the reasons for your recommendation.

 Stop

Preparation Time – 20 seconds
Response Time – 60 seconds

QUESTION 4

In this question, you will listen to part of a lecture. You will then be asked to summarize important information from the lecture. After you hear the question, you have 20 seconds to prepare your response and 60 seconds to speak.

 Album 7, Track 12

> Using points and examples from the lecture, explain some of the common causes of insomnia.

 Stop

Preparation Time – 20 seconds
Response Time – 60 seconds

Key points for Speaking Quiz 6 are on page 665.

Record your score on the Progress Chart on page 792.

PROGRESS – 3.1 through 3.10

QUIZ 7 *Time – approximately 20 minutes*

There are six questions in this quiz. You may take notes, and you may use your notes to help prepare your responses. Record your responses. Each response will earn a score of 1, 2, 3, or 4, with 4 the highest score. Add the six scores to obtain your total score.

QUESTION 1

In this question, you will be asked to talk about a familiar topic. After you hear the question, you will have 15 seconds to prepare your response and 45 seconds to speak.

 Album 7, Track 13

> What book have you read that you would recommend to others? Explain why you think other people should read this book. Include details and examples to support your explanation.

 Stop

Preparation Time – 15 seconds
Response Time – 45 seconds

QUESTION 2

In this question, you will be asked to give your opinion about a familiar topic. After you hear the question, you will have 15 seconds to prepare your response and 45 seconds to speak.

 Album 7, Track 14

> Some people have a few favorite foods that they eat most of the time. Others are always trying new dishes and styles of cooking. Which do you prefer and why? Include details and examples in your explanation.

 Stop

Preparation Time – 15 seconds
Response Time – 45 seconds

QUESTION 3

In this question, you will read a short passage about a campus situation, listen to a conversation, and then speak in response to a question about what you have read and heard. After you hear the question, you have 30 seconds to prepare your response and 60 seconds to speak.

Read the following announcement from the dean's office.

Reading Time – 45 seconds

PROPOSAL TO LIMIT STUDENT COURSE LOAD

The dean's office has proposed placing a limit on the number of credit hours for which students are allowed to register in a term. Currently, there is no limit on how many credits a student may pursue in a single semester. The proposal would impose a maximum course load per semester of 20 credit hours, with 12 to 20 credit hours indicating full–time status. This proposal comes in response to an increase in the number of students with heavy loads who either withdraw from courses or do not complete courses. The dean will speak about the proposal on Wednesday at 12:30 p.m. in Lecture Hall 2.

Now cover the passage and listen to the recording. When you hear the question, begin preparing your response.

 Album 7, Track 15

> The woman expresses her opinion about the proposal. State her opinion and explain the reasons she gives for holding that opinion.

 Stop

Preparation Time – 30 seconds
Response Time – 60 seconds

QUESTION 4

In this question, you will read a short passage, then listen to a lecture on the same topic, and then speak in response to a question about what you have read and heard. After you hear the question, you have 30 seconds to prepare your response and 60 seconds to speak.

Read the following information from a textbook.

Reading Time – 50 seconds

COEVOLUTION

Coevolution is the joint evolution of two species that are dependent on each other. Each species influences the other, so they evolve at the same time. Coevolution is a result of complex interactions involving mutual evolutionary changes. A change in one species acts as a selective force on another species, which adapts in response. The adaptation in the second species, in turn, is a selective force on the first species. Hence, the two species trade adaptations and evolve together. Coevolution often occurs when both species receive a benefit, such as a higher rate of survival.

Now cover the passage and listen to the recording. When you hear the question, begin preparing your response.

 Album 7, Track 16

Use the examples from the lecture to explain the concept of coevolution.

 Stop

Preparation Time – 30 seconds
Response Time – 60 seconds

QUESTION 5

In this question, you will listen to a conversation. You will then be asked to talk about the information in the conversation and to give your opinion about the ideas presented. After you hear the question, you have 20 seconds to prepare your response and 60 seconds to speak.

 Album 7, Track 17

> The speakers discuss possible solutions to the man's problem. Briefly describe the problem. Then state which solution you prefer and explain why.

 Stop

Preparation Time – 20 seconds
Response Time – 60 seconds

QUESTION 6

In this question, you will listen to part of a lecture. You will then be asked to summarize important information from the lecture. After you hear the question, you have 20 seconds to prepare your response and 60 seconds to speak.

 Album 7, Track 18

> Using points and examples from the lecture, explain the three main ways that manufacturers sell goods to consumers.

 Stop

Preparation Time – 20 seconds
Response Time – 60 seconds

Key points for Speaking Quiz 7 are on pages 665–666.

Record your score on the Progress Chart on page 792.

PROGRESS – 3.1 through 3.10

QUIZ 8

Time – approximately 20 minutes

There are six questions in this quiz. You may take notes, and you may use your notes to help prepare your responses. Record your responses. Each response will earn a score of 1, 2, 3, or 4, with 4 the highest score. Add the six scores to obtain your total score.

QUESTION 1

In this question, you will be asked to talk about a familiar topic. After you hear the question, you will have 15 seconds to prepare your response and 45 seconds to speak.

 Album 7, Track 19

> What is the best gift you have ever received? Describe this gift and explain its importance to you. Include details and examples in your explanation.

 Stop

Preparation Time – 15 seconds
Response Time – 45 seconds

QUESTION 2

In this question, you will be asked to give your opinion about a familiar topic. After you hear the question, you will have 15 seconds to prepare your response and 45 seconds to speak.

 Album 7, Track 20

> Some students like to study for a long period of hours at a time. Others divide their study time into many shorter sessions. Which method do you think is better for studying and why? Include details and examples in your explanation.

 Stop

Preparation Time – 15 seconds
Response Time – 45 seconds

QUESTION 3

In this question, you will read a short passage about a campus situation, listen to a conversation, and then speak in response to a question about what you have read and heard. After you hear the question, you have 30 seconds to prepare your response and 60 seconds to speak.

Read the following information from a college bulletin.

Reading Time – 45 seconds

SCHOLARSHIP PROGRAMS

A variety of scholarship programs at Middleton College enable deserving students to attend college and lessen their financial burden. Most scholarships are available only for full–time students. Scholarships are generally awarded to prospective students who have excelled in their previous studies or made distinguished contributions in their community or other work. A separate application is required for each scholarship applied for. Scholarship applications are due in the Financial Aid Office by May 1 for the academic year beginning the following September.

Now cover the passage and listen to the recording. When you hear the question, begin preparing your response.

 Album 7, Track 21

> The man expresses his opinion on applying for scholarships. State his opinion and explain the reasons he gives for holding that opinion.

 Stop

Preparation Time – 30 seconds
Response Time – 60 seconds

QUESTION 4

In this question, you will read a short passage, then listen to a lecture on the same topic, and then speak in response to a question about what you have read and heard. After you hear the question, you have 30 seconds to prepare your response and 60 seconds to speak.

Read the following information from a textbook.

Reading Time – 50 seconds

THE CONVOY

The term "convoy" describes the network of social relationships that everyone carries forward through life. The convoy provides valuable social support because it forms a protective layer of family and friends who help a person manage the challenges of life. The members of one's convoy are the individuals with whom one has close and intimate relationships. The convoy does not remain static as it moves through time. Rather, membership changes over the years. New members are added, and members are lost, but the core members of the convoy tend to remain constant over long periods.

Now cover the passage and listen to the recording. When you hear the question, begin preparing your response.

 Album 7, Track 22

Explain the convoy and how the examples given by the professor illustrate the concept.

 Stop

Preparation Time – 30 seconds
Response Time – 60 seconds

QUESTION 5

In this question, you will listen to a conversation. You will then be asked to talk about the information in the conversation and to give your opinion about the ideas presented. After you hear the question, you have 20 seconds to prepare your response and 60 seconds to speak.

 Album 7, Track 23

> Briefly summarize the problem the speakers are discussing. Then state which solution you would recommend. Explain the reasons for your recommendation.

 Stop

Preparation Time – 20 seconds
Response Time – 60 seconds

QUESTION 6

In this question, you will listen to part of a lecture. You will then be asked to summarize important information from the lecture. After you hear the question, you have 20 seconds to prepare your response and 60 seconds to speak.

 Album 7, Track 24

> Using points and examples from the lecture, explain how various abiotic factors in ecosystems affect plants and animals.

 Stop

Preparation Time – 20 seconds
Response Time – 60 seconds

Key points for Speaking Quiz 8 are on page 666.

Record your score on the Progress Chart on page 792.

PART 4 — WRITING

The Writing section of the TOEFL measures your ability to plan and write responses to questions in essay format. You must be able to select and convey relevant information, organize and support ideas, and demonstrate that you can use English effectively.

There are two questions in the Writing section. The first question is an integrated reading–listening–writing task, in which you will read a short passage, listen to a short lecture, and then write a response based on what you have read and heard. The second question is an independent writing task, in which you will write a response based on your own knowledge and experience. Both writing questions are about topics that are appropriate for international students. You do not need special knowledge of any subject to respond to the questions.

WRITING SECTION			
Question	**Reading Time**	**Listening Time**	**Writing Time**
Integrated task	3 minutes	2 minutes	20 minutes
Independent task	—	—	30 minutes

The entire Writing section takes approximately one hour to complete. This includes the time that you spend reading the directions, reading the passage, listening to the lecture, and writing your responses to both questions. A clock at the top of the screen shows how much writing time is left for each question. For the integrated writing task, you will use headphones to listen to the lecture. You will be able to change the volume of the sound. The clock does not count down while you are listening to the lecture.

The test supervisor will give you paper for taking notes. You may take notes during both writing tasks, and you may use your notes to help you write your responses. However, at the end of the test you must give all of your notes to the test supervisor. Your notes will not be scored; only what you type on the computer will be scored.

You must type your responses to both writing questions in the typing box on the computer screen. You will not be allowed to write your responses by hand.

THE INTEGRATED WRITING TASK

The integrated–skills writing task measures your ability to understand key ideas from an academic reading passage and a short lecture, and to write a response to a question about them. You must determine what information in the lecture relates in some way to information in the reading. Then you must organize and compose a response in standard written English. The task does *not* require you to express your personal opinion.

In your response, you must demonstrate your ability to:

- organize ideas effectively in answering the question;
- draw requested connections between the lecture and the reading;
- develop ideas with appropriate examples and explanation;
- display unity and coherence; and
- use English words and sentences effectively.

Your response is expected to have about 150 to 225 words. It will be read by two qualified evaluators who will score it on a scale of 1 to 5, with 5 being the highest score possible. You will receive a score of 0 if you do not write a response, do not write about the given question, or do not write in English. Your score on the integrated writing task will be combined with your score on the independent writing task. The total number of points you earn for both writing questions will be converted to a Writing section score of 0 to 30.

First, you have three minutes to read a passage that is 250 to 300 words long. Here is an example:

The discovery of penicillin and other antibiotic drugs was the most dramatic medical development of the twentieth century. These new drugs quickly became known as "wonder drugs" because of their ability to cure major forms of bacterial infection quickly and completely. Antibiotics made it possible for hospital patients to survive during and after surgery. No longer did patients have to depend largely on their body's own immune system to fight off infections. These infections could be attacked directly with antibiotics.

Antibiotics have given the medical profession powerful tools to fight a wide range of specific diseases. The development of antibiotics in the 1930s rested on the belief in the existence of certain chemicals that had the power to destroy specific microorganisms without injuring the human body at the same time. Advances in chemistry and in the study of bacteria quickened the discovery of such chemical wonders. The development of penicillin in the 1940s laid the foundation for even more powerful weapons against specific diseases. Since that time, researchers have identified hundreds of antibiotic substances that are effective against one or another type of bacteria.

Among the most spectacular effects of antibiotics are reductions in the number of deaths from pneumonia and tuberculosis. Penicillin, one of the earliest of the wonder drugs, is a highly successful cure for pneumonia. Just ten thousand units of penicillin four times a day will be enough to cure bacterial pneumonia in most patients. Another important antibiotic is streptomycin, which is potent against tuberculosis. As a result, tuberculosis is no longer the life-threatening illness it once was.

Then the passage will disappear temporarily while you listen to a short lecture on the same topic. The passage will reappear later and be available to you during the writing time.

While you are listening, you will see a picture of the professor and the class:

(Narrator)   Now listen to part of a lecture on the topic you just read about.

(Professor) Several facts refute the idea that antibiotics are wonder drugs. First, as soon as we developed antibiotics, new strains of bacteria appeared that were resistant to some or all of the drugs. For example, hospitals started using antibiotics in the 1950s, but today many drug–resistant hospital infections make it safer for some people to stay home than go to the hospital. The rise in dangerous hospital infections is clear evidence that antibiotics are not the wonder drugs they used to be.

Second, bacteria can create very effective weapons against antibiotics. It happens like this. If you douse a colony of bacteria with an antibiotic, the colony will be killed—that is, all except for a few cells that carry a resistance gene for that particular antibiotic. The surviving cells quickly multiply, and soon you have a new strain of bacteria that's resistant to that drug. Some bacteria develop enzymes to counteract every antibiotic we throw at them. So, no matter what antibiotic we use, the bacteria will come up with a way to make it useless.

Third, antibiotics are no longer effective cures for some infections. For example, today you could treat a pneumonia patient with 24 million units of penicillin a day, but the patient might still die. This is because several strains of bacteria are now completely resistant to penicillin. Another consequence is the reappearance of tuberculosis as a major illness. Twenty years ago, doctors thought tuberculosis was a defeated disease. Since then, however, new cases of tuberculosis have increased by 20 percent, and several strains of the disease are resistant to any drug we attack them with.

(Narrator)   Summarize the points made in the lecture, being sure to explain how they cast doubt on specific points made in the reading passage.

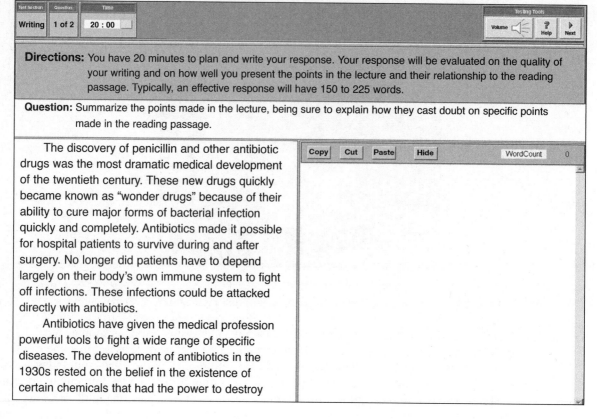

Directions: You have 20 minutes to plan and write your response. Your response will be evaluated on the quality of your writing and on how well you present the points in the lecture and their relationship to the reading passage. Typically, an effective response will have 150 to 225 words.

Question: Summarize the points made in the lecture, being sure to explain how they cast doubt on specific points made in the reading passage.

The discovery of penicillin and other antibiotic drugs was the most dramatic medical development of the twentieth century. These new drugs quickly became known as "wonder drugs" because of their ability to cure major forms of bacterial infection quickly and completely. Antibiotics made it possible for hospital patients to survive during and after surgery. No longer did patients have to depend largely on their body's own immune system to fight off infections. These infections could be attacked directly with antibiotics.

Antibiotics have given the medical profession powerful tools to fight a wide range of specific diseases. The development of antibiotics in the 1930s rested on the belief in the existence of certain chemicals that had the power to destroy

Copy | Cut | Paste | Hide | WordCount | 0

After the lecture, you will both *hear* and *see* the writing question. Then you have 20 minutes to plan, write, and revise your response. The reading passage is available during this time. You may use your notes from the lecture to help you write your response.

As you type, the computer will show your word count—how many words you have written. An effective response usually has approximately 150 to 225 words.

THE INDEPENDENT WRITING TASK

The independent writing task measures your ability to write an essay in response to a given topic. You must be able to generate and organize ideas, to develop and support these ideas, and to compose in standard written English.

In your essay, you must demonstrate your ability to:

- organize ideas effectively in answering the question;
- state and support an opinion;
- develop ideas with appropriate reasons, examples, and personal experience;
- display unity and coherence; and
- use English words and sentences effectively.

Your essay is expected to have a minimum of about 300 words. It will be read by two qualified evaluators who will score it on a scale of 1 to 5, with 5 being the highest score possible. You will receive a score of 0 if you do not write an essay, do not write about the assigned topic, or do not write in English. Your score on the independent writing task will be combined with your score on the integrated writing task. The total number of points you earn for both writing questions will be converted to a Writing section score of 0 to 30.

Here is an example of an independent writing task:

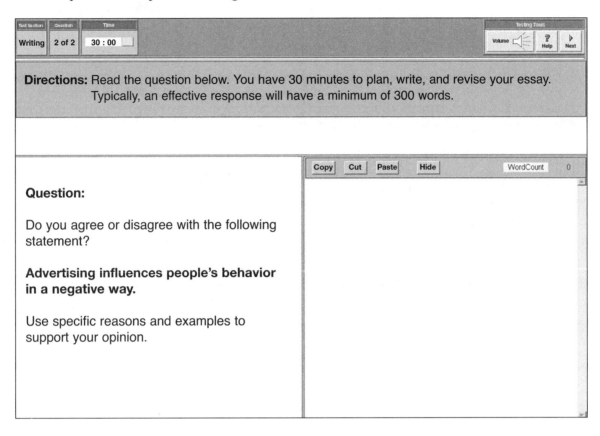

STRATEGIES FOR THE WRITING SECTION

Before the Test

- Listen to a variety of recorded materials that use academic English, such as university lectures, documentaries, educational television programs, and in–depth radio news programs. Practice taking notes as you listen. Practice identifying main ideas and supporting details in your notes.

- Work on building your vocabulary. Practice using transitions—connecting words and expressions— to make your writing more coherent.

- Become familiar with the types of writing questions that appear on the TOEFL.

- Become familiar with the English keyboard, and practice typing on it.

- Become familiar with the TOEFL testing tools, such as **Copy**, **Cut**, and **Paste**. Practice using these keys to move text and make corrections.

- Your own best strategy: _____

During the Test—Integrated Task

✐ While you are reading the passage, think about its general message and organization. Notice key words and phrases that appear throughout the passage.

✐ While you are listening to the lecture, focus on major ideas. Listen for terms and concepts that are repeated throughout the lecture. Take notes only about the information that will be important to remember: key points, examples, and reasons. Do not try to write down everything you hear. Do not allow your writing to detract from your listening.

✐ When the integrated writing question is presented, take a few minutes to plan your response before you start writing. Think about everything the question requires you to do. Review your notes and the reading passage. Select and organize appropriate information to answer each part of the question.

✐ Organize your response logically into paragraphs. Generally, each paragraph should develop one major point. Answer all parts of the question, using appropriate ideas and information from the lecture and reading. Use your own words. Do not just copy sentences from the reading passage.

✐ Use your time wisely. You have 20 minutes to plan and write your response. Allow a few minutes at the end to read and revise what you have written. Check and correct your grammar, word choice, spelling, and punctuation.

✐ Your own best strategy: _____

_____

During the Test—Independent Task

✐ When the independent writing question is presented, take a few minutes to plan your essay before you start writing. Read the question carefully and make sure you understand everything it asks you to do. Organize your ideas by making an outline.

✐ Write only about the given topic. Clearly state your opinion about the topic. Support all of your points with evidence: examples, facts, reasons, personal experiences, and other details.

✐ Use grammatical structures and vocabulary that you are familiar with. Use transitions to make your sentences and paragraphs coherent.

✐ Use your time wisely. You have 30 minutes to plan and write your essay. Allow a few minutes at the end to read and revise what you have written. Check and correct your grammar, word choice, spelling, and punctuation.

✐ Do not be concerned about whether the essay readers will agree with your opinion. Be concerned about whether your essay states your opinion clearly, supports your opinion with appropriate details, shows organization and development, and uses appropriate sentence structure and vocabulary.

✐ Your own best strategy: _____

_____

4.1 Integrated Writing: Connecting Information

🔍 FOCUS

Imagine you are enrolled in a university course. Your professor asks you to read an article for homework as preparation for the lecture on the following day. What do you expect from this assignment? Check all of the statements that might be true.

___ The reading will be a waste of time.

___ The reading will give background information for the lecture.

___ The lecture will be about a completely different topic from that of the reading.

___ The lecture will present an opposing view of ideas in the reading.

___ The lecture will give examples to illustrate concepts in the reading.

___ You will have to demonstrate your understanding of the reading and lecture.

Because your professor assigned the reading as preparation for the lecture, you can expect the reading to give background information about the lecture topic. You can expect that your professor will discuss the reading—perhaps by presenting an opposing view, or by providing examples to illustrate concepts in the reading. You can expect that you will have to demonstrate your understanding of ideas in the reading and the lecture.

This type of activity is common in university study. You will read course material, listen to a professor talk about the material, and then demonstrate your understanding of the material by responding to questions in essay format. This type of activity also occurs on the TOEFL in the form of the integrated reading–listening–writing task.

 STUDY

1. The Integrated Writing Task

The TOEFL integrated writing task involves the three language skills of reading, listening, and writing. In the integrated writing task, you will:

⤳ read a short passage about an academic topic;
⤳ listen to a short lecture about the same topic; and
⤳ write a response that connects information from the lecture and the reading.

You have 20 minutes to plan and write your response to the integrated writing task. Your response will be evaluated on the quality of your writing and on how well you convey the key points in the lecture and their relationship to information in the reading. An effective response usually has 150 to 225 words.

WRITING

2. Connecting Information from Two Sources

The reading passage provides information on an academic topic. The lecture expands on the same topic or presents a different perspective on the topic. The lecture will not merely repeat the points in the reading passage; rather, it will react to the reading in a particular way. For example, the lecture may contradict or challenge ideas in the reading.

The integrated writing task is more about the lecture than the reading, but it requires you to draw a connection between the two. Among the possible types of connections between the two texts, you might be asked to explain how points in the lecture:

- oppose, contradict, refute, challenge, or cast doubt on points in the reading;
- present an alternate view of the reading topic; or
- support or illustrate points in the reading.

The written response should contain key ideas from the lecture and the reading.

3. Sample Task

Reading Time – 3 minutes

> The plow is one of our greatest inventions because it makes large–scale agriculture possible. The practice of turning the soil before planting is very old, but until the plow was invented, farming was limited to what humans could do by hand. The plow has enabled us to cultivate larger and larger areas of land, and in places where farming was previously impossible. Advances in plowing technology have made it possible to convert native grasslands into huge fields of corn and wheat.
>
> Tilling the soil with a plow improves the soil in numerous ways. The plow turns over the upper layer of soil, bringing fresh nutrients to the surface. This also loosens and aerates the soil, improving its ability to hold moisture and nutrients. Freshly turned soil is darker in color, which enhances soil warming and thereby promotes seed germination. Turning the soil buries crop residues—the stalks, leaves, and roots remaining from the previous year's harvest—allowing them to break down more quickly. Plowing incorporates these residues into the soil, along with any manure, limestone, and commercial fertilizers that are applied. In addition, plowing creates a pattern of low and high ridges in the soil, forming water channels that allow the soil to drain properly.
>
> The plow reduces the costs and labor requirements of agriculture. With the introduction of animal–drawn plows, fewer people were needed to till the same amount of land. In time, mechanized plowing further reduced labor requirements, permitting the labor of a few people to sustain many. The plow greatly reduced the amount of time needed to prepare a field, consequently allowing a farmer to work a larger area of land. This, in turn, increased each farmer's crop yields.

The key points in the reading are:

- The plow is a great invention.
- The plow has enabled large–scale agriculture.
- Plowing improves the soil in numerous ways.
- The plow reduces the costs and labor requirements of agriculture.

Listening and Writing

 Album 8, Track 1

(Narrator)

Now listen to part of a lecture on the topic you just read about.

(Professor)

The plow is responsible for larger crop yields, but there are also some problems with it. For one thing, simply producing large amounts of food is not enough. Food has to be produced in a sustainable way so natural resources are conserved for future generations. No–till agriculture—farming without the plow—has the potential to help develop a more sustainable agriculture.

Another problem is that overuse of the plow is a major cause of damage to the land. Plowing leaves the soil vulnerable to erosion by wind and water. An example is the Dust Bowl disaster, when extensive plowing, combined with long periods of no rain, caused the dry topsoil to be blown away in dust storms. Plowing also increases erosion by water, and the channels in fields promote the runoff of soil and fertilizers into lakes, rivers, and oceans.

In contrast, no–till farming minimizes soil damage. Instead of plowing under the remains of last year's crop—stalks and other litter—farmers leave it on the fields, where it acts as mulch to conserve water and protect the soil from erosion. Leaving crop residue in place increases levels of organic matter and improves soil productivity.

Finally, overuse of the plow is a threat to rural livelihoods, particularly in the developing world. No–till farming has economic advantages. For example, the number of passes over a field needed to grow and harvest a crop decreases from seven or more to about four, thereby saving fuel and labor costs. In fact, no–till farming uses 50 percent less fuel, and 30 to 50 percent less labor than plow–based farming. This means a significantly lower production cost per acre.

(Narrator)

Summarize the points made in the lecture, being sure to explain how they challenge specific points made in the reading passage.

 Stop

The task requires you to do two things: (1) summarize the points made in the lecture, and (2) explain how they challenge specific points made in the reading. To respond to the question completely, you must connect information from the lecture with information in the reading.

The lecture discusses disadvantages of the plow and advantages of no–till farming. The key points in the lecture are:

- Producing large amounts of food is not enough; food production must be sustainable.
- Overuse of the plow is a major cause of soil damage; no–till farming minimizes soil damage.
- Overuse of the plow is a threat; no–till farming has economic advantages.

Generally, the points made in this lecture challenge or oppose those made in the reading. An effective response would connect information from the two sources like this:

- The lecture states that producing large amounts of food is not enough; food production must be sustainable. This challenges the point in the reading that large–scale agriculture and the plow are good.

- The lecture states that overuse of the plow is a major cause of soil damage. This challenges the point in the reading that plowing improves the soil in numerous ways.

- The lecture states that overuse of the plow is a threat; no–till farming has economic advantages. This challenges the point in the reading that the plow reduces the costs and labor requirements of agriculture.

4. Things to Consider

- In the integrated writing task, the lecture will either oppose or support the reading. Typically, both the reading and the lecture will contain three major points.

- The task will require you to describe the relationship between the two sources. The question will contain a key verb that tells you the kind of relationship to describe: opposition or support.

- The following key verbs in the question signal a relationship of opposition:

cast doubt on	contradict	differ from
challenge	contrast with	oppose
conflict with	deny	refute

- The following key verbs in the question signal a relationship of support:

compare with	illustrate	support

 PRACTICE

Exercise 4.1.A

For this task, you will write a response to a question about a reading passage and a lecture. You may take notes, and you may use your notes to help you write your response. Your response will be scored on the quality of your writing and on how well you connect the points in the lecture with points in the reading. Typically, an effective response will have 150 to 225 words.

Reading Time – 3 minutes

> Pruning is removing dead or living branches of a tree to improve the tree's health and structure. Careful pruning will control the size of a tree and hold the tree within bounds. Tree size is maintained through crown reduction pruning, the removal of larger branches at the top of the tree to reduce its height. When done properly, crown reduction only removes branches immediately above the joint with other branches, leaving no stubs.
>
> Pruning invigorates trees and keeps them healthy. In general, a tree will be more vigorous with a few healthy branches than with many weak ones. Crowded branches never develop to full size. Large branches compete with small branches, and the small ones become targets for disease and breakage. Pruning encourages trees to develop a strong structure, which reduces the likelihood of damage during severe weather. Pruning should always be done sparingly; removing too many branches in one season can damage the tree's capability for photosynthesis.
>
> The aim of pruning is to enhance the natural shape and beauty of a tree. Most hardwood trees have rounded crowns that lack a strong leader and may have several lateral, or side, branches. Branches grow from stems at nodes, and cuts are always made just above the stem–branch node so that the wound heals effectively. Cuts should not be made in the middle of a branch or near the end of a branch. After a mature tree reaches the desirable shape, pruning should be done only to remove broken or diseased branches and to thin occasionally to avoid overcrowding.

Now listen to the recording. When you hear the question, begin your response. You may look at the reading passage during the writing time.

 Album 8, Track 2

> Summarize the points made in the lecture, being sure to explain how they contrast with specific points made in the reading passage.

 Stop

Writing Time – 20 minutes

Exercise 4.1.B

For this task, you will write a response to a question about a reading passage and a lecture. You may take notes, and you may use your notes to help you write your response. Your response will be scored on the quality of your writing and on how well you connect the points in the lecture with points in the reading. Typically, an effective response will have 150 to 225 words.

Reading Time – 3 minutes

> People who are especially talented in solving problems that concern an understanding of space are said to have visual–spatial intelligence, a superior visual sense. People with visual–spatial intelligence are able to perceive patterns. They will notice immediately when a building, painting, or face is not symmetrical. They can recognize objects, both when the objects are seen in their original setting and when some part of the original setting has changed. Their ability to perceive patterns enables them to draw whatever object they see, usually after seeing the object for only a short time.
>
> Typically, visual–spatial intelligence involves several related capacities, such as the ability to create and transform mental imagery, the ability to mentally rotate complex forms and "see" objects from various angles, and the ability to draw a picture or map of spatial information. Visual–spatial skills are used when an individual works with graphic depictions—two–dimensional or three–dimensional versions of real–world scenes—as well as other symbols, such as maps, diagrams, or geometrical forms.
>
> People with visual–spatial intelligence have a superior visual memory, or visual imagination, but this memory is abstract rather than pictorial—a kind of geometrical memory. A visual imagination involves the ability to predict and plan ahead. People with a visual imagination are skilled at understanding patterns, including patterns of mental reasoning, which enables them to predict actions and their consequences before these actions occur. For this reason, many people with visual–spatial intelligence love to play games.

Now listen to the recording. When you hear the question, begin your response. You may look at the reading passage during the writing time.

 Album 8, Track 3

> Summarize the points made in the lecture, being sure to explain how they illustrate specific points made in the reading passage.

 Stop

Writing Time – 20 minutes

Key points for Exercises 4.1.A and 4.1.B are on page 667.

EXTENSION

1. With your teacher and classmates, discuss situations in which it is necessary to write about information from different types of sources. On the board, write a list of as many situations as you can think of. (Possible situations: research papers; open–book tests; business reports.) What types of sources might be used for each writing situation?

2. Review your response to the writing question in Exercise 4.1.A or 4.1.B. Analyze and evaluate your response by answering the following questions:

    a. What important points from the lecture does my response convey?
    b. What examples and explanation does my response include?
    c. How can I improve my responses for this type of question in the future?

3. Share and discuss your response to the writing question in Exercise 4.1.A or 4.1.B. Work in a group of three students. Make copies of your response, and give a copy to everyone in your group. Read and discuss each student's writing. Answer the following questions about each:

    a. What important points from the lecture does the response convey?
    b. What examples and explanation does the response include?
    c. Does the response answer the question effectively?

Make suggestions that will help each student improve in the future.

WRITING

4.2 Integrated Writing: Taking and Using Notes

 FOCUS

Listen to part of a university lecture. While you are listening, write down some words and phrases from the lecture that you think are important. It is impossible to write down everything that the professor says, so concentrate on the most important things.

 Album 8, Track 4

_____

_____

_____

 Stop

What were the most important ideas in the lecture? Some important words and phrases you may have heard are:

> overuse
> damage
> erosion – dust bowl
> by water

While listening to a lecture, your most important task is to listen carefully for important information. Listen for the speaker's main idea. What points does the speaker make? Write down key words and phrases that will help you remember these points. Limit your notes to key terms, concepts, examples, and reasons that will help you recall the major points in the lecture.

 STUDY

1. Taking Notes

Your response to the integrated writing task must include the key points from the lecture and the reading. For this reason, it is important to take good notes.

Taking notes, or ***note taking***, is writing down important information that you hear. Taking notes is an essential academic skill. During your university experience, you must take notes to help you remember important ideas and details from lectures and class discussions. You will have to study and understand the information in your notes. You will have to explain this information when you write answers to essay questions on examinations.

Just before the TOEFL begins, the test supervisor will give you paper to write on. You may use the paper to take notes, and you may use your notes to help you answer the integrated writing question. Your notes will not be scored. Only what you type on the keyboard will be scored.

For the integrated writing question, you will have three minutes to read a passage of 250 to 300 words. As you read the passage, think about its main idea. Notice how the passage is divided into paragraphs. Each paragraph will state a major point. It is not necessary to take notes now because you will be able to see the passage again later. However, if you have time remaining during the three minutes allowed, write a short note about the main idea of the passage.

The writing task will be mainly about the points in the lecture, so focus your attention on taking good notes during the lecture. After the lecture, you will be able to see the reading passage again. Then you will be able to compare points made in the lecture with specific points made in the reading.

2. Listening for Key Information

While you are listening to the lecture, focus on the major ideas, and take notes about them. Do not try to write down everything. Limit your note taking to examples and reasons concerning the speaker's major points. Use symbols and abbreviations to help you write more quickly. Do not allow your writing to detract from your listening.

Sometimes the speaker will call attention to important information. The speaker may emphasize certain words or repeat ideas throughout the lecture. Listen for words that the speaker emphasizes or repeats.

Generally, the speaker will make three major points. The speaker may use *signposts*, expressions that call attention to the points. For example, the speaker may use the following signposts:

> There are three types/kinds/groups/classes of _____.
> The key feature of _____ is _____.
> The main role of _____ is _____.
> _____ is interesting/important because _____.
> For one thing, _____.
> One example is _____.
> For instance, _____.
> The primary reason for this is _____.
> Another reason is _____.
> This is because _____.
> What this means is _____.
> First, _____.
> Second, _____.
> Third, _____.
> In fact, _____.
> Furthermore, _____.
> Finally, _____.
> Most importantly, _____.
> In short, _____.

If the speaker emphasizes or repeats certain words, or if the speaker uses signposts to call attention to important ideas, take notes about these.

3. Sample Notes

Listen again to the sample lecture from unit 4.1. Listen for key words and ideas that the professor emphasizes or repeats. Take notes on paper. Then compare your notes with the sample notes below.

 *Album 8, Track 1*

```
plow incr crops – but problems
must conserve – future
no till – no plow
over use plow – damage
erosion        wind            dust bowl
        no rain, dust storm
        water – run off soil        lake, river
no till        conserve, prot.
            imprv soil
threat – rural
no till econ adv        # pass over field ↓
        save fuel        50% low
        labor
```

 Stop

4. Preparing Your Response

Preparing your response begins with reading the question carefully. The integrated writing task requires you to do two things: (1) demonstrate understanding of the key points from the lecture, and (2) explain how these points relate to information in the reading. Your response must address each part of the task.

You will have 20 minutes to plan, write, and revise your response.

PLAN	Plan what points to present, and in what order.
WRITE	Write a paragraph to develop each major point. Support each point with information from the lecture and reading.
REVISE	Allow time to correct grammar and vocabulary errors.

5. Using Your Notes

The integrated writing task will state the type of relationship between the lecture and reading that your response should address. Generally, the points made in the lecture will either support or oppose those made in the reading.

The task is more about the lecture than the reading, so focus on the points in the lecture. Usually, the speaker makes three major points. After you hear the task, review the notes you took during the lecture. Select information that you can use to answer the question. What were the speaker's major points? Underline, circle, or number parts of your notes that you can use in your response.

You will be able to see the reading passage during the writing time. Scan the passage, and identify the points that you can connect to the points made in the lecture.

Once you have identified the key points from the lecture, you have the outline of your response. Generally, it is good to present these points in the same order in which the speaker discusses them. Here is a general plan for organizing your response:

Introduction	Relationship of the lecture to the reading
Paragraph 1	First point from the lecture • Examples or explanation • Connection to the reading
Paragraph 2	Second point from the lecture • Examples or explanation • Connection to the reading
Paragraph 3	Third point from the lecture • Examples or explanation • Connection to the reading

6. Sample Outline

The sample notes on page 390 could be organized into the following outline:

Plow – no plow

1   Plow incr crop but not conserve
      No plow better
      r – plow great, large–scale ag

2   Over use plow cause damage
      erosion – wind – dust bowl
              – water
      r – Tilling w/plow improves soil

3   No till econ advantage
      save fuel – 50%
      save labor, # pass
      r – Plow reduces costs

7. Things to Consider

- You must type your response on the computer keyboard. Do not write your entire response on paper and then try to type it into the computer; you will not have enough time to do this. Organize your notes on paper, and plan your response. Then type your response directly into the typing box on the screen.

- It is not necessary for your response to have a conclusion. Rather, it should focus on stating and developing three points, with a paragraph devoted to each point. Each paragraph should connect a point from the lecture with a point from the reading.

- When you state points from the reading passage, paraphrase the points in your own words as much as possible. Do not just copy whole sentences from the reading. You may quote parts of sentences, but keep quotations to a minimum, and put quotation marks around the parts that you copy directly.

- The integrated writing task does not ask for your opinion about the topic. For this task, your opinion is irrelevant and should not be included in your response. Your response should be based only on what you hear in the lecture and read in the passage. Your response will include a summary of the major ideas from the lecture and an explanation of how they relate to ideas in the reading passage.

 PRACTICE

Exercise 4.2.A

For this task, you will write a response to a question about a reading passage and a lecture. You may take notes, and you may use your notes to help you write your response. Your response will be scored on the quality of your writing and on how well you connect the points in the lecture with points in the reading. Typically, an effective response will have 150 to 225 words.

Reading Time – 3 minutes

Members of the city council of a small city are considering a plan to develop a strip of land in the downtown area, between a lake and bay. Currently, the area contains several unoccupied buildings scheduled for demolition, vacant lots between buildings, and a small wooded area on the lakeside. The plan calls for the construction of several blocks of mixed–use buildings up to six stories in height. All street–level spaces will be for commercial and retail use. The upper stories will be devoted mainly to residential use. City planners have determined that development of the land will beautify and improve the area, which will motivate people to live and shop downtown.

The development will help solve the city's growing need for residential space by providing much–needed housing in the downtown core. The plan includes more than one hundred condominiums, two apartment buildings, and four blocks of townhouses. Many of the residential buildings will have the added attraction of rooftop recreational facilities, such as swimming pools, tennis courts, and restaurants. The project will rejuvenate the area and turn it into a desirable place to live, thereby attracting more people to live downtown.

The project will benefit the city economically in several ways. The construction phase will create numerous jobs in the building trades. Upon completion of construction, the area will attract a variety of small businesses, such as restaurants, bookstores, art galleries, clothing boutiques, and specialty shops. These businesses will provide hundreds of new jobs, as well as attract residents and tourists to the downtown area. This growth in economic activity will benefit the city through additional revenue from the sales tax.

Now listen to the recording. When you hear the question, begin your response. You may look at the reading passage during the writing time.

 Album 8, Track 5

Summarize the points made in the lecture, being sure to explain how they oppose specific points made in the reading passage.

 Stop

Writing Time — 20 minutes

Exercise 4.2.B

For this task, you will write a response to a question about a reading passage and a lecture. You may take notes, and you may use your notes to help you write your response. Your response will be scored on the quality of your writing and on how well you connect the points in the lecture with points in the reading. Typically, an effective response will have 150 to 225 words.

Reading Time – 3 minutes

Psychology is a natural science that describes and explains the physiological and sensory aspects of human behavior. It studies the causes, conditions, and immediate consequences of sensations and emotions. Psychologists view the human mind as a function of the brain. Thought is a result of chemical and mechanical laws that govern brain action. All human cognition is the result of physiological processes that can be observed and measured. A variety of computational models provide tools for studying the functional organization of the mind.

Because psychology is a natural science, it is based on objectively verified facts and the application of the scientific method. Psychologists conduct controlled experiments in a laboratory in order to support their basic assumptions and develop theories. Experimenters use several types of measurements, such as rate of response, reaction time, and level of neural activity in various areas of the brain. Psychologists use inductive methods to derive general principles from specific facts. They aim to acquire a body of facts and laws about the human mind.

Psychology has a number of related subfields, all of which are primarily concerned with the biological bases of behavior and mental states. For example, behavioral neuroscientists use animal models, typically rats, to develop theories about the neural and cellular mechanisms of human behavior. Cognitive neuroscientists study the neural aspects of psychological processes in humans. Neuropsychologists study specific aspects of mental impairment caused by brain damage or disease.

Now listen to the recording. When you hear the question, begin your response. You may look at the reading passage during the writing time.

 Album 8, Track 6

Summarize the points made in the lecture, being sure to explain how they contrast with specific points made in the reading passage.

 Stop

Writing Time – 20 minutes

Key points for Exercises 4.2.A and 4.2.B are on page 667.

 EXTENSION

1. With your teacher and classmates, discuss symbols, shortcuts, and abbreviations that will help you take notes quickly while you are listening.

2. Review your response to the writing question in Exercise 4.2.A or 4.2.B. Analyze and evaluate your response by answering the following questions:

    a. What important points from the lecture does my response convey?

    b. What examples and explanation does my response include?

    c. How can I improve my responses for this type of question in the future?

3. Share and discuss your response to the writing question in Exercise 4.2.A or 4.2.B. Work in a group of three students. Make copies of your response, and give a copy to everyone in your group. Read and discuss each student's writing. Answer the following questions about each:

    a. What important points from the lecture does the response convey?

    b. What examples and explanation does the response include?

    c. Does the response answer the question effectively?

Make suggestions that will help each student improve in the future.

4. Obtain permission to make a recording of a real college or university lecture. (Topics in history, anthropology, sociology, and psychology are good choices.) Bring your recording to class. In class, everyone listens to three minutes of the recording. While listening, everyone takes notes about the important information in the lecture. Don't try to write down everything. Write only the key words and phrases that you think are important to remember.

Then break into groups of three or four students each. Compare your notes with the notes taken by the other students in your group. Listen again to the same three–minute recording. In your group, try to agree on the key points of the lecture. Write a summary of the lecture. Choose a student to read your group's summary to the whole class.

WRITING

4.3 Integrated Writing: Developing Your Response

 FOCUS

Imagine you are enrolled in a university course that is studying the history of agriculture. Your class has read an article about the plow, and your professor has given a lecture on the same topic. Now your professor gives an assignment and announces that it is an "open–book" quiz. Here is the quiz:

Directions:	You have 20 minutes to plan and write your response. You may use your lecture notes and the article you read. The length of your response should be about 150 to 225 words.
Question:	Summarize the information about the plow, explaining differences between points in the article and the lecture.

What would you do? Check all of the things that you would do:

___ Start writing quickly and stop when you have 150 words.

___ Read the question carefully and think about what it asks you to do.

___ Review the notes that you took during the lecture.

___ Write about a topic that you like better.

___ Plan what facts to present, and in what order.

___ Select three points and write a paragraph about each.

___ Develop important points with examples or reasons.

Is it a good idea to just start writing and stop when you have 150 words? Very few people can do that and have good results. It is better to read the question carefully and think about what it asks you to do.

Should you review your notes from the lecture? Of course! Should you write about a topic that you like better? Probably not, if you want a good score on the quiz.

Should you plan what facts to present, and in what order? Definitely yes! Should you select three points and write a paragraph about each? Good idea! Should you develop your ideas with examples and reasons? Absolutely!

 STUDY

1. Addressing the Task

There is no single correct response to the integrated writing question. There are several ways to address the task effectively. A successful response usually has between 150 and 225 words. A longer response is not always better than a shorter response. It is better to write a shorter response that answers the question completely than it is to write a longer response that does not answer the question completely, is filled with repetition, or contains many language errors.

2. Organization and Development

Your response will be evaluated on its organization, so you should present the information in a logical order. Begin with a short introduction stating the relationship of the lecture to the reading.

Each paragraph in the body of your response should convey one major point from the lecture and the reading. State the source of each point. Develop the points with relevant details. Be as thorough as you can, but use your time wisely. It is better to develop all points with minimal detail than to have an incomplete answer because you spent too much time on the first point. If you write three paragraphs, you have approximately five minutes to spend on each paragraph.

State one major point clearly in the first sentence of each paragraph. Then use the rest of the paragraph to provide examples, reasons, or other supporting details. Include at least one sentence about a relevant point from the reading. Paraphrase points from the reading in your own words as much as possible.

Your response should be clearly organized into paragraphs of approximately equal length. You can indicate the division into paragraphs in either of two ways:

- indent the first line of each paragraph; or
- leave a blank space between paragraphs.

3. Two Sample Plans

Here is one way to develop your response to the integrated writing task:

Introduction	State the relationship of the lecture to the reading.
Paragraph 1	State the first key point from the lecture. • Give supporting details from the lecture. • Explain how this relates to the reading.
Paragraph 2	State the second key point from the lecture. • Give supporting details from the lecture. • Explain how this relates to the reading.
Paragraph 3	State the third key point from the lecture. • Give supporting details from the lecture. • Explain how this relates to the reading.

Here is another way to organize and develop your response:

Introduction	State the relationship of the lecture to the reading.
Paragraph 1	Compare/contrast the first key point from the lecture with a point from the reading. • Compare/contrast details from the lecture and reading.
Paragraph 2	Compare/contrast the second key point from the lecture with a point from the reading. • Compare/contrast details from the lecture and reading.
Paragraph 3	Compare/contrast the third key point from the lecture with a point from the reading. • Compare/contrast details from the lecture and reading.

4. Writing Coherently

A well–organized response is coherent. *Coherence* is the quality of unity and order in a piece of writing. Writing is coherent when all of the ideas are connected logically. The following *transitions* and other expressions will help you express relationships between ideas and give your writing unity and coherence.

Connect Lecture to Reading

The lecture states that ___, while the reading states that ___.

The lecture ___. However, the reading ___.

The points in the lecture contradict/oppose/challenge/refute/cast doubt on the points in the reading.

The points in the lecture support/illustrate ideas in the reading.

Introduce Key Points

According to the lecture, ___.

The professor makes the point that ___.

The reading states that ___.

The lecture states that ___. This contradicts/opposes/challenges/refutes/casts doubt on the point in the reading that ___.

The lecture states that ___. This supports/illustrates the idea in the reading that ___.

First, ___.   Second, ___.   Third, ___.   Finally, ___.

Introduce Examples or Reasons

because	for example	one example is
first	for instance	such as

Add Examples or Reasons

also	furthermore	next
another example is	in addition	second, third...

Show Contrast between Ideas

although	in contrast	on the contrary
but	is contrary to	on the other hand
however	is the opposite of	while

---

5. Sample Task and Responses

Read the passage and listen to the lecture and question. Then read the sample responses.

Reading Time – 3 minutes

> The plow is one of our greatest inventions because it makes large–scale agriculture possible. The practice of turning the soil before planting is very old, but until the plow was invented, farming was limited to what humans could do by hand. The plow has enabled us to cultivate larger and larger areas of land, and in places where farming was previously impossible. Advances in plowing technology have made it possible to convert native grasslands into huge fields of corn and wheat.
>
> Tilling the soil with a plow improves the soil in numerous ways. The plow turns over the upper layer of soil, bringing fresh nutrients to the surface. This also loosens and aerates the soil, improving its ability to hold moisture and nutrients. Freshly turned soil is darker in color, which enhances soil warming and thereby promotes seed germination. Turning the soil buries crop residues—the stalks, leaves, and roots remaining from the previous year's harvest—allowing them to break down more quickly. Plowing incorporates these residues into the soil, along with any manure, limestone, and commercial fertilizers that are applied. In addition, plowing creates a pattern of low and high ridges in the soil, forming water channels that allow the soil to drain properly.
>
> The plow reduces the costs and labor requirements of agriculture. With the introduction of animal–drawn plows, fewer people were needed to till the same amount of land. In time, mechanized plowing further reduced labor requirements, permitting the labor of a few people to sustain many. The plow greatly reduced the amount of time needed to prepare a field, consequently allowing a farmer to work a larger area of land. This, in turn, increased each farmer's crop yields.

 Album 8, Track 7

Writing Task

> Summarize the points made in the lecture, being sure to explain how they challenge specific points made in the reading passage.

 Stop

SAMPLE RESPONSE 1   Word count: 174

The points in the lecture challenge points in the reading. According to the lecture, the plow increases crops, but does not conserve for the future. The professor discussed no till farming, which is better. This challenges the point in the reading that the plow is a great invention because it makes large–scale agriculture possible.

Over use of the plow causes damage to the land. For example, it causes erosion by the wind. The dust bowl happened because there was no rain. As a result, the dry soil blew away in dust storms. The plow also causes erosion by water. It causes the run off of soil into lakes and rivers. This challenges the point in the reading that tilling the soil with a plow improves the soil.

Finally, the professor mentioned the economic advantages of no till farming. It saves fuel and labor costs. It requires 50% less fuel and a lower number of passes over a field. However, the reading passage states that the plow reduces the costs and labor requirements of agriculture.

SAMPLE RESPONSE 2   Word count: 208

The lecture criticizes the plow, while the reading passage discusses benefits of the plow. The lecture discusses benefits of farming without the plow.

First, the lecture states that farming without the plow can help develop sustainable agriculture. However, the reading passage emphasizes benefits of the plow for large–scale agriculture. Advances in plowing technology have made it possible to develop larger areas of land, where farming was previously impossible.

Second, the lecture states that the plow damages the soil, but the passage states that the plow improves the soil. The lecture mentions erosion; for example, the plow causes water to carry soil and fertilizer from the field. However, the passage states that plowing creates a pattern of low and high ridges in the soil, and channels allow the soil to drain properly.

Third, the lecture states that no till farming leaves crop residues on the field, and this improves the soil. However, the passage states that plowing incorporates these residues into the soil. Furthermore, plowing loosens and aerates the soil.

Finally, the lecture states that farming without the plow will save fuel and labor costs. In contrast, the reading states that the plow reduces costs. With the plow, fewer people were needed to till the same amount of land.

Both sample responses effectively address the task. Both responses accurately connect information from the lecture and reading. Both develop key points with details from the two sources. Both use transitions to make the writing coherent. Both would receive a high score on the TOEFL.

6. Things to Consider

↝ An effective response will generally have at least three paragraphs and a total word count of 150 to 225 words. On the TOEFL, the computer will keep a current count of how many words you write.

↝ As you complete each writing task in the Practice exercises of this book, count the words in your response. Most word processing software has a tool for word count. Try to write at least 150 words, with body paragraphs of approximately equal length. Write more if you can, but make sure you have at least 150 words.

 PRACTICE

Exercise 4.3.A

For this task, you will write a response to a question about a reading passage and a lecture. You may take notes, and you may use your notes to help you write your response. Your response will be scored on the quality of your writing and on how well you connect the points in the lecture with points in the reading. Typically, an effective response will have 150 to 225 words.

Reading Time – 3 minutes

In recent decades, space–based observations have led astronomers to change their previous view that Pluto was the ninth planet in the solar system. By a strong majority, the International Astronomical Union voted to change the definition of what it means to be a planet. The new definition states that, in order to be called a planet, an object must meet three criteria. First, it must orbit the sun. Second, it must be large enough to have a round shape due to the force of its own gravity. Third, it must dominate the neighborhood of its orbit by clearing the region of other large bodies.

Pluto meets the first two criteria. It orbits the sun, is round in shape, and has an estimated diameter of 2,400 kilometers. However, Pluto does not meet the third criterion because it does not dominate the region of its orbit. As a planet forms, it becomes the strongest gravitational body in its orbit, and this gravity causes it to sweep up asteroids, comets, and other debris around it. Pluto's orbit remains crowded with other objects, many of which are nearly as large as Pluto itself. The new definition of planet is clear and precise, and Pluto does not qualify.

Astronomers now agree that Pluto is not a true planet. Instead, Pluto and its moons are part of a collection of objects called the Kuiper Belt. Astronomers have redefined Pluto as a dwarf planet, an object too small to be a real planet but too large to be a space rock. Unless Pluto gains mass by crashing into and absorbing the other objects in its orbit, it will remain a dwarf planet and not a true planet.

Now listen to the recording. When you hear the question, begin your response. You may look at the reading passage during the writing time.

 Album 8, Track 8

> Summarize the points made in the lecture, being sure to explain how they contradict specific points made in the reading passage.

 Stop

Writing Time – 20 minutes

Exercise 4.3.B

For this task, you will write a response to a question about a reading passage and a lecture. You may take notes, and you may use your notes to help you write your response. Your response will be scored on the quality of your writing and on how well you connect the points in the lecture with points in the reading. Typically, an effective response will have 150 to 225 words.

Reading Time – 3 minutes

> Research has taught us a lot about job satisfaction and the motivation of workers. First, workers are more motivated if their job offers a sense of community. A sense of community grows when workers get recognition for their accomplishments and when they believe their skills are being well used. Social organization in the workplace is important. Supervisors and co–workers have a tremendous influence on job satisfaction. When workers are asked what they like or do not like about their job, around 80 percent will mention the people they work with.
>
> Second, while workers value traditional economic incentives such as pay and promotions, they also have needs and expectations that go beyond economic concerns. Workers need a sense of security in the workplace. Security comes from confidence in the system that they are part of, the quality of the product or service they provide, and the reputation of the company. Security comes from the personal satisfaction of knowing that their skills are being utilized in a way that contributes to the company's success.
>
> Third, the most satisfying jobs are those with a high level of autonomy, in which employees can make their own decisions about the pacing and sequence of work with minimal supervision. Job autonomy is most often found in high–pay and high–prestige occupations. In jobs in the middle or lower levels of pay and prestige, workers generally have less autonomy. The lower the occupational status, the more heavily supervised the workers are, and the fewer decisions they can make on their own.

Now listen to the recording. When you hear the question, begin your response. You may look at the reading passage during the writing time.

 Album 8, Track 9

> Summarize the points made in the lecture, being sure to explain how they support specific points made in the reading passage.

 Stop

Writing Time – 20 minutes

Exercise 4.3.C

For this task, you will write a response to a question about a reading passage and a lecture. You may take notes, and you may use your notes to help you write your response. Your response will be scored on the quality of your writing and on how well you connect the points in the lecture with points in the reading. Typically, an effective response will have 150 to 225 words.

Reading Time – 3 minutes

The term "alternative medicine" describes healing practices that are used in place of conventional "Western" medicine. Alternative medicine often rejects science–based medicine and includes therapies that developed out of religious and cultural traditions. Examples are naturopathy, herbalism, meditation, biofeedback, hypnosis, homeopathy, and nutritional–based therapies. Advocates of alternative medicine believe that the various alternative methods are more effective than conventional medicine in treating a wide range of medical conditions.

Dissatisfaction with conventional medicine leads many people to seek alternative therapies. Some people choose alternative medicine because they do not trust traditional authority figures, such as the physician, or they dislike the current delivery methods of scientific medicine, particularly the over–reliance on synthetic drugs. Some patients prefer alternative therapies because they are averse to the painful or dangerous side effects of biomedical treatments. The majority of alternative medicine users find health–care alternatives to be more in agreement with their own values, beliefs, and philosophy about health. Many have a holistic orientation to health, a belief that the body, mind, and spirit are connected.

To meet the growing demand for alternative treatments, a variety of schools and colleges offer courses in alternative medicine. Even conventional medical colleges have started offering courses. Most alternative medicine programs take a holistic approach to health that explores the interconnection between the mind and body. Mind–body medicine works under the premise that the mind can affect bodily functions and symptoms. Other alternative medicine programs emphasize the study of substances found in nature such as herbs, foods, vitamins, and minerals.

Now listen to the recording. When you hear the question, begin your response. You may look at the reading passage during the writing time.

 Album 8, Track 10

> Summarize the points made in the lecture, being sure to explain how they challenge specific points made in the reading passage.

 Stop

Writing Time – 20 minutes

Key points for Exercises 4.3.A through 4.3.C are on page 667.

 EXTENSION

1. Review your response to one of the writing questions in Exercise 4.3.A through 4.3.C. Analyze and evaluate your response by answering the following questions:

    a. How is my response organized? How many paragraphs are there?
    b. What key points does my response convey?
    c. How is each point developed?
    d. What transitions and expressions make my writing coherent?
    e. Does my response answer the question effectively? How can I improve my responses for this type of question in the future?

2. Share and discuss your response to one of the writing questions in Exercises 4.3.A through 4.3.C. Work in a group of three students. Make copies of your response, and give a copy to everyone in your group. Read and discuss each student's writing. Answer the following questions about each:

    a. How is the response organized?
    b. What key points does the writer convey?
    c. How does the writer support and develop each point?
    d. What transitions and expressions make the writing coherent?
    e. Does the response answer the question effectively?

Make suggestions that will help each student improve in the future.

4.4 Integrated Writing: Sentence Structure

🔍 FOCUS

Read the following paragraph from a response to an integrated writing question:

> The plow he was a great invention made large–scale agriculture possible.
> However some problems. For example, a major cause of damage to the land. Long
> periods no rain and causing erosion, topsoil might to blow away in dust storms. In
> contrast, no–till farming he doesn't a plow, is a better for the soil because not cause
> soil damage as much. Farmers they are leaving crop litter on fields, actually built up
> soil levels also not erosion.

The response contains many errors in sentence structure. Some errors obscure meaning, making the writer's message unclear. Can you identify the errors?

Now read the same paragraph without errors.

> The plow was a great invention that made large–scale agriculture possible.
> However, there are some problems. For example, plowing is a major cause of damage
> to the land. Long periods of no rain cause erosion; topsoil might blow away in dust
> storms. In contrast, no–till farming does not use a plow and is better for the soil because
> it does not cause as much damage. Farmers leave crop litter on fields, which actually
> builds up soil levels and prevents erosion.

On the TOEFL, your response to the integrated writing task can have a few minor language errors and still earn a high score—if the errors do not obscure meaning. However, if your response has too many errors that make the meaning unclear, the result will be a lower score.

 STUDY

1. Checking Your Writing

You have 20 minutes to plan, write, and revise your response to the integrated writing question. After you are satisfied that you have answered the question, allow a few minutes near the end to check and correct your grammar, vocabulary, and spelling.

Your response will be evaluated on how well you use English to convey important ideas from the lecture and the reading. Use only grammatical structures that you know well. It is better to keep most of your sentences fairly simple than to write long, complicated sentences that might confuse your readers. Use appropriate vocabulary—your own words and key words from the lecture. Do not just copy whole sentences from the reading passage. Use mainly your own words.

2. Common Sentence Errors

Every sentence must have a subject and a verb. A sentence can have one or more clauses, but the clauses must be joined correctly with a semicolon (;), a semicolon and a subordinating conjunction (such as *however* or *therefore*), or a comma and a coordinating conjunction (such as *and*, *but*, or *so*).

A verb must agree in number with its subject. A pronoun must agree in number with the noun it replaces.

When you check your response to the writing task, make sure your sentences do not contain any of the problems below.

PROBLEM: INCOMPLETE SENTENCE (FRAGMENT)

Incorrect	Correct
Because Earth is our home.	Because Earth is our home, we need to protect our natural resources.
For example, television and computers.	For example, television and computers have impacted family life.

PROBLEM: RUN–ON SENTENCE (INCORRECTLY JOINED CLAUSES)

Incorrect	Correct
Conventional medical training involves a degree from a medical school alternative medicine may require no formal training.	Conventional medical training involves a degree from a medical school; however, alternative medicine may require no formal training.
Plowing increases erosion by water, the channels in fields carry soil away.	Plowing increases erosion by water, and the channels in fields carry soil away.

PROBLEM: DUPLICATE SUBJECT

Incorrect	Correct
Private companies they should spend more money to clean up pollution.	Private companies should spend more money to clean up pollution.
The professor she stated that farming without the plow, it saves fuel and labor costs.	The professor stated that farming without the plow saves fuel and labor costs.

PROBLEM: INCORRECT VERB FORM

Incorrect	Correct
Overuse of the plow leading to loss of the soil by erosion.	Overuse of the plow leads to loss of the soil by erosion.
The majority of workers generally be satisfied with their jobs.	The majority of workers are generally satisfied with their jobs.
Astronomers changed their opinion about Pluto, so they vote for a new definition of planet.	Astronomers changed their opinion about Pluto, so they voted for a new definition of planet.

PROBLEM: NO SUBJECT–VERB AGREEMENT

Incorrect

The unity of all parts are the main feature of this style.

Community, security, and autonomy promotes a higher level of job satisfaction.

Correct

The unity of all parts is the main feature of this style.

Community, security, and autonomy promote a higher level of job satisfaction.

PROBLEM: NO PRONOUN AGREEMENT

Incorrect

The purpose of pruning a tree is to improve their health and beauty.

Alternative medicine is a set of practices who are not based on science.

Correct

The purpose of pruning a tree is to improve its health and beauty.

The purpose of pruning trees is to improve their health and beauty.

Alternative medicine is a set of practices that are not based on science.

 PRACTICE

Exercise 4.4.A

Check the sentence structure of the following paragraphs. Cross out errors and write corrections above them. There may be more than one way to correct an error.

1.

The speaker talk about a maple tree that was topping. This not a good pruning practice. Because topping cause a lot of damage to trees. The first reason was topping cause leaves and branches grew fast. The growth rate of a tree speed up when they are topping. Branches became crowded and dangerous could crush a car. Another reason, topping remove too many leaves, which the tree's food source. The tree will starve also more likely to infected by disease. Topping cause a lot of stress for the tree therefore not good pruning practice.

2.

The lecture mention reasons for choose alternative medicine. For example, an increase in conspiracy theories. Some people belief conventional medicine be causing their depend on drugs. The reading that dissatisfaction with conventional medicine, for example people did not trust the physician. Also, the professor he talking about alternative medicine how to mislead people and encourage him choose treatments who not base on science.

3.

The professor made many points about the motivation and needs of workers they support points made in the reading. First, the professor say the small work group important for workers about 3 to 15 people with one leader. The work group fill needs of workers the reason is they can participate and a sense of respect. The small work group also give workers the ability for make decisions. This point agreed with the reading it said the most satisfying jobs are those with a high level of autonomy this gave workers a voice can make their own decisions.

Corrected paragraphs for Exercise 4.4.A are on page 668.

 EXTENSION

1. Review the responses you wrote for the writing tasks in units 4.1 through 4.3. Check your sentences for correct grammar and usage. Ask yourself the following questions:

   a. Are all of my sentences complete?
   b. Does every sentence have a correctly formed subject and verb?
   c. Are all subjects and verbs in agreement?
   d. Are there any run–on sentences that need correcting?
   e. Do all pronouns agree with the nouns they replace?
   f. Are there any misspelled words that need correcting?
   g. What improvements can I make to clarify meaning?

4.5 Evaluating Integrated Writing

🔍 FOCUS

What are the characteristics of good writing? What is it that successful writers do?

Circle **T** if the statement is true. Circle **F** if the statement is false.

T	**F**	Good writers do not have to answer the question that is asked.
T	**F**	The best writers support key ideas with relevant details and examples.
T	**F**	An explanation can be successful even if the key points are missing.
T	**F**	Writing is more interesting if the reader must guess what it means.
T	**F**	Successful writers make their meaning clear with the right words.
T	**F**	Good writing is easy to read because the information is organized.

Which statements are true? If you circled **T** for these sentences...

The best writers support key ideas with relevant details and examples.
Successful writers make their meaning clear with the right words.
Good writing is easy to read because the information is organized.

...you would find that most people agree with you.

Good writers make themselves understood to their readers. They state key ideas clearly and give appropriate supporting details. They provide all of the information that is necessary to fulfill the writing task. Good writers use the right words to make their meaning clear. Their writing is easy to understand because the information is organized into logical paragraphs and grammatical sentences.

 STUDY

1. How Your Response Will Be Evaluated

When you take the TOEFL, two trained evaluators will read your response to the integrated writing task. They will judge your response on the quality of your writing and on how well and how completely you answer the question by presenting key points from the lecture and relating them to information in the reading passage.

Among other things, your writing will be evaluated on how well you:

- draw requested connections between the lecture and the reading;
- organize ideas effectively in addressing the task;
- develop ideas with appropriate examples and explanation;
- display unity and coherence; and
- use English appropriately.

The evaluators will assign a score of 1 to 5, with 5 the highest score possible. To score your writing, they will use criteria similar to those in the following table.

	INTEGRATED WRITING TASK **Description of Score Levels**
5	**A response at this level** ⤳ effectively addresses the task by conveying relevant information from the lecture; and ⤳ accurately relates key information from the lecture to information in the reading; and ⤳ is well organized and coherent; and ⤳ contains appropriate grammar and vocabulary, with only occasional minor language errors.
4	**A response at this level** ⤳ generally conveys relevant information from the lecture, but may have minor omissions; and ⤳ is generally good in relating information from the lecture to information in the reading, but may have minor inaccuracies or vagueness of some content or connections among ideas; and ⤳ is generally well organized; and ⤳ contains appropriate grammar and vocabulary, but may have noticeable minor language errors or occasional lack of clarity.
3	**A response at this level** ⤳ contains some relevant information from the lecture, but may omit one key point; or ⤳ conveys some connections between the lecture and the reading, but some content or connections among ideas may be incomplete, inaccurate, or vague; or ⤳ contains errors in grammar or usage that result in vagueness of some content or connections among ideas.
2	**A response at this level** ⤳ contains some relevant information from the lecture, but may have significant omissions or inaccuracies of key points; or ⤳ omits or largely misrepresents the connections between the lecture and the reading; or ⤳ contains language errors that obscure meaning of key ideas or connections among ideas.
1	**A response at this level** ⤳ contains little or no relevant content from the lecture; or ⤳ fails to connect points from the lecture and reading; or ⤳ contains language errors that greatly obscure meaning; or ⤳ is too brief to allow evaluation of writing proficiency.
0	**A response at this level** ⤳ only copies sentences from the reading; or ⤳ is not related to the given topic; or ⤳ is written in a language other than English; or ⤳ is blank.

 PRACTICE

Exercise 4.5.A

Read the passage and answer the question below. Then listen to the recording and answer the rest of the questions.

Reading Time – 3 minutes

The discovery of penicillin and other antibiotic drugs was the most dramatic medical development of the twentieth century. These new drugs quickly became known as "wonder drugs" because of their ability to cure major forms of bacterial infection quickly and completely. Antibiotics made it possible for hospital patients to survive during and after surgery. No longer did patients have to depend largely on their body's own immune system to fight off infections. These infections could be attacked directly with antibiotics.

Antibiotics have given the medical profession powerful tools to fight a wide range of specific diseases. The development of antibiotics in the 1930s rested on the belief in the existence of certain chemicals that had the power to destroy specific microorganisms without injuring the human body at the same time. Advances in chemistry and in the study of bacteria quickened the discovery of such chemical wonders. The development of penicillin in the 1940s laid the foundation for even more powerful weapons against specific diseases. Since that time, researchers have identified hundreds of antibiotic substances that are effective against one or another type of bacteria.

Among the most spectacular effects of antibiotics are reductions in the number of deaths from pneumonia and tuberculosis. Penicillin, one of the earliest of the wonder drugs, is a highly successful cure for pneumonia. Just ten thousand units of penicillin four times a day will be enough to cure bacterial pneumonia in most patients. Another important antibiotic is streptomycin, which is potent against tuberculosis. As a result, tuberculosis is no longer the life–threatening illness it once was.

1. What is the main idea of the passage? What points support the main idea?

Now listen to the recording. Take notes on the important information.

 Album 8, Track 11

> Summarize the points made in the lecture, being sure to explain how they cast doubt on specific points made in the reading passage.

 Stop

2. What are the major points made in the lecture?

3. How do the key points in the lecture cast doubt on specific points in the reading?

Exercise 4.5.B

Read the sample responses to the writing task in Exercise 4.5.A. Evaluate each response according to the description of the five score levels on page 410. What score should each response receive? Why?

> Summarize the points made in the lecture, being sure to explain how they cast doubt on specific points made in the reading passage.

Response A   Score: _____

      The lecture casts doubt on the main idea of the reading, which states that antibiotics are wonder drugs.

      The professor discusses resistance to antibiotics. He makes the point that new types of bacteria appeared soon after hospitals started to use antibiotics. There has a rise in hospital infections, which means that antibiotics are not wonder drugs. However, the passage states the antibiotics have made it possible for hospital patients to survive during and after surgery because antibiotic are wonder drugs.

      The professor explains how bacteria develop resistance to antibiotics. If you use an antibiotic, it will kill the bacteria. However, a few cells will not killed because they carry a gene, which the bacteria resistant to the drug. However, the passage states that antibiotic are powerful tools to fight disease. They are chemicals with the power to destroy specific microorganisms.

      Finally, the professor states that resistance has caused several diseases to return. Two examples are pneumonia and tuberculosis. Penicillin is no longer a cure for pneumonia. You can give a patient a large amount of penicillin, but he might die anyway. However, the passage states that just ten thousand units of penicillin four times a day will cure pneumonia in most patients.

Response B   Score: _____

I will describe how the resistance of bacteria to antibiotics. First, it's big problem in the hospitals. Hospitals used antibiotics in 1950, but resistance appearing a problem. The reason is danger of hospital infection is very bad so people had better stay home.

Second, penicillin was a wonder drug in the past. You gave a man 10 thousand penicillin and he cured the disease. But today you give 24 millions penicillin but he might die. The reason is resistant so very difficult treat pnemunia. Several people die – because the resistance of the bacteria to antibiotics.

Third, how does this happen is you dose a bacteria with antibiotic. The colony killed except a few cells. This is a dangerous problem in a hospital because people may die. Doctors think tuberculosos was a defeated disease but the increase is by 20%.

The changes the view of antibiotics as wonder drugs by resistance of bacteria to antibiotics. It's a big problem today and doctors can't find drugs to cure the disease such as tuberculoses. Penicillin and other antibiotic drugs were wonder drugs in 1940s but necessary to have a different view of antibiotics today

Response C   Score: _____

Professor talk about antibiotics. These new drugs as wonder drugs saving many lifes many people who very sick the diseases. Professor he describe penicilin as wonder drug it causing many people cure after sick. The discovery of penicillin and other antibiotic drugs was the most dramatic medical development of the twenteth century quickly become known as 'wonder drugs. Antibiotics given the medical profession powerful tools to fight a wide range of specific diseases. Professor he gave example the antibiotics make to survive during and after surgery. For example, infections, pneumonia and tuberculosis. As a result, reductions in the number of death.

Response D   Score: _____

In general, the lecture contradicts the idea that antibiotics are "wonder drugs" as the reading states. On the contrary, antibiotics are not wonder drugs because the resistance of bacteria to antibiotics.

According the lecture, bacteria have developed effective wepons against some drugs, for example, penicillin. They create resistance against antibiotics. It happens when a few cells of bacteria survive because they have the resistance. Then new strains of bacteria appeared. After that, antiboitics may attack but they do not kill all disease infections. This serious problem today is the resistance of bacteria to antibiotics.

According to the reading, the discovery of penicillin and other antitiotic drugs saved many lives that were threatened by dangerous diseases such a penumonia and tuberculosis. In the twentieth century, penicillin was first a wonder drug because it can cure pneumonia. In addition, streptomycin is potent against tuberculosis. However, the lecture made the point that this is not true today. Tuberculoss is a major illness again because the new strain of bacteria is resistant to antibiotics.

In the past, antibiotic drugs could attack and kill diseases, but this is not true today. Therefore, it is necessary to develop new wonder drugs to fight disease.

WRITING

Response E   Score: _____

The resistance of bacteria to antibiotics changes the view of wonder drugs. One example is penicillin. The discovery of penicillin the foundation for even more powerful drugs, for example, antiobiotics. Another example is streptomycin, against tuberculosis. Many diseases cured by penicillin.

The resistance of bacteria to antibiotics to some of the drugs. First example is pnemonia. In the past penicillin cure him, however today he still die.

Second example is tuberculosis. The most effects of antibiotics were reductions in the number of deaths, however, since tuberculosis increase 20 precent deaths. It describes the resistance of bacteria to antiobiotics. In the past, it was no problem, however, today it is serious problem. It's changes the view of antiobitics as wonder drugs which saved so many lives. Because today people can still die in a hospital.

Answers for Exercises 4.5.A and 4.5.B are on page 668.

 EXTENSION

1. Study the descriptions of the five score levels on page 410. Make sure you understand the description for each level. Check your understanding of the meaning of these words and phrases:

effectively addresses	minor omissions	significant omissions
accurately relates	inaccuracies	misrepresents
coherent	vagueness	obscure meaning
occasional	lack of clarity	writing proficiency

2. Review the responses you wrote for units 4.1 through 4.3. Evaluate each response according to the descriptions of the five levels on page 410. What are the areas of strength in your writing? What are your most serious problems? What can you do to improve your writing and earn a high score for the integrated writing task on the TOEFL?

PROGRESS – 4.1 through 4.5

QUIZ 1

Time – approximately 25 minutes

For this task, you will write a response to a question about a reading passage and a lecture. You may take notes, and you may use your notes to help you write your response. Your response will be scored on the quality of your writing and on how well you connect the points in the lecture with points in the reading. Typically, an effective response will have 150 to 225 words.

Reading Time – 3 minutes

Evidence that some animals possess self–awareness comes from a series of experiments in which animals appear to recognize themselves in mirrors.

Researchers have repeatedly demonstrated the mirror–recognition ability of chimpanzees by using a procedure called the "mark test." For several days, chimpanzees were exposed to a mirror so they would become used to it. Then, one day they were given a sleeping drug, and while the chimps were asleep the researchers marked one eyebrow and one ear on each animal with a bright red dye. The researchers then watched the chimpanzees to see what they would do when they woke up and noticed the red mark. At first the chimps were placed in their cage without the mirror. On average, they touched the marked areas only once during a half–hour. Then the mirror was brought in, and the chimpanzees on average touched the marked spots seven times in a half–hour.

The mark test clearly showed that the chimps touched their heads and faces more when the mirror was present. Some of them touched the marked spots while they looked at their image in the mirror, and then sniffed or examined their fingers. The researchers concluded that the chimpanzees recognized the red mark as being on their own bodies, suggesting that chimpanzees are self–aware.

When the chimpanzees recognized themselves in the mirror, they would often groom themselves. They used the mirror to explore the insides of their mouths. They made faces and stuck out their tongues. These results strengthened the hypothesis that chimpanzees have a concept of self and are able to recognize the image in the mirror as their own.

Now listen to the recording. When you hear the question, begin your response. You may look at the reading passage during the writing time.

 Album 8, Track 12

> Summarize the points made in the lecture, being sure to explain how they cast doubt on specific points made in the reading passage.

 Stop

Writing Time – 20 minutes

Key points for Writing Quiz 1 are on page 668.

Record your score on the Progress Chart on page 793.

PROGRESS – 4.1 through 4.5

QUIZ 2

Time – approximately 25 minutes

For this task, you will write a response to a question about a reading passage and a lecture. You may take notes, and you may use your notes to help you write your response. Your response will be scored on the quality of your writing and on how well you connect the points in the lecture with points in the reading. Typically, an effective response will have 150 to 225 words.

Reading Time – 3 minutes

Compared to other energy sources, wind energy is available, abundant, affordable, and clean. The wind is a renewable natural resource that is available everywhere. In the United States, the wind supply is abundant. Wind power could provide 20 percent of the electricity in the United States, with turbines installed on less than one percent of the nation's land area. Within that area, less than five percent of the land would be occupied by wind equipment; the remaining 95 percent could continue to be used for farming or ranching.

Wind energy is one of the lowest–priced renewable energy technologies available today. It is affordable enough to compete with coal, oil, and gas. The wind is free, and with modern technology it can be captured efficiently. Better turbine technology has helped reduce the cost of wind energy by more than 80 percent since the 1980s. In several places around the world, energy companies offer wind–generated electricity at a cost that is almost half the cost for coal power, and around one–fifth the cost for nuclear power.

Most importantly, wind power is safe and environmentally friendly. Once the wind turbine is built, the energy it produces does not cause greenhouse gases or other pollutants. Wind is a much cleaner source of fuel than coal, oil, and gas, so there are fewer emissions of carbon dioxide, sulfur, and other gases that cause global warming, smog, and acid rain. Wind power will decrease our dependence on fossil fuels, which is critical to the health of all living things.

Now listen to the recording. When you hear the question, begin your response. You may look at the reading passage during the writing time.

 Album 8, Track 13

> Summarize the points made in the lecture, being sure to explain how they challenge specific points made in the reading passage.

 Stop

Writing Time – 20 minutes

Key points for Writing Quiz 2 are on page 669.

Record your score on the Progress Chart on page 793.

PROGRESS – 4.1 through 4.5

QUIZ 3

Time – approximately 25 minutes

For this task, you will write a response to a question about a reading passage and a lecture. You may take notes, and you may use your notes to help you write your response. Your response will be scored on the quality of your writing and on how well you connect the points in the lecture with points in the reading. Typically, an effective response will have 150 to 225 words.

Reading Time – 3 minutes

Abstract Expressionism was a movement in painting that emerged in New York City in the 1940s and attained prominence in the following decade. It emphasized personal expression, individuality, and freedom from convention.

Abstract Expressionism valued the act of painting itself, including the accidents and discoveries that can occur during the process of painting. For this reason, it is sometimes called action painting. The expressive method of painting was considered as important as the finished product. Artists typically applied paint rapidly and with force. They valued improvisation and painted spontaneously, without planning or sketching in advance.

Abstract expressionists gave special attention to surface qualities of paint, such as brushstroke and texture. They sometimes applied paint with large brushes—dripping, splattering, or even throwing it onto a canvas. They used various tools, including their hands, to spread the paint. Some artists applied multiple layers of paint, filling the entire canvas with broad brushstrokes and thick globs of color.

Abstract expressionists had a preference for dramatically large canvases. Painters rejected easel–bound canvases for over–sized surfaces that were often placed upon the floor. Their approach to space meant that all parts of the canvas played an equally important role in the total work. Huge canvases suited the heavyweight, tragic, and emotional themes. Bold use of color and texture contributed to a painting's sense of power and movement.

Now listen to the recording. When you hear the question, begin your response. You may look at the reading passage during the writing time.

 Album 8, Track 14

> The lecture discusses the painter Jackson Pollock. Summarize the points made in the lecture, being sure to explain how they illustrate specific points made in the reading passage.

 Stop

Writing Time – 20 minutes

Key points for Writing Quiz 3 are on page 669.

Record your score on the Progress Chart on page 793.

COMPLETE SKILL PRACTICE

4.6 Independent Writing: Prewriting

 FOCUS

Imagine you are taking an essay examination, and you see the following question:

> Do you agree or disagree with the following statement?
>
> **Teachers are responsible for motivating students to learn.**
>
> Use specific reasons and examples to support your opinion.

What would you do to answer this question? Check all of the things that you would do:

____ Just start writing as quickly as you can.

____ Think about everything the question asks you to do.

____ Write about a topic that you think is more interesting.

____ Decide whether you agree or disagree with the given statement.

____ Try to guess the opinion of the person who will grade the essay.

____ Make a list of your favorite teachers.

____ Organize your thoughts in the form of an outline.

Most people cannot just start writing quickly and produce a good essay, so that is not a good idea. It is better to start by thinking about everything the question asks you to do.

Writing about a different topic, even a more interesting one, is not a good idea. On the TOEFL, your essay will receive a score of zero if you do not write about the assigned topic. For this question, you must either agree or disagree with the given statement. Do you believe it is true that teachers are responsible for motivating students to learn? Or do you believe it is not true? Your position on the topic will be the main idea of your essay.

Some students think their opinion must agree with the opinion of the person who will grade the essay. This is not true. On the TOEFL, you should not be concerned about whether the essay readers will agree with your opinion. Rather, you should be concerned about whether the essay readers will understand your opinion because it is stated clearly and is well supported with specific reasons and examples.

Should you make a list of your favorite teachers? Maybe. Some of your own teachers might be good examples to help you support your position. Should you organize your thoughts in the form of an outline? Yes, because this will help you write a better, more organized essay.

 STUDY

1. The Independent Writing Task

The independent writing task requires you to write an essay in response to a given topic. You have 30 minutes to plan, write, and revise your essay. Your essay will be evaluated on the quality of your writing, including the development of your ideas, the organization of your essay, and the quality and accuracy of the language you use. An effective essay usually has at least 300 words.

2. The Essay

An *essay* is a written work that contains three or more paragraphs. The function of an essay is to communicate to a reader an opinion about a topic and to provide information that supports or defends this opinion. An essay has three parts: introduction, body, and conclusion.

Introduction	The *introduction* is the first paragraph of the essay. The introductory paragraph tells your readers what the essay is about. It restates the question in your own words and expresses the main idea, which is called the *thesis* or *thesis statement*. The thesis statement is often the last sentence of the introductory paragraph.
Body	The *body* is the center of the essay. Each body paragraph contains one *supporting point* that develops the thesis. The body paragraphs are sometimes called *developmental paragraphs*. They contain specific examples, reasons, and other details that support the thesis.
Conclusion	The *conclusion* is the last paragraph of the essay. The concluding paragraph can restate your thesis, summarize your points, or make a recommendation. The conclusion completes the essay.

3. Prewriting

Prewriting is the planning that you do before you start writing your essay. Prewriting includes:

- reading and thinking about the question;
- brainstorming and making notes on paper;
- deciding what your thesis or main idea will be; and
- writing an outline of your essay.

Brainstorming is quickly generating ideas—examples, reasons, personal experiences, and other details—in the form of notes, a list, or a diagram. Brainstorming is thinking on paper. It is writing down as many ideas as possible in a short amount of time.

In the independent writing task, your *thesis* will be your opinion about the topic that is assigned in the question. For example, your thesis may:

- state that you agree with a given statement; or
- state that you disagree with a given statement; or
- state which of two positions you hold on a given issue.

WRITING

An *outline* is a simple plan of your essay. Sometimes it is a short list of your points. Sometimes it is a diagram of each paragraph. Before you write your outline, decide what your thesis will be. Then choose ideas from your brainstorming that will support this position. Choose two to four of your best examples or reasons and discard the rest. Decide the most effective order for arranging these ideas, and write your outline. Your outline should be short. It does not have to be written in complete sentences, but the ideas should be in an order that makes sense.

4. Sample Task and Prewriting

> Do you agree or disagree with the following statement?
>
> **Teachers are responsible for motivating students to learn.**
>
> Use specific reasons and examples to support your opinion.

Brainstorming

Disagree—Student is responsible, not teacher
- <u>self–motivated</u>
- S not motivated, T can't help
- People <u>naturally</u> want to learn
- my teacher – grade 5
- work/<u>whole life</u>
- learning – <u>no teacher</u>

Outline

- Natural love of learning
- Learning during whole life
- Develop self–motivation

Thesis

Although many people believe it is the teacher's responsibility to motivate students to learn, students will not learn much unless they are self–motivated.

5. Sample Task and Prewriting

> Some people like to spend their leisure time doing activities with a lot of people. Others prefer to spend their leisure in quiet ways by themselves or with one other person. Which do you prefer? Use specific reasons and examples to support your answer.

Brainstorming

<u>Activities with people</u>
    reason – desk job, alone (computer)
active things/play <u>tennis</u> & <u>basketball</u>
    good for exercise, health, social
    time with friends/go <u>bowling</u>
college <u>basketball</u> team
enjoy – <u>rafting</u>/teamwork important
    safety

Outline

1. Intro
2. Enjoyment and exercise:
    bowling
    tennis
3. Teamwork:
    basketball
    rafting

Thesis

Since I work mainly by myself in my job as a computer specialist, I prefer leisure activities with other people that provide enjoyment, exercise, and teamwork.

 PRACTICE

Exercise 4.6.A

For each writing question below, plan how you will write an essay that will:

- answer the question;
- show organization and development; and
- support a thesis.

Brainstorm and make any notes that will help you plan an essay. Write an outline and thesis statement for each topic. In this exercise, you do not have to write the essay. Focus on writing a good thesis and outline in five minutes.

Time – 5 minutes each

1. Do you agree or disagree with the following statement?
    Children should not have to work or help with household tasks; their only responsibility should be to study.
    Use specific reasons and examples to support your opinion.

2. Some people argue for a broad university education in which students learn about many different subjects. Others argue for a specialized university education in which students learn only about a specific field of study. Which position do you agree with? Use specific reasons and examples to support your opinion.

3. Do you agree or disagree with the following statement?
    You should not believe everything that you read in the newspaper.
    Use specific reasons and examples to support your opinion.

4. Some people think that their friends are the most influential people in their lives. Others think that members of their family have a stronger influence. Who has more influence in your life: friends or family members? Use specific and reasons and examples to support your choice.

5. Do you agree or disagree with the following statement?
    It is better to give than to receive.
    Use specific reasons and examples to support your answer.

Answers to Exercise 4.6.A will vary.

EXTENSION

1. Choose one outline and thesis statement that you wrote for Exercise 4.6.A. Work in a group of three students. Make copies of your outline and thesis, and give a copy to everyone in your group. Read and discuss each student's paper. Answer the following questions about each:

    a. Will the finished essay answer the question?

    b. Will the finished essay show organization and development?

    c. Will the finished essay support the thesis?

    Make suggestions that will help each student improve in the future.

2. Choose one outline and thesis statement that you wrote for Exercise 4.6.A and complete the essay. Allow 25 minutes to write your essay. Then analyze and evaluate your essay by answering the following questions:

    a. Does my essay answer the question?

    b. Does my essay show organization and development? Does it support my thesis?

    c. How can I improve my essay writing in the future?

3. Choose one outline and thesis statement that you wrote for Exercise 4.6.A and complete the essay. Allow 25 minutes to write the essay. Then share and discuss your essay in a group of three students. Make copies of your outline, thesis, and essay, and give a copy to everyone in your group. Read and discuss each student's paper. Answer the following questions about each:

    a. Does the essay answer the question?

    b. Does the essay show organization and development?

    c. Does the essay support the thesis?

    Make suggestions that will help each student improve in the future.

4.7 Independent Writing: Stating and Supporting an Opinion

 FOCUS

Read the following essay question and the first paragraph of a response:

> Some people think that government should spend as much money as possible on developing space technology for the exploration of the moon and other planets. Others think that this money should be spent on solving the basic problems of society on Earth. Which view do you agree with? Use specific reasons and examples to support your answer.

Society is often divided on major issues involving government spending. One group believes that we should spend as much money as possible on space exploration, while another group thinks that we should spend this money on solving basic social problems on Earth. I believe there are stronger reasons for spending on space technology because this leads to knowledge that will benefit society on Earth.

The first sentence introduces the general topic of the essay: how the government should spend money.

Society is often divided on major issues involving government spending.

The next sentence restates the question in the writer's own words.

One group believes that we should spend as much money as possible on space exploration, while another group thinks that we should spend this money on solving basic social problems on Earth.

The last sentence states the writer's opinion. This is the ***thesis statement***, the main idea of the essay. The rest of the essay must support this idea.

I believe there are stronger reasons for spending on space technology because this leads to knowledge that will benefit society on Earth.

 STUDY

1. Addressing the Task

The independent writing question requires you to do more than one thing. For example, it may ask you to (1) state your position on a given topic, and (2) support this position with specific reasons and examples. You must answer all parts of the question.

A very important part of the question is *Use specific reasons and examples to support your opinion*. The readers who rate your essay are *not* interested in what your opinion is, but they *are* interested in how you support your opinion with appropriate ideas and details.

You will have 30 minutes to plan, write, and revise your essay.

PLAN	*5 minutes*	• Decide what your thesis will be.
		• Plan what information to present, and in what order.
WRITE	*20 minutes*	• Write a separate paragraph to develop each major point.
		• Each point should directly support your thesis.
REVISE	*5 minutes*	• Allow time to correct grammar and vocabulary errors.

A well–organized essay has an introduction, a body, and a conclusion. The introduction communicates your opinion about the topic. The body contains supporting ideas that develop your opinion. The conclusion completes the essay.

2. The Introduction

The *introduction* is the first paragraph of an essay. The introduction tells your readers what the essay is about. It focuses on the topic and expresses your *thesis*, or *controlling idea*. The thesis is an essential part of your essay because it expresses your opinion about the topic. The thesis is often stated in the last sentence of the introductory paragraph. The thesis statement may preview the points you will make in the body of your essay, in the same order in which they will be discussed.

A good introduction contains two or more sentences.

Sentence 1	• introduces the topic.
	• may restate the question in your own words.
Sentences 2 – 3	• state your thesis.
	• may preview your supporting points in the order in which you will discuss them.

3. The Body

The *body* of the essay consists of the middle paragraphs, which are sometimes called *developmental paragraphs* because they contain ideas that develop the thesis. Each body paragraph should have a *topic sentence* that expresses the main point of the paragraph. The topic sentence of the paragraph should also directly support the thesis; for this reason, it is called a *supporting point*. The rest of the sentences should give appropriate examples, reasons, facts, personal experiences, or other *supporting details*.

Your essay for the independent writing task should contain two to four body paragraphs. Each body paragraph should contain four or more sentences.

Topic Sentence	• states the main idea of the paragraph.
	• supports the thesis of the essay.
Other Sentences	• provide specific examples, reasons, or other details to support the topic sentence.

4. The Conclusion

The *conclusion* is the last paragraph of an essay. The conclusion is often very short and may contain only one or two sentences. The conclusion should leave your readers with a feeling of completion. It can do one or more of the following:

- restate your thesis in different words (paraphrase);
- summarize your supporting points;
- draw a conclusion;
- make a prediction; or
- make a recommendation.

5. Sample Task and Essay

> Some people think that government should spend as much money as possible on developing space technology for the exploration of the moon and other planets. Others think that this money should be spent on solving the basic problems of society on Earth. Which view do you agree with? Use specific reasons and examples to support your answer.

SAMPLE ESSAY   Word count: 271

Society is often divided on major issues involving government spending. One group believes that we should spend as much money as possible on space exploration, while another group thinks that we should spend this money on solving basic social problems on Earth. I believe there are stronger reasons for spending on space technology because this leads to knowledge that will benefit society on Earth.

Spending money on space technology can lead to better ways to produce food and clothing. Space travel requires special ways to preserve and store food for a long journey. Scientists also work on ways to grow vegetables and fruits in space so that astronauts can have fresh food. Scientists must develop new types of clothing made from new materials. Many of these new methods of food and clothing production also benefit people on Earth.

Space exploration has led to important developments in communications technology. One of the first government projects in space technology was for satellite communications. Today, this technology benefits everyone who uses satellite television or telephones.

The most important reason for spending money on space technology is that it promotes international cooperation. When the governments of several different countries work together on space projects, there is better communication between countries. The international space station is a good example of international cooperation that benefits everyone on Earth. Not only does it lead to scientific progress, but it also promotes international understanding.

In conclusion, several developments in space technology have already helped society on Earth. If we spend money on space programs, we may discover even greater knowledge that will improve our life and promote world peace.

The writer has chosen the position that government should spend as much money as possible on developing space technology. The thesis is stated in the last sentence of the introduction:

> I believe there are stronger reasons for spending on space technology because this leads to knowledge that will benefit society on Earth.

The writer makes three supporting points. Each supporting point is the topic sentence of one of the body paragraphs. Each body paragraph develops its topic sentence with examples and reasons. Each body paragraph therefore supports and develops the thesis of the essay:

Supporting Point / Topic Sentence	Supporting Details
Spending money on space technology can lead to better ways to produce food and clothing.	ways to preserve and store food; ways to grow vegetables and fruits; new types of clothing
Space exploration has led to important developments in communications technology.	satellite communications; television; telephones
The most important reason for spending money on space technology is that it promotes international cooperation.	better communication between countries; international space station

In the conclusion, the writer restates the thesis:

> In conclusion, several developments in space technology have already helped society on Earth.

The writer also makes a prediction:

> If we spend money on space programs, we may discover even greater knowledge that will improve our life and promote world peace.

The sample essay is a bit short, but it effectively addresses the task. It is well organized, with an introduction, a body, and a conclusion. It clearly states an opinion and supports the opinion with reasons and examples. The essay would receive a high score on the TOEFL.

6. Things to Consider

- An effective essay will generally have four or more paragraphs and a minimum of 300 words. On the TOEFL, the computer will keep a count of how many words you write.

- As you complete each writing task in the Practice exercises, count the words in your response. Most word processing software has a tool for word count. Try to write at least 300 words. Include an introductory paragraph, two or more body paragraphs of approximately equal length, and a conclusion.

 **PRACTICE**

Exercise 4.7.A

Read the following independent writing question and sample essay:

> Do you agree or disagree with the following statement?
>
> **The best things in life do not cost money.**
>
> Use specific reasons and examples to support your opinion.

       Many of our favorite activities require us to spend money. Some important things in life, such as getting a good education and buying a home, cost a lot of money. However, it does not cost money to experience the best things in life: enjoying nature and being with our friends and family.

       We can relax and enjoy the beauty of nature without spending money. Walking in the park, looking at the colorful leaves, and watching the snow falling are good ways to relax. Listening to the beautiful songs of birds does not cost money, but it can make us feel peaceful. Also, we can enjoy nature by having a garden. When I was a child, I helped my grandmother in her vegetable garden. We pulled up carrots and ate them, and we watched the butterflies and birds. I have many beautiful memories of sunshine and happiness in my grandmother's garden.

       It does not cost money to spend time with our friends and family. We can visit friends and have a good time by talking and laughing. Sometimes we need a little money to go to a movie. However, our time together is more important than the money that we spend. We can do a lot of things that are free. For example, we can go to the library. When I was little, I used to walk to the library with my mother and sister every week to borrow books. When we got home, we sat on the porch and read to each other. Many of our best memories result from these simple things.

       Money is necessary in our lives, but having a lot of money does not always lead to happiness. The most important things in life do not require a lot of money. If we learn to enjoy simple things, we will have many wonderful memories, and our memories are entirely free.

Now answer the following questions. Discuss your answers with your teacher and classmates.

1. How many parts does the question have? What does each part ask you to do?

2. Does the essay address all parts of the question?

3. How is the essay organized?

4. What does the writer do in the introduction?

5. What is the thesis or main idea of the essay?

6. How does the writer support the thesis?

7. What is the topic sentence of each body paragraph?

8. What specific examples, reasons, and other details are given? What is their purpose?

9. What does the writer do in the conclusion?

10. Does the essay effectively address the topic and task?

Answers to Exercise 4.7.A are on page 669.

Exercise 4.7.B

Your teacher will assign one of the following essay questions. Read the question carefully, and then plan and write a response. To make this practice more like the real test, allow 30 minutes to complete the essay. Use your time like this:

> ✏ 5 minutes – to brainstorm and write an outline;
> ✏ 20 minutes – to write the introduction, body, and conclusion; and
> ✏ 5 minutes – to check your essay and make corrections.

1. Do you agree or disagree with the following statement?
   A student must like a teacher in order to learn from the teacher.
   Use specific reasons and examples to support your opinion.

2. Do you agree or disagree with the following statement?
   Youth is wasted on the young.
   Use specific reasons and examples to support your opinion.

3. Do you agree or disagree with the following statement?
   We should pay attention to the opinions of famous people.
   Use specific reasons and examples to support your opinion.

4. Some people think that teachers and education professionals should make all of the important decisions about what subjects are taught in schools. Others think that business and industry professionals should make all of the major decisions. Which view do you agree with? Use specific reasons and examples to support your opinion.

5. Do you agree or disagree with the following statement?
   In any society, the contributions of scientists and engineers are more important than the contributions of artists and writers.
   Use specific reasons and examples to support your opinion.

6. Some students prefer to live on campus in a dormitory. Others prefer to live in an apartment or house off campus. Which do you prefer? Use specific reasons and examples to support your opinion.

7. Do you agree or disagree with the following statement?
   Some things are too serious to be the subject of jokes or comedy.
   Use specific reasons and examples to support your answer.

8. Some people would rather be very successful professionally and have a personal life that is comfortable but unexciting. Other people would rather have an extremely happy private life and an unexciting professional life. Which kind of life would you rather have? Use specific reasons and examples to support your choice.

Answers to Exercise 4.7.B will vary.

 EXTENSION

1. Review the essay that you wrote for Exercise 4.7.B. Analyze and evaluate your essay by answering the following questions:

    a. How is my essay organized?
    b. Does my introduction include a thesis statement? What is my thesis?
    c. What is the topic sentence of each body paragraph?
    d. What supporting details are given?
    e. How does my essay conclude?
    f. How can I improve my essay writing in the future?

2. Share and discuss the essay that you wrote for Exercise 4.7.B. Work in a group of three students. Make copies of your essay, and give a copy to everyone in your group. Read and discuss each student's essay. Answer the following questions about each:

    a. How is the essay organized?
    b. What does the writer do in the introduction?
    c. What is the thesis or main idea of the essay?
    d. What is the topic sentence of each body paragraph?
    e. What supporting details does the writer give?
    f. What does the writer do in the conclusion?

Make suggestions that will help each student improve in the future.

4.8 Independent Writing: Unity and Coherence

 FOCUS

Read the following essay question and a paragraph from the body of an essay:

> Do you agree or disagree with the following statement?
>
> **The things we learn from our friends are more important than what we learn from our family.**
>
> Use specific reasons and examples to support your opinion.

     While my friends have taught me to enjoy my life, my family has taught me to be strong. My friends have taught me how to feel independent. They have encouraged me to be myself, to have a lot of fun, and to find happiness in life. On the other hand, my mother has taught me to be independent in a very different way. When I was a child, she gave me advice such as "Fight your own battles." She said that so I would be strong because she could not always protect me. Sometimes this was very difficult for me when I wanted my mother to help me, even though I knew her advice was important.

This paragraph is easy to read and understand. What makes it so? Check all of the statements that are true:

____ All of the sentences in the paragraph are simple.

____ The topic sentence is stated clearly at the beginning.

____ The sentences are written in a logical order.

____ All of the ideas in the paragraph support the topic sentence.

____ The writer uses appropriate transitions to connect ideas.

All of the statements are true except the first one. All of the sentences in the paragraph are *not* simple, but they *are* easy to understand. This is because the topic sentence is stated clearly at the beginning, the sentences are written in a logical order, and all of the ideas in the paragraph support the topic sentence. Moreover, the writer uses appropriate transitions to connect ideas.

The paragraph is well organized and coherent. When a piece of writing is **coherent**, it is easy for readers to understand.

 STUDY

1. Unity and Coherence

A well–organized essay has an introduction, a body, and a conclusion. Each body paragraph contains one major point that is developed with examples, reasons, and other supporting details. Each body paragraph supports the thesis of the essay. When all of the ideas and information in the essay support the thesis, the essay is said to have *unity*.

The body paragraphs should be arranged in the order that will best support the thesis. This is why having an outline is important. Sometimes the body paragraphs are best arranged from the most important point to the least important point. Sometimes it is more effective to put the most important point last, just before the conclusion. Sometimes the points are previewed in the introduction. When the body paragraphs are arranged effectively and logically, the essay is said to have *coherence*.

An essay is *coherent* when all of the ideas within paragraphs and between paragraphs are connected logically. The following *transitions* will help you express relationships between ideas and give your essay unity and coherence.

Introduce examples or reasons	because first	for example for instance	one reason is such as
Add examples or reasons	also and another example is as well as	finally furthermore in addition moreover	next not only…but also second, third… similarily
Show contrast between ideas	although but by contrast even though however	in contrast instead on the contrary on the one hand… on the other hand	nevertheless rather though while yet
Emphasize or show importance	clearly certainly indeed	in fact moreover most importantly	the best example the most important surely
Make a conclusion	consequently in conclusion	in short in summary	therefore thus

WRITING

2. Sample Task and Essay

Here is an example of an independent writing question and a sample essay. The thesis statement appears in bold text in the introduction. Notice how the transitions make the essay more coherent and easier to understand:

Do you agree or disagree with the following statement?

The things we learn from our friends are more important than what we learn from our family.

Use specific reasons and examples to support your opinion.

SAMPLE ESSAY   Word count: 340

   When I think about the lessons I have learned in my life, I find many similarities in what I learned from my friends and from my family. There are also differences. Both kinds of lessons have been very important to me. *However*, when I consider them carefully, **I know that the lessons from my family are more important**.

   While my friends have taught me to enjoy my life, my family has taught me to be strong. My friends have taught me how to feel independent. They have encouraged me to be myself, to have a lot of fun, *and* to find happiness in life. *On the other hand*, my mother has taught me to be independent in a very different way. When I was a child, she gave me advice *such as* "Fight your own battles." She said that so I would be strong *because* she could not always protect me. Sometimes this was very difficult for me when I wanted my mother to help me, *even though* I knew her advice was important.

   Furthermore, my family has taught me compassion and forgiveness. My younger brother taught me these qualities. I will never forget that once I was cruel to him *because* I was angry. My brother was afraid of the dark, *but* I turned off the lights to scare him. He was only six years old, *and* he was afraid and cried. *But* later he asked me to read a book to him until he fell asleep. It was his way to forgive me. I can never forget how my little brother taught me how to forgive.

   I believe that our family teaches us the most important things *because* the lessons from family last longer. My family has taught me to be independent and strong, *and* this will help me during my whole life. *Moreover*, they have taught me how to forgive, which is necessary for getting along with other people. *In short*, the lessons from my family were not always enjoyable, *yet* they are deeper in my heart.

The sample essay effectively addresses the task. It clearly states an opinion and supports the opinion with reasons and examples. It uses transitions appropriately to build unity and coherence. The essay would receive a high score on the TOEFL.

3. Things to Consider

- You must type your essay on the computer keyboard. Do not write your essay on paper and then try to type it into the computer; you will not have enough time to do this. You may plan your essay and write an outline on paper. Then type your essay directly into the typing box on the screen.

 PRACTICE

Exercise 4.8.A

Read the following independent writing question and sample essay:

> Some people learn by reading about things. Others learn by doing things. Which of these methods of learning is better for you? Use specific reasons and examples to support your choice.

Although some people learn better by reading about things, I learn better by doing things. There are several important skills that I learned through action.

I learned how to ride a bicycle and drive a car by experience. I rode a bicycle when I was six years old. Because I could not read about it, I had to get on the bicycle and use my feet and hands. I could also learn from my mistake when I fell off my bicycle. Similarly, I earned to drive a car by doing it. Although I had to study a driving manual and take a test on a computer, I could not learn driving well until I practiced driving in a car.

Learning mathematics is another example of learning by doing things. When I was in sixth grade, my teacher made the students measure our classroom. We measured the length and width of the room. Therefore, we learned how to calculate the area of our classroom or any other room. This experience made mathematics become real for me.

Finally, I learned how to use a computer by doing it. I tried to read the computer manual, but this was difficult for me because the book was very complex. I learned more when I sat at the keyboard and tried using several keys. Of course, my teacher explained some things about the computer. However, I could learn best when I experienced it.

It is true that I have to learn some things by reading, such as history and literature. Reading gives me important knowledge. However, for most skills that I need for my life, such as driving a car and using a computer, I must experience using them in order to learn the skills well. Therefore, I prefer to learn through action.

Now answer the following questions. Discuss your answers with your teacher and classmates.

1. What does the question ask you to do?

2. What does the writer do in the introduction?

3. What is the thesis or main idea of the essay?

4. How is the essay organized?

5. What is the topic sentence of each body paragraph?

6. Does the essay have unity? Why or why not?

7. What transitions help give the essay coherence?

8. Does the essay effectively address the topic and task?

Answers to Exercise 4.8.A are on page 669.

Exercise 4.8.B

Your teacher will assign one of the following essay questions. Read the question carefully, and then plan and write a response. To make this practice more like the real test, allow 30 minutes to complete the essay. Use your time like this:

   ⟋° 5 minutes – to brainstorm and write an outline;

   ⟋° 20 minutes – to write the introduction, body, and conclusion; and

   ⟋° 5 minutes – to check your essay and make corrections.

1. Do you agree or disagree with the following statement?
    All high school students should be required to have three years of studying a foreign language.
    Use specific reasons and examples to support your opinion.

2. Do you agree or disagree with the following statement?
    The automobile is destroying our quality of life.
    Use specific reasons and examples to support your opinion.

3. Some people like to be the leader of a group. Others like to be a member of a group in which another person is the leader. Which do you prefer? Use specific reasons and examples to support your answer.

4. Do you agree or disagree with this statement?
    Employers should be required to provide smoking areas for their employees who smoke cigarettes.
    Use specific reasons and examples to support your opinion.

5. Some students prefer to study at a large university that has several thousand students. Other students prefer studying at a small school that has only a few hundred students. Which of these two types of schools do you prefer? Use specific reasons and examples to support your answer.

6. Do you agree or disagree with the following statement?
    The use of electronic mail (e–mail) makes people become better writers.
    Use specific reasons and examples to support your opinion.

Answers to Exercise 4.8.B will vary.

 EXTENSION

1. Share and discuss the essay that you wrote for Exercise 4.8.B. Work in a group of three students. Make copies of your essay, and give a copy to everyone in your group. Read and discuss each student's essay. Answer the following questions about each:

    a. What is the thesis or main idea of the essay?
    b. Is the essay easy to understand? Why or why not?
    c. What supporting points does the writer make?
    d. What supporting details does the writer give?
    e. Does the essay have unity and coherence? Why or why not?
    f. What transitions does the writer use? Are they used correctly?

    Make suggestions that will help each student improve in the future.

4.9 Independent Writing: Sentence Variety and Word Choice

 FOCUS

Read the following essay question and a paragraph from a student's essay:

> Do you agree or disagree with the following statement?
> **You will not learn much about life if you are always comfortable.**
> Use specific reasons and examples to support your opinion.

> Children must learning about life in a comfortable place. If a child is no safe, the child can't learn nothing. I wanna have children in the future. My duty is for keep my children safety and protection from bad experiences. I gonna give my children food, clothes, and other stuffs. Because my child is comfortable, they will learn alot of things about life. On the contrary, I disagree with the statement.

The writer makes several errors in word choice. Can you identify them? Underline words and phrases that are incorrect or confusing.

Look at these words and phrases in the paragraph. How many did you underline?

must learning	is for keep	stuffs
no safe	safety	Because my child is
can't learn nothing	protection	alot
wanna	I gonna	On the contrary

Now read the same paragraph without errors.

> Children must learn about life in a comfortable place. If a child is not safe, the child can't learn anything. I want to have children in the future. My duty will be to keep my children safe and protect them from bad experiences. I am going to give my children food, clothes, and other things. If my children are comfortable, they will learn a lot of things about life. Therefore, I disagree with the statement.

On the TOEFL, an essay can have a few language errors and still earn a high score—if the errors are minor and do not obscure meaning. However, frequent or serious errors in word choice will result in a lower score.

 STUDY

1. Checking Your Writing

On the TOEFL, you have 30 minutes to plan, write, and revise your response to the independent writing task. Allow around 5 minutes at the end to check and correct your sentence structure, sentence variety, word choice, and spelling.

Your essay will be easier to read, more interesting, and more effective if you:

- use a variety of short and long sentences;
- avoid common sentence errors; and
- use appropriate word choice and word forms.

2. Sentence Variety

Your essay should contain a variety of short and long sentences. If a sentence has more than one clause, the clauses must be joined correctly with a conjunction, subordinator, or conjunctive adverb.

Conjunctions				
and	but	or	so	yet
Subordinators				
although	if	since	unless	where
because	just as	though	when	while
Conjunctive Adverbs				
as a result	furthermore	in addition	moreover	therefore
consequently	however	instead	similarly	thus

There are several ways to combine two or more short sentences into one long sentence. Here are some examples:

Short	Living off campus is exciting. Living off campus is more independent. I prefer the convenience of living on campus.
Long	Living off campus is exciting *and* more independent, *but* I prefer the convenience of living on campus.
Short	Teachers are important for motivating children. Parents are even more important.
Long	*Although* teachers are important for motivating children, parents are even more important.
Short	Athletes are such great entertainers. People like to watch athletes play.
Long	*Since* athletes are such great entertainers, people like to watch them play.
Short	Children should grow up in the country. Children can experience nature.
Long	Children should grow up in the country, *where* they can experience nature.

Short	You are always comfortable. You will never have to struggle. You will not learn much about life.
Long	*If* you are always comfortable, you will never have to struggle; *as a result*, you will not learn much about life.

Short	Students are responsible for their own learning. Students should be self–motivated.
Long	Students are responsible for their own learning, *so* they should be self–motivated.
Long	*Because* students are responsible for their own learning, they should be self–motivated.
Long	Students are responsible for their own learning; *therefore*, they should be self–motivated.

Short	Some people like living in a rural area. I prefer the urban lifestyle.
Long	Some people like living in a rural area, *but* I prefer the urban lifestyle.
Long	*While* some people like living in a rural area, I prefer the urban lifestyle.
Long	Some people like living in a rural area; *however*, I prefer the urban lifestyle.

3. Word Choice

Inappropriate word choice and incorrect word forms may obscure meaning, making your essay difficult to understand. It is best to use vocabulary you are familiar with, but avoid slang and other words that are too informal for an academic essay.

Inappropriate	Parents have to get kids food and other stuff.
Appropriate	Parents have to provide children with food and other necessities.

Inappropriate	Join a hobby club helping you make new friends.
Appropriate	Joining a hobby club will help you make new friends.

Inappropriate	People driving more careful the children are walking to school.
Appropriate	People should drive more carefully when children are walking to school.

Inappropriate	I'm gonna go for a job in broadcast communications.
Appropriate	I am going to look for a job in broadcast communications.

Inappropriate	Competitive sports are totally cool.
Appropriate	Competitive sports benefit us in several important ways.

Inappropriate	I'm exciting about my decision apply to film school.
Appropriate	I am excited about my decision to apply to film school.

Inappropriate	I no like crazy idea.
Appropriate	I do not like strange or confusing ideas.

4. Useful Words for Essays

advantage	contribute	examine	prefer
benefit	controversy	factor	produce
cause	dilemma	influence	provide
characteristic	effect	issue	solution
consequence	essential	necessary	view

WRITING

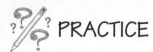 PRACTICE

Exercise 4.9.A

Read the following paragraphs. Check sentence structure, sentence variety, and word choice. Make any corrections that will improve the paragraphs. There may be more than one way to correct an error.

1.

I decide not to get married two years ago. I could finish my university studies. My father he wanted me to get married. My parents they allow me decide. I had married, I have to stay in my husband's home. Because in my culture, married woman, she has a duty to her husband, it's our tradition. I choose finishing my degree instead. I will to be a graduate student in Toronto. I will earning my master's degree in business economics.

2.

I prefer students should have several short vacations throughout the year instead to one long vacation. Students work hardly and need a brake often. Students in my country have several short holidays while every seasons. On the contrast, American students have one long vacation in a summer. I read a paper say that American students forgetting what they learned because the long vacation. This why I belief several short vacations is good than one long vacation.

3.

There are many advantage in having friends that different to me. Such as my friend who is from Turkey learns me alot about his culture. His family is so big and my family is not big. As a result, I like to go to his house to visiting his family. I enjoy the good food. I enjoy the talking because is really cool and interesting. Other friend is an artist. My friend makes pictures and does other arts. It's really cool. In conclusion, my artist friend is not alike me, I learn good things about art from him.

Exercise 4.9.B

Read the following independent writing question and a student's essay. Check sentence structure, sentence variety, and word choice. Make any corrections that will improve the essay. There may be more than one way to correct an error.

> Some people prefer occupations in which they work primarily with machines. Others prefer occupations in which they work mainly with people. Which type of occupation do you prefer? Use specific reasons and examples to support your opinion.

Occupations are mainly two kinds. Some occupations require your work primarily with machines. Other need working with other people. My job is working with machines, especial computers, so I prefer this kind.

Computers are important in the society. I am a computer programmer at a medical university. I like to solving the problems of medical record system. Computer has improved business, research, educational, and many the field of study. Many occupations require specialization in computers. People need specialization training. It's in area of computer operations.

On the other hand, some occupations work mainly with people. It's also neccesary for my job. Because I work a team with two other people. Therefore we must help each one. We solve the problems.

In conclusion, I prefer to working with machines. Because machines need people to operate. In addition, machines improve peoples life. Many occupations need specialization, such as computer programmer. But also need ability for communication to other people. Therefore I believe to work with both machines and people are best kind of job.

Corrections for Exercises 4.9.A and 4.9.B are on pages 669–670.

WRITING

Exercise 4.9.C

Your teacher will assign one of the following essay questions. Read the question carefully, and then plan and write a response. To make this practice more like the real test, allow 30 minutes to complete the essay. Use your time like this:

>   5 minutes – to brainstorm and write an outline;

>   20 minutes – to write the introduction, body, and conclusion; and

>   5 minutes – to check your essay and make corrections.

1. Do you agree or disagree with the following statement?
    You can learn a lot about people by the clothes they wear.
    Use specific reasons and examples to support your opinion.

2. Some people prefer working for a very large company that has several hundred employees. Others prefer working for a small company where they know all of their co–workers. Which do you prefer? Use specific reasons and examples to support your opinion.

3. Do you agree or disagree with the following statement?
    Leaders must pay attention to the advice and opinions of other people.
    Use specific reasons and examples to support your opinion.

4. Do you agree or disagree with the following statement?
    Every child should be raised in a home with two parents.
    Use specific reasons and examples to support your opinion.

5. Some people believe that in high school, boys should be in classes with only boys, and girls should be in classes with only girls. Other people believe that high school classes should be coeducational, with students of both genders studying together. Which view do you agree with? Use specific reasons and examples to support your opinion.

6. Do you agree or disagree with the following statement?
    Technological progress has made us lazy.
    Use specific reasons and examples to support your opinion.

7. Do you agree or disagree with the following statement?
    Children should always be happy, so they should be sheltered from unhappiness.
    Use specific reasons and examples to support your answer.

8. Some people think that science and technology are most important to society. Others think that art, literature, and music are most important. Which position do you favor? Use specific reasons and examples to support your opinion.

9. Do you agree or disagree with the following statement?
    It is always important to support your friends even if they do something illegal.
    Use specific reasons and examples to support your answer.

10. When governments make decisions, some people think it is most important to consider the effect of the decision on the economy. Others think the effect on the environment is more important. Which position do you agree with? Use specific reasons and examples to support your opinion.

Answers to Exercise 4.9.C will vary.

 EXTENSION

1. Review the essay you wrote for one of the essay questions in units 4.7 through 4.9. Check your sentence structure, sentence variety, and vocabulary. Ask yourself the following questions:

    a. Are all of my sentences complete, with correctly formed subjects and verbs?
    b. Are there any grammar errors that need correcting?
    c. Does my essay have a variety of short and long sentences?
    d. Does my essay use appropriate word choice and correct word forms?
    e. Are there any misspelled words that need correcting?
    f. What changes can I make to improve the essay?

2. Share and discuss your essay for one of the essay questions in units 4.7 through 4.9. Work in a group of three students. Make copies of your essay, and give a copy to everyone in your group. Read and discuss each student's essay. Answer the following questions about each:

    a. Is the essay easy to read and understand? Why or why not?
    b. Does the essay have unity and coherence? Why or why not?
    c. Are there any sentences in which the meaning is unclear? If so, what makes them unclear?
    d. Does the essay have a variety of short and long sentences?
    e. Does the essay use appropriate word choice and correct word forms?
    f. What improvements would you make?

Make suggestions that will help each student earn a high score on the independent writing task.

4.10 Evaluating the Essay

FOCUS

Read the following independent writing task and sample essay:

> Do you agree or disagree with the following statement?
>
> **Students learn more in large lecture classes than in small discussion classes.**
>
> Use specific reasons and examples to support your answer.

Students can learn in both large lecture classes and small discussion classes. However, I beleive that students learn more in small discussion classes because they can practice skills that need in their profession.

First, a small class allows students improve their speaking skills. Students give alot of oral reports, and they discuss ideas with their instructor and classmates. They express their own opinions and learn about classmate's opinions. Class discussions give students confidence in speaking a group, that is a skill required in many professions.

Second, a small class is like a work situation. Many professions require people work in teams to solve problems and making decisions. A small class give students valuable practice in teamworks. In a small class, students responsible for participation, just as in a team in a work situation.

Finally, students can get more help from the instructor in a small class. Usually, it is not possible in a large class, students can not ask quetions. However, in a small class, students can ask questions and get better helps from the instructor.

In summary, students learn more useful skills in a small class. Therefore, I recommend small classes for students who want experience for their profession.

How would you rate the essay? Check the appropriate space between WEAK and STRONG:

Organization	WEAK __ __ __ __ __ STRONG
Thesis and support	WEAK __ __ __ __ __ STRONG
Unity and coherence	WEAK __ __ __ __ __ STRONG
Grammar and vocabulary	WEAK __ __ __ __ __ STRONG

On the TOEFL, this essay would receive a score of 3. It is well organized. It has a thesis and some supporting details; however, the essay is also short and lacks development. It is written coherently with appropriate use of transitions. However, there are many errors in grammar, vocabulary, and spelling.

 STUDY

1. How Your Essay Will Be Evaluated

When you take the TOEFL, two trained evaluators will read your response to the independent writing task. Your writing will be evaluated on how well you organize and develop ideas, display unity and coherence, and use English appropriately. The evaluators will assign a score of 1 to 5, with 5 the highest score possible. To score your essay, they will use criteria similar to those in the following table.

	INDEPENDENT WRITING TASK **Description of Score Levels**
5	**An essay at this level** ⤳ effectively addresses the task by clearly stating an opinion; and ⤳ is well organized and well developed with appropriate examples, reasons, or details; and ⤳ displays unity and coherence; and ⤳ uses language effectively, with sentence variety and appropriate word choice and only occasional minor language errors.
4	**An essay at this level** ⤳ addresses the task well, but some points may not be fully supported; and ⤳ is generally well organized and sufficiently developed with examples, reasons, or details; and ⤳ displays unity and coherence, but may have some redundancy or lack of clarity; and ⤳ contains sentence variety and a range of vocabulary, but may have noticeable minor language errors that do not interfere with meaning.
3	**An essay at this level** ⤳ addresses the task with some development and some appropriate supporting details; or ⤳ displays unity and coherence, but connections among ideas may be occasionally unclear; or ⤳ is inconsistent in using language effectively, with errors in grammar and vocabulary that occasionally obscure meaning; or ⤳ contains an accurate but limited range of sentence structures and vocabulary.
2	**An essay at this level** ⤳ displays limited development in response to the task, with inappropriate or insufficient supporting details; or ⤳ contains inadequate organization or connections among ideas; or ⤳ contains an accumulation of errors in grammar and usage.
1	**An essay at this level** ⤳ is flawed by serious disorganization or underdevelopment; or ⤳ contains little or no detail, or details that are irrelevant to the task; or ⤳ contains serious and frequent errors in grammar and usage.
0	**An essay at this level** ⤳ is not related to the given topic; or ⤳ is written in a language other than English; or ⤳ is blank.

PRACTICE

Exercise 4.10.A

Read the independent writing question and the five essays that follow. Evaluate each essay according to the descriptions of the five levels on page 443. Assign each response a score of 5, 4, 3, 2 or 1.

> Do you agree or disagree with the following statement?
> **Advertising influences people's behavior in a negative way.**
> Use specific reasons and examples to support your opinion.

Response A   Score: _____

People see a lot of advertising in newspapers and magazines, on signs, and on television. Today people even see ads in the movie theater! All of this advertising influences people's behavior in a negative way. It influences how people spend their money, how they look at themselves, and how they communicate with other people.

Advertising influences how people spend their money. People sometimes buy things they can't afford or don't need. I read a story of a family that bought a computer for their children, but they were living in a tent. They didn't even have electricity for the computer. People spend too much because they have to be better than everyone else. In my country, weddings are a big industry, and families spend too much money because of advertising. This is a negative influence of advertising.

Advertising affects how people view themselves. Sometimes it makes people feel bad if they can't buy something. For example, a lot of sports and movie stars advertise shoes, clothes, and so on. Children see this on television and pressure their parents to buy it. There are a lot of crimes because teenagers kill to get designer jackets. Advertising makes them feel like they are nobody without designer clothes. Also, teenagers start to smoke because they think this looks cool. Moreover, some girls want to be thin like girls in the ads.

Finally, advertising changes people's communication. I hear a lot of little children saying the phrases they hear on television. They also sing the songs from the commercials. Also, advertising influences spelling. I have seen "night" spelled like "nite." Therefore, advertising has a negative effects on the ways that people speak and write English.

Advertising has a lot of good points. It is a way to sell things in a capitalist country. However, there are also a lot of bad influences on people's behavior because of advertising.

Response B   Score: _____

We can see advertising in many places. For example, on TV also on buildings, magazines and junk mail. The purpose of advertising is showing people to buy things. We can't avoid a negative way for advertising even we are educated. Many advertising is a lie so we don't always know it's true. It's a negative behavior for people tell a lie in advertising. But it's too bad because people don't know and buy things even it's a lie. This is illegal in many countries. We had better to find the answer to the problem.

I used to watch TV and saw many advertising on TV. I saw lot of negative behavior. Many TV shows are very stupid advertising. Sometimes is a lie, animals don't talk. Advertising—it's good but some is a lie and not real. But still people's belief, and so it's a problem.

Response C   Score: _____

Advertising is a large part of our culture, so of course advertising influences people's behavior. But I disagree with the statement, advertising influences behavior in a negative way. On the contrary, I think the effect of advertising is positive for society.

One effect of advertising is a way for people to learn about new products to buy. We learn about new types of products and service by seeing it on television. For example, I learned about a special price for a travel to Florida from advertising on television. This had a positive effect on my behavior because I could enjoyed a beautiful week in Florida. Other things I learned are a new restaurant of health food, a movie, and places for automobile service. All these advertising had a positive effect of helping me have a better life.

Another effect of advertising is a way to compare the prices and the quality of service. This is a positive because we can think carefully before we buy something. Also, we can save money. We can find a better quality. So advertising has a positive effect of critical thinking and making smarter shoppers.

Also, another positive effect of advertising is a way to get ideas for living more interesting life. We learn many interesting ideas from television advertising and also in magazines. For example, I read magazines and see intresting ideas to decorate my apartment in advertising. Also, I learn about new kinds of food and places to visit. So advertising has a positive effect of helping me, not a negative influence on my behavior.

Of course, some advertising influence behavior in a negative way, such as smoking. But I think the general influence on people's behavior is positive. Advertising helps people learn about products, compare the prices, and to get interesting ideas for better life.

Response D   Score: _____

Advertising influences people's behavior in a negative way. I disagree with the statement. The statement is not true.

Sometimes advertising is very interesting. I am interesting by the ads on the bus and train. Some advertising is beautiful art and it's not negative influence, it's very creativity. The advertising industry gives jobs to artists and writers. My two cousins and his friend they have a job in advertising company where draw pictures and design posters. Some posters on the bus and train where many people can see the posters. My cousin he studied at art college and his degree in commercial art. He got a job where make advertising posters. On the other hand, some advertising on television gives jobs to actors and musicians. Sometimes famous actors they make ad for television advertising, then later get a job in movies and so on. Some actor he doesn't act, he uses voice narration on the television ads. I can hear the voice of some famous actors in the advertising, it's not negative influence. The advertising industry has jobs for many people, it's the reason I disagree with the statement. Also, I am interesting by the ads on clothing, such as T–shirts and caps. These pictures they are very beautiful by artists. Some ads in the print media, newspaper and magazine, also, they are very good. My second cousin sometime she designs ads for the print media.

Response E   Score: _____

> People influenced by the world around them. Advertising has many ways
influencing people's behavior. I agree with the statement. Most the influences of
advertising are negative. I will discuss advertising on television and Internet.
> Advertising on television is too much. Every hour has too many comercials.
Advertising is for cars, lifestyle, cloths, liquer, diamonds, and many other things. People
don't need all these things. These things are espensive, so influence is negative. People
want too many things. They see the comercial on television. They want rich lifestyle.
So they spend too much money can't afford.
> Some advertising is for medicine and drugs such as asprin. People need some
medicine. However, they take too many drugs don't need them. Some advertising is for
food, such as pizza, cookies, candy, coke, and beer. People need food to live. However,
many people get very fat. They eat too much junk food. Therefore, advertising is mainly
a negative influence. Advertising cause people spend too much money. Moreover, people
eat too much junk food. It's bad for health.
> Also, people influenced by the Internet advertising. It's too much! Every kind of
picture and spam on email—it's too much comercial on Internet. In the past, Internet was
for study and learning. But now Internet is mainly way for sell things. People see
advertising. They want too many things. It's a pity. It's mainly influences people's behavior
in a negative way. Moreover, some Internet advertising is false.

Answers to Exercise 4.10.A are on page 670.

EXTENSION

1. Study the descriptions of the five score levels on page 443. Make sure you understand the
    description for each level. Check your understanding of the meaning of these words and phrases:

effectively addresses	redundancy	limited range
unity	lack of clarity	limited development
coherence	range of vocabulary	accumulation of errors
minor language errors	obscure meaning	usage

2. Review the essays you wrote for the writing questions in units 4.6 through 4.9. Evaluate each essay
    according to the descriptions of the five levels on page 443. What are the areas of strength in your
    writing? What are your most serious problems? How can you improve your writing to earn a high
    score on the independent writing task?

PROGRESS – 4.6 through 4.10

QUIZ 4

Time – 30 minutes

For this task, you will write an essay in response to a question that asks you to state and support your opinion on a topic. Your essay will be scored on the quality of your writing, including how well you organize and develop your ideas and how well you use language to express your ideas. Typically, an effective essay will have a minimum of 300 words.

Read the question below and make any notes that will help you plan your response. Then begin typing your essay.

Do you agree or disagree with the following statement?

It is more important for students to read books about real events than it is for them to read novels.

Use specific reasons and examples to support your opinion.

Writing Time – 30 minutes

Record your score on the Progress Chart on page 793.

PROGRESS – 4.6 through 4.10

QUIZ 5

Time – 30 minutes

For this task, you will write an essay in response to a question that asks you to state and support your opinion on a topic. Your essay will be scored on the quality of your writing, including how well you organize and develop your ideas and how well you use language to express your ideas. Typically, an effective essay will have a minimum of 300 words.

Read the question below and make any notes that will help you plan your response. Then begin typing your essay.

> Some people want to have a job where they can make or do things with their hands. Other people prefer having a job where they can work with their heads and think. Which type of job do you prefer? Use specific reasons and examples to support your answer.

Writing Time – 30 minutes

Record your score on the Progress Chart on page 793.

PROGRESS – 4.6 through 4.10

QUIZ 6

Time – 30 minutes

For this task, you will write an essay in response to a question that asks you to state and support your opinion on a topic. Your essay will be scored on the quality of your writing, including how well you organize and develop your ideas and how well you use language to express your ideas. Typically, an effective essay will have a minimum of 300 words.

Read the question below and make any notes that will help you plan your response. Then begin typing your essay.

> Do you agree or disagree with the following statement?
>
> **Solitude, spending time alone, is one of our best teachers.**
>
> Use specific reasons and examples to support your opinion.

Writing Time – 30 minutes

WRITING

Record your score on the Progress Chart on page 793.

PROGRESS – 4.1 through 4.10

QUIZ 7

Time – approximately 55 minutes

There are two questions in this quiz. Question 1 is an integrated writing task. Question 2 is an independent writing task. Your response to each task will earn a score of 1, 2, 3, 4, or 5, with 5 the highest possible score. Add the two scores to obtain your total score.

QUESTION 1

For this task, you will write a response to a question about a reading passage and a lecture. You may take notes, and you may use your notes to help you write your response. Your response will be scored on the quality of your writing and on how well you connect the points in the lecture with points in the reading. Typically, an effective response will have 150 to 225 words.

Reading Time – 3 minutes

When we experience acute stress, a hormonal response triggers our body either to stand and fight or to flee as quickly as possible. It is an ancient survival mechanism, common to all humans, which evolved when our prehistoric ancestors were chased by saber–toothed tigers. This mechanism is known as the acute stress response, or the "fight or flight" response. During the fight/flight response, our bodies get a boost of adrenaline, a hormone that stimulates the heart rate. This, in turn, provides the strength to fight or the speed to flee.

The fight response is expressed as aggressive behavior. For example, when threatened by a potential attack from an enemy, a human will respond with a show of force: a display of weapons or actual fighting. The fight response can take various forms. Instead of physical fighting, it may take the form of angry, argumentative behavior. A heated verbal argument increases the flow of adrenaline, which can cause an argument to become a physical attack.

The flight response causes humans to withdraw from situations where stress occurs. When our prehistoric ancestors encountered a predator, they had to avoid being killed. If they could not fight the predator, they had to flee. The flight response provided a burst of speed that enabled a fast escape. Today, the flight response may take the form of withdrawal from social activities, abuse of alcohol or drugs, or other forms of escape. In the workplace, a stressed person might go into his office to work alone, avoiding co–workers. Outside work, he might escape by watching television, surfing the Internet, or playing electronic games.

Now listen to the recording. When you hear the question, begin your response. You may look at the reading passage during the writing time.

 Album 8, Track 15

> Summarize the points made in the lecture, being sure to explain how they differ from specific points made in the reading passage.

 Stop

Writing Time – 20 minutes

QUESTION 2

For this task, you will write an essay in response to a question that asks you to state and support your opinion on a topic. Your essay will be scored on the quality of your writing, including how well you organize and develop your ideas and how well you use language to express your ideas. Typically, an effective essay will have a minimum of 300 words.

Read the question below and make any notes that will help you plan your response. Then begin typing your essay.

> Some students like to work in a group with other students when doing assignments and projects. Other students prefer to work independently. Which do you prefer? Use specific reasons and examples to support your answer.

Writing Time – 30 minutes

Key points for Writing Quiz 7 are on page 670.

Record your total score on the Progress Chart on page 793.

WRITING

PROGRESS – 4.1 through 4.10

QUIZ 8

Time – approximately 55 minutes

There are two questions in this quiz. Question 1 is an integrated writing task. Question 2 is an independent writing task. Your response to each task will earn a score of 1, 2, 3, 4, or 5, with 5 the highest possible score. Add the two scores to obtain your total score.

QUESTION 1

For this task, you will write a response to a question about a reading passage and a lecture. You may take notes, and you may use your notes to help you write your response. Your response will be scored on the quality of your writing and on how well you connect the points in the lecture with points in the reading. Typically, an effective response will have 150 to 225 words.

Reading Time – 3 minutes

Contemporary method acting is a style of acting that emphasizes an individualized, psychological approach. "The Method" requires an actor to bring realism and depth to a part with his own emotions and experiences. Actors use techniques such as sense and memory to achieve realism. They delve into their own past to discover feelings that are similar to those of the character. Method acting is the opposite of the "wooden" acting of earlier periods. Characters are shown to have a complex interior life, rather than being stereotyped figures, such as hero or villain, which represent a single concept.

"The Method" develops an actor's ability to use the subtext of a script to convey the complexity of inner feelings. Training involves long rehearsal periods where actors "go into character" and analyze all the specifics of a scene. They must explore the subtext, the deeper, unwritten meaning in the script, the source of conflict and contradiction. The subtext is where actors discover how to structure motion around conflicting emotions so the character can be shown as a complex human being with multiple and contradictory desires.

Method acting is one of the most difficult styles to learn because there are no technical forms that can be practiced. Spoken language is secondary to emotions, so no training in voice or movement is necessary. Emotions shape how a character speaks and moves. Method acting requires a strong commitment from actors, who are encouraged to "live the part," to become the character and allow the character to develop naturally. Some actors become so immersed in a role that they remain in character even when they are not acting.

Now listen to the recording. When you hear the question, begin your response. You may look at the reading passage during the writing time.

 Album 8, Track 16

> Summarize the points made in the lecture, being sure to explain how they oppose specific points made in the reading passage.

 Stop

Writing Time – 20 minutes

QUESTION 2

For this task, you will write an essay in response to a question that asks you to state and support your opinion on a topic. Your essay will be scored on the quality of your writing, including how well you organize and develop your ideas and how well you use language to express your ideas. Typically, an effective essay will have a minimum of 300 words.

Read the question below and make any notes that will help you plan your response. Then begin typing your essay.

> Do you agree or disagree with the following statement?
> **Television has had a mostly positive effect on society.**
> Use specific reasons and examples to support your opinion.

Writing Time – 30 minutes

Key points for Writing Quiz 8 are on page 670.

Record your total score on the Progress Chart on page 793.

READING SECTION DIRECTIONS

The Reading section measures your ability to understand academic passages in English. You will read passages and answer questions about them. Answer all questions based on what is stated or implied in the passages.

You will read three passages. You have 60 minutes to read the passages and answer the questions.

Most questions are worth one point, but the last question in each set is worth more than one point. The directions indicate how many points you may receive.

Some passages include a word or phrase in **bold** type. For these words and phrases, you will see a definition in a glossary at the end of the passage.

THE MOON

1   The moon is the closest natural body and the single natural satellite of the earth. The orbit of the moon around the earth is not circular but elliptical. Thus, the distance of the moon from the earth varies from a maximum distance of 406,685 kilometers to a minimum of 356,410 kilometers. In one day, the moon moves about 12 degrees along its orbit. The moon completes one revolution of the earth in 27.3 days, a period known as a sidereal month.

2   The moon rotates slowly on its axis, making one complete rotation in a period of time exactly equal to its orbit around the earth. Thus, the moon keeps the same hemisphere or face turned toward the earth at all times. We do not, however, always see only half of the moon's surface from the earth. The eccentricity of the moon's orbit allows us to see additional lunar surface through irregular movements called librations, which expose an extra 18 percent of the moon's surface at one time or another.

3   In 1969, the first humans landed on the moon's surface in the Sea of Tranquility. Subsequent lunar landings were on the Ocean of Storms and the Sea of Serenity. Despite these watery names, the astronauts had to cope with an environment devoid of water. The dark areas on the moon's surface are called seas and oceans because early observers assumed the moon was much like the earth. We now know that the seas are dark because they are volcanic basalt flows, mostly of iron silicate. The brighter parts, the mountains, consist of igneous deposits of aluminum and calcium silicates.

4   Like the earth, the moon has no light of its own; its daylight side reflects the light of the sun. The moon goes through phases, apparent changes in its shape, because it orbits the earth in nearly the same plane as the earth orbits the sun. The eight phases of the moon arise from its changing position in relation to the earth. At the new moon, the start of the first phase, the dark side of the moon is turned toward the earth, so the moon cannot be seen. A few nights later, a thin crescent hangs in the evening twilight. At this time, the dark side of the moon is faintly visible because it is illuminated by earthshine, the light of the sun reflected from the earth to the moon, then back again.

5   The second phase is a waxing crescent moon, followed by the third phase, when the moon forms a right angle with the earth–sun line, and a half moon appears at sunset. During the fourth phase, the moon is more than half but less than fully illuminated, known as a waxing gibbous moon. The waxing gibbous moon is followed by a full moon (fifth phase), which occurs when the sun, earth, and moon are in opposition, or roughly aligned. At full moon, the rising disk of the moon appears to balance the setting sun in the evening sky. When the moon is just past full, a lunar twilight—seen as a glow in the eastern sky—will precede moonrise.

6   After the full moon, the moon begins to wane, through a waning gibbous moon (sixth phase), a waning half moon (seventh phase), and a waning crescent moon (eighth phase). Toward the end of the eighth phase, a thin crescent appears at morning twilight, again accompanied by earthshine. Finally, the cycle ends and another begins with a dark moon: another new moon. The lunar cycle takes 29.5 days to complete—a period known as a synodic month or the moon's synodic period.

7   At its full phase, the moon's intensity is about one millionth that of the sun, and it is possible to read a newspaper by the light of the moon. The full moon nearest the autumnal equinox in September is called the Harvest Moon. The Harvest Moon ushers in a period of several successive days when the moon rises in the northeast soon after sunset. This phenomenon gives farmers in temperate latitudes extra hours of light in which to harvest their crops before frost and winter come. The full moon following the Harvest Moon is called the Hunter's Moon and is accompanied by a similar but less marked phenomenon of early moonrise.

1. Which sentence below best expresses the essential information in the highlighted sentence in paragraph 1? Incorrect choices change the meaning in important ways or leave out essential information.

   (A) The only object circling the earth that is not man–made is the moon, our closest satellite.
   (B) The earth has several natural satellites, but the moon has only one natural satellite.
   (C) The moon is closer to the earth's surface than are other moons to other planets' surfaces.
   (D) At some times during its orbit, the moon is closer to the earth than it is at other times.

2. The word eccentricity in paragraph 2 is closest in meaning to

   (A) speed
   (B) beauty
   (C) abnormality
   (D) distance

3. The phrase devoid of in paragraph 3 is closest in meaning to

   (A) similar to
   (B) without any
   (C) covered by
   (D) colder than

4. Which of the following can be inferred from paragraph 3 about the naming of the dark areas on the moon's surface?

   (A) People once thought the moon contained large bodies of water.
   (B) The moon's oceans and seas are named after places on the earth.
   (C) The dark areas are the result of underwater volcanic eruptions.
   (D) The first astronauts named the body of water in which they landed.

5. All of the following occur during a lunar cycle EXCEPT:

   (A) The dark side of the moon faces the earth.
   (B) A thin crescent moon appears in the evening.
   (C) The moon forms a right angle with the earth–sun line.
   (D) All sides of the moon are seen from the earth.

6. Which statement is true of a gibbous moon?

   (A) A gibbous moon cannot be seen from the earth.
   (B) A gibbous moon is more than halfway full.
   (C) A gibbous moon has its own source of light.
   (D) A gibbous moon immediately follows a new moon.

7. The word wane in paragraph 6 is closest in meaning to

   (A) glow brightly
   (B) appear smaller
   (C) change color
   (D) rise earlier

8. The period of time between successive new moons is known as

   (A) an elliptical orbit
   (B) moonrise
   (C) a waxing moon
   (D) a synodic month

9. At what point in the lunar cycle is the dark side of the moon faintly illuminated?

   (A) When the moon is just past full
   (B) When the sun, earth, and moon are aligned
   (C) Just before and just after the new moon
   (D) During the fifth and sixth phases

10. The phrase ushers in in paragraph 7 is closest in meaning to

    (A) prevents
    (B) invades
    (C) separates
    (D) introduces

11. According to the passage, which of the following is a benefit of the Harvest Moon?

    (A) The moon forecasts clear weather for several days.
    (B) The moon indicates the best time to harvest crops.
    (C) Farmers are able to work by moonlight.
    (D) The beginning of winter is delayed.

12. Look at the four squares, **A**, **B**, **C**, and **D**, which indicate where the following sentence could be added to the passage. Where would the sentence best fit?

This is because tidal distortion by the earth over time has slowed the moon's rotation period to match its orbital period.

    A The moon rotates slowly on its axis, making one complete rotation in a period of time exactly equal to its orbit around the earth. **B** Thus, the moon keeps the same hemisphere or face turned toward the earth at all times. We do not, however, always see only half of the moon's surface from the earth. **C** The eccentricity of the lunar orbit allows us to see additional lunar surface through irregular movements called librations, which expose an extra 18 percent of the moon's surface at one time or another. **D**

13. An introductory sentence for a brief summary of the passage is provided below. Complete the summary by selecting the THREE answer choices that express the most important ideas in the passage. Some sentences do not belong in the summary because they express ideas that are not presented in the passage or are minor ideas in the passage. ***This question is worth 2 points.***

Several important features characterize the moon.

•
•
•

Answer Choices

(A) The moon makes one complete rotation on its axis in the same time it makes one revolution around the earth.

(B) The moon's librations are revealed through systematic mapping of the moon during a lunar month.

(C) The first astronauts walked on the moon's surface in the Sea of Tranquility in 1969.

(D) The same hemisphere of the moon always faces the earth, although it changes in appearance during a lunar cycle.

(E) The moon's different phases are a result of its changing position in relation to the earth.

(F) The Harvest Moon is the name given to the full moon nearest the autumnal equinox.

How to Score 2–Point Question	
Answers Correct	**Points Earned**
3	2
2	1
0 – 1	0

ORIGINS OF THE NATURE MOVEMENT

1   The nature preservation movement is based on the belief that we should respect the natural environment and work to protect it for others to enjoy. The movement had its origins in a nineteenth–century geological study of the American West. In 1871 the director of the United States Geological Survey invited a painter named Thomas Moran to join a government expedition that would explore the Yellowstone area of Wyoming. At that time, Yellowstone was largely unknown except for the tales of mysterious mud lakes and geysers. Moran's role in the expedition was funded partly by the Northern Pacific Railroad, whose directors thought that an artist's images of Yellowstone might help create a new tourist destination. Besides Moran, the expedition included a photographer who provided an objective record of Yellowstone's geothermal wonders. Moran's watercolors supplied the color the photographs could not, and the photographs confirmed the reality of Moran's strange sketches of geysers and steaming lakes.

2   The expedition was the turning point in Thomas Moran's career. Lacking formal training, he was essentially self–taught, spending his early career copying the works of English landscape painters. Then the expedition allowed the artist to combine his personal vision with his public role as educator of a national audience. His watercolors of Yellowstone portrayed its glorious features in a way that increased their emotional impact. Yet in the majestic Western landscape there were some scenes that neither a photograph nor a watercolor could adequately convey. One of these was the view down into the deep chasm of the Yellowstone River, toward the waterfall. As soon as Moran returned east, he painted the scene in oil from memory and imagination on an eight–by–fourteen–foot canvas. *The Grand Canyon of the Yellowstone* became the first landscape by an American artist ever bought by the U.S. government.

3   Meanwhile, the expedition leader and the railroad had been lobbying Congress to set aside Yellowstone as a national park. To prove Yellowstone's uniqueness and beauty, Moran's watercolor sketches were displayed in the U.S. Capitol. In 1872, President Grant signed a law preserving the whole Yellowstone area, thirty–five hundred square miles, as the world's first national park. Artists rarely have such an immediate impact on the political process, and the accomplishment is a tribute to the passion of Moran's vision.

4   Another person who influenced the public's perception of nature was the Canadian wildlife artist and writer Ernest Thompson Seton. During his long life as a naturalist, explorer, and educator, Seton promoted the idea that nature is something to be respected and preserved. He was a fascinating storyteller who wrote and illustrated over 60 books and several hundred articles and short stories.

5   Seton was born in England in 1860 and immigrated to Canada at the age of six. Active in art from an early age, at twenty–one he joined two older brothers on their farm in Manitoba, Canada. Seton was always interested in his natural surroundings and devoted much of his time to studying and drawing wild animals, sometimes counting every feather on the wing of a bird. Self–trained as a biologist, he started out as a naturalist and scientific illustrator for the government of Manitoba. Around the same time, he began writing as well. One of Seton's most popular and dramatic wilderness stories, "Lobo," told of his hunt for a legendary gray wolf in New Mexico. The story of Lobo was first published in a popular magazine, and later with other stories in book form as *Wild Animals I Have Known*. This book has never been out of print since it first appeared in 1898. Seton also wrote a series of magazine articles that taught children about nature, camping, hiking, and woodcraft. As a key figure in the woodcraft movement and in the early history of the Boy Scouts of America, Seton inspired thousands of children to appreciate the natural world.

6   The enduring message of both Thomas Moran and Ernest Thompson Seton was that nature is beautiful, noble, and deserving of our respect and protection. They believed that people should become close with nature and educate others about it. The remarkable extent to which we have become a society of nature lovers can be attributed to their vision and influence.

14. According to paragraph 1, the primary purpose of the 1871 expedition to Yellowstone was to

   (A) search for suitable land to build a railroad
   (B) study a region that was not well known
   (C) provide an artist with new subjects to paint
   (D) preserve the area as a national park

15. Which sentence below best expresses the essential information in the highlighted sentence in paragraph 1? Incorrect choices change the meaning in important ways or leave out essential information.

   (A) Moran asked the directors of the railroad to finance the expedition so tourists would want to visit Yellowstone by train.
   (B) Yellowstone was not a popular tourist destination until Moran created images that convinced the railroad that this was a good idea.
   (C) The railroad helped pay for Moran to join the expedition because its directors wanted pictures to promote tourism in Yellowstone.
   (D) The directors of the railroad believed that Moran was the best artist for the expedition because his paintings were very famous.

16. The word objective in paragraph 1 is closest in meaning to

   (A) opposing
   (B) realistic
   (C) creative
   (D) blurry

17. Why does the author use the phrase turning point in discussing Moran's career in paragraph 2?

   (A) To show that Moran became successful because of the expedition
   (B) To explain why Moran changed his focus to landscape painting
   (C) To describe how public opinion about art education changed
   (D) To state that at first Moran did not want to go on the expedition

18. The word glorious in paragraph 2 is closest in meaning to

   (A) dangerous
   (B) hidden
   (C) wonderful
   (D) simple

19. What is The Grand Canyon of the Yellowstone?

   (A) A watercolor sketch
   (B) An early photograph
   (C) An oil painting
   (D) A book title

20. It can be inferred from paragraph 3 that

   (A) there were many art lovers in the U.S. government in 1872
   (B) President Grant visited Yellowstone before signing the law
   (C) politicians knew more about art than the general public did
   (D) Moran's artistry helped inspire the national park concept

21. The word perception in paragraph 4 is closest in meaning to

   (A) view
   (B) exploitation
   (C) fear
   (D) memory

22. The word figure in paragraph 5 is closest in meaning to

   (A) hunter
   (B) student
   (C) leader
   (D) statue

23. All of the following statements are true of both Moran and Seton EXCEPT:

   (A) They created influential images of nature.
   (B) They were self–trained in some areas of study.
   (C) They informed a wide audience about nature.
   (D) They formed a wilderness protection society.

24. Which of the following statements most accurately reflects the author's opinion of Moran and Seton?

(A) Moran and Seton had different ideas about how to portray nature.

(B) The work of Moran and Seton inspired the nature preservation movement.

(C) Seton's illustrations show that he was influenced by Moran's paintings.

(D) Moran was important in his time, but Seton is more influential today.

25. Look at the four squares, **A**, **B**, **C**, and **D**, which indicate where the following sentence could be added to the passage. Where would the sentence best fit?

Seton thought wolves were the noblest of creatures, and he developed an almost mystical reverence for them.

Seton was born in England in 1860 and immigrated to Canada at the age of six. Active in art from an early age, at twenty–one he joined two older brothers on their farm in Manitoba, Canada. **A** Seton was always interested in his natural surroundings and devoted much of his time to studying and drawing wild animals, sometimes counting every feather on the wing of a bird. **B** Self–trained as a biologist, he started out as a naturalist and scientific illustrator for the government of Manitoba. Around the same time, he began writing as well. One of Seton's most popular and dramatic wilderness stories, "Lobo," told of his hunt for a legendary gray wolf in New Mexico. **C** The story of Lobo was first published in a popular magazine, and later with other stories in book form as *Wild Animals I Have Known*. This book has never been out of print since it first appeared in 1898. Seton also wrote a series of magazine articles that taught children about nature, camping, hiking, and woodcraft. **D** As a key figure in the woodcraft movement and in the early history of the Boy Scouts of America, Seton inspired thousands of children to appreciate the natural world.

26. Select the appropriate phrases from the answer choices and match them to the person that they describe. TWO of the answer choices will NOT be used. *This question is worth 3 points.*

Answer Choices

(A) Began his career as a naturalist and scientific illustrator

(B) Painted watercolor sketches of geological features

(C) Learned to paint by copying the works of landscape painters

(D) Produced art that inspired a social reform movement in cities

(E) Wrote a collection of stories that is still being printed as a book

(F) Took photographs of Yellowstone's natural wonders

(G) Influenced the process that created the world's first national park

Thomas Moran

-
-
-

Ernest Thompson Seton

-
-

How to Score 3–Point Question	
Answers Correct	**Points Earned**
5	3
4	2
3	1
0 – 2	0

THE ATLANTIC COD FISHERY

1   Off the northeastern shore of North America, from the island of Newfoundland in Canada south to New England in the United States, there is a series of shallow areas called banks. Several large banks off Newfoundland are together called the Grand Banks, huge shoals on the edge of the North American continental shelf, where the warm waters of the Gulf Stream meet the cold waters of the Labrador Current. As the currents brush each other, they stir up minerals from the ocean floor, providing nutrients for plankton and tiny shrimp–like creatures called krill, which feed on the plankton. Herring and other small fish rise to the surface to eat the krill. Groundfish, such as the Atlantic cod, live in the ocean's bottom layer, congregating in the shallow waters where they prey on krill and small fish. This rich environment has produced cod by the millions and once had a greater density of cod than anywhere else on Earth.

2   Beginning in the eleventh century, boats from the ports of northwestern Europe arrived to fish the Grand Banks. For the next eight centuries, the entire Newfoundland economy was based on Europeans arriving, catching fish for a few months in the summer, and then taking fish back to European markets. Cod laid out to dry on wooden "flakes" was a common sight in the fishing villages dotting the coast. Settlers in the region used to think the only sea creature worth talking about was cod, and in the local speech the word "fish" became synonymous with cod. Newfoundland's national dish was a pudding whose main ingredient was cod.

3   By the nineteenth century, the Newfoundland fishery was largely controlled by merchants based in the capital at St. John's. They marketed the catch supplied by the fishers working out of more than 600 villages around the long coastline. In return, the merchants provided fishing equipment, clothing, and all the food that could not be grown in the island's thin, rocky soil. This system kept the fishers in a continuous state of debt and dependence on the merchants.

4   Until the twentieth century, fishers believed in the cod's ability to replenish itself and thought that overfishing was impossible. However, Newfoundland's cod fishery began to show signs of trouble during the 1930s, when cod failed to support the fishers and thousands were unemployed. The slump lasted for the next few decades. Then, when an international agreement in 1977 established the 200–mile offshore fishing limit, the Canadian government decided to build up the modern Grand Banks fleet and make fishing a viable economic base for Newfoundland again. All of Newfoundland's seafood companies were merged into one conglomerate. By the 1980s, the conglomerate was prospering, and cod were commanding excellent prices in the market. Consequently, there was a significant increase in the number of fishers and fish–processing plant workers.

5   However, while the offshore fishery was prospering, the inshore fishermen found their catches dropping off. In 1992 the Canadian government responded by closing the Grand Banks to groundfishing. Newfoundland's cod fishing and processing industries were shut down in a bid to let the vanishing stocks recover. The moratorium was extended in 1994, when all of the Atlantic cod fisheries in Canada were closed, except for one in Nova Scotia, and strict quotas were placed on other species of groundfish. Canada's cod fishing industry collapsed, and around 40,000 fishers and other industry workers were put out of work.

6   Atlantic cod stocks had once been so plentiful that early explorers joked about walking on the backs of the teeming fish. By 2008, cod stocks were still at historically low levels and showed no signs of imminent recovery, even after drastic conservation measures and severely limited fishing. Some fishermen blamed the diminished stocks on seals, which prey on cod and other species, but scientists believe that decades of overfishing are to blame. There have been occasional signs of hope. For example, studies on fish populations show

that cod disappeared from Newfoundland at the same time that stocks started rebuilding in Norway, raising the possibility that the cod had simply migrated to a different region. Still, in the early twenty–first century, it remains uncertain whether or when the cod will return to the Grand Banks or the moratorium will end.

27. The word shoals in paragraph 1 is closest in meaning to

  (A) shallows
  (B) currents
  (C) mountains
  (D) islands

28. What physical process occurs in the region of the Grand Banks?

  (A) Underwater hot springs heat the water.
  (B) Warm and cold currents come together.
  (C) Nutrient–rich water flows in from rivers.
  (D) Tides transport plankton and small fish.

29. Which sentence below best expresses the essential information in the highlighted sentence in paragraph 1? Incorrect choices change the meaning in important ways or leave out essential information.

  (A) Millions of cod come to the Grand Banks every year to feed on the abundant supplies of herring and other small fish.
  (B) The Grand Banks used to have the world's largest concentration of cod because of favorable natural conditions.
  (C) The Grand Banks is the only place on Earth where cod are known to come together in extremely large groups.
  (D) The environmental resources of the Grand Banks have made many people wealthy from cod fishing.

30. The word common in paragraph 2 is closest in meaning to

  (A) messy
  (B) colorful
  (C) plain
  (D) familiar

31. Why does the author mention Newfoundland's national dish in paragraph 2?

  (A) To encourage the development of tourism in Newfoundland
  (B) To describe the daily life of people in Newfoundland
  (C) To stress the economic and cultural significance of cod
  (D) To show that Newfoundland used to be a separate country

32. All of the following statements characterized Newfoundland's cod fishery in the past EXCEPT:

  (A) Fishers were dependent on merchants in the capital.
  (B) Cod were the foundation of the island's economy.
  (C) Fishers competed with farmers for natural resources.
  (D) Cod were placed on wooden "flakes" for drying.

33. The word replenish in paragraph 4 is closest in meaning to

  (A) defend
  (B) repair
  (C) reproduce
  (D) improve

34. What event first signaled the overfishing of the Atlantic cod?

  (A) The failure of cod to support thousands of fishers in the 1930s
  (B) The merging of seafood companies into one huge conglomerate
  (C) An increase in the number of fishers and fish–processing plants
  (D) The government moratorium on cod fishing during the 1990s

35. Why did the Canadian government decide to build up the Grand Banks fishing fleet?

  (A) The 200–mile limit was seen as an economic opportunity.
  (B) There had not been enough boats to handle all the fish.
  (C) The shipbuilding sector of the economy was in a slump.
  (D) Canada faced stiff competition from other fishing nations.

36. The word commanding in paragraph 4 is closest in meaning to

  (A) suggesting
  (B) missing
  (C) defying
  (D) receiving

37. It can be inferred from paragraph 6 that the author most likely believes which of the following about the future of the Atlantic cod fishery?

  (A) The fishery will improve if the government lifts the fishing ban.
  (B) It may be a long time before cod stocks recover from overfishing.
  (C) The center of the Atlantic cod fishery will shift to Norway.
  (D) The cod will return to the Grand Banks if seal hunting is allowed.

38. The word teeming in paragraph 6 is closest in meaning to

  (A) endangered
  (B) numerous
  (C) delicious
  (D) mysterious

39. Look at the four squares, **A**, **B**, **C**, and **D**, which indicate where the following sentence could be added to the passage. Where would the sentence best fit?

They suspected this was because the offshore draggers were taking so many cod that the fish did not have a chance to migrate inshore to reproduce.

However, while the offshore fishery was prospering, the inshore fishermen found their catches dropping off. **A** In 1992 the Canadian government responded by closing the Grand Banks to groundfishing. **B** Newfoundland's cod fishing and processing industries were shut down in a bid to let the vanishing stocks recover. **C** The moratorium was extended in 1994, when all of the Atlantic cod fisheries in Canada were closed, except for one in Nova Scotia, and strict quotas were placed on other species of groundfish. **D** Canada's cod fishing industry collapsed, and around 40,000 fishers and other industry workers were put out of work.

40. An introductory sentence for a brief summary of the passage is provided below. Complete the summary by selecting the THREE answer choices that express the most important ideas in the passage. Some sentences do not belong in the summary because they express ideas that are not presented in the passage or are minor ideas in the passage. ***This question is worth 2 points.***

**The Atlantic cod fishery has shaped
Newfoundland's economy for centuries.**

•
•
•

Answer Choices

(A) Atlantic cod stocks were once plentiful in the rich environment around the Grand Banks.

(B) The Atlantic cod is a groundfish that preys on herring and small fish that eat krill.

(C) Cod fishing was so successful that few people considered the possibility of overfishing until fish stocks fell.

(D) The Canadian government tried to diversify Newfoundland's economy in the 1980s.

(E) Despite severe limits on fishing, cod stocks remain at low levels and show few signs of recovery.

(F) Newfoundland exports millions of dollars worth of crab and other shellfish every year.

How to Score 2–Point Question	
Answers Correct	**Points Earned**
3	2
2	1
0 – 1	0

Answers to Test 1 – Reading are on pages 671–672.

Record your total Reading score on page 794.

LISTENING SECTION DIRECTIONS

The Listening section measures your ability to understand conversations and lectures in English. You will hear each conversation and lecture only one time. After each conversation or lecture, you will answer some questions about it. The questions typically ask about the main idea and supporting details. Some questions ask about a speaker's purpose or attitude. Answer the questions based on what the speakers state or imply.

You may take notes while you listen. You may use your notes to help you answer the questions. Your notes will not be scored.

In some questions, you will see this icon: 🎧. This means that you will hear, but not see, part of the question.

Some questions have special directions, which appear in a gray box. Most questions are worth one point. If a question is worth more than one point, the directions will indicate how many points you can receive.

You will now begin part 1 of the Listening section.

PART 1

 Album 9, Track 2

QUESTIONS 1 – 5

Conversation

1. What is the purpose of the conversation?

   (A) The man is interviewing the woman for a job in the office.
   (B) The woman wants to enroll in the communications program.
   (C) The man wants to discuss a change in the course schedule.
   (D) The woman is requesting an interview with the dean.

2. Why does the man say this:

   (A) To express regret that the dean is not available
   (B) To state that the dean cannot change his schedule
   (C) To let the woman know the dean is very busy
   (D) To apologize for the dean's confusing behavior

3. Why does the woman want to meet with the dean?

   (A) To learn about his ideas and vision
   (B) To ask for a letter of recommendation
   (C) To request a change in the school calendar
   (D) To tell him that she enjoyed his lecture

4. What can be inferred about the dean?

   (A) He is in his office two days a week.
   (B) He has been dean for only a short time.
   (C) He generally does not give interviews.
   (D) He is an excellent public speaker.

5. When will the meeting with the dean take place?

   (A) The next day
   (B) The next week
   (C) In two weeks
   (D) In three weeks

Album 9, Track 3

QUESTIONS 6 – 11

Economics

opportunity cost

TEST 1

6. What are the students mainly discussing?

   (A) Various costs that businesses face
   (B) The concept of opportunity cost
   (C) The rising costs of owning a business
   (D) Differences between economics and accounting

7. How does the man help the woman understand a concept that she finds difficult?

   (A) He illustrates the concept with an example.
   (B) He makes a list of terms for her to study.
   (C) He asks her to explain a similar concept.
   (D) He reads a passage from their textbook.

8. Listen again to part of the conversation. Then answer the question.

   Why does the man ask this:

   (A) To find out how much money the woman made
   (B) To evaluate the food at a restaurant
   (C) To suggest that the profit is less than it seems
   (D) To express his concerns about owning a business

9. According to the man, how does an economist's view of costs differ from that of an accountant?

   (A) An economist's definition of costs never changes.
   (B) An economist uses a computer to calculate costs.
   (C) An economist tries to lessen the effect of costs.
   (D) An economist looks at a broader range of costs.

10. What can be inferred about the true cost of a college education?

    (A) It includes the cost of lost income.
    (B) It is more than the woman can afford.
    (C) It is not as expensive as it appears.
    (D) It continues to increase every year.

11. Why does the man say this:

    (A) To help the woman make a decision
    (B) To show that choice has an opportunity cost
    (C) To complain about the cost of education
    (D) To imply that college is not a wise choice

QUESTIONS 12 – 17

Botany

pine sap
dogwood
sassafras

12. According to the speaker, what did European explorers notice as they sailed toward the shores of North America?

    (A) The strength of the wind
    (B) The density of the forests
    (C) The fragrance of the trees
    (D) The Native American villages

13. According to the speaker, why was pine sap a valuable commodity?

    (A) It could make wooden ships waterproof.
    (B) It was an effective cure for headaches.
    (C) It provided an aromatic spice for food.
    (D) It was a good material for starting fires.

14. How was the flowering dogwood used?

    (A) As a flavoring for candy and soft drinks
    (B) As a spring tonic for pioneer children
    (C) As a treatment for fevers and malaria
    (D) As an ingredient in soaps and perfumes

15. Why does the speaker say this:

    (A) She is demonstrating how to brew tea.
    (B) She needs someone to help her lift a heavy tree.
    (C) She wants the students to smell a piece of wood.
    (D) She is giving a recipe for a medicinal tonic.

16. Why was sassafras once considered a wonder tree?

    (A) Its fragrance was the sweetest of any American tree.
    (B) Its sap could be made into a tar to seal wooden ships.
    (C) It provided more board timber than any other tree.
    (D) It was thought to be a cure for almost every disease.

17. Listen again to part of the talk. Then answer the question.

What does the speaker imply about sassafras?

    (A) It is probably not harmful to humans.
    (B) It is no longer a legal medicine.
    (C) It is too expensive for most people.
    (D) It is available only in drugstores.

PART 2

Album 9, Track 5

QUESTIONS 1 – 5

Conversation

1. Why does the student go see his professor?

  (A) He needs extra help with a difficult statistics course.
  (B) He requests her permission to substitute one class for another.
  (C) He would like an advanced copy of the seminar reading list.
  (D) He lacks the prerequisite for a class that he wants to take.

2. What is the professor's initial response to the student's request?

  (A) She offers to speak to the professor who will teach the seminar.
  (B) She explains the importance of the advanced statistics class.
  (C) She recommends taking a different course as the prerequisite.
  (D) She regrets that she does not have time to give students extra help.

3. Why does the student say this: 🎧

  (A) To express disappointment that she will not teach next year
  (B) To persuade the professor to allow him into her seminar
  (C) To learn what actions he should take to graduate early
  (D) To show his appreciation for the professor's help in the past

4. What does the professor mean when she says this: 🎧

  (A) She warns him that having a tutor will not necessarily be enough.
  (B) She believes that teaching assistants are rarely good tutors.
  (C) She suggests that he relax rather than study during spring break.
  (D) She predicts that no teaching assistant will be available to help him.

5. What does the professor insist that the student do?

  Click on 2 answers.

  [A] Register early for her Spring Quarter seminar
  [B] Find a tutor for help with advanced statistics
  [C] Go to the beach during spring break
  [D] Join a study group that will meet every week

Album 9, Track 6

QUESTIONS 6 – 11

Philosophy

Plato

6. What aspect of Plato's philosophy does the professor mainly discuss?

   (A) Plato's teachings about culture
   (B) Plato's rules for good government
   (C) Plato's effect on other philosophies
   (D) Plato's views on education

7. Why does the professor mention the mathematical concept of 2 + 2 = 4?

   (A) To compare philosophy and mathematics
   (B) To give an example of a lasting truth
   (C) To show the simplicity of Plato's philosophy
   (D) To discover which students like mathematics

8. What do idealists believe about higher–level thinking?

   Click on 2 answers.

   [A] It develops a person's character.
   [B] It makes all people equal.
   [C] It benefits the whole society.
   [D] It gives teachers too much power.

9. Listen again to part of the discussion. Then answer the question. 🎧

   What is the woman's attitude toward the idealist view of education?

   (A) She thinks it does not give students useful knowledge.
   (B) She finds it complex and difficult to understand.
   (C) She disagrees with its emphasis on truth.
   (D) She considers it the most liberal system of education.

10. Listen again to part of the discussion. Then answer the question. 🎧

    What does the professor mean when he says this: 🎧

    (A) Idealism has been criticized unfairly.
    (B) Idealism changes how people think.
    (C) Idealism has diminished in influence.
    (D) Idealism remains the only true philosophy.

11. According to the professor, what do critics say about idealism?

    (A) It gives students immoral ideas about learning.
    (B) It discourages student creativity and questioning.
    (C) It is overly concerned with economic development.
    (D) Its focus on abstract thinking is unfair to many students.

QUESTIONS 12 – 17

Physics

Energy and Work

Conservation of Energy
1st Law of Thermodynamics

12. How does the field of physics define "work"?

  (A) Work is the research done by physicists in a laboratory.
  (B) Work is the change in speed of a falling object.
  (C) Work is the amount of energy in the solar system.
  (D) Work is the ability to move an object.

13. Listen again to part of the lecture. Then answer the question.

  Why does the professor talk about a plow?

  (A) To describe recent improvements in agricultural technology
  (B) To explain what happens when a moving object meets resistance
  (C) To show that a plow is the least efficient piece of farm equipment
  (D) To give reasons for the failure of agriculture in some areas

14. Which statement best reflects the first law of thermodynamics?

  (A) Energy can change forms, but it cannot disappear.
  (B) If a machine slows an object, energy will be conserved.
  (C) The amount of energy in a system tends to increase over time.
  (D) Nuclear energy must be regulated by international law.

15. Which two sentences illustrate the conversion of energy from one form to another?

  Click on 2 answers.

  A A car changes the chemical energy in gasoline to motion.
  B A tractor engine stops when the fuel tank is empty.
  C An electric stove converts electricity to heat energy.
  D A light bulb burns out after being on for one hundred hours.

16. Listen again to part of the lecture. Then answer the question.

  Why does the professor say this:

  (A) To support the idea of giving food aid to needy people
  (B) To explain why organisms must create their own energy
  (C) To recommend the development of new energy sources
  (D) To show that both machines and living things need energy

17. What can be inferred about the energy in the earth as a whole system?

  (A) The system gradually gains energy in the form of heat.
  (B) If there is no sunlight, the earth makes its own energy.
  (C) No new energy is created, and no energy is destroyed.
  (D) Plants contribute more energy than animals contribute.

 Stop

Answers to Test 1 – Listening are on pages 672–674.

Record your total Listening score on page 794.

 *Album 9, Track 8*

SPEAKING SECTION DIRECTIONS

The Speaking section measures your ability to speak in English about a variety of topics. There are six questions in this section.

In questions 1 and 2, you will speak about familiar topics. Your responses will be scored on your ability to speak clearly and coherently about the topics.

In questions 3 and 4, you will first read a short text and then listen to a talk on the same topic. You will then be asked a question about what you have read and heard. You will need to combine appropriate information from the text and the talk to provide a complete answer to the question. Your responses will be scored on your ability to speak clearly and coherently and on your ability to accurately convey information about what you have read and heard.

In questions 5 and 6, you will listen to part of a conversation or lecture. You will then be asked a question about what you have heard. Your responses will be scored on your ability to speak clearly and coherently and on your ability to accurately convey information about what you have heard.

You may take notes while you read and while you listen to the conversations and lectures. You may use your notes to help prepare your responses.

 Stop

QUESTION 1

In this question, you will be asked to talk about a familiar topic. After you hear the question, you will have 15 seconds to prepare your response and 45 seconds to speak.

 Album 9, Track 9

> What game do you enjoy playing? Describe the game, and explain why you like to play it. Include details and examples in your explanation.

 Stop

Preparation Time – 15 seconds
Response Time – 45 seconds

QUESTION 2

In this question, you will be asked to give your opinion about a familiar topic. After you hear the question, you will have 15 seconds to prepare your response and 45 seconds to speak.

 Album 9, Track 10

> Some people drive their own car to school or work. Others ride a bus, train, or other form of public transportation. Which do you think is better and why? Include details and examples in your explanation.

 Stop

Preparation Time – 15 seconds
Response Time – 45 seconds

QUESTION 3

In this question, you will read a short passage about a campus situation, listen to a conversation, and then speak in response to a question about what you have read and heard. After you hear the question, you have 30 seconds to prepare your response and 60 seconds to speak.

Read the following information from a college catalog.

Reading Time – 45 seconds

DISTANCE EDUCATION COURSES

Distance education courses at Valley Community College are regularly scheduled classes that must be completed by the end of the quarter. All online courses are taught by college faculty in conjunction with the related academic departments. Students will be required to participate in a "virtual classroom" online, conduct research, and complete assignments. Students must have daily access to a personal computer with word processing software and connection to the Internet. Students should expect to spend approximately 12–15 hours a week for any online course.

Now cover the passage and listen to the recording. When you hear the question, begin preparing your response.

 Album 9, Track 11

> The adviser expresses her opinion about online courses. State her opinion and explain the reasons she gives for holding that opinion.

 Stop

Preparation Time – 30 seconds
Response Time – 60 seconds

QUESTION 4

In this question, you will read a short passage, then listen to a lecture on the same topic, and then speak in response to a question about what you have read and heard. After you hear the question, you have 30 seconds to prepare your response and 60 seconds to speak.

Read the following information from a textbook.

Reading Time – 50 seconds

HOMEOSTASIS

Homeostasis is the tendency toward balance. In zoology, homeostasis is an animal's ability to maintain body equilibrium by adjusting its physiological processes. It is the body's continuous balancing and re–balancing of the processes that maintain stability and restore the body's normal state when it has been disturbed. Homeostatic systems keep an animal's internal environment within acceptable limits, even though the external environment may change. Homeostatic systems protect an animal's body from harmful changes, such as changes in temperature or water level.

Now cover the passage and listen to the recording. When you hear the question, begin preparing your response.

 Album 9, Track 12

> The professor describes the large ears of a rabbit. Explain how the rabbit's ears are used in homeostasis.

 Stop

Preparation Time – 30 seconds
Response Time – 60 seconds

QUESTION 5

In this question, you will listen to a conversation. You will then be asked to talk about the information in the conversation and to give your opinion about the ideas presented. After you hear the question, you have 20 seconds to prepare your response and 60 seconds to speak.

 Album 9, Track 13

> The students discuss possible solutions to the man's problem. Describe the problem. Then state which solution you prefer and explain why.

 Stop

Preparation Time – 20 seconds
Response Time – 60 seconds

QUESTION 6

In this question, you will listen to a short lecture. You will then be asked to summarize important information from the lecture. After you hear the question, you have 20 seconds to prepare your response and 60 seconds to speak.

 Album 9, Track 14

> Using points and examples from the lecture, explain how the communication between babies and mothers is musical in nature.

 Stop

Preparation Time – 20 seconds
Response Time – 60 seconds

Key points for Test 1 – Speaking are on page 674.

Each response earns a score of 1, 2, 3, or 4.

Record your total Speaking score on page 794.

 *Album 9, Track 15*

WRITING SECTION DIRECTIONS

The Writing section measures your ability to use writing to communicate in an academic environment. There are two writing questions.

Question 1 is a writing task based on reading and listening. You will read a passage, listen to a lecture, and then write a response to a question about the relationship between the lecture and the reading. You have 20 minutes to plan and write your response.

Question 2 is writing based on knowledge and experience. You will write an essay in response to a question that asks you to state, explain, and support an opinion on an issue. You have 30 minutes to plan and write your essay.

 Stop

DELTA'S KEY TO THE TOEFL IBT®

QUESTION 1

For this task, you will write a response to a question about a reading passage and a lecture. You may take notes, and you may use your notes to help you write your response. Your response will be scored on the quality of your writing and on how well you connect the points in the lecture with points in the reading. Typically, an effective response will have 150 to 225 words.

Reading Time – 3 minutes

The solution to most problems that societies confront is a higher level of political sophistication that results from more education. When people have the facts about the issues, they will be clearer thinkers and better citizens.

Most people depend on broadcast news and print media for information about current issues. However, in addition to good information, the media contain rumors, misinformation, and politically motivated variations on the truth. The most effective remedy for misinformation is fact checking. If the information people have is incorrect, the corrected facts will enlighten them. Knowing the truth will help people reject misinformation because they will have a better understanding of the issues.

When people have all of the available information, they are able to develop intelligent, informed opinions about issues. People base their opinions on facts, and the more information they have, the more informed their opinions will be. Listening to opposing opinions is an important component of being informed. Therefore, political debate will benefit society by ensuring that citizens understand all sides of an issue.

Accurate information is necessary for solving the problems societies face. When people feel threatened, they will search for the truth. Their natural instinct is to seek information that will help them to make decisions about potential solutions to problems. They will listen to the opinions of experts and look to their elected officials for leadership. When the people are well informed, everyone will benefit: the people, the leaders, and the society as a whole.

Now listen to the recording. When you hear the question, begin your response. You may look at the reading passage during the writing time.

 Album 9, Track 16

> Summarize the points made in the lecture, being sure to explain how they contradict specific points made in the reading passage.

 Stop

Writing Time – 20 minutes

QUESTION 2

For this task, you will write an essay in response to a question that asks you to state and support your opinion on a topic. Your essay will be scored on the quality of your writing, including how well you organize and develop your ideas and how well you use language to express your ideas. Typically, an effective essay will have a minimum of 300 words.

Read the question below and make any notes that will help you plan your response. Then begin typing your essay.

Do you agree or disagree with the following statement?

Subjects such as art, music, and drama should be a part of every child's basic education.

Use specific reasons and examples to support your opinion.

Writing Time – 30 minutes

Key points for Test 1 – Writing are on page 674.

Each response earns a score of 1, 2, 3, 4 or 5.

Record your total Writing score on page 794.

READING SECTION DIRECTIONS

The Reading section measures your ability to understand academic passages in English. You will read passages and answer questions about them. Answer all questions based on what is stated or implied in the passages.

You will read three passages. You have 60 minutes to read the passages and answer the questions.

Most questions are worth one point, but the last question in each set is worth more than one point. The directions indicate how many points you may receive.

Some passages include a word or phrase in **bold** type. For these words and phrases, you will see a definition in a glossary at the end of the passage.

THE UNDERGROUND RAILROAD

1   Slavery was legal for over 200 years in some parts of North America, particularly the southern states of the United States, where the plantation system of agriculture depended on the labor of slaves, most of whom came from Africa. Slaves had no rights or freedoms because they were thought of as property. From the time of its origin, slavery had opponents. The abolitionist movement began in the 1600s when the Quakers in Pennsylvania objected to slavery on moral grounds and wanted to abolish the institution.

2   In 1793, Canada passed a law abolishing slavery and declared that any escaped slaves who came to Canada would be free citizens. Slavery was already illegal in most northern states; however, slaves captured there by slave hunters could be returned to slavery in the South. Canada refused to return runaway slaves or to allow American slave hunters into the country. It is estimated that more than 30,000 runaway slaves immigrated to Canada and settled in the Great Lakes region between 1830 and 1865.

3   The American antislavery movement was at the height of its activity during the 1800s, when abolitionists developed the Underground Railroad, a loosely organized system whereby runaway slaves were passed from safe house to safe house as they fled northwards to free states or Canada. The term was first used in the 1830s and came from an Ohio clergyman who said, "They who took passage on it disappeared from public view as if they had really gone to ground." Because the Underground Railroad was so secret, few records exist that would reveal the true number of people who traveled it to freedom. The most active routes on the railroad were in Ohio, Indiana, and western Pennsylvania.

4   Runaway slaves usually traveled alone or in small groups. Most were young men between the ages of 16 and 35. The fugitives hid in wagons under loads of hay or potatoes, or in furniture and boxes in steamers and on rafts. They traveled on foot through swamps and woods, moving only a few miles each night, using the North Star as a compass. Sometimes they moved in broad daylight. Boys disguised themselves as girls, and girls dressed as boys. In one well–known incident, twenty–eight slaves escaped by walking in a funeral procession from Kentucky to Ohio.

5   The "railroad" developed its own language. The "trains" were the large farm wagons that could conceal and carry a number of people. The "tracks" were the backcountry roads that were used to elude the slave hunters. The "stations" were the homes and hiding places where the slaves were fed and cared for as they moved north. The "agents" were the people who planned the escape routes. The "conductors" were the fearless men and women who led the slaves toward freedom. The "passengers" were the slaves who dared to run away and break for liberty. Passengers paid no fare and conductors received no pay.

6   The most daring conductor was Harriet Tubman, a former slave who dedicated her life to helping other runaways. Tubman made 19 trips into the South to guide 300 relatives, friends, and strangers to freedom. She was wanted dead or alive in the South, but she was never captured and never lost a passenger. A determined worker, she carried a gun for protection and a supply of drugs to quiet the crying babies in her rescue parties.

7   A number of white people joined the effort, including Indiana banker Levi Coffin and his wife Catherine, who hid runaways in their home, a "station" conveniently located on three main escape routes to Canada. People could be hidden there for several weeks, recovering their strength and waiting until it was safe to continue on their journey. Levi Coffin was called the "president of the Underground Railroad" because he helped as many as 3,000 slaves to escape.

8   The people who worked on the railroad were breaking the law. Although the escape network was never as successful or as well organized as Southerners thought, the few thousand slaves who made their way to freedom in this way each year had a symbolic

significance out of proportion to their actual numbers. The Underground Railroad continued operating until slavery in the United States was finally abolished in 1865.

1. The word abolish in paragraph 1 is closest in meaning to

   (A) defend
   (B) end
   (C) legalize
   (D) expand

2. Why did thousands of runaway slaves immigrate to Canada?

   (A) They preferred the climate of the Great Lakes region.
   (B) Working conditions for slaves were better in Canada.
   (C) Canada had no laws restricting immigration.
   (D) Former slaves could live as free citizens in Canada.

3. Which sentence below best expresses the essential information in the highlighted sentence in paragraph 3? Incorrect choices change the meaning in important ways or leave out essential information.

   (A) The Underground Railroad kept secret records in which all of the passengers and trips were documented.
   (B) Few people understood why the Underground Railroad would not reveal how many people chose to travel in this way.
   (C) The Underground Railroad's records were not accurate, so the true number of travelers is difficult to estimate.
   (D) We do not know exactly how many slaves escaped on the Underground Railroad because it was a secret organization.

4. The word fugitives in paragraph 4 is closest in meaning to

   (A) leaders
   (B) old men
   (C) runaways
   (D) brave ones

5. All of the following are mentioned as methods of escape on the Underground Railroad EXCEPT

   (A) hiding in a hay wagon
   (B) wearing a disguise
   (C) riding in a railcar
   (D) walking in a procession

6. The author discusses the language of the Underground Railroad in paragraph 5 in order to

   (A) trace the history of American English words
   (B) illustrate the secret nature of the escape network
   (C) point out that some words have more than one meaning
   (D) compare the Underground Railroad to other railways

7. The word elude in paragraph 5 is closest in meaning to

   (A) avoid
   (B) follow
   (C) find
   (D) assist

8. The phrase break for in paragraph 5 is closest in meaning to

   (A) hide from
   (B) support
   (C) escape to
   (D) ignore

9. Which of the following statements is true about passengers on the Underground Railroad?

  (A) Their destination was in the northern states or Canada.
  (B) They were not allowed to make stops during the journey.
  (C) Their babies were disguised to look like baggage.
  (D) They paid the conductors at the end of the journey.

10. In stating that She was wanted dead or alive in the South in paragraph 6, the author means that Harriet Tubman

  (A) was responsible for the deaths of several passengers
  (B) refused to return the runaway slaves that she captured
  (C) was sought by the authorities for helping escaped slaves
  (D) was an outlaw who carried a gun and sold drugs

11. The author points out that workers on the Underground Railroad

  (A) became wealthy from the fees that they charged
  (B) could have been arrested as criminals
  (C) never knew whether their passengers arrived
  (D) developed a highly organized network

12. It can be inferred from paragraph 8 that the author most likely believes which of the following about the Underground Railroad?

  (A) The people who worked on the railroad should have been arrested.
  (B) The railroad was unsuccessful because it could not help every slave.
  (C) Southerners did not know about the railroad until after it closed.
  (D) The railroad represented a psychological victory for abolitionists.

13. Look at the four squares, **A**, **B**, **C**, and **D**, which indicate where the following sentence could be added to the passage. Where would the sentence best fit?

Women and children also escaped, but they were more easily captured.

  Runaway slaves usually traveled alone or in small groups. Most were young men between the ages of 16 and 35. **A** The fugitives hid in wagons under loads of hay or potatoes, or in furniture and boxes in steamers and on rafts. **B** They traveled on foot through swamps and woods, moving only a few miles each night, using the North Star as a compass. Sometimes they moved in broad daylight. **C** Boys disguised themselves as girls, and girls dressed as boys. In one well–known incident, twenty–eight slaves escaped by walking in a funeral procession from Kentucky to Ohio. **D**

DELTA'S KEY TO THE TOEFL iBT®

14. An introductory sentence for a brief summary of the passage is provided below. Complete the summary by selecting the THREE answer choices that express the most important ideas in the passage. Some sentences do not belong in the summary because they express ideas that are not presented in the passage or are minor ideas in the passage. *This question is worth 2 points.*

The Underground Railroad was a secret network that helped thousands of people escape slavery.

-
-
-

Answer Choices

(A) Most slaves were captured in West Africa and transported to North America on slave ships.

(B) The railroad was part of the American abolitionist movement that opposed slavery for moral reasons.

(C) Slaves that were captured in the North could be returned to slavery in the South.

(D) The railroad was a loosely organized system that provided guides, hiding places, and food to runaway slaves.

(E) "Conductors" and "agents" led "passengers" north to free states and Canada.

(F) The president of the Underground Railroad was an Indiana banker named Levi Coffin.

| How to Score 2–Point Question ||
Answers Correct	Points Earned
3	2
2	1
0 – 1	0

TEST 2

Tornado Formation

1   Tornadoes are one of the most violent of all weather systems. A tornado can produce tremendous destructive power in a restricted area as it passes by, sweeping the ground clear of all movable objects. Fortunately, tornadoes are short–lived and often strike sparsely populated regions. Occasionally, however, a major tornado outbreak causes incredible devastation. A tornado's powerful blasts of wind put all human life in jeopardy, sending debris flying and lifting buildings from their foundations.

2   The formation of tornadoes has been the subject of increasingly fruitful research. Nevertheless, some mystery still surrounds tornadoes, and their formation cannot be predicted with absolute accuracy, even when conditions for their occurrence seem just right. Most tornadoes are created by, and travel with, intense thunderstorm cells. Because tornadoes require moist air, they favor the warmest part of the day, when solar heating and thunderstorm development are at their maximum.

3   Probably the most striking characteristic of a tornado is its spinning funnel cloud, a lowering of cloud base into a column that narrows as it reaches down to the ground from a parent cloud that is part of an active thunderstorm. The funnel cloud forms in response to the steep air pressure directed from the storm's outer edge toward its center. Humid air expands and cools as it is drawn inward toward the center of the system. The cooling of air below its dewpoint causes water vapor to condense into cloud droplets.

4   The actual tornadic circulation covers a much wider area than the funnel cloud suggests. The funnel may range in diameter from a few meters to 3.2 kilometers (2 miles). However, the diameter of a funnel cloud is typically only about one–tenth that of the associated tornadic circulation. Several funnels may develop in a mature tornado system, with small **vortexes** continually forming and then disappearing while whirling around the central core of the main tornado. The funnels may be made visible by the presence of dust and debris. A funnel can assume a variety of forms, from a thin, writhing, ropelike pendant of grayish white to a thick mass of menacing black.

5   The central United States is one of only a few places in the world where the spring weather conditions and flat terrain are ideal for tornado development. Although tornadoes have been reported in all 50 states and throughout southern Canada, most occur in "tornado alley," a level corridor that stretches from eastern Texas northward through the open plains of Oklahoma, Kansas, and Nebraska.

6   Almost three–quarters of the tornadoes in North America occur from March to July. The months of peak tornado activity are April (13%), May (12%), and June (21%). During that time of year, weather conditions are optimal for causing the severe thunderstorms that produce tornadoes. One contributing factor is the relative instability of the lower atmosphere. During the transition from winter to summer, days lengthen, thereby warming the ground. Heat is transferred from the ground into the **troposphere**, but it takes time for the entire troposphere to adjust to receiving heat from below. The upper troposphere, in fact, usually retains its winter cold into the spring months. The result is an imbalance of cold air and warm ground that favors the development of rotating thunderstorms known as supercells.

7   In the Northern Hemisphere, tornadoes almost always spin counterclockwise. Around 87 percent of all tornadoes and their parent cells travel from southwest to northeast, but any direction is possible. Tornado trajectories are often irregular, with many tornadoes exhibiting a hopscotch pattern of destruction as they alternately touch down and lift off the ground. Some have been known to move in circles and even to describe figure eights. Tornadoes may track along paths from several meters to more than 320 kilometers (200 miles) long. Average forward speed is around 48 kilometers (30 miles) per hour, although there are reports of tornadoes racing along at speeds approaching 120 kilometers (75 miles) per hour. During part of its course, the great Tri–State Tornado on March 18, 1925, moved at the astonishing

rate of 117 kilometers (73 miles) per hour, killing 695 people in Missouri, Illinois, and Indiana, and making it one of the most deadly tornadoes on record.

Glossary:

> **vortexes:** spiraling masses of air or water that suck everything toward their center
> **troposphere:** the lowest region of the atmosphere

15. According to the passage, tornadoes are one of the most violent weather systems because they

- (A) frequently occur with very little warning
- (B) cause tremendous damage in a short time
- (C) move very quickly and change direction
- (D) kill more people than any other weather system

16. The word jeopardy in paragraph 1 is closest in meaning to

- (A) motion
- (B) shock
- (C) confusion
- (D) danger

17. Which sentence below best expresses the essential information in the highlighted sentence in paragraph 2? Incorrect choices change the meaning in important ways or leave out essential information.

- (A) Some tornadoes are mysterious because they develop when the wrong conditions are present.
- (B) Tornadoes are difficult to predict accurately because they can occur for different reasons at different times.
- (C) Despite the presence of the right conditions, we cannot predict with certainty the formation of every tornado.
- (D) We will never be able to predict tornadoes until we understand the mystery of what causes them.

18. Tornado formation is usually associated with

- (A) heavy rainfall
- (B) thunderstorms
- (C) cold air currents
- (D) solar flares

19. The word mature in paragraph 4 is closest in meaning to

- (A) cooling
- (B) harmless
- (C) large
- (D) dying

20. The word whirling in paragraph 4 is closest in meaning to

- (A) falling
- (B) spinning
- (C) pushing
- (D) sliding

21. Paragraph 4 supports which of the following statements about tornadoes?

- (A) Tornado formation signals the end of a thunderstorm.
- (B) Tornadoes have the smallest diameter of any storm system.
- (C) When several funnels form, each is smaller than the previous one.
- (D) Tornadoes can differ greatly in size, shape, and color.

22. According to the passage, all of the following contribute to tornado formation EXCEPT

- (A) movement of the ground
- (B) a moist stream of air
- (C) warm temperatures
- (D) a flat landscape

23. In discussing peak tornado activity in paragraph 6, the author means that in April, May, and June tornadoes

- (A) move the fastest
- (B) are very irregular
- (C) occur most frequently
- (D) can not be predicted

24. According to paragraph 7, most tornadoes move

   (A) in a clockwise direction
   (B) toward the northeast
   (C) faster than 75 miles per hour
   (D) forward and backward

25. Why does the author mention hopscotch, circles, and figure eights in paragraph 7?

   (A) To show that tornadoes can move in different ways
   (B) To emphasize the destructive power of tornadoes
   (C) To describe the stages of an average tornado
   (D) To give examples of informal names for tornadoes

26. Look at the four squares, ▣, ▣, ▣, and ▣, which indicate where the following sentence could be added to the passage. Where would the sentence best fit?

   For this reason, more than half of all tornadoes develop between 10:00 a.m. and 6:00 p.m.

   The formation of tornadoes has been the subject of increasingly fruitful research. ▣ Nevertheless, some mystery still surrounds tornadoes, and their formation cannot be predicted with absolute accuracy, even when conditions for their occurrence seem just right. ▣ Most tornadoes are created by, and travel with, intense thunderstorm cells. ▣ Because tornadoes require moist air, they favor the warmest part of the day, when solar heating and thunderstorm development are at their maximum. ▣

27. An introductory sentence for a brief summary of the passage is provided below. Complete the summary by selecting the THREE answer choices that express the most important ideas in the passage. Some sentences do not belong in the summary because they express ideas that are not presented in the passage or are minor ideas in the passage. *This question is worth 2 points.*

Several factors contribute to the formation of tornadoes, one of the most violent of all weather systems.

•
•
•

Answer Choices

(A) Severe thunderstorms are responsible for the creation of most tornadoes.

(B) Predicting the formation of tornadoes has become more accurate.

(C) Tornadoes have been recorded on every continent except Antarctica.

(D) A funnel cloud forms when humid air is pulled toward the center of the storm.

(E) Tornadoes are likely to form on warm spring days over level plains.

(F) The Tri–State Tornado of 1925 moved at 117 kilometers per hour.

How to Score 2–Point Question	
Answers Correct	**Points Earned**
3	2
2	1
0 – 1	0

TEST 2

MARY COLTER AND FRANK LLOYD WRIGHT

1   In the early twentieth century, the thrust in American architecture was toward a style rooted in the American landscape and based on American rather than European forms. Two architects who worked independently yet simultaneously at endorsing an American architecture were Mary Colter (1869–1958) and Frank Lloyd Wright (1867–1959). Both developed regional styles that paralleled the regionalism seen in the other visual arts. Colter created a uniquely Southwestern idiom incorporating desert landscapes with Native American arts; Wright and his followers in Chicago developed the Prairie style of domestic architecure that reflected the natural landscape of the Midwest.

2   Mary Colter's hotels and national park buildings are rooted so masterfully in the history of the Southwest that they seem to be genuine pieces of that history. Her magnificent Watchtower, overlooking the Grand Canyon in Arizona, was built to suggest an ancient Native American ruin preserved for the delight of the present–day traveler.

3   Colter was a lifelong student of art history, natural history, and human civilization. Her well–rounded artistic talents empowered her to work historical references into buildings constructed with modern methods and materials. She preferred to use materials **indigenous** to the region, such as Kaibab limestone and yellow pine. She took great stock in materials and setting, gathering many of her materials on–site and incorporating them in their natural state into her projects. She treated building and site as integral halves of a single composition and merged them seamlessly. Her Lookout Studio, for example, appears to rise straight from the rim of the Grand Canyon because its layering of stonework matches the texture, pattern, and color of the canyon wall below it.

4   When Colter designed the Watchtower, she wanted the building to be a part of its environment while also enhancing the view of the surrounding desert and the canyon and river below. She decided to recreate a Native American watchtower because it would provide the necessary height while assuming the appearance of a prehistoric building. Colter was familiar with the architectural remains of ancient villages scattered about the Southwest and was especially fascinated by the stone towers—round, square, and oval monoliths. The ancient Round Tower at Mesa Verde became the direct inspiration for the form and proportions of the Watchtower. The Twin Towers ruin at Hovenweep, whose stone was closer to that available at the Grand Canyon, was the model for the Watchtower's masonry. The Watchtower is perhaps the best example of Colter's integration of history, architecture, and landscape in a unified work of art.

5   Like Mary Colter, Frank Lloyd Wright believed that architecture was an extension of the natural environment. Wright was appalled by much of what he saw in the industrialized world. He was not fond of cities, and although he designed office buildings and museums, his favorite commissions were for homes, usually in the country. Wright is associated with the Prairie style of residential architecture, whose emphasis on horizontal elements reflected the prairie landscapes of the Midwest. Most Prairie–style homes have one or two stories and are built of brick or timber covered with stucco. The eaves of the low–pitched roof extend well beyond the walls, enhancing the structure's horizontality.

6   Wright's own studio–residence in Wisconsin was completely integrated with the surrounding landscape. He nestled his house in the brow of a hill and gave it the name Taliesin, which means "shining brow" in Welsh. Every element of the design corresponded to the surounding landscape. The yellow stone came from a quarry a mile away, so Taliesin looked like the outcroppings on the local hills. The exterior wood was the color of gray tree trunks. The stucco walls above the stone had the same tawny color as the sandbanks in the river below.

7   Wright's most famous house, Fallingwater, was built right over a waterfall in Pennsylvania. The house blends harmoniously with its surroundings, yet it departs from the Prairie philosophy of being a completely integrated extension of the natural landscape. Some features of the house are more like those of the simple, unadorned International style, particularly the interlocking geometry of the planes and the flat, textureless surface of the horizontal elements.

Glossary:
    indigenous: originating or growing in an area; native

28. The word thrust in paragraph 1 is closest in meaning to

(A) movement
(B) criticism
(C) accident
(D) education

29. According to the passage, both Mary Colter and Frank Lloyd Wright designed buildings that

(A) reflected the history of the region
(B) emphasized the architect's individuality
(C) relied on the assistance of other artists
(D) blended into the natural environment

30. The author mentions Kaibab limestone and yellow pine in paragraph 3 as examples of

(A) materials with high artistic value
(B) references to art history and natural history
(C) materials that are native to the Southwest
(D) traditional materials that are now scarce

31. Which sentence below best expresses the essential information in the highlighted sentence in paragraph 3? Incorrect choices change the meaning in important ways or leave out essential information.

(A) Colter valued materials and location, so she blended into her works many natural materials collected from the building site.
(B) Because Colter used various types of materials, it was often difficult to combine them in a way that would look natural.
(C) Colter bought stock in corporations that made building materials and delivered them directly to the project site.
(D) Materials and setting were equally important to Colter, who was very skilled at choosing the right materials for the job.

32. The word merged in paragraph 3 is closest in meaning to

(A) contrasted
(B) outlined
(C) joined
(D) painted

33. What was the main inspiration for Mary Colter's design of the Watchtower?

(A) The beautiful views of the American Southwest
(B) The ancient Round Tower at Mesa Verde
(C) The colorful stone cliffs of the Grand Canyon
(D) Architectural remains of masonry homes

34. What can be inferred from paragraph 4 about the Watchtower?

(A) The Watchtower was the only building Colter designed at the Grand Canyon.
(B) The Watchtower's purpose was to help people appreciate the desert scenery.
(C) Colter used landscape design to enhance the beauty of the Watchtower.
(D) The Watchtower's success inspired other architects to design tall buildings.

35. The word appalled in paragraph 5 is closest in meaning to

(A) inspired
(B) relieved
(C) amused
(D) shocked

36. All of the following characterize the Prairie style of architecture EXCEPT

(A) a concern for the surrounding landscape
(B) a direct reference to the region's history
(C) an emphasis on horizontal elements
(D) a low roof that extends beyond the walls

37. The word nestled in paragraph 6 is closest in meaning to

(A) set comfortably
(B) built daringly
(C) painted brightly
(D) buried deeply

38. Why does the author mention Fallingwater in paragraph 7?

(A) To criticize Wright's most famous house design
(B) To provide the best illustration of the Prairie style
(C) To give an example of an artistic use of a waterfall
(D) To show that Wright did not work in just one style

39. Look at the four squares, **A**, **B**, **C**, and **D**, which indicate where the following sentence could be added to the passage. Where would the sentence best fit?

Taliesin's rough stone facades and low–slung roofs blurred the distinction between the manmade and the natural.

Wright's own studio–residence in Wisconsin was completely integrated with the surrounding landscape. **A** He nestled his house in the brow of a hill and gave it the name Taliesin, which means "shining brow" in Welsh. **B** Every element of the design corresponded to the surrounding landscape. The yellow stone came from a quarry a mile away, so Taliesin looked like the outcroppings on the local hills. **C** The exterior wood was the color of gray tree trunks. **D** The stucco walls above the stone had the same tawny color as the sandbanks in the river below.

40. Select the appropriate sentences from the answer choices and match them to the architect to which they refer. TWO of the answer choices will NOT be used. *This question is worth 3 points.*

Answer Choices

(A) Others followed the architect in developing a style that would suit the landscape of the prairies.

(B) The architect improved the designs of famous architects of the past.

(C) The architect developed a style integrating the history and landscape of the American Southwest.

(D) The architect preferred designing country residences.

(E) Native American culture provided the architect with ideas and inspiration.

(F) The architect worked exclusively with modern materials and methods.

(G) The architect designed structures that would blend into the desert environment.

Mary Colter

-
-
-

Frank Lloyd Wright

-
-

How to Score 3–Point Question	
Answers Correct	**Points Earned**
5	3
4	2
3	1
0 – 2	0

Answers to Test 2 – Reading are on pages 675–676.

Record your total Reading score on page 794.

TEST 2

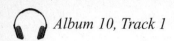 *Album 10, Track 1*

LISTENING SECTION DIRECTIONS

The Listening section measures your ability to understand conversations and lectures in English. You will hear each conversation and lecture only one time. After each conversation or lecture, you will answer some questions about it. The questions typically ask about the main idea and supporting details. Some questions ask about a speaker's purpose or attitude. Answer the questions based on what the speakers state or imply.

You may take notes while you listen. You may use your notes to help you answer the questions. Your notes will not be scored.

In some questions, you will see this icon: 🎧. This means that you will hear, but not see, part of the question.

Some questions have special directions, which appear in a gray box. Most questions are worth one point. If a question is worth more than one point, the directions will indicate how many points you can receive.

You will now begin part 1 of the Listening section.

PART 1

Album 10, Track 2

QUESTIONS 1 – 5

Conversation

1. What are the speakers mainly discussing?

    (A) The classes the woman is taking
    (B) The theater program at the university
    (C) The woman's interest in an internship
    (D) The importance of work experience

2. What does the woman like about theater?

    (A) The chance to meet interesting people
    (B) The opportunity to improve her acting
    (C) The efficiency of theater management
    (D) The entire atmosphere of theater

3. What is the woman's opinion of her own acting ability?

    (A) She thinks she needs more acting experience.
    (B) She is excited about learning new acting skills.
    (C) She thinks she is not very skilled at acting.
    (D) She thinks she is better at acting than directing.

4. Why does the man say this:

    (A) To state what he likes about the theater
    (B) To learn more about the woman's interests
    (C) To imply that the woman should be a director
    (D) To compliment the woman on her abilities

5. What does the man suggest the woman do?

    Click on 2 answers.

    [A] Gather some of her drawings
    [B] Observe the theater director
    [C] Enroll in an acting class
    [D] Write to the theater manager

QUESTIONS 6 – 11

Biology

Carbon

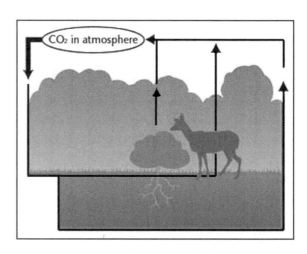

TEST 2

6. What is the main purpose of the lecture?

  (A) To describe the process of photosynthesis
  (B) To explain how the carbon cycle works
  (C) To link carbon and global warming
  (D) To compare carbon dioxide and energy

7. What point does the professor make about the cycling of carbon dioxide in the atmosphere?

  (A) It is disrupted when animals eat the leaves of trees.
  (B) It provides a link between Earth's atmosphere and outer space.
  (C) It occurs globally through the respiration of plants and animals.
  (D) It is a subject of disagreement among scientists.

8. Listen again to part of the lecture. Then answer the question.

  Why does the professor say this:

  (A) To show that environmental conditions have changed over time
  (B) To explain how carbon can be removed from the cycle for long periods
  (C) To point out that coal and petroleum are the oldest organic substances
  (D) To compare the carbon content of coal with that of petroleum

9. According to the professor, what factors affect the amount of carbon dioxide in the atmosphere?

  Click on 2 answers.

  [A] The season of year
  [B] The species of vegetation
  [C] The burning of fossil fuels
  [D] The amount of precipitation

10. According to the professor, why is the level of atmospheric carbon dioxide lowest during the summer?

  (A) Carbon separates from oxygen in warm temperatures.
  (B) Respiration by animals exceeds respiration by plants.
  (C) Plant–eating animals eat less during the summer.
  (D) Plants use more carbon dioxide for photosynthesis.

11. What does the professor mean when she says this:

  (A) There is disagreement over the effects of changes to the carbon cycle.
  (B) Tomorrow the class will participate in a scientific debate.
  (C) The increase in carbon dioxide is the most serious scientific issue.
  (D) The disadvantages of burning fossil fuels exceed the advantages.

Album 10, Track 4

QUESTIONS 12 – 17

Anthropology

12. What is the main idea of the lecture?

   (A) Every human society is interested in sports.
   (B) Rules were developed to make sports fair.
   (C) Sports contain many elements of hunting.
   (D) Complex cultures have violent sports.

13. Listen again to part of the discussion. Then answer the question.

   Why does the professor say this:

   (A) To find out if the student did her homework
   (B) To contradict the student's answer
   (C) To learn about what food the student likes
   (D) To encourage the student to elaborate

14. According to the professor, why did the ancient Romans build the Coliseum?

   (A) To make the hunt an entertainment for spectators
   (B) To compete with other cities in sports architecture
   (C) To put Rome at the center of Olympic sports
   (D) To shock and offend the enemies of Rome

15. What point does the professor make about track and field sports?

   (A) They were performed in the Coliseum of Rome.
   (B) They are shocking because an animal is killed.
   (C) They are the most popular sporting events today.
   (D) They involve skills originally used by hunters.

16. Which sports contain a symbolic element of the kill?

   Click on 2 answers.

   A Fencing
   B Running
   C Baseball
   D Boxing

17. What does the professor imply about the negative element of sports?

   (A) People prefer sports with a strong negative element.
   (B) The concept of sportsmanship makes sports less negative.
   (C) Today, only blood sports contain a negative element.
   (D) Sports will become even more negative in the future.

PART 2

 Album 10, Track 5

QUESTIONS 1 – 5

Conversation

1. Why does the student go to see the professor?

   (A) He needs advice about a problem with his house.
   (B) He wants to discuss an idea for a paper.
   (C) He is confused about an article that he read.
   (D) He would like to enroll in her geology course.

2. What topic is the man mainly interested in?

   (A) Some houses that are sliding
   (B) Effects of groundwater removal
   (C) How to build a sturdy home
   (D) Why a famous tower is leaning

3. Why does the student say this:

   (A) He would like to visit the Leaning Tower of Pisa.
   (B) He thinks the local slide may have a similar cause.
   (C) He wants to work as an engineer of tall buildings.
   (D) He needs information that he missed due to absence.

4. According to the professor, where are mudslides most common?

   (A) 30 feet beneath the earth's surface
   (B) On slopes of 27 to 45 degrees
   (C) In places where frozen ground melts
   (D) In the San Joaquin Valley of California

5. What will the man probably include in his research?

   Click on 2 answers.

   A An article about groundwater removal
   B A visit to a leaning tower
   C A study of the area's geology
   D A search for other mudslides in the area

Album 10, Track 6

QUESTIONS 6 – 11

Astronomy

6. What is the discussion mainly about?

  Ⓐ Objects that crash into planets
  Ⓑ How meteors become meteorites
  Ⓒ Properties of meteors and comets
  Ⓓ How comets form in outer space

7. What happens when a meteor strikes the atmosphere?

  Ⓐ The meteor breaks into dust that falls to the earth.
  Ⓑ The atmosphere deflects the meteor back into space.
  Ⓒ The meteor changes direction in its path around the sun.
  Ⓓ The impact releases a large amount of nuclear energy.

8. Why does the student say this:

  Ⓐ He thinks the professor said something incorrect.
  Ⓑ He is amused by the professor's previous statement.
  Ⓒ He does not agree with the professor's statement.
  Ⓓ He wants the professor to give more explanation.

9. What does the professor imply when she says this: 🎧

  Ⓐ The student has asked an interesting question.
  Ⓑ The material they are discussing will be on the test.
  Ⓒ The class will have another discussion on Friday.
  Ⓓ The professor might not be in class on Friday.

10. What does the professor say about comets?

  Ⓐ They fall to Earth as showers or shooting stars.
  Ⓑ They are composed of a nucleus, a coma, and a tail.
  Ⓒ They are formed from the debris of dying meteors.
  Ⓓ They have a relatively low surface temperature.

11. Listen again to part of the conversation. Then answer the question. 🎧

  What can be inferred about Halley's Comet?

  Ⓐ It will pass Earth again several decades from now.
  Ⓑ It is named for the constellation from which it came.
  Ⓒ It can be seen from only a few places on Earth.
  Ⓓ It has an irregular pattern of orbit around Earth.

Album 10, Track 7

QUESTIONS 12 – 17

Music Education

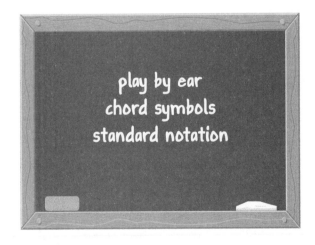

play by ear
chord symbols
standard notation

12. What is playing by ear?

    (A) Listening to music through ear phones
    (B) Playing an instrument that is held up to the ear
    (C) Paying attention to what the teacher says
    (D) Learning to play music without reading notation

13. Listen again to part of the talk. Then answer the question.

    Why does the professor ask this:

    (A) To suggest that all children should study music
    (B) To introduce the main point he wants to make
    (C) To find out if everyone in class can read music
    (D) To review material for an examination

14. According to the professor, when should children learn to read musical notation?

    Click on 2 answers.

    [A] When they first learn how to play an instrument
    [B] When a group of children play music together
    [C] When the music is too complex to learn by ear
    [D] When they are ready to play in front of an audience

15. According to the professor, why should a music teacher play the score for a child the first time?

    (A) To demonstrate how the printed notes translate into music
    (B) To suggest that the score can be played in different styles
    (C) To allow the child to memorize the score by listening
    (D) To show the child that the teacher is an excellent player

16. According to the professor, what is the natural order for children to learn music?

    (A) Play music alone, play with a teacher, play with other children
    (B) Learn chord symbols, learn standard notation, learn to play by ear
    (C) Play an instrument by ear, learn chord symbols, learn standard notation
    (D) Learn standard notation, learn chords, listen to others play music

17. What does the professor imply about the three methods of playing music?

    (A) Each method is appropriate for some students.
    (B) There is no reason to learn all three methods.
    (C) The best method is playing by standard notation.
    (D) Students should use the teacher's favorite method.

Stop

Answers to Test 2 – Listening are on pages 676–678.

Record your total Listening score on page 794.

 *Album 10, Track 8*

 Stop

QUESTION 1

In this question, you will be asked to talk about a familiar topic. After you hear the question, you will have 15 seconds to prepare your response and 45 seconds to speak.

 Album 10, Track 9

> Describe a person who has influenced you in an important way. Explain why this person has had an effect on your life. Include details and examples in your explanation.

 Stop

Preparation Time – 15 seconds
Response Time – 45 seconds

QUESTION 2

In this question, you will be asked to give your opinion about a familiar topic. After you hear the question, you will have 15 seconds to prepare your response and 45 seconds to speak.

 Album 10, Track 10

> Some people get most of their news from the radio or television. Others read news on the Internet. Which source of news do you think is better and why? Include details and examples in your explanation.

 Stop

Preparation Time – 15 seconds
Response Time – 45 seconds

QUESTION 3

In this question, you will read a short passage about a campus situation, listen to a conversation, and then speak in response to a question about what you have read and heard. After you hear the question, you have 30 seconds to prepare your response and 60 seconds to speak.

Read the following information from a student handbook.

Reading Time – 45 seconds

ATTENDANCE POLICY

Students are expected to attend all classes for which they are registered, including the first class session. Courses for which attendance is mandatory from the first session will be so noted in the class schedule. Instructors may set an attendance policy for each course, and it is the student's responsibility to know and comply with individual course attendance policies. Students who fail to comply with the established attendance policy for a course forfeit the right to continue in the course and will be subject to an administrative withdrawal.

Now cover the passage and listen to the recording. When you hear the question, begin preparing your response.

 Album 10, Track 11

The woman expresses her opinion about the attendance policy. State her opinion and explain the reasons she gives for holding that opinion.

 Stop

Preparation Time – 30 seconds
Response Time – 60 seconds

QUESTION 4

In this question, you will read a short passage, then listen to a lecture on the same topic, and then speak in response to a question about what you have read and heard. After you hear the question, you have 30 seconds to prepare your response and 60 seconds to speak.

Read the following information from a textbook.

Reading Time – 45 seconds

THE GESTURAL THEORY OF LANGUAGE

Language is the systematic communication of ideas or feelings through symbols, gestures, or sounds. The production of speech sounds is not necessary for language. Many scientists believe that language developed earlier than speech. The gestural theory of language argues that human language evolved from gestures that were used for simple communication. Most people still use hand and facial gestures when they speak. Both gestural language and spoken language depend on similar neural systems. In fact, the area of the brain responsible for hand movements borders the area controlling the mouth.

Now cover the passage and listen to the recording. When you hear the question, begin preparing your response.

 Album 10, Track 12

> Explain the gestural theory of language and how the examples given by the professor support the theory.

 Stop

Preparation Time – 30 seconds
Response Time – 60 seconds

QUESTION 5

In this question, you will listen to a conversation. You will then be asked to talk about the information in the conversation and to give your opinion about the ideas presented. After you hear the question, you have 20 seconds to prepare your response and 60 seconds to speak.

 Album 10, Track 13

> The students discuss possible solutions to a problem that the man has. Describe the problem. Then state what you think the man should do, and explain why.

 Stop

Preparation Time – 20 seconds
Response Time – 60 seconds

QUESTION 6

In this question, you will listen to a short lecture. You will then be asked to summarize important information from the lecture. After you hear the question, you have 20 seconds to prepare your response and 60 seconds to speak.

 Album 10, Track 14

> Using points and examples from the lecture, explain direct and indirect competition in bird populations.

 Stop

Preparation Time – 20 seconds
Response Time – 60 seconds

Key points for Test 2 – Speaking are on page 678.

Each response earns a score of 1, 2, 3 or 4.

Record your total Speaking score on page 794.

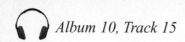

WRITING SECTION DIRECTIONS

The Writing section measures your ability to use writing to communicate in an academic environment. There are two writing questions.

Question 1 is a writing task based on reading and listening. You will read a passage, listen to a lecture, and then write a response to a question about the relationship between the lecture and the reading. You have 20 minutes to plan and write your response.

Question 2 is writing based on knowledge and experience. You will write an essay in response to a question that asks you to state, explain, and support an opinion on an issue. You have 30 minutes to plan and write your essay.

 Stop

QUESTION 1

For this task, you will write a response to a question about a reading passage and a lecture. You may take notes, and you may use your notes to help you write your response. Your response will be scored on the quality of your writing and on how well you connect the points in the lecture with points in the reading. Typically, an effective response will have 150 to 225 words.

Reading Time – 3 minutes

   Parents and teachers generally believe it is best for children to study and play with other children of the same age. For this reason, same–age peer groups are the norm for children, both in and out of school, and at all ages, from infancy through adolescence. When children are organized into groups with their peers, it encourages tolerance and cooperation and discourages conflict and competition.

   Peer groups build tolerance and decrease conflict because the children are equals in terms of status and power. Even when peers tease each other, the teasing is acceptable because it occurs among equals. Joking and teasing will actually build toleration among peers, who are able to work out any differences without the intervention of adults.

   Because peers are at the same stage of mental and physical development, structured competition is a positive experience for them. The healthy competition of team sports, games, and other contests will challenge individuals to perform well in order to benefit the group. Contests and competition between same–age peer groups will reduce conflict because the competition is structured and managed in a healthy, enjoyable manner. Competitive games build teamwork and group pride because winning the game is a shared success.

   Cooperation comes naturally to children of the same age because they experience the same events and issues at the same level of development. Peers are friends, classmates, and teammates who learn together in a healthy, sharing environment. Same–age peer groups play an important positive role in children's socialization because they promote cooperation and group identity.

Now listen to the recording. When you hear the question, begin your response. You may look at the reading passage during the writing time.

 Album 10, Track 16

> Summarize the points made in the lecture, being sure to explain how they challenge specific points made in the reading passage.

 Stop

Writing Time – 20 minutes

QUESTION 2

For this task, you will write an essay in response to a question that asks you to state and support your opinion on a topic. Your essay will be scored on the quality of your writing, including how well you organize and develop your ideas and how well you use language to express your ideas. Typically, an effective essay will have a minimum of 300 words.

Read the question below and make any notes that will help you plan your response. Then begin typing your essay.

Do you agree or disagree with the following statement?

There are times when it is acceptable not to tell the truth.

Use specific reasons and details to support your answer.

Writing Time – 30 minutes

Key points for Test 2 – Writing are on page 678.

Each response earns a score of 1, 2, 3, 4 or 5.

Record your total Writing score on page 794.

TEST 3

ECTOTHERMY AND ENDOTHERMY

1   Many biological systems are based on the process of homeostasis, which means "steady state." Homeostasis is the ability to maintain balance. Homeostatic mechanisms enable animals to survive changes in their external environment by regulating conditions within their bodies. Conditions in the external environment, such as temperature, may vary widely, but conditions in the internal environment can vary only within a narrow range necessary for survival.

2   Temperature is a constraint for animals, all of which must maintain biochemical stability. When an animal's body temperature drops too low, its metabolism slows, thus reducing the amount of energy the animal can use for activity. If body temperature rises too high, metabolic reactions become unbalanced, and enzyme activity is hindered. Animals can succeed only in a limited range of body temperatures, and for most, this is between 0 and 40 degrees Celsius.

3   One way to classify animals is to emphasize their source of body heat. For instance, "cold–blooded" animals are those that must warm their body with heat from the surrounding environment, and "warm–blooded" animals are those that can heat themselves. However, these traditional terms are inaccurate and misleading. Some "cold–blooded" animals, such as lizards, have higher body temperatures when active than many "warm–blooded" animals have when **hibernating**. Physiologists prefer the terms "ectotherm" and "endotherm" because they reflect the fact that an animal's body temperature is a balance between heat loss and heat gain.

4   All animals produce heat from cellular metabolism, but in most the heat is conducted away as fast as it is produced, so the amount of heat obtained from metabolism is very small. In these animals, the ectotherms, body temperature is determined almost entirely by their surroundings. Most invertebrates, fishes, amphibians, and reptiles are ectotherms. In contrast, some animals are able to generate and retain enough heat from metabolism to elevate their own body temperature to the optimum level. These animals are called the endotherms because the source of their body heat is internal. Mammals, birds, some fishes, and numerous insects are endotherms.

5   Ectotherms warm their body mainly by absorbing heat from their environment. Ectotherms cannot control their body temperature physiologically, yet many are able to regulate it behaviorally by selecting areas of the environment with a more favorable temperature. Some, such as desert lizards, exploit hour–to–hour changes in solar radiation to keep their body temperature relatively constant. In the morning, the lizard absorbs the sun's heat through its head, while keeping the rest of its body protected from the cool air. Later, the lizard will emerge to bask in the sun. At noon, with its body temperature high, it seeks shade under a rock. When the air temperature drops in the late afternoon, it emerges and lies parallel to the sun's rays.

6   Endotherms, on the other hand, derive most or all of their body heat from their own metabolism. A consistently warm body temperature requires active metabolism, which includes oxidation of foods, cellular respiration, and muscular contraction. Conversely, a warm body temperature contributes to the high levels of metabolism required for extended periods of intense physical activity. This is one reason endotherms can generally endure vigorous activity longer than ectotherms. However, being endothermic is energetically expensive, especially in a cold environment. Because much of an endotherm's daily intake of calories is used to generate heat, the endotherm must eat more food than an ectotherm of the same size.

7   Endothermy allows birds and mammals to stabilize their internal temperature so that biochemical processes and nervous system functions can proceed at steady levels of activity. These animals maintain a constant body temperature through a delicate balance between heat

production and heat loss. This is why endotherms can remain active in winter and exploit habitats denied to ectotherms. If the animal becomes too cool, it can generate heat by increasing muscular activity (exercise or shivering), or it can decrease heat loss by increasing insulation. In general, birds and mammals are warmer than their surroundings, but they also have mechanisms for cooling the body in a hot environment. If the animal becomes too warm, it decreases heat production and increases heat loss by evaporative cooling (sweating or panting).

Glossary:
   hibernating: passing the winter in an inactive state

1. In using the term internal environment in paragraph 1, the author is talking about

   (A) the animal's den
   (B) the animal's body
   (C) the animal's genetic code
   (D) the animal's social position

2. The word constraint in paragraph 2 is closest in meaning to

   (A) restriction
   (B) reward
   (C) certainty
   (D) comfort

3. Why can animals survive only in a limited range of body temperatures?

   (A) Body temperature is a key contributor to metabolic stability.
   (B) Animals cannot maintain necessary body fluids at extreme temperatures.
   (C) Body temperature is linked to an animal's ability to reproduce.
   (D) Most environmental temperatures fall between 0 and 40 degrees Celsius.

4. According to paragraph 3, why are the terms "cold–blooded" and "warm–blooded" inaccurate for classifying animals?

   (A) They imply that warm blood is better.
   (B) They incorrectly identify blood as important in body temperature.
   (C) They suggest that some animals do not like heat.
   (D) They imply that the animal's blood is always cold or warm.

5. The word optimum in paragraph 4 is closest in meaning to

   (A) environmental
   (B) opposite
   (C) most common
   (D) most favorable

6. The word exploit in paragraph 5 is closest in meaning to

   (A) get away with
   (B) get used to
   (C) take advantage of
   (D) take care of

7. Which of the following statements can be inferred about ectotherms?

   (A) They can engage in physical activity for long periods of time.
   (B) They are the most intelligent animals that live in the desert.
   (C) They must eat all day long to maintain their body temperature.
   (D) They are likely to live where heat from the sun is available.

8. Why does the author use the term energetically expensive in paragraph 6?

   (A) To point out that intense physical exercise is difficult for animals
   (B) To stress that generating internal body heat requires a lot of calories
   (C) To explain why there are many more ectotherms than endotherms
   (D) To show that endotherms consume too many environmental resources

9. Which sentence below best expresses the essential information in the highlighted sentence in paragraph 7? Incorrect choices change the meaning in important ways or leave out essential information.

(A) Because endotherms can maintain their body temperature, they can live in cold habitats.

(B) In winter, endotherms do not allow ectotherms access to the resources they need for survival.

(C) Endotherms are naturally warmer than ectotherms, so the two kinds of animals prefer different habitats.

(D) Ectotherms thrive in cold habitats, but they must compete with endotherms for survival.

10. All of the following are mentioned as advantages of endothermy EXCEPT

(A) endurance of intense physical activity
(B) survival in cold surroundings
(C) high level of intelligence
(D) ability to cool the body

11. Which of the following is a mechanism that promotes heat loss?

(A) Shivering
(B) Insulation
(C) Exercise
(D) Panting

12. Look at the four squares, **A**, **B**, **C**, and **D**, which indicate where the following sentence could be added to the passage. Where would the sentence best fit?

Many endotherms maintain a consistent internal temperature even as the temperature of their surroundings fluctuates.

    A All animals produce heat from cellular metabolism, but in most the heat is conducted away as fast as it is produced, so the amount of heat obtained from metabolism is very small. In these animals, the ectotherms, body temperature is determined almost entirely by their surroundings. **B** Most invertebrates, fishes, amphibians, and reptiles are ectotherms. **C** In contrast, some animals are able to generate and retain enough heat from metabolism to elevate their own body temperature to the optimum level. These animals are called the endotherms because the source of their body heat is internal. **D** Mammals, birds, some fishes, and numerous insects are endotherms.

13. Select the appropriate phrases from the answer choices and match them to the class of animal that they describe. TWO of the answer choices will NOT be used. *This question is worth 3 points.*

Answer Choices

(A) Are cold–blooded when active and warm–blooded when inactive

(B) Generate heat internally to achieve the correct body temperature

(C) Use the environment as their primary source of body heat

(D) Survive by hibernating when their body becomes too warm

(E) Need a large amount of food to regulate metabolism and body temperature

(F) Maintain body temperature behaviorally, by seeking sun or shade

(G) Have bodily mechanisms for controlling heat production and heat loss

Ectotherms

-
-

Endotherms

-
-
-

How to Score 3–Point Question	
Answers Correct	**Points Earned**
5	3
4	2
3	1
0 – 2	0

CANADIAN ENGLISH

1   Canadian English is a regional variety of North American English that spans almost the entire continent. Canadian English became a separate variety of North American English after the American Revolution, when thousands of Loyalists, people who had supported the British, left the United States and fled north to Canada. Many Loyalists settled in southern Ontario in the 1780s, and their speech became the basis for what is called General Canadian, a definition based on the norms of urban middle–class speech.

2   Modern Canadian English is usually defined by the ways in which it resembles and differs from American or British English. Canadian English has a great deal in common with the English spoken in the United States, yet many Americans identify a Canadian accent as British. Many American visitors to Canada think the Canadian vocabulary sounds British—for example, they notice the British "tap" and "braces" instead of the American "faucet" and "suspenders." On the other hand, many British people identify a Canadian accent as American, and British visitors think the Canadians have become Americanized, saying "gas" and "truck" for "petrol" and "lorry."

3   People who live outside North America often find it difficult to hear the differences between Canadian and American English. There are many similarities between the two varieties, yet they are far from identical. Canadian English is instantly recognizable to other Canadians, and one Canadian in a crowded room will easily spot the other Canadian among the North Americans.

4   There is no distinctive Canadian grammar. The differences are mainly in pronunciation, vocabulary, and idioms. Canadian pronunciation reflects the experience of a people struggling for national identity against two strong influences. About 75 percent of Canadians use the British "zed" rather than the American "zee" for the name of the last letter of the alphabet. On the other hand, 75 percent of Canadians use the American pronunciation of "schedule," "tomato," and "missile." The most obvious and distinctive feature of Canadian speech is probably its vowel sound, the **diphthong** "ou." In Canada, "out" is pronounced like "oat" in nearby U.S. accents. There are other identifying features of Canadian vowels; for example, "cot" is pronounced the same as "caught" and "collar" the same as "caller."

5   An important characteristic of the vocabulary of Canadian English is the use of many words and phrases originating in Canada itself, such as "kerosene" and "chesterfield" ("sofa"). Several words are borrowed from North American Indian languages, for example, "kayak," "caribou," "parka," and "skookum" ("strong"). The name of the country itself has an Indian origin; the Iroquois word "kanata" originally meant "village." A number of terms for ice hockey—"face–off," "blue–line," and "puck"—have become part of World Standard English.

6   Some features of Canadian English seem to be unique and are often deliberately identified with Canadian speakers in such contexts as dramatic and literary characterizations. Among the original Canadian idioms, perhaps the most famous is the almost universal use of "eh?" as a tag question, as in "That's a good movie, eh?" "Eh" is also used as a filler during a narrative, as in "I'm walking home from work, eh, and I'm thinking about dinner. I finally get home, eh, and the refrigerator is empty."

7   The traditional view holds that there are no dialects in Canadian English and that Canadians cannot tell where other Canadians are from just by listening to them. The linguists of today disagree with this view. While there is a greater degree of homogeneity in Canadian English compared with American English, several dialect areas do exist across Canada. Linguists have identified distinct dialects for the Maritime Provinces, Newfoundland, the Ottawa Valley, southern Ontario, the Prairie Provinces, the Arctic North, and the West.

Glossary:
     diphthong: a speech sound that begins with one vowel and changes to another vowel

14. According to the passage, how did Canadian English become a distinct variety of North American English?

   (A) Linguists noticed that Canadians spoke a unique dialect.
   (B) A large group of Loyalists settled in one region at the same time.
   (C) Growth of the middle class led to a standard school curriculum.
   (D) Canadians declared their language to be different from U.S. English.

15. The word norms in paragraph 1 is closest in meaning to

   (A) patterns
   (B) history
   (C) words
   (D) ideas

16. The phrase a great deal in common with in paragraph 2 is closest in meaning to

   (A) different words for
   (B) the same problems as
   (C) many similarities to
   (D) easier pronunciation than

17. In paragraph 2, what point does the author make about Canadian English?

   (A) Canadian English is more similar to American than to British English.
   (B) American and British visitors define Canadian English by their own norms.
   (C) Canadian English has many words that are not in other varieties of English.
   (D) Canadians speak English with an accent that Americans cannot understand.

18. The word spot in paragraph 3 is closest in meaning to

   (A) describe
   (B) ignore
   (C) prefer
   (D) find

19. Which sentence below best expresses the essential information in the highlighted sentence in paragraph 4? Incorrect choices change the meaning in important ways or leave out essential information.

   (A) Canadian English has been strongly influenced by both British and American English.
   (B) Canada is the only nation where people can deliberately choose which pronunciation they prefer.
   (C) Canadians have tried to distinguish themselves as a nation, and this effort is shown in their pronunciation.
   (D) Many newcomers to Canada must work hard to master the national style of pronouncing English.

20. All of the following words originated in North American Indian languages EXCEPT

   (A) kerosene
   (B) parka
   (C) Canada
   (D) kayak

21. Which of the following can be inferred from paragraph 5?

   (A) Vocabulary is the most distinctive feature of Canadian English.
   (B) World Standard English has a very large vocabulary.
   (C) Canadians use more North American Indian words than Americans do.
   (D) Much of the vocabulary for ice hockey originated in Canada.

22. The author discusses the expression "eh" in paragraph 6 as an example of

(A) an idiom that uniquely characterizes Canadian speech
(B) an expression that few people outside Canada have heard
(C) a style of Canadian drama and literature
(D) a word that cannot be translated into other languages

23. The word homogeneity in paragraph 7 is closest in meaning to

(A) accent
(B) change
(C) creativity
(D) sameness

24. According to paragraph 7, dialects in Canadian English

(A) have rarely been a subject of study
(B) are identified primarily through pronunciation
(C) are linked to different geographic regions
(D) are the same as those in American English

25. Look at the four squares, **A**, **B**, **C**, and **D**, which indicate where the following sentence could be added to the passage. Where would the sentence best fit?

Thus, "out" rhymes with "boat," so the phrase "out and about in a boat" sounds like "oat and aboat in a boat" to American ears.

There is no distinctive Canadian grammar. The differences are mainly in pronunciation, vocabulary, and idioms. Canadian pronunciation reflects the experience of a people struggling for national identity against two strong influences. About 75 percent of Canadians use the British "zed" rather than the American "zee" for the name of the last letter of the alphabet. On the other hand, 75 percent of Canadians use the American pronunciation of "schedule," "tomato," and "missile." **A** The most obvious and distinctive feature of Canadian speech is probably its vowel sound, the diphthong "ou." **B** In Canada, "out" is pronounced like "oat" in nearby U.S. accents. **C** There are other identifying features of Canadian vowels; for example, "cot" is pronounced the same as "caught" and "collar" the same as "caller." **D**

26. An introductory sentence for a brief summary of the passage is provided below. Complete the summary by selecting the THREE answer choices that express the most important ideas in the passage. Some sentences do not belong in the summary because they express ideas that are not presented in the passage or are minor ideas in the passage. *This question is worth 2 points.*

Canadian English is a variety of North American English that contains several distinguishing features.

-
-
-

Answer Choices

(A) Canadian English contains elements of both British and American English.

(B) Several unique varieties of English have evolved in North America.

(C) Canadians pronounce most words the same way as Americans do.

(D) Canadian English asserts its distinctiveness through pronunciation.

(E) Words and idioms originating in Canada also help to define Canadian English.

(F) Most Canadians cannot identify where other Canadians are from.

How to Score 2–Point Question	
Answers Correct	**Points Earned**
3	2
2	1
0 – 1	0

HUMAN MIGRATION

1   The long–term movement of individuals, families, or larger groups to a new location outside their community of origin is known as migration. Human migration occurs on various geographic scales: from one continent or country to another, between regions within a single country, and from one city neighborhood to another. Several factors stimulate migration, including economic conditions, political conflict, war, cultural circumstances, and environmental factors.

2   People migrate from source to destination in well–defined streams. Many migration streams actually consist of a series of stages, a phenomenon known as step migration. For example, a peasant family from the countryside is likely to move first to a village, then to a nearby town, later to a city, and finally to a metropolis—the capital or the largest city in the region. The intensity of a migration stream depends on such factors as the physical distance and the degree of difference between the source and the destination. It also depends on the flow of information from the destination back to the source. People are likely to have more complete and accurate information about nearby places than about places that are farther away.

3   The decision to move is the result of various stimuli, which social scientists classify as "push" and "pull" factors. Push factors are the conditions that impel people to leave their home communities. The lack of jobs or educational opportunities, political fear, ethnic or religious discrimination, and natural disasters are all examples of push factors. Pull factors are the circumstances that attract people to certain destinations, such as better living standards, the chance of getting a job, and family connections. The circumstances that induce people to move from one part of the world to another—economic, political, and environmental conditions—usually involve a combination of push and pull factors. Because people are usually more familiar with their home community than with a desired destination, they are likely to understand push factors more accurately than pull factors. Pull factors tend to be more vague, and people often have overly optimistic expectations of their destination.

4   Economic conditions are a leading factor in human migration. Throughout history, poverty has driven millions of people from their homelands. Industrialization has attracted populations to urban areas in search of economic opportunity. The flow from farms or villages to the expanding metropolitan and industrial centers has occurred both within and between countries. During the twentieth century, Russians moved into the new industrial centers in Siberia, Chinese migrated to Manchuria and Southeast Asia, and Africans moved from tribal areas into the mining regions of South Africa and Congo. Today, perceived opportunities in destinations such as Western Europe and North America encourage numerous migrants to search for a better life. Some workers migrate only seasonally or temporarily. Especially in newly industrializing areas, workers tend to retain their village roots and return home after a period of earning in a factory or mine. However, most migrants relocate permanently, and the growing urban populations worldwide are composed of people who have cut themselves off from their roots.

5   The twentieth century saw an increase in migratory flows caused by the push factors of political oppression, revolution, and war. Refugees fled from Russia after the 1917 revolution, from Germany and Italy during the Nazi and Fascist regimes, and from Eastern Europe after the Second World War. Millions of people were uprooted as a result of political, cultural, and religious conflict. The partition of India and Pakistan in 1947 led to the uprooting and resettlement of around 14 million Muslims and Hindus—the largest single movement of people in a short period. The armed conflict in the former Yugoslavia during the 1990s drove as many as three million people from their homes. In the same decade, a civil war in Rwanda forced more than two million Rwandans from their homeland.

6   Reasons for migration include environmental conditions, often in combination with economic and political problems. A major historical example is the Irish famine of the 1840s, when prolonged rains and **blight** destroyed the potato crop. The resulting famine, along with the oppressive political system, caused hundreds of thousands of peasants to migrate from Ireland to North America. In recent decades, a series of droughts resulting from successive rainless seasons in sub–Saharan Africa, combined with such factors as ethnic strife and civil war, have caused large–scale migrations and a growing refugee crisis in the region.

Glossary:
   blight: severe plant disease

27. In paragraph 1, the author makes the point that

   (A) there are similarities between human migration and animal migration
   (B) most people who migrate move to another region in their home country
   (C) human migration varies in the distance traveled and the factors involved
   (D) we understand only some of the conditions that cause people to migrate

28. Which statement best describes step migration?

   (A) A family systematically lists their reasons for leaving home.
   (B) A village man moves to the city to work to support his family.
   (C) Workers migrate seasonally to wherever jobs are available.
   (D) A family moves a relatively short distance several times.

29. The word impel in paragraph 3 is closest in meaning to

   (A) force
   (B) dare
   (C) permit
   (D) invite

30. All of the following are identified as conditions that may push people to move away from their place of origin EXCEPT

   (A) the inability to find employment
   (B) prejudice based on religion
   (C) a high standard of living
   (D) environmental disasters

31. Which sentence below best expresses the essential information in the highlighted sentence in paragraph 3? Incorrect choices change the meaning in important ways or leave out essential information.

   (A) Only when conditions at home become unbearable will people migrate to another country.
   (B) Push factors are more powerful than pull factors in stimulating human migration.
   (C) The three leading causes of migration are economics, politics, and environmental change.
   (D) The decision to migrate a great distance normally results from both push and pull factors.

32. The word vague in paragraph 3 is closest in meaning to

   (A) serious
   (B) unclear
   (C) difficult
   (D) simple

33. It can be inferred from paragraph 3 that

   (A) governments encourage migration by describing push and pull factors
   (B) few migrants fully understand why they leave their home communities
   (C) people may overestimate the chance of finding work in their chosen destination
   (D) the same factors that pull people to one place may push away other people

34. What is the main purpose of paragraph 4?

    (A) To present some economic causes of migration
    (B) To describe the long–term effects of poverty
    (C) To explain why some migration is only temporary
    (D) To compare past and present causes of migration

35. In stating in paragraph 4 that the growing urban populations worldwide are composed of people who have cut themselves off from their roots, the author means that these people

    (A) come from a variety of cultural backgrounds
    (B) have chosen not to return to their villages
    (C) will eventually forget their native language
    (D) feel homesick and regret moving to the city

36. Paragraph 5 supports which of the following statements about migration?

    (A) More people migrated during the twentieth century than in any other period.
    (B) Most migration is the product of our human desire to find meaning in life.
    (C) Political circumstances are a major factor driving numerous migration streams.
    (D) International migration will continue to increase because of war and revolution.

37. The word strife in paragraph 6 is closest in meaning to

    (A) tradition
    (B) education
    (C) advancement
    (D) conflict

38. In paragraph 6, the author provides two examples to illustrate that

    (A) other factors join environmental factors in causing migration
    (B) famine and drought are caused by political corruption
    (C) push and pull factors in migration can not easily be separated
    (D) migration caused by environmental conditions will increase

39. Look at the four squares, **A**, **B**, **C**, and **D**, which indicate where the following sentence could be added to the passage. Where would the sentence best fit?

Consequently, the majority of migrants move only a short distance.

   People migrate from source to destination in well–defined streams. **A** Many migration streams actually consist of a series of stages, a phenomenon known as step migration. For example, a peasant family from the countryside is likely to move first to a village, then to a nearby town, later to a city, and finally to a metropolis—the capital or the largest city in the region. **B** The intensity of a migration stream depends on such factors as the physical distance and the degree of difference between the source and the destination. It also depends on the flow of information from the destination back to the source. **C** People are likely to have more complete and accurate information about nearby places than about places that are farther away. **D**

40. An introductory sentence for a brief summary of the passage is provided below. Complete the summary by selecting the THREE answer choices that express the most important ideas in the passage. Some sentences do not belong in the summary because they express ideas that are not presented in the passage or are minor ideas in the passage. ***This question is worth 2 points.***

Humans migrate on a variety of geographic scales and for several reasons.

-
-
-

Answer Choices

(A) Migration can occur as a long stream to a distant location or as a series of short moves to a nearby destination.

(B) People are more likely to migrate a short distance than they are to migrate to another continent.

(C) Migration results from circumstances that either push people to leave their homes or pull them to new destinations.

(D) The largest migration in history occurred when 14 million people relocated after the partition of India and Pakistan.

(E) Environmental disaster and political factors caused the large flow of migrants from Ireland to North America.

(F) Economic, political, cultural, and environmental conditions are major factors in human migration.

| How to Score 2–Point Question ||
Answers Correct	Points Earned
3	2
2	1
0 – 1	0

Answers to Test 3 – Reading are on pages 679–680.

Record your total Reading score on page 794.

TEST 3

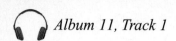

LISTENING SECTION DIRECTIONS

The Listening section measures your ability to understand conversations and lectures in English. You will hear each conversation and lecture only one time. After each conversation or lecture, you will answer some questions about it. The questions typically ask about the main idea and supporting details. Some questions ask about a speaker's purpose or attitude. Answer the questions based on what the speakers state or imply.

You may take notes while you listen. You may use your notes to help you answer the questions. Your notes will not be scored.

In some questions, you will see this icon: 🎧. This means that you will hear, but not see, part of the question.

Some questions have special directions, which appear in a gray box. Most questions are worth one point. If a question is worth more than one point, the directions will indicate how many points you can receive.

You will now begin part 1 of the Listening section.

PART 1

Album 11, Track 2

QUESTIONS 1 – 5

Conversation

1. What topics do the speakers mainly discuss?

   Click on 2 answers.

   [A] Their summer plans
   [B] Their mutual acquaintances
   [C] Their musical interests
   [D] Their work experience

2. What does the professor mean when she says this: 🎧

   (A) He is one of the best teachers available.
   (B) You should ask for a different teacher.
   (C) Some teachers are more effective than others.
   (D) Students are not allowed to select their teachers.

3. Why does the professor say this: 🎧

   (A) To praise the excellent food at Silverwood
   (B) To comment on the man's summer workload
   (C) To predict which courses the student will like
   (D) To explain why the summer program is popular

4. What does the professor do for relaxation?

   (A) Teach music theory
   (B) Conduct the orchestra
   (C) Play in a jazz band
   (D) Coach voice students

5. What can be inferred from the conversation?

   (A) The professor used to be on the faculty at Silverwood.
   (B) The summer program at Silverwood is not well known.
   (C) The student wants to study music in graduate school.
   (D) The professor recommended the student for a scholarship.

 *Album 11, Track 3*

QUESTIONS 6 – 11

Geology

Fossils

correlation

fossil succession

6. What is the main idea of the lecture?

   (A) Fossils are important indicators of a region's economic potential.
   (B) Fossils make it possible for us to form opinions about evolution.
   (C) Fossils help geologists predict where climate change will occur.
   (D) Fossils provide clues to our geologic and environmental history.

7. According to the lecture, what important contribution came from a nineteenth–century British canal builder?

   (A) The development of a more efficient method of digging canals
   (B) The first detailed scientific writings about the existence of fossils
   (C) The discovery that each rock layer held a distinctive fossil content
   (D) The invention of a simple system of classifying and naming fossils

8. According to the professor, how does the correlation of rocks in different places contribute to scientific understanding?

   (A) Correlation helps us identify the best locations for building canals.
   (B) Correlation provides information about the geologic history of Earth.
   (C) Correlation encourages geologists and other scientists to work together.
   (D) Correlation reveals that certain organisms lived only on one continent.

9. Why does the professor talk about the principle of fossil succession?

   (A) To explain how fossils can indicate the age of rock layers
   (B) To show that the study of fossils is very complex
   (C) To compare fossil succession with other theories about fossils
   (D) To state that fossil succession occurred differently around the world

10. Listen again to part of the lecture. Then answer the question.

What does the professor mean by this statement:

   (A) Fossils of extinct species will not appear in higher layers of rock.
   (B) It takes a very long time for fossils to disappear from solid rock.
   (C) Geologists have never been able to explain the absence of some fossils.
   (D) The fossil record is a permanent description of the earth's history.

11. Why does the professor say this:

   (A) To describe some of the most beautiful fossils ever discovered
   (B) To compare the fossils found in two different layers of rock
   (C) To illustrate how fossils are clues about the past environment
   (D) To explain why water must be present for the formation of fossils

Album 11, Track 4

QUESTIONS 12 – 17

Biology

12. What is the talk mainly about?

  Ⓐ The economic importance of bees
  Ⓑ A decline in pollinator populations
  Ⓒ How flowers are pollinated
  Ⓓ Nature's services to farmers

13. According to the professor, what factors have affected pollinator populations?

  Click on 2 answers.

  Ⓐ Parasites
  Ⓑ Air pollution
  Ⓒ Hunting
  Ⓓ Farm chemicals

14. Listen again to part of the talk. Then answer the question. 🎧

  Why does the professor say this: 🎧

  Ⓐ To show the effect of agriculture on pollinators
  Ⓑ To describe nectar–producing plants
  Ⓒ To show how stones improve a garden
  Ⓓ To describe effects of plant disease

15. Listen again to part of the talk. Then answer the question. 🎧

  What can be inferred about monarch butterflies?

  Ⓐ They are the most common butterflies in North America.
  Ⓑ Their population has been reduced because of herbicides.
  Ⓒ They have lived on Earth for several million years.
  Ⓓ Their diet consists mainly of other butterflies.

16. According to the professor, which pollinator feeds on the nectar of cactus flowers?

  Ⓐ Honeybee
  Ⓑ Parasitic mite
  Ⓒ Monarch butterfly
  Ⓓ Long–nosed bat

17. How does the professor support his main point about the pollinator crisis?

  Ⓐ He describes problems in specific pollinator populations.
  Ⓑ He presents some possible ways to address the crisis.
  Ⓒ He traces the evolution of pollinators and plants.
  Ⓓ He explains why ranchers must poison a species of bat.

PART 2

 Album 11, Track 5

QUESTIONS 1 – 5

Conversation

1. What is the woman's problem?

   (A) The physics course she is required to take is very difficult.
   (B) She is not sure whether she needs the physics book right now.
   (C) The bookstore does not have any copies of the book she needs.
   (D) She does not have enough money to pay for the physics book.

2. What does the man say about students who are put on the waiting list for a class?

   (A) They are informed immediately when they are enrolled in the class.
   (B) They may not attend the class as long as they are on the waiting list.
   (C) Their name is kept on the waiting list until the following quarter.
   (D) They must have the professor's permission to be on the waiting list.

3. Why does the woman say this: 🎧

   (A) To show that she does not believe what the man said
   (B) To ask why the physics book costs more than other books
   (C) To express displeasure about the store's return policy
   (D) To complain about the high cost of a university education

4. On which two points do the speakers probably agree?

   Click on 2 answers.

   [A] Engineering textbooks are too expensive.
   [B] The bookstore's return policy is very strict.
   [C] Students on the waiting list rarely get into the class.
   [D] The physics professor is an excellent teacher.

5. What will the woman probably do?

   (A) Ask the registrar's office to remove her from the waiting list
   (B) Search elsewhere for a less expensive copy of the book
   (C) Complain to the bookstore manager about the refund policy
   (D) Purchase the book now so she can start reading it

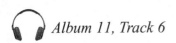

Album 11, Track 6

QUESTIONS 6 – 11

Art

6. What is the discussion mainly about?

    (A) Factors that influence the application of paint

    (B) How to determine the quality of various paints

    (C) Techniques that improve the permanence of paint

    (D) The three most popular styles of paintbrushes

7. According to the discussion, what factors affect an artist's ability to control the paint?

    Click on 2 answers.

    [A] The temperature of the room
    [B] The coarseness of the painting surface
    [C] The quality of the brush
    [D] The brightness of the color

8. Listen again to part of the discussion. Then answer the question. 🎧

What does the professor imply about the paper on which paint is applied?

    (A) The absorbency of the paper affects the artist's control of the paint.

    (B) Paint dries faster on smooth paper than it does on coarse paper.

    (C) Coarse papers are usually of lower quality than are smooth papers.

    (D) The type of paper determines which shape of brush to use.

9. Why does one of the students say this: 🎧

    (A) To show that thick paints are difficult to control

    (B) To describe a painting technique that he invented

    (C) To explain why he does not like using oil paints

    (D) To illustrate the importance of quality in brushes

10. According to the professor, what is one sign of a high–quality brush for oil painting?

    (A) The brush costs more than the paper or canvas.

    (B) The ends of the brush's hairs are trimmed evenly.

    (C) The tip contains the natural split ends of hog's hair.

    (D) The bristles are arranged in a perfect circle.

11. In discussing the three types of brushes, how does the professor distinguish them?

    (A) By listing them from lowest to highest quality

    (B) By comparing their prices

    (C) By giving the best painting surface for each type

    (D) By describing the shape and length of the bristles

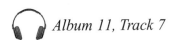

QUESTIONS 12 – 17

United States History

Mathew Brady

TEST 3

12. What is the main idea of the lecture?

  Ⓐ People should protest against war photography.
  Ⓑ Photographers recorded the fighting at Antietam.
  Ⓒ The battlefield is too dangerous for photographers.
  Ⓓ Photography changed the nature of war reporting.

13. Listen again to part of the lecture. Then answer the question.

  What does the professor mean by this statement:

  Ⓐ More Americans died on that day than on any other day.
  Ⓑ Antietam was the only battle in which Americans died.
  Ⓒ Deaths were counted for the first time at Antietam.
  Ⓓ Antietam was the shortest battle of the Civil War.

14. Who was Mathew Brady?

  Ⓐ A military leader during the Civil War
  Ⓑ A portrait painter in New York
  Ⓒ The owner of a photography business
  Ⓓ The inventor of photography

15. Listen again to part of the lecture. Then answer the question.

  Why does the professor say this:

  Ⓐ To warn students not to look at the pictures
  Ⓑ To encourage students to study photography
  Ⓒ To contrast different photographic styles
  Ⓓ To emphasize the power of photography

16. What were some of the limitations of photography during the Civil War?

  Click on 2 answers.

  A The slow exposure time did not allow action shots.
  B Photographers were not permitted near the battlefield.
  C Newspapers were not able to reproduce photographs.
  D There were only a few schools that taught photography.

17. What does the professor imply about Mathew Brady?

  Ⓐ He was unfairly criticized for his photographs of the dead.
  Ⓑ His work had a lasting effect on photography and journalism.
  Ⓒ He took more photographs during his life than anyone else did.
  Ⓓ His Civil War photographs are worth a lot of money today.

 Stop

Answers to Test 3 – Listening are on pages 681–682.

Record your total Listening score on page 794.

 *Album 11, Track 8*

SPEAKING SECTION DIRECTIONS

The Speaking section measures your ability to speak in English about a variety of topics. There are six questions in this section.

In questions 1 and 2, you will speak about familiar topics. Your responses will be scored on your ability to speak clearly and coherently about the topics.

In questions 3 and 4, you will first read a short text and then listen to a talk on the same topic. You will then be asked a question about what you have read and heard. You will need to combine appropriate information from the text and the talk to provide a complete answer to the question. Your responses will be scored on your ability to speak clearly and coherently and on your ability to accurately convey information about what you have read and heard.

In questions 5 and 6, you will listen to part of a conversation or lecture. You will then be asked a question about what you have heard. Your responses will be scored on your ability to speak clearly and coherently and on your ability to accurately convey information about what you have heard.

You may take notes while you read and while you listen to the conversations and lectures. You may use your notes to help prepare your responses.

 Stop

QUESTION 1

In this question, you will be asked to talk about a familiar topic. After you hear the question, you will have 15 seconds to prepare your response and 45 seconds to speak.

 Album 11, Track 9

> Describe an event such as a holiday or other occasion that you enjoy celebrating. Explain why the event is significant to you. Include details and examples to support your explanation.

 Stop

Preparation Time – 15 seconds
Response Time – 45 seconds

QUESTION 2

In this question, you will be asked to give your opinion about a familiar topic. After you hear the question, you will have 15 seconds to prepare your response and 45 seconds to speak.

 Album 11, Track 10

> Some people keep in touch with friends and family by letter or e–mail. Others keep in touch by telephone. Which method do you prefer to use, and why? Include details and examples in your explanation.

 Stop

Preparation Time – 15 seconds
Response Time – 45 seconds

QUESTION 3

In this question, you will read a short passage about a campus situation, listen to a conversation, and then speak in response to a question about what you have read and heard. After you hear the question, you have 30 seconds to prepare your response and 60 seconds to speak.

Read the following information from a university's course catalog.

Reading Time – 45 seconds

REQUIRED DISCUSSION SECTION

All students who are enrolled in a lecture course in the Social Sciences division must also register for a one–credit discussion section for that course. In the past, this requirement applied only to lecture courses in the History and Political Science departments. However, beginning next quarter, the requirement also applies to lecture courses in Sociology, Anthropology, and Economics. Each discussion section will be taught by a graduate teaching assistant. Students will receive a grade for the discussion section that is separate from their final examination grade for the lecture course.

Now cover the passage and listen to the recording. When you hear the question, begin preparing your response.

 Album 11, Track 11

> The man expresses his opinion about the required discussion section. State his opinion and explain the reasons he gives for holding that opinion.

 Stop

Preparation Time – 30 seconds
Response Time – 60 seconds

QUESTION 4

In this question, you will read a short passage, then listen to a lecture on the same topic, and then speak in response to a question about what you have read and heard. After you hear the question, you have 30 seconds to prepare your response and 60 seconds to speak.

Read the following information from a textbook.

Reading Time – 50 seconds

DEHYDRATION

Dehydration is the condition in which body water output exceeds water input. Dehydration may develop with either water deprivation or excessive water loss. Symptoms include thirst, dry skin and mouth, rapid heartbeat, low blood pressure, weakness, exhaustion, and delirium. If not corrected, dehydration will end in death. When water intake is inadequate, the blood becomes concentrated. The mouth becomes dry, and the brain initiates drinking behavior. The first signal is thirst. Thirst drives one to seek water, but lags behind the body's need because by the time thirst is felt the body has already lost some of its water.

Now cover the passage and listen to the recording. When you hear the question, begin preparing your response.

 Album 11, Track 12

Explain dehydration and how the example given by the professor illustrates the condition.

 Stop

Preparation Time – 30 seconds
Response Time – 60 seconds

QUESTION 5

In this question, you will listen to a conversation. You will then be asked to talk about the information in the conversation and to give your opinion about the ideas presented. After you hear the question, you have 20 seconds to prepare your response and 60 seconds to speak.

 Album 11, Track 13

> Briefly summarize the problem the speakers are discussing. Then state which solution
> you would recommend. Explain the reasons for your recommendation.

 Stop

Preparation Time – 20 seconds
Response Time – 60 seconds

QUESTION 6

In this question, you will listen to a short lecture. You will then be asked to summarize important information from the lecture. After you hear the question, you have 20 seconds to prepare your response and 60 seconds to speak.

 Album 11, Track 14

> Using points and details from the lecture, explain the characteristics of theater that define
> it as a separate art.

 Stop

Preparation Time – 20 seconds
Response Time – 60 seconds

Key points for Test 3 – Speaking are on pages 682–683.

Each response earns a score of 1, 2, 3 or 4.

Record your total Speaking score on page 794.

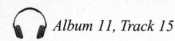 *Album 11, Track 15*

WRITING SECTION DIRECTIONS

The Writing section measures your ability to use writing to communicate in an academic environment. There are two writing questions.

Question 1 is a writing task based on reading and listening. You will read a passage, listen to a lecture, and then write a response to a question about the relationship between the lecture and the reading. You have 20 minutes to plan and write your response.

Question 2 is writing based on knowledge and experience. You will write an essay in response to a question that asks you to state, explain, and support an opinion on an issue. You have 30 minutes to plan and write your essay.

 Stop

QUESTION 1

For this task, you will write a response to a question about a reading passage and a lecture. You may take notes, and you may use your notes to help you write your response. Your response will be scored on the quality of your writing and on how well you connect the points in the lecture with points in the reading. Typically, an effective response will have 150 to 225 words.

Reading Time – 3 minutes

Dog breeds developed as humans intentionally mated dogs with certain desirable traits to encourage those traits in the next generation. Through this process, dogs developed into distinct groups, with each group specializing in a skill such as hunting, herding, or guarding. Today, dog breeders apply the science of canine genetics to produce purebred dogs with characteristics suitable for the dog's intended purpose. Purebred dogs are registered with a canine association such as the American Kennel Club. Breed registries ensure breed purity by documenting each dog's ancestry, achievements, and working qualities.

The aim of dog breeding is to benefit dogs by enhancing their desirable traits. Breeders choose to mate dogs that best represent the breed in appearance, performance, or some other specific point. Careful selection increases the probability that the favorable characteristics will be conveyed genetically. Professional breeders love dogs and care about each dog they bring into the world. Breeders are experts in their breed and know the genetic history of each individual dog. They support and participate in programs that collect and maintain standardized information on the health of dogs. For these reasons, dog breeders not only improve dog breeds but also contribute to the welfare of all dogs.

Popular culture, dog shows, and other media foster public appreciation of various breeds. The films *Rin Tin Tin* and *101 Dalmatians* made the German shepherd and the dalmatian popular breeds for pets. Television has done the same for the collie, the chihuahua, and the Jack Russell terrier. Dog shows educate the public and promote dog breeds. Websites and social media provide information about popular breeds and their suitability for various contexts. All of these things encourage responsible dog ownership.

Now listen to the recording. When you hear the question, begin your response. You may look at the reading passage during the writing time.

 Album 11, Track 16

> Summarize the points made in the lecture, being sure to explain how they contradict specific points made in the reading passage.

 Stop

Writing Time – 20 minutes

QUESTION 2

For this task, you will write an essay in response to a question that asks you to state and support your opinion on a topic. Your essay will be scored on the quality of your writing, including how well you organize and develop your ideas and how well you use language to express your ideas. Typically, an effective essay will have a minimum of 300 words.

Read the question below and make any notes that will help you plan your response. Then begin typing your essay.

Do you agree or disagree with the following statement?

It is more important to work at a job that you enjoy, even if the salary is low, than it is to have a high–paying job that you do not enjoy.

Use specific reasons and details to support your answer.

Writing Time – 30 minutes

Key points for Test 3 – Writing are on page 683.

Each response earns a score of 1, 2, 3, 4 or 5.

Record your total Writing score on page 794.

READING SECTION DIRECTIONS

The Reading section measures your ability to understand academic passages in English. You will read passages and answer questions about them. Answer all questions based on what is stated or implied in the passages.

You will read three passages. You have 60 minutes to read the passages and answer the questions.

Most questions are worth one point, but the last question in each set is worth more than one point. The directions indicate how many points you may receive.

Some passages include a word or phrase in bold type. For these words and phrases, you will see a definition in a glossary at the end of the passage.

Musical Talent

1   Among all the abilities with which an individual may be endowed, musical talent appears earliest in life. Very young children can exhibit musical precocity for different reasons. Some develop exceptional skill as a result of a well–designed instructional regime, such as the Suzuki method for the violin. Some have the good fortune to be born into a musical family in a household filled with music. In a number of interesting cases, musical talent is part of an otherwise disabling condition such as autism or mental retardation. A musically gifted child has an inborn talent; however, the extent to which the talent is expressed publicly will depend upon the environment in which the child lives.

2   Musically gifted children master at an early age the principal elements of music, including pitch and rhythm. Pitch—or melody—is more central in certain cultures, for example, in Eastern societies that make use of tiny quarter–tone intervals. Rhythm, sounds produced at certain auditory frequencies and grouped according to a prescribed system, is emphasized in sub–Saharan Africa, where the rhythmic ratios can be very complex.

3   All children have some aptitude for making music. During infancy, normal children sing as well as babble, and they can produce individual sounds and sound patterns. Infants as young as two months can match their mother's songs in pitch, loudness, and melodic shape, and infants at four months can match rhythmic structure as well. Infants are especially predisposed to acquire these core aspects of music, and they can also engage in sound play that clearly exhibits creativity.

4   Individual differences begin to emerge in young children as they learn to sing. Some children can match large segments of a song by the age of two or three. Many others can only approximate pitch at this age and may still have difficulty in producing accurate melodies by the age of five or six. However, by the time they reach school age, most children in any culture have a **schema** of what a song should be like and can produce a reasonably accurate imitation of the songs commonly heard in their environment.

5   The early appearance of superior musical ability in some children provides evidence that musical talent may be a separate and unique form of intelligence. There are numerous tales of young artists who have a remarkable "ear" or extraordinary memory for music and a natural understanding of musical structure. In many of these cases, the child is average in every other way but displays an exceptional ability in music. Even the most gifted child, however, takes about ten years to achieve the levels of performance or composition that would constitute mastery of the musical sphere.

6   Every generation in music history has had its famous prodigies—individuals with exceptional musical powers that emerge at a young age. In the eighteenth century, Wolfgang Amadeus Mozart began composing and performing at the age of six. As a child, Mozart could play the piano like an adult. He had perfect pitch, and at age nine he was also a master of the art of modulation—transitions from one key to another—which became one of the hallmarks of his style. By the age of eleven, he had composed three symphonies and 30 other major works. Mozart's well–developed talent was preserved into adulthood.

7   Unusual musical ability is a regular characteristic of certain **anomalies** such as **autism**. In one case, an autistic girl was able to play "Happy Birthday" in the style of various composers, including Mozart, Beethoven, Verdi, and Schubert. When the girl was three, her mother communicated with her by playing incomplete melodies, which the child would complete with the appropriate tone in the proper octave. For the autistic child, music may be the primary mode of communication, and the child may cling to music because it represents a haven in a world that is largely confusing and frightening.

Glossary:

schema: a mental outline or model
anomaly: departure from what is normal; abnormal condition
autism: a developmental disorder involving impaired communication and emotional separation

1. The word precocity in paragraph 1 is closest in meaning to

   (A) strong interest
   (B) good luck
   (C) advanced skill
   (D) personal style

2. Which sentence below best expresses the essential information in the highlighted sentence in paragraph 1? Incorrect choices change the meaning in important ways or leave out essential information.

   (A) Children may be born with superior musical ability, but their environment will determine how this ability is developed.
   (B) Every child is naturally gifted, and it is the responsibility of the public schools to recognize and develop these talents.
   (C) Children with exceptional musical talent will look for the best way to express themselves through music–making.
   (D) Some musically talented children live in an environment surrounded by music, while others have little exposure to music.

3. The author makes the point that musical elements such as pitch and rhythm

   (A) distinguish music from other art forms
   (B) vary in emphasis in different cultures
   (C) make music difficult to learn
   (D) express different human emotions

4. The word predisposed in paragraph 3 is closest in meaning to

   (A) inclined
   (B) gifted
   (C) pushed
   (D) amused

5. According to the passage, when does musical talent usually begin to appear?

   (A) When infants start to babble and produce sound patterns
   (B) Between the ages of two and four months
   (C) When children learn to sing at two or three years old
   (D) Between ten years old and adolescence

6. According to the passage, which of the following suggests that musical talent is a separate form of intelligence?

   (A) Exceptional musical ability in an otherwise average child
   (B) Recognition of the emotional power of music
   (C) The ability of all babies to acquire core elements of music
   (D) Differences between learning music and learning language

7. Why does the author discuss Mozart in paragraph 6?

   (A) To compare past and present views of musical talent
   (B) To give an example of a well–known musical prodigy
   (C) To list musical accomplishments of the eighteenth century
   (D) To describe the development of individual musical skill

8. In music, the change from one key to another is known as

   (A) rhythm
   (B) prodigy
   (C) perfect pitch
   (D) modulation

9. All of the following are given as examples of exceptional musical talent EXCEPT

   (A) a remarkable "ear" or perfect memory for music
   (B) ability to compose major works at a young age
   (C) appreciation for a wide variety of musical styles
   (D) playing a single song in the style of various composers

10. The word haven in paragraph 7 is closest in meaning to

   (A) beautiful art
   (B) safe place
   (C) personal goal
   (D) simple problem

11. It can be inferred from the passage that exceptional musical ability

   (A) occurs more frequently in some cultures than in others
   (B) is evidence of a superior level of intelligence in other areas
   (C) has been documented and studied but is little understood
   (D) is the result of natural talent and a supportive environment

12. Look at the four squares, **A**, **B**, **C**, and **D**, which indicate where the following sentence could be added to the passage. Where would the sentence best fit?

They can even imitate patterns and tones sung by other people.

    All children have some aptitude for making music. **A** During infancy, normal children sing as well as babble, and they can produce individual sounds and sound patterns. **B** Infants as young as two months can match their mother's songs in pitch, loudness, and melodic shape, and infants at four months can match rhythmic structure as well. **C** Infants are especially predisposed to acquire these core aspects of music, and they can also engage in sound play that clearly exhibits creativity. **D**

13. An introductory sentence for a brief summary of the passage is provided below. Complete the summary by selecting the THREE answer choices that express the most important ideas in the passage. Some sentences do not belong in the summary because they express ideas that are not presented in the passage or are minor ideas in the passage. **This question is worth 2 points.**

Musical talent usually appears early in life.

•
•
•

Answer Choices

(A) Very young children can develop exceptional skill in playing the violin by the Suzuki method.

(B) While all children have a basic ability to make music, some exhibit extraordinary skill at a very early age.

(C) Prodigies have a natural understanding of musical structure that enables them to play and compose music with great skill.

(D) Wolfgang Amadeus Mozart had composed several major works and symphonies by the age of eleven.

(E) Autistic children cannot relate to their environment realistically and therefore have difficulty in communicating.

(F) Exceptional musical ability is often part of an otherwise disabling condition such as autism.

How to Score 2–Point Question	
Answers Correct	**Points Earned**
3	2
2	1
0 – 1	0

CLOTHING AND COSTUME

1 The ancient Greeks and the Chinese believed that we first clothed our bodies for some physical reason, such as protecting ourselves from the elements. Ethnologists and psychologists have invoked psychological reasons: modesty, taboo, magical influence, or the desire to please. Anthropological research indicates that the function of the earliest clothing was to carry objects. Our hunting–gathering ancestors had to travel great distances to obtain food. For the male hunters, carrying was much easier if they were wearing simple belts or animal skins from which they could hang weapons and tools. For the female gatherers, more elaborate carrying devices were necessary. Women had to transport food back to the settlement and also had to carry babies, so they required bags or slings.

2 Another function of early clothing—providing comfort and protection—probably developed at the same time as utility. As human beings multiplied and spread out from the warm lands in which they evolved, they covered their bodies more and more to maintain body warmth. Today, we still dress to maintain warmth and to carry objects in our clothes. And like our hunting–gathering ancestors, most men still carry things on their person, as if they still needed to keep their arms free for hunting, while women tend to have a separate bag for carrying, as if they were still food–gatherers. But these two functions of clothing are only two of many uses to which we put the garments that we wear today.

3 There is a clear distinction between attire that constitutes "clothing" and attire that is more aptly termed "costume." We might say that clothing has to do with covering the body, and costume concerns the choice of a particular form of garment for a particular purpose. Clothing depends primarily on such physical conditions as climate, health, and textile, while costume reflects social factors such as personal status, religious beliefs, aesthetics, and the wish to be distinguished from or to emulate others.

4 Even in early human history, costume fulfilled a function beyond that of simple utility. Costume helped to impose authority or inspire fear. A chieftain's costume embodied attributes expressing his power, while a warrior's costume enhanced his physical superiority and suggested he was superhuman. Costume often had a magical significance such as investing humans with the attributes of other creatures through the addition of ornaments to identify the wearer with animals, gods, or heroes. In more recent times, professional or administrative costume is designed to distinguish the wearer and to express personal or delegated authority. Costume communicates the status of the wearer, and with very few exceptions, the aim is to display as high a status as possible. Costume denotes power, and since power is often equated with wealth, costume has come to be an expression of social class and material prosperity.

5 A uniform is a type of costume that serves the important function of displaying membership in a group: school, sports team, occupation, or armed force. Military uniform denotes rank and is intended not only to express group membership but also to protect the body and to intimidate. A soldier's uniform says, "I am part of a powerful machine, and when you deal with me, you deal with my whole organization." Uniforms are immediate beacons of power and authority. If a person needs to display power—a police officer, for example—then the body can be virtually transformed. Height can be exaggerated with protective headgear, thick clothing can make the body look broader and stronger, and boots can enhance the power of the legs. Uniforms also convey low social status; at the bottom of the scale, the uniform of the prisoner denotes membership in the society of convicted criminals.

6 Religious costume signifies spiritual or superhuman authority and possesses a significance that identifies the wearer with a belief or god. A successful clergy has always displayed impressive vestments of one kind or another that clearly demonstrate the religious leader's dominant status.

14. According to the passage, psychological reasons for wearing clothing include

  (A) protection from cold weather
  (B) the availability of materials
  (C) prevention of illness
  (D) the wish to give pleasure

15. The word elaborate in paragraph 1 is closest in meaning to

  (A) primitive
  (B) modest
  (C) complex
  (D) attractive

16. According to the passage, what aspect of humanity's hunting–gathering past is reflected in the clothing of today?

  (A) People cover their bodies because of their modesty.
  (B) Most men still carry objects on their person.
  (C) Women like clothes that are beautiful and practical.
  (D) Men wear pants, but women wear skirts or pants.

17. Which sentence below best expresses the essential information in the highlighted sentence in paragraph 3? Incorrect choices change the meaning in important ways or leave out essential information.

  (A) Clothing protects the body, and costume involves selecting clothing for a specific intention.
  (B) We like clothing to fit our body well, but different costumes fit differently depending on the purpose.
  (C) Both clothing and costume are types of attire, but it is often difficult to distinguish between them.
  (D) People spend more time in choosing special costumes than they do in selecting everyday clothing.

18. According to paragraph 4, early humans used costume to

  (A) maintain body warmth
  (B) carry weapons
  (C) attract a potential spouse
  (D) convey social position

19. The word ornaments in paragraph 4 is closest in meaning to

  (A) layers
  (B) words
  (C) feathers
  (D) decorations

20. It can be inferred from paragraph 4 that the author most likely believes which of the following about costume?

  (A) We can learn about a society's social structure by studying costume.
  (B) Costume used to serve a simple function, but now it is very complex.
  (C) The main purpose of costume is to force people to obey their leaders.
  (D) Costume is rarely a reliable indicator of a person's material wealth.

21. The word beacons in paragraph 5 is closest in meaning to

  (A) signals
  (B) lights
  (C) inventions
  (D) reversals

22. Why does the author discuss the police officer's uniform in paragraph 5?

  (A) To describe the aesthetic aspects of costume
  (B) To identify the wearer with a hero
  (C) To suggest that police are superhuman
  (D) To show how costume conveys authority

23. All of the following are likely to be indicated
by a person's costume EXCEPT

- (A) playing on a football team
- (B) being a prisoner
- (C) having a heart condition
- (D) leading a religious ceremony

24. Look at the four squares, **A**, **B**, **C**, and **D**, which indicate where the following sentence could
be added to the passage. Where would the sentence best fit?

Such power is seen clearly in the judge's robes and the police officer's uniform.

Even in early human history, costume fulfilled a function beyond that of simple utility.
A Costume helped to impose authority or inspire fear. A chieftain's costume embodied
attributes expressing his power, while a warrior's costume enhanced his physical superiority
and suggested he was superhuman. Costume often had a magical significance such as
investing humans with the attributes of other creatures through the addition of ornaments
to identify the wearer with animals, gods, or heroes. **B** In more recent times, professional
or administrative costume is designed to distinguish the wearer and to express personal or
delegated authority. **C** Costume communicates the status of the wearer, and with very few
exceptions, the aim is to display as high a status as possible. Costume denotes power, and
since power is often equated with wealth, costume has come to be an expression of social
class and material prosperity. **D**

25. Select the appropriate phrases from the answer choices and match them to the type of attire that they describe. TWO of the answer choices will NOT be used. *This question is worth 4 points.*

Answer Choices

(A) Reflects social factors such as personal status or material prosperity

(B) Makes it legal for people to perform dangerous work

(C) Provides comfort, warmth, and protection from the weather

(D) Shows that a person is a member of a particular group

(E) Depends on physical conditions such as climate and health

(F) Conveys personal, administrative, or superhuman authority

(G) Enabled early humans to carry the objects needed to obtain food

(H) Serves as a symbol that unites all people on the earth

(I) Indicates the dominant status of religious leaders

Clothing

-
-
-

Costume

-
-
-
-

| How to Score 4–Point Question ||
Answers Correct	Points Earned
7	4
6	3
5	2
4	1
0 – 3	0

TEST 4

THE GREENHOUSE EFFECT

1   In the nineteenth century, scientists discovered that certain gases in Earth's atmosphere behave like the panes of glass in a greenhouse. These gases admit visible radiation from the sun but prevent the escape of infrared radiation from Earth's surface. Because of their radiative properties, the action of these atmospheric gases is known as the greenhouse effect, and the gases are known as greenhouse gases. Water vapor is the principal greenhouse gas. Others are carbon dioxide, ozone, methane, and nitrous oxide.

2   Window glass is relatively transparent to visible radiation but slows the transmission of infrared radiation. Plant greenhouses are designed to take advantage of this property of glass by being constructed almost entirely of glass panes. Visible radiation—light from the sun—enters the greenhouse, and is absorbed by the dark plants. Thus, light energy is converted to heat. The plants use some of the heat and re–radiate the rest as infrared radiation, most of which cannot escape the greenhouse because it is trapped by the solid glass. The atmosphere inside the greenhouse therefore becomes heated, and the temperature can rise well above that of the outside air. Similarly, greenhouse gases in Earth's atmosphere keep infrared radiation from escaping into space, thereby keeping the planet warm.

3   However, the greenhouse analogy is not completely accurate because the trapping of infrared radiation by glass is only part of the reason that most plant greenhouses retain internal heat. Greenhouses cut heat loss mainly by acting as a shelter from the wind, thereby reducing heat loss due to **conduction** and **convection**. As a rule, the thinner the greenhouse glass and the stronger the external wind speed, the more important the shelter effect is. Still, the greenhouse analogy remains relevant in most discussions of radiation balance in Earth's atmospheric system.

4   The effect of a greenhouse gas can be seen by comparing the typical summer weather of the American Southwest with that of the coast along the Gulf of Mexico. Both areas are at about the same latitude and therefore receive about the same intensity of solar radiation. In both places, afternoon temperatures typically exceed 30 degrees Celsius. At night, however, air temperatures often differ remarkably due to the absence or presence of the leading greenhouse gas, water vapor. In the desert Southwest, there is less water vapor in the air to impede the escape of infrared radiation; therefore, heat is readily lost to space. Air temperatures on the surface of the Southwest desert may fall below 15 degrees Celsius. In contrast, along the more humid Gulf Coast, infrared radiation does not escape to space as readily, and minimum temperatures may fall only into the 20s Celsius.

5   Clouds produce a greenhouse effect because they are composed of radiation–absorbing water droplets or ice crystals. Nights are usually warmer when the sky is cloud–covered than when the sky is clear. However, clouds can affect climate in two opposing ways. On the one hand, clouds warm the planet's surface by absorbing and re–radiating infrared radiation; on the other hand, they cool the surface by reflecting solar radiation away from Earth. Analyses of satellite measurements of radiation indicate that clouds have a net cooling effect on global climate. Thus, a more extensive cloud cover would tend to cool the planet.

6   The greenhouse effect also operates on other planets. On both Mars and Venus, the principal atmospheric gas, carbon dioxide, is also the main greenhouse gas. Earth has an abundance of plants to absorb carbon dioxide, but Mars and Venus do not possess living organisms. Consequently, Earth's two closest neighbors have extremely high concentrations of atmospheric carbon dioxide. The atmosphere of Mars is considerably thinner than the atmosphere on Earth, so its greenhouse effect raises the average surface temperature by only about 10 degrees Celsius. In contrast, the atmosphere of Venus is about 90 times denser than Earth's, and its greenhouse warming is estimated at 523 degrees Celsius. The hot, thick, cloud–filled atmosphere shrouding Venus is composed of 97 percent carbon dioxide.

7   Some scientists believe that Venus used to be similar to Earth, with liquid water on
the surface. Then, billions of years ago, Venus started to heat up. Eventually, all its surface
water evaporated into the atmosphere, and planetary warming became self–sustaining and
unstoppable. Venus provides a warning for what could happen on Earth if the greenhouse
effect continued unchecked and a high percentage of surface water became water vapor. If
that happened, global warming would reach the point of no return, as it did on Venus.

Glossary:
   conduction: the transmission of heat through a heat–conveying substance
   convection: the transfer of heat by the movement of air currents

26. Which of the following statements can be inferred from paragraph 1?

   Ⓐ The greenhouse effect did not occur on Earth before the nineteenth century.
   Ⓑ The discovery of the greenhouse effect led to better greenhouse designs.
   Ⓒ Changes in atmosphere's composition cannot stop the greenhouse effect.
   Ⓓ The main cause of the greenhouse effect is water vapor in the atmosphere.

27. According to paragraph 2, why does the air inside a plant greenhouse stay warm?

   Ⓐ The glass lets in visible radiation but does not let out infrared radiation.
   Ⓑ The walls are insulated with compartments filled with greenhouse gases.
   Ⓒ The doors and windows are kept closed when the sun is not shining.
   Ⓓ The furnace converts greenhouse gases into infrared radiation.

28. The word transmission in paragraph 2 is closest in meaning to

   Ⓐ observation
   Ⓑ warming
   Ⓒ escape
   Ⓓ creation

29. Which sentence below best expresses the essential information in the highlighted sentence in paragraph 3? Incorrect choices change the meaning in important ways or leave out essential information.

   Ⓐ iMost greenhouses retain heat because their windows have a special type of glass that can trap infrared radiation.
   Ⓑ The greenhouse comparison is not perfect because greenhouses retain heat only partly as a result of radiation trapping.
   Ⓒ Greenhouses are used for many purposes, but most importantly for collecting radiant heat with greenhouse gases.
   Ⓓ The greenhouse is a good analogy for a number of reasons; one is that a greenhouse has its own source of internal heat.

30. According to paragraph 3, the main way that greenhouses prevent heat loss is by

   Ⓐ controlling the amount of light
   Ⓑ converting heat to electricity
   Ⓒ keeping the wind out
   Ⓓ using a special type of glass

31. Why does the author discuss the weather of the American Southwest and the coast along the Gulf of Mexico in paragraph 4?

   Ⓐ To illustrate the role of water vapor in the greenhouse effect
   Ⓑ To describe the weather's influence on the culture of each area
   Ⓒ To show that the greenhouse effect can occur on a small scale
   Ⓓ To explain why these two places attract tourists in the summer

32. The word impede in paragraph 4 is closest in meaning to

- (A) cause
- (B) reverse
- (C) prevent
- (D) increase

33. What can be inferred from paragraph 5 about the effect of clouds on climate?

- (A) Clouds have the greatest effect on climate in the summer.
- (B) The cooling effect of clouds exceeds their warming effect.
- (C) The effect of clouds on climate has diminished over time.
- (D) Clouds are the leading cause of global climate change.

34. According to paragraph 6, what factors contribute to the greenhouse effect on Mars and Venus?

- (A) The size of the planet and its distance from the sun
- (B) The atmospheric gases and the length of the day
- (C) The surface temperature and the number of volcanoes
- (D) The absence of plants and the density of the atmosphere

35. The word shrouding in paragraph 6 is closest in meaning to

- (A) poisoning
- (B) rubbing
- (C) melting
- (D) covering

36. In paragraph 7, the author implies that planetary warming on Venus is

- (A) a phenomenon that requires further research
- (B) an optimistic view of the greenhouse effect
- (C) a model for a possible outcome on Earth
- (D) a creative idea for a science fiction story

37. In stating in paragraph 7 that global warming would reach the point of no return, the author means that

- (A) it could change Earth's orbit
- (B) it could not be stopped
- (C) it would make Earth cooler
- (D) it would have no major effect

38. Look at the four squares, **A**, **B**, **C**, and **D**, which indicate where the following sentence could be added to the passage. Where would the sentence best fit?

Even a high, thin cloud cover can raise the temperature at the planet's surface by several degrees.

Clouds produce a greenhouse effect because they are composed of radiation–absorbing water droplets or ice crystals. Nights are usually warmer when the sky is cloud–covered than when the sky is clear. **A** However, clouds can affect climate in two opposing ways. **B** On the one hand, clouds warm the planet's surface by absorbing and re–radiating infrared radiation; on the other hand, they cool the surface by reflecting solar radiation away from Earth. **C** Analyses of satellite measurements of radiation indicate that clouds have a net cooling effect on global climate. **D** Thus, a more extensive cloud cover would tend to cool the planet.

39. An introductory sentence for a brief summary of the passage is provided below. Complete the summary by selecting the THREE answer choices that express the most important ideas in the passage. Some sentences do not belong in the summary because they express ideas that are not presented in the passage or are minor ideas in the passage. *This question is worth 2 points.*

The atmosphere functions as a giant greenhouse that warms the surface of the planet.

-
-
-

Answer Choices

(A) Sunlight enters a greenhouse and is absorbed by the dark plants, which convert light energy to energy for growth.

(B) Some atmospheric gases have a warming effect because they slow the escape of infrared radiation into space.

(C) Rising sea levels and shifts in climatic zones are probable effects of global warming.

(D) In the American Southwest, a high level of solar radiation reaches the planet's surface.

(E) Water vapor and clouds are greenhouse gases because they absorb and re-radiate infrared radiation.

(F) There is also a greenhouse effect on Mars and Venus, where carbon dioxide is the main greenhouse gas.

| How to Score 2–Point Question ||
Answers Correct	Points Earned
3	2
2	1
0 – 1	0

Answers to Test 4 – Reading are on page 683–685.

Record your total Reading score on page 794.

TEST 4

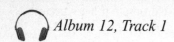
Album 12, Track 1

LISTENING SECTION DIRECTIONS

The Listening section measures your ability to understand conversations and lectures in English. You will hear each conversation and lecture only one time. After each conversation or lecture, you will answer some questions about it. The questions typically ask about the main idea and supporting details. Some questions ask about a speaker's purpose or attitude. Answer the questions based on what the speakers state or imply.

You may take notes while you listen. You may use your notes to help you answer the questions. Your notes will not be scored.

In some questions, you will see this icon: 🎧. This means that you will hear, but not see, part of the question.

Some questions have special directions, which appear in a gray box. Most questions are worth one point. If a question is worth more than one point, the directions will indicate how many points you can receive.

You will now begin part 1 of the Listening section.

PART 1

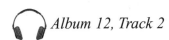 *Album 12, Track 2*

QUESTIONS 1 – 5

Conversation

1. What is the purpose of the conversation?

   (A) The man needs information for a
      research project.
   (B) The man wants to change his housing
      situation.
   (C) The man wants to move to a house
      off campus.
   (D) The man wants to know why his rent
      was raised.

2. What are some features of the suites in
   the villages?

      Click on 2 answers.

   [A] A full refrigerator
   [B] Two study rooms
   [C] A fireplace
   [D] Two to four bedrooms

3. Listen again to part of the conversation. Then
   answer the question.

   Why does the woman say this:

   (A) To show her concern for the man's situation
   (B) To suggest that she is sad about leaving her
      suite
   (C) To express regret at not being able to help
      the man
   (D) To apologize for not answering the man's
      question

4. What does the man think of the cost of rent in
   the villages?

   (A) The rent should be lower for such old
      buildings.
   (B) The rent is reasonable for the features
      included.
   (C) The rent is higher than he hoped it would
      be.
   (D) The rent is similar to that of a house off
      campus.

5. Listen again to part of the conversation. Then
   answer the question.

   Select the sentence that best expresses how the
   man probably feels.

   (A) He does not think he will be able to get a
      room in the villages.
   (B) He is surprised at the number of people
      who live there.
   (C) He does not like the idea of living with 27
      people.
   (D) He is confused about why there is a waiting
      list.

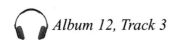 *Album 12, Track 3*

QUESTIONS 6 – 11

World History

6. What is the main purpose of the lecture?

  (A) To instruct in the cultivation of wild squash
  (B) To describe how hunter–gatherers found food
  (C) To compare agriculture around the world
  (D) To explain how early people started farming

7. What is probably true about the origins of agriculture?

  (A) The process of gathering wild food led naturally to farming.
  (B) Agriculture and written language developed at the same time.
  (C) People around the world tried similar experiments with squash.
  (D) The cultivation of vegetables occurred before that of grains.

8. According to the professor, which of the following occurred as plants were first being domesticated?

  Click on 2 answers.

  [A] Plants grew from seeds that were dropped accidentally.
  [B] People chose to grow squash to feed their animals.
  [C] Attempts to domesticate some plants led to their extinction.
  [D] People started tending and protecting wild gardens.

9. Why did the people begin to use digging sticks?

  (A) They found that water would fill the holes they made.
  (B) They noticed that seeds grew better in turned–over soil.
  (C) They dug trenches around the garden to keep out animals.
  (D) They discovered that food could be stored underground.

10. Listen again to part of the lecture. Then answer the question.

  Why does the professor say this:

  (A) To show that people could not work in their gardens at night
  (B) To emphasize the amount of effort it took to protect the plants
  (C) To point out that agriculture developed over a very long time
  (D) To explain why squash was a particularly successful crop

11. What point does the professor make about the transition from hunting–gathering to agriculture?

  (A) The process probably followed a similar pattern around the world.
  (B) The transition to agriculture eliminated the need for hunting.
  (C) Agriculture developed everywhere in the world at the same time.
  (D) The rapid move to agriculture led to environmental devastation.

Album 12, Track 4

QUESTIONS 12 – 17

Biology

12. What is the discussion mainly about?

    (A) Science as a process of discovery
    (B) How science and technology are connected
    (C) Ways that technology has harmed society
    (D) Responsibilities of scientists to society

13. What does the electron microscope provide an example of?

    (A) How technology applies scientific knowledge
    (B) How inventions improve our standard of living
    (C) How governments control science and technology
    (D) How science can advance without technology

14. Why does the professor mention tools, pottery, and musical instruments?

    (A) To compare past technology with current technology
    (B) To list inventions that scientists helped to design
    (C) To show that art and science are not separate activities
    (D) To give examples of technology that came before science

15. Why does one of the students say this:

    (A) To blame humans for not developing better technology
    (B) To contradict the idea that human activity has consequences
    (C) To list additional consequences of technology
    (D) To suggest that some topics are too unpleasant to discuss

16. What does the professor mean by this statement:

    (A) Technology has created powerful weapons.
    (B) Technology will cure every human problem.
    (C) Technology has both helped and harmed us.
    (D) Technology cannot exist without science.

17. Why does one of the students plan to get a master's degree in public policy?

    (A) He wants to convince the government to support technology.
    (B) He believes scientists should inform people about technology.
    (C) He would like to teach in a graduate school of technology.
    (D) He has idea for new technology that will improve society.

PART 2

 *Album 12, Track 5*

QUESTIONS 1 – 5

1. Why does the student go to see the professor?

   (A) She is requesting extra time to finish her project.
   (B) She might have to leave school to get a job.
   (C) She is concerned about the difficulty of the course.
   (D) She needs time off to recover from surgery.

2. Why does the professor say this: 🎧

   (A) To disagree with the student's decision to go home
   (B) To imply that the student should study harder
   (C) To express concern for the student's family
   (D) To encourage the student to explain what she will do

3. What does the student say she will do to complete the course?

   Click on 2 answers.

   [A] Ask her father to help her
   [B] Watch the lectures online
   [C] Email the professor for advice
   [D] Study extra hard for the test

4. What does the professor suggest the student do?

   (A) Change her method of doing research for her project
   (B) Complete her project by the end of the current quarter
   (C) Accept a grade of Incomplete and finish her work later
   (D) Transfer to another school closer to her home

5. What does the professor imply when he says this: 🎧

   (A) He thinks the student will regret leaving the class.
   (B) He believes the student will succeed in another school.
   (C) He is offering to recommend the student for a job.
   (D) He trusts that the student will finish her project.

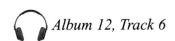 *Album 12, Track 6*

QUESTIONS 6 – 11

Canadian Studies

Art

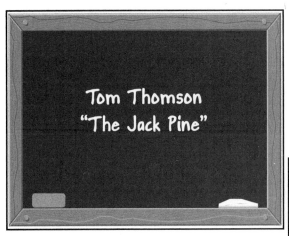

6. Which of the following best describes the organization of the lecture?

   Ⓐ A list of influential painters
   Ⓑ A history of an art movement
   Ⓒ A comparison of schools of art
   Ⓓ A description of a painting

7. What is the professor's point of view concerning the Group of Seven?

   Ⓐ They created a distinctive Canadian art inspired by Canada itself.
   Ⓑ They produced a style of painting that was crude and barbaric.
   Ⓒ They deserve more attention than they have received.
   Ⓓ They influenced new trends in Canadian literature and music.

8. Listen again to part of the lecture. Then answer the question.

Why does the professor say this:

   Ⓐ To explain why the Group's work was misunderstood
   Ⓑ To state that the Group earned very little money
   Ⓒ To contrast the methods of different artists in the Group
   Ⓓ To show how one artist inspired the Group's direction

9. What subjects did the Group of Seven paint?

Click on 2 answers.

   Ⓐ Active street scenes
   Ⓑ Jack pine trees
   Ⓒ Sailing ships
   Ⓓ Uninhabited landscapes

10. What does the professor mean by this statement:

   Ⓐ Art lovers pay high prices for the Group's paintings.
   Ⓑ Canada has more painters now than at any time in the past.
   Ⓒ Much of the Group's work has come to represent Canada.
   Ⓓ People come from all over the world to study Canadian art.

11. Listen again to part of the lecture. Then answer the question.

What can be concluded about the Group of Seven's style of painting?

   Ⓐ The Group did not share a single style of painting.
   Ⓑ All artists in the Group followed the style of Jackson.
   Ⓒ Three artists are responsible for the Group's style.
   Ⓓ The Group started the abstract style of painting.

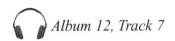

QUESTIONS 12 – 17

Ecology

The Hydrologic Cycle

climatology
hydrology

12. What is the hydrologic cycle?

   (A) The economic issues concerning water
   (B) The movement of water through the earth and atmosphere
   (C) The changes in the amount of rain throughout the year
   (D) The absorption of water vapor into the atmosphere

13. Which of the following statements describes climatology?

   (A) It studies how water is used as a solvent in biological processes.
   (B) It studies the origin, history, and structure of solid matter.
   (C) It studies the movement of groundwater to the earth's surface.
   (D) It studies how solar energy moves water through the atmosphere.

14. What do hydrologists mainly study?

   (A) The role of solar energy in the cycle
   (B) Water movement and storage on land
   (C) Biological reactions that use water
   (D) Atmospheric circulation of water

15. What happens to water that falls to the earth as precipitation?

   Click on 2 answers.

   [A] It is stored in lakes or underground.
   [B] It evaporates before reaching the ground.
   [C] It eventually flows back to the ocean.
   [D] It raises the temperature of the soil.

16. Why does the professor say this:

   (A) To describe the importance of runoff and groundwater
   (B) To compare the amount of runoff with that of groundwater
   (C) To show similarities between runoff and groundwater
   (D) To explain how runoff eventually becomes groundwater

17. What can be inferred about plants in the hydrologic cycle?

   (A) Plants remove excess water from the cycle.
   (B) Water moves quickly through plants.
   (C) Plants perform the function of water storage.
   (D) Plants recycle more water than animals do.

 Stop

Answers to Test 4 – Listening are on pages 685–686.

Record your total Listening score on page 794.

 *Album 12, Track 8*

SPEAKING SECTION DIRECTIONS

The Speaking section measures your ability to speak in English about a variety of topics. There are six questions in this section.

In questions 1 and 2, you will speak about familiar topics. Your responses will be scored on your ability to speak clearly and coherently about the topics.

In questions 3 and 4, you will first read a short text and then listen to a talk on the same topic. You will then be asked a question about what you have read and heard. You will need to combine appropriate information from the text and the talk to provide a complete answer to the question. Your responses will be scored on your ability to speak clearly and coherently and on your ability to accurately convey information about what you have read and heard.

In questions 5 and 6, you will listen to part of a conversation or lecture. You will then be asked a question about what you have heard. Your responses will be scored on your ability to speak clearly and coherently and on your ability to accurately convey information about what you have heard.

You may take notes while you read and while you listen to the conversations and lectures. You may use your notes to help prepare your responses.

 Stop

QUESTION 1

In this question, you will be asked to talk about a familiar topic. After you hear the question, you will have 15 seconds to prepare your response and 45 seconds to speak.

 Album 12, Track 9

> What foreign country would you like to visit? Choose a country and explain why you would like to go there. Include details and examples to support your explanation.

 Stop

Preparation Time – 15 seconds
Response Time – 45 seconds

QUESTION 2

In this question, you will be asked to give your opinion about a familiar topic. After you hear the question, you will have 15 seconds to prepare your response and 45 seconds to speak.

 Album 12, Track 10

> In some schools, teachers decide what classes students must take. Other schools allow students to select their own classes. Which system do you think is better and why? Include details and examples in your explanation.

 Stop

Preparation Time – 15 seconds
Response Time – 45 seconds

QUESTION 3

In this question, you will read a short passage about a campus situation, listen to a conversation, and then speak in response to a question about what you have read and heard. After you hear the question, you have 30 seconds to prepare your response and 60 seconds to speak.

A university has changed the hours that the swimming pool will be open to students. Read the following notice about the change.

Reading Time – 45 seconds

NOTICE OF CHANGE TO SWIMMING POOL HOURS

Due to an increase in the number of swimming classes being offered to both university students and the general public, the university must reduce the hours that the pool is open for the personal use of students. The main change is that the pool will be closed to university students on Monday and Wednesday evenings after 3:00 p.m. The pool will be available to university students from 9:00 a.m. to 3:00 p.m. seven days a week, and from 7:00 p.m. to 10:00 p.m. on Tuesday, Thursday, and Friday evenings. The new pool hours will go into effect beginning on January 5.

Now cover the passage and listen to the recording. When you hear the question, begin preparing your response.

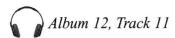 *Album 12, Track 11*

> The man expresses his opinion about the change in swimming pool hours. State his opinion and explain the reasons he gives for holding that opinion.

 Stop

Preparation Time – 30 seconds
Response Time – 60 seconds

QUESTION 4

In this question, you will read a short passage, then listen to a lecture on the same topic, and then speak in response to a question about what you have read and heard. After you hear the question, you have 30 seconds to prepare your response and 60 seconds to speak.

Read the following information from a textbook.

Reading Time – 45 seconds

SOCIAL NORMS AND BEHAVIOR

Human behavior is motivated by social norms. Social norms are the "rules" that describe what is typical or normal for most people. Social norms motivate people by providing evidence of what behavior will be best. In other words, if everyone is doing it, it must be the thing to do. Social pressure to conform offers a shortcut to deciding how to act in a given situation. By seeing what other people do, and by imitating their actions, one can usually choose efficiently. The perception of what most others are doing influences one to behave similarly.

Now cover the passage and listen to the recording. When you hear the question, begin preparing your response.

Album 12, Track 12

Use the examples from the lecture to explain how social norms influence human behavior.

Stop

Preparation Time – 30 seconds
Response Time – 60 seconds

QUESTION 5

In this question, you will listen to a conversation. You will then be asked to talk about the information in the conversation and to give your opinion about the ideas presented. After you hear the question, you have 20 seconds to prepare your response and 60 seconds to speak.

 Album 12, Track 13

> Briefly summarize the problem the speakers are discussing. Then state which solution you would recommend. Explain the reasons for your recommendation.

 Stop

Preparation Time – 20 seconds
Response Time – 60 seconds

QUESTION 6

In this question, you will listen to a short lecture. You will then be asked to summarize important information from the lecture. After you hear the question, you have 20 seconds to prepare your response and 60 seconds to speak.

 Album 12, Track 14

> Using points and examples from the lecture, describe fears that young children experience, and explain how these fears help children.

 Stop

Preparation Time – 20 seconds
Response Time – 60 seconds

Key points for Test 4 – Speaking are on page 687.

Each response earns a score of 1, 2, 3 or 4.

Record your total Speaking score on page 794.

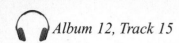

WRITING SECTION DIRECTIONS

The Writing section measures your ability to use writing to communicate in an academic environment. There are two writing questions.

Question 1 is a writing task based on reading and listening. You will read a passage, listen to a lecture, and then write a response to a question about the relationship between the lecture and the reading. You have 20 minutes to plan and write your response.

Question 2 is writing based on knowledge and experience. You will write an essay in response to a question that asks you to state, explain, and support an opinion on an issue. You have 30 minutes to plan and write your essay.

 Stop

QUESTION 1

For this task, you will write a response to a question about a reading passage and a lecture. You may take notes, and you may use your notes to help you write your response. Your response will be scored on the quality of your writing and on how well you connect the points in the lecture with points in the reading. Typically, an effective response will have 150 to 225 words.

Reading Time – 3 minutes

Earthworms have a beneficial effect on the physical and chemical properties of soil. Earthworms change the structure of the soil and improve its ability to cycle nutrients. The burrowing of earthworms aerates the soil and improves water drainage. As earthworms dig through compacted soil, they ingest the soil and grind it up. They move organic matter from the surface and mix it deeper into the soil. In the forest, this organic matter is called duff, mostly litter from fallen leaves and decaying branches.

Earthworms benefit plants in every conceivable way. Their burrowing creates channels through which plant roots may more easily penetrate the soil. Earthworms aid in the formation of humus, the organic matter in soil. A high level of humus is associated with soil fertility, so worms are beneficial to forests, agriculture, and gardens. Worm excretions are a valuable source of nitrogen, which assists in plant growth. The bodies of earthworms are rich in proteins, minerals, and vitamins, and when worms die these nutrients are released into the soil.

Earthworms are an important link in the food web because they are a food source for numerous species of animals. They are preyed upon by many species of birds, snakes, and mammals, as well as invertebrates such as beetles and snails. Earthworms are also used as bait in sports fishing and as animal feed in poultry farming. With the help of gardeners and sports fishermen, earthworm populations continue to spread, sometimes at the speed of ten meters a year. Wherever they go, earthworms are a positive force in the ecosystem.

Now listen to the recording. When you hear the question, begin your response. You may look at the reading passage during the writing time.

 Album 12, Track 16

Summarize the points made in the lecture, being sure to explain how they refute specific points made in the reading passage.

 Stop

Writing Time – 20 minutes

QUESTION 2

For this task, you will write an essay in response to a question that asks you to state and support your opinion on a topic. Your essay will be scored on the quality of your writing, including how well you organize and develop your ideas and how well you use language to express your ideas. Typically, an effective essay will have a minimum of 300 words.

Read the question below and make any notes that will help you plan your response. Then begin typing your essay.

> Some people think that we learn our most important lessons in school. Others think that the knowledge we acquire outside of school is the most important. Which view do you agree with? Use specific reasons and examples to support your opinion.

Writing Time – 30 minutes

Key points for Test 4 – Writing are on page 687.

Each response earns a score of 1, 2, 3, 4 or 5.

Record your total Writing score on page 794.

TEST 5

TEST 5

EARTH'S INTERIOR

1   Earth's immense interior has never been explored directly, and its mysteries have long been a subject of imagination and conjecture. One seventeenth–century map depicted the planet's interior as a cavern with numerous chambers, each filled with air, water, or fire. Two centuries later, in the novel *Journey to the Center of the Earth*, Jules Verne described the subterranean world as a yawning abyss filled with giant sea serpents and other horrifying creatures. Many prominent scientists proposed hypotheses about Earth's structure, including Edmond Halley, who in 1692 described the interior as mostly hollow, with three concentric shells rotating around a core. According to Halley, each shell had its own magnetic poles, and gaseous atmospheres separated the shells.

2   Today, scientists believe that Earth has a solid iron core, approximately the size of the moon, with an outer core of liquid iron and nickel, surrounded by a solid mantle and a crust of tectonic plates. Most knowledge about the interior comes from analysis of variations in the speed of seismic waves recorded during earthquakes. The invention of the seismograph in 1875 was critical in the development of a detailed picture of the planet's structure. By the early twentieth century, a global network of seismographs allowed scientists to record earthquake activity around the world. When an earthquake occurs, it releases seismic waves that race through the planet's body. These waves are measured by the thousands of seismographs worldwide. Seismic waves tend to travel in a straight line and at an unchanging velocity as long as they pass through a homogeneous medium at constant temperature and pressure. Changes in speed indicate that the waves are passing through materials of varied composition and structure at different temperatures and pressures.

3   During an earthquake, some seismic waves move across the surface, causing great damage. Other, less destructive waves travel through the body of the planet. Those traveling through the body are classified as either primary waves (P–waves) or secondary waves (S–waves). The speeds and paths of both types of body waves vary with the density and elasticity of the materials they encounter. P–waves travel very quickly and are the first waves to reach seismographs. Solid, liquid, or gaseous materials conduct P–waves at different rates. When P–waves pass through solid rock, an elastic medium, the rock is compressed and then quickly returns to its original volume, which causes the waves to accelerate in velocity. In contrast, when P–waves enter a liquid or a gas, which are not elastic, the waves decrease in speed. S–waves move at about half the speed of P–waves and are slower in reaching seismographs. As S–waves undulate through the planet, they create shear forces that tear rocks apart. S–waves can pass only through solid materials. Liquids are not elastic, and hence cannot deform and then return to their original shape; they simply flow away from the shearing stress.

4   Earth's interior is filled with layers of rocks and metals, which are subjected to increasing heat and pressure at deeper levels. By analyzing the data from seismic waves, scientists have been able to identify the materials that compose each layer. When seismic waves move between layers, their paths suddenly change. When they meet a boundary between regions differing in density, the waves are deflected from their paths. As waves travel deeper through the interior, they increase in velocity, and the deeper segment of a wave front travels faster than segments that are less deep. Any given layer becomes more rigid with increasing depth, and the velocity of seismic waves increases with the rigidity of the materials composing the layer. Seismic waves increase in speed as they pass through colder regions, where the rocks are more rigid than surrounding rocks. Conversely, waves slow down when they pass through warmer regions, where the rocks are less rigid than surrounding rocks.

5   Through the process of seismic tomography, which uses seismic waves to provide three–dimensional images, scientists now have a detailed map of Earth's interior. By synthesizing data from hundreds of thousands of earthquakes, computers have generated a sequence of cross–

sectional views, which together form a three–dimensional image of the planet. Seismic tomography reveals that the outer surface of Earth's core is not smooth and featureless, as scientists once believed. In some places the outer core projects upward into the mantle, while in other places the mantle extends downward into the liquid outer core.

1. The word conjecture in paragraph 1 is closest in meaning to

   (A) ear
   (B) dispute
   (C) inference
   (D) poetry

2. According to the passage, past depictions of Earth's interior include all of the following EXCEPT

   (A) separate chambers of air, water, and fire
   (B) a liquid core with a solid outer core
   (C) a deep hole inhabited by dangerous creatures
   (D) three gas–filled shells moving around a core

3. According to the passage, one current belief about Earth's interior that differs from past beliefs is that

   (A) the interior is mostly solid instead of hollow
   (B) heat and pressure decrease at deeper levels
   (C) the interior atmosphere is lit by a subterranean sun
   (D) scientists may soon be able to explore the interior directly

4. According to paragraph 2, current scientific knowledge of Earth's interior is mainly based on

   (A) a rejection of Edmond Halley's hypothesis
   (B) variations in the density of rocks near the surface
   (C) direct evidence obtained through deep drilling
   (D) analyzing data recorded during earthquakes

5. What is the main purpose of paragraph 3?

   (A) To describe the destruction caused by earthquakes
   (B) To explain how the seismograph has advanced scientific knowledge
   (C) To define conduction rates of solids, liquids, and gases
   (D) To compare properties of different types of seismic waves

6. According to paragraph 3, an elastic material is one that

   (A) contracts and then returns to its initial shape
   (B) is composed over a long period of time
   (C) causes seismic waves to decrease in speed
   (D) changes from a solid to a liquid state

7. The word deform in paragraph 3 is closest in meaning to

   (A) cause stress
   (B) change shape
   (C) tear rocks apart
   (D) become cooler

8. It can be inferred from paragraph 3 that shear forces

   (A) are more destructive than surface waves
   (B) have no effect on elastic materials
   (C) do not exist in liquids
   (D) move very quickly through gases

TEST 5

9. Which sentence below best expresses the essential information in the highlighted sentence in paragraph 4? Incorrect choices change the meaning in important ways or leave out essential information.

(A) With increasing depth, materials become more rigid and seismic waves travel faster.
(B) The deeper segments of a layer are more rigid, which causes seismic waves to change direction.
(C) The materials composing each layer undergo sudden temperature changes as seismic waves pass through.
(D) The speed of seismic waves increases in cold regions and decreases in warm regions.

10. Paragraph 4 supports which of the following statements?

(A) Knowledge obtained from seismic data proves the accuracy of Halley's model.
(B) Scientists still have many unanswered questions about Earth's internal structure.
(C) Heat from Earth's core creates a magnetic field that changes the paths of seismic waves.
(D) Analysis of seismic data has increased scientific knowledge of Earth's interior.

11. The word synthesizing in paragraph 5 is closest in meaning to

(A) combining
(B) sorting
(C) naming
(D) reducing

12. According to paragraph 5, one result of seismic tomography is

(A) the ability to predict when earthquakes will occur
(B) the discovery that Earth's outer core is irregular in shape
(C) a slight reduction in importance of the seismograph
(D) confirmation of Halley's hypothesis about Earth's interior

13. Look at the four squares, **A**, **B**, **C**, and **D**, which indicate where the following sentence could be added to the passage. Where would the sentence best fit?

However, comparisons of seismic data show that sometimes seismic waves decrease or increase in velocity.

Today, scientists believe that Earth has a solid iron core, approximately the size of the moon, with an outer core of liquid iron and nickel, surrounded by a solid mantle and a crust of tectonic plates. Most knowledge about the interior comes from analysis of variations in the speed of seismic waves recorded during earthquakes. The invention of the seismograph in 1875 was critical in the development of a detailed picture of the planet's structure. **A** By the early twentieth century, a global network of seismographs allowed scientists to record earthquake activity around the world. **B** When an earthquake occurs, it releases seismic waves that race through the planet's body. These waves are measured by the thousands of seismographs worldwide. **C** Seismic waves tend to travel in a straight line and at an unchanging velocity as long as they pass through a homogeneous medium at constant temperature and pressure. **D** Changes in speed indicate that the waves are passing through materials of varied composition and structure at different temperatures and pressures.

14. An introductory sentence for a brief summary of the passage is provided below. Complete the summary by selecting the THREE answer choices that express the most important ideas in the passage. Some sentences do not belong in the summary because they express ideas that are not presented in the passage or are minor ideas in the passage. ***This question is worth 2 points.***

> **Although Earth's interior has never been explored directly, scientists have other ways to learn about its structure and composition.**

•
•
•

Answer Choices

(A) Jules Verne and Edmond Halley made significant contributions to an understanding of the interior.

(B) Measuring seismic waves during earthquakes has been essential in developing scientific knowledge of the interior.

(C) Variations in the speed and direction of seismic waves indicate properties of the materials through which the waves pass.

(D) Some seismic waves travel over Earth's surface, while others travel through the interior of the planet.

(E) Analysis of rocks expelled to the surface during earthquakes suggests that the composition of the interior varies with depth.

(F) The seismograph and seismic tomography have given scientists a detailed map of the planet's interior.

How to Score 2–Point Question	
Answers Correct	**Points Earned**
3	2
2	1
0 – 1	0

TROPICAL AND TEMPERATE RAINFORESTS

1   Earth's oldest living ecosystems, rainforests are areas of high humidity, abundant rainfall, and lush vegetation. Tropical rainforests cover a large part of the planet, while temperate rainforests occur in only a few regions. In the Western Hemisphere, tropical rainforests are found in equatorial Central and South America, where rainfall is greater than 250 centimeters per year. Temperate rainforests occur in the mid–latitudes on the western edge of North and South America, where moist air from the Pacific Ocean drops between 150 and 500 centimeters of rain in a year. Tropical rainforests are characterized by a warm, wet climate with an even distribution of rainfall annually, often two wet seasons and two dry seasons, with dry periods lasting only a few months. There is only slight temperature variation throughout the year. Temperate rainforests, in contrast, have seasonal variation: typically one long wet winter or spring, followed by a dry summer. In the American temperate zones, a range of mountains traps moisture from the ocean, protecting the forests from severe weather extremes. Winter temperatures rarely drop below freezing, and summer temperatures seldom exceed 27 degrees Celsius.

2   The tropical rainforests of Central and South America are characterized by luxuriant vegetation: tall, dense jungle, with thick vines covering the trees. The most common trees are broad–leaf evergreens including palm, bamboo, and tree ferns. Tropical rainforests are typically divided into four layers, each with different plants and animals adapted for life in that particular area. At the top is the emergent layer, which contains a small number of very tall trees. Next is the canopy, a nearly continuous cover of foliage formed by the treetops. The canopy is the densest area of biodiversity, home to around half of the forest's plant species, including large trees 30 to 45 meters in height. Below the canopy is the understory, filled with large–leaf plants, vines, and shrubs, and home to many insects, birds, reptiles, and mammals. The bottom layer, the forest floor, is relatively clear of vegetation because only a small amount of sunlight penetrates the forest's upper layers.

3   The temperate rainforests of North America have a less complex ecology. The topmost layer is dominated by a few species of tall coniferous evergreens such as spruce, hemlock, cedar, and fir, along with deciduous big–leaf maples. The understory consists of small, shade–loving trees such as dogwood. The temperate forest has a jungle–like appearance, but ferns and mosses are more common than vines. The forest floor is littered with needles, leaves, twigs, and fallen trees—all of which lie on and under a thick carpet of mosses, lichens, grasses, and small plants. The low–growing plants are shade tolerant because little sunlight extends down to the forest floor. The mild climate has produced an ecosystem in which change occurs slowly, giving the illusion that time itself moves slowly. Trees in the temperate rainforest live very long lives and grow to immense sizes. When fully grown, some trees reach heights of 85 meters.

4   When trees and plants die, their nutrients are recycled to maintain the forest. Nutrients in rainforests are recycled at various rates, due to differences in rates of decomposition and variations in soil chemistry. In tropical rainforests, the warm temperatures and abundant precipitation cause most organic material to decompose in a few months to a few years. Because decomposition is so rapid, relatively little organic material accumulates on the floor of tropical forests. As the vegetation dies and decays, the roots of the trees quickly absorb the nutrients. Most of the nutrients supporting the rainforest—about 75 percent of those in the ecosystem—are stored in the woody trunks of trees, while only about 10 percent are contained in the soil. The relatively low concentrations of nutrients in the soil are a result of the fast cycling time rather than a shortage of these elements in the ecosystem.

5   In temperate rainforests, decomposition is much slower, taking four to six years. More dead plant material accumulates as litter on the forest floor, where it is slowly digested by fungi, insects, and bacteria. The abundance of organic matter on the ground creates soil rich in nutrients, with the soil containing as much as 50 percent of all the nutrients in the ecosystem. The nutrients in the forest litter and soil may remain there for long periods of time before being absorbed by the trees.

The nutrient–rich soil makes the temperate rainforest less vulnerable to the effects of destruction and the recovery period faster than it is for the tropical rainforest.

15. According to paragraph 1, one similarity between the tropical and temperate rainforests of the Americas is

(A) the latitudes where they occur
(B) the abundance of rainfall in a year
(C) the diversity of species they contain
(D) the degree of seasonal variation in temperature

16. The word traps in paragraph 1 is closest in meaning to

(A) catches
(B) limits
(C) dries
(D) repels

17. In paragraph 2, what does the author state about the layers of tropical rainforests?

(A) The uppermost layer is habitat for a variety of birds.
(B) The canopy is the layer that most defines the tropical rainforest.
(C) The middle layers contain resources that are valuable to humans.
(D) Each layer contains species that are most suited for life there.

18. The word luxuriant in paragraph 2 is closest in meaning to

(A) beautiful
(B) valuable
(C) unusual
(D) abundant

19. Which sentence below best expresses the essential information in the highlighted sentence in paragraph 2? Incorrect choices change the meaning in important ways or leave out essential information.

(A) Sunlight dries the forest floor in places where trees have been cut.
(B) Little sunlight reaches the forest floor, so few plants grow there.
(C) People clear away most of the vegetation that grows on the forest floor.
(D) Tall trees in the forest's upper layers capture most of the sunlight.

20. The word littered in paragraph 3 is closest in meaning to

(A) darkened
(B) degraded
(C) covered
(D) contaminated

21. In stating that the low–growing plants are shade tolerant in paragraph 3, the author means that the plants

(A) require only a small amount of light
(B) do not produce colorful flowers
(C) would be taller if they had more light
(D) grow only in open areas between trees

22. Which of the following is given to illustrate the apparent slow passage of time in temperate rainforests?

(A) The length of the wet winter and spring
(B) The great age and great height of trees
(C) The slow evolution of ferns and mosses
(D) The low concentration of nutrients in the soil

23. What can be inferred from paragraphs 4 and 5 about the rate of decomposition in rainforests?

  (A) The rate of decomposition can be controlled by human activity.

  (B) Temperature and availability of water affect decomposition rates.

  (C) Areas richer in biodiversity have a slower rate of decomposition.

  (D) Ecosystems with rapid decomposition are poor in total nutrients.

24. Paragraph 4 supports which statement about tropical rainforests?

  (A) The biodiversity of tropical rainforests creates a high demand for nutrients.

  (B) Tropical rainforests are richer in nutrients than are temperate rainforests.

  (C) New species of trees evolve quickly in tropical rainforests.

  (D) Trees in tropical rainforests have a key role in the cycle of nutrients.

25. What is the main purpose of paragraph 5?

  (A) To contrast decomposition in temperate rainforests with that in tropical forests

  (B) To explain the importance of small organisms in the temperate rainforest

  (C) To describe the natural history, destruction, and recovery of temperate rainforests

  (D) To warn of the consequences of destroying rainforest ecosystems

26. Look at the four squares, **A**, **B**, **C**, and **D**, which indicate where the following sentence could be added to the passage. Where would the sentence best fit?

For this reason, even though the vegetation may be lush, the soil itself contains few available nutrients.

When trees and plants die, their nutrients are recycled to maintain the forest. **A** Nutrients in rainforests are recycled at various rates, due to differences in rates of decomposition and variations in soil chemistry. In tropical rainforests, the warm temperatures and abundant precipitation cause most organic material to decompose in a few months to a few years. **B** Because decomposition is so rapid, relatively little organic material accumulates on the floor of tropical forests. As the vegetation dies and decays, the roots of the trees quickly absorb the nutrients. **C** Most of the nutrients supporting the rainforest—about 75 percent of those in the ecosystem—are stored in the woody trunks of trees, while only about 10 percent are contained in the soil. The relatively low concentrations of nutrients in the soil are a result of the fast cycling time rather than a shortage of these elements in the ecosystem. **D**

27. Select the appropriate phrases from the answer choices and match them to the type of rainforest that they describe. TWO of the answer choices will NOT be used. *This question is worth 3 points.*

Answer Choices

(A) There is little variation in temperature and rainfall throughout the year.

(B) Temperatures typically range from very cold in the winter to hot in the summer.

(C) The trees grow extremely tall, and low–lying plants include ferns, mosses, and grasses.

(D) The middle two layers are characterized by dense plant growth and rich biodiversity.

(E) The nutrients in decaying organic matter are slowly recycled through the ecosystem.

(F) Even though the soil is nutrient–poor, small plants grow profusely on the sun–lit floor.

(G) A greater portion of the forest's nutrients are stored in the trees than in the soil.

Tropical Rainforest

-
-
-

Temperate Rainforest

-
-

| How to Score 3–Point Question ||
Answers Correct	Points Earned
5	3
4	2
3	1
0 – 2	0

TEST 5

SUSPENSION BRIDGES

1   The suspension bridge is a very ancient device that has long been used for foot traffic in many regions of the world. These simple foot bridges are of the type called catenary, a term referring to the curve or sag that a hanging cable takes under its own weight when supported only at its ends. In catenary foot bridges, the footway follows the natural curve assumed by the hanging cables. By the fifteenth century, the Chinese started using the catenary concept to suspend a level roadway, often using iron chains instead of bamboo rope in bridge construction.

2   The main parts of the suspension bridge are the roadway, the cables, the towers, and the cable anchorages. The level roadway hangs from the cables, which bear the load of the roadway and the bridge traffic. The cables pass over the towers and connect to the cable anchorages. If the cables were to end at the tops of the towers, their own weight combined with the weight of the roadway and the traffic would bend the towers toward each other. To prevent this from happening, the cables extend beyond the towers and are attached to concrete anchorages that are embedded in solid rock. The weight of the cables creates a strong vertical force that is transferred into the ground at the anchorages and down through the tower foundations.

3   Suspension bridges of great size did not appear in the West until the nineteenth century. The first major suspension bridge in Europe was built across the Menai Strait in Wales. Designed by Thomas Telford and completed in 1826, the Menai Bridge is a massive structure in which the suspension units are heavy iron bars and rods. Sixteen huge chain cables, each made of 935 iron bars, support the bridge's 176–meter span. On either side of the strait, towers constructed of limestone support the cables and the roadway. The original wooden roadway was later replaced with a steel deck.

4   In North America, the great pioneer of the suspension bridge was John Roebling, who designed the Brooklyn Bridge in New York. Completed in 1883, the Brooklyn Bridge was the longest suspension bridge in the world at that time, with a span of 486 meters, steel cables, two enormous granite towers, and a total length of 1,825 meters. The Brooklyn Bridge is a hybrid of the suspension bridge and the cable–stayed bridge, one of the oldest examples of either type in the United States. A cable–stayed bridge has one or more towers, each with a number of cables connected to the bridge deck on both sides. The primary load–bearing structures are the towers, which transmit the bridge load down into the ground, with less force placed on the anchorages.

5   In the twentieth century, suspension bridges achieved greater spans and more graceful designs. One of the best known examples is San Francisco's magnificent Golden Gate Bridge, completed in 1937. Several engineers worked on the project, although Charles Ellis is given credit as the principal designer. The scale of the Golden Gate Bridge is greater than that of any other suspension bridge at the time. The length of the main span is 1,300 meters, the height of the towers is 64 meters from the surface of the water, and the width of the roadway is an impressive 27 meters. Each of the cable anchorages has three main components: the base block, which is set in the bedrock; the anchor block, which is keyed into the base block; and a weight block, which rests on top of the anchor block. The great weight of the anchorages counteracts the pull of the cables.

6   The bridge designers created a structure that would control, rather than try to prevent, the movement caused by high winds and extreme temperatures. Each of the two towers is constructed with cross–bracing to stiffen the structure against the force of the wind. The ends of the roadway assembly are hinged to the towers, enabling the entire structure to rotate slightly on a horizontal plane. Sets of trusses along the roadway serve to stiffen the curvature of the cables and to minimize bending caused by wind pressure. The bottom corners of the stiffening trusses rest on flexible vertical columns called rocker arms. In very hot weather, the roadway will expand, and the ends of the bridge will slide toward the towers. To prevent this movement from affecting cars on the bridge, expansion joints are built into the road surface on both sides of each tower.

28. In paragraph 1, the author states that the earliest suspension bridges

    (A) were supported by bamboo poles
    (B) had a curving surface for traffic
    (C) spanned only short distances
    (D) used cables made of iron chains

29. The word assumed in paragraph 1 is closest in meaning to

    (A) formed
    (B) hidden
    (C) raised
    (D) surrounded

30. Which sentence below best expresses the essential information in the highlighted sentence in paragraph 2? Incorrect choices change the meaning in important ways or leave out essential information.

    (A) The great height of the towers prevents the cables from bending excessively under the weight of the bridge traffic.
    (B) The length and weight of the cables will determine the height of the towers and the location of the cable anchorages.
    (C) To allow for heavier loads, the cables are supported by towers built of concrete and anchorages made of hard rock.
    (D) To keep the towers from bending, the cables pass over the towers and connect to anchorages set in rock.

31. According to the passage, all of the following are features of the suspension bridge EXCEPT

    (A) a design originating in the catenary concept
    (B) a roadway supported by posts and beams
    (C) a system of cables, towers, and anchorages
    (D) towers that transmit a vertical force

32. Which of the following statements applies to the Menai Bridge in Wales?

    (A) It is the oldest bridge in Europe based on the catenary model.
    (B) Each limestone tower has an interior metal frame.
    (C) The suspension cables are large, heavy iron chains.
    (D) It was the first suspension bridge with a steel roadway.

33. In paragraph 4, the author makes the point that the Brooklyn Bridge

    (A) was the first suspension bridge in North America
    (B) required several years to complete
    (C) is a combination of two bridge designs
    (D) is still the longest bridge in New York

34. It can be inferred from the passage that a suspension bridge and a cable–stayed bridge differ in

    (A) the length of the span that can be supported
    (B) how much of the load is carried by the anchorages
    (C) where the towers are located in relation to the anchorages
    (D) the materials used in tower construction

35. The word graceful in paragraph 5 is closest in meaning to

    (A) expensive
    (B) controversial
    (C) modern
    (D) elegant

36. The author uses the word impressive in paragraph 5 in order to

    (A) classify the Golden Gate as a suspension bridge
    (B) explain the bridge's historical importance
    (C) emphasize the great scale of the bridge
    (D) compare the bridge with others of its time period

37. The phrase keyed into in paragraph 5 is closest in meaning to

    (A) connected to
    (B) divided by
    (C) hanging from
    (D) heavier than

38. Paragraph 6 supports which of the following statements about the Golden Gate Bridge?

   (A) The bridge was built to tolerate severe weather conditions.
   (B) The designers used controversial techniques to strengthen the bridge.
   (C) The distribution of weight prevents the bridge from movement.
   (D) The bridge has rarely experienced extreme environmental stress.

39. Look at the four squares, **A**, **B**, **C**, and **D**, which indicate where the following sentence could be added to the passage. Where would the sentence best fit?

   To protect the cables from weakening under stress, the designers added features to maintain a constant sag.

   The bridge designers created a structure that would control, rather than try to prevent, the movement caused by high winds and extreme temperatures. Each of the two towers is constructed with cross–bracing to stiffen the structure against the force of the wind. **A** The ends of the roadway assembly are hinged to the towers, enabling the entire structure to rotate slightly on a horizontal plane. **B** Sets of trusses along the roadway serve to stiffen the curvature of the cables and to minimize bending caused by wind pressure. The bottom corners of the stiffening trusses rest on flexible vertical columns called rocker arms. **C** In very hot weather, the roadway will expand, and the ends of the bridge will slide toward the towers. **D** To prevent this movement from affecting cars on the bridge, expansion joints are built into the road surface on both sides of each tower.

40. An introductory sentence for a brief summary of the passage is provided below. Complete the summary by selecting the THREE answer choices that express the most important ideas in the passage. Some sentences do not belong in the summary because they express ideas that are not presented in the passage or are minor ideas in the passage. *This question is worth 2 points.*

Beginning with simple foot bridges, the suspension bridge has undergone many developments throughout its history.

-
-
-

Answer Choices

(A) The Chinese were the first to suspend roadways, but the suspension bridge also developed independently in the West.

(B) The basic design includes a roadway suspended from cables, which pass over the tops of towers and are fastened to the ground at cable anchorages.

(C) The Brooklyn Bridge in New York was the world's longest suspension bridge when it was completed in 1883.

(D) In the nineteenth century, suspension bridges of great size and strength were constructed with stone, iron, and steel.

(E) Suspension bridges achieved even longer spans and acquired features to control the movement caused by environmental factors.

(F) The road surface on the Golden Gate Bridge has expansion joints so that bridge traffic will not be affected when the road expands during hot weather.

| How to Score 2–Point Question ||
Answers Correct	Points Earned
3	2
2	1
0 – 1	0

Answers to Test 5 – Reading are on pages 688–690.

Record your total Reading score on page 794.

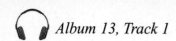

LISTENING SECTION DIRECTIONS

The Listening section measures your ability to understand conversations and lectures in English. You will hear each conversation and lecture only one time. After each conversation or lecture, you will answer some questions about it. The questions typically ask about the main idea and supporting details. Some questions ask about a speaker's purpose or attitude. Answer the questions based on what the speakers state or imply.

You may take notes while you listen. You may use your notes to help you answer the questions. Your notes will not be scored.

In some questions, you will see this icon: 🎧. This means that you will hear, but not see, part of the question.

Some questions have special directions, which appear in a gray box. Most questions are worth one point. If a question is worth more than one point, the directions will indicate how many points you can receive.

You will now begin part 1 of the Listening section.

PART 1

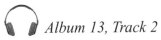

Album 13, Track 2

QUESTIONS 1 – 5

Conversation

1. What are the speakers mainly discussing?

   (A) How to place a hold on a book
   (B) Books that are available online
   (C) A book that the student requested
   (D) Copy services available in the library

2. What does the man say about the book?

   (A) The book is rare, so there are special conditions for its use.
   (B) The book is heavy, so the student should be careful handling it.
   (C) The book must be sent to another library after one month.
   (D) The book has been scanned and is available online.

3. According to the man, what is one rule for using the book?

   (A) The book can be checked out for only one month.
   (B) Students may not remove the book from the library.
   (C) Only library employees can scan pages from the book.
   (D) Students are not allowed to write in the book.

4. Listen again to part of the conversation. Then answer the question. 🎧

   What can be inferred from the conversation?

   (A) There are restrictions on how many pages can be copied.
   (B) The student needs the book for longer than one month.
   (C) Both speakers are concerned about damaging the book.
   (D) Students are not allowed to photocopy books.

5. What will the student probably do?

   (A) Write her name inside the book cover
   (B) Check out the book from the library
   (C) Read an online copy of the book
   (D) Try photographing the book with her camera

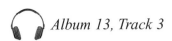 *Album 13, Track 3*

QUESTIONS 6 – 11

Biology

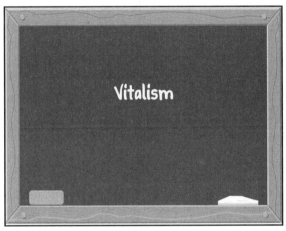

Vitalism

TEST 5

6. What is the main topic of the discussion?

   (A) Past and present uses of the scientific method
   (B) How scientists approach facts and new information
   (C) The difference between a fact and a hypothesis
   (D) Important facts in the field of cell biology

7. Why does the professor discuss the concept of vitalism?

   (A) To illustrate how previously held facts can be replaced
   (B) To emphasize the value of studying chemistry and physics
   (C) To show that living matter is controlled by a vital force
   (D) To explain one of the three tenets of cell biology

8. What does the professor imply when she says this: 🎧

   (A) Scientists easily understand facts that other people can not understand.
   (B) Some facts are more difficult to understand than others.
   (C) Facts are only valid until they are replaced by a better understanding.
   (D) Not all scientists agree on what can be considered a fact.

9. According to the discussion, how do scientists deal with new information?

   (A) They revise previous explanations that no longer make sense.
   (B) They state opinions and debate them with other scientists.
   (C) They use the scientific method to form and test a hypothesis.
   (D) They consult other scientists to learn if the information is useful.

10. What two statements about a hypothesis do the speakers make in the discussion?

   Click on 2 answers.

   A A hypothesis replaces an idea that was previously believed to be a fact.
   B A hypothesis appears to provide a reasonable explanation for a phenomenon.
   C A hypothesis is useful to scientists only if it can be tested.
   D A hypothesis is widely accepted by most scientists in the field.

11. Listen again to part of the discussion. Then answer the question. 🎧

   What can be inferred about the three tenets of cell biology?

   (A) They are based on the fact that living and nonliving matter are composed of different substances.
   (B) They are a subject of conflict and controversy outside the scientific community.
   (C) They will eventually be replaced by a better explanation after new technology becomes available.
   (D) They have been thoroughly and repeatedly tested and are consistently supported by the evidence.

Album 13, Track 4

QUESTIONS 12 – 17

History

Aboriginal Canadians

12. How does the professor organize the information that he presents?

    (A) By tracing the settlement of aboriginal peoples in North America
    (B) By explaining relationships among various aboriginal groups
    (C) By describing the development of trade routes in Canada
    (D) By classifying aboriginal cultures according to region

13. What does the professor say about the economies of aboriginal Canadians?

    (A) Their economies depended on trade with Europeans.
    (B) The economy of each tribe was very different from all others.
    (C) Their economies developed around the food supply.
    (D) The economy of each tribe was centered on one main resource.

14. Which of the following were characteristics of the hunting–gathering tribes of the forests?

    Click on 3 answers.

    [A] Living in small bands that migrated in search of food
    [B] The sharing of a common language and belief system
    [C] The cultivation of corn, beans, and squash
    [D] Making tools and other objects from locally available materials
    [E] Skill in hunting and trapping fur–bearing animals

15. Listen again to part of the lecture. Then answer the question. 🎧

    What can be inferred about the societies the professor is describing?

    (A) Their political organization grew from a basis in agriculture.
    (B) War rarely occurred between the societies based on kinship and trade.
    (C) Their political systems were more complex than those in Europe.
    (D) The largest societies were the most economically independent.

16. What does the professor mean when he says this: 🎧

    (A) The Plains people suffered from famine and disease during the winter.
    (B) The bison was essential to the wealth and survival of the Plains people.
    (C) The Plains people hunted other animals during the bison's winter migration.
    (D) The economy of the Plains people depended on trade with other tribes.

17. According to the professor, what cultural characteristic was shared by the aboriginal peoples all over Canada?

    (A) An ability to understand and speak the same language
    (B) An economic system based on agriculture
    (C) A close relationship with the natural environment
    (D) A highly complex political system

PART 2

 Album 13, Track 5

QUESTIONS 1 – 5

Discussion

1. What do the speakers mainly discuss?

   (A) The origin of the Milky Way galaxy
   (B) The formation of new stars
   (C) Interactions between galaxies
   (D) New models used by astronomers

2. According to the discussion, what can happen when two galaxies collide?

   Click on 2 answers.

   A   Stars crash into other stars and explode.
   B   The galaxies pass through one another.
   C   The distance between stars increases.
   D   A single larger galaxy starts to form.

3. According to the discussion, what have astronomers concluded from computer models?

   (A) When spiral galaxies collide, they tend to form very large elliptical galaxies.
   (B) The most massive galaxies have a strong gravitational pull on smaller galaxies.
   (C) The stars in spiral galaxies are closest to one another near the galaxy's center.
   (D) The first stars had short, violent lives before creating later generations of stars.

4. Listen again to part of the discussion. Then answer the question.

   What does the tutor imply?

   (A) Not all astronomers agree about the Milky Way's true shape.
   (B) He is not certain if there is an answer to the student's question.
   (C) The Milky Way has definitely never collided with other galaxies.
   (D) He does not want to start an argument with the student.

5. Why does the student say this:

   (A) To suggest they move to a quieter place
   (B) To complain about the exam
   (C) To state that she must leave soon
   (D) To signal a shift in topic

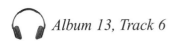

Album 13, Track 6

QUESTIONS 6 – 11

Communications

TEST 5

6. What is the discussion mainly about?

    (A) Why some people are immune to the message of advertising

    (B) The language and techniques of advertising claims

    (C) How the celebrity endorsement works to sell products

    (D) The elements of a creative advertising campaign

7. Why does the professor say this: 🎧

    (A) To classify ads by the quality of the products they sell

    (B) To criticize ads that make false claims about products

    (C) To explain how advertising uses language to mislead

    (D) To illustrate the concept of immunity to advertising

8. Which statement accurately describes parity products?

    (A) Parity products appeal to a class of consumers who share the same values.

    (B) Parity products are not popular, so advertisers do little to promote them.

    (C) Parity products are expensive, so they make consumers feel special.

    (D) Parity products have several brands that are all similar in quality.

9. According to the professor, how do advertisers promote parity products?

    (A) They use a few basic techniques to create an illusion of superiority.

    (B) They rely on consumers to tell other consumers about the product.

    (C) They focus on the consumers who have the most money to spend.

    (D) They do very little advertising because people buy the product anyway.

10. Which advertising techniques do the speakers discuss?

    Click on 2 answers.

    [A] Appeal to patriotism
    [B] Endorsement by a famous person
    [C] Promotion in social media
    [D] Statistical claim

11. Listen again to part of the discussion. Then answer the question. 🎧

    What does the professor imply when he says this: 🎧

    (A) People are more likely to remember ads with a positive message.

    (B) Advertising affects even intelligent people, whether they know it or not.

    (C) Most consumers know the difference between lies and the truth.

    (D) If an advertising claim is false, smart consumers will criticize it.

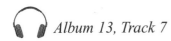

QUESTIONS 12 – 17

Geology

Streams

graded stream

plunge pool

TEST 5

12. What is the main point the professor makes in the lecture?

  (A) Streams exist in a continuous state of geological change.
  (B) During periods of glacial melting, streams deposit more sediment.
  (C) The force of falling water creates a pool at the base of a waterfall.
  (D) Niagara Falls is the most famous waterfall in North America.

13. According to the professor, which environmental factors cause streams to respond?

  Click on 2 answers.

  [A] Heavy rainfall during a storm
  [B] An increase in pollution from runoff
  [C] Seasonal changes in water temperature
  [D] A change in the amount of sediment

14. Why does the professor say this:

  (A) To explain that evolutionary change sometimes occurs suddenly
  (B) To state that graded streams constantly adjust to changing conditions
  (C) To stress the importance of equilibrium in the physical sciences
  (D) To contrast the life spans of graded streams and waterfalls

15. What happens when faulting lowers or raises part of a stream bed?

  (A) A number of fish will die.
  (B) The water rises quickly and flows more rapidly.
  (C) A waterfall immediately forms.
  (D) The water flow is blocked by debris.

16. Listen again to part of the lecture. Then answer the question.

  What point does the professor illustrate?

  (A) A plunging waterfall is a subject of great aesthetic beauty.
  (B) Erosion continuously changes the profile of a waterfall.
  (C) The ultimate base level for most streams is sea level.
  (D) A graded stream responds to an increase in the volume of water.

17. According to the professor, what factor contributes to the retreat of Niagara Falls?

  (A) The annual freezing and thawing of ice
  (B) The changing weather conditions due to global warming
  (C) The increase in earthquake activity in the region
  (D) The erosion of softer rock beneath a cap of harder rock

PART 3

 Album 13, Track 8

QUESTIONS 1 – 5

Conversation

1. Why does the student speak to the professor?

(A) He needs her advice about a counseling position.
(B) He would like her opinion about a summer program.
(C) He is excited about something he read on a website.
(D) He wants to thank her for helping him get a job.

2. What does the professor say about the student's news?

(A) The student should share his news in an interview next week.
(B) The professor did not expect to hear from the student so soon.
(C) The student will benefit from working in an excellent program.
(D) The professor first learned the news from the program director.

3. What will the student's summer job include?

Click on 2 answers.

[A] Teaching young students about the environment
[B] Supervising production of a brochure
[C] Contributing stories to a blog
[D] Using a boat to catch fish for tagging

4. Listen again to part of the conversation. Then answer the question. 🎧

What can be inferred about the student?

(A) He enjoys going fishing with friends.
(B) He knows how to operate a fishing boat.
(C) He is interested in designing a website.
(D) He is an accomplished photographer.

5. Why does the professor say this: 🎧

(A) To introduce the topic of her lecture
(B) To signal an end to the conversation
(C) To suggest that the student attend a lecture
(D) To invite the student to visit again

Album 13, Track 9

QUESTIONS 12 – 17

Psychology

TEST 5

6. What is the discussion mainly about?

  (A) Various methods in psychological research
  (B) The brain as the center of consciousness
  (C) Differences between the self and consciousness
  (D) The physical location of the self

7. What issues and questions do the students raise in the discussion?

  Click on 2 answers.

  [A] How the self is defined
  [B] Why the self is an important topic for research
  [C] Which group of interview subjects gave the correct answer
  [D] Whether the self is located in different places for different people

8. Which statement best states the main finding of the research described by the professor?

  (A) People define consciousness in a number of different ways.
  (B) Most people believe the self is located in one of two places in the body.
  (C) The self is made of different substances from those in the body.
  (D) If the self exists, it most likely resides in the action center of the brain.

9. Listen again to part of the discussion. Then answer the question

   What does the professor mean when he says this:

  (A) The most important part of research is how the subjects are selected.
  (B) The responses of the subjects suggest that the researchers made mistakes.
  (C) How a study is conducted has a bearing on the accuracy of results.
  (D) Some studies use tools and procedures that cause controversy.

10. According to the professor, what was significant about the results of the study that used a physical pointer?

  (A) The study was the first attempt by researchers to locate the self in the body.
  (B) The responses of the subjects depended on the direction that the pointer moved.
  (C) The pointer succeeded in producing results that the researchers had expected.
  (D) The results prove that consciousness emerges from all of the body's activity.

11. Why does the professor say this:

  (A) To argue for a better definition of the self
  (B) To emphasize the difficulty of locating the self
  (C) To summarize the results of the research
  (D) To imply that more research is needed in this area

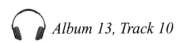

Album 13, Track 10

QUESTIONS 12 – 17

Music Appreciation

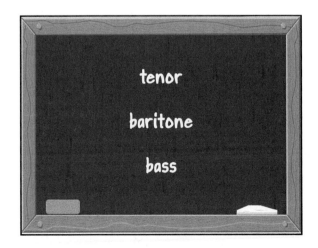

tenor

baritone

bass

12. Which of the following best describes the organization of the lecture?

(A) A history of Western classical music
(B) A classification of singing voices
(C) A comparison of themes in opera
(D) An explanation of sound frequency

13. What accounts for the generally lower singing voices of men compared to women?

(A) Men are not trained to sing in the higher frequencies.
(B) Men's voices have a peak frequency of 250 Hz.
(C) Men must extend their voices downward to sing opera.
(D) Men's vocal cords are longer and thicker.

14. According to the professor, how did the tenor become the standard voice for leading male roles in opera?

(A) The title role in the earliest surviving opera was written for the tenor.
(B) More performers can sing in the tenor range than in any other voice.
(C) Audiences have generally favored the lyrical quality of the tenor.
(D) The tenor is the so-called "normal" range of the male voice.

15. Which two statements describe the tenor voice?

Click on 2 answers.

[A] This voice is often used for villains and father figures in opera.
[B] In early choral music, it held all of the other voices together.
[C] The most demanding heroic roles in opera are sung in this voice.
[D] This voice is the intermediate class of the male voice.

16. Listen again to part of the lecture. Then answer the question.

What does the professor imply?

(A) Men who sing in their normal range are easier to understand.
(B) The baritone is the best male voice to pair with the female voice.
(C) Many roles for baritone singers can result in voice strain.
(D) A singing actor must be able to extend his voice upward.

17. Listen again to part of the lecture. Then answer the question.

What can be inferred about the bass voice?

(A) The bass is the most demanding voice for heroic roles in opera.
(B) Composers rarely write for the bass voice because it is difficult to sing.
(C) The bass voice is frequently used in comedy and musical theater.
(D) Both audiences and singers value leading roles for the bass voice.

 Stop

Answers to Test 5 – Listening are on pages 690–692.

Record your total Listening score on page 794.

 *Album 13, Track 11*

SPEAKING SECTION DIRECTIONS

The Speaking section measures your ability to speak in English about a variety of topics. There are six questions in this section.

In questions 1 and 2, you will speak about familiar topics. Your responses will be scored on your ability to speak clearly and coherently about the topics.

In questions 3 and 4, you will first read a short text and then listen to a talk on the same topic. You will then be asked a question about what you have read and heard. You will need to combine appropriate information from the text and the talk to provide a complete answer to the question. Your responses will be scored on your ability to speak clearly and coherently and on your ability to accurately convey information about what you have read and heard.

In questions 5 and 6, you will listen to part of a conversation or lecture. You will then be asked a question about what you have heard. Your responses will be scored on your ability to speak clearly and coherently and on your ability to accurately convey information about what you have heard.

You may take notes while you read and while you listen to the conversations and lectures. You may use your notes to help prepare your responses.

 Stop

QUESTION 1

In this question, you will be asked to talk about a familiar topic. After you hear the question, you will have 15 seconds to prepare your response and 45 seconds to speak.

 Album 13, Track 12

> Describe a product or crop that is important to your country or region. Explain why this product is important. Include details and examples to support your explanation.

 Stop

Preparation Time – 15 seconds
Response Time – 45 seconds

QUESTION 2

In this question, you will be asked to give your opinion about a familiar topic. After you hear the question, you will have 15 seconds to prepare your response and 45 seconds to speak.

 Album 13, Track 13

> Some students learn better when they attend a class in a room with a teacher. Other students learn more from online courses. Which system of learning do you think is better for students, and why? Include details and examples to support your explanation.

 Stop

Preparation Time – 15 seconds
Response Time – 45 seconds

QUESTION 3

In this question, you will read a short passage about a campus situation, listen to a conversation, and then speak in response to a question about what you have read and heard. After you hear the question, you have 30 seconds to prepare your response and 60 seconds to speak.

Read the following e–mail message to students at a university.

Reading Time – 45 seconds

NEW FEE FOR COMPUTER LAB

The Director of Student Services announces a new fee concerning the computer lab in the Meade Technology Center. Beginning in the fall semester, all full–time and part–time students will be assessed an additional $50 per semester on their tuition bill. The fee will help to defray the cost of upgrading and remodeling the computer lab, including installation of 60 new work stations, a fully–equipped conference room, and the hiring of additional support staff. There will also be extended hours of operation, starting on September 1, when the lab will be open from 6:00 a.m. to 12:00 midnight, seven days per week.

Now cover the passage and listen to the recording. When you hear the question, begin preparing your response.

 Album 13, Track 14

> The man expresses his opinion about the new fee. State his opinion and explain the reasons he gives for holding that opinion.

 Stop

Preparation Time – 30 seconds
Response Time – 60 seconds

QUESTION 4

In this question, you will read a short passage, then listen to a lecture on the same topic, and then speak in response to a question about what you have read and heard. After you hear the question, you have 30 seconds to prepare your response and 60 seconds to speak.

Read the following information from a textbook.

Reading Time – 50 seconds

AESTIVATION

Aestivation is a state of dormancy in which an animal's metabolism decreases in response to high temperatures and arid conditions. Also known as summer torpor, aestivation is characterized by inactivity, a slow heart rate, and slow respiration. Animals enter aestivation in order to survive long periods of high temperatures and scarce water supplies. The primary physiological concerns for an aestivating animal are to conserve energy, to regulate body temperature, to retain water in the body, and to prevent extreme drying of the cells and tissues. Aestivation is common in many invertebrates, but also occurs in some vertebrates during periods of heat and dryness.

Now cover the passage and listen to the recording. When you hear the question, begin preparing your response.

 Album 13, Track 15

Explain aestivation and how the examples given by the professor illustrate the concept.

 Stop

Preparation Time – 30 seconds
Response Time – 60 seconds

QUESTION 5

In this question, you will listen to a conversation. You will then be asked to talk about the information in the conversation and to give your opinion about the ideas presented. After you hear the question, you have 20 seconds to prepare your response and 60 seconds to speak.

 Album 13, Track 16

> Briefly summarize the man's problem. Then state which solution you would recommend. Explain the reasons for your recommendation.

 Stop

Preparation Time – 20 seconds
Response Time – 60 seconds

QUESTION 6

In this question, you will listen to a short lecture. You will then be asked to summarize important information from the lecture. After you hear the question, you have 20 seconds to prepare your response and 60 seconds to speak.

 Album 13, Track 17

> Using points and examples from the lecture, explain some of the reasons for including engineering in the basic education of children.

 Stop

Preparation Time – 20 seconds
Response Time – 60 seconds

Key points for Test 5 – Speaking are on pages 692–693.

Each response earns a score of 1, 2, 3, or 4.

Record your total Speaking score on page 794.

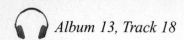

WRITING SECTION DIRECTIONS

The Writing section measures your ability to use writing to communicate in an academic environment. There are two writing questions.

Question 1 is a writing task based on reading and listening. You will read a passage, listen to a lecture, and then write a response to a question about the relationship between the lecture and the reading. You have 20 minutes to plan and write your response.

Question 2 is writing based on knowledge and experience. You will write an essay in response to a question that asks you to state, explain, and support an opinion on an issue. You have 30 minutes to plan and write your essay.

 Stop

QUESTION 1

For this task, you will write a response to a question about a reading passage and a lecture. You may take notes, and you may use your notes to help you write your response. Your response will be scored on the quality of your writing and on how well you connect the points in the lecture with points in the reading. Typically, an effective response will have 150 to 225 words.

Reading Time – 3 minutes

     In the typical customer–service call center, operators speak with customers who are often demanding and sometimes rude. Operator burnout is high and productivity can decline. To address the problem, some companies are exploring what makes a happy workplace. Research shows that the social patterns of workers influence their job satisfaction and productivity. To promote interactions among workers, there are a few positive changes that companies can make.

     One way to increase social interaction is to stagger break times so that each worker interacts with as many co–workers as possible. Staggering breaks means scheduling a team's rest time in alternating or overlapping periods. Thus, workers have an opportunity to socialize with co–workers from other teams. This arrangement will promote interactions within a larger, more diverse network of people and expose workers to multiple viewpoints.

     Another change is to move the location where workers can meet and interact. For example, consider the communal coffee pots and the break room. To get different groups of workers talking to each other, the best location for a coffee pot is between the groups. The break room should be in a central location as well. If the company occupies multiple floors of a building, the ideal location for the break room is on a middle floor.

     A third change is to adopt an open seating plan, in which workers choose their desks randomly each day. This will encourage initiative because workers have the freedom to choose where they sit. It will also increase interaction because each worker has an opportunity to talk with different co–workers. In this way, an open seating plan improves the flow of information and the exchange of ideas.

Now listen to the recording. When you hear the question, begin your response. You may look at the reading passage during the writing time.

 Album 13, Track 19

> Summarize the points made in the lecture, being sure to explain how they contradict specific points made in the reading passage.

 Stop

Writing Time – 20 minutes

QUESTION 2

For this task, you will write an essay in response to a question that asks you to state and support your opinion on a topic. Your essay will be scored on the quality of your writing, including how well you organize and develop your ideas and how well you use language to express your ideas. Typically, an effective essay will have a minimum of 300 words.

Read the question below and make any notes that will help you plan your response. Then begin typing your essay.

Some people think it is very important to look back and remember the past. Others think it is more important to look ahead and focus on the future. Which view do you agree with? Use specific reasons and examples to support your opinion.

Writing Time – 30 minutes

Key points for Test 5 – Writing are on page 693.

Each response earns a score of 1, 2, 3, 4 or 5.

Record your total Writing score on page 794.

For each answer, there is a short explanation followed by a number in parentheses. The number refers to the relevant unit in this book, where you will find discussion and examples of that specific skill or question type.

PRE-TEST

READING (p. 9)

1. **B** Clues: *The work of life depends on the ability of cells to use energy...; Energy enables cells to cause specific changes that are necessary for life.* (1.1)

2. **D** Clues: *The changes caused by cellular activities involve the transformation of energy from one type to another.* (1.1)

3. **A** The paragraph supports the statement that life is characterized by various kinds of change. Clues: *...specific changes that are necessary for life. Many cells move or change their shapes. They grow and reproduce. Cells organize small organic molecules into proteins and DNA. Cells pump substances across membranes. They export products...; The changes caused by cellular activities....* (1.4)

4. **A** The author's purpose is to illustrate how a cell can move through its environment. Clues: *...the movement of a cell in relation to its environment. Such movement requires the presence of some sort of appendage, such as the long, thread–like structure called...; ...they wag these tail–like structures to push themselves through the environment.* (1.5)

5. **B** *Propelled* means *pushed* in this context. Clues: *...the movement of chromosomes...; ...move apart and are ----- along the surface of the nucleus by the lengthening spindle fibers between them; ...eventually travel to opposite poles of the cell.* The prefix *pro–* = forward. (1.3)

6. **C** The organization of small molecules into proteins is not given as an example of mechanical work; it is synthetic work. All of the other answers are examples of mechanical work: *The human trachea is lined with cilia that beat upward...; An example of mechanical work that involves not just a single cell but a large number of cells is muscle contraction; Still another example of mechanical work occurs within a cell, and this is the movement of chromosomes during cell division.* (1.2)

7. **D** The main purpose of the paragraph is to explain the function of synthetic work. Clues: *Synthetic work involves changes in chemical bonds; ...the important work of biosynthesis, which causes the formation of new bonds and the generation of new molecules; ...making energy–rich organic molecules from simpler starting materials...activating these molecules for incorporation into larger molecules.* (1.5)

8. **C** *This activity* in the highlighted sentence refers to *biosynthesis* in the previous sentence. *This activity can be observed...* is paraphrased in *Biosynthesis occurs.... ...as additional molecules are being synthesized* is paraphrased in *...when new molecules are generated.... ...in a population of growing cells...where the cells increase in size, number, or both...* is paraphrased in *...as cells grow in size, number, or both.* (1.6)

9. **D** *Turnover* means *replacement* in this context. Clues:

...a state of constant...; ...continuously being degraded and replaced. (1.3)

10. **A** The author implies that moving the substances requires the use of force. Clues: *...the transport of substances across a membrane or boundary....* A major idea in the passage is that energy is required for cells to perform work. Pumping substances against the direction of spontaneous (natural) movement requires using energy to apply force in pushing the substances. (1.4)

11. **C** You can infer that some concentration work generates electrical impulses. Clues: *A specialized case of concentration work is electrical work...; Electrical work is important in the mechanism whereby impulses are conducted in nerve and muscle cells.* (1.4)

12. **D** In the added sentence, *The result* develops the idea *movement of ions across a membrane against an electrical gradient* in the previous sentence. The added sentence introduces the idea *establishment of an electrical potential*, which the next sentence develops. (1.7)

13. **A, C, F** Key information: *Mechanical work involves a physical change in the position of a cell or some part of the cell; ...the movement of a cell in relation to its environment; ...another example of mechanical work occurs within a cell...; Synthetic work involves changes in chemical bonds; Almost every cell is continuously engaged in the important work of biosynthesis, which causes the formation of new bonds and the generation of new molecules; Concentration work is the transport of substances across a membrane or boundary...; ...to accumulate substances within a cell...; A specialized case of concentration work is electrical work, which involves the movement of ions across a membrane against an electrical gradient.* Answers (B) and (D) are minor ideas. Answer (E) is not mentioned. (1.8, 1.9)

LISTENING (p. 14)

1. **D** The speakers mainly discuss a report that the student is preparing. The student says: *Could I talk to you about the presentation next week; I need your advice on what I still need to do.* The professor says: *Okay. Tell me what you've got.* (2.1)

2. **B** The professor's purpose is to inform the student that he has only a little time to talk. The student wants advice, but the professor has less than a half hour before he must go to a meeting. (2.5)

3. **A, D** The student plans to use a summary of volcanic eruptions: *...I thought I'd give a history of the eruptions in that area; I won't go over every little eruption, just the six or seven major ones.* She also will use a series of pictures of a mountain: *A set of photographs...; I have some good shots of the mountain...; ...the color photo...and after that, the black–and–white photos....* (2.2)

4. C   The student's opinion is that the photographs show the mountain's changes very clearly. She says: *I have some good shots of the mountain—you can really see how much the bulge has grown; The changes really show up well, much better in black and white.* (2.3)

5. A   The professor means that the audience is very likely to ask about the meaning of the bulge. He says: *Your pictures of the bulge and the cause of its formation—you are going to talk about that, right?* He says that she is *bound* (very likely) to be asked about the bulge. (2.4)

6. A   The professor mainly discusses how nature's color signals can help us understand climate change. He says: *...there's another relationship I'd like to talk about, one that can help in our understanding of climate change...; The current research in phenology looks at how nature's color signals can help us understand the feedback between plants and our changing climate; Nature's colors are already responding to changing weather due to climate change.* (2.1)

7. C   The professor's purpose is to illustrate the concept of phenology. He gives examples of the responses of animals to seasonal changes in their environment. (2.3)

8. B   The professor's purpose is to signal that he will eventually address the student's question. The student asks about how researchers collect data, and the professor says he is *getting to* her question, implying that he is leading into it. (2.5)

9. D   The professor implies that the students should read the explanations in the textbook. The professor gives a brief explanation of color pigments, then mentions their textbook, where the students can find further explanation. (2.4)

10. B   The professor says: *...a web camera on top of a tower that captures high–resolution images of the forest canopy; The camera then uploads these images to an online database. This huge collection of color data....* (2.2)

11. A   The professor says: *We're already seeing this in color data from the camera; ...we can use this data to develop better models of how weather and phenology are related. We can compare these models against the climate forecasts. This will improve our ability to predict how the forests might change in the future.* (2.2)

12. B   The main idea is that farm management is a complex job with responsibility for all of a farm's resources. The professor says: *Farm managers have a complicated job in a complicated world; ...farm managers are responsible for the resources under their control; In short, farm management is a complex and demanding job. Farm managers are responsible for the physical, financial, and human resources of the farm.* (2.1)

13. D   The talk is mainly a list of the requirements and responsibilities of farm management. The professor says: *...farm managers are responsible for the resources under their control; ...a farm manager needs to have knowledge in a variety of subjects; Farm managers are responsible for the physical, financial, and human resources of the farm; ...a farm manager is responsible for all of the management and business functions...; ...farm managers always have to monitor and adjust their strategies. They have to be experts at strategic thinking; ...there should always be a business plan.* (2.6)

14. B, D, E   A farm manager must be knowledgeable in biological sciences: *...a farm manager needs scientific knowledge about soil structure and soil microbiology; ...animal nutrition, genetics, crop growth, plant and animal diseases, and insect control.* A farm manager must be knowledgeable in communication: *...a farm manager needs leadership and communication skills; Writing a business plan....* He or she must be knowledgeable in strategic planning: *...a farm manager needs an understanding of... strategic planning...; They have to be experts at strategic thinking; ...a farm business needs a structured approach to planning.* (2.2)

15. A   The professor's purpose is to introduce the topic of preparing a business plan. According to the professor, farm managers must be *experts at strategic thinking*, and farms must have *a structured approach to planning.* She is leading into discussion of the business plan. (2.3)

16. A, C   The business plan for a farm should include a description of the farm and its goals: *The business plan includes a general description of the farm...; The plan also describes the farm's vision—both short– and long–term goals.* It should also include plans for production and marketing: *It includes a plan for production and operations, a marketing plan....* (2.2)

17. D   The professor describes the profession of farm management. She says: *This course will introduce you to all the management skills you need to plan, organize, and direct the farm business. You'll also learn how to prepare a business plan. In fact, your major course assignment will be to research, write, and revise a business plan for a farm—either a farm you manage now, or one you'd like to manage in the future.* You can infer that the students in this class are interested in farm management as a career. (2.4)

SPEAKING (p. 20)

1. Responses will vary. (3.1–3.4)
2. Responses will vary. (3.1–3.4)
3. Key points:
   - The man supports the new block schedule; he thinks it is a good idea.
   - One reason he gives is that it seems like a more efficient use of time, both in class and outside class. Reading topics would be integrated. Study time would be more focused and interesting.

- Another reason is that it seems like a better way to meet people in your interest area. You would get to know your classmates and professor better. (3.5, 3.7, 3.10)
4. Key points:
   - A proverb is an expression that conveys traditional wisdom or offers advice on how to live. The language of a proverb is simple and direct. The images refer to everyday objects and experiences.
   - The speaker gives the example of this proverb: Look before you leap. This proverb illustrates the effectiveness of simplicity and memorability. It is easy to remember because it uses alliteration, the repetition of the "l" sound in "look" and "leap."
   - The speaker also gives this example: A friend in need is a friend indeed. This proverb is effective because it is about the everyday experience of friendship. It contains rhythm (friend, need, friend, deed), rhyme (need, deed), and parallelism (friend in need, friend indeed). It also uses alliteration in the repetition of the "f" sound in "friend." (3.6, 3.7, 3.10)
5. Key points:
   - The woman's problem is that she wants to go to a party for a professor, but she must work in the lab at the time of the party. Her professor is retiring, and she wants to say good–bye to him.
   - One possible solution is to find another person who will agree to work her shift in the lab.
   - Another solution is to visit the professor at another time, for example, to go to the professor's office.
   - Opinions about the preferred solution will vary. (3.8, 3.10)
6. Key points:
   - Advertising portrays the future in bright colors and strong lines. Colors attract us. Examples: red, blue, a golden sunset, a rainbow of colors. Strong lines direct our attention forward. Examples: triangles, arrows, tall buildings.
   - Advertising shows the future as a kinetic force, something moving at a very high speed. Examples: fast–paced cars, computer technology, a person leaping across space, a dynamic city, a high–speed train.
   - Advertising portrays the future as something positive: brighter, promising, full of potential, something we can control. Examples: universities, financial securities, insurance, teaching children, saving energy, protecting the environment. (3.9, 3.10)

WRITING (p. 25)
1. Key points:
   - The lecture states that lentic ecosystems have standing or stationary water; the water does not flow. This contrasts with the point in the reading that lotic ecosystems have water that is moving continually.
   - The lecture states that in lentic ecosystems, the oxygen content varies with the depth of the water. This contrasts with the point in the reading that lotic ecosystems typically have high oxygen levels because water flowing over objects oxygenates the water.
   - The lecture states that in lentic ecosystems, a greater share of the production of organic matter occurs in the body of water. This contrasts with the point in the reading that in lotic ecosystems, most of the production of organic matter comes from surrounding land habitats. (4.1–4.5)
2. Responses will vary. (4.6–4.10)

PART 1 – READING

EXERCISE 1.1.A (p. 40)
1. A Clues: *Each tissue system is continuous throughout the plant's body.*
2. C Clues: *The dermal system, or epidermis, is a single layer of cells covering the entire body of the plant.*
3. D Clues: *The third system—the ground tissue—makes up the bulk of a plant, filling all of the spaces between the dermal and vascular tissue systems.*
4. B Clues: *Because of the rising demand for cotton from the mills of England,... the cotton production of the South increased tremendously; ...by the 1850s, output had soared to five million bales.*
5. A Clues: *Northern farmers would boast of... machinery....*
6. C Clues: *...just before the Civil War of the 1860s, the Southern states had developed an economic culture distinct from that of the North; The economic differences between the two regions would ultimately lead to armed conflict....*
7. B Clues: *the most playful...are also the most intelligent and sociable.*
8. C Clues: *...the most playful—such as dolphins and monkeys....*
9. D Clues: *A kitten that grows up separated from other kittens becomes both a social misfit and a poor hunter, largely because it is deprived of play.*
10. B Clues: *Early play consists of mock attacks with the mother and littermates, clearly previewing the territorial behavior of adult life; They recognize these patterns as being playful, even though the same signals in adult life may have a more serious meaning.*

EXERCISE 1.1.B (p. 43)
1. D Clues: *The child develops a sense of industry; If the child is encouraged to make and do things, allowed to finish tasks, and praised for trying, a sense of industry is the result.*
2. D Clues: *...if the child's efforts are unsuccessful, or if they are criticized or treated as bothersome, a sense of inferiority is the result.*
3. A Clues: *Erik Erikson believed that personality development is a series of turning points, which he described in terms of the tension between desirable qualities and dangers; ...Erikson called the period from age six to eleven Industry vs. Inferiority.*
4. C Clues: *In the storytelling traditions of West Africa, the tiny rabbit appears frequently as a rascal who teases or plays jokes on bigger animals.*
5. C Clues: *Joel Chandler Harris, a journalist in Georgia...; Harris wrote down and published many of the stories, popularizing them for the general public.*
6. B Clues: *...a trickster rabbit in the character of Brer Rabbit; ...similar versions of the same stories in southern Louisiana, where the rabbit character was known as Compair Lapin...; ...Bugs Bunny—a rascally rabbit who causes trouble, tricks the hunter....*

7. B Clues: *A hot spot is a giant underground caldron of molten rock in one of the world's many volcanically active areas.*

8. B Clues: *Annually, more than 200 geysers erupt in Yellowstone, making this one of the most interesting places in the world for geologists.*

9. C Clues: *The rock heats the water, and the boiling water and steam often make their way back up to the surface in the form of a geyser...; ...pressure builds up, eventually forcing the superheated water to burst to the surface as a geyser.*

10. A Clues: *If the water does not make it all the way to the surface, steam and gases may dissolve rocks and form a bubbling mud pot instead.*

EXERCISE 1.1.C (p. 46)

1. A Clues: *Organic compounds contain atoms of the element carbon, usually combined with itself and with atoms of one or more other elements....*

2. C Clues: *Important organic polymers include carbohydrates, proteins, and nucleic acids.*

3. D Clues: *Most animals, including humans, can manufacture about ten of these amino acids in their cells, but the other ten, called essential amino acids, must be obtained from food ....*

4. C Clues: *The oldest of the resource commodities, fish, was traditionally associated with Newfoundland....*

5. D Clues: *...the fur trade was of tremendous value politically because it provided the means for Great Britain to retain its claim over much of Canada....*

6. A Clues: *By the 1840s, British North America had developed a vibrant commercial economy based on its abundant natural resources....; Fish, furs, timber, and grains represented over 90 percent of all economic activity.*

7. B Clues: *...she worked at Johns Hopkins in the laboratories...; Reed's research in pathology....*

8. A Clues: *In 1906, her marriage...took Reed away from the research laboratory; For ten years, she remained at home....*

9. C Clues: *...she concluded that she could not imagine life without her husband and sons, but she hoped for a future when marriage would not have to end a career of laboratory research.*

10. C Clues: *Reed's research in pathology established conclusively that Hodgkin's disease...was a distinct disorder characterized by a specific blood cell, which was named the Reed cell after her.*

EXERCISE 1.2.A (p. 52)

1. C The passage does not mention writing dialogue for characters. All the other answers are mentioned: *Another aspect is costumes...; ...a presentation by performers in front of an audience...; ...drama involves storytelling....*

2. D The passage does not give sun avoidance as a factor that can cause skin cancer; rather, sun avoidance is given as the most effective preventative measure against skin cancer. All the other answers are given: *...exposure to x–rays...; Chronic sun exposure— especially when it causes sunburn or blistering— results in more skin cancer...; ...family history of the disease.*

3. B Laughter does not increase the body's vulnerability to illness; rather, it is stress hormones that increase vulnerability to illness. All the other answers are given: *...boosts brain chemicals that fight pain; ...increase hormones that have been shown to help produce restful sleep; ...diminish feelings of tension, anger....*

4. A The author does not recommend playing tricks on family and friends. All the other answers are recommended: *...create a weekly fun time...; ...spending time with children and animals; ...try keeping a humor journal in which you record some of the amusing things that happen to you.*

5. C The passage does not describe fleas as self–aware. All the other answers are self–aware animals: *Horses know how much room they have around them when they move through narrow spaces; A dog, for example, has no trouble knowing where to scratch itself to kill a flea; While looking at itself in a mirror, an elephant may move its trunk over different parts of its body.*

6. B Using sign language to communicate is not given as an example of self–awareness. All the other answers are given: *A horse can run between two trees...in a way that clearly shows the horse's knowledge of its own body size; Animals show self–awareness in how they respond to discomfort. A dog...has no trouble knowing where to scratch itself...; A chimpanzee will make faces...in front of a mirror.*

7. A The passage does not state that the films of Satyajit Ray are characterized by adventure. All the other answers are given: *Ray's films are known for their compassion, honesty, and quiet dignity.*

8. C The third film of the Apu Trilogy does not deal with struggle against poverty—that is a theme of the first film. All the other answers are themes of the third film: *...the young man...fails at his life's ambitions, and then, after losing his wife, he wanders across the country for several years before returning home....*

9. C The passage does not mention diaries as something studied by archaeologists. All the other answers are mentioned: *...weapons...; ...items used in religious ceremonies...; ...ruins of buildings....*

10. A Archaeologists do not plan and design more efficient uses for objects and materials. All the other answers are given: *...archaeologists establish the sequence of events that occurred in a given place and time period; ...these objects lie buried in the ground, so our image of the archaeologist is of a scientist who is always digging; ...document how big changes occurred in the way peoples exploited their environment and one another.*

EXERCISE 1.2.B (p. 55)

1. A Cold weather is not given as a cause of the Dust Bowl. All the other answers are given: *The Dust Bowl was the result of human activity and bad weather that led to soil erosion; ...farmers had plowed millions of acres of grassland...; ...when a period of dry weather struck the region, there were no native grasses to hold the soil in place.*

2. B Clues: *The enlargement of the electorate...has increased the importance of parties to the point where it is practically impossible for a candidate to get elected without the support of a party organization.* (1.1)

3. D   The passage does not state that voters prefer candidates that express the values of an established party. All the other answers are given: *The job of influencing popular opinion through newspapers, television, the Internet, and other mass media is too complicated...; ...the variety of issues facing nation states has complicated the problem of creating an informed electorate...; Building political support on a nation–wide scale carries a high cost....*

4. C   The passage does not state that dance bands in northern cities invented the blues. All the other answers are given: *These work songs and "field hollers"...helped to pass the time; The blues spread from its birthplace in the Mississippi Delta...; The blues contributed to the development of other types of music, such as the big–band jazz....*

5. B   The passage does not state that coral reefs have caused sea–surface temperatures to rise. All the other answers are given: *Coral reefs are one of the earth's most ancient ecosystems...; The brilliant blue, purple, green, gold, and pink have begun to disappear as a disease called bleaching drains the color and the life from the reefs; The huge cities built by corals provide shelter and food for billions of other marine animals.*

6. D   Rising water level is not given as an effect of the bleaching of coral reefs. All the other answers are given: *...bleaching drains the color...; Millions of aquatic animals that depend directly or indirectly on corals have died as well...; Bleaching has killed more corals....*

7. D   Clues: *...so different from one another...their use of animals; The Native Americans' relationship to the deer, moose, and beaver...was far different from that of the Europeans to the pigs, cows, sheep, and horses....* (1.1)

8. B   Burning the woods was not an agricultural practice of the Europeans; it was a practice of the Native Americans. All the other answers are given: *...the Europeans were responsible for a host of changes in the New England landscape: endless miles of fences...; ...the plow...characteristics of European agricultural practices; ...new fields covered with grass, clover....*

9. C   Landscape architects do not draw or paint scenes from the natural environment. All the other answers are given: *Landscape architects design landscapes in residential areas, public parks, and commercial zones; They usually plan the arrangement of vegetation, walkways, and other natural features of open spaces.*

10. B   The passage does not list building a fence around the construction site as a stage in the landscape design process. All the other answers are listed: *...landscape architects first consider the nature and purpose of the project, the funds available...; ...they prepare working drawings to show all existing and proposed features; They outline the methods of constructing features and draw up lists of building materials.*

Quiz 1 (p. 59)

1. B   Clues: *...small, relatively harmless amounts of ionizing radiation, known as background radiation...; However, other types of ionizing radiation...have the potential to harm the human body.* (1.1)

2. A   Clues: *Most damage occurs in tissues with rapidly dividing cells....* (1.1)

3. A   Genetic defects are not an example of somatic damage; they are an example of genetic damage. All the other answers are examples of somatic damage: *The second type of damage is somatic, which causes victims direct harm in the form of burns...eye cataracts...cancers of the...lung.* (1.2)

4. D   Clues: *Exposure to a large dose of ionizing radiation over a short time can be fatal within a few minutes to a few months later.* (1.1)

5. C   Clues: *...the populations of most North American canids...have decreased greatly. The coyote, however, has thrived alongside humans, increasing in both numbers and range.* (1.1)

6. B   The passage does not state that the coyote uses its distinctive call to trick and catch prey. All the other answers are given: *This call keeps the band alert to the locations of its members; One voice usually prompts others to join in, resulting in the familiar chorus...; ...its scientific name, canis latrans, means "barking dog."* (1.2)

7. D   Clues: *In feeding, the coyote is an opportunist, eating rabbits, mice...and carrion—whatever is available.* (1.1)

8. D   Clues: *Often a badger serves as involuntary supplier of smaller prey: while it digs for rodents at one end of their burrow, the coyote waits for any that may emerge from an escape hole at the other end.* (1.1)

9. C   Clues: *Man is the major enemy....* (1.1)

10. A   The passage does not state that the coyote is a serious threat to human activities. All the other answers are given: *The best runner among the canids...a strong swimmer...does not hesitate to enter water after prey; ...the coyote may team up with one or two others, running in relays to tire prey...; ...the coyote population continues to grow, despite efforts at trapping, shooting, and poisoning the animals.* (1.2)

Quiz 2 (p. 62)

1. D   Clues: *However, a more accurate view shows that rural Canadians had access to considerable information.* (1.1)

2. B   Clues: *The postal service was efficient and inexpensive and connected rural Canadians with the outside world. Many farm families received at least one newspaper through the mail....* (1.1)

3. A   Clues: *...especially during the winter, when work on the farm was much lighter and people had more time for a variety of social and cultural events.* (1.1)

4. B   The passage does not state that the rural school provided public health clinics. All the other answers are given: *The local school served other functions besides providing formal education...; ...school districts were often the only sign of political organization...; ...one–room schoolhouse as a meeting place...a variety of social and cultural events.* (1.2)

5. C   Clues: *...there was a growing exodus from farms to the city, mainly because smaller farms...were no longer able to support the entire family.* (1.1)

6. A   Clues: *...artists and writers romanticized the family farm. In the novel Anne of Green Gables....* (1.1)

7. D   Clues: *...the novel Anne of Green Gables...about a young woman who strove to reconcile the beauty and peace of the rural landscape with the need to leave it in order to fulfill her ambitions. For large numbers of young Canadians, growing up meant leaving the farm to find work in the city.* (1.1)

8. D   Clues: *Two conditions are necessary for the formation of ice: the presence of water and temperatures below freezing. Ice in the atmosphere...can assume various forms, depending on the conditions under which water is converted to its solid state.* (1.1)

9. A   Clues: *Ice in the atmosphere and on the ground can assume various forms...; ...snow, sleet, or hail.* (1.1)

10. C   Clues: *Ice that forms in the atmosphere can fall to the ground as...hail; Hail consists of rounded or jagged lumps of ice, often in layers....* (1.1)

11. A   Sleet does not form on bodies of water; it forms in the atmosphere. All the other answers are forms of ice that form on bodies of water: *...the first ice to form is a thin surface layer of slush...; ...eventually grows into small floes of pancake ice; If the lake is small enough...the floes may freeze together into a fairly solid sheet of pack ice.* (1.2)

12. B   Clues: *On very large bodies of water, it may not form until late winter because there must be several months of low temperatures to chill such large amounts of water.* (1.1)

13. D   Clues: *On puddles and small ponds, ice first freezes in a thin layer with definite crystal structure....* (1.1)

14. C   Clues: *...small floes of pancake ice. If the lake is small enough or the weather cold enough, the floes may freeze together into a fairly solid sheet of pack ice.* (1.1)

15. D   Clues: *...ice is less dense than liquid water and therefore floats rather than sinks in water; Without the insulating effect of floating ice sheets, surface water would lose heat more rapidly....* (1.1)

16. C   The passage does not mention the rate at which ice melts. All the other answers are mentioned: *Ice in the atmosphere and on the ground can assume various forms...; ...flakes...pellets; ...rounded or jagged lumps...layers...; Ice also forms directly on the ground or on bodies of water; As ice floats on the surface of a lake, ocean, or river, it acts as an insulator and is thus important in maintaining the balance of the ecosystem.* (1.2)

17. A   Clues: *Because most people do not volunteer to pay taxes or police their own financial affairs...; To accomplish these things, governments have to pass laws.* (1.1)

18. C   Clues: *...governments cannot influence economic activity simply by asking people to pollute less, to give money to the poor, or to be innovative. To accomplish these things, governments have to pass laws.* (1.1)

19. C   Clues: *...large–scale organizations—corporations, labor unions, and government structures—that have grown in importance...; Their presence and growing dominance have shifted capitalist economies... toward government administration of markets.* (1.1)

20. D   Clues: *...the individual states and the federal government have passed laws to shield investors against fraud; Another important area of law concerns the labor force....* (1.1)

21. B   Clues: *...laws for the conduct of economic activity that attempts to make it serve the public interest. For instance...laws to shield investors against fraud.* (1.1)

22. A   The passage does not give stock ownership as an issue concerning the labor force. All the other answers are given: *...concerns the labor force, such as regulation of work hours...health and safety conditions...and the rights of workers...to strike....* (1.2)

23. B   Clues: *...governments everywhere deal with essentially the same issues and participate in economic activity.* (1.1)

24. D   Clues: *Even governments that are reluctant to regulate commerce directly have undertaken large–scale projects...and other public services.* (1.1)

25. B   The passage does not give small business ownership as an example of government participation in economic activity. All the other answers are given: *...governments...have been playing an increasing role in economics. This can be seen in the growth of government taxation and spending, in the growing share of national income devoted to income–support payments...; Even governments that are reluctant to regulate commerce directly have undertaken... transportation networks....* (1.2)

EXERCISE 1.3.A (p. 76)

1. D   *Obstructed* means *blocked* in this context. Clues: *...what we consider taste is actually smell. If the sense of smell is -----, as by a head cold, the perception of taste is sharply reduced;* the prefix *ob–* = against; the stem *–struct–* = build.

2. A   *Accounts for* means *explains* in this context. Clues: *...120 degrees—the same angle as the angles of a hexagon—which ----- the characteristic six–sided structure....*

3. B   *Compile* means *put together* in this context. Clues: *...preparing the report...; ...how the report will be used...;* the prefix *com–* = together.

4. A   *Split off* means *separated* in this context. Clues: *...had common origins but then ----- from one another several hundred thousand years ago.*

5. A   *Indulge* means *participate* in this context. Clues: *...travel for pleasure was limited to the wealthy, but since then, improved standards of living and the availability of transportation have allowed more people to -----;* the prefix *in–* = into.

6. B   *Exploded* means *expanded rapidly* in this context. Clues: *...the development of commercial jet airlines enabled fast international travel; Today, airports in nearly every country can accommodate jumbo jets full of tourists...;* the prefix *ex–* = out.

7. A   *Grasp* means *understanding* in this context. Clues: *...must broaden and deepen their understanding...; ...some comprehension of...; ...must gain an understanding of....*

8. D   *Pitfalls* means *hazards* in this context. Clues: *...its negative aspects, such as the sources of human conflict and the ----- of power.*

9. C   *Foliage* means *mass of leaves* in this context. Clues: *...autumn leaves...; Red leaves...; Leaves that appear yellow....*

10. D   *Masked* means *concealed* in this context. Clues: *Leaves that appear yellow in autumn are no less yellow in spring and summer. However, in spring and summer the yellow pigments...are ----- by the green pigment chlorophyll....* The yellow pigments do not appear in spring and summer because the green pigment conceals them.

EXERCISE 1.3.B (p. 79)

1. D   *Crude* means *simple* in this context. Clues: *The moon with its earthshine acts as a ----- weather satellite by reporting, in a very simple way, the general state of terrestrial cloudiness.*

2. B   *Glare* means *bright light* in this context. Clues: *As the phase of the moon progresses beyond a thin crescent...; ...the increasing ----- of the moon's growing crescent...; ... irradiation.*

3. A   *Fleeting* means *temporary* in this context. Clues: *...withstood the ----- nature of most slang; ...has been around a long time. Most slang is temporary,* meaning it changes rapidly, but *cool has lasted a long time.*

4. C   *Carry the same weight* means *have the same importance. Weight* means *heaviness* or, in this context, *importance.* Clues: *As long as...Birth of the Cool remains one of the best–selling jazz recordings of all time, cool will stay cool—it will ----- as it did more than 50 years ago.*

5. D   *Scouring* means *scraping* in this context. Clues: *...removing most of the existing soil, and hollowing out countless lakes.*

6. C   *Sustained* means *supported* in this context. Clues: *...attempts to bring them into agricultural use have been largely unsuccessful. However, the region's mineral wealth ----- both temporary and permanent settlements...;* the prefix *sus–* = under.

7. C   *Talk over* means *explore* in this context. Clues: *...small–group discussions allow them to develop healthier ways to think about work; ...ways to make workplaces more ethical and just.*

8. A   *In lockstep* means *alike* in this context. Clues: *Groups work best when they consist of people who have similar duties, responsibilities, and missions. This does not mean, however, that everyone in the group must think -----.*

9. B   *Fuel* means *stimulate* in this context. Clues: *Finding the right subject matter...; ...several ways to ----- the discussion...; ...the company's mission statement...; ...readings on work and ethics...; ...specific workplace incidents....*

10. A   *Overwhelm* means *dominate* in this context. Clues: *...the dynamics of the group should be balanced...; ...the discussion leader must not be allowed to ----- the conversation or the agenda; ...when the same person is not always in charge;* the prefix *over–* = too much.

EXERCISE 1.3.C (p. 82)

1. A   *Wreak havoc on* means *disrupt* in this context. Clues: *...has a sharp impact on...; ...changes that can ----- precipitation patterns...; ...both delay and stimulate the fall of precipitation....*

2. C   *Drenching* means *thoroughly wetting* in this context. Clues: *...both delay and stimulate the fall of precipitation, depriving some areas of rain while ----- others. While* shows contrast between *depriving some areas of rain* and *drenching.*

3. A   *Hoisted* means *lifted* in this context. Clues: *...heavy amounts of heat and pollution rising from cities...; ...up in the sky....*

4. D   *Torrential* means *heavy* in this context. Clues: *...a precipitation shortage...; By contrast...invigorate summer storm activity...allowing clouds to build higher and fuller.... By contrast* shows contrast between *precipitation shortage* and *torrential rains.*

5. C   *Sentimentality* means *feeling* in this context. Clues: *So much ----- is attached to the rose...it is difficult to separate the original mythological and folkloric beliefs from the emotional excess....*

6. B   *Invoked* means *called on* in this context. Clues: *...symbol of romantic love ----- by every minor poet and painter;* the prefix *in–* = on; the stem *–vok–* = call.

7. C   *Decked* means *decorated* in this context. Clues: *...roses were to be planted on the grave.*

8. D   *Plucking* means *picking* in this context. Clues: *...equated the rose with life, and they believed that when a child died, the figure of death could be seen ----- a rose outside the house.*

9. A   *Token* means *symbol* in this context. Clues: *...association with female beauty; ...a ----- of all that is lovely and good; ...on the other hand, the rose was a symbol not of feminine but of masculine beauty.* The parallel use of *token* and *symbol* shows that they are similar in meaning.

10. C   *Sub rosa* means *secretly* in this context. Clues: *...a sign of secrecy and silence; ...the intention of secrecy.*

EXERCISE 1.3.D (p. 84)

1. A   Clues: *When "period" furniture became popular, American furniture factories attempted to duplicate various styles of French and English furniture of the seventeenth and eighteenth centuries.* A reproduction is a duplicate (copy) of something. (1.1)

2. C   *Revolt* means *break* in this context. Clues: *...based not only on individualism but also on a return to simplicity and practicality...; represented a ----- from mass–produced furniture; ...departed greatly from the ornate and pretentious factory–made "period" furniture.... Individualism* is the opposite of *mass–produced,* so *revolt* must indicate a change or break.

3. D   *Primitive* means *simple* in this context. Clues: *...a return to simplicity and practicality; ...simple, straight lines....*

4. A   *Hallmarks* means *features* in this context. Clues: *...possess the essential qualities of...; ...plain and unornamented...; ...simple, straight lines were the ----- of its construction.*

5. B   *Ornate* means *complex* in this context. Clues: *Craftsman furniture was plain...; The severity of the style departed greatly from the ----- and pretentious factory–made "period" furniture....* The phrase *departed greatly from* shows contrast between *plain* Craftsman furniture and *ornate* "period" furniture.

6. B   *Vitality* means *energy* in this context. Clues: *...rhythms of speech...; ...daring...; ...movement, and color of rural black culture;* the stem *–vita–* = life.

7. A   *Calling* means *profession* in this context. Clues: *...continued her fieldwork...but eventually followed her most cherished -----, that of fiction writer.*

8. A   *Autonomy* means *independence* in this context. Clues: *...freedom, -----, and self–realization, while also being...attached to a man;* the prefix *auto–* = self.

9. C   *Out of touch* means that Hurston's opinions differed from those of most other people. Clues: *Hurston was criticized for not writing fiction in the protest tradition. Her conservative views....*

10. D   *Revere* means *honor* in this context. Clues: *...it was only afterward that later generations...were to rediscover and ----- her celebrations of black culture. It was only afterward* shows contrast with Hurston's dying in poverty and obscurity, indicating that *revere* has a positive meaning.

Quiz 3 (p. 87)

1. C   *Sparsely populated* means that few people lived in the region. Clues: *...still two years away from becoming the state of Ohio; ...settlers of the Ohio frontier...; ...prepared the way for farms and towns...; When Chapman started his "apple seeding" in 1801, the population of Ohio was 45,000....* (1.3)

2. B   *Pacifist* means *peace advocate* in this context. Clues: *He was a ----- in a time of warfare and brutality against the Indians, treating Indians and settlers alike with respect. Peace advocate* contrasts with *warfare* and *brutality.* (1.3)

3. B   *Marching* means *advancing* in this context. Clues: *...agricultural development...; ...ever–increasing pace...; ...more than forty percent of the land had been cleared of trees and converted to farms.* (1.3)

4. D   *Subside* means *decrease* in this context. Clues: *Not until 1880 did the cutting of trees -----. By then, three–quarters of Ohio had been cleared, and people were becoming aware of the limits of expansion;* the prefix *sub–* = below, under. (1.3)

5. A   *Primeval* means *original* in this context. Clues: *...the universe began...; ...yet even now...may be present; ...original universe....* (1.3)

6. D   *Transition* means *change* in this context. Clues: *...gradually differentiated it...; ...expanded and cooled...;* the prefix *trans–* = across. (1.3)

7. C   *Uniform* means *consistent* in this context. Clues: *...not completely...; ...some regions that were slightly denser and capable of generating stronger gravitational fields than others;* the prefix *uni–* = one; *uniform* = one form or type. (1.3)

8. B   *Compact* means *dense* in this context. Clues: *Since gravity tends to pull matter together, the denser regions tended to become even more -----; evolved into denser clouds....* Gravity pulled the dense regions together, making them denser than before. (1.3)

9. A   *Luminous* means *light–emitting* in this context. Clues: *...glow...; ...stars...;* the stem *–lum–* = light. (1.3)

10. C   *Merged* means *blended* in this context. Clues: *...accumulated most of their mass later through collisions...; ...smaller galaxies were pulled together over time...; into larger and larger structures, eventually forming massive galaxies.* (1.3)

Quiz 4 (p. 90)

1. C   Clues: *Car registrations in the United States rose from one million in 1913 to ten million in 1923. By 1927...some twenty–six million automobiles....* (1.1)

2. B   *The lifeblood* means *an important part* in this context. Clues: *The growth of roads and the automobile industry made cars ----- of the petroleum industry...; The automobile caused expansions in....* (1.3)

3. A   *Frenzied* means *intense* in this context. Clues: *...automobile industry reached new heights...; ...new roads...; ...road building...; ...largest public works program in history.* (1.3)

4. C   Clues: *After 1945...new roads led out of the city to the suburbs...; The result was a network of federally subsidized highways connecting major urban centers.* (1.1)

5. B   *Scant* means *barely sufficient* in this context. Clues: *...75 percent of federal funds for transportation has been spent on highways, while a ----- one percent has gone to buses, trains, or subways; ...worst public transit system. While* shows contrast between 75 percent for highways and one percent for public transit. (1.3)

6. C   The passage does not state that the growth in the number of cars had a positive impact on subway systems; in fact, there was a negative impact on subways and other forms of public transit. All the other answers are given as positive impacts: *The automobile caused expansions in outdoor recreation, tourism...service stations...; ...two–car families transported children to...shopping malls.* (1.2)

7. A   Clues: *...the American bias was clear, which is why the United States has the world's best road system and nearly its worst public transit system.* (1.1)

8. C   *Range* means *variety* in this context. Clues: *Some species are restricted to a single song...while other species have a ----- of songs and dialects.... While* shows contrast between *single song* and *range.* (1.3)

9. D   Clues: *For all bird species, there is a prescribed path to development of the final song...; This process is similar to the steps through which young children pass as they first babble and then mimic pieces of the songs they hear....* (1.1)

10. A   *Mimic* means *imitate* in this context. Clues: *The most important auditory stimuli for birds are the sounds of other birds...; This process is similar to... young children...as they first babble and then ----- pieces of the songs they hear around them....* (1.3)

11. D   *Underlying* means *supporting* in this context. Clues: *...all avian vocal activity is the syrinx...; ...the syrinx is a...sound–producing mechanism that can create sound...;* the prefix *sup–* = under. (1.3)

12. D   Clues: *...compared to the human larynx, which uses only about two percent of exhaled air, the syrinx is a far more efficient sound–producing mechanism that can create sound from nearly all the air passing through it.* (1.1)

13. B Clues: *Song is a complex activity that young birds must learn, and learning implies that higher–brain activity must be complex in the control of song.* (1.1)

14. A *Lateralized* means *linked to a specific area of the brain*. Clues: *...the song–control centers are located in the left side of the avian brain.* (1.3)

15. B The passage does not state that birds are born with the full ability to sing their species song; in fact, birds must learn the species song. All other answers are given: *The most important auditory stimuli for birds are the sounds of other birds...; Underlying all avian vocal activity is the syrinx, an organ...linked to the brain; Possibly the most interesting aspect of bird song...is its foundation in the central nervous system.* (1.2)

16. A Clues: *Machiavelli was a product of Renaissance Florence, a city–state that was struggling for expansion and survival among a competing group of similar states; Machiavelli came to understand power politics by observing the spectacle around him....* (1.1)

17. B *Illusions* means *false beliefs* in this context. Clues: *...came to understand power politics by observing the spectacle around him without any -----;* the prefix *il–* = not; the stem *–lus–* = light. (1.3)

18. A *Potent* means *influential* in this context. Clues: *...classics in political theory...; ...little book that would shock readers for centuries.* (1.3)

19. C Clues: *In his most famous work, The Prince (1532), Machiavelli described the means by which a leader may gain and maintain power.* (1.1)

20. A *Pessimistic* means *negative* in this context. Clues: *...all men were brutal, selfish, and cowardly...; ...thought that his own time was too corrupt...; Machiavelli's philosophy arose more from a deeply ----- view of human nature....* (1.3)

21. C Machiavelli's political philosophy did not include the belief that people must organize to fight against evil and corruption in politics. All the other answers are given: *Politics was simply the battle of men in search of power, and since all men were brutal, selfish...; The ideal prince was the man who had studied his fellow men...and was willing to exploit their weaknesses; Machiavelli saw politics as an affair separate from religion and ethics, an activity to be practiced and studied for its own sake.* (1.2)

22. D Clues: *He was, and still is, misunderstood to have promoted...treachery and criminality over other means of governing.* (1.1)

23. B *Lucidity* means *clarity* in this context. Clues: *...saw the world more clearly than others...; ...honesty;* the stem *–luc–* = light. (1.3)

24. A *Monologues* means *speeches* in this context. Clues: *...to comment on his own wickedness...;* the prefix *mono–* = one; the stem *–log–* = study. *Comment* indicates speaking; a monologue is a speech by one person. (1.3)

25. D Complex motivation is not a characteristic of the Machiavel character. All the other answers are given: *...contempt for goodness; The Machiavel had a habit of using humorous monologues to comment on his own wickedness...; ...delight in evil...* (1.2)

EXERCISE 1.4.A (p. 100)

1. B You can infer that people have long been aware of links between music and mathematics. Clues: *In classical and medieval times, the study of music shared many features with the discipline of mathematics....*

2. A You can infer that corvids are a family of birds. Clues: *...stay in their flocks all year round; ...synchronized flight test; ...adaptability and intelligence of this family....*

3. C You can infer that the author believes trees, plants, and organic matter can store solar energy. Clues: *Major indirect forms of solar energy include... biomass—solar energy converted to chemical energy in trees, plants, and other organic matter.*

4. C You can infer that women did not acquire property through inheritance. Clues: *The family members who would not inherit a share in the property were exploited by the laws of inheritance. The system was particularly hard on women, who usually did not share in the ownership of the farm....*

5. B *Embark on* means *begin* in this context. Clues: *When the family's first child is born, the parents ----- a sequence of experiences....* (1.3)

6. D You can infer that the family life cycle shapes several years in the lives of most adults. Clues: *...from infancy and toddlerhood...and eventually, to departure from the nest. Each of these periods in the child's life makes a different set of demands on the parents.*

7. B You can infer that aromatherapy is the use of certain scents to promote health. Clues: *...odors and fragrances affect the body and mind and are capable of healing anxiety, stress, and other sources of disease; Some popular essential oils and their uses in aromatherapy include....*

8. B The passage does not state that jasmine is believed to reduce stress. All the other answers are believed to reduce stress: *...lavender and chamomile, which are reputed to ease stress...; Orange eases anxiety....* (1.2)

9. D You can infer that social interactions related to teaching and learning provide evidence that orangutans have culture. Clues: *Some orangutan parents teach their young...while others demonstrate the technique...; Such social interactions lead researchers to conclude that if orangutans have culture....*

10. C You can infer that primate culture may be older than scientists used to believe. Clues: *The discovery of orangutan culture suggests that early primates... might have developed the ability to invent new behaviors...approximately 6 million years earlier than once believed.*

EXERCISE 1.4.B (p. 104)

1. A You can infer that the sources of immigrants shifted to different parts of Europe. Clues: *In the early nineteenth century, most of the Europeans who immigrated to the United States were from northern and western European countries...; However, most of the fifteen million Europeans arriving between 1890 and 1914 came from southern and eastern Europe....*

2. C   You can infer that the Doukhobors mainly settled in the Canadian prairies. Clues: *The Doukhobors... established communal settlements in Saskatchewan. Together with other immigrants, they arrived in such numbers that...the population of the prairies had increased....*

3. D   *Vigor* means *strength* in this context. Clues: *...iron... power...the industrial age.* (1.3)

4. B   You can infer that David Smith's childhood exposed him to the uses and possibilities of iron. Clues: *His iron sculptures flowed naturally out of the mechanized heart of America, a landscape of railroads and factories. As a child, Smith played on trains and around factories....*

5. D   You can infer that the *Sentinels* and the *Cubis* each consist of a number of pieces placed in outdoor settings. Clues: *...two series of sculptures...the Sentinels...and the Cubis...; He also began placing his sculptures outdoors...; In the late afternoon sun, the steel planes of the Cubis reflect a golden color....*

6. C   You can infer that the author believes David Smith's pieces capture the power of industry and the beauty of natural light. Clues: *To Smith, iron spoke of the power, mobility, and vigor of the industrial age; He also began placing his sculptures outdoors, in natural light, where the highly reflective stainless steel could bring sunlight and color into the work.*

7. A   You can infer that constellations have interested people for a very long time. Clues: *Long ago, people looked up in the sky...; ...constellations...part of human culture for thousands of years; Astronomers identified many constellations only a few centuries ago.*

8. D   You can infer that the ancient Greeks and Romans acquired knowledge of constellations from earlier cultures. Clues: *Ancient Syrians and Babylonians named many constellations and created stories about them. The Greeks and Romans later adopted these constellations and translated their names and stories into their own language.*

9. B   You can infer that scientists today continue to study constellations. Clues: *Today's astronomers view constellations simply as areas of the sky where interesting objects await observation and study; Scientists...still refer to many constellations by their popular names....*

10. C   You can infer that a constellation's alpha star is the one that is easiest to see. Clues: *...the "alpha star" is the brightest star of that constellation.*

Exercise 1.4.C (p. 107)

1. B   You can infer that the organs for hearing and balance both send nerve impulses to the brain. Clues: *Both organs involve fluid–filled channels containing hair cells that produce electrochemical impulses...; To perform the function of hearing, the ear converts the energy of pressure waves moving through the air into nerve impulses that the brain perceives as sound; When the position of the head changes...the force on the hair cells changes its output of nerve impulses. The brain then interprets these changes....*

2. A   Hearing does not involve motion of the vocal cords so that they vibrate; this is an aspect of speaking, not hearing. All the other answers are given as part of hearing: *...fluid–filled channels containing hair cells that produce electrochemical impulses when the hairs are stimulated...; ...bones of the middle ear amplify and transmit the vibrations...; the ear converts the energy of pressure waves moving through the air into nerve impulses....* (1.2)

3. D   You can infer that the cochlea is a part of the inner ear. Clues: *The inner ear is a network of channels containing fluid...; ...the cochlea, the organ of hearing; ...the fluid inside the cochlea. Hair cells in the cochlea convert the energy of the vibrating fluid....*

4. A   You can infer that gravity has an essential role in the sense of balance. Clues: *Hair cells in the inner ear respond to changes in head position with respect to gravity and movement. Gravity is always pulling down on the hairs, sending a constant series of impulses to the brain.*

5. C   *Fashioned* means *made* in this context. Clues: *...the canoe cedar...the raw material for their seagoing dugout canoes; ...from a single tree trunk....* (1.3)

6. A   Clues: *...keeping the sections below the waterline thickest and heaviest to help keep the canoe upright in stormy seas.* (1.1)

7. D   You can infer that canoes were important cultural artifacts of the Haida. Clues: *The canoes were often painted with elaborate designs of cultural significance to the tribe.*

8. B   *Staunch* means *strong* in this context. Clues: *...the canoe's stability...; ...sturdy wooden thwarts...; ...utility....* (1.3)

9. D   You can infer that trees provided essential tools for obtaining food. Clues: *...harpoons of yew wood, baited hooks of red cedar, and lines of twisted and braided bark fibers, they fished...and hunted....*

10. C   You can infer that Haida canoes were of great value in the regional economy. Clues: *...neighboring tribes were willing to exchange quantities of hides, meats, and oils for a Haida canoe. These graceful vessels became the island–dwelling tribe's chief item of export.*

Exercise 1.5.A (p. 114)

1. A   The author's purpose is to point out that financial measurements are not always precise. Clues: *In economics and finance, nothing can be measured with the precision...; ...approximate measurement is often sufficient....*

2. D   The author's purpose is to warn potential buyers of the possibility of accounting abuses. Clues: *Accounting scandals occur...; Although the accounting profession and government agencies have attempted to reform some of these abuses....*

3. B   The author's purpose is to provide biographical information about the author. Clues: *...Stephen Leacock's masterpiece, Sunshine Sketches of a Little Town...; ...one of the founders of Canadian literature....*

4. A   The author's purpose is to describe the tone of the book. Clues: *...a portrait of small–town Canadian life in the early twentieth century; ...a past to be cherished, a pastoral and idyllic town....*

5. C The author's purpose is to illustrate the behavior required of certain social roles. Clues: ...*certain types of behavior from people who play certain social roles; Anyone occupying a given position is expected to adopt a specific attitude.*

6. D The author's purpose is to emphasize the value of informal roles to a group. Clues: ...*a group's health and happiness....*

7. C Clues: ...*the family historian...relays valuable cultural information that maintains both the family and the larger society.* (1.1)

8. C The author's purpose is to compare how various surfaces transfer heat into the atmosphere. Clues: *Thus, the different types of surfaces transfer heat into the atmosphere at different rates.*

9. A Clues: ...*we depend on our perceptions of the data...; Human perception must be included if our understanding of climatic processes is to be translated into societal actions.* (1.1)

10. C The author's purpose is to give examples of dangerous effects of climate. Clues: ...*the harmful effects of climate....*

Exercise 1.5.B (p. 118)

1. A The author's purpose is to emphasize Pinchot's contributions to the field. Clues: ...*promoting forestry as a profession. Foremost was Gifford Pinchot...; ...chief of the Forest Service...; ...professor of forestry and founder of the Pinchot School of Forestry....*

2. D The author's purpose is to introduce the types of work done by professional foresters. Clues: ...*plan and supervise the growth, protection, and utilization of trees; ...make maps of forest areas...manage timber sales; ...protect the trees...; ...may be responsible for other duties...; ...do research, provide information...teach in colleges and universities.*

3. B The passage does not mention how to select a good school of forestry. All the other answers are mentioned: *Some foresters may be responsible for other duties, ranging from...; Several men have been responsible for promoting forestry as a profession; ...estimate the amount of standing timber and future growth, and manage timber sales.* (1.2)

4. B The passage does not state that fashions serve the purpose of signaling a change in personal beliefs. All the other answers are given: *By keeping up with fashions...members of a group both satisfy their desire for novelty...; ...demonstrating their membership in the group; ...obey the rules....* (1.2)

5. D The author's purpose is to explain how high status may involve an inverted status display. Clues: *Some people...consider themselves of such high status that they do not need to display it with their clothing; ...an inverted status display is most likely to occur where the person's high status....*

6. A The author's purpose is to give an example of an item that conveys one's actual status. Clues: ...*a subtle but important signal, such as an expensive -----, will prevail over the message of the casual dress.*

7. A The author's purpose is to show how the war for independence affected the economy. Clues: *The war for independence from Britain was a long and economically costly conflict.*

8. C Clues: *The most serious consequences were felt in the cities, whose existence depended on commercial activity.* (1.1)

9. C The author's purpose is to emphasize the great short–term cost of the war for New York. Clues: *The population...declined from 21,000 in 1774 to less than half that number only nine years later in 1783.*

10. D You can infer that shortages of money and manufactured goods occurred during the years right after the war for independence. Clues: ...*the loss of established markets for manufactured goods...the loss of sources of credit...the lack of new investment all created a period of economic stagnation that lasted for the next twenty years.* (1.4)

Quiz 5 (p. 122)

1. B The author's purpose is to identify the freezing point of water. Clues: *Because many foods contain large amounts of water, they freeze solidly at or just below....* (1.5)

2. B The author's purpose is to warn that not blanching will harm the food's nutritional value. Clues: ...*avoid this step...; The result would be a product largely devoid of vitamins and minerals.* (1.5)

3. A You can infer that enzyme action in vegetables eventually causes vegetables to spoil. Clues: ...*enzyme action, which vegetables require during their growth and ripening but which continues after maturation and will lead to decay....* (1.4)

4. C You can infer that underblanched vegetables would lack vitamins and minerals. Clues: ...*to avoid this step would be an expensive mistake. The result would be a product largely devoid of vitamins and minerals; Underblanching is like no blanching at all....* (1.4)

5. D You can infer that the French colonies had fewer people than did other North American colonies. Clues: ...*there were never enough French settlers to make French North America a large center of population.* (1.4)

6. A The author's purpose is to emphasize the competition among European groups. Clues: ...*the lead...; ... early losses....* (1.5)

7. B You can infer that England was a leading European power. Clues: *England's commercial and political growth at home soon gave it the lead in the colonial race....* (1.4)

8. D The author's purpose is to illustrate England's growing power in North America. Clues: *England's commercial and political growth at home soon gave it the lead in the colonial race...; ...there were 2,000 in the English colonies; ...the English had absorbed the Dutch colonies; ...the English colonies had a quarter of a million.* (1.5)

9. C You can infer that the Dutch and the English competed for land, and the English prevailed. Clues: *The Dutch settlements suffered a lot of competition from the English, and eventually, the Dutch governor was forced to surrender all Dutch lands to the English; ...the English had absorbed the Dutch colonies.* (1.4)

10. B Clues: *The conflicts...were mostly over commercial interests and signaled the intense rivalry for control of North American land and resources.* (1.1)

Quiz 6 (p. 125)

1. **D** The name is curious because it did not originate in America. Clues: *The name was, in fact, a historical accident, originating with fashionable architects in Victorian England who coined it....* (1.5)

2. **D** *Asymmetrical* means *unbalanced* in this context. Clues: *...how drastically different the right and left sides are....* (1.3)

3. **A** The passage does not mention decorative windows as a characteristic of Queen Anne houses. All the other answers are mentioned: *...the wood shingle siding...; ...the inviting wraparound porch...; ...the unusual roof shape—a steeply pitched....* (1.2)

4. **C** You can infer that the Queen Anne style was elaborate and ornate. Clues: *...unusual roof shape...; ...the detailing, shown in the wood shingle siding cut into fanciful decorative patterns of scallops, curves, diamonds, or triangles.* (1.4)

5. **C** Clues: *Queen Anne houses faded from fashion early in the twentieth century as the public's taste shifted toward the more modern Prairie and Craftsman style houses.* (1.1)

6. **A** *Buffs* means *experts* in this context. Clues: *...painstakingly and lovingly restored...; ...reproduced by builders who give faithful attention to the distinctive shapes and detailing....* (1.3)

7. **A** *Arenas* means *settings* in this context. Clues: *...such public ----- as political ceremonies, parades, funerals, fashion shows, and cooking demonstrations. Such...as introduces examples of public settings where commentary is used.* (1.3)

8. **C** *Background* means *knowledge* in this context. Clues: *...provides the audience with...interpretation... evaluation.* (1.3)

9. **D** Clues: *..."color" commentary provides the audience with pre–event background, during–event interpretation, and post–event evaluation.* (1.1)

10. **B** Clues: *Play–by–play commentary...is unlike other kinds of narrative, which are typically reported in past tense. Play–by–play commentary is reported in present tense.* (1.1)

11. **A** The author's purpose is to describe the uniqueness of radio play–by–play. Clues: *It is these characteristics that make this kind of commentary unlike any other type of speech situation.* (1.5)

12. **A** "He pitched for Chicago" is not an example of play–by–play commentary; rather, it is an example of background information that is part of color commentary. All the other answers are examples of play–by–play commentary: "Junior out of bounds" eliminates the verb; "Straight away it's Owens" has inverted word order and is spoken in present tense; "He can't make the shot" is spoken in present tense. (1.2)

13. **D** *Pace* means *speed* in this context. Clues: *...very fluent, keeping up with the ----- of the action. The rate is steady....* (1.3)

14. **B** *Crucial* means *important* in this context. Clues: *...informing the listener...; ..."state of play" summary...; ...for listeners or viewers who have just tuned in.* (1.3)

15. **C** You can infer that the author believes commentary enhances the excitement and enjoyment of sports. Clues: *"Play–by–play" commentary narrates the sports event, while "color–adding" or "color" commentary provides the audience with... background...interpretation...evaluation; Play–by–play commentary is very fluent, keeping up with the pace of the action.* (1.4)

16. **B** Clues: *...the circulatory system, consisting of two cellular pipelines...; One pipeline, called the xylem...; The other, the phloem....* (1.1)

17. **D** Clues: *This is the tree's major growth organ, responsible for the outward widening of the trunk, branches, twigs, and roots; ...the vascular cambium produces new phloem cells...and new xylem cells....* (1.1)

18. **B** You can infer that the xylem is located inside the phloem and the vascular cambium. Clues: *...the vascular cambium produces new phloem cells on its outer surface and new xylem cells on its inner surface.* (1.4)

19. **A** You can infer that xylem sap is composed mainly of water. Clues: *Xylem cells in the roots draw water molecules into the tree...; The xylem pipeline transports this life–sustaining mixture upward as xylem sap...; ...bringing xylem sap to thirsty cells. Leaves depend on this delivery system for their water supply....* (1.4)

20. **D** *Wilt* means *sag* in this context. Clues: *Unless the transpired water is replaced...the leaves will ----- and eventually die.* The leaves will sag and die because they have lost water. (1.3)

21. **C** Clues: *Water moves through the tree because it is driven by negative pressure—tension...; Transpiration, the evaporation of water from leaves, creates the tension that drives long–distance transport up through the xylem pipeline.* (1.1)

22. **B** *Adhere to* means *stick to* in this context. Clues: *...cohesion of water due to hydrogen bonding...; ...water molecules ----- each other and are pulled upward...; the prefix ad– = to, toward.* (1.3)

23. **A** *Gummy* means *sticky* in this context. Clues: *... become clogged...; ...can no longer transport fluids... Gummy* is the adjective form of *gum,* a sticky substance. (1.3)

24. **C** The author's purpose is to compare what happens in two aging circulatory systems. Clues: *Over time the innermost xylem cells become clogged with hard or gummy waste products and can no longer transport fluids. A similar situation occurs in the clogging of -----.* (1.5)

25. **A** Transporting food from the leaves to the trunk is not a function of the xylem; it is a function of the phloem. All the other answers are functions of the xylem: *Xylem cells in the roots draw water molecules into the tree... carrying chemical nutrients from the soil; ...the dead xylem cells become part of the central column of heartwood, the supportive structure of the tree; ...Within the xylem cells, water molecules...are pulled upward through the trunk.* (1.2)

EXERCISE 1.6.A (p. 134)

1. D *Some general preparation may be in order...* is paraphrased in *As general preparation.... ...participants may want to take into the conference materials or data that might be useful if a matter comes up* is paraphrased in *...participants can bring materials or data that might be a part of the discussion.*

2. A *This* in the highlighted sentence refers to *Ectotherms heat directly with solar energy*, stated in the previous sentence, and paraphrased in *...a reptile heats with solar energy.... ...a reptile can survive on less than 10 percent of the calories required by a mammal of equivalent size* is paraphrased in *...it requires less than 10 percent of the calories that a mammal of the same size needs.*

3. C *Sometimes the designer disregards the context...* is paraphrased in *...they ignore them. ...the assumption that surrounding structures will later be replaced* is paraphrased in *Architects often believe that nearby structures will not always be there....*

4. B *They* in the highlighted sentence refers to *folkways* in the previous sentence and is paraphrased in *Canada's folkways.... ...provided evidence of the everyday life of the people...* is paraphrased in *...give us a much better description of daily life.... ...far richer than that in most other historical texts* is paraphrased in *...much better...than most histories do.*

5. D *The ruminant periodically returns the cud to its mouth...* is paraphrased in *The cud is sent back to the ruminant's mouth.... ...chewed at length...* is paraphrased in *...chewed extensively.... ...to crush the fibers, making them more accessible to further bacterial action* is paraphrased in *...so that the fibers can be digested more easily.*

6. B *...urbanism...can be considered a trait of all modern societies at a high level of technological development* is paraphrased in *Urbanism characterizes all highly developed societies.... ...not restricted to city dwellers...* is paraphrased in *...not just people who live in cities.*

7. C *...humans drove alligators to near extinction...* is paraphrased in *People almost destroyed the native alligator population.... ...many of their marsh and swamp habitats in North America* is paraphrased in *...many North American environments.*

8. A *...it is still protected from excessive harvesting by hunters...* is paraphrased in *Alligators are still protected.... ...limited hunting is allowed...* is paraphrased in *...hunters are allowed to kill a certain number.... ...to keep the population from growing too large* is paraphrased in *...to control their population.*

9. D *Current archaeological theory holds...* is paraphrased in *Archaeologists believe.... ...the first humans in the Americas were bands of advanced Stone Age people...* is paraphrased in *...groups of Stone Age humans first came to the Americas.... ...crossed over from what is now Siberia in Asia sometime between 12 and 30 thousand years ago* is paraphrased in *...came to the Americas from Asia about 12 to 30 thousand years ago.*

10. C *In South America, where the glaciers from the ice age melted first...* is paraphrased in *The ice age glaciers melted earliest in South America.... ...the migrants took strong root...* is paraphrased in *...the migrants settled.... ...the fertile soil and warm climate of Patagonia* is paraphrased in *...the warm, fertile region of Patagonia.*

EXERCISE 1.6.B (p. 139)

1. D *Whenever these differences lead to exclusion or discrimination...* is paraphrased in *...when these people face discrimination. ...subcultures develop as a shield to protect members from the negative attitudes of others* is paraphrased in *Subcultures form to protect people who differ from the majority....*

2. A A desire to join the dominant culture is not given as a characteristic of subcultures. All the other answers are given: *...differ from the mainstream...; ...own special language and customs; ...a "we" feeling among members....* (1.2)

3. C *These variations are close enough for the subgroup to remain under the societal umbrella...* is paraphrased in *A subculture's values...resemble the majority's values enough to keep the subgroup within the larger society. ...different enough to reflect the unique experience of subgroup members* is paraphrased in *A subculture's values show its separateness....*

4. B *Each hemisphere has four discrete lobes...* is paraphrased in *The brain's two hemispheres each have four separate parts.... ...researchers have identified a number of functional areas within each lobe* is paraphrased in *...each part controls several functions.*

5. C Clues: *Without the corpus callosum to function as a switchboard...; The link between sensory input and spoken response was disconnected.* (1.1)

6. A *Without the corpus callosum to function as a switchboard between the two sides of the brain...* is paraphrased in *...because the corpus callosum did not provide the link. ...the subject's knowledge of the size, texture, and function of the key...* is paraphrased in *Information about the key.... ...could not be transferred from the right to the left hemisphere* is paraphrased in *...could not travel from one side of the brain to the other....*

7. B *The microorganisms secrete enzymes...* is paraphrased in *...microorganisms produce certain enzymes. ...break down the cells of the dead vegetation and animal matter* is paraphrased in *Nonliving plant and animal matter is digested....*

8. D *Cements* means *combines* in this context. Clues: *...the glue that ----- the soil particles into larger, coarser grains.* (1.3)

9. B You can infer that organic compost relies on the digestive processes of microorganisms. Clues: *The microorganisms secrete enzymes that break down the cells...; This partially digested mixture is compost.* (1.4)

10. A *...the terms "compost" and "humus" are often used interchangeably...* is paraphrased in *...people sometimes confuse the two words. ...they are not synonymous* is paraphrased in *Compost and humus are different substances....*

EXERCISE 1.7.A (p. 149)

1. A In the added sentence, *Most of them* refers to *Kindergartners*, the subject of the previous sentence. The added sentence introduces the idea of talking in front of a group, which the next sentence develops with the example of "sharing time."

2. B In the added sentence, *However* is a transition that shows contrast between *appear relatively dry* in the previous sentence and *spongy and wet to the touch* in the added sentence.

3. C In the added sentence, *narrower leaves of trees like willows and mimosa* logically follows *broad leaves of deciduous trees like oaks and maples* in the previous sentence.

4. D In the added sentence, *This* refers to the oboe's rasping, "sawtooth" sound, mentioned in the previous sentence. The added sentence gives the reason for this sound.

5. C In the added sentence, *It* refers to *Carbonizing*, the subject of the previous sentence. Also, *method* in the added sentence restates *technique* in the previous sentence. The added sentence gives additional information about carbonizing.

6. D The added sentence further develops the idea that *no one can find another trade to improve his situation,* mentioned in the previous sentence.

7. C The added sentence discusses the study mentioned in the previous sentence. The added sentence introduces the idea of bright and dark colors, which the next sentence develops with specific examples.

8. A In the added sentence, *This irritation* refers to *an inflammation of the bronchial tubes* in the previous sentence.

9. D The added sentence gives examples of courses included *in the curriculum from a variety of ethnic sources* mentioned in the previous sentence.

10. B The added sentence gives another example of two types of oceanographers, *Both biological and chemical oceanographers*, that logically follows the example of *Both physical oceanographers and ocean engineers* given in the previous sentence.

EXERCISE 1.7.B (p. 152)

1. C *Flourished* means *lived* in this context. Clues: *Their mound construction was especially intensive in this area; ...evidence...; ...five hundred years.* (1.3)

2. A *Likenesses* means *forms* in this context. Clues: *...pipes...are remarkable for their... workmanship... realism in the ----- of animals and birds....* (1.3)

3. C The added sentence introduces the idea that objects found in particular mounds indicate the status and occupation of the deceased. The next sentence develops this idea with a description of the *pipes found in one mound* that probably belonged *to a chief or priest.*

4. B You can infer that a 60–centimeter fish can swim faster than a 30–centimeter fish. Clues: *Generally speaking, the larger the fish the faster it can swim.* (1.4)

5. D *Thrust is used to propel the fish forward...* is paraphrased in *Thrust pushes the fish forward.... ...lateral force tends to make the fish's head deviate from the course in the same direction as the tail* is paraphrased in *...lateral force pushes both its head and its tail to the same side.* (1.6)

6. B The added sentence further describes the undulations mentioned in the previous sentence. The added sentence introduces the idea of the bending of the body, which the next sentence develops with more details.

7. B *Although the wealthier classes used money for major transactions...* is paraphrased in *Rich people used money for important purchases, but.... ...ordinary people continued to barter for most things in their daily lives* is paraphrased in *...common people traded goods and services directly.* (1.6)

8. C *Grasped* means *understood* in this context. Clues: *Paper money had a lot of advantages...; ...the difference between money as a symbol and money as something that was worth only the actual cost of the paper and ink...; Because paper money made trade easier and more efficient, its use quickly caught on throughout the world.* (1.3)

9. D In the added sentence, *However* is a transition that shows contrast between *traders worked out different rates of exchange* in the previous sentence and *this was a long, slow process* in the added sentence. In the added sentence, *this* refers to *rates of exchange* in the previous sentence.

10. A The added sentence introduces the topic of paper money, which the rest of the paragraph develops with facts and details.

QUIZ 7 (p. 157)

1. C *In evolutionary history, the development of language...* is paraphrased in *The emergence of language.... ...set humans apart from the rest of the animal kingdom* is paraphrased in *...distinguished early humans from other animals.* (1.6)

2. D *The expansion of humanity from an oral society to one that also used the written word for communication...* is paraphrased in *...writing was added to speaking as a form of communication. ...a defining point in human civilization* is paraphrased in *An important development in human history....* (1.6)

3. A The added sentence introduces the topic of written language, which the rest of the paragraph develops with facts and details. (1.7)

4. B *It is one of the most important sensations...* is paraphrased in *The ability to sense pain is extremely important.... ...because it is translated into a negative reaction, such as withdrawal from danger* is paraphrased in *...because pain signals the body to respond to a threat.* (1.6)

5. A In the added sentence, *They* refers to *Pain receptors*, the subject of the previous sentence. In the added sentence, *such as* is a transition that introduces examples of *a variety of stimuli*, mentioned in the previous sentence. (1.7)

6. D In the added sentence, *Thus* is a transition that shows result by linking the idea of *decreasing the perception of pain* in the previous sentence with *natural painkillers* in the added sentence. In the added sentence, *they* refers to *peptides*, the subject of the previous sentence. (1.7)

7. B   *Prestige is a valued resource for people at all levels of a society...* is paraphrased in *People at all social levels value prestige... ...this can be seen among inner–city youth...* is paraphrased in *...for example, among urban youth. ...to disrespect or "diss" someone has negative consequences* is paraphrased in *...to disrespect another is punished...* (1.6)

8. D   The added sentence gives the examples of *wisdom, old age, warriors,* and *youth,* which illustrate qualities that are respected in different societies, an idea mentioned in the previous sentence. (1.7)

9. C   *Prestige is linked to income, but there are exceptions...* is paraphrased in *...an exception to the rule that prestige and income are related. ...college professors, who have high prestige but relatively low salaries compared to physicians and lawyers* is paraphrased in *...college professors have high prestige but relatively low incomes....* (1.6)

10. A   The added sentence introduces the topic of occupational status, which the rest of the paragraph develops with facts and examples. (1.7)

Quiz 8 (p. 162)

1. B   *Palisades* means *fences* in this context. Clues: *...fortified villages...; ...easy to defend...; Twenty–foot ----- surrounded a group of longhouses and acted as a defensive wall....* (1.3)

2. D   The author's purpose is to show that villages varied in population. Clues: *A number of families were housed within each longhouse, which varied in size...; ...huge multiple family structures...; In the more populous villages....* (1.5)

3. D   *The longhouse was more than just a shelter...* is paraphrased in *The longhouse not only provided housing.... ...the basic unit upon which the entire society was constructed* is paraphrased in *...formed the foundation of the whole society.* (1.6)

4. C   Clues: *In building the longhouse, a row of forked wooden poles...; Cross poles were lashed to the forked uprights to form an arched roof; Slender poles or rafters were then secured to the roof frame....* (1.1)

5. A   *Secured* means *attached* in this context. Clues: *Cross poles were lashed to the forked uprights...; Slender poles or rafters were then ----- to the roof frame...; Large pieces of bark were then tied to the frame.* The paragraph describes how the parts of the longhouse were attached to each other. (1.3)

6. A   The passage does not state that each longhouse was a separate village. All the other answers are given: *Two families shared the stone–lined hearth... Corn, dried fish, and other foods hung from overhead; A number of families were housed within each longhouse...; ...carved images of clan symbols represented the families living there.* (1.2)

7. C   The added sentence gives examples of trees that were sources of bark, which the previous sentence mentions. (1.7)

8. B   You can infer that the Harlem Renaissance is the name of a literary movement. Clues: *...African American writers...; ...poetry and storytelling...; ...written form....* (1.4)

9. D   *Prolific* means *productive* in this context. Clues: *...literary career...; ...his first book; ...his poetry, plays, screenplays, novels, and short stories;* the prefix *pro–* = forward. (1.3)

10. C   Clues: *...the incorporation of the rhythms of black music into his poetry...; ...a collection of poems on African American themes set to rhythms from jazz and blues.* (1.1)

11. A   The passage does not state that Langston Hughes taught university courses. All the other answers are given: *His first novel...screenplays...novels...; ...founded African American theaters...; ...The Weary Blues, a collection of poems on African American themes set to rhythms from jazz and blues.* (1.2)

12. A   *Sham* means *falsehood* in this context. Clues: *...a wise fool, an honest man who saw through ----- and spoke plainly.* (1.3)

13. D   *Overshadowed* means *dominated* in this context. Clues: *...readers preferred themes that reflected the struggles of the times...;* the prefix *over–* = too much. Readers preferred the writings of a younger generation of poets. The writings of the younger poets became more influential; they dominated the writings of Hughes. (1.3)

14. B   *His poetry and stories remain an enduring legacy of the Harlem Renaissance...* is paraphrased in *...his writings represent the accomplishments of the Harlem Renaissance. ...his position in the American canon is secure* is paraphrased in *Hughes attained prominence in American literature....* (1.6)

15. D   In the added sentence, *this book* refers to *The Weary Blues* in the previous sentence. (1.7)

16. C   The author's purpose is to clarify the distinctions between the two terms. Clues: *...often used interchangeably, but there are actually differences between them. One difference is....* (1.5)

17. D   *Submerged* means *underwater* in this context. Clues: *...every part of it is sometimes underwater; ...extends seaward to the edge of the continental shelf...; ...extends down into deep water;* the prefix *sub–* = under. (1.3)

18. B   The passage does not state that a coast extends to the continental shelf and a shore extends inland to a highland. All the other answers accurately describe coasts and shores: *A shore is the zone at the edge of an ocean, lake, or river...A coast is the land just inland from the shore...; ..."coast" applies only to oceans, but "shore" can apply to other bodies of water as well; A coast is...beyond the usual reach of high water; The shore is the area between the high–water mark and the low–water mark, and thus every part of it is sometimes underwater.* (1.2)

19. C   Clues: *Many coasts are sea bottoms uplifted by earthquakes to become dry land, so they may show some features of shores....* (1.1)

20. A   You can infer that the Oregon coast is relatively straight. Clues: *If the grain is mostly parallel to the coast, as along the Oregon coast, the mouths of few rivers will indent the coastline...; Such coastlines... are likely to be smooth, straight, or gently curving.* (1.4)

21. A   Clues: *The direction of the structural "grain" of the coastal rock affects the shape of the coastline; If the grain is mostly parallel to the coast...called Pacific type...; ...if the grain of the rock is at an angle to the coast...Atlantic type.* (1.1)

22. C *These forces* in the highlighted sentence refers to *tides, waves, and currents* in the previous sentence. *These forces erode rocky shores...* is paraphrased in *Tides, waves, and currents wear away shores....* *...transport sand and debris from place to place, depleting some beaches...* is paraphrased in *...wear away shores in some places.* *...building up others* is paraphrased in *...deposit sand and rock elsewhere along the shore.* (1.6)

23. B *Batter* means *strike* in this context. Clues: *...waves crash against sea cliffs...; Storm waves ----- beaches and...rush beyond them....* (1.3)

24. D Clues: *...coastal processes change as tectonic activity raises, lowers, and disrupts the terrain and the sea bottoms near shores.* (1.1)

25. A The added sentence introduces the idea of the straightness or irregularity of coastlines, which the rest of the paragraph develops with facts and description. (1.7)

EXERCISE 1.8.A (p. 172)

1. A, C, F Key information: *Homer was a master of watercolor...understood and exploited the requirements of watercolor...the recording of immediate experience; ...Homer's watercolors of the Adirondack woods...are demonstrations of masterful completeness; In one particular Adirondack painting...all elements come together with perfect unity.* Answers (B) and (D) are not mentioned; answer (E) is a minor idea.

2. B, E, F Key information: *The debris transported by a glacier is produced either by erosion of the rock beneath the glacier or by erosion on the slopes rising above the surface of the glacier; ...moraine debris remains unsorted both during its transport and after it has been deposited...; Once the glacial ice has retreated, the moraine deposits are left exposed...The various landforms—moraines....* Answer (A) is not mentioned; answers (C) and (D) are minor ideas.

3. B, D, E Key information: *Cultural evolution has occurred in stages...; ...new technology has escalated exponentially, and so has the human impact on the planet; Cultural evolution has enabled us to...shortcut biological evolution. We no longer have to wait to adapt to our environment through natural selection; we simply change the environment to meet our needs.* Answers (A) and (F) are not mentioned; answer (C) is a minor idea.

4. A, B, E Key information: *...the central theme of love serves as the trigger for extraordinary adventures...fantastic journeys to exotic lands...; ...and other elements of tragedy...but everything is resolved in the traditional happy ending of comedy; Love is subjected to abnormal strains, often involving separation, jealousy...separation and reunion of loved ones....* Answer (C) is not mentioned; answers (D) and (F) are minor ideas.

5. A, C, E Key information: *Humans lose water by evaporation from respiratory and body surfaces and must replenish such losses...; With enough water to drink, the human body can withstand extremely high temperatures...the body's internal environment responds to this change by the evaporative cooling method of sweating; Without water to drink, the body will continue to sweat and lose water...water deficit...collapse occurs...death occurs.* Answers (B) and (D) are minor ideas; answer (F) is not mentioned.

EXERCISE 1.8.B (p. 177)

1. D *Mathematicians are motivated by the belief...* is paraphrased in *...what motivates mathematicians. ...they may be able to create a pattern that is entirely new, one that changes forever the way that others think about the mathematical order* is paraphrased in *The idea of establishing a completely new way of understanding mathematics...* (1.6)

2. A Clues: *An extended chain of reasoning may be intuitive...However, even when guided by intuition, they must eventually work out the solution in exact detail if they are to convince others of its validity.* (1.1)

3. C *Insoluble* means *impossible to solve* in this context. Clues: *...finding the solution to a problem that has long been considered -----;* the prefix *in-* = not. (1.3)

4. B, C, E Key information: *At the center of mathematical talent lies the ability to recognize significant problems and then to solve them; ...an exceptional ability to manage long chains of reasoning...develop theories from very simple contexts and then apply them to very complex ones; They must demonstrate the solution without any errors or omissions in definition or in line of reasoning... The mathematician must be rigorous....* Answer (A) is a minor idea; answers (D) and (F) are not mentioned.

5. B The author's purpose is to give an example of a very large case of white–collar crime. Clues: *...there are some very large cases of white–collar crime, such as....* (1.5)

6. C *Line one's pockets* means *take money illegally* in this context. Clues: *White–collar crime...; Government employment...also provides opportunities to -----. For example, building inspectors accept bribes and kickbacks....* (1.3)

7. A *It is likely that there are more criminals in the office suites than in the streets...* is paraphrased in *White–collar criminals may be more numerous than street criminals.* *...yet the nature of white–collar crime makes it difficult to uncover the offenses and pursue the offenders* is paraphrased in *...but are difficult to catch because the crimes often go unnoticed.* (1.6)

8. A, C, F   Key information: *The majority of cases involve low–level employees...Their crimes are usually never discovered because the amounts of money are small...; White–collar crime is not confined to the business sector. Government employment...also provides opportunities...it involves far more money and harm to the public...; ...the nature of white–collar crime makes it difficult to uncover the offenses and pursue the offenders...extremely difficult and expensive to prosecute.* Answers (B) and (E) are minor ideas; answer (D) is not mentioned.

EXERCISE 1.8.C (p. 181)

1. C   The author's purpose is to give examples of groupings that do not represent social behavior. Clues: *...not all aggregations of animals are social; Clusters of moths...or trout gathering...are groupings of animals responding to environmental signals. Social aggregations, on the other hand....* (1.5)

2. B   A group of turtles sunning on a log is not an example of social behavior; it is a grouping of animals responding to an environmental signal. All the other answers illustrate social behavior: *...an individual fighting to defend a territory; Musk oxen that form a passive defensive circle...; ...cooperation in hunting for food....* (1.2)

3. A   *Huddling* means *gathering* in this context. Clues: *...protection from severe weather....* (1.3)

4. B, D, E   Key information: *Social behavior includes any interaction that is a consequence of one animal's response to another of its own species...; ...not all social to the same degree...reproduction...defense... cooperation in hunting for food...huddling for protection...transmitting information...; One obvious benefit of social organization is defense...from predators.* Answer (A) is inaccurate; answers (C) and (F) are minor ideas.

5. A   You can infer that the best coffee would come from a mountainous region close to the equator. Clues: *The perfect climate for coffee production exists between the latitudes of 25 degrees north and 25 degrees south of the equator; The best–tasting coffees are grown at between five and eight thousand feet in elevation....* (1.4)

6. B   *Bearing* means *influence* in this context. Clues: *Nitrogen in soil gives rise to...; ...potassium produces...; ...phosphorus, while having no ----- on coffee in the final cup, helps the tree to develop....* (1.3)

7. D   *Caring for the coffee tree...* is paraphrased in *...the care given to the tree. ...critical to the character of the final product* is paraphrased in *The quality of the finished coffee depends on....* (1.6)

8. A, D, F   Key information: *The perfect climate for coffee production exists between the latitudes of 25 degrees north and 25 degrees south of the equator...The best–tasting coffees are grown at between five and eight thousand feet in elevation...; ...soil chemistry is carefully watched in commercial operations...soil rich in nitrogen, phosphorus, and potassium...the more balanced the soil, the better the coffee; Caring for the coffee tree is critical... seedlings...require careful eplanting... transfer from nursery to plantation is a critical part of the process....* Answers (B) and (E) are minor ideas; answer (C) is not mentioned.

EXERCISE 1.9.A (p. 189)

1. B, E   Enlightenment: *...the Enlightenment... dictated that the discipline of formal structure was beneficial to artistic expression; ...human society could reach perfection through rational thought....*

    A, C, F   Romanticism: *...celebrated emotions and the senses...Romantic philosophy reveled in the beauty and unpredictable power of Nature; Romanticism found inspiration in death as an "other kingdom" and in the supernatural...; Romanticism believed in democracy and the common people, reviving folk traditions...that made heroes of rural characters.* Answers (D) and (G) are not mentioned.

2. A, D, F   Rock floor: *The floor of the river channel lies in the bedrock...; As the stream swings across the valley floor, it deposits material on the insides of the bends in the channel; In a rock-floored valley, the valley slopes are undercut and steepened by the sideways erosion.*

    C, G   Accumulation floor: *An accumulation valley floor is created by the continuous deposition of gravel and sand...; Both the channel floor and the floodplain...are composed entirely of these gravel and sand deposits.* Answers (B) and (E) are not mentioned.

3. B, F, H   Plants: *...construct organic molecules from inorganic chemicals as plants can during photosynthesis; ...plants store their food as starch; ...two types of tissues that plants do not have. The first is nervous tissue...and the other is muscle tissue.*

    A, D, E, I   Animals: *...animals cannot manufacture their own food; Nerves and muscles, which control active behavior, are unique to animals; Animal life began...with the evolution of multi-cellular forms that lived by eating other organisms; Animal cells lack the cell walls....* Answer (C) is not mentioned; answer (G) is inaccurate.

Exercise 1.9.B (p. 192)

1. B, D   Arcade: *The Arcade's pitched glass roof sheltered a large open space surrounded by tiered shops; ...the entire focus of large commercial blocks....*

    C, E, G   Department store: *...an array of goods were organized under a single management; The origins of the department store...in 1829, a new kind of building...featured a four–story rotunda beneath a huge dome...; ...large plate glass display windows...easily lured in the city's wealthy customers.* Answer (A) is inaccurate; answer (F) is not mentioned.

2. D, G   Cross–sectional: *...each subject is tested or interviewed only once; ...groups of subjects at different age levels...Cross–sectional studies...can provide information about possible age differences.*

    A, E, F   Longitudinal: *...a relatively small group of subjects who are all about the same age at the beginning of the study and then look at them repeatedly over a period of time; One advantage of longitudinal studies is that any changes found are real changes, not just age-group differences; Longitudinal studies...allow us to look at consistency or change within the same individual.* Answers (B) and (C) are not mentioned.

3. B   *These two types of questions* in the highlighted sentence refers to *proximate and ultimate causation*, discussed in the passage and stated in the answer choice. *...very independent approaches to behavior* is paraphrased in *...distinct ways of thinking about behavior.* (1.6)

4. B, C, G   Proximate: *The biological sciences that address proximate causes...use the experimental method...; The "how" questions seek to understand the proximate or immediate causes... For example, a biologist might want to explain the singing of a male white-throated sparrow in the spring...; ...the proximate or immediate causes underlying a behavior at a particular time and place.*

    A, E   Ultimate: *These are "why" questions that focus on ultimate causation, the evolutionary origin and purpose of behavior; Researchers compare characteristics...among related species to identify patterns of variation.* Answers (D) and (F) are not mentioned.

Quiz 9 (p. 196)

1. B, E, F   Key information: *...life expectancy, the average number of years a person can expect to live...rose dramatically, from about 47 years in 1900 to about 76 years in 2000; ...several factors increased life expectancy, most notably improvements in public health...Advances in medical practice...; Large numbers of elderly, many with chronic diseases, become a burden on the health care system and on their families.* Answer (A) is inaccurate; answers (C) and (D) are not mentioned. (1.8)

2. C, E, G   Oil paints: *...special manipulative properties of oil colors...smoothly blended tones...; ...the latter remains the standard because the majority of painters find...that in optical quality oil paints surpass all others; ...the principal defect of oil painting is the darkening of the oil over time....*

    B, F   Acrylic paints: *Acrylic paints are thinned with water...; ...a painting can be completed in one session that might have taken days in oil because of the drying time required....* Answers (A) and (D) are not mentioned. (1.9)

3. C, D, F   At the equator: *The large input of heat at and near the equator warms large masses of air; ...near the equator evaporates huge amounts of water from the earth's surface into the troposphere; ...at the equator (zero latitude), where the sun is almost directly overhead....*

    A, E   At the poles: *...at the high-latitude poles, where the sun is lower in the sky and strikes the earth at a low angle; At the poles, the warm air becomes cool and falls to the earth.* Answers (B) and (G) are inaccurate for both the equator and the poles. (1.9)

4. A, B, E   Key information: *One major factor determining the uneven patterns of world climates is the variation in the amount of solar energy striking different parts of the earth; ...carrying heat from the equator toward the poles...the warm air becomes cool...cool air masses then flow back toward the equator...This general air circulation pattern...; Two major factors cause seasonal changes in climate. One is the earth's annual orbit around the sun; the other is the earth's daily rotation around its tilted axis....* Answers (C) and (F) are not mentioned; answer (D) is a minor idea. (1.8)

Quiz 10 (p. 200)

1. A   The paragraph supports the statement that the North American prairie biome covers a large area with varying weather conditions. Clues: *...one of the most extensive grasslands in the world, extending from...in the west to...in the east, and from...in the south to...in the north; Average annual rainfall ranges from...in the west to...in the east; ...temperatures can vary widely from very hot in summer to bitter cold in winter.* (1.4)

2. C   *Tangled* means *dense* in this context. Clues: *...many-branched grass roots; ...a dense mat of roots; Even after the roots die, their ----- mass holds the soil together....* (1.3)

3. D   Clues: *Colonies of prairie dogs, large burrowing rodents, dig extensive underground tunnel systems that aerate the soil and allow water to reach below the surface.* (1.1)

4. B   Clues: *Much of the prairie is now farmland, the most productive agricultural region in the world; Monocultures of wheat, barley, soybeans, corn, and sunflowers occupy the land that was once prairie.* (1.1)

5. C   Clues: *The potholes were formed during the most recent Ice Age...; ...the retreating glaciers created about 25 million depressions...; As the ice blocks melted, much of the water was left behind, forming wetlands....* (1.1)

6. B   The passage does not state that an unbroken prairie now extends from the western mountains to the eastern forest. All of the other answers are given: *...temperatures can vary widely from very hot in summer to bitter cold in winter; The wetlands were soon surrounded by waves of grasses: shortgrass, mixed grass, and tallgrass; An important feature of the northern Great Plains grasslands is the presence of millions of glacial depressions that are now small ponds known as prairie potholes.* (1.2)

7. D   *Today these small wetlands still cover the prairies...* is paraphrased in *...the small ponds remain. ...although much of the landscape, including both native grasses and potholes, has been transformed to cropland and grassland for grazing* is paraphrased in *Even though a large portion of the prairies is used for crops and grazing....* (1.6)

8. A   *Dot* means *cover* in this context. Clues: *Today these small wetlands still cover the prairies...; ...the seasonal wetlands that ----- portions of Minnesota, Iowa....* (1.3)

9. D   The author's purpose is to emphasize the region's value as a breeding ground for ducks. Clues: *...an important breeding area for more than 300 bird species...; Four to six million birds come to breed and feed in the seasonal wetlands...; Prairie pothole country produces half of North America's 35 to 40 million ducks....* (1.5)

10. D   The added sentence introduces the idea that the original communities of plants and animals have been destroyed. The next sentences develops this with *The landscape is now dominated by monocultures, the cultivation of a single variety of plant....* (1.7)

11. A, B, E   Key information: *The prairie soil is rich in nutrients derived mainly from the decomposition of the deep, many-branched grass roots; ...the decaying matter provides nutrients for living plants; Much of the prairie is now farmland...; Monocultures of wheat, barley, soybeans, corn, and sunflowers occupy the land that was once prairie; ...given over to grazing lands for cattle and sheep, virtually all of the major native grasses have been replaced by nonnative species; ...much of the landscape, including both native grasses and potholes, has been transformed to cropland and grassland for grazing; An important feature of the northern Great Plains grasslands is the presence of millions of glacial depressions that are now small ponds known as prairie potholes; ...an important breeding area for more than 300 bird species...; Four to six million birds come to breed and feed in the seasonal wetlands...; The potholes also have an important role in flood control.* Answer (C) is not mentioned; Answers (D) and (F) are minor ideas. (1.8)

12. D   *Truth cannot be separated from experience...* is paraphrased in *...the two are necessarily connected. ...in order to understand truth, we have to study experience itself* is paraphrased in *We must study experience to know the meaning of truth....* (1.6)

13. A   *Sequential* means *continuous* in this context. Clues: *... "stream" of experience...; ...course of events in our lives*; the stem *-sequ-* = follow. (1.3)

14. A   The author's purpose is to describe how thoughts and feelings flow into each other. Clues: *...a stream of thoughts and feelings...; One wave dissolves into another gradually, like the ripples of water in....* (1.5)

15. C   *"Workable"* means *capable of being learned* in this context. Clues: *An incoming thought is ----- only if it is meaningful and can be associated with something already in the person's mind; ...associative learning...new learning involves activating previous learning....* (1.3)

16. B   *Reconstructive* means *creative* in this context. Clues: *...experience and knowledge building on each other*; the stem *-struct-* = build. (1.3)

17. D   Clues: *Dewey believed that experience is an interaction between what a person already knows and the person's present situation.* (1.1)

18. C   Dewey's theory does not include the idea that every experience is educative; in fact, he believed that an experience is miseducative if it distorts the growth of further experience. All the other answers are given: *...experience is an interaction between what a person already knows and the person's present situation; ...together they lead to new knowledge that in turn will influence future experience; Experience is educative only when it contributes to the growth of the individual.* (1.2)

19. D   Clues: *Furthermore, truly progressive education must involve the participation of the learner in directing the learning experience.* (1.1)

20. B   You can infer that William James and John Dewey would probably agree that our life experiences are a very important part of our education. Clues: *In James's theory, thought and experience are connected; James's theory supports later theories of associative learning...; Dewey asserted that experience is central to education...; ...productive experience is both the means and the goal of education.* (1.4)

21. B   The added sentence further develops the idea that incoming thoughts and outgoing thoughts *become associated with each other*, mentioned in the previous sentence. (1.7)

22. C, E   William James: *He believed that human consciousness is a stream of thoughts and feelings...waves of bodily sensations...memories of past experiences...; An incoming thought is "workable" only if it is meaningful and can be associated with something already in the person's mind.*

    A, D, F   John Dewey: *...learning is more than the amassing and retention of information; learning is learning how to think; Dewey felt that education should be problem–centered and interdisciplinary...productive experience is both the means and the goal of education; Dewey viewed life as a continuously reconstructive process, with experience and knowledge building on each other.* Answers (B) and (G) are not mentioned. (1.9)

PART 2 – LISTENING

Exercise 2.1.A (p. 219)

1. C   The woman is confused by her professor's response to her paper. She says: *So I'm really confused. This is the first time I ever got a paper back with no grade on it.*

2. C   The speakers mainly discuss their plans for spring break, a school vacation. The woman says: *I sure am ready for spring break!* The man asks: *Are you doing anything special?*

3. B   The woman is mainly discussing her internship at a children's agency. She says: *I'll be doing an internship...; It's a nonprofit agency that works on children's issues....*

4. A   The man has difficulty remembering some terms. He says: *...if only I could remember the difference between xylem and phloem. I can't seem to get it straight....*

5. D   The woman suggests that he imagine a tree with key letters on it. She says: *I always think of a tree and imagine a "P" at the top, up in the branches, and an "X" at the bottom.... Now just imagine your tree tomorrow during the quiz!*

Exercise 2.1.B (p. 220)

1. B   The speaker mainly discusses services of the Safety and Security Office. She says: *The place to go for... is the Safety and Security Office; Safety and Security also provides....*

2. A   The professor mainly discusses the origins of bread. She says: *...primitive forms of bread. Primitive bread wasn't like the bread we know today...; Leavened breads and cakes...were also a discovery of the ancient Egyptians; News of this new wonder food spread....*

3. C   The professor mainly discusses the high use of water by irrigation. He says: *One of our greatest concerns is the very high use of water by irrigation; The least efficient types of irrigation...field flooding. It takes a lot of water to flood a field.*

4. D   The speaker mainly discusses how sand dunes shift position. She says: *The dunes of Spirit Sands are constantly changing...; Here's how it works; ...the dune sort of walks downwind; It will reverse direction....*

5. A   The speaker mainly discusses research in pain management. He says: *There've been several influential studies in pain management.* He then gives examples of research studies.

Exercise 2.1.C (p. 221)

1. A   The speaker's main point is that attitudes toward aging can affect how long a person lives. She says: *...the key to a longer life might be the way you think about yourself as you get older...; ...people who view aging positively live longer than people who view it negatively.*

2. D   The speaker mainly discusses diversity in the workplace. He says: *...racial, ethnic, gender, or cultural differences; ...increasingly diverse workforce; ...diversity training...; ...differences in perspective.*

3. B   The speaker's main point is that responding to a diverse workforce is an economic decision. He says: *There is a growing economic need to respond to diversity, as organizations must manage and train this increasingly diverse workforce; For most organizations, the decision to provide diversity training is a business rather than a moral decision.*

4. C   The professor mainly discusses characteristics of marshes. She says: *A marsh is a wetland where the soil is regularly or permanently saturated with water; ...marsh vegetation is...; Animal life is...; The water in marshes may become tea-colored or dark brown...; ...the ecological importance of marshes....*

5. A   The professor's main point is that marshes are energy-rich, ecologically important areas. She says: *Marshes are among the richest of all biomes; Much of this energy-rich biomass...; ...we recognize the ecological importance of marshes....*

6. A   The speakers mainly discuss the beans of the cocoa tree. They say: *The primary ingredient of chocolate is cocoa, which comes from the beans of the cacao, or cocoa tree...; The tree's fruit is a pod...with several beans inside...; Could you say more about how the beans are processed; After the beans have fermented enough...; This is when the beans start to acquire the rich flavor we associate with chocolate.*

7. D   The professor mainly discusses steps in processing the beans. The professor says: *...cut open the mature pods and remove the seeds by hand; ...piled on the ground and allowed to dry in the sun for several days; During fermentation, the beans...; ...they're stripped of the remaining pulp; ...the beans are sent to the processing plant to be roasted...; ...the beans start to acquire the rich flavor we associate with chocolate.*

8. B   The professor's main point is that there are important factors in the production of top quality cocoa. The professor says: *Certain key factors govern the production of high quality cocoa. For example...; ...only the mature pods can be harvested because only they will produce top quality ingredients; ...this air-drying is another important step in the process; The roasting process causes a browning reaction...; ...this is the magic moment.*

Exercise 2.2.A (p. 226)

1. A   The woman says: *You should check out the job board in the student center.*

2. B   The man says: *I'd like a quiet job that would allow me to get some reading done.*

3. C   The man says: *...we need extra cashiers...why not volunteer to help us out?* The woman says: *I guess I could spare a few hours; I'll be there around noon.*

4. D   The man says: *The library will give you ten dollars in book credit for every hour you work. You have to use the credit at this sale....*

5. B   The woman says: *I'll be there around noon.*

6. B   The woman says: *Her assignments are challenging but useful. And she has the most interesting stories to illustrate her lectures. She really makes us think; ...I'm starting to figure things out as a result of this class.*

7. D   The man says: *We had to write a lot of papers; ...she really makes you work in her class!*

8. B The professor says: *These are all journal articles that I need to go through for my research. It would really help if they were arranged more logically. Can you help me?*

9. A The professor says: *Most are about primate behavior, but a few deal with other mammals or birds, or with behavioral psychology in general.*

10. B The woman says: *I have some free time tomorrow afternoon. Would that be all right?*

EXERCISE 2.2.B (p. 227)

1. C The man says: *The hunting season began in the fall and continued until midwinter.*
2. C, D The man says: *Moose, deer...were the animals sought.*
3. A The man says: *The women often accompanied their husbands on hunting parties. Their job was to take charge of the camps.*
4. B, D Women controlled clan leadership: *...a woman headed each clan, and these women were respected for their role as keepers of the clan.* Women also controlled agriculture: *...women managed all of the agricultural operations.*
5. B, D Talent is an important factor for a career in the arts: *...there are a number of factors to consider. Whether your goal is to be an actor or an animator, a saxophonist or a sculptor, talent is an essential consideration.* Experience is another important factor: *...you also need training, experience...; ...experience is the best way to get a feel for the field.*
6. B The professor says: *...a career in the arts requires a personal sense of commitment—a calling—because art does have a history of insecure employment.*
7. C The woman asks: *...how do we get started?* The professor replies: *Experience doesn't have to be formal. It can be part–time or volunteer work; The important thing is getting started—spending time doing something in your chosen medium.*
8. B The instructor says: *The first step, of course, is to realize the importance of the speech to you.*
9. A, C The speakers mention the purpose of informing others about your subject: *...decide on your purpose. Do you simply want to inform us about your subject?* The speakers also mention making your audience laugh: *Your purpose could be to make your audience laugh.*
10. B The instructor says: *Why don't you all just take the next few minutes to start brainstorming? Jot down ideas that come to mind....*

EXERCISE 2.2.C (p. 228)

1. C The instructor says: *...it's the pigment that gives the paint its color.*
2. D The instructor says: *A pigment should not exert a harmful chemical reaction upon the medium, or upon other color pigments it is mixed with.*
3. A The instructor says: *Generally, pigments are classified according to their origin, either natural or synthetic.*
4. C The instructor says: *...Tyrian purple, the imperial purple the Romans prepared from a shellfish native to the Mediterranean.*

5. A, D Synthetic pigments are superior because they last for a longer time: *Inorganic synthetic colors...are generally the most permanent for all uses. In contrast, pigments from natural sources are less permanent than the average synthetic color.* They also provide stronger, brighter colors: *Synthetic organic pigments provide colors of unmatched intensity and tinting strength. The synthetic counterparts of the yellow and red earths are more brilliant and...are superior in all other respects to the native products.*
6. D The professor mainly talks about the relationship of gender and toy preferences in young children. She says: *...pick their toys based on gender; ...two of the girls usually went straight to the kitchen area...; One girl usually sat at the table, coloring...; The boys usually spent most of the hour with blocks...; ...the research supports the idea that most boys and girls are naturally drawn to different types of toys....* (2.1)
7. B The professor says: *Research shows that two–year–old boys like to play with dolls and kitchen sets as much as little girls do; ...younger children of both sexes play with both dolls and trucks, with no apparent thought of being a boy or girl.*
8. A The professor says: *...male monkeys spent more time playing with cars and balls....*
9. B The professor says: *...by age five or so, most will tell you those toys are for girls; ...around age five, the boys start moving away from kitchen play, and the girls start ignoring cars and trucks.*
10. D The professor's main point is that boys and girls naturally prefer different types of toys. She says: *I believe—and research supports this—that a child's choice of toys is a natural occurrence, not a sexist plot by society; ...the research supports the idea that most boys and girls are naturally drawn to different types of toys....* (2.1)

EXERCISE 2.2.D (p. 229)

1. A The students are discussing terms from a lecture. They say: *...history lecture...; ...meant by "partible inheritance"...; ...what's "primogeniture"; ...the word "primogeniture."* (2.1)
2. C The woman asks: *...what's "primogeniture"?* The man answers: *That's when all the property goes to the eldest son.*
3. D The professor says: *So, why do so many small businesses fail each year? Well, for one thing, they usually face stiff competition from larger, more established companies. Large companies generally have cash reserves that enable them to absorb losses more easily than small firms can.*
4. D The professor says: *It's absolutely essential to be a competent manager...; Your primary responsibilities center on planning, management, and marketing, so organizational skills are a must.*
5. B, C One responsibility of a store owner is keeping track of inventory: *To run a store, for example, you need to know how to keep track of your inventory....* Another responsibility is promoting the store's products: *To keep your store in business, you have to adapt to changing market conditions. This means improving services or promoting your products in innovative ways.*

6. C   The woman says: *...I saw something happen—on a hike I did last weekend....*

7. D   The woman says: *I was hiking with my friend—on the desert canyon trail—and we ran into these two guys sitting by the side of the trail. ...it turns out that one of them was sort of having trouble.*

8. A, D   The young man received water from the woman: *...we gave them one of our water bottles....* He also received food from his teacher: *We asked if they had water and food, and they said a little, but their teacher went back to get some more; ...the teacher and the ranger were there. The guy was eating saltine crackers.*

9. B   The woman says: *I wondered if his muscle cramps were...because lactic acid ferments when the cell has no oxygen; ...human muscle cells make ATP by lactic acid fermentation when oxygen is scarce; This means lactate collects in the muscle as a waste product, and that causes muscle pain.*

10. A   The teaching assistant says: *Well, Julie, it looks like you saw biology in action!*

Quiz 1 (p. 232)

1. B   The speakers mainly discuss health dangers in the workplace. The instructor says: *The computerized workplace can be hazardous to your health...; Today we'll go over what some of these hazards are....* (2.1)

2. B   The instructor says: *A good way to relieve eyestrain is to look away from the screen frequently. Focus your eyes on objects that are far away....* (2.2)

3. D   The instructor says: *Neck and back pain are a big problem for computer people. Always make sure your screen, keyboard, and chair are at the right height for you.* The man says: *...it's important to have a comfortable chair; I put a cushion on my chair, and that really helps my lower back.* (2.2)

4. C   The instructor says: *Photocopy machines aren't a health hazard for people who use them only occasionally. But for people who use them a lot, there can be bad effects. For example, people who handle the toners can get skin rashes.* (2.2)

5. C   The instructor says: *Another problem—if the machines are in an area that's not well ventilated—is ozone; Almost all photocopiers give off some ozone.* (2.2)

6. B   The professor mainly discusses past and present reasons for traveling. She says: *Many centuries ago, the reasons for travel were...; While the earliest tourists traveled in search of..., later tourists took trips for...; The tourists of today take trips purely for....* (2.1)

7. A   The professor says: *Many centuries ago, the reasons for travel were primarily economic or political; Early hunting–gathering people migrated in search of resources to sustain themselves; ...the search for resources...; While the earliest tourists traveled in search of resources....* (2.2)

8. B, D   Traveling for scientific purposes originated in the past two centuries: *Beginning in the nineteenth century, naturalists like Charles Darwin studied animal and plant species in exotic places. Darwin's travels created interest in traveling for scientific advancement.* Traveling for recreation also originated in the past two centuries: *The tourists of today take trips purely for pleasure, recreation....* (2.2)

9. D   The professor says: *Ethnic tourism helps preserve aboriginal cultures that might otherwise be endangered....* (2.2)

10. C   The main point made in the lecture is that the reasons for traveling have changed over the centuries. The professor says: *Many centuries ago, the reasons for travel were primarily economic or political; While the earliest tourists traveled in search of resources, later tourists took trips for cultural, educational, and scientific purposes; The tourists of today take trips purely for pleasure, recreation, adventure, and...personal growth.* (2.1)

Exercise 2.3.A (p. 237)

1. B   The student must leave school for a family emergency. He says: *...I have a problem. My father had to have surgery, and I have to go to Oklahoma. I don't know how long I'll be gone.*

2. A   The professor says: *...you can take a grade of Incomplete. It means you would have six weeks to make up the term paper and the final exam.* (2.2)

3. D   The man would like a different meal arrangement. He says: *I'd like to change my meal plan.*

4. C   The woman's purpose is to emphasize the importance of breakfast because the man says he doesn't have time to eat breakfast in the cafeteria.

5. B   The woman's purpose is to give the man another choice of meal plan in case he would like a plan that would give him lunch and dinner.

6. A   The student wants to take a quiz that she missed. She says: *I was wondering—could I make up the quiz?*

7. C   The professor suggests that the student write about what she learned. The professor says: *...give me a one–page report, summarizing the most important thing you got out of the chapter.* (2.2)

8. C   The speakers are mainly discussing a guest speaker. They say: *...he'd be happy to visit our class; ...assignment to invite a guest speaker....* (2.1)

9. A   The man's purpose is to emphasize the professor's qualifications as a guest speaker in their seminar.

10. B   The man's opinion is that the assignment will help them meet people in their field. He says: *Look at all the professional contacts we're making!*

Exercise 2.3.B (p. 238)

1. A   The professor is giving a writing assignment. The professor says: *...it would be a good idea if this week's journal theme were along the same lines. What I'd like you to do is think and write about a time....*

2. D   The woman finds the assignment boring. She says: *But isn't this the same topic as last week? I mean, I feel I've already written a lot about it. I had to do something like this in two of my other classes too. Can't we write about something else for a change?; I mean, I'm getting tired of writing about my life.*

3. A   The main purpose of the talk is to contrast Native American and European concepts of resources. The professor says: *...the Native Americans—compared to the European colonists—had a far greater knowledge of what resources in the environment could be eaten or made useful; For the European colonists, on the other hand, resources in the environment were seen more as commodities, as goods that could be exchanged in markets.*

4. C   The professor says: *Native Americans used a wide range of resources for economic subsistence....* (2.2)

5. D   The professor's purpose is to define the Native American concept of wealth, in response to the student's question.

6. A   The professor's purpose is to illustrate the colonists' view of commodities by giving examples of things that could be sold for a profit.

7. D   The purpose of the talk is to define what culture is. The professor says: *What would human life be without culture; ...these aspects of our cultures...; ...what anthropologists call student culture; In a way a culture is like a club...; Culture isn't a thing. It's an idea.*

8. A   The professor's purpose is to illustrate how culture involves shared ideas and behaviors. The professor says: *If you could take all the ideas and behaviors, all the tools and technology, all the things that college students share...you'd have what anthropologists call student culture.*

9. C   The woman thinks student culture is similar to a club. She says: *So, what you're saying is culture is sort of like a club. College students are a club; This is why—that's what we have in common with other students—it's why our culture makes us feel like part of a club, right?*

10. B   The professor thinks that the comparison is imperfect. The professor says: *In a way a culture is like a club...; But the comparison doesn't completely cut it. Think about it. A club has borders that we can define—but we run into trouble if we try to draw borders around a culture.*

EXERCISE 2.3.C (p. 239)

1. D   The main purpose of the talk is to discuss ways of dealing with stress. The professor says: *... managers have to deal with stress. Some handle it by...; Most have some favorite place or pastime...;. It's important to have some form of rest and relaxation....*

2. B   The professor's opinion is that activity and exercise are forms of rest. She says: *It's important to have some form of rest and relaxation—creating art, working with your hands, gardening, playing sports—the list goes on. Rest doesn't always mean inactivity. For some people, exercise is rest.*

3. B   The purpose of the lecture is to describe how psychologists diagnose problems. The professor says: *...the clinical psychologist has to know what causes the client to behave the way he or she does; Identifying the cause is called diagnosis; In diagnosis a psychologist uses two basic tools....*

4. B, C   The professor says: *In diagnosis a psychologist uses two basic tools: interviews and psychological tests.* (2.2)

5. A   The professor's purpose is to show that a client's past behavior assists in diagnosis. The professor says: *In a diagnostic interview, the psychologist takes the client's case history. This means learning how the client got along with parents, teachers, and friends, as well as how the person handled difficult situations in the past.*

6. D   The professor says: *Personality tests can reveal unconscious feelings the person is unable to talk about.* (2.2)

7. C   The main purpose of the talk is to give advice about contact with bats. The speaker says: *...if you encounter a bat like that, you should...; If you have bats in your attic or house, contact...; If you should come in physical contact with a bat, it's important to....*

8. C   The speaker's purpose is to give an example of how bats benefit us. She says: *Bats are a normal part of our environment and can even be a good thing.*

9. A   The speaker says: *To avoid having bats in your house altogether, find all possible entry points into the house and close them by caulking or screening the gap.* (2.2)

10. D   The speaker recommends getting medical attention because the bat might be carrying a fatal disease. She says: *Bats are the most likely carriers of rabies in our area, and almost one hundred percent of rabies cases are fatal; If possible, catch the bat so it can be tested for rabies.*

EXERCISE 2.3.D (p. 240)

1. B   The professor says: *...a mechanism that releases tension. For most people, a good laugh is welcome—and worth looking for—because it brings pleasure and relief.* (2.2)

2. A   The professor's purpose is to give examples of stress that is carefully controlled. He says: *This causes the child to experience mild stress, but in a secure setting because the stress is carefully controlled by the parent.*

3. D   The professor says: *This element of shock in an otherwise safe situation is a universal characteristic of situations where people laugh.* (2.2)

4. C   The professor's purpose is to show that humor is a safe way to bring about social change. He says: *Social rules and conventions provide us with a range of situations that we can turn into humor; Humor gives us the power to think about changing the rules. Therefore, comedians...are agents of social change.*

5. B   The professor's purpose is to emphasize the importance of humor in managing anxiety. If we had no sense of humor, it would be more difficult to deal with the anxiety of failure, fear, pain, and death.

EXERCISE 2.3.E (p. 241)

1. C   The main purpose of the talk is to explain how erosion shaped certain landforms. The professor says: *All of these spectacular forms are the result of the erosion of rocks of differing hardness; On a mesa, conditions are optimal for erosion; Further erosion can change a butte into a tower or spire; Further erosion of the softer rock may reduce the spire to some interesting and really weird forms.*

2. D   The professor's purpose is to preview what students will see on a field trip. Just before that the professor said: *On our next field trip, we'll see several of the formations called mesas. The students will also see a variety of other formations....*

3. A, D   One reason for the erosion of a mesa is that the rock on the sides is softer than that on the top: *The sides of a mesa are often made of shale or softer sandstone.* Another reason is that the force of water cuts away the softer rock: *The slope of the sides will increase the water's speed and force as it runs down; Debris carried by the running water cuts away the softer surface rock.* (2.2)

4. B   The professor's purpose is to describe the appearance of spires by comparing them to chimneys.

5. B   The professor's purpose is to show that erosion continually changes the shape of rock. She explains how erosion reduces spires to other forms and eventually to pebbles.

QUIZ 2 (p. 246)

1. B   The student is concerned about material that will be on a test. He says: *There's a lot we have to remember for the test on Monday; ...I have a hard time keeping them all straight; I think I'll go downtown and look at both of those buildings before the test.* (2.3)

2. D   The speakers mainly discuss differences between two architectural styles, Art Deco and Art Moderne. They say: *They're not the same...; ...Art Deco appeared a little earlier...; ...Art Deco has more decoration than Art Moderne; ...Art Moderne is simpler than Art Deco; Moderne is more streamlined than Deco.* (2.1)

3. A, C   Geometric designs are characteristics of Art Deco: *Art Deco has facades with geometric designs...; ... a geometric pattern in the tile on the floor....* Sleek lines and slender forms are also characteristics: *Deco buildings have straight lines and slender forms. "Sleekness" is the word.* (2.2)

4. B   The professor says: *Both styles are what we call modernistic, but Art Moderne is simpler than Art Deco; Moderne is more streamlined than Deco.* (2.2)

5. A   The professor is confirming that the building's style is Art Deco. She says: *...you know what style it is*, to which the student responds, *It's Art Deco!* (2.3)

6. A   The main purpose of the talk is to describe some of the functions of banks. The professor says: *Banks manage money...; Banks provide a number of important services...; ...banks also lend money; Banks provide these services...; ...their main function is to....* (2.3)

7. C, D   Individuals take out bank loans to pay for education: *Ordinary people take out bank loans for a number of reasons—to pay for college...* They also take out loans to purchase a home: *...to buy or remodel a home....* (2.2)

8. C   The professor says: *For a bank to make a profit, it has to collect more interest than it pays out.* (2.2)

9. D   The professor's purpose is to explain how bank failures have occurred. In the past, banks failed because they did not have enough available money to give to people who wanted to withdraw all of their money. The money was not available because the banks had lent it out or invested it. (2.3)

10. B   The professor says: *Bank failures...were especially common during the Great Depression of the 1930s. When Franklin Roosevelt became president in 1933, one of the first things he did was close all the banks, so depositors wouldn't panic and try to take all their money out.* (2.2)

QUIZ 3 (p. 248)

1. B   The professor mainly discusses the formation of coal. She says: *Coal has formed only since land plants evolved on Earth. Large amounts were formed in the Carboniferous period...; Coal started to form when huge quantities of vegetable matter collected and decomposed in swamps.* (2.1)

2. C   The professor says: *Coal is a substance of plant origin; Coal has formed only since land plants evolved on Earth; ...there were a lot of plants on Earth, and these plants contained carbon that later hardened into coal.* (2.2)

3. A, C, D   One step in coal formation is when plant matter collects and decays under water: *Coal started to form when huge quantities of vegetable matter collected and decomposed in swamps.* Another step is when sediments accumulate upon beds of peat: *...layers of sand, rock, and other mineral sediments accumulated on top of the peat beds.* Another step is when peat undergoes pressure and heat: *...the pressure and heat of the sediment forced out much of the volatile matter in the peat.* (2.2)

4. D   The professor's purpose is to give an example of where coal is forming today. Coal forms where plant debris collects, sinks, and experiences pressure and heat. This is what is happening in the Mississippi Delta today. (2.3)

5. A   The professor's purpose is to argue that coal is linked to air pollution and global warming. The professor says that the use of coal is *our number one environmental concern* because it sends soot and smoke into the air and releases greenhouse gases that contribute to global warming. (2.3)

6. C   The main idea is that television promotes a culture of consumerism. The professor says: *The American television industry is controlled by people who are more interested in the culture of consumerism...; Television promotes consumerism.* (2.1)

7. D   The professor says: *Researchers study television to understand its effects on viewers and to measure its effectiveness in selling products.* (2.2)

8. B   The professor says: *The television industry depends on advertising money to survive, and this relationship influences what television offers viewers; This means advertisers have a lot of control over what programs are made and when they are shown.* (2.2)

9. A   The professor's purpose is to argue that television images of life lack depth and meaning. The professor suggests that television's images of affluence have less meaning than personal relationships have. (2.3)

10. B   The professor's opinion is that television has had a mostly negative effect on society. He says: *...I tend to agree with critics of the media; Television promotes consumerism; It encourages greed and envy. Television helps create a wasteful society....* (2.3)

EXERCISE 2.4.A (p. 254)

1. D   The student wants to obtain advice about dropping a class. He says: *...I'm having a hard time keeping up in geometry. I think I'd better get out of the class and try again next quarter.* (2.3)

2. C   The adviser says: *...why not drop your history class?* The student says: *Oh, all right. If I drop history, maybe then I'll be able to catch up in geometry.* You can predict that the student will not continue in his history class.

3. B   The man has an unpaid charge on his account. He says: *I ran into a problem when I tried to register by telephone. I got a message that said I had an outstanding charge on my account that needed to be paid....* (2.1)

4. C   The woman says: *You'd better go to the accounting office and try to clear it up.* The man says: *Yeah, and I'd better make sure my roommate pays for the damage.* You can predict that the man will speak to someone in the accounting office.

5. B   The student will miss the beginning of the summer term. She says: *I registered for your psychology course for summer session. But I have to go to Vancouver and won't be back until June 25.* (2.3)

6. A   The professor implies that it is not acceptable to miss class time. He says: *...we'll cover the important basics during the first week; Summer session is only six weeks, and you can't afford to get a late start.*

7. A   The student says: *That's OK. I understand. Will you teach this course again in the fall?* You can predict that the student will take the course during the fall.

8. B   The students are mainly discussing off–campus apartments for students. The woman says: *I live off campus now, in Forest Glen.* The man says: *Oh, those are the apartments in Glenwood....* (2.1)

9. C   The man says: *But how did you manage to get in Forest Glen? I thought it was just for married students.* The woman says: *Three of the buildings are for married people only, but anyone can live in the rest.* You can infer that the woman is not married.

10. D   The man says: *Maybe I'll look into that.* You can predict that he will find out more about the apartments.

EXERCISE 2.4.B (p. 255)

1. A   The instructor implies that composition in painting is similar to composition in writing. He says: *The elements of composition—line, shape, tone, and color—need to be well arranged, need to be ordered. They need to be coherent...just like the words and phrases and sentences in a piece of writing.*

2. C   The instructor says: *The artist's message is strongest when it's clear. A composition is better if it says one thing strongly than if it tries to say too many things.* You can infer that the professor would agree that a successful composition conveys a single message.

3. D   The main purpose of the talk is to introduce students to the course. The professor says: *Over the next fifteen weeks, we will be observing the science of biology; This course has something for all of you to discover.* (2.3)

4. A, C   Biology studies complex living systems: *In many ways, biology is the most demanding of all sciences. This is partly because living systems are so complex.* Biology also requires knowledge of other sciences: *It requires knowledge of chemistry, physics, and mathematics.* (2.2)

5. D   The professor implies that scientists are enthusiastic in their study of nature. She says: *Scientists are people who ask questions about nature and who believe that these questions can be answered. Scientists are explorers who are passionate about discovery.*

6. C   The professor says: *If you're a biology major or a pre–medical student...; If you're a physical science or engineering major...; And if you're a non–science major....* You can infer that the students in this course are pursuing various fields of study.

7. C   The professor says: *A hormone is a chemical signal. ...it triggers responses in cells and tissues.* (2.2)

8. B   The professor says: *The growth of a plant toward light is called phototropism; Later experiments by other scientists studying phototropism led to the discovery of chemical messengers that stimulated growth in the stem. These chemical messengers were hormones.* You can infer that phototropism relies on hormones produced by the plant.

9. B, C   You can infer that a seedling with the tip cut off would not bend toward light: *The Darwins observed that a grass seedling could bend toward light only if the tip of the shoot was present. If the tip was removed, the shoot would not curve toward light.* You can also infer that a seedling wearing a black cap would not bend toward light: *The seedling would also fail to grow toward light if the tip was covered with an opaque cap.*

10. D   The professor says: *The Darwins proposed the hypothesis that some signal was transmitted downward from the tip into the part of the stem that controlled growth; These chemical messengers were hormones.* You can infer that the tip of a plant's stem produces a hormone that affects the stem's growth.

EXERCISE 2.4.C (p. 256)

1. C   The man cannot think of a topic for his paper. He says: *I'm having trouble coming up with a good idea.* (2.1)

2. A   The woman says: *What about the culture of...your hometown?* The man says: *I grew up in a small town where almost everyone works in the orchards; Well, why not? It's something I know a lot about.* You can predict that the man will describe his hometown culture.

3. C   There was a death in the student's family. The student says: *My great aunt passed away and her funeral is tomorrow.* (2.3)

4. A   The student asks: *...would it be possible for me to take the test next week?* The professor says: *Of course. Eric handles all make–ups; Can you stop by the office today and make an appointment with him?* You can predict that the student will arrange to take the test next week.

5. C   The books that the man needs are a strain on his finances. The man says: *I can't believe how much my books cost this semester; It's a little more than my budget can handle at the moment.* (2.1)

6. D   The man says: *And I still need the book for chemistry; I wonder if they'd have my chemistry book.* You can infer that he is taking a chemistry course.

7. A   The woman says: *...did you know there's another bookstore...? They carry used copies of most of the textbooks for the university.* The man says: *That's not a bad idea. Where did you say that was again?* You can predict that the man will look for a cheaper copy of the chemistry book.

8. A   The man implies that the medication may be dangerous if taken incorrectly. He says: *Now, this is a powerful drug, so you need only—no more than two capsules every six hours. And you shouldn't drink alcohol, drive a car, or operate machinery.*

9. B   The woman says she has a big test the next day. She says: *...if this is going to make me drowsy...* to express concern about feeling drowsy (sleepy) during the test. You can infer that she is concerned about taking the drug before her test.

10. D   The man says: *...you could take two capsules three or four hours before your test.* The woman says: *Okay. Well, I guess I have no choice.* You can predict that the woman will take the medicine a few hours before the test.

EXERCISE 2.4.D (p. 258)

1. B, C   The speaker discusses a change in the design of human settlements: *As human settlements evolved from simple groups of huts to larger villages, and then to towns and cities, their basic pattern changed.* He also discusses the significance of trees in urban spaces: *The rest is covered by trees and grass—foresters call it the urban forest...; The extent of this forest is sort of amazing—two-thirds of our urban space.* (2.1)

2. A   The speaker says: *The early rural villages grew naturally—sort of organically...; ...buildings were clustered near water sources...; Our city planners and architects have converted the organic pattern of the village into a geometrically perfect grid.* (2.2)

3. D   The speaker says: *...foresters call it the urban forest—meaning all the trees in city parks, the trees planted along streets and highways, and the trees in people's yards.* (2.2)

4. A   The speaker's purpose is to give an example of an urban park project. He says: *...one of North America's first public parks—that was sort of created as a unified project—was Central Park in New York City.* (2.3)

5. D   The speaker implies that New York's Central Park contributes to the quality of life in the city. He says: *...an oasis in the middle of steel and stone. Central Park has been called "the city's lung" because of its purifying effect on the air, not to mention its effect on the human psyche.*

6. B   The speaker's opinion is that the city is a symbol of human achievement. He says: *...the city is our most spectacular creation...; ...the finest evidence of our civilization is the city. The city is a symbol of experimentation and creation....* (2.3)

EXERCISE 2.4.E (p. 259)

1. B   The professor says: *Various species of Pacific salmon make a round trip from the small streams where they hatch, to the sea, and then back to the stream of their origin, where they spawn and die; Pacific salmon hatch...; As fry...; When mature....* (2.1)

2. A   The professor means that reproduction is the goal of the salmon's run. The salmon's run ends with *the beginning of the next generation,* when young salmon hatch.

3. B, D   Salmon find their way home by seeing the sun's position: *...they navigate by the position of the sun.* They also smell the water: *...their keen sense of smell takes over; The water flowing from each stream carries a unique scent.* (2.2)

4. C   The sight of leaping salmon amazed the student. She was surprised to see a fish jump up a waterfall, and then she was amazed to see several others also jump. (2.3)

5. D   The professor says: *Salmon provide an important link in the food web; When they make their return journey, they carry nutrients from the ocean back to the rivers and streams.* (2.2)

6. A   You can conclude that baby salmon eat the bodies of dead salmon. After salmon spawn, they die. Their dead bodies, or *carcasses,* become the food source for many organisms, including newly hatched baby salmon.

QUIZ 4 (p. 262)

1. D   The speakers mainly discuss an opportunity for the man to work at a television station. The man says: *There's an opening at channel 12 that kind of interests me—an internship. I was kind of thinking of applying for it.* The woman asks: *You mean the television station? What sort of job?* (2.1)

2. B, D   The man would like television work in the future: *Some day I'd like to write, or produce.* Also, the man will gain production experience: *It's a part–time internship for production assistant. Production work, general stuff...; It's the experience—the chance to work in television....* (2.2)

3. C   The man implies that he is not confident he will get the internship. He says: *I probably don't stand much of a chance...* to express doubt about the likelihood of getting the internship when other, more qualified people will probably also apply. (2.4)

4. A   The woman's purpose is to reassure the man about his chance of getting the position. The woman says: *You never know. Sometimes it's not the credentials but the person who matters.* (2.3)

5. D   The woman asks: *You want a recommendation?* The man says: *Uh, yeah, like I said, I need all the help I can get.* You can infer that the man wants the woman to write a letter of recommendation. (2.4)

6. A   The speakers mainly discuss hiking safely in bear habitat. The speakers are a naturalist and members of a hiking club. The naturalist says: *One or two bear attacks occur each year in Glacier Park; In bear country, noise is good for you. Hiking quietly endangers you, the bear, and other hikers; Some trail conditions make it hard for bears to see, hear, or smell approaching hikers.* (2.1)

7. A   The naturalist thinks bear bells are not effective in keeping away bears. The naturalist says: *Most bells—even the so-called bear bells—are not loud enough. Calling out or clapping hands at regular intervals are better ways to make your presence known.* (2.3)

8. C   The naturalist's purpose is to warn that bears many not notice you in certain conditions in which they cannot see, hear, or smell you approaching. (2.3)

9. A   The naturalist says: *They may appear to tolerate you, and then attack without warning.* You can infer that bears may respond to people suddenly. (2.4)

10. B, D   Hikers should avoid approaching a bear: *The most important advice I can give you is never to approach a bear intentionally.* Hikers should also avoid hiking when it is dark: *...avoid hiking early in the morning, late in the day, or after dark, when bears are more likely to be active.* (2.2)

Quiz 5 (p. 264)

1. C   The professor mainly discusses how leadership and power are related. She says: *...leaders always have some degree of power; Both leadership and power involve the ability to...; Although leadership and power are different things, they're related in important ways.* (2.1)

2. A   The professor's purpose is to show that having power does not imply leadership. She says: *The headwaiter has power to some degree—for example, the power to seat you at the best table by the window—but he doesn't necessarily have the qualities we associate with leadership.* (2.3)

3. B   The professor's purpose is to distinguish between leaders and power holders. A military dictator and a robber have power, but they may lack leadership skills. (2.3)

4. D   The professor says: *Both leadership and power involve the ability to...bring about the results you want....* (2.2)

5. A   The professor implies that successful managers know how and when to use their power. She says: *Remember, both leadership and power... successful managers understand how the two work together....* (2.4)

6. A, C   The speakers mainly discuss forestry as a profession: *...professional forester; ...our professional organization...; ...over 700 job categories.* They also discuss where foresters work: *Foresters...do work in the woods...they also work in laboratories, classrooms, planning agencies, corporate offices....* (2.1)

7. A   The forester says: *Managing a forest is both a science and an art, which is why my education included courses in the biological, physical, and social sciences, as well as the humanities.* You can infer that the profession of forestry is a broad field requiring diverse skills. (2.4)

8. B   The student wants to understand how national parks and forests are different. He knows of similarities between them, but is confused about the differences. (2.3)

9. D   The forester says: *National parks...are set aside and preserved in a near-natural state...; National forests, on the other hand....are managed for their many benefits, including...wood products....* You can infer that national parks do not supply commercial wood products. (2.4)

10. C   The forester's purpose is to show that foresters and biologists have shared interests and often work together to preserve forest habitats. (2.3)

Exercise 2.5.A (p. 269)

1. D   The man says that some scholarship applications require an essay. The woman responds with *Oh, great...my favorite thing*, but her tone of voice conveys the opposite. You can infer that she does not enjoy writing essays.

2. A   The woman is asking for clarification. The man says: *You don't even have to write a different essay for each application.* However, earlier he said: *Each scholarship has its own requirements.* The woman wants him to clarify the essay requirement.

3. B   The man says: *If an essay isn't required, write one anyway and attach it to your application.* You can infer that he thinks an essay will strengthen her application.

4. C   The student is concerned about his grade for the course. He says: *It's about my midterm grade. I...I'm surprised it's so low.* (2.3)

5. A   The professor implies that the student does not have to drive his brother all the time. The student says that he is helping his brother find a place to live. His brother does not have a car, so he must drive him everywhere. The professor mentions the bus system to suggest an alternative solution.

6. B   The student's purpose is to convince the professor that he will complete the work. He asks if he may make up some assignments, and the professor agrees, but he needs to do the work as soon as possible.

Exercise 2.5.B (p. 270)

1. B   The student's purpose is to suggest that the professor said something incorrect. The professor mistakenly named one of the flower parts. The professor says: *Oh, sorry, I believe I misspoke. Thank you for noticing.*

2. D   The professor's purpose is to shift attention to her next point. *All right now, moving on* means that she is moving on to the next thing she wants to say.

3. D   The student asks for clarification of a point, and the professor gives further explanation. The professor asks: *Does that help?* Then she states that it *will make more sense in the lab this afternoon.* You can infer that the students will learn more in the lab.

4. A   The professor's purpose is to illustrate a point with a personal story. He makes the point that clothing styles are an example of cultural norms, which he then illustrates with a personal story about the clothing styles where he once worked.

5. C   The woman finds the man's example amusing. The man mentions the company colors at his mother's workplace: *They also have company colors that everyone wears...my mother has a lot of blue and gold outfits.* The woman expresses amusement by saying *You're kidding!*

6. B   The professor draws a conclusion about what the student said. The student describes the *laid-back* (relaxed) culture where her brother works. The professor concludes that her example is *an informal workplace culture where there are no fixed traditions to follow.*

EXERCISE 2.6.A (p. 274)

1. C   The talk is mainly a classification of insurance. The speaker says: *Each kind of insurance...; Life insurance...; Health insurance...; Another kind, property–liability insurance....*

2. C   The speaker mainly discusses educational programs for engineers. He says: *...typical four–year engineering program...; ...general engineering curriculum...; ...five–year master's degree programs....* (2.1)

3. D   The speaker mainly gives examples of undergraduate and graduate programs. He says: *...typical four–year engineering program...; ...programs, for example, where a student spends three years in a liberal arts college...; ...five–year master's degree programs...; ...five– or six–year cooperative programs....*

4. B   The instructor mainly discusses causes and effects of RSI. She says: *RSI is brought on by...; RSI affects different people differently.*

5. D   The instructor describes symptoms of RSI. She says: *...an inflammation of the sheathing around the tendons in the hand...; ...makes your fingers painful and hard to straighten; The swelling causes a numbness or tingling sensation in the hand, and pain shoots up from the wrist....*

6. B   The professor mainly discusses avalanche control on a mountain highway. He says: *...the highway now has a sophisticated defense system; ...it's important to control an avalanche...so a slide is set off while it's still small...; When the time is right, they close the road...; Slides are set off, one by one.* (2.1)

7. A   The lecture is mainly a summary of a procedure. The professor says: *A team of snow technicians monitors the snowpack; ...try to predict when it's likely to slide; ...they close the road and remove all traffic from the pass; Then the army comes in. A ten–man artillery crew...firing shells into the slopes. This sends out shock waves that trigger the avalanches. Slides are set off, one by one. The technicians direct the action...; Then they have to check and see if the avalanche has released well enough.*

8. A, C   Technicians determine when the snow is ready to slide: *A team of snow technicians monitors the snowpack. They sort of "read" the snow and try to predict when it's likely to slide.* A large gun fires shells into the snow slopes: *A ten–man artillery crew operates a mobile 105 mm howitzer, firing shells into the slopes; ... telling the troops where to aim the gun.* (2.2)

EXERCISE 2.6.B (p. 275)

1. C   The talk is mainly a set of instructions for drawing. The speaker says: *...start off with a light pencil sketch; Take a few minutes to study your subject...; Once you are ready to begin drawing, define the shape of the chair with clean straight lines. Then add contrast by drawing the outline...; When you have drawn the outlines of both objects, add in the finer details....*

2. D   The speaker classifies drums by shape. She says: *Drums can be divided according to shape. Some of the types are...; A lot of long drums are cylindrical—they have the same diameter from top to bottom...; ...a pot or vessel body; The frame is shallow....*

3. A   The professor mainly discusses the process of making a film. He says: *The part of filmmaking...the production phase...; ...plan the film; ...develop a script for the film; Then comes the production, when the filming takes place; After the filming...; ...the post-production phase...editing the film.* (2.1)

4. C   The professor mainly describes the major steps in filmmaking. He says: *...plan the film; ...develop a script...; ...the storyboard, an important step in the planning; ...the filming takes place; ...editing the film; ...the sound and special effects are added....*

5. D   The instructor mainly describes each leaf arrangement and gives an example. She says: *...the one called alternate, each leaf is attached at a different level on the stem. This poppy is a good example; Another type is the opposite arrangement; The bee plant's leaves are paired on opposite sides of the stem; This one's called basal, and our example is the amaryllis.*

6. ✓   Opposite: The plant's leaves are paired on the opposite sides of the stem: *The bee plant's leaves are paired on opposite sides of the stem.*
    ✓   Basal: All of the plant's leaves are at ground level: *Notice how all the leaves are at ground level, at the stem's base.*
    ✓   Alternate: Each leaf is attached at a different level on the stem: *...the one called alternate, each leaf is attached at a different level on the stem.*
    ✓   Opposite: The leaves are attached at the same level on the stem, but on different sides: *...they're attached at the same level of the stem, but on opposite sides.*

7. B   The instructor says: *I have some lovely samples to share with you today. I'd like you all to come up and examine the contents of...these two tables. Many of them are specimens of the sunflower family....* You can predict that the students will look at flower samples. (2.4)

Quiz 6 (p. 277)

1. **B, C** The speakers discuss a missing article of clothing: *I left my jacket in the cafeteria...; If anyone turned in your jacket, they would probably have it there. You can also report it missing.* They also discuss the menu in the cafeteria: *Are you the person who decides what's on the menu in the cafeteria; We try to serve what people want; We have a vegetarian pizza on the menu; I know it's on the menu...; ...I'd still like to see more healthy options.* (2.1)

2. **B** The man's purpose is to lead into a complaint about the cafeteria food. Much of the conversation consists of the man complaining about the cafeteria menu and expressing a desire for more healthy food choices. (2.5)

3. **A** The man's opinion is that there is too much fried food and not enough nutritious options. He says: *There's a lot of fried food and some pretty unhealthy things...; ...I'd still like to see more healthy options; How about adding more fresh vegetables....* (2.3)

4. **D** The woman says: *We can fix that. I'll talk to the chef; ...we can do a better job with what we have— more fresh vegetables, for instance; ...I'm sure we can get fresh produce during most of the year; ...I'll check into the pizza situation.* (2.2)

5. **C** The woman implies that her actions are limited by the amount of money she has to spend. She mentions *the budget* to inform the man that she has a specific amount of money to spend, which restricts what she is able to do. (2.4)

6. **C** The speaker mainly discusses how epidemiologists gather data. She says: *We gather data in a variety of ways. One way is through what we call descriptive epidemiology...; A second approach is observational epidemiology...; A third approach is experimental epidemiology....* (2.1)

7. **B** The speaker explains different research methods. She says: *We gather data in a variety of ways. One way is through what we call descriptive epidemiology, or looking at the trends of diseases over time...; A second approach is observational epidemiology, where we observe what people do; A third approach is experimental epidemiology, sometimes called an intervention study.* (2.6)

8. **A** The speaker says: *We take a group of people who have a disease and a group of people who don't have a disease; We also take a group of people who've been exposed to something...and a group of people who haven't, and then observe them over time to see whether they develop a disease or not.* (2.2)

9. **D** The speaker says: *...experimental epidemiology, sometimes called an intervention study; Experimental research is the only type of research that directly attempts to influence a particular variable...as a way to test a hypothesis about cause and effect.* (2.2)

10. **A** The speaker's purpose is to show how one organization uses various approaches to epidemiology. She says: *From these different approaches—descriptive, observational, and experimental—we can judge whether a particular factor causes or prevents the disease that we're looking at.* (2.3)

Quiz 7 (p. 279)

1. **A** The student is concerned about the assigned group project. She says: *...I have a question about the group project; I wanted to ask you if it has to be with a group; ...actually, I don't feel good about it being a group grade; That just doesn't seem fair.* (2.3)

2. **C** The student means that she does not want to work on her project with other students. She says: *I'd rather do mine solo*, meaning she wants to work on her project alone. (2.4)

3. **B** The professor says: *In life, in the workplace— whatever your job is—you will have to work in a team; ...whatever you end up doing, you'll have to work on projects with other people. So this assignment is experience for life.* (2.2)

4. **B** The professor says: *Why don't you talk to a few of your classmates? Find out what kind of project they're thinking about; I recommend you meet with some classmates in the coffee shop.* (2.2)

5. **D** The student expresses doubt about what the professor said. She wants to work alone and is not convinced that working with a partner is a good idea. (2.5)

6. **D** The main idea is that children go through stages of mental and social development. The professor says: *...mental development is related to social development...; ...children gradually acquire...; the egocentric stage of social development; the multiple role–taking stage.* (2.1)

7. **A** The professor says: *...at around four to six years old, they can focus on only one thought at a time; ... don't yet understand that other people may see the same event differently from the way they see it. They don't reflect on the thoughts of others.* (2.2)

8. **B** The professor's purpose is to illustrate how children must experience something directly to understand it because they cannot yet think abstractly at six to ten years old. (2.3)

9. **A** The professor says: *Children can now manage various social roles...; Because they can play multiple roles, this stage is known as the multiple role–taking stage.* You can infer that children in the multiple role–taking stage know that different social roles require certain behavior. (2.4)

10. **A, D** One stage in the social development of children is when the child understands actions as others see them: *...on a social level, children can now understand actions as an outsider might see them.* Another stage is when the child can judge actions as they affect all people: *...the young teenager is now able to judge actions by how they might influence all individuals....* (2.2)

11. **C** The professor says: *In their social development, children gradually acquire interpersonal reasoning skills. They learn to understand the feelings of other people...; When children first start school...; ...they can understand only their own perspective...; ...children at this age are self–centered...; Sometime between twelve and fifteen years old, a societal perspective begins to develop.* You can infer that the professor would agree that children progress from being self–centered to being able to understand how others feel. (2.4)

12. D   The speakers mainly discuss the meaning of improvisation. They say: *Every jazz player knows what he or she means by improvisation. And all writers know what they mean by improvisation; What does it all mean; My dictionary says improvise means...; Maybe a better definition is...; In the beginning, music was largely improvisational, supplied on the spur of the moment....* (2.1)

13. A, B   Improvisation is difficult to define because there are several kinds of it: *We hear about the different types of improvisation—free improvisation and controlled improvisation and collective improvisation.* Also, people disagree about what improvisation is: *Every jazz player knows what he or she means by improvisation. And all writers know what they mean by improvisation. The result, of course, is a lot of confusion and disagreement about what improvisation really is.* (2.2)

14. C   The professor discusses the history of improvisation. He says: *Let's try to understand it more by looking at history.* (2.6)

15. B   The professor's purpose is to provide historical examples of improvisation, that of ancient Greeks and sixteenth–century Italian organists. (2.3)

16. ✓   Prehistoric people: Improvised music for work, play, and war: *In the beginning, music was largely improvisational, supplied on the spur of the moment by prehistoric people who "made" music for work, play, war....*
    ✓   Jazz musicians: Combined their own music with stock melodies: *...the early jazz musicians were very similar to the ancient Greeks in the ways they were making a music that was partly their own and partly derived from the stock melodies....*
    ✓   Prehistoric people: Used music as a force to show relationships: *...music was a force that communicated the relationship of people to nature, and people to each other.*
    ✓   Jazz musicians: Improvised on the music of other bands: *...African–American jazz musicians improvised on the European melodies they heard popular white bands playing.* (2.2)

17. D   The professor says: *There were a number of jazz musicians who had played in army bands, and they had training of one kind or another. It was these trained military bandsmen who were responsible for the rise of jazz improvisation.* (2.2)

Quiz 8 (p. 282)

1. C   The woman wants to talk about ideas for her project. She says: *I was hoping...we could talk about the project that's due at the end of May; I have an idea...it's something that interests me.* (2.3)

2. B   The woman asks: *...the project plan...that part's due next week, right?* The professor replies: *Uh...yes, that's right, the first due date—the project plan—is due next week, on Monday, May 3.* (2.2)

3. B   The woman says: *I'm a little—I'm not sure about what you want.* You can infer that she does not understand the assignment. (2.5)

4. A, C   You can predict that the woman will write about an economic development organization: *...she works for economic development...; ...a case study of an economic development organization....* You can also predict that she will write about how an organization promotes social change: *...also for social change because it's work that affects women and their role in society; I could do a case study about a group that works for both economic and social change.* (2.4)

5. C, D   The woman will include an interview with her boss: *...I'd like to interview my boss...; ...combine the interview data....* She will also include description of a product catalog: *...their product catalog...; ...an analysis and evaluation of their catalog.* (2.2)

6. D   The professor mainly compares the two main divisions of the science of anthropology. She says: *The science of anthropology has two major divisions: physical and cultural. Physical anthropology studies...; Physical anthropologists study...; Cultural anthropology studies...; Like physical anthropologists, cultural anthropologists study...; However, cultural anthropologists also look at....* (2.6)

7. A   The professor's purpose is to request that the student be patient. The professor wants the student to listen to everything she is going to say. *Just hear me out* implies that she will eventually address the student's concerns. (2.5)

8. B   The professor says: *The Leakeys are a well–known family of physical anthropologists. Their research... showed us that human evolution centered there, in East Africa...; They discovered stone tools and other hominid evidence....* (2.2)

9. B   The professor says: *Physical anthropology studies human evolution...; Physical anthropologists study the fossils and organic remains of once–living primates; They discovered stone tools and other hominid evidence that pushed back the dates of the earliest humans....* (2.2)

10. A   The professor says: *...cultural anthropologists study clues about human life in the distant past. However, cultural anthropologists also look at similarities and differences among human communities today.* You can infer that cultural anthropology is concerned with all human cultures of the past and present. (2.4)

11. C   The professor's purpose is to encourage student interest in the course. The course is a two–quarter introduction to anthropology, and the professor has given a preview of both quarters. She says *I hope you will all stay and enjoy the ride* to encourage students to remain in the course for both quarters. (2.3)

12. C   The professor mainly discusses a specific period of volcanic activity. He says: *Mount St. Helens has a long history of volcanic activity, so the eruptions of 1980...; In March of 1980...; All during April...; By early May...; On the morning of May 18....* (2.1)

13. A   The professor says: *The eruption cycle had sort of a harmless beginning. In March of 1980, seismologists picked up signs of earthquake activity below the mountain. And during the next week, the earth¬quakes increased rapidly, causing several avalanches.* (2.2)

14. C   The professor's purpose is to show that the eruptions interested a lot of people, including tourists and hikers who were not scientists. (2.3)

15. D   The professor means that the small eruptions paused briefly just before the major eruption. There were a few days with no volcanic activity, and then the major eruption occurred. (2.4)

16. B, C   One effect of the eruption was that large numbers of animals and people were killed: *The blast killed the mountain's goats, millions of fish and birds, thousands of deer and elk—and around sixty people.* Another effect was that an ash cloud affected weather around the world: *The ash cloud drifted around the world, disrupting global weather patterns.* (2.2)

17. D   The professor says: *...geologists who've studied the mountain believe she won't stay asleep forever. The Cascade Range is volcanically active. Future eruptions are certain and—unfortunately—we can't prevent them.* You can conclude that Mount St. Helens is likely to erupt in the future. (2.4)

PART 3 – SPEAKING

EXERCISE 3.4.A (p. 304)

1. Opinion: *I would like to learn how to play the guitar.* Supporting details and examples: *I could take my guitar to parties and play music for my friends; ...I could join a band and play songs with other musicians; ...I could make money...the most important reason is because I enjoy music and want to understand it better.*

2. The response would receive a score of 4 on the TOEFL. It effectively addresses the task. It states an opinion clearly, supports it with appropriate details, and expresses ideas coherently.

EXERCISE 3.5.A (p. 311)

Key points:
 • The university is offering a training course for students who want to be tutors. The woman thinks that the man should enroll in the course.
 • One reason she gives is that the course will give him valuable experience for being a teaching assistant in graduate school.
 • Another reason is that he would learn some practical theories about teaching and learning.
 • Another reason is that the course might give him skills that could be useful for whatever kind of work he does later.

EXERCISE 3.5.B (p. 312)

Key points:
 • The man does not support the proposal to increase the physical education requirement.
 • One reason he gives is that students should make the choice to get exercise, and it is not the college's responsibility to require it.
 • Another reason is that students' main job is to study and exercise their brains, not their bodies.
 • Another reason is that he already gets a lot of exercise outside of school.

EXERCISE 3.5.C (p. 313)

Key points:
 • The woman's opinion of the childcare center is that the service is not satisfactory.
 • One reason she gives is that the center does not have enough space, and many children are on the waiting list for a long time.
 • Another reason is that the lack of space prevents a lot of parents from going to college.
 • Another reason is that the center closes too early for some parents who take evening classes.

EXERCISE 3.6.A (p. 318)

Key points:
 • Emotional intelligence consists of self–awareness, self–control, self–motivation, enthusiasm, and social ability.
 • The professor discusses a study in which many of the subjects were active in the performing arts, student government, and community service. This illustrates how people with emotional intelligence have social ability and are successful in cooperation and leadership.

•One subject described himself as a very sensitive and emotional person. This illustrates how people with emotional intelligence are self–aware and understand their feelings.
•All of the subjects reported having at least one close friend and a good relationship with their parents. This illustrates how people with emotional intelligence succeed at relationships.

EXERCISE 3.6.B (p. 319)
Key points:
•Role conflict occurs when our different role partners expect different behavior from us.
•The professor discusses the role of student and the different expectations of parents and friends. Parents expect students to study, but friends want to go out and party.
•The professor discusses role conflict over choosing an academic major. Parents and friends may expect different choices. Both examples illustrate conflict between the expectations of different role partners—parents and friends.

EXERCISE 3.6.C (p. 320)
Key points:
•Spatial memory is the ability to remember objects based on their relationship to other things in the environment.
•The professor describes how some birds bury food and later remember the hiding place. The birds use landscape features to remember where the food is buried.
•When researchers moved an object, such as a log or a rock, the birds appeared to search for their food in a particular spatial relationship to the object. This illustrates how birds use landmarks to indicate where their food is buried.

EXERCISE 3.7.A (p. 326)
Key points:
•The woman wants to share a dormitory room on campus with her best friend from high school. The man's opinion is that the woman should consider not sharing a room with her best friend.
•One reason he gives is that it can destroy a friendship because knowing someone isn't the same as living together.
•Another reason is that having someone else for a roommate will allow her to meet new and interesting people.
•Another reason is that she might benefit by living in a dormitory with other students of her academic major.

EXERCISE 3.7.B (p. 327)
Key points:
•SAD is a type of mild depression that is linked to the change in the amount of daylight during the fall and winter.
•The symptoms of SAD are like those of other types of depression, including sadness, sleepiness, lack of energy, and weight gain.
•The symptoms disappear when the hours of daylight increase in the spring. In cases of mild or situational depression, the symptoms usually decline once the problem that caused the depression disappears.

EXERCISE 3.7.C (p. 328)
Key points:
•The woman's opinion is that she will not like seminars.
•One reason she gives is that seminars seem similar to class discussions in her high school, which were boring because a few students always did all the talking.
•Another reason is that she would rather listen to the professor because the professor has all the knowledge, not the students.

EXERCISE 3.7.D (p. 329)
Key points:
•Boycotts are a form of nonviolent protest to achieve a goal. A boycott is a refusal to buy, sell, or trade with a business that one believes is doing something morally wrong.
•The professor discusses a grape boycott in which workers refused to pick grapes. The boycott got a lot of attention and forced grape growers to allow their workers to join the labor union.
•The professor discusses a lettuce boycott in which people refused to buy lettuce. Both boycotts called attention to a wrong, punished the growers, and forced them to improve working conditions.

EXERCISE 3.7.E (p. 330)
Key points:
•The college is offering a course in theater production to members of the community who are not college students. The man's opinion is that the course is not fair because it discriminates against college students who are not in the Theater Arts program.
•One reason he gives is that students pay tuition and fees, so they should be allowed to take any course they want.
•Another reason is that students may want to take the course just to have fun and learn about theater.

EXERCISE 3.7.F (p. 331)
Key points:
•Sleep unifies and protects memories from loss. Sleep helps recover lost memories. Sleep promotes higher–level learning.
•The professor discusses research showing that sleep improved the ability of students to retain knowledge about computer speech. This supports the point that sleep promotes the ability to learn.
•The study showed that when students learned in the morning and were tested at night, they forgot much of what they had learned. However, after sleeping and being retested in the morning, their scores improved. This supports the point that sleep helps to restore memories.

EXERCISE 3.8.A (p. 337)
Key points:
•The man's elbow is sore. He thinks he hurt it, but he doesn't want to miss baseball practice. He has already missed too much practice and is concerned the coach will put him off the team.
•One possible solution is to go to the clinic and see a doctor, but then he would miss baseball practice.
•Another solution is to go to practice, but also tell his coach about his elbow.
•Opinions about the preferred solution will vary.

EXERCISE 3.8.B (p. 338)

Key points:
- The woman needs another course to fill a social science requirement, but she can't find a course to fit her schedule for winter.
- One possible solution is to take an evening course.
- Another solution is to wait until Spring Quarter. However, she will be doing a full–time internship in the spring.
- Opinions about the preferred solution will vary.

EXERCISE 3.8.C (p. 338)

Key points:
- The man's problem is that his learning partner is lazy and has not done any work on a project for which they will be graded together.
- One possible solution is for the man to have a serious talk with his partner and lay out a plan for completing the project.
- Another solution is to talk to his professor about working on the project with a different group.
- Opinions about the preferred solution will vary.

EXERCISE 3.8.D (p. 339)

Key points:
- The woman's problem is that her car does not always start; she needs to have it checked out, but her regular mechanic is expensive, and she still must pay her tuition.
- One possible solution is to take her car to the community college program in automotive technology, where students can have their cars fixed for less money than it usually would cost.
- Another solution is to check the bulletin board in the Student Center to find a mechanic that is not expensive.
- Opinions about the preferred solution will vary.

EXERCISE 3.8.E (p. 339)

Key points:
- The man's problem is that he will miss an upcoming test. He has already missed one test and is in danger of not receiving credit for the course (failing).
- One possible solution is for the man to do something to raise his grade, such as get a tutor or a study partner to help him.
- Another solution is to consider dropping the course.
- Opinions about the preferred solution will vary.

EXERCISE 3.9.A (p. 347)

Key points:
- Hotel managers are responsible for the overall operation of the hotel and for seeing that guests receive good service.
- The general manager is the top executive in a hotel. The general manager directs the work of other managers in the hotel. General managers must be skilled in leadership and financial decision making.
- Hotel controllers are responsible for the management of money. Controllers manage the accounting and payroll departments, find ways to improve efficiency, and interpret financial statements.
- Sales managers market the services of the hotel. Sales managers have constant contact with customers and know what selling points appeal to the public. Sales managers must be skilled in business, marketing, and advertising.

EXERCISE 3.9.B (p. 348)

Key points:
- Two features of the earth's surface that influence climate are ocean currents and landforms.
- There are two large, circular ocean currents, one in each hemisphere. These currents move warm water from the equator to the north and south.
- Warm and cold ocean currents affect the climates of nearby coastal areas; for example, the Gulf Stream warms the climate of northwestern Europe.
- Landforms affect climate. Mountains are cooler, windier, and wetter than valleys; one example is Mount Kilimanjaro, which is near the equator but always covered with snow.
- Mountains interrupt the flow of winds and storms. When moist winds blow toward mountains, the air on the slope facing the wind is cool and moist, causing rain and snow to fall there. The air on the other side of the mountain is warmer and drier.

EXERCISE 3.9.C (p. 348)

Key points:
- Crowd behavior can be unpredictable because crowds have the potential for several different outcomes.
- Crowds have an expressive quality. Crowds show strong emotions that can be either positive or negative. Crowds can become out of control.
- Some crowds are organized. Demonstrations have rules for behavior, such as marching and chanting. However, the mood can change quickly.
- A crowd can have a feeling that something should be done, but uncertainty about what to do. Uncertainty may lead to breaking the rules.

EXERCISE 3.9.D (p. 349)

Key points:
- The Flatiron Building was the first true skyscraper in New York. It is an office tower that stands apart from other buildings on all sides.
- The Flatiron Building is twenty–two stories tall, has a steel frame covered on the outside with stone, and is decorated with geometric patterns, columns, arches, and a crown of carved stone.
- The Flatiron Building is built on an irregular, triangle–shaped site, giving it an unusual shape.
- The building got its name from a joke about its shape. People thought it looked like a flatiron, a triangle–shaped piece of iron used for pressing clothes.

EXERCISE 3.9.E (p. 349)

Key points:
- One physical difference between water and land is that oxygen is more abundant in air than in water. Land animals can get oxygen more easily than water animals can, but first land animals had to evolve lungs.
- Another physical difference is that air is less dense than water and provides less support against gravity than water does. Therefore, land animals had to develop strong legs and a stronger skeleton for moving in air.
- Another difference is that the temperature of the air on land changes more easily than it does in water. Therefore, land animals had to develop strategies to survive in warm and cold temperatures, such as the ability to maintain a constant body temperature.

Exercise 3.10.A (p. 354)

The response would receive a score of 4 on the TOEFL. The response effectively addresses the task. It explains agents of socialization and gives relevant examples from the lecture. It expresses ideas coherently and develops points with appropriate details. It accurately conveys information from the lecture and the reading, including the following key points:

- Agents of socialization teach us how to live in our society. They give us important knowledge and opportunities to practice the social roles we will occupy.
- The professor gives the example of parents, who teach us the first lessons in how to behave in society. Parents act as role models for adulthood and give guidance on long–term goals.
- The professor also discusses peers as agents of socialization. Peers teach us the social role of friend and influence our lifestyle choices.

Exercise 3.10.B (p. 355)

1. The response accurately summarizes the problem. It includes relevant details from the conversation: the woman lives off campus; she rides the bus; her class begins at 7:00; the bus leaves at 6:00; and she arrives at campus too early.
2. The response states the opinion that the solution of a bicycle is better. The reasons given are that the woman can arrive at campus at a better time and she can ride her bicycle on a path by the river.
3. The response would receive a score of 4 on the TOEFL. It effectively addresses all parts of the task and gives relevant details from the conversation.

Key points:

- The woman's problem is that she lives off campus and the bus schedule does not work out well for her early morning class. She arrives at campus too early.
- One possible solution is to use the extra time to eat breakfast on campus.
- Another possible solution is to get a bicycle so she can leave home whenever she wants.
- Opinions about the preferred solution will vary.

Exercise 3.10.C (p. 356)

Key points:

- The woman opposes the plan for having a new building in that particular location.
- One reason she gives is that the space is a natural wooded area where students can enjoy nature. She goes there for peace and quiet. Art and film students go there to work.
- Another reason is that the construction project will destroy an existing green space. Adding a parking lot will only encourage more people to drive to campus. She believes that the university should promote green technology, not destroy green space.

Exercise 3.10.D (p. 357)

Key points:

- Spider webs are flexible, strong, and able to span great distances. Spider silk is stronger than steel of the same weight. It can stretch to almost double its length.
- Spider webs perform the function of gathering food. They are efficient at catching prey. When webs are rebuilt, the spider recycles the old web by eating it.
- Webs function as homes for spiders. Webs are a place to mate and lay eggs. Webs collect dew for spiders to drink. Webs are a place to store food.
- Webs function as a communication medium. Webs convey vibrations, and spiders can interpret the meaning and act in response.

Quiz 4 (p. 358)

1. Key points:
   - The man's opinion is that the woman should attend a free career workshop.
   - One reason he gives is that there will be several people to talk to about working in her field.
   - Another reason is that the university has only one career workshop each year and she shouldn't miss it.
   - Another reason is that the workshop is a good way to start looking for a job after graduation. (3.5, 3.7, 3.10)
2. Key points:
   - Reciprocity is a relationship between parties that benefits both sides equally. It is based on sharing and balance. Both sides give and receive equal value.
   - The professor discusses friendship as a reciprocal relationship. Close friendships involve the sharing of emotions. This illustrates how reciprocity is based on sharing.
   - Friendship involves giving and receiving. When giving and receiving are not in balance, the friendship is less reciprocal and less satisfying. This illustrates how reciprocity is based on balance. (3.6, 3.7, 3.10)
3. Key points:
   - The woman's problem is that she has two midterms on Monday, but she will have little time to study that weekend because her parents are coming to visit.
   - One possible solution is for the woman to join a study group that night to review for the midterm.
   - Another solution is for the woman to explain the problem to her parents and give them a list of places to go during the day.
   - Opinions about the preferred solution will vary. (3.8, 3.10)
4. Key points:
   - Humans have more than one hundred separate gestures and facial expressions that are nonverbal signals in communication.
   - Body language communicates how people perceive a social situation; for example, strangers meeting at a party will lift their eyebrows to communicate friendly feelings.
   - Hand or arm gestures, such as a salute or a handshake, signal involvement.
   - Eye movement and eye contact are used to regulate the rhythm of conversation. In Western society, friends look at each other often during conversation. A speaker looks away to signal his intention to speak; a listener looks at the speaker and nods his head to signal his interest and attention.
   - The smile has a tremendous power to generate friendly feelings. The smile has the same meaning in every culture and is first seen in babies when they are very young. (3.9, 3.10)

QUIZ 5 (p. 361)

1. Key points:
   - The man will be taking a writing course that includes a peer feedback group. He does not want to attend the peer feedback group.
   - One reason he gives is that he was in a student writing group before, but it didn't help with his writing.
   - Another reason is that he can't learn from other students if they don't know how to write.
   - Another reason is that he can learn better from a teacher because a teacher has more education and experience. (3.5, 3.7, 3.10)

2. Key points:
   - A cohort is a group of people who were born around the same time. Members of the same cohort experience historical events together.
   - The professor discusses two cohorts that were influenced by the Great Depression of the 1930s, but in different ways. People who were young children in the 1930s were affected negatively, while people who were teenagers had more positive effects.
   - The examples show how historical events and developmental issues interact in influencing cohorts. (3.6, 3.7, 3.10)

3. Key points:
   - The woman's problem is that she has to drive to school and needs to park on campus, but the parking lots are not big enough, and a parking permit does not guarantee a space.
   - One possible solution is for the woman to register for classes that meet in the afternoon, when the parking lots are less full.
   - Another solution is to park in the park–and–ride lot a mile from campus and ride the free shuttle bus from there to campus.
   - Opinions about the preferred solution will vary. (3.8, 3.10)

4. Key points:
   - Organizational charts reveal a company's management structure and how information flows.
   - The pyramid chart reveals a hierarchy, a formal chain of command with management on the top and the labor force on the bottom. Information flows up, and orders flow down. The pyramid is logical and orderly, but decision–making can take a long time.
   - The wheel chart reveals an integrated company, with management at the hub and the labor force on the rim. Information flows around the rim in both directions. The wheel chart implies a policy of open communication. (3.9, 3.10)

QUIZ 6 (p. 364)

1. Key points:
   - The woman's opinion about volunteering for the conference is that it will be a great opportunity.
   - One reason she gives is that volunteers can go to the reception and meet a lot of prominent scientists from around the world.
   - Another reason is that volunteers will learn how a conference is organized; this interests her because she plans to be involved in environmental issues.
   - Another reason is to get a free T–shirt. (3.5, 3.7, 3.10)

2. Key points:
   - The chase film was a popular form of comedy that told a simple story of someone being chased by others.
   - The lecture describes a film about a rich man who is looking for a wife and ends up being chased by a crowd of women. This example illustrates the humorous nature of the chase film.
   - The lecture describes the chase films about the Keystone Kops, clownish policemen who chased villains and bank robbers. These examples illustrate the fast action, excitement, and comedy of the chase film. (3.6, 3.7, 3.10)

3. Key points:
   - The woman must take a course during the summer in order to transfer to the university in the fall. However, she had planned to take a sailboat trip in the summer.
   - One solution is to go on the sailboat trip and delay the transfer to the university.
   - Another solution is to cancel the sailboat trip and take the course in the summer so she can go to the university in the fall.
   - Opinions about the preferred solution will vary. (3.8, 3.10)

4. Key points:
   - Insomnia is difficulty falling asleep or staying asleep.
   - Insomnia can be caused by emotional distress. It can be caused by stress from a single event, such as job loss or change, death of a loved one, or moving. Long–term insomnia may be caused by chronic stress or depression.
   - Insomnia can have physical causes, such as discomfort or pain due to illness or injury. The consumption of coffee or alcohol may cause insomnia.
   - Insomnia can be related to environmental factors such as noise, light, or extreme temperatures. Other causes are jet lag and a change in work shift. (3.9, 3.10)

QUIZ 7 (p. 367)

1. Responses will vary. (3.1–3.4)
2. Responses will vary. (3.1–3.4)
3. Key points:
   - The dean's office has proposed limiting the student course load to 20 credit hours per semester. The woman does not like the idea.
   - One reason she gives is that she has taken more than 20 credits before and did not have any problem finishing the work.
   - Another reason is that she needs only 21 more credits to graduate and hopes to graduate this spring.
   - Another reason is that if she has to take a class this summer, she will have to pay more tuition, and she does not want to ask her family for more money. (3.5, 3.7, 3.10)
4. Key points:
   - Coevolution is the evolution of two species at the same time. Coevolution occurs when the interaction between two species benefits both species.
   - The professor discusses the coevolution of insects and flowers. Insects benefit flowers by pollinating them. Flowers provide food to insects. In turn, each evolves features to attract the other.
   - The professor gives the example of the yucca flower, which evolved its shape to benefit a specific pollinator, the yucca moth.
   - The professor also gives the example of the snapdragon, which evolved features that benefit a specific bee. (3.6, 3.7, 3.10)

5. Key points:
- The man's problem is that he has trouble remembering the material from class, and he can't understand his notes when he looks at them later.
- One possible solution is to review his lecture notes as soon as possible after class, when the material is still fresh in his mind.
- Another solution is to take a short nap or get a good night's sleep after studying because sleeping will help him remember what he just studied.
- Opinions about the preferred solution will vary. (3.8, 3.10)

6. Key points:
- One way that manufacturers sell goods to consumers is direct sales. Direct sales take place in the customer's home or in a business setting. Examples are door–to–door sales, catalog shopping, telemarketing, and Internet shopping.
- Another way to sell goods is retail sales, which take place in stores. Examples are department stores, discount chains, supermarkets, hardware stores, car dealerships, drugstores, and convenience stores. Retail stores are a convenient way for consumers to buy.
- Another way to sell goods is wholesaling, where goods are sold at lower prices because customers buy in large quantities or in a low overhead setting. Examples are outlet stores and selling to retail stores. Wholesaling is the most practical method for the widespread distribution of goods. (3.9, 3.10)

QUIZ 8 (p. 371)

1. Responses will vary. (3.1–3.4)
2. Responses will vary. (3.1–3.4)
3. Key points:
- The man is encouraging the woman to apply for scholarships.
- One reason he gives is that the woman has leadership skills. He thinks her volunteer work with the elderly will impress the scholarship committee.
- Another reason is that applying for a scholarship is good experience. It will make the woman think about her accomplishments. It is good practice for job hunting. (3.5, 3.7, 3.10)

4. Key points:
- The convoy is a network of social relationships that provide social support throughout one's life. The convoy changes in size and membership, but core members remain for a long time.
- The professor gives the example of friends, who are added and lost throughout life. Close friends are core members of the convoy.
- The professor gives the example of spouses or partners, who may be added or lost through marriage, divorce, or death. They are core members of the convoy.
- Other examples are parents, siblings, and pets. All of the examples illustrate how one's convoy moves through time and changes in membership. (3.6, 3.7, 3.10)

5. Key points:
- The woman has too much work to do. She has many student papers to grade by the end of the week, in addition to her own coursework.
- One possible solution is to ask Dr. Carter for more time to grade the papers.
- Another solution is to set a strict time limit for grading each paper.
- Opinions about the preferred solution will vary. (3.8, 3.10)

6. Key points:
- Sunlight is an abiotic factor. Sunlight provides the energy for plants to make food. The amount of sunlight affects seasonal events, such as the flowering of plants and the migration of birds.
- Rainfall and temperature affect plants, which in turn affect the availability of food, nest sites, and shelter for animals. Air temperature affects the ability of plants and animals to regulate their body temperature.
- Wind is an abiotic factor. Wind increases the effects of air temperature. Wind chill increases heat loss in organisms. Wind causes water loss in animals and plants. (3.9, 3.10)

PART 4 – WRITING

EXERCISE 4.1.A (p. 385)

Key points:
- The lecture describes a poor pruning practice known as topping.
- The lecture states that topping does not keep a tree small; topping increases a tree's growth rate. This contrasts with the point in the reading that careful pruning will control the size of a tree.
- The lecture states that topping is very stressful for trees. This contrasts with the point in the reading that pruning invigorates trees and keeps them healthy.
- The lecture states that topping destroys a tree's natural shape. This contrasts with the point in the reading that pruning should enhance the natural shape and beauty of a tree.

EXERCISE 4.1.B (p. 386)

Key points:
- The lecture illustrates visual–spatial intelligence by explaining its importance in the game of chess.
- The lecture states that chess masters can draw a picture of a chessboard they have seen for just a few seconds if the pieces are set in meaningful positions. This illustrates the point in the reading that people with visual–spatial intelligence are able to perceive patterns and draw objects after seeing them for only a short time.
- The lecture states that a blindfolded chess player has to remember the movements of the chess pieces and hold a picture of the chessboard in his mind. This illustrates the point in the reading that people with visual–spatial intelligence have the ability to create and transform mental imagery.
- The lecture states that chess players remember plans, strategies, and patterns of reasoning of important games they have played. This illustrates the point in the reading that people with visual–spatial intelligence have superior visual memory and the ability to predict and plan ahead.

EXERCISE 4.2.A (p. 393)

Key points:
- The lecture states that the development plan would destroy the view; critics want to preserve the land as a park for the entire community to enjoy. This opposes the point in the reading that the development plan will beautify and improve the area and attract people downtown.
- The lecture states that the proposed new housing would benefit only upper income people. This opposes the point in the reading that the project will help solve the city's need for more residential space.
- The lecture states that the plan would benefit only a few people economically at the expense of the environment. This opposes the point in the reading that the project will benefit the city economically in several ways.

EXERCISE 4.2.B (p. 394)

Key points:
- The lecture states that psychology is a social science. This contrasts with the point in the reading that psychology is a natural science.
- The lecture states that psychology studies the overall processes of mental activity, including how these processes influence human behavior and society. This contrasts with the point in the reading that psychology focuses on the physiological and sensory aspects of human behavior.
- The lecture states that psychology is based on the subjective interpretation of phenomena and on knowledge by description. This contrasts with the point in the reading that psychology is based on objectively verified facts and the application of the scientific method.
- The lecture states that all subfields of psychology study the interaction of mental processes and social behavior. This contrasts with the point in the reading that all subfields of psychology study the biological bases of behavior and mental states.

EXERCISE 4.3.A (p. 401)

Key points:
- The lecture states that the decision to change Pluto's status was controversial; scientists disagree about the decision. This contradicts the point in the reading that the decision was reached by a strong majority vote.
- The lecture states that critics think the new definition of planet is not adequate or realistic. This contradicts the point in the reading that the new definition is clear and precise.
- The lecture states that calling Pluto a dwarf planet causes controversy and confusion. This contradicts the point in the reading that astronomers agree that Pluto is a dwarf planet and not a true planet.

EXERCISE 4.3.B (p. 402)

Key points:
- The lecture states that the small work group fills important social and emotional needs of workers. This supports the point in the reading that workers are more motivated if their job offers a sense of community.
- The lecture states that the work group improves worker motivation because it promotes an atmosphere of security. This supports the point in the reading that workers need a sense of security in the workplace.
- The lecture states that the small work group gives individuals a sense of autonomy; workers need to feel in control of what happens during the workday. This supports the point in the reading that the most satisfying jobs are those with a high level of autonomy.

EXERCISE 4.3.C (p. 403)

Key points:
- The lecture states that health–care practices should be based solely on scientific evidence. This challenges the point in the reading that alternative medicine often rejects science–based medicine.
- The lecture states that people turn to alternative therapies because they are misinformed or misled. This challenges the point in the reading that people seek alternative therapies because they are dissatisfied with conventional medicine.
- The lecture states that alternative medicine does not require practitioners to have any formal training or professional credentials. This challenges the point in the reading that a variety of schools and colleges offer courses in alternative medicine.

EXERCISE 4.4.A (p. 407)

1. The speaker talks about a maple tree that was topped. This is not a good pruning practice because topping causes a lot of damage to trees. The first reason is topping causes leaves and branches to grow fast. The growth rate of a tree speeds up when it is topped. Branches become crowded and dangerous and could crush a car. Another reason is topping removes too many leaves, which are the tree's food source. The tree will starve, and it is also more likely to be infected by disease. Topping causes a lot of stress for the tree; therefore, it is not a good pruning practice.

2. The lecture mentions reasons for choosing alternative medicine. For example, there has been an increase in conspiracy theories. Some people believe conventional medicine causes them to depend on drugs. The reading discusses dissatisfaction with conventional medicine; for example, people do not trust the physician. Also, the professor talks about how alternative medicine misleads people and encourages them to choose treatments that are not based on science.

3. The professor made many points about the motivation and needs of workers that support points made in the reading. First, the professor said that the small work group, about 3 to 15 people with one leader, is important for workers. The work group fills needs of workers because they can participate and have a sense of respect. The small work group also gives workers the ability to make decisions. This point agrees with the reading, which said the most satisfying jobs are those with a high level of autonomy. This gives workers a voice so they can make their own decisions.

EXERCISE 4.5.A (p. 411)

1. Main idea of the passage: The discovery of antibiotics was the most dramatic medical development of the twentieth century.
   Supporting points:
   • Antibiotics became known as wonder drugs because of their ability to cure major forms of bacterial infection quickly and completely.
   • Antibiotics have given the medical profession powerful tools to fight a wide range of specific diseases.
   • The most spectacular effects of antibiotics include reductions in the number of deaths from pneumonia and tuberculosis.

2. Major points in the lecture:
   • As soon as antibiotics were developed, new strains of bacteria appeared that were resistant to the drugs.
   • Bacteria can create very effective weapons against antibiotics.
   • Antibiotics are no longer effective cures for some infections.

3. Generally, the key points in the lecture refute the idea that antibiotics are wonder drugs. The lecture casts doubt on the reading by presenting examples of antibiotic resistance, including the rise in drug–resistant hospital infections, the resistance of pneumonia bacteria to penicillin, and the reappearance of tuberculosis as a major illness.

EXERCISE 4.5.B (p. 412)

Response A: Score: 5
The response accurately conveys relevant information from the lecture and the reading. It is well organized and coherent and contains only minor language errors. It effectively links points from the lecture to those in the reading, including the following key points:
• The lecture states that as soon as antibiotics were developed, new strains of bacteria appeared that were resistant to the drugs. The rise in dangerous hospital infections is evidence that antibiotics are not the wonder drugs they used to be. This casts doubt on the point in the reading that antibiotics are wonder drugs that can cure major forms of infection quickly and completely.
• The lecture states that bacteria can create effective weapons against antibiotics. This casts doubt on the point in the reading that antibiotics have given the medical profession powerful tools to fight a wide range of specific diseases.
• The lecture states that antibiotics are no longer effective cures for pneumonia and tuberculosis. This casts doubt on the point in the reading that antibiotics have reduced the number of deaths from pneumonia and tuberculosis.

Response B: Score: 3
The response contains some relevant information from the lecture, but some points are incomplete, inaccurate, or vague, particularly in the second and third paragraphs. The response contains errors of grammar and usage that result in vagueness.

Response C: Score: 1
The response contains little relevant content from the lecture. It includes some information from the reading, but fails to connect points from the lecture and reading. It contains numerous language errors, such as run–on sentences and incorrect word forms, which greatly obscure meaning.

Response D: Score: 4
The response generally conveys relevant information from the lecture. It is generally good in relating information from the lecture to that in the reading, but some points are vague. The response is generally well organized. The grammar is generally accurate, but some minor language errors result in occasional lack of clarity.

Response E: Score: 2
The response contains some relevant information from the lecture but has significant omissions, such as an explanation of how bacteria became resistant to antibiotics. It contains language errors, such as incomplete sentences and incorrect word forms, which largely obscure the meaning of key ideas.

QUIZ 1 (p. 415)

Key points:
• The lecture states that the mark test was repeated many times, but some of the results were inconsistent. This casts doubt on the point in the reading that the mark test has repeatedly demonstrated that chimpanzees recognize themselves in a mirror.
• The lecture states that all chimpanzees touch their heads and faces a lot, with or without a mirror. This casts doubt on the point in the reading that the mark test clearly showed that the chimps touched their heads and faces more when the mirror was present.
• The lecture states that self–grooming in chimpanzees is a social behavior. This casts doubt on the point in the reading that chimps would groom themselves because they recognized their own image in a mirror. (4.1–4.5)

QUIZ 2 (p. 416)

Key points:

- The lecture states that the amount of energy produced from the wind is unpredictable. This challenges the point in the reading that wind energy is available and abundant.
- The lecture states that wind energy is expensive to develop. This challenges the point in the reading that wind energy is low priced and affordable.
- The lecture states that wind energy has some negative impacts on the environment. This challenges the point in the reading that wind energy is safe and environmentally friendly. (4.1–4.5)

QUIZ 3 (p. 417)

Key points:

- The lecture states that Jackson Pollock painted as a form of self–expression. This illustrates the point in the reading that Abstract Expressionism emphasized personal expression, individuality, and freedom.
- The lecture states that Pollock was influential for his process of creating art; his devotion to the act of painting led to the term "action painting." This illustrates the point in the reading that Abstract Expressionism valued the act of painting itself.
- The lecture states that Pollock controlled the drip to give his paintings a special character. This illustrates the point in the reading that artists gave special attention to surface qualities of paint, such as brushstroke and texture.
- The lecture states that Pollock's "all–over" paintings filled the entire canvas. This illustrates the point in the reading that all parts of the canvas played an equally important role in the total work. (4.1–4.5)

EXERCISE 4.7.A (p. 427)

1. The question has two parts. The first part asks you to state whether you agree or disagree with the given statement. The second part asks you to support your opinion with specific reasons and examples.
2. Yes.
3. The essay is organized into an introduction, a body, and a conclusion. The two body paragraphs develop the two supporting points.
4. In the introduction, the writer states the thesis and previews the supporting points.
5. *It does not cost money to experience the best things in life: enjoying nature and being with our friends and family.*
6. The writer supports the thesis with two supporting points, which are developed in the body paragraphs with examples, reasons, and personal experience.
7. Body paragraph 1: *We can relax and enjoy the beauty of nature without spending money.* Body paragraph 2: *It does not cost money to spend time with our friends and family.*
8. Answers will vary, but may include the following: walking in the park; looking at the leaves; watching the snow falling; listening to the birds; having a garden; visiting friends; going to the library; reading; and spending time with family. Their purpose is to support and develop the thesis.
9. In the conclusion, the writer restates the thesis.
10. Yes. The essay would receive a score of 5 on the TOEFL.

EXERCISE 4.8.A (p. 433)

1. The question asks you to do two things: (1) state your position on the given topic, and (2) support your choice with specific reasons and examples.
2. In the introduction, the writer restates the question and states the thesis of the essay.
3. *There are several important skills that I learned through action.*
4. The essay is organized into an introduction, a body, and a conclusion. The three body paragraphs develop the three supporting points.
5. Body paragraph 1: *I learned how to ride a bicycle and drive a car by experience.* Body paragraph 2: *Learning mathematics is another example of learning by doing things.* Body paragraph 3: *Finally, I learned how to use a computer by doing it.*
6. Yes, the essay has unity because all of the ideas and information support the thesis.
7. Answers will vary, but may include *or, because, and, also, similarly, although, another example, therefore, finally, but, however,* and *such as.*
8. Yes. The essay would receive a score of 5 on the TOEFL.

EXERCISE 4.9.A (p. 438)

1. I decided not to get married two years ago so I could finish my university studies. My father wanted me to get married, but my parents allowed me to decide. If I had married, I would have had to stay in my husband's home because in my culture, a married woman has a duty to her husband. It is our tradition. I chose to finish my degree instead. I will be a graduate student in Toronto, where I will earn my master's degree in business economics.
2. I think students should have several short vacations throughout the year instead of one long vacation because they work hard and need breaks often. Students in my country have several short holidays during every season. In contrast, American students have one long vacation in the summer. I read a paper saying that American students forget what they learn because of the long vacation. This is why I believe several short vacations are better than one long vacation.
3. There are many advantages in having friends that are different from me. For example, my friend from Turkey teaches me a lot about his culture. His family is very big, and my family is not big, so I like to go to his house to visit his family. I enjoy the good food and the conversation because it is really wonderful and interesting. Another friend is an artist who paints pictures and creates other art that is very good. My artist friend is not like me, and I learn interesting things about art from him.

EXERCISE 4.9.B (p. 439)

There are mainly two kinds of occupations. Some occupations require you to work primarily with machines, while others require you to work with other people. My job is working with machines, especially computers, so I prefer this kind of occupation.

Computers are important in our society. I am a computer programmer at a medical university, and I like to solve the problems of the medical record system. Computers have improved business, research, education, and many other fields of study. Many occupations require specialization in computers, so people need specialized training in an area of computer operations.

ANSWER KEY

On the other hand, in some occupations you work mainly with people. This is also necessary for my job because I work on a team with two other people. Therefore, we must help each other solve problems.

In conclusion, I prefer working with machines because machines need people to operate them, and machines improve people's lives. Many occupations, such as computer programmer, require specialization but also the ability to communicate with other people. Therefore, I believe that working with both machines and people is the best kind of job.

EXERCISE 4.10.A (p. 444)

Response A: Score: 5
The essay effectively addresses the task by clearly stating the thesis. It is well organized and well developed with appropriate reasons and examples. The essay has unity and coherence, with appropriate use of transitions. There are only occasional minor language errors.

Response B: Score: 1
The essay is seriously disorganized and underdeveloped. The thesis is not clear, and the essay contains little detail that is relevant to the task.

Response C: Score: 4
The essay addresses the task well, although the point in paragraph 3 is not fully elaborated. The thesis is clearly stated, and the essay is generally well organized and sufficiently developed. The essay has unity and coherence, with appropriate use of transitions, but there are noticeable minor language errors.

Response D: Score: 2
The essay displays limited development in response to the task. The thesis is stated, but there is little organization. There are few connections among ideas to support the thesis. The essay also contains an accumulation of errors in grammar and usage.

Response E: Score: 3
The essay addresses the task by stating a thesis and developing it with some reasons and examples. There is some use of transitions, but connections among ideas are occasionally unclear. The essay contains errors in grammar and a limited range of sentence structures.

QUIZ 7 (p. 450)

1. Key points:
   - The lecture states that men and women deal with stressful situations differently. While men have a "fight or flight" reaction, women have a "tend and befriend" reaction. This differs from the point in the reading that the fight–flight response is common to all humans.
   - The lecture states that women under stress will attack a problem rather than another person; women will avoid fighting with another person. This differs from the point in the reading that the fight response is expressed as aggressive behavior.
   - The lecture states that women under stress seek help and support from friends. This differs from the point in the reading that the flight response results in withdrawal from social activities. (4.1–4.5)
2. Responses will vary. (4.6–4.10)

QUIZ 8 (p. 452)

1. Key points:
   - The lecture states that it is not the actor's job to look for deeper meaning in the subtext. This opposes the point in the reading that actors must explore and use the subtext to convey the complexity of inner feelings.
   - The lecture states that it is unrealistic for actors to depend on their own emotions and experiences. This opposes the point in the reading that an actor must bring realism and depth to a part with his own emotions and experiences.
   - The lecture states that good acting requires skill training. This opposes the point in the reading that method acting has no technical forms that can be practiced.
   - The lecture states that good acting does not require an actor to live the part. This opposes the point in the reading that an actor should become the character and be immersed in the role. (4.1–4.5)
2. Responses will vary. (4.6–4.10)

TEST 1

READING (p. 457)

1. **A** *The moon is the closest natural body...* is paraphrased in *...the moon, our closest satellite. ...the single natural satellite of the earth* is paraphrased in *The only object circling the earth that is not man–made....* (1.6)

2. **C** *Eccentricity* means *abnormality* in this context. Clues: *We do not...always see only half of the moon's surface from the earth; ...allows us to see additional lunar surface through irregular movements...which expose an extra 18 percent of the moon's surface at one time or another.* (1.3)

3. **B** *Devoid of* means *without any* in this context. Clues: *Despite these watery names, the astronauts had to cope with an environment devoid of water. Despite* shows contrast between the watery names and the fact that the astronauts had to cope with an environment without any water. (1.3)

4. **A** You can infer that people once thought the moon contained large bodies of water. Clues: *Despite these watery names, the astronauts had to cope with an environment devoid of water. The dark areas on the moon's surface are called seas and oceans because early observers assumed the moon was much like the earth.* (1.4)

5. **D** The passage does not state that all sides of the moon are seen from the earth during a lunar cycle; in fact, the passage states that *the moon keeps the same hemisphere or face turned toward the earth at all times.* All the other answers are given: *...the dark side of the moon is turned toward the earth...; ...a thin crescent hangs in the evening twilight; ...the moon forms a right angle with the earth–sun line....* (1.2)

6. **B** Clues: *...the moon is more than half but less than fully illuminated, known as a waxing gibbous moon; After the full moon, the moon begins to wane, through a waning gibbous moon....* (1.1)

7. **B** *Wane* means *appear smaller* in this context. Clues: *After the full moon, the moon begins to -----, through a waning gibbous moon...a waning half moon...and a waning crescent moon...; Finally, the cycle ends and another begins with a dark moon....* The moon appears smaller as its phase goes from full to dark. (1.3)

8. **D** Clues: *...the cycle ends and another begins with a dark moon: another new moon. The lunar cycle takes 29.5 days to complete—a period known as a synodic month....* (1.1)

9. **C** Clues: *At the new moon.... A few nights later.... At this time, the dark side of the moon is faintly visible because it is illuminated by earthshine...; Toward the end of the eighth phase, a thin crescent appears at morning twilight, again accompanied by earthshine.* (1.1)

10. **D** *Ushers in* means *introduces* in this context. Clues: *...a period of several successive days when the moon rises in the northeast soon after sunset. This phenomenon gives farmers in temperate latitudes extra hours of light....* An *usher* is a person who leads or escorts another; *to usher in* is to lead into or to introduce; in this context, it means to introduce a period of several successive days of extra moonlight. (1.3)

11. **C** Clues: *This phenomenon gives farmers in temperate latitudes extra hours of light in which to harvest their crops....* (1.1)

12. **B** In the added sentence, *This* refers to the moon's *making one complete rotation in a period of time exactly equal to its orbit around the earth,* mentioned in the previous sentence. In the added sentence, *because* introduces the reason that the moon's rotation period matches its orbital period. (1.7)

13. **A, D, E** Key information: *The moon rotates slowly on its axis, making one complete turn in a period of time exactly equal to its revolution around the earth; ...the moon keeps the same hemisphere or face turned toward the earth at all times; The eight phases of the moon, the apparent changes in the moon's shape, arise from its changing position in relation to the earth; ...thin crescent...; ...half moon...; ...gibbous moon...; ...full moon...; ...dark moon....* Answer (B) is not mentioned; answers (C) and (F) are minor ideas. (1.8)

14. **B** Clues: *...a government expedition that would explore the Yellowstone area of Wyoming. At that time, Yellowstone was largely unknown....* (1.1)

15. **C** *Moran's role in the expedition was funded partly by the Northern Pacific Railroad...* is paraphrased in *The railroad helped pay for Moran to join the expedition.... ...whose directors thought that an artist's images of Yellowstone might help create a new tourist destination* is paraphrased in *...because its directors wanted pictures to promote tourism in Yellowstone.* (1.6)

16. **B** *Objective* means *realistic* in this context. Clues: *...a photographer who provided an ----- record of...; ...the photographs confirmed the reality....* (1.3)

17. **A** The author's purpose is to show that Moran became successful because of the expedition. A turning point is a time when a significant change occurs. Clues: *The expedition was the ----- in Thomas Moran's career; ...the expedition allowed the artist to combine his personal vision with his public role as educator of a national audience; The Grand Canyon of the Yellowstone became the first landscape by an American artist ever bought by the U.S. government.* (1.5)

18. **C** *Glorious* means *wonderful* in this context. Clues: *...watercolors of Yellowstone...increased their emotional impact; ...majestic Western landscape....* (1.3)

19. **C** Clues: *...there were some scenes that neither a photograph nor a watercolor could adequately convey; ...painted the scene in oil....* (1.1)

20. **D** You can infer that Moran's artistry helped inspire the national park concept. Clues: *To prove Yellowstone's uniqueness and beauty, Moran's watercolor sketches were displayed in the U.S. Capitol; ...a law preserving the whole Yellowstone area...as the world's first national park; ...the accomplishment is a tribute to the passion of Moran's vision.* (1.4)

21. **A** *Perception* means *view* in this context. Clues: *...influenced the public's ----- of nature...; ...promoted the idea that nature is something to be respected and preserved.* One's perception of something is one's way of seeing it. (1.3)

22. **C** *Figure* means *leader* in this context. Clues: *...wrote a series of magazine articles that taught children...; ...inspired thousands of children....* (1.3)

23. **D** The passage does not state that Moran and Seton formed a wilderness protection society. All the other answers are given: *(Moran's) watercolors of Yellowstone portrayed its glorious features in a way that increased their emotional impact; Another person who influenced the public's perception of nature was the Canadian wildlife artist and writer Ernest Thompson Seton; Lacking formal training, (Moran) was essentially self–taught...; Self–trained as a biologist, (Seton)...; (Moran's) public role as educator of a national audience; ...Seton inspired thousands of children to appreciate the natural world.* (1.2)

24. **B** You can infer that the author's opinion is that the work of Moran and Seton inspired the nature preservation movement. Clues: *The enduring message of both Thomas Moran and Ernest Thompson Seton was that nature is beautiful, noble, and deserving of our respect and protection; ...can be attributed to their vision and influence.* (1.4)

25. **C** The added sentence gives Seton's opinion of wolves, which further develops the topic of *his hunt for a legendary gray wolf*, mentioned in the previous sentence. The next sentence gives more information about *the story of Lobo.* (1.7)

26. **B, C, G** Thomas Moran: *Moran's watercolors...strange sketches of geysers and steaming lakes; His watercolors of Yellowstone portrayed its glorious features...; ...he was essentially self– taught, spending his early career copying the works of English landscape painters; ...a law preserving the whole Yellowstone area...as the world's first national park. Artists rarely have such an immediate impact on the political process, and the accomplishment is a tribute to the passion of Moran's vision.*

    A, E Ernest Thompson Seton: *...he started out as a naturalist and scientific illustrator...; ...with other stories in book form as Wild Animals I Have Known. This book has never been out of print since it first appeared....* Answers (D) and (F) describe neither Moran nor Seton. (1.9)

27. **A** *Shoals* means *shallows* in this context. Clues: *...a series of shallow areas....* (1.3)

28. **B** Clues: *...the Grand Banks...where the warm waters of the Gulf Stream meet the cold waters of the Labrador Current. As the currents brush each other....* (1.1)

29. **B** *This rich environment...* is paraphrased in *The Grand Banks...favorable natural conditions. ...has produced cod by the millions and once had a greater density of cod than anywhere else on Earth* is paraphrased in *...used to have the world's largest concentration of cod....* (1.6)

30. **D** *Common* means *familiar* in this context. Clues: *...the entire Newfoundland economy was based on... catching fish for a few months in the summer....* (1.3)

31. **C** The author's purpose is to stress the economic and cultural significance of cod. Clues: *...the entire Newfoundland economy was based on...catching fish...; ...the only sea creature worth talking about was cod...; ...a pudding whose main ingredient was cod.* (1.5)

32. **C** The passage does not state that fishers competed with farmers for natural resources. All the other answers are given: *...controlled by merchants based in the capital...This system kept the fishers in a continuous state of debt and dependence on the merchants; ...the entire Newfoundland economy was based on Europeans arriving, catching fish... and then taking fish back to European markets; Cod laid out to dry on wooden "flakes"....* (1.2)

33. **C** *Replenish* means *reproduce* in this context. Clues: *...fishers believed in the cod's ability to ----- itself and thought that overfishing was impossible;* the prefix *re–* = *again.* (1.3)

34. **A** Clues: *Until the twentieth century, fishers...thought that overfishing was impossible. However, Newfoundland's cod fishery began to show signs of trouble during the 1930s, when cod failed to support the fishers and thousands were unemployed.* (1.1)

35. **A** Clues: *...when an international agreement in 1977 established the 200–mile offshore fishing limit, the Canadian government decided to build up the modern Grand Banks fleet and make fishing a viable economic base for Newfoundland again.* (1.1)

36. **D** *Commanding* means *receiving* in this context. Clues: *...the conglomerate was prospering, and cod were ----- excellent prices in the market.* (1.3)

37. **B** You can infer that the author believes it may be a long time before cod stocks recover from overfishing. Clues: *By 2008, cod stocks were still at historically low levels and showed no signs of imminent recovery...; ...it remains uncertain whether or when the cod will return....* (1.4)

38. **B** *Teeming* means *numerous* in this context. Clues: *Atlantic cod stocks had once been so plentiful....* (1.3)

39. **A** In the added sentence, *They* refers to *inshore fishermen*, the main subject of the previous sentence. The added sentence develops the idea of *catches dropping off*, mentioned in the previous sentence, by discussing a possible reason for this. (1.7)

40. **A, C, E** Key information: *This rich environment has produced cod by the millions and once had a greater density of cod than anywhere else on Earth; Until the twentieth century, fishers believed in the cod's ability to replenish itself and thought that overfishing was impossible... Newfoundland's cod fishery began to show signs of trouble...when cod failed to support the fishers...; By 2008, cod stocks were still at historically low levels and showed no signs of imminent recovery, even after drastic conservation measures and severely limited fishing; ...it remains uncertain whether or when the cod will return.* Answers (B) and (D) are minor ideas; answer (F) is not mentioned. (1.8)

LISTENING — Part 1 (p. 470)

1. **D** The woman is requesting an interview with the dean. The woman says: *Our class is doing a radio program, and we'll have interviews with a lot of people from all parts of campus life. We'd like to interview the new Dean of Students, if he's willing.* (2.3)

2. **C** The man's purpose is to let the woman know that the dean is very busy and that his schedule is already full. (2.3)

3. A   The woman says: *I hope Dean Evans will agree to meet with us…. It would be a way for the whole community to get to know him, get to know his ideas and everything…like the kind of vision he has for the university.* (2.2)

4. B   The woman says: *This will be a great way for everyone to learn about our new dean.* You can infer that the dean has been dean for only a short time. (2.4)

5. C   The meeting will take place in two weeks, the week after next week. The man says: *…it looks like he's got a lot of meetings this week, and, well, most of next week, too, but what about the week after that?* The woman says: *Um, yeah, I think so.* (2.2)

6. B   The students are mainly discussing the concept of opportunity cost. The woman says: *Let's start with "opportunity cost."* The man says: *Opportunity cost—that's when…; You have an opportunity cost when….; This is the opportunity cost….* (2.1)

7. A   The man illustrates the concept with an example. The man says: *Say you want to have your own business, so you, so you open a restaurant.* He then explains how the concept of opportunity cost applies in the restaurant example. (2.1)

8. C   The man's purpose is to suggest that the restaurant's profit is less than it seems because of the opportunity cost. (2.3)

9. D   The man says: *…an economist tries to look at all the factors, all the costs; An economist's definition of costs is broader than an accountant's.* (2.2)

10. A   The woman says: *…it's more than what we pay for tuition and books! We have to subtract the income we lose by not working full time.* You can infer that the true cost of a college education includes the cost of lost income. (2.4)

11. B   The man's purpose is to show that choice has an opportunity cost. Opportunity cost includes the cost of something that must be given up. (2.3)

12. C   The speaker says: *When European explorers first approached the coast of North America, …the first thing they noticed was the pungent aroma…; …the agreeable smells didn't come from spices; they came from the lush vegetation of the North American forests.* (2.2)

13. A   The speaker says: *Pine sap was a valuable commodity to the sailors who explored the coast; …what were known as naval stores—pitch and pine tar; Sailors used naval stores for caulking and waterproofing their wooden ships, which kept them seaworthy.* (2.2)

14. C   The speaker says: *The Native Americans already knew about the medicinal properties of the dogwood, and they used its bark and roots to treat malaria and other fevers; European settlers also used the dogwood to relieve attacks of malaria.* (2.2)

15. C   The speaker wants the students to smell a piece of wood after scraping it with their thumbnail to release the scent. The speaker says: *I have a sassafras twig with me here, which I'll pass around so you can all enjoy its smell.* (2.3)

16. D   The speaker says: *Other Native American tribes used sassafras tonic as a cure for everything from fever to stomachache; For centuries, sassafras enjoyed a fantastic reputation as a cure for almost every disease.* (2.2)

17. B   The speaker implies that sassafras is no longer a legal medicine. She says: *…sassafras has been banned for human consumption.* (2.4)

LISTENING — Part 2 (p. 476)

1. D   The student lacks the prerequisite for a class that he wants to take. He says: *I'd like to take your seminar…; But I don't have the prerequisite that's listed in the college catalog, you know, Statistics 210.* (2.3)

2. B   The professor says: *That statistics course is necessary before you can take the seminar. The reading list for the seminar assumes you've got a solid understanding of numerical data; You need the course before you begin the seminar. Unless you have a good grasp of advanced statistics, you'll find the quantitative analyses very difficult, if not impossible.* (2.2)

3. B   The student's purpose is to persuade the professor to allow him into her seminar. The student says …*I guess I could wait till next fall to take your seminar,* but the professor tells him that she is …*not going to be teaching next year.* He then tells her how much he had looked forward to being in her seminar. He asks …*is there any way I can still do this* to show his determination and persuade her to let him take the seminar. (2.3)

4. A   The professor warns him that having a tutor will not necessarily be enough for him to learn advanced statistics. She has already told him that he needs the prerequisite course Statistics 210 for advanced statistics. The student wants to start studying statistics during spring break, and he asks the professor for help in finding a tutor. However, the professor is …*not convinced it's the best way to study advanced statistics.* (2.4)

5. B, D   The professor insists that the student find a tutor for help with advanced statistics: *I'll consider making an exception in your case, that is, if you get a tutor….* She also insists that he join a study group that will meet every week: *…and if you also join my TA's study group; They meet for three hours each week…. I strongly recommend—in fact, I require you to join the group….* (2.2)

6. D   The professor mainly discusses Plato's views on education. The professor says: *Plato believed the state should take an active role in education…the state should create a curriculum that leads students from thinking about concrete information toward thinking about abstract ideas; Plato believed our most important goal was the search for truth.* (2.1)

7. B   The professor's purpose is to give an example of a lasting truth. He says: *Plato believed the only true reality consists of ideas; For instance, the mathematical concept of two plus two equals four— this is an idea that's always existed.* (2.3)

8. A, C   Idealists believe that higher–level thinking develops a person's character and benefits the whole society: *Higher–level thinking would develop the individual student's character, and thus ultimately benefit the larger society.* (2.2)

9. A   The woman thinks that the idealist view of education does not give students useful knowledge. The woman says: *But isn't that kind of impractical? I mean, most of us go to college because we want knowledge about certain subjects, not the whole universe.* (2.3)

10. C The professor means that idealism has diminished in influence. He says: *...it's questions like this that have led to a weakening of idealism today.* He says that developments in science and technology have changed our way of thinking about what is true. (2.4)

11. B The professor says: *Critics of idealism would agree with you that "character development" comes at the expense of creativity, and that too much emphasis on traditional values can be harmful—if it makes students stop questioning what they're being taught.* (2.2)

12. D The professor says: *In physics, work means moving an object when there is some resistance to its movement. Every time we lift an object, push it, pull it, or carry it, we are doing work.* (2.2)

13. B The professor's purpose is to explain what happens when a moving object meets resistance. The plow meets resistance in the soil, requiring the tractor's engine to use more energy. (2.3)

14. A The professor says: *Energy can change forms, but it cannot be created or destroyed; The law states that energy can be converted from any form to any other form, but...none of the energy disappears when it changes form.* (2.2)

15. A, C A car changing chemical energy to motion illustrates the conversion of energy from one form to another: *Machines do work by converting one form of energy to another. For example, a car converts the chemical energy in gasoline to kinetic energy—to motion.* An electric stove converting electricity to heat is another illustration: *A stove converts electrical energy or chemical energy into heat energy that cooks our food.* (2.2)

16. D The professor's purpose is to show that both machines and living things need energy. Both must convert one form of energy to another in order to work. If there is no energy, the machine stops or the organism dies. (2.3)

17. C The professor says: *The first law of thermodynamics—conservation of energy—says the earth must end up with the same amount of energy it started out with. The energy changes forms, but no energy is lost or gained.* You can infer that in the earth as a whole system, no new energy is created, and no energy is destroyed. (2.4)

SPEAKING (p. 482)

1. Responses will vary. (3.1–3.4)
2. Responses will vary. (3.1–3.4)
3. Key points:
   • The man is thinking of registering for an online course.
   • The adviser's opinion about online courses is that they are not right for all students.
   • One reason she gives is that online courses require students to be self–motivated and able to learn on their own, mainly by reading.
   • Another reason is that online courses have a fairly high dropout rate.
   • Another reason is that some students prefer going to class and interacting face–to–face with the professor and other students. (3.5, 3.7, 3.10)

4. Key points:
   • The rabbit's ears are part of a homeostatic system that maintains the rabbit's body temperature.
   • The rabbit can adjust the amount of blood flowing through its ears to increase or decrease heat loss.
   • When the rabbit's body temperature increases, the blood vessels in the ears expand and fill with blood so that heat can escape from the ears. This cools the rabbit's body.
   • When the rabbit's body temperature decreases, the blood vessels in the ears constrict, sending blood to deeper parts of the body. This reduces heat loss. (3.6, 3.7, 3.10)
5. Key points:
   • The man is concerned about his grade in geology. He needs to pass the course, but he does not have enough time to study.
   • One possible solution is to get a tutor. The woman recommends her former tutor.
   • Another solution is for the man to reduce the amount of time spent on other activities, such as sports.
   • Opinions about the preferred solution will vary. (3.8, 3.10)
6. Key points:
   • The communication between babies and mothers is musical because there is a shared sense of timing.
   • A baby can make sounds with a musical inflection when he's "talking" with his mother.
   • Just as one musician will lead another in a performance, a child will often lead the earliest "conversations" with his mother.
   • Babies and mothers use a special musical language called baby talk.
   • Babies develop a large vocabulary of meaningful sounds. Different meanings are expressed by changes in intonation, rhythm, and timing—all characteristics of music. (3.9, 3.10)

WRITING (p. 487)

1. Key points:
   • The lecture states that education alone is not the solution to society's problems. This contradicts the point in the reading that the solution to most problems societies face is a higher level of political sophistication that comes from more education.
   • The lecture states that facts do not change minds; facts do not cure misinformation. This contradicts the point in the reading that fact checking is effective in correcting misinformation.
   • The lecture states that people often base their opinions on their beliefs rather than on facts. This contradicts the point in the reading that people base their opinions on facts.
   • The lecture states that if people feel threatened, they will not listen to new information. This contradicts the point in the reading that when people feel threatened, they will seek the truth. (4.1–4.5)
2. Responses will vary. (4.6–4.10)

TEST 2

READING (p. 491)

1. **B** *Abolish* means *end* in this context. Clues: *...objected to slavery...; ...wanted to ----- the institution; ...Canada passed a law abolishing slavery and declared that any escaped slaves who came to Canada would be free citizens*; the prefix *ab–* = away. (1.3)

2. **D** Clues: *In 1793, Canada passed a law abolishing slavery and declared that any escaped slaves who came to Canada would be free citizens.* (1.1)

3. **D** *Because the Underground Railroad was so secret...* is paraphrased in *...it was a secret organization. ...few records exist that would reveal the true number of people who traveled it to freedom* is paraphrased in *We do not know exactly how many slaves escaped on the Underground Railroad....* (1.6)

4. **C** *Fugitives* means *runaways* in this context. Clues: *Runaway slaves...; ...hid in wagons...; ...traveled on foot...; ...escaped...* (1.3)

5. **C** The passage does not mention riding in a railcar as a method of escape on the Underground Railroad. All the other answers are mentioned: *The fugitives hid in wagons under loads of hay...; Boys disguised themselves as girls, and girls dressed as boys; ...twenty–eight slaves escaped by walking in a funeral procession....* (1.2)

6. **B** The author's purpose is to illustrate the secret nature of the escape network. Clues: *...the Underground Railroad was so secret...; ...developed its own language; ...elude the slave hunters; ...hiding places...; ...slaves who dared to run away and break for liberty.* (1.5)

7. **A** *Elude* means *avoid* in this context. Clues: *...backcountry roads that were used to ----- the slave hunters; ...hiding places....* The runaway slaves had to avoid being caught by the slave hunters. (1.3)

8. **C** *Break for* means *escape to* in this context. Clues: *...slaves who dared to run away and ----- liberty.* The purpose of the Underground Railroad was to help slaves escape to liberty in areas where slavery was illegal. (1.3)

9. **A** Clues: *...the Underground Railroad, a loosely organized system whereby runaway slaves were passed from safe house to safe house as they fled northwards to free states or Canada.* (1.1)

10. **C** The author means that Harriet Tubman was sought by the authorities for helping escaped slaves. Clues: *...Harriet Tubman, a former slave who dedicated her life to helping other runaways; ...but she was never captured....* (1.3)

11. **B** Clues: *The people who worked on the railroad were breaking the law.* (1.1)

12. **D** You can infer that the author believes the railroad represented a psychological victory for abolitionists. Clues: *...the few thousand slaves who made their way to freedom in this way each year had a symbolic significance...; ...slavery in the United States was finally abolished in 1865.* (1.4)

13. **A** The added sentence adds the example of women and children escaping, which logically follows the example of young men given in the previous sentence. (1.7)

14. **B, D, E** Key information: *The abolitionist movement...objected to slavery on moral grounds...; The American antislavery movement was at the height of its activity during the 1800s, when abolitionists developed the Underground Railroad, a loosely organized system whereby runaway slaves were passed from safe house to safe house as they fled northwards to free states or Canada; ...hiding places where the slaves were fed and cared for...; The "agents" were the people who planned the escape routes. The "conductors" were the fearless men and women who led the slaves toward freedom. The "passengers" were the slaves who dared to run away and break for liberty.* Answer (A) is not mentioned; answers (C) and (F) are minor ideas. (1.8)

15. **B** Clues: *A tornado can produce tremendous destructive power in a restricted area as it passes by...; ...tornadoes are short–lived....* (1.1)

16. **D** *Jeopardy* means *danger* in this context. Clues: *...violent...; ...incredible devastation; ...powerful blasts of wind put all human life in -----, sending debris flying and lifting buildings from their foundations.* (1.3)

17. **C** *Nevertheless, some mystery still surrounds tornadoes, and their formation cannot be predicted with absolute accuracy...* is paraphrased in *...we cannot predict with certainty the formation of every tornado. ...even when conditions for their occurrence seem just right* is paraphrased in *Despite the presence of the right conditions....* (1.6)

18. **B** Clues: *Most tornadoes are created by, and travel with, intense thunderstorm cells; ...favor the warmest part of the day, when solar heating and thunderstorm development are at their maximum.* (1.1)

19. **C** *Mature* means *large* in this context. Clues: *The actual tornadic circulation covers a much wider area than the funnel cloud suggests; ...the diameter of a funnel cloud is typically only about one–tenth that of the associated tornadic circulation.* (1.3)

20. **B** *Whirling* means *spinning* in this context. Clues: *...spinning funnel cloud...; ...small vortexes... around the central core....* (1.3)

21. **D** The paragraph supports the statement that tornadoes can differ greatly in size, shape, and color. Clues: *The funnel may range in diameter from a few meters to 3.2 kilometers...; A funnel can assume a variety of forms, from a thin, writhing, ropelike pendant of grayish white to a thick mass of menacing black.* (1.4)

22. **A** The passage does not state that movement of the ground contributes to tornado formation. All the other answers are given: *Because tornadoes require moist air, they favor the warmest part of the day...; ...spring weather conditions and flat terrain are ideal for tornado development.* (1.2)

23. **C** The author means that tornadoes occur most frequently in April, May, and June. Clues: *Almost three–quarters of the tornadoes in North America occur from March to July.* (1.3)

24. B   Clues: *Around 87 percent of all tornadoes and their parent cells travel from southwest to northeast....* (1.1)

25. A   The author's purpose is to show that tornadoes can move in different ways. Clues: *...any direction is possible. Tornado trajectories are often irregular...a hopscotch pattern of destruction as they alternately touch down and lift off the ground; ...move in circles and even to describe figure eights.* (1.5)

26. D   In the added sentence, *For this reason* is a transition that indicates a cause–result relationship. *For this reason* links the idea that tornadoes *favor the warmest part of the day,* mentioned in the previous sentence, with the time expression *between 10:00 a.m. and 6:00 p.m.* in the added sentence. (1.7)

27. A, D, E   Key information: *Most tornadoes are created by, and travel with, intense thunderstorm cells; The funnel cloud forms in response to the steep air pressure directed from the storm's outer edge toward its center. Humid air...is drawn inward toward the center of the system; ...the spring weather conditions and flat terrain are ideal for tornado development.* Answers (B) and (F) are minor ideas. Answer (C) is not mentioned. (1.8)

28. A   *Thrust* means *movement* in this context. Clues: *...toward a style...; ...endorsing an American architecture...; ...developed regional styles....* (1.3)

29. D   Clues: *Her Lookout Studio...appears to rise straight from the rim of the Grand Canyon...; ...she wanted the building to be a part of its environment...; Like Mary Colter, Frank Lloyd Wright believed that architecture was an extension of the natural environment; Wright's own studio–residence in Wisconsin was completely integrated with the surrounding landscape.* (1.1)

30. C   Clues: *Colter created a uniquely Southwestern idiom...; She preferred to use materials indigenous to the region, such as Kaibab limestone and yellow pine.* (1.1)

31. A   *She took great stock in materials and setting...* is paraphrased in *Colter valued materials and location.... ...gathering many of her materials on–site...* is paraphrased in *...many natural materials collected from the building site. ...incorporating them in their natural state into her projects* is paraphrased in *...she blended into her works many natural materials....* (1.6)

32. C   *Merged* means *joined* in this context. Clues: *...integral halves of a single composition... seamlessly; ...Lookout Studio...appears to rise straight from the rim of the Grand Canyon....* (1.3)

33. B   Clues: *She decided to recreate a Native American watchtower...; The ancient Round Tower at Mesa Verde became the direct inspiration for the form and proportions of the Watchtower.* (1.1)

34. B   You can infer that the Watchtower's purpose was to help people appreciate the desert scenery. Clues: *Her magnificent Watchtower, overlooking the Grand Canyon in Arizona, was built to suggest an ancient Native American ruin preserved for the delight of the present–day traveler; ...enhancing the view of the surrounding desert and the canyon and river below.* (1.4)

35. D   *Appalled* means *shocked* in this context. Clues: *...by much of what he saw in the industrialized world. He was not fond of cities....* (1.3)

36. B   The passage does not state that a direct reference to the region's history characterizes the Prairie style of architecture. All the other answers are given: *Every element of the design corresponded to the surrounding landscape; ...the Prairie style of residential architecture, whose emphasis on horizontal elements...; The eaves of the low–pitched roof extend well beyond the walls, enhancing the structure's horizontality.* (1.2)

37. A   *Nestled* means *set comfortably* in this context. Clues: *...integrated with the surrounding landscape; ...in the brow of a hill....* (1.3)

38. D   The author's purpose is to show that Wright did not work in just one style. Clues: *...yet it departs from the Prairie philosophy...; Some features of the house are more like those of the simple, unadorned International style....* (1.5)

39. B   The added sentence develops the topic of Taliesin, mentioned in the previous sentence. The added sentence discusses the idea of blurring the distinction between the manmade and the natural, which the rest of the paragraph develops with examples. (1.7)

40. C, E, G   Mary Colter: *Colter created a uniquely Southwestern idiom incorporating desert landscapes with Native American arts...; ...Colter's integration of history, architecture, and landscape in a unified work of art; She decided to recreate a Native American watchtower...; The ancient Round Tower at Mesa Verde became the direct inspiration...; She treated building and site as integral halves of a single composition and merged them seamlessly. Her Lookout Studio...appears to rise straight from the rim of the Grand Canyon....*

A, D   Frank Lloyd Wright: *Wright and his followers in Chicago developed the Prairie style of domestic architecture that reflected the natural landscape of the Midwest; ...his favorite commissions were for homes, usually in the country.* Answer (B) is not mentioned; answer (F) is inaccurate for both Mary Colter and Frank Lloyd Wright. (1.9)

LISTENING — Part 1 (p. 504)

1. C   The speakers are mainly discussing the woman's interest in an internship. The woman says: *I'm hoping to do something in the arts, maybe some sort of work experience or internship.* The man says: *Then it sounds like an internship might be a good move for you.* (2.1)

2. D   The woman says: *It's the whole atmosphere of the theater that I find exciting.* (2.2)

3. C   The woman thinks she is not very skilled at acting. She says: *...I took drama in high school, but I was awful on stage.* (2.3)

4. B   The man's purpose is to learn more about the woman's interests in theater, specifically whether directing or lighting interests her. (2.3)

5. A, D   The man suggests that the woman gather some of her drawings: *Why don't you put together a portfolio of your drawings?* He also suggests that she write to the theater manager: *You should also write a letter to the manager of the theater.* (2.2)

6. B   The main purpose of the lecture is to explain how the carbon cycle works. The professor says: *The movement of carbon through an ecosystem parallels the movement of energy, as carbon is cycled through a number of life processes; In the carbon cycle, the processes of photosynthesis and respiration balance each other and provide a link between the atmosphere and the earth environments.* (2.3)

7. C   The professor says: *Respiration by all organisms—plants and animals—returns carbon dioxide to the atmosphere. The cycling of carbon dioxide in the atmosphere is essentially global.* (2.2)

8. B   The professor's purpose is to explain how carbon can be removed from the cycle for long periods. During the formation of coal and petroleum, carbon is *locked away, buried in the earth, for millions of years.* (2.3)

9. A, C   The season of year affects the amount of carbon dioxide in the atmosphere: *The amount of carbon dioxide in the atmosphere varies slightly with the seasons.* The burning of fossil fuels also affects the amount of carbon dioxide: *Another factor affecting atmospheric carbon levels is our burning of fuels; We're burning it as fossil fuels and turning it into carbon dioxide. The combustion of wood, coal, and petroleum adds more carbon dioxide to the atmosphere.* (2.2)

10. D   The professor says: *In the Northern Hemisphere, concentrations are lowest during the summer and highest during the winter. This is because in summer plants reach their highest level of photosynthetic activity, reducing the amount of carbon dioxide in the atmosphere.* (2.2)

11. A   The professor means that there is disagreement over the effects of changes to the carbon cycle. According to the professor, the consequences of the increase in carbon dioxide are *a cause of conflict between scientists and policy makers*, meaning that scientists and policy makers do not agree. (2.4)

12. C   The main idea is that sports contain many elements of hunting. The professor says: *...the ancient pattern of killing prey is kept alive...; Think of how many Olympic sports there are that involve aiming, throwing, and running—which are all hunting skills; In some sports, there's still a strong symbolic element of the kill.* (2.1)

13. D   The professor's purpose is to encourage the student to elaborate, to give a more detailed answer. (2.3)

14. A   The professor says: *The ancient Romans brought the hunt to the people by confining it to an arena—the Coliseum. The Coliseum made the hunting field smaller, and this sort of intensified the activity for the entertainment of the spectators.* (2.2)

15. D   The professor says: *Take track and field sports. These don't involve animals, but they did originate in hunting; Think of how many Olympic sports there are that involve aiming, throwing, and running—which are all hunting skills.* (2.2)

16. A, D   Fencing and boxing contain a symbolic element of the kill. The professor says: *In some sports, there's still a strong symbolic element of the kill. ...boxing, fencing...examples of ritualized fighting.* (2.2)

17. B   The professor implies that the concept of sportsmanship makes sports less negative. He says: *Because sports contain such a powerful negative element, most have an ideal of acceptable behavior—something we call "sportsmanship."* (2.4)

Listening — Part 2 (p. 510)

1. B   The student wants to discuss an idea for a paper. The student says: *...just an idea I have. I've been thinking—um, I was reading about what's been going on with those houses on Fox Point; ...I was sort of thinking I could write a paper on it.* (2.3)

2. A   The man is mainly interested in some houses that are sliding. The man says: *...I was reading about what's been going on with those houses on Fox Point; ...I was sort of thinking I could write a paper on it.* (2.1)

3. B   The student thinks the local slide may have a similar cause to that of the Leaning Tower of Pisa, which was caused by settlement. The student says: *I thought maybe...the slide on Fox Point was a case of subsidence...when the earth sinks 'cause there's a weakening of support. I was thinking this might be an example of settlement.* (2.3)

4. B   The professor says: *Mudslides are most common on intermediate slopes—27 to 45 degrees....* (2.2)

5. C, D   You can predict that the man will include in his research a study of the area's geology: *One suggestion I have is to take a look at the county's Web site. There's a page on the geology of the region.* You can also predict that he will include a search for other mudslides in the area: *This area has a history of slides. There was one on Johnson Island about ten, twelve years ago.* (2.4)

6. C   The speakers mainly discuss the properties of meteors and comets. The professor says: *Meteors are tiny bits of mineral or rock that strike the atmosphere; Comets, on the other hand, don't enter the atmosphere; A meteor shower appears to radiate from a single point in the sky; Comets actually have three distinct components...; All comets are periodic because they complete their orbits in a certain interval of time.* (2.1)

7. A   The professor says: *Meteors are tiny bits of mineral or rock that strike the atmosphere. Billions of them crash into the atmosphere every day, and they're vaporized, and they drop tons of cosmic dust on the earth.* (2.2)

8. D   The student wants the professor to give more explanation about the connection between meteors and comets, specifically whether meteors come from comets. (2.3)

9. B   The professor implies that the material they are discussing will be on the test. The class is reviewing for a test on Friday. The professor suggests that the student reread a section of the chapter because he might see the material from that section again on Friday. (2.5)

10. B   The professor says: *Comets actually have three distinct components: the nucleus... the coma...and the tail....* (2.2)

11. A   The student says that her *parents saw Halley's Comet the last time it passed by Earth.* The professor hopes that the students will be watching it with their great–grandchildren. You can infer that Halley's Comet will pass Earth again several decades from now. (2.4)

12. D   The professor says: *A child's first experience with playing an instrument should be by ear, without the distraction of printed music.* (2.2)

13. B   The professor's purpose is to introduce the main point he wants to make about when and how children should learn to read music. (2.3)

14. B, C   The professor says children should learn to read musical notation when a group of children play music together: *A good time to teach notation is when a group of children play together. The printed score is a way to help them sort of keep track of who plays what and when.* Also, they should learn how to read when the music is too complex to learn by ear: *Another good time is when the child wants to play music that's so complex it would be difficult to learn by ear.* (2.2)

15. A   The professor says: *The teacher should play the score for the child the first time through, and demonstrate how the notes on the page are transformed into music.* (2.2)

16. C   The professor says: *After children can play by ear, and then by chord symbols, the next step is to read standard music notation.* (2.2)

17. A   The professor implies that each method of playing music is appropriate for some students. He says: *The three methods of playing music...are all valuable in their own way. Some children will always prefer...; Others will like...; And still others will find their musical home....* (2.4)

Speaking (p. 516)

1. Responses will vary. (3.1–3.4)
2. Responses will vary. (3.1–3.4)
3. Key points:
   •The woman's opinion about the attendance policy is that it is fair and justified.
   •One reason she gives is that the instructor has the right to set the attendance policy.
   •Another reason is that the instructor has to be there every day, and so should the students.
   •Another reason is that participating in class is an important part of learning.
   •Another reason is that students need to go to class because they can't always understand everything on their own. (3.5, 3.7, 3.10)
4. Key points:
   •The gestural theory of language states that language first evolved as a gesture system before becoming vocal.
   •The professor gives the example of primates that use gestures to communicate. This supports the idea that gestures are a form of language because they convey meaning.

•The professor discusses a study of dance, which showed a similarity between brain activity associated with leg movement and speech. This suggests that dance was an early form of language. Dance can communicate ideas and feelings, as language does. (3.6, 3.7, 3.10)
5. Key points:
   •The man's problem is that his parents want him to take an internship at a bank, but he would rather accept an internship as a research assistant to his sociology professor.
   •One solution is to take the internship at the bank to please his parents.
   •Another solution is to explain to his father why he wants to accept the research internship.
   •Opinions about the preferred solution will vary. (3.8, 3.10)
6. Key points:
   •Competition is the struggle over scarce resources. The lecture discusses direct and indirect competition.
   •Direct competition is when a bird actively excludes others from getting resources. Examples are stealing food, establishing territories, and fighting.
   •Indirect competition is when birds simply use up a resource so others can not use that resource. An example is a flock of geese eating all the food in an area. (3.9, 3.10)

Writing (p. 521)

1. Key points:
   •The lecture discusses negative aspects of same–age peer groups, while the reading focuses on positive aspects.
   •The lecture discusses a study showing that dividing eleven–year–old boys into two groups led to negative attitudes between the groups. Structured contests increased the teasing and insults between the groups. This challenges the point in the reading that peer groups build tolerance and decrease conflict.
   •The lecture states that contests increased conflict between the two groups, but when the groups were put back together and given a cooperative task, conflict was reduced. This challenges the point in the reading that contests and competition between same–age peer groups will reduce conflict.
   •The lecture states that when children of the same age are divided into groups, competition comes more naturally than cooperation. This challenges the point in the reading that cooperation comes naturally to children of the same age. (4.1–4.5)
2. Responses will vary. (4.6–4.10)

TEST 3

READING (p. 525)

1. **B** *Internal environment* means *the animal's body* in this context. Clues: *...biological systems...; ...conditions within their bodies.* (1.3)

2. **A** *Constraint* means *restriction* in this context. Clues: *Animals can succeed only in a limited range of body temperatures....* (1.3)

3. **A** Clues: *Temperature is a constraint for animals, all of which must maintain biochemical stability. When body temperature drops too low, metabolism slows...; If body temperature rises too high, metabolic reactions become unbalanced....* (1.1)

4. **D** The terms "cold–blooded" and "warm–blooded" are inaccurate because they imply that the animal's blood is always cold or warm. Clues: *Some "cold–blooded" animals, such as lizards, have higher body temperatures when active than many "warm–blooded" animals have when hibernating.* (1.1)

5. **D** *Optimum* means *most favorable* in this context. Clues: *...generate and retain enough heat from metabolism to elevate their own body temperature to the optimum level.* Endotherms can produce and store enough heat to maintain the most favorable body temperature for their survival. (1.3)

6. **C** *Exploit* means *take advantage of* in this context. Clues: *...regulate it behaviorally by selecting areas of the environment with a more favorable temperature; ...exploit hour–to–hour changes in solar radiation to keep their body temperature relatively constant.* The lizard changes its behavior at different times of day to take advantage of the amount of solar heat available. (1.3)

7. **D** You can infer that ectotherms are likely to live where heat from the sun is available. Clues: *Ectotherms warm their body mainly by absorbing heat from their environment; Some, such as desert lizards, exploit hour–to–hour changes in solar radiation...; ...the lizard absorbs the sun's heat...; ...the lizard will emerge to bask in the sun.* (1.4)

8. **B** The author's purpose is to stress that generating internal body heat requires a lot of calories. Clues: *Because much of an endotherm's daily intake of calories is used to generate heat, the endotherm must eat more food than an ectotherm of the same size.* (1.5)

9. **A** *This is why...* is paraphrased in *Because endotherms can maintain their body temperature.... ...endotherms can remain active in winter and exploit habitats denied to ectotherms* is paraphrased in *...they can live in cold habitats.* (1.6)

10. **C** The passage does not state that high level of intelligence is an advantage of endothermy. All the other answers are given: *...endotherms can generally endure vigorous activity...; ...endotherms can remain active in winter and exploit habitats denied to ectotherms; ...they also have mechanisms for cooling the body in a hot environment.....* (1.2)

11. **D** Clues: *If the animal becomes too warm, it decreases heat production and increases heat loss by evaporative cooling (sweating or panting).* (1.1)

12. **D** The added sentence gives more information about *endotherms*, mentioned in the previous sentence, further developing the idea that *the source of their body heat is internal.* (1.7)

13. **C, F** Ectotherms: *...the ectotherms, body temperature is determined almost entirely by their surroundings; Ectotherms warm their body mainly by absorbing heat from their environment; ...many are able to regulate it behaviorally by selecting areas of the environment with a more favorable temperature; ...will emerge to bask in the sun; ...seeks shade under a rock.*

    B, E, G Endotherms: *...some animals are able to generate and retain enough heat from metabolism to elevate their own body temperature...; These animals are called the endotherms because the source of their body heat is internal; Because much of an endotherm's daily intake of calories is used to generate heat, the endotherm must eat more food...; ...can generate heat by increasing muscular activity (exercise or shivering)...; ...can decrease heat loss by increasing insulation; ...decreases heat production and increases heat loss by evaporative cooling (sweating or panting).* Answers (A) and (D) describe neither ectotherms nor endotherms. (1.9)

14. **B** Clues: *Canadian English became a separate variety of North American English...when thousands of Loyalists...fled north to Canada. Many Loyalists settled in southern Ontario in the 1780s....* (1.1)

15. **A** *Norms* means *patterns* in this context. Clues: *...their speech became the basis...; ...a definition based on the ----- of urban middle–class speech.* (1.3)

16. **C** *A great deal in common with* means *many similarities to* in this context. Clues: *...the ways in which it resembles....* (1.3)

17. **B** Clues: *Modern Canadian English is usually defined by the ways in which it resembles and differs from American or British English; ...many Americans identify a Canadian accent as British; ...many British people identify a Canadian accent as American....* (1.1)

18. **D** *Spot* means *find* in this context. Clues: *...instantly recognizable...; ...one Canadian in a crowded room will easily ----- the other Canadian among the North Americans.* (1.3)

19. **C** *Canadian pronunciation reflects the experience of a people struggling...* is paraphrased in *...this effort is shown in their pronunciation. ...struggling for national identity against two strong influences* is paraphrased in *Canadians have tried to distinguish themselves as a nation.* (1.6)

20. **A** *Kerosene* did not originate in a North American Indian language. All the other answers did originate in Indian languages: *Several words are borrowed from North American Indian languages, for example, "kayak,"... "parka,"...; The name of the country itself has an Indian origin; the Iroquois word "kanata" originally meant "village."* (1.2)

21. **D** You can infer that much of the vocabulary for ice hockey originated in Canada. Clues: *...many words and phrases originating in Canada itself...; A number of terms for ice hockey...have become part of World Standard English.* (1.4)

22. A   Clues: *Some features of Canadian English...are often deliberately identified with Canadian speakers...; Among the original Canadian idioms, perhaps the most famous is the almost universal use of "eh?"....* (1.1)

23. D   *Homogeneity* means *sameness* in this context. Clues: *While there is a greater degree of ----- in Canadian English...several dialect areas do exist across Canada. Linguists have identified distinct dialects....* (1.3)

24. C   Clues: *...several dialect areas...across Canada; ...distinct dialects for the Maritime Provinces, Newfoundland, the Ottawa Valley, southern Ontario, the Prairie Provinces, the Arctic North, and the West.* (1.1)

25. C   In the added sentence, *Thus* is a transition that shows result by linking *"out" is pronounced like "oat"* in the previous sentence with *"out" rhymes with "boat"* in the added sentence. (1.7)

26. A, D, E   Key information: *Canadian English has a great deal in common with the English spoken in the United States...; About 75 percent of Canadians use the British "zed"...; ...75 percent of Canadians use the American pronunciation of...; The differences are mainly in pronunciation...; Canadian pronunciation reflects the experience of a people struggling for national identity...; An important characteristic of the vocabulary of Canadian English is the use of many words and phrases originating in Canada itself....* Answers (B), (C), and (F) are minor ideas. (1.8)

27. C   Clues: *Human migration occurs on various geographic scales...; Several factors stimulate migration, including....* (1.1)

28. D   Clues: *Many migration streams actually consist of a series of stages, a phenomenon known as step migration. For example, a peasant family from the countryside is likely to move first to a village, then to a nearby town, later to a city, and finally to a metropolis....* (1.1)

29. A   *Impel* means *force* in this context. Clues: *...leave their home communities; ...lack of jobs or educational opportunities, political fear, ethnic or religious discrimination, and natural disasters....* (1.3)

30. C   The passage does not identify a high standard of living as a condition that may push people to move away from their place of origin. All of the other answers are given: *The lack of jobs ... religious discrimination, and natural disasters are all examples of push factors.* (1.2)

31. D   *The circumstances that induce people to move from one part of the world to another—economic, political, and environmental conditions...* is paraphrased in *The decision to migrate a great distance.... ...usually involve a combination of push and pull factors* is paraphrased in *...normally results from both push and pull factors.* (1.6)

32. B   *Vague* means *unclear* in this context. Clues: *...they are likely to understand push factors more accurately than pull factors; ...overly optimistic....* (1.3)

33. C   You can infer that people may overestimate the chance of finding work in their chosen destination. Clues: *Pull factors are the circumstances that attract people to certain destinations, such as...the chance of getting a job...; Pull factors tend to be more vague, and people often have overly optimistic expectations of their destination.* (1.4)

34. A   The main purpose is to present some economic causes of migration. The given economic causes include *poverty, industrialization, expanding metropolitan and industrial centers, perceived opportunities, to search for a better life,* and *earning in a factory or mine.* (1.5)

35. B   The author means that the people have chosen not to return to their villages. In this context, *roots* means native village or cultural background. To cut oneself off from one's roots is to end the relationship with one's native village. Clues: *Some workers migrate only seasonally or temporarily; ...tend to retain their village roots and return home...; However, most migrants relocate permanently.... However* shows contrast between workers who migrate temporarily and those who relocate permanently. (1.3)

36. C   The paragraph supports the statement that political circumstances are a major factor driving numerous migration streams, which is the implied main idea. Clues: *...migratory flows caused by the push factors of political oppression, revolution, and war; Millions of people were uprooted as a result of political, cultural, and religious conflict; ...the armed conflict in the former Yugoslavia...; ...a civil war in Rwanda....* (1.4)

37. D   *Strife* means *conflict* in this context. Clues: *...in combination with economic and political problems; ...ethnic...civil war...refugee crisis....* (1.3)

38. A   Clues: *Reasons for migration include environmental conditions, often in combination with economic and political problems; ...famine, along with the oppressive political system...; ...a series of droughts...combined with such factors as ethnic strife and civil war....* (1.1)

39. D   In the added sentence, *Consequently* is a transition that shows effect. *Consequently* shows that *the majority of migrants move only a short distance* is the logical effect of *People are likely to have more complete and accurate information about nearby places,* stated in the previous sentence. (1.7)

40. A, C, F   Key information: *Human migration occurs on various geographic scales: from one continent or country to another, between regions within a single country, and from one city neighborhood to another; Many migration streams actually consist of a series of stages, a phenomenon known as step migration; Push factors are the conditions that impel people to leave their home communities; Pull factors are the circumstances that attract people to certain destinations...; Several factors stimulate migration, including economic conditions, political conflict, war, cultural circumstances, and environmental factors.* Answers (B), (D), and (E) are minor ideas. (1.8)

LISTENING — Part 1 (p. 538)

1. **A, C** The speakers discuss their summer plans. The professor asks: *So are you ready for summer?* The student then describes his plans for the summer program at Silverwood. The student asks: *What will you be doing this summer?* The professor then discusses her teaching. The speakers also discuss their musical interests. The student says: *I'll be studying oboe with him, and also orchestra…and I'm hoping to do the French horn, too, and maybe take up the krummhorn….* The professor says: *I'll be teaching Theory I and II, and coaching voice; I play piano and sing.* (2.1)

2. **A** The professor means that he is one of the best teachers available. *Couldn't ask for a better teacher* means that there is no better teacher to ask for. (2.4)

3. **B** The professor's purpose is to comment on the man's summer workload. A *full plate* is a busy schedule with a lot of activities. (2.3)

4. **C** The professor says: *Yes, I am—a jazz quintet. We do mostly standards. I play piano and sing. For me, that's fun and relaxation time.* (2.2)

5. **D** The professor says: *I heard you got the scholarship for the summer program at Silverwood.* The student says: *…I'm sure your recommendation helped me a lot; And thanks again for the recommendation.* You can infer that the professor recommended the student for a scholarship. (2.4)

6. **D** The main idea is that fossils provide clues to our geologic and environmental history. The professor says: *…their significance as geologic tools became evident; Correlation gives us a better understanding of geologic history; Fossils are the most useful means of correlating rocks of similar age in different regions; In addition to being important time indicators, fossils are important environmental indicators.* (2.1)

7. **C** The professor says: *That was when a British engineer and canal builder made an interesting discovery. He noticed that each rock layer in the canals he worked on contained fossils that were unlike those in the rocks either above or below. Each layer held fossils of different types of ancient plants or animals.* (2.2)

8. **B** The professor says: *Correlation gives us a better understanding of geologic history. By correlating the rocks from one place to another, we've been able to develop a geologic time scale that applies to the whole planet.* (2.2)

9. **A** The professor's purpose is to explain how fossils can indicate the age of rock layers. The professor says: *The principle of fossil succession states that fossil organisms succeed one another in a definite order; Thus, fossils document the evolution of life through time. Therefore, we can identify the time period of rock layers by the types of fossils we find there.* (2.3)

10. **A** The professor means that fossils of extinct species will not appear in higher layers of rock. The professor says: *The fossils at the bottom don't appear at the top…; …certain fossils disappeared from the record.* Fossils disappear from the record in the rock layers after those species become extinct. (2.4)

11. **C** The professor's purpose is to illustrate how fossils are clues about the past environment. The professor gives the example of *sandstone with ripple marks*, indicating *the action of the water.* These fossils are a clue that the environment once contained *a shallow sea.* The professor mentions *fossils of oyster shells and water–loving plants such as ferns*, which are clues about the past environment. (2.3)

12. **B** The professor mainly discusses a decline in pollinator populations. He says: *…pollinator scarcity; …the worst pollinator crisis in history; …a steep decline in North American populations of honeybees.* (2.1)

13. **A, D** Parasites have affected pollinator populations: *An outbreak of parasitic mites has caused a steep decline in North American populations of honeybees.* Farm chemicals have also affected pollinator populations: *In California, farm chemicals are killing around ten percent of all the honeybee colonies.* (2.2)

14. **A** The professor's purpose is to show the effect of agriculture on pollinators. Large–scale agriculture has reduced the areas of nectar–producing plants that pollinators depend on. (2.3)

15. **B** The professor says: *Unfortunately, the herbicides used on the milkweed in the Great Plains are taking a toll on monarchs, and fewer of them are reaching their winter grounds in Mexico.* You can infer that the population of monarch butterflies has been reduced because of herbicides. (2.4)

16. **D** The professor says: *…the long–nosed bat. These amazing animals feed on cactus flowers; …they lap up the nectar at the bottom of the flower, and then when the bat flies off to another cactus….* (2.2)

17. **A** The professor describes problems in specific pollinator populations: honeybees, monarch butterflies, and long–nosed bats. He says: *An outbreak of parasitic mites has caused a steep decline in North American populations of honeybees; Both wild and domesticated bees are in serious trouble because of pesticides; …the herbicides used on the milkweed in the Great Plains are taking a toll on monarchs, and fewer of them are reaching their winter grounds…; …the long–nosed bat is having a tough time, too. Some desert ranchers mistake them for vampire bats, and they've tried to poison them, or dynamite the caves where they roost.* (2.6)

LISTENING — Part 2 (p. 544)

1. **B** The woman is not sure whether she needs the physics book right now because she is on the waiting list for the class. She says: *I don't know if I'll actually end up in the class, so I don't know if I should buy the book yet.* (2.1)

2. **A** The man says: *If you do get in the class, the registrar's office will let you know right away. As soon as there's an opening in the class, if someone drops out, then whoever's next on the waiting list gets in automatically. They'll let you know as soon as that happens.* (2.2)

3. C   The woman's is expressing displeasure about the store's return policy. She does not like that the bookstore will give a full refund only if the book is returned during the first week of the quarter and that only half of the amount will be refunded in the second and third weeks. (2.5)

4. B, D   You can infer that the speakers agree that the bookstore's return policy is very strict. When the man explains the policy, the woman says: *That seems kind of stiff.* The man says: *I know, I know. But unfortunately, that's the bookstore's policy. I know…it's kind of unfair in your situation. Sorry.* You can also infer that both speakers think the physics professor is an excellent teacher. The woman says: *Doctor Kelly teaches the class I want to get into! He's the best professor in the whole department.* The man replies: *It's true. I've heard other people say that too.* (2.4)

5. D   The woman says: *…I think I want to buy the textbook now—assuming I will get into the class—so I can get started on the reading.* Later the man says: *…you'll have gotten an early start on reading the book, that is, if you buy it today.* The woman says: *Right. You talked me into it. Thanks for your help.* You can predict that she will probably purchase the book now so she can start reading it. (2.4)

6. A   The discussion is mainly about factors that influence the application of paint. The professor says: *Today I want to talk about the act of painting…controlling and manipulating the paint as you apply it. There are several elements that contribute to the ease or difficulty you have in controlling paint as you're brushing it on paper or canvas.* (2.1)

7. B, C   The coarseness of the painting surface affects the artist's ability to control the paint: *Another is the nature of the surface to which it's applied; The coarseness of the surface—and this is true for both paper and canvas—the coarseness is related to how the paint is absorbed.* Another factor is the quality of the brush: *Another important thing is the quality of the brush you use; A good brush makes all the difference in the world.* (2.2)

8. A   The professor implies that the absorbency of the paper affects the artist's control of the paint. Smooth, low–absorbency paper causes the paint to *flow easily across the surface.* Coarse, high–absorbency paper causes the paint to be taken into the paper more quickly. The topic of the discussion is the artist's ability to control the application of paint; the absorbency of the paper is an important factor in controlling the paint. (2.4)

9. D   The student's purpose is to illustrate the importance of quality in brushes. He describes the difficulty he had when he used *cheaper brushes.* (2.3)

10. C   The professor says: *A high–quality oil painting brush is made from the best grades of bleached animal hair: hogs' bristles; The tip of a high–quality paintbrush is made up of the natural split ends of the hair or bristle of a hog. The tips are never cut or trimmed.* (2.2)

11. D   The professor describes the shape and length of the bristles. He says: *Bristle brushes come in three major shapes: rounds, flats, and brights. The shape, of course, refers to the shape of the bristles…; The third type of brush, the bright, is sometimes confused with the flat brush because the bristles are actually flat, but much shorter.* (2.6)

12. D   The main idea is that photography changed the nature of war reporting. The professor says: *…a series of photographs that ushered in a new era in the visual documentation of war; …the first time most people had ever seen the carnage of the war; …the battlefield was no longer comfortably distant—the camera was bringing it closer…; …photography made a huge impact, and media coverage of war—and public opinion about war—would never be the same again.* (2.1)

13. A   The professor means that more Americans died on that day than on any other day in American history. Several thousand men died or were wounded in one day, and there has never been another day like that. (2.4)

14. C   The professor says: *…Mathew Brady, a leading portrait photographer of the time. Brady owned studios in New York and in Washington….* (2.2)

15. D   The professor's purpose is to emphasize the power of photography in making people aware of the effects of the war. The images had *a sensational impact.* (2.3)

16. A, C   One limitation of photography was that the slow exposure time did not allow action shots: *…the exposure time of the camera was slow…; …it was not possible for photographers to take action pictures.* Another limitation was that newspapers were not able to reproduce photographs: *…newspapers couldn't yet reproduce photographs.* (2.2)

17. B   The professor implies that Mathew Brady's work had a lasting effect on photography and journalism. She says: *Mathew Brady's work was the first instance of the comprehensive photo–documentation of a war—the Civil War—which as a result became the first media war; …media coverage of war—and public opinion about war—would never be the same again.* (2.4)

SPEAKING (p. 550)

1. Responses will vary. (3.1–3.4)
2. Responses will vary. (3.1–3.4)
3. Key points:
   - A new policy requires that students who take a lecture course in social science also take a discussion section.
   - The man's opinion about the required discussion section is favorable.
   - One reason he gives is that three hours of lecture time is not long enough for the professor to cover all the material they need to know for the examination.
   - Another reason is that the discussion section will give students a chance to talk to the teacher and other students and thus to learn more.
   - Another reason is that it is easy to get a high grade in the discussion section. (3.5, 3.7, 3.10)

4. Key points:
- Dehydration is the condition in which too much water is lost from the body and not replaced.
- The professor gives the example of a woman who had symptoms of dehydration, but failed to notice. The woman was too busy to notice thirst, which is the first sign of dehydration.
- The woman also experienced weakness, confusion, fast heart rate, and low blood pressure, which are all symptoms of dehydration. Her condition improved when she received fluids. (3.6, 3.7, 3.10)

5. Key points:
- The woman's problem is that she needs an official copy of her transcript, but she cannot get one because there is an unpaid charge on her student account. She was charged for something that her roommate did (a broken window).
- One possible solution is to pay the charge to clear her account. She could pay it herself (then have her roommate pay her back) or send her roommate in to pay it.
- Another solution is to talk to the dean's secretary about releasing the transcript.
- Opinions about the preferred solution will vary. (3.8, 3.10)

6. Key points:
- The subject matter of theater is always human beings and human concerns. Other arts can deal with any subject, but theater always focuses on human experiences.
- Theater is universal. It exists in every society. Theater always consists of a story presented by performers to an audience.
- Theater is transitory in nature. A performance changes from moment to moment, but is always in the present tense. Theater shares this quality with music and dance. Theater is not a fixed object, like a novel or a painting. Theater is an event, an experience. (3.9, 3.10)

WRITING (p. 555)

1. Key points:
- The lecture states that too many dog breeders are unqualified; backyard breeders exploit animals for profit. This contradicts the point in the reading that breeders love dogs and contribute to their welfare.
- The lecture states that the focus on breed purity leads to inbreeding and genetic disorders. This contradicts the point in the reading that dog breeders use genetics beneficially, to produce dogs with desirable traits. The lecture criticizes of the role of breed registries in promoting breed purity; the reading speaks favorably of breed registries.
- The lecture states that the culture of dog breeding is responsible for the proliferation of puppy mills that produce an overpopulation of dogs, leading to more unwanted dogs. This contradicts the point in the reading that the promotion of dog breeds encourages responsible dog ownership. (4.1–4.5)

2. Responses will vary. (4.6–4.10)

TEST 4

READING (p. 559)

1. C *Precocity* means *advanced skill* in this context. Clues: *...abilities...; ...talent...; ...exceptional skill...; ...gifted....* (1.3)

2. A *A musically gifted child has an inborn talent...* is paraphrased in *Children may be born with superior musical ability.... ...the extent to which the talent is expressed publicly...* is paraphrased in *...how this ability is developed. ...will depend upon the environment in which the child lives* is paraphrased in *...their environment will determine....* (1.6)

3. B Clues: *Pitch—or melody—is more central in certain cultures...; Rhythm ...is emphasized in sub–Saharan Africa....* (1.1)

4. A *Predisposed* means *inclined* in this context. Clues: *All children have some aptitude for making music; Infants are especially ----- to acquire these core aspects of music...;* the prefix *pre-* = before; the stem *–pos–* = put. (1.3)

5. C Clues: *Individual differences begin to emerge in young children as they learn to sing. Some children can match large segments of a song by the age of two or three. Many others can only approximate pitch at this age....* (1.1)

6. A Clues: *The appearance of superior musical ability in some children provides evidence that musical talent may be a separate and unique form of intelligence; In many of these cases, the child is average in every other way but displays an exceptional ability in music.* (1.1)

7. B The author's purpose is to give an example of a well–known musical prodigy. Clues: *Every generation in music history has had its famous prodigies...; In the eighteenth century, Wolfgang Amadeus Mozart began composing and performing at the age of six.* (1.5)

8. D Clues: *...modulation—transitions from one key to another....* (1.1)

9. C Appreciation for a wide variety of musical styles is not given as an example of exceptional musical talent. All the other answers are given: *...a remarkable "ear" or extraordinary memory for music...; By the age of eleven, he had composed three symphonies and 30 other major works; ...able to play "Happy Birthday" in the style of various composers....* (1.2)

10. B *Haven* means *safe place* in this context. Clues: *...the child may cling to music because it represents a ----- in a world that is largely confusing and frightening.* (1.3)

11. D You can infer that exceptional musical ability is the result of natural talent and a supportive environment. Clues: *...exceptional skill as a result of a well–designed instructional regime...; ...the good fortune to be born into a musical family in a household filled with music; A musically gifted child has an inborn talent; however, the extent to which the talent is expressed publicly will depend upon the environment in which the child lives.* (1.4)

12. B   In the added sentence, *They* refers to *normal children*, the subject of the previous sentence. The added sentence develops the idea that children *can produce individual sounds and sound patterns*, mentioned in the previous sentence. The added sentence introduces *patterns and tones sung by other people*, which the next sentence develops with *their mother's songs*. (1.7)

13. B, C, F   Key information: *Musically gifted children master at an early age the principal elements of music...; All children have some aptitude for making music; The early appearance of superior musical ability in some children...; ...a natural understanding of musical structure; ...prodigies— individuals with exceptional musical powers...; ...began composing and performing at the age of six; ...musical talent is part of an otherwise disabling condition such as autism...; Unusual musical ability is a regular characteristic of certain anomalies, such as autism.* Answers (A) and (D) are minor ideas; answer (E) is not mentioned. (1.8)

14. D   Clues: *...psychological reasons: modesty, taboo, magical influence, or the desire to please.* (1.1)

15. C   *Elaborate* means *complex* in this context. Clues: *For the male hunters...simple belts or animal skins...; For the female gatherers, more ----- were necessary; ...transport food...carry babies....* (1.3)

16. B   Clues: *And like our hunting–gathering ancestors, most men still carry things on their person....* (1.1)

17. A   *We might say that clothing has to do with covering the body...* is paraphrased in *Clothing protects the body.... ...costume concerns the choice of a particular form of garment for a particular purpose* is paraphrased in *...costume involves selecting clothing for a specific intention.* (1.6)

18. D   Clues: *...costume fulfilled a function beyond that of simple utility. Costume helped to impose authority...; A chieftain's costume...a warrior's costume....* (1.1)

19. D   *Ornaments* means *decorations* in this context. Clues: *...a function beyond that of simple utility; ...the addition of....* (1.3)

20. A   You can infer that the author believes we can learn about a society's social structure by studying costume. Clues: *...costume fulfilled a function beyond that of simple utility; Costume communicates the status of the wearer...; Costume denotes power...; ...costume has come to be an expression of social class and material prosperity.* (1.4)

21. A   *Beacons* means *signals* in this context. Clues: *...uniform says, "I am part of a powerful machine..."; Uniforms are immediate ----- of power and authority. If a person needs to display power....* (1.3)

22. D   The author's purpose is to show how costume conveys authority. Clues: *Uniforms are immediate beacons of power and authority. If a person needs to display power—a police officer, for example...; Height can be exaggerated...thick clothing can make the body look broader and stronger, and boots can enhance the power of the legs.* (1.5)

23. C   The passage does not state that having a heart condition is likely to be indicated by a person's costume. All the other answers are given: *A uniform is a type of costume that serves the important function of displaying membership in a group... sports team...; ...the uniform of the prisoner...; Religious costume signifies spiritual or superhuman authority....* (1.2)

24. C   The added sentence gives examples of *professional or administrative costume*, mentioned in the previous sentence; *the judge's robes and the police officer's uniform* are examples that express authority and power. (1.7)

25. C, E, G   Clothing: *Another function of early clothing—providing comfort and protection...; ...covered their bodies more and more to maintain body warmth; ...we first clothed our bodies for some physical reason, such as protecting ourselves from the elements; ...the function of the earliest clothing was to carry objects; ...carrying was much easier if they were wearing simple belts or animal skins from which they could hang weapons and tools; ...transport food back to the settlement....*

     A, D, F, I   Costume: *...costume reflects social factors such as personal status, religious beliefs...; A uniform is a type of costume that serves the important function of displaying membership in a group...; Costume helped to impose authority...; ...enhanced his physical superiority and suggested he was superhuman...; ...professional or administrative costume is designed to distinguish the wearer and to express personal or delegated authority; Religious costume signifies spiritual or superhuman authority....* Answers (B) and (H) are not mentioned. (1.9)

26. D   You can infer that the main cause of the greenhouse effect is water vapor in the atmosphere. Clues: *...the action of these atmospheric gases is known as the greenhouse effect...; Water vapor is the principal greenhouse gas.* (1.4)

27. A   Clues: *Window glass is relatively transparent to visible radiation but slows the transmission of infrared radiation; Visible radiation...enters the greenhouse...; ...infrared radiation...cannot escape the greenhouse because it is trapped by the solid glass.* (1.1)

28. C   *Transmission* means *escape* in this context. Clues: *...slows the ----- of infrared radiation; ...infrared radiation...cannot escape the greenhouse because it is trapped....* (1.3)

29. B   *However, the greenhouse analogy is not completely accurate...* is paraphrased in *The greenhouse comparison is not perfect.... ...because the trapping of infrared radiation by glass...* is paraphrased in *...as a result of radiation trapping. ...is only part of the reason that most greenhouses retain internal heat* is paraphrased in *...because greenhouses retain heat only partly....* (1.6)

30. C   Clues: *Greenhouses cut heat loss mainly by acting as a shelter from the wind....* (1.1)

31. A   The author's purpose is to illustrate the role of water vapor in the greenhouse effect. Clues: *The effect of a greenhouse gas can be seen by comparing the typical summer weather...; ...air temperatures often differ remarkably due to the absence or presence of the leading greenhouse gas, water vapor.* (1.5)

32. C   *Impede* means *prevent* in this context. Clues: *...there is less water vapor in the air to ----- the escape of infrared radiation; therefore, heat is readily lost to space.* The radiation is not slowed or stopped by water vapor, so the heat from the radiation escapes into space. (1.3)

33. B   You can infer that the cooling effect of clouds exceeds their warming effect. Clues: *...clouds have a net cooling effect on global climate; ...a more extensive cloud cover would tend to cool the planet.* (1.4)

34. D   Clues: *Earth has an abundance of plants to absorb carbon dioxide, but Mars and Venus do not possess living organisms; The atmosphere of Mars is considerably thinner than the atmosphere on Earth...; ...the atmosphere of Venus is about 90 times denser than Earth's....* (1.1)

35. D   *Shrouding* means *covering* in this context. Clues: *...thick, cloud-filled atmosphere....* An atmosphere surrounds or covers a planet. (1.3)

36. C   The author implies that planetary warming on Venus is a model for a possible outcome on Earth. Clues: *Some scientists believe that Venus used to be similar to Earth...; Venus provides a warning for what could happen on Earth if the greenhouse effect continued unchecked....* (1.4)

37. B   The author means that global warming could not be stopped if the greenhouse effect continued unchecked on Earth. When all the surface water evaporated from Venus, *planetary warming became self-sustaining and unstoppable.* The author states that Venus provides a warning for what could happen on Earth. (1.3)

38. A   In the added sentence, *a high, thin cloud cover can raise the temperature* develops the idea that *Nights are usually warmer when the sky is cloud-covered,* stated in the previous sentence. (1.7)

39. B, E, F   Key information: *...certain gases in Earth's atmosphere behave like the panes of glass in a greenhouse. These gases admit visible radiation from the sun but prevent the escape of infrared radiation...; ...greenhouse gases in Earth's atmosphere keep infrared radiation from escaping into space, thereby keeping the planet warm; ...the leading greenhouse gas, water vapor; Clouds produce a greenhouse effect...; ...clouds warm the planet's surface by absorbing and re-radiating infrared radiation...; On both Mars and Venus, the principal atmospheric gas, carbon dioxide, is also the main greenhouse gas.* Answers (A) and (D) are minor ideas. Answer (C) is not mentioned. (1.8)

LISTENING — Part 1 (p. 572)

1. B   The man wants to change his housing situation. He says: *I'd kind of like to live in a smaller building. I'm thinking of moving next semester.* (2.3)

2. A, D   A full refrigerator and two to four bedrooms are features of the suites. The woman says: *The suites have two to four bedrooms...and a full refrigerator.* (2.2)

3. D   The woman's purpose is to apologize for not answering the man's question. The man asks about the rent more than once before the woman answers him. (2.5)

4. C   The man thinks the rent in the villages is higher than he hoped it would be. He says: *Wow. That's more than I expected; ...I was hoping it'd be a lot less.* (2.3)

5. A   The man says: *Number twenty-seven...oh...wow.* He is the 27th person on the waiting list. You can infer that he does not think he will be able to get a room in the villages. (2.5)

6. D   The main purpose of the lecture is to explain how early people started farming. The professor says: *What led these people to invent agriculture, a completely different way of life; ...ancient people changed from hunters and gatherers to farmers when they began to domesticate wild plants and animals.* (2.3)

7. A   The professor says: *The people brought the squash seeds back to their camp. As they ate the seeds, some seeds fell to the ground all around the camp. Later, some of these seeds germinated and produced new plants. Thus, the hunter-gatherers became farmers sort of by accident.* You can infer that the process of gathering wild food led naturally to farming. (2.4)

8. A, D   As plants were first being domesticated, they grew from seeds that were dropped accidentally: *...some seeds fell to the ground all around the camp. Later, some of these seeds germinated and produced new plants.* Also, people started tending and protecting wild gardens: *Now the people had a wild garden of squash plants at their campsite; They tried to protect the plants in practical ways.* (2.2)

9. B   The professor says: *Eventually, the people realized that seeds grew better when they were planted in earth that was turned over. So they began to scratch the earth with a digging stick....* (2.2)

10. C   The professor's purpose is to point out that agriculture developed over a very long time. When something doesn't happen overnight, it takes a long time. The professor says: *The process probably took thousands of years.* (2.3)

11. A   The professor says: *...it's very likely that the change from a hunting-gathering society to an agricultural society followed a similar pattern in different regions of the world.* (2.2)

12. B   The speakers mainly discuss how science and technology are connected. The professor says: *Today we'll focus on science and technology; ...technology often applies the discoveries of science; Science and technology are partners; The relationship between science and technology is very important.* (2.1)

13. A   The professor says: *The electron microscope is an excellent example of applied science.* (2.2)

ANSWER KEY

14. D   The professor's purpose is to give examples of technology that came before science. She says: *In fact, technology came before science in human prehistory. In prehistoric times, technology was driven by inventive humans who built tools, made pottery, designed musical instruments, and so on, all without science....* (2.3)

15. C   The student's purpose is to list additional consequences of technology. His examples are meant to show that technology can not always save us.

16. C   The professor means that technology has both helped and harmed us. A double–edged sword cuts in two directions, and so does technology. Technology helps us: *It's kept us healthier and enabled us to live longer lives.* It also harms us: *...environmental repercussions.* (2.4)

17. B   The student says: *I think scientists have a responsibility to educate politicians and the public about the consequences of certain technologies...; This is why...I've decided to get a master's degree in public policy.* (2.2)

LISTENING — Part 2 (p. 578)

1. A   The student is requesting extra time to finish her project. She explains that she must go home to help her parents. She says: *So I need to ask you for an . extension on my project.* (2.3)

2. D   The professor's purpose is to encourage the student to explain what she will do to finish her coursework because she has just told him that she must go home to help her parents *for a few weeks or maybe longer.* (2.5)

3. B, C   The student says she will watch the lectures online: *I'll watch the online versions of your lectures.* She also says she will email the professor for advice: *...I might need to email you sometimes, if I have questions or need help.* (2.2)

4. C   The professor suggests that the student accept a grade of Incomplete and finish her work later. He says: *I suggest that you take a grade of Incomplete. That would give you two months after the end of the quarter to complete your project.* (2.2)

5. D   The professor implies that he trusts the student to finish her project. He grants her an extension to complete her project because he knows that she is a good student. (2.4)

6. B   The lecture is mainly a history of an art movement. The professor says: *The Group's origins date back to the 1911 showing...; ...a new direction for Canadian art, a distinctly Canadian style of painting; Their 1920 exhibition was an important moment in Canadian art.* (2.6)

7. A   The professor's view is that the Group of Seven created a distinctive Canadian art inspired by Canada itself. He says: *...a generation of artists set out to create a school of painting that would record the Canadian scene and reinforce a distinctive Canadian identity; Their 1920 exhibition was an important moment in Canadian art. It proclaimed that Canadian art must be inspired by Canada itself.* (2.3)

8. D   The professor's purpose is to show how one artist, Tom Thomson, inspired the Group's direction in seeking a distinctly Canadian art. (2.3)

9. B, D   The Group of Seven painted jack pine trees and uninhabited landscapes: *... "The Jack Pine," one of the nation's best–loved pictures; ...they all captured the essence of wilderness Canada—a bleak, somber, incredibly beautiful landscape of rock outcroppings, storm–driven lakes, and jack pine trees—a land totally uninhabited by people.* (2.2)

10. C   The professor means that much of the Group's work has come to represent Canada. An *icon* is a symbol, a representation of something else. (2.4)

11. A   The professor says: *A.Y. Jackson was influential for his...; Arthur Lismer's work has an intensity all its own...; Lawren Harris went further than the rest....* You can conclude that the Group did not share a single style of painting. (2.4)

12. B   The professor says: *Water continuously circulates from the ocean to the atmosphere, to the land, and back to the ocean, providing us with a renewable supply of purified water. This complex cycle—known as the hydrologic cycle—balances the amount of water in the ocean, in the atmosphere, and on the land.* (2.2)

13. D   The professor says: *Climatologists study the role of solar energy in the cycle. They're mainly concerned with the atmospheric phase of the cycle—how solar energy drives the cycle....* (2.2)

14. B   The professor says: *The land phase of the cycle is the concern of hydrologists. Hydrologists study the vast quantities of water in the land phase of the cycle, how water moves over and through the land, and how it's stored on or within the earth.* (2.2)

15. A, C   Water that falls to earth as precipitation is stored in lakes or underground: *The water that falls to earth is stored on the surface in lakes, or it penetrates the surface....* The water eventually flows back to the ocean: *Eventually, all of the water falling on land makes its way back to the ocean.* (2.2)

16. A   The professor's purpose is to describe the importance of runoff and groundwater. The amount of runoff and groundwater equals the amount of water from the ocean that falls on the land as precipitation. (2.3)

17. C   The professor says: *Trees and plants circulate and store water...; ...plants...are also part of the cycle, since water is a large part of the mass of most organisms. Living organisms store and use water....* You can infer that plants perform the function of water storage. (2.4)

SPEAKING (p. 584)

1. Responses will vary. (3.1–3.4)
2. Responses will vary. (3.1–3.4)
3. Key points:
   - Because of an increase in the number of swimming classes, the university will reduce the hours that the swimming pool is open for students' personal use.
   - The man does not like the change in swimming pool hours.
   - One reason he gives is that the change will eliminate late afternoon hours, when he likes to swim.
   - Another reason is that swimming classes don't take up the whole pool; he suggests keeping half of the pool open for other people.
   - Another reason is that it is not fair for the university to take away pool time; he suggests extending the morning hours to make up for the loss. (3.5, 3.7, 3.10)
4. Key points:
   - Social norms are rules that describe what is typical for most people. Social norms motivate human behavior.
   - The professor talks about a study in hotels, in which two different bathroom signs influenced whether guests would reuse their towels. The social–norm message was more effective than the environmental message. This illustrates how social norms influence behavior in a given situation.
   - Another study showed that people were even more likely to reuse their towels when they were told that other guests in the same room had done so. This illustrates how social pressure motivates people to conform. (3.6, 3.7, 3.10)
5. Key points:
   - The woman is considering which math class to take. She would like a statistics course, but the class is full. She may have to take calculus instead.
   - One possible solution is to register for both statistics and calculus and get on the waiting list for statistics.
   - Another solution is to talk to the instructor of the statistics class and try to persuade the instructor to let her in.
   - Opinions about the preferred solution will vary. (3.8, 3.10)
6. Key points:
   - Fears in young children are normal. Fears help children solve issues of change and development, and get attention and help from parents when needed.
   - The fear of falling is shown as a clasping motion that the baby makes when he is uncovered, surprised, or dropped. The baby cries out, which attracts a parent's attention and gets help.
   - The fear of strangers alerts the child to a new situation.
   - Fears appear during periods of new and rapid learning, such as when children learn to walk. New independence brings new things to fear, such as dogs, loud noises, and strange places.
   - By overcoming fears, children acquire confidence in their own new abilities. (3.9, 3.10)

WRITING (p. 589)

1. Key points:
   - The lecture states that earthworms are causing significant damage to some forests by destroying the soil cover. This refutes the point in the reading that earthworms have a beneficial effect on the soil.
   - The lecture states that earthworms are a threat to wildflowers. This refutes the point in the reading that earthworms benefit plants in every conceivable way.
   - The lecture states that worms have a negative effect on animals and, in turn, the whole forest ecosystem. This refutes the point in the reading that worms are a food source for animals and a positive force in the ecosystem. (4.1–4.5)
2. Responses will vary. (4.6–4.10)

TEST 5

READING (p. 593)

1. **C** *Conjecture* means *inference* in this context. Clues: *...has never been explored directly...mysteries...a subject of imagination....* (1.3)

2. **B** The passage does not state that Earth's interior was ever depicted as a liquid core with a solid outer core. All of the other answers are given: *One seventeenth–century map depicted the planet's interior as a cavern with numerous chambers, each filled with air, water, or fire; ...Jules Verne described the subterranean world as a yawning abyss filled with giant sea serpents and other horrifying creatures; ...Edmond Halley, who in 1692 described the interior as mostly hollow, with three concentric shells rotating around a core.* (1.2)

3. **A** Clues: *Today, scientists believe that Earth has a solid iron core....* However, past beliefs were that the interior was hollow: *...a cavern with numerous chambers...; ...a yawning abyss...; ...mostly hollow....* (1.1)

4. **D** Clues: *Most knowledge about the interior comes from analysis of variations in the speed of seismic waves recorded during earthquakes.* (1.1)

5. **D** The main purpose of the paragraph is to compare properties of different types of seismic waves. Clues: *...some seismic waves move across the surface...; Other, less destructive waves travel through the body of the planet; The speeds and paths of both types of body waves vary with the density and elasticity of the materials they encounter.* (1.5)

6. **A** Clues: *...solid rock, an elastic medium, the rock is compressed and then quickly returns to its original volume...; Liquids are not elastic, and hence cannot deform and then return to their original shape....* (1.1)

7. **B** *Deform* means *change shape* in this context. Clues: *Liquids are not elastic, and hence cannot ----- and then return to their original shape....* The prefix *de–* = away, from; *deform* is to move away from form (change shape). Substances that are not elastic do not change shape when met with seismic waves. (1.3)

8. **C** You can infer that shear forces do not exist in liquids. Clues: *S–waves...create shear forces...; S–waves can pass only through solid materials; Liquids...simply flow away from the shearing stress.* (1.4)

9. **A** *Any given layer becomes more rigid with increasing depth...* is paraphrased in *With increasing depth, materials become more rigid.... ...and the velocity of seismic waves increases with the rigidity of the materials composing the layer* is paraphrased in *...and seismic waves travel faster.* (1.6)

10. **D** The paragraph supports the statement that analysis of seismic data has increased scientific knowledge of Earth's interior. Clues: *By analyzing the data from seismic waves, scientists have been able to identify the materials that compose each layer. From the data on direction and speed of seismic waves, scientists have located layer boundaries and identified the rocks and metals in each layer.* (1.4)

11. **A** *Synthesizing* means *combining* in this context. Clues: *...data from hundreds of thousands of earthquakes...; ...together form....* The prefix *syn–* = with, together. (1.3)

12. **B** Clues: *Seismic tomography reveals that the outer surface of Earth's core is not smooth and featureless...; In some places the outer core projects upward into the mantle, while in other places the mantle extends downward....* (1.1)

13. **D** In the added sentence, *However* is a transition that shows contrast between *Seismic waves tend to travel...at an unchanging velocity...* in the previous sentence and *...sometimes seismic waves decrease or increase in velocity* in the added sentence. The next sentence develops this idea with *Changes in speed indicate....* (1.7)

14. **B, C, F** Key information: *Most knowledge about the interior comes from analysis of variations in the speed of seismic waves recorded during earthquakes; The invention of the seismograph in 1875 was critical in the development of a detailed picture of the planet's structure; Changes in speed indicate that the waves are passing through materials of varied composition and structure at different temperatures and pressures; The speeds and paths of both types of body waves vary with the density and elasticity of the materials they encounter; By analyzing the data from seismic waves, scientists have been able to identify the materials that compose each layer; Through the process of seismic tomography, which uses seismic waves to provide three–dimensional images, scientists now have a detailed map of Earth's interior.* Answers (A) and (D) are minor ideas. Answer (E) is not mentioned. (1.8)

15. **B** Clues: *...rainforests are areas of...abundant rainfall...; ...tropical rainforests are found in equatorial Central and South America, where rainfall is greater than 250 centimeters per year; Temperate rainforests occur in the mid–latitudes... where moist air from the Pacific Ocean drops between 150 and 500 centimeters of rain in a year.* (1.1)

16. **A** *Traps* means *catches* in this context. Clues: *...moist air from the Pacific Ocean drops between 150 and 500 centimeters of rain in a year; ...a range of mountains ----- moisture from the ocean....* The mountains catch moist air from the ocean, and this moisture falls as rain. (1.3)

17. **D** Clues: *Tropical rainforests are typically divided into four layers, each with different plants and animals adapted for life in that particular area.* (1.1)

18. **D** *Luxuriant* means *abundant* in this context. Clues: *...vegetation: tall, dense jungle, with thick vines covering the trees; ...nearly continuous cover of foliage...; ...filled with large–leaf plants, vines, and shrubs....* (1.3)

19. **B** *The bottom layer, the forest floor, is relatively clear of vegetation because...* is paraphrased in *...so few plants grow there. ...only a small amount of sunlight penetrates the forest's upper layers* is paraphrased in *Little sunlight reaches the forest floor....* (1.6)

20. **C** *Littered* means *covered* in this context. Clues: *The forest floor is ----- with needles, leaves, twigs, and fallen trees—all of which lie on and under a thick carpet....* (1.3)

21. A The author means that the plants require only a small amount of light. Clue: *...because little sunlight extends down to the forest floor.* (1.3)

22. B Clues: *...an ecosystem in which change occurs slowly, giving the illusion that time itself moves slowly. Trees in the temperate rainforest live very long lives and grow to immense sizes. When fully grown, some trees reach heights of 85 meters.* (1.1)

23. B You can infer that temperature and availability of water affect decomposition rates. Clues: *In tropical rainforests, the warm temperatures and abundant precipitation cause most organic material to decompose in a few months to a few years; In temperate rainforests, decomposition is much slower, taking four to six years.* (1.4)

24. D The paragraph supports the statement that trees in topical rainforests have a key role in the cycle of nutrients. Clues: *...the roots of the trees quickly absorb the nutrients. Most of the nutrients supporting the rainforest—about 75 percent of those in the ecosystem—are stored in the woody trunks of trees....* (1.4)

25. A The main purpose of the paragraph is to contrast decomposition in temperate rainforests with that in tropical forests; tropical rainforests are discussed in the previous paragraph. Clues: *In temperate rainforests, decomposition is much slower...; More dead plant material accumulates as litter on the forest floor....* (1.5)

26. C In the added sentence, *For this reason* refers to *the roots of the trees quickly absorb the nutrients*, stated in the previous sentence. The added sentence introduces the idea that *the soil itself contains few available nutrients*, which the next sentence develops with *only about 10 percent are contained in the soil.* (1.7)

27. A, D, G Tropical Rainforest: *Tropical rainforests are characterized by a warm, wet climate with an even distribution of rainfall annually...; There is only slight temperature variation throughout the year; Next is the canopy, a nearly continuous cover of foliage...; The canopy is the densest area of biodiversity, home to around half of the forest's plant species...; Below the canopy is the understory, filled with large–leaf plants, vines, and shrubs, and home to many insects, birds, reptiles, and mammals; Most of the nutrients supporting the rainforest—about 75 percent of those in the ecosystem—are stored in the woody trunks of trees, while only about 10 percent are contained in the soil.*

    C, E Temperate Rainforest: *The topmost layer is dominated by a few species of tall coniferous evergreens...; Trees in the temperate rainforest...grow to immense sizes; ...ferns and mosses...; The forest floor...mosses...grasses...; The low–growing plants...; In temperate rainforests, decomposition is much slower, taking four to six years; The nutrients in the forest litter and soil may remain there for long periods of time before being absorbed by the trees.* Answers (B) and (F) describe neither type of rainforest. (1.9)

28. B Clues: *The suspension bridge is a very ancient device that has long been used for foot traffic...; ...of the type called catenary, a term referring to the curve or sag...; ...the footway follows the natural curve....* (1.1)

29. A *Assumed* means *formed* in this context. Clues: *...the curve or sag that a hanging cable takes under its own weight...; ...the footway follows the natural curve ----- by the hanging cables.* (1.3)

30. D *This* in the highlighted sentence refers to *bend the towers toward each other* in the previous sentence. *To prevent this from happening...* is paraphrased in *To keep the towers from bending.... ...the cables extend beyond the towers...* is paraphrased in *...the cables pass over the towers.... ...and are attached to concrete anchorages that are embedded in solid rock* is paraphrased in *...and connect to anchorages set in rock.* (1.6)

31. B The passage does not state that a roadway supported by posts and beams is a feature of the suspension bridge. All of the other answers are given: *...the Chinese started using the catenary concept to suspend a level roadway...; The main parts of the suspension bridge are the roadway, the cables, the towers, and the cable anchorages; ...a strong vertical force that is transferred into the ground... down through the tower foundations.* (1.2)

32. C Clues: *...the Menai Bridge is a massive structure in which the suspension units are heavy iron bars and rods. Sixteen huge chain cables....* (1.1)

33. C Clues: *The Brooklyn Bridge is a hybrid of the suspension bridge and the cable–stayed bridge....* (1.1)

34. B You can infer that the suspension bridge and the cable–stayed bridge differ in how much of the load is carried by the anchorages. Clues: *The weight of the cables creates a strong vertical force that is transferred into the ground at the anchorages and down through the tower foundations* (paragraph 2); *A cable–stayed bridge...; ...the towers, which transmit the bridge load down into the ground, with less force placed on the anchorages* (paragraph 4). (1.4)

35. D *Graceful* means *elegant* in this context. Clues: *One of the best known examples...magnificent....* (1.3)

36. C The author's purpose is to emphasize the great scale of the bridge. Clues: *The scale of the Golden Gate Bridge is greater than that of any other suspension bridge at the time; ...length of the main span... height of the towers...width of the roadway....* (1.5)

37. A *Keyed into* means *connected to* in this context. Clues: *Each of the cable anchorages has three main components: the base block, which is set in the bedrock; the anchor block, which is ----- the base block....* The author explains how the main components of the anchorage are connected to each other and to the ground. (1.3)

38. A The paragraph supports the statement that the bridge was built to tolerate severe weather conditions. Clues: *...a structure that would control, rather than try to prevent, the movement caused by high winds and extreme temperatures; ...constructed with cross–bracing to stiffen the structure against the force of the wind; In very hot weather, the roadway will expand...; ...expansion joints are built into the road surface....* (1.4)

39. B   The added sentence introduces the topic of *features to maintain a constant sag*, which the next sentence develops with *Sets of trusses along the roadway serve to stiffen the curvature of the cables....* (1.7)

40. B, D, E   Key information: *The main parts of the suspension bridge are the roadway, the cables, the towers, and the cable anchorages. The level roadway hangs from the cables...; The cables pass over the towers and connect to the cable anchorages; Suspension bridges of great size did not appear in the West until the nineteenth century; ...completed in 1826, the Menai Bridge is a massive structure in which the suspension units are heavy iron bars and rods; ...towers constructed of limestone...; ...steel deck; Completed in 1883, the Brooklyn Bridge was the longest suspension bridge in the world at that time...steel cables, two enormous granite towers...; In the twentieth century, suspension bridges achieved greater spans...; The length of the main span is 1,300 meters...; The bridge designers created a structure that would control, rather than try to prevent, the movement caused by high winds and extreme temperatures.* Answer (A) is not mentioned. Answers (C) and (F) are minor ideas. (1.8)

LISTENING — PART 1 (p. 606)

1. C   The speakers mainly discuss a book that the student requested. The student says: *I placed a book on hold, and I got an e–mail saying that the book was here at the reference desk.* The man says: *Sorry it took a while to get this book. It had to be shipped from another library.* (2.1)

2. A   The man says: *Now, as you know, this book is rare, so there are conditions for using it.* (2.2)

3. B   The man says: *Because it's a rare book, you can't check it out. You have to use it here in the library.* (2.2)

4. C   The man says: *...because the book is so old, you need to be careful with the binding. You don't want to crack it.* The student says: *Yikes,* an expression of alarm. You can infer that both speakers are concerned about damaging the book. (2.4)

5. D   The student says: *...could I take pictures with my own camera? That might be safer than putting it on the copy machine; I'm not even sure the images would be clear enough. I'll have to experiment.* You can predict that she will try photographing the book with her camera. (2.4)

6. B   The discussion is mainly about how scientists approach facts and new information. The professor says: *To a scientist, a "fact" is simply a statement of our current understanding; And a fact is only valid until it's revised or replaced by a new understanding; To scientists, facts are not hard and fast truths. So, how does new information change our understanding? Well, scientists usually follow a systematic approach to new information; The scientific method: how scientists deal with new information.* (2.1)

7. A   The professor's purpose is to illustrate how previously held facts can be replaced. She says: *The field of cell biology is full of "facts" that were once widely held as true, but were later revised when biologists acquired a better understanding of cells. For example...; Wohler's work undermined the previously held "facts" of vitalism.* (2.3)

8. C   The professor implies that facts are only valid until they are replaced by a better understanding. *Hard and fast truths* would not be subject to change. However, scientists do not view facts as hard and fast. Facts are subject to change with new information that leads to a better understanding. (2.4)

9. C   The professor says: *The scientific method: how scientists deal with new information. The scientific method begins as a researcher makes observations...and then formulates a hypothesis; ...a hypothesis must be testable.* (2.2)

10. B, C   One statement is that a hypothesis appears to provide a reasonable explanation for a phenomenon: *Sometimes a hypothesis takes the form of a model that appears to provide a reasonable explanation for a phenomenon.* Another statement is that a hypothesis is useful to scientists only if it can be tested: *...to be useful, a hypothesis must be testable.* (2.2)

11. D   The professor says: *And when a hypothesis has been tested critically, under many different conditions, by many different researchers, using a variety of approaches, and the hypothesis is consistently supported by the evidence, it gradually acquires the status of a theory; For example, there's little or no disagreement about the three tenets of cell biology.* You can infer that the three tenets of cell biology have been thoroughly and repeatedly tested and are consistently supported by the evidence. (2.4)

12. D   The professor mainly classifies aboriginal cultures according to region. He says: *Let's take a look at some of the cultural characteristics of the aboriginal peoples. Generally, we can divide aboriginal Canadians into five major groups, based on geography; First, across most of Canada, from the Yukon to the Atlantic...; Second, to the north...; The third major group lived to the south...; The fourth group...lived on the western plains; Finally, in the far west....* (2.6)

13. C   The professor says: *Their economies were organized around the food supply.* (2.2)

14. A, D, E   One characteristic of the hunting–gathering tribes of the forests was living in small bands that migrated in search of food: *They lived in small bands that migrated frequently.* Another characteristic was making tools and other objects from locally available materials: *They made tools, weapons, clothing, and ceremonial objects from materials that were available locally.* Another characteristic was skill in hunting and trapping fur–bearing animals: *They were skilled in trapping fur–bearing animals and in curing animal skins....* (2.2)

15. A   The professor says: *Agriculture enabled thousands of people to live together in societies and develop complex political systems.* You can infer that their political organization grew from a basis in agriculture. (2.4)

16. **B** The professor means that the bison was essential to the wealth and survival of the Plains people. The bison was the basis of their economy and of their ability to survive in harsh conditions. (2.4)

17. **C** The professor says: *Aboriginal Canadians lived in a close relationship with nature. Wherever they lived, the people were well adapted to their environment.* (2.2)

LISTENING — PART 2 (p. 612)

1. **C** The speakers mainly discuss interactions between galaxies. The student says: *...galaxies don't act alone. They can influence each other and even collide with other galaxies; ...small galaxies can be pulled together by gravity, and then they can blend to form more massive galaxies....* The tutor says: *...yeah, galaxies can be pulled together by their mutual gravitational attraction; So, we can say that the interaction between the galaxies has the effect of—it sort of plays a role in their evolution.* (2.1)

2. **B, D** When two galaxies collide, the galaxies can pass through one another: *...when galaxies collide, they actually pass through one another; ...they sort of collide, but the stars just pass by each other, and what really happens is, the galaxies don't actually crash.* Also, a single larger galaxy can start to form: *...small galaxies can be pulled together by gravity, and then they can blend to form more massive galaxies...; Eventually, two smaller galaxies become a large elliptical galaxy.* (2.2)

3. **A** The tutor says: *The models suggest that collisions between spiral galaxies tend to make elliptical ones. The Milky Way is expected to collide with the Andromeda Galaxy in the next few billion years, and this will create an even huger elliptical galaxy.* (2.2)

4. **B** The tutor implies that he is not certain if there is an answer to the student's question about spiral galaxies. He says: *Astronomers argue and speculate about this stuff all the time. They don't know everything about the evolution of galaxies.* (2.4)

5. **D** The student's purpose is to signal a shift in topic. They have been discussing galaxies and then mention the Big Bang. The student thinks the Big Bang will be on the exam and suggests they also review that topic. (2.5)

6. **B** The speakers mainly discuss the language and techniques of advertising claims. The professor says: *To understand how ads work, we need to analyze the language used in the advertising claim. The claim is the spoken or text part of an ad...; ...advertisers depend on a handful of basic techniques; One technique is...; Another technique...; Another advertising technique is....* (2.1)

7. **C** The professor's purpose is to explain how advertising uses language to mislead. He says that most advertising claims are neither true nor false, but they use *a careful choice of words* to make people believe that a product is superior. (2.3)

8. **D** The student says: *A parity product is something just like everything else; ...there are lots of different brands for the same product...and they're all basically the same.* The professor says: *...all parity products, with several brands that are all similar in quality.* (2.2)

9. **A** The professor says: *But for a product that's merely the same quality as others, the advertising has to create the illusion of being superior. To create this illusion, advertisers depend on a handful of basic techniques.* (2.2)

10. **B, D** The speakers discuss the technique of endorsement by a famous person: *Another technique...is the celebrity endorsement; Somebody famous...appears in the ad to give his or her endorsement to the product.* They also discuss the statistical claim: *Another advertising technique is the scientific or statistical claim.* (2.2)

11. **B** The professor implies that advertising affects even intelligent people, whether they know it or not. The professor says: *...smart consumers aren't influenced by ads*, but he means the opposite. A major idea in the discussion is that advertising works even on people who think they are immune to its message. (2.4)

12. **A** The main point is that streams exist in a continuous state of geological change. The professor says: *Streams are the most dynamic agents of geological change on the surface of the planet; Streams respond immediately to changes in their environment; A stream's environment is always changing; The equilibrium of any graded stream is only temporary. It lasts only until the next change in the environment.* (2.1)

13. **A, D** One environmental factor that causes streams to respond is heavy rainfall during a storm: *For example, when a heavy storm drops 25 centimeters of rain on a drainage basin, the streams in that region will rise quickly and flow more rapidly.* Another factor is a change in the amount of sediment: *...there may be a sudden increase in sediment load...and this increase in sediment will upset the stream's equilibrium. Any change in sediment load will force the stream to adjust.* (2.2)

14. **B** The professor's purpose is to state that graded streams constantly adjust to changing conditions. The equilibrium of a graded stream is temporary; it does not last forever. A change in environmental conditions will change the equilibrium and cause the stream to respond. (2.3)

15. **C** The professor says: *...if normal faulting occurs across a stream channel, and the downstream section drops during an earthquake, a waterfall will form immediately.* (2.2)

16. **B** The professor illustrates the point that erosion continuously changes the profile of a waterfall. Erosion creates a plunge pool; erosion causes the waterfall to migrate upstream; erosion changes a waterfall to rapids; erosion eventually returns a stream to its graded state. (2.4)

17. **D** The professor says: *The plunging water erodes the shale bed below the resistant cap of dolostone, and this continues to undercut the falls. In the past, the falls retreated at a rate of approximately one meter per year.* (2.2)

LISTENING — PART 3 (p. 618)

1. D   The student wants to thank the professor for helping him get a job. The student says: *...I wanted to thank you again for your recommendation...you know, the camp counselor position; I just wanted to let you know I got the job. And thanks again. I really mean that.* (2.3)

2. C   The professor says: *I know you'll do a great job, and this is an excellent way to get started in environmental education; The summer youth program is one of the best in the country.* (2.2)

3. A, C   The student's summer job will include teaching young students about the environment: *Mainly I'll be working with the kids, supervising hikes...teaching ecology....* It will also include contributing stories to a blog: *...the director asked if I'd write for their blog, and I said, of course...; They have a great website, and I look forward to contributing.* (2.2)

4. D   The student says: *...did you see my photograph in the new brochure...; I submitted five images, and that was the one the editor picked.* You can infer that he is an accomplished photographer. (2.4)

5. B   The professor's purpose is to signal an end to the conversation. She says: *I have a lecture in five minutes*, implying that she must leave soon. (2.5)

6. D   The speakers mainly discuss the physical location of the self. The professor says: *Where in your body is this entity known as the "self"; ...various methods to find out where people believe their selves to be...; Where do you think the self is; The research shows that the vast majority of people say their self is located either in their heart or their head.* (2.1)

7. A, D   The students raise the issue of how the self is defined: *How did they define the self; ...there are different things we could mean when we talk about the self.* They also raise the question of whether the self is located in different places for different people: *Maybe there just isn't one right answer to the question. What if the self really does exist in different places for different people?* (2.2)

8. B   The professor says: *The research shows that the vast majority of people say their self is located either in their heart or their head; ...these three studies suggest that people lean toward the idea of a specific place where their self resides. One place is in the head. Another is in the heart.* (2.2)

9. C   The professor means that how a study is conducted has a bearing on the accuracy of results. *Methodology* means the methods and procedures that researchers use in conducting a study. To say that *methodology is key* is to emphasize the importance of procedures in producing good results, that is, results that accurately answer the question. (2.4)

10. B   The professor says: *Their results were interesting and significant. They found that if they started from the top, subjects were more likely to respond when the pointer hit the upper face. However, when they started from the bottom, at the person's feet, the same subjects were more likely to call out when the pointer reached the upper torso, the chest. So, depending on the direction the pointer moved, the subjects said that both locations—the head and the chest—felt right.* (2.2)

11. C   The professor's purpose is to summarize the results of the research. The professor has described three different studies, then states the conclusion that is common to all three: *that people lean toward the idea of a specific place where their self resides.* (2.3)

12. B   The lecture is mainly a classification of singing voices. The professor says: *In Western classical music, singing voices are classified for male and female singers; The high and low female voices are the soprano and the alto, with the mezzo–soprano as an intermediate class. The high and low male voices are the tenor and the bass, with baritone as an intermediate class; ...I'll talk more about the male voices: the tenor, the baritone, and the bass.* (2.6)

13. D   The professor says: *In general, men have deeper voices than women do. This is because men have longer and thicker vocal cords.* (2.2)

14. A   The professor says: *The earliest surviving opera that's still widely performed is Monteverdi's Orfeo. The title role of the character Orfeo was written for the tenor. The role of Orfeo set the standard for leading male roles to be taken by the tenor voice.* (2.2)

15. B, C   In early choral music, the tenor voice held all of the other voices together: *In early choral music, the tenor was the middle voice that held all of the other voices together.* The most demanding heroic roles in opera are sung in the tenor voice: *...some of Wagner's roles are the most demanding ever for the tenor voice. Italian opera, too, has a multitude of heroic roles for a tenor voice....* (2.2)

16. A   The professor implies that men who sing in their normal range are easier to understand. The professor says that the baritone is the normal range of the male voice. She also says: *...a man singing in his natural range can articulate words more clearly than a singer who is in some way extending his voice...*, implying that the words are easier for audiences to understand. (2.4)

17. D   The professor says: *...leading roles for the deep and powerful bass have become especially prized by performers and opera lovers everywhere.* You can infer that both audiences and singers value leading roles for the bass voice. (2.4)

SPEAKING (p. 624)

1. Responses will vary. (3.1–3.4)
2. Responses will vary. (3.1–3.4)
3. Key points:
   • The man opposes the new fee. The fee will help to pay for the cost of remodeling the computer lab.
   • One reason he gives is that all students have to pay the fee, whether or not they use the lab. He does not use the lab. He believes it is not fair to charge students who do not use the lab.
   • Another reason is that there are already too many fees. Tuition just increased, and parking fees will also increase. (3.5, 3.7, 3.10)
4. Key points:
   • Aestivation is a state of dormancy (inactivity) in which an animal's metabolism decreases in response to hot, dry conditions. Aestivation conserves energy, regulates body temperature, prevents water loss, and enables survival.

•The professor gives the example of land snails, which escape heat by moving into the shade or by climbing tall plants, posts, or walls. The snails remain inactive until moisture returns.

•The professor gives the example of the burrowing frog, which buries itself in the ground and enters a state of dormancy. Some frogs cover their skin with waterproof mucus to prevent water loss. Some frogs store water in their bladder.

•The professor gives the example of a desert lizard that escapes the heat by moving to an underground burrow. It remains inactive to conserve energy when food and water are not available. (3.6, 3.7, 3.10)

5. Key points:

•The man's problem is that he would like to change his academic major to communications, but his current school does not have a communications department. He does not want to move to another city.

•One possible solution is to design his own program at his current school. He could do independent study in communications with the help of a faculty adviser.

•Another solution is to consider the communications program at the art college in a nearby city.

•Opinions about the preferred solution will vary. (3.8, 3.10)

6. Key points:

•One reason for including engineering in the basic education of children is that the problem–solving   • perspective of engineering matches how children naturally learn. When young children play, they build things, test things, and take things apart to understand them. Children are natural engineers.

•Another reason is that problem–solving skills are necessary for the twenty–first century. Students need experiences with engineering and technology. They need to know how things are made and how things work. Studying problem solving and the design process will prepare students for their careers and for life. (3.9, 3.10)

WRITING (p. 629)

1. Key points:

•The lecture states that workers who share breaks with teammates are happier and more productive; teammates with staggered breaks have little opportunity to share tips or vent about angry customers. This contradicts the point in the reading that staggered break times are a positive change that will increase social interaction within a large, diverse network.

•The lecture states that there should be no barriers to interaction within groups; the best place for the coffee pot is in the middle of a group; a flight of stairs is a psychological barrier. This contradicts the point in the reading that the coffee pots and the break room should be in a central location, between groups or on a middle floor of the building.

•The lecture states that an open seating plan had a negative effect on how information was shared. This contradicts the point in the reading that an open seating plan improves the flow of information and the exchange of ideas. (4.1–4.5)

2. Responses will vary. (4.6–4.10)

ALBUM 1 — PRE-TEST

Album 1, Track 1

PRE-TEST — LISTENING SECTION DIRECTIONS (p. 12)

The Listening section measures your ability to understand conversations and lectures in English. You will hear each conversation and lecture only one time. After each conversation or lecture, you will answer some questions about it. Answer the questions based on what the speakers state or imply.

You may take notes while you listen. You may use your notes to help you answer the questions. Your notes will not be scored.

In some questions, you will see this icon: 🎧. This means that you will hear, but not see, part of the question. Some questions have special directions, which appear in a gray box.

You will now begin the Listening section.

Album 1, Track 2

PRE-TEST — LISTENING QUESTIONS 1–5 (p. 13)

Listen to a conversation between a student and a professor.

W: Hi, Professor Rivera! Could I talk to you about the presentation next week?

M: Uh …

W: I need your advice on what I still need to do.

M: Okay, sure … uh … but I have a meeting in half an hour.

W: This won't take long.

M: Do you have much left to do? I thought you were almost ready.

W: I've got data, photos and graphs of the mountain. I just want to know if that's going to be enough.

M: Okay. Tell me what you've got.

W: For my introduction … uh … first, I'll talk about how the geologists at Volcano Watch detected another earthquake—a tiny one—two weeks ago. They think that quake could be part of a series of small quakes that precede an eruption.

M: Hmm. All right.

W: Then I thought I'd give a history of the eruptions in that area.

M: How far are you going back?

W: Two thousand years. That's the last time Stone Peak erupted. I won't go over every little eruption, just the six or seven major ones. Then I guess at that point I'll show my graphs—no, maybe the pictures first, at least the one of the bulge. Uh, does that sound like a good way to do it?

M: So far, so good. What pictures do you have?

W: A set of photographs that George Davidson at the observatory gave me. One thing I still have to do is make slides out of 'em—and of my graphs, too—but that won't take me long. I have some good shots of the mountain—you can really see how much the bulge has grown.

M: Interesting. How much has it grown?

W: A few inches a year, for the past six years. He—I mean George—said the bulge is forming 'cause a chamber of magma below the surface is growing. Earth's crust is being bent and bent—a few inches each year—and sooner or later, it'll start to break open.

M: That could get very interesting.

W: Really. Anyway … uh … first I'll show them the color photo, then the graphs showing the eruptions over the past six years … and after that, the black–and–white photos showing the bulge. The changes really show up well, much better in black and white.

M: Yes, I can imagine they do. So … um … after you show your slides, you want to make sure you allow time for discussion. Your pictures of the bulge and the cause of its formation—you are going to talk about that, right?

W: Of course.

M: That's good, because you're bound to get some questions.

W: Do I need more? I mean, do I have enough material?

M: It all sounds good to me. Just finish your slides and practice what you want to say.

W: Okay.

M: See? You're almost set to go.

1. What is the conversation mainly about?
2. Listen again to part of the conversation. Then **answer the question.**
   "I need your advice on what I still need to do."
   "Okay, sure … uh … but I have a meeting in half an hour."
   Why does the professor say this:
   "Okay, sure … uh … but I have a meeting in half an hour."
3. What types of data does the student plan to use?
4. What is the student's opinion of the photographs?
5. Listen again to part of the conversation. Then **answer the question.**
   "So … um … after you show your slides, you want to make sure you allow time for discussion. Your pictures of the bulge and the cause of its formation—you are going to talk about that, right?"
   "Of course."
   "That's good, because you're bound to get some questions."
   What does the professor mean when he says this:
   "That's good, because you're bound to get some questions."

Album 1, Track 3

PRE-TEST — LISTENING QUESTIONS 6–11 (p. 15)

Listen to part of a lecture in an ecology class.

M1: While we're on the topic of relationships in ecosystems, there's another relationship I'd like to talk about, one that can help in our understanding of climate change … and this is the link between weather patterns and the periodic biological phenomena related to climatic conditions …

phenomena like the seasonal changes in trees. This is the science of phenology. Okay. We're all familiar with the changing colors of the seasons: summer green, autumn red and gold, white snow cover, and bright new green in the spring. These colors mark the rhythmic cycles of weather. We know that animals have adapted to the seasonal color changes. Think about it. Animals have their young just as green plants are sprouting in the spring. Some animals change their color during the year to blend in with the seasonal colors. These changes, these physiological responses to the environment—it's all like a dance, a complex interaction called phenology. The current research in phenology looks at how nature's color signals can help us understand the feedback between plants and our changing climate. One way this is done … is … uh … by … um … by analyzing the forest as a collection of numbers … numbers like the mix of colors in the leaves … also, the amount of carbon inhaled from the atmosphere … and … uh … yes, Sophie?

W: Could you … um … maybe say more about how the researchers collect these numbers?

M1: I'm getting to that. Okay … uh … we measure how much a tree's leaves reflect different wavelengths of light—a very precise way of measuring color. Different wavelengths can indicate different levels of stress experienced by the tree.

W: So, how exactly does color relate to stress?

M1: Sure. Okay, an example … well … uh … different pigments in leaves … uh … have different functions. Green is chlorophyll, which dominates during the growing season when photosynthesis takes place. Then, when the amount of daylight decreases in autumn, red and yellow pigments take control to help guard against stress. This is all in your textbook, by the way.

W: Okay. This is interesting.

M1: Good. And you asked how we get the numbers. Well, one very important instrument is a web camera on top of a tower that captures high–resolution images of the forest canopy. The camera collects these images every 30 minutes, during the hours of daylight. The camera then uploads these images to an online database. This huge collection of color data will increase our understanding of how ecosystems respond to climate change and, we hope, will make us better able to predict the effects.

M2: Leaves change color during the year, right? That's pretty normal. So, how do we know if the changes are just normal seasonal changes or whether it's the result of climate change?

M1: Nature's colors are already responding to changing weather due to climate change. This is because phenology is sensitive to weather. For example, when spring is unusually warm, the leaves come earlier. We're already seeing this in color data from the camera. We have data about warm years, cold years, wet years, and dry years. As we build up our color record, we can use this data to develop better models of how weather and phenology are related. We can compare these models against the climate forecasts. This will improve our ability to predict how the forests might change in the future. We'll be able to put together a picture of landscapes in a world of warmer temperatures and changes in precipitation.

6. What is the lecture mainly about?

7. Why does the professor say this:
"Animals have their young just as green plants are sprouting in the spring. Some animals change their color during the year to blend in with the seasonal colors. These changes, these physiological responses to the environment—it's all like a dance, a complex interaction called phenology."

8. Listen again to part of the discussion. Then answer the question.
"Could you … um … maybe say more about how the researchers collect these numbers?"
"I'm getting to that. Okay … uh … we measure how much a tree's leaves reflect different wavelengths of light—a very precise way of measuring color."
Why does the professor say this:
"I'm getting to that."

9. Listen again to part of the discussion. Then answer the question.
"Green is chlorophyll, which dominates during the growing season when photosynthesis takes place. Then, when the amount of daylight decreases in autumn, red and yellow pigments take control to help guard against stress. This is all in your textbook, by the way."
What does the professor imply when he says this:
"This is all in your textbook, by the way."

10. What does the professor say about a method of data collection that uses a camera?

11. According to the professor, how will color data about forests be useful to researchers?

Album 1, Track 4

PRE–TEST — LISTENING QUESTIONS 12–17 (p. 17)

Listen to part of a talk in an agricultural management class.

Managers do many things, but mainly they're responsible for seeing that an organization accomplishes what it's supposed to. Managers direct resources to achieve the goals of the business. They're responsible for managing an organization called a farm. Farm managers have a complicated job in a complicated world. Like other types of managers, farm managers are responsible for the resources under their control. But unlike many other managers, a farm manager needs to combine information from the biological, physical, and social sciences.

Depending on the type of farm, a farm manager needs to have knowledge in a variety of subjects. For example, a farm manager needs scientific knowledge about soil structure and soil microbiology. A farm manager has to understand animal nutrition, genetics, crop growth, plant and animal diseases, and insect control. A farm manager has to understand ecology. A farm manager has to know about farm machinery. In the social sciences, a farm manager needs leadership and communication skills. He or she has to understand human psychology. A farm is a business, so a farm manager needs an understanding of business organization, business law, strategic planning, and operations management. A farm manager also needs a firm grasp of economics and international food markets.

In short, farm management is a complex and demanding job. Farm managers are responsible for the physical, financial, and human resources of the farm.

In general business terms, a farm manager is a general manager, that is, a manager who is responsible for many—if not all—parts of the business. As a general manager, a farm manager is responsible for all of the management and business functions, although he or she may not personally perform all those functions. For example, some farm managers select a capable farm operator who performs the management tasks of running the farm, such as planning which crops to grow, directing production, managing farm workers, and so on. Some farm managers just concentrate on the financial aspects of managing the farm. For example, they may supervise product marketing or be the one who projects the budget for the next year.

The farm business is characterized by changing conditions. Farming is full of uncertainties—changing prices, changing government regulations, and the uncertainty caused by the weather—so farm managers always have to monitor and adjust their strategies. They have to be experts at strategic thinking. In such an uncertain environment, a farm business needs a structured approach to planning. This is why there should always be a business plan. Having a written business plan forces a manager to make and defend choices. It also provides a document to show interested parties such as creditors, investors, and customers.

Writing a business plan ensures that important points are considered. The business plan includes a general description of the farm—where the farm is located physically, economically, and historically. The plan also describes the farm's vision—both short– and long–term goals. It includes a plan for production and operations, a marketing plan, a financial plan, and a plan for organizing and staffing the business.

What I've just given you is a basic outline of farm management. This course will introduce you to all the management skills you need to plan, organize, and direct the farm business. You'll also learn how to prepare a business plan. In fact, your major course assignment will be to research, write, and revise a business plan for a farm—either a farm you manage now, or one you'd like to manage in the future.

12. What is the main idea of the talk?
13. Which of the following best describes the organization of the talk?
14. According to the professor, in which subjects must a farm manager be knowledgeable?
15. Listen again to part of the lecture. Then answer the question.
    "Farming is full of uncertainties—changing prices, changing government regulations, and the uncertainty caused by the weather—so farm managers always have to monitor and adjust their strategies. They have to be experts at strategic thinking. In such an uncertain environment, a farm business needs a structured approach to planning."
    Why does the professor say this:
    "In such an uncertain environment, a farm business needs a structured approach to planning."
16. According to the professor, what should be included in the business plan for a farm?
17. What can be inferred about the students in this class?

Album 1, Track 5

PRE–TEST — SPEAKING SECTION DIRECTIONS (p. 19)

The Speaking section measures your ability to speak in English about a variety of topics. There are six questions. Record your response to each question.

In questions 1 and 2, you will speak about familiar topics.

In questions 3 and 4, you will first read a short text and then listen to a talk on the same topic. You will then be asked a question about what you have read and heard.

In questions 5 and 6, you will listen to part of a conversation or lecture. You will then be asked a question about what you have heard.

You may take notes while you read and while you listen to the conversations and lectures. You may use your notes to help prepare your responses.

Your responses will be scored on your ability to speak clearly and coherently about the topics. For some questions, your responses will be scored on your ability to accurately convey information about what you have read and heard.

Album 1, Track 6

PRE–TEST — SPEAKING QUESTION 1 (p. 20)

What city would you like to visit? Explain why you would like to go there. Include details and examples in your explanation.

Album 1, Track 7

PRE–TEST — SPEAKING QUESTION 2 (p. 20)

Some people enjoy having a pet animal. Other people do not want a pet. What is your opinion about having a pet? Include details and examples in your explanation.

Album 1, Track 8

PRE–TEST — SPEAKING QUESTION 3 (p. 21)

Now listen to two students as they discuss the block schedule.

M: Hey, did you hear about the new block schedule for next year?
W: Yes, I did. I've never taken classes that way before, in three–hour blocks instead of separate one–hour classes. What about you?
M: I've never done it either, but I think it's a great idea. It sounds like a more efficient use of time—not just in class, but outside of class too. I mean, if all your reading is integrated, sort of based on related topics, then your study time would be more focused and more interesting. You wouldn't have to spend time on subjects you don't care about.
W: Hmmm. Yeah, it does seem like a more efficient way to study … things more coordinated and all.
M: It also seems like a better way to meet people in your interest area, you know, because there are different tracks for science, business, and humanities. Everyone in your block would be focused on the same content. You could get to know your classmates better, and your professor too, because you'd all be together for three hours a day.
W: That does seem like a plus. I hardly know any of my professors this quarter.
M: You'd probably like the block schedule.
W: Yeah, I might.

The man expresses his opinion about the block schedule. State his opinion and explain the reasons he gives for holding that opinion.

Album 1, Track 9

PRE–TEST — SPEAKING QUESTION 4 (p. 22)

Now listen to part of a talk in a linguistics class.

Look before you leap. A friend in need is a friend indeed. What do these statements have in common? Well, they're both proverbs, and they're both very old. They've been around for hundreds, maybe thousands, of years, in one version or another, in different cultures.

Look before you leap.

The message is simple. Open your eyes and understand a situation before you act. Look before you leap. Don't act—don't leap—before you see where you're going. It's good advice. Look before you leap. Why is this statement so effective? Why will you be able to remember it? Think about the language, both the sound and the meaning.

Okay. Let's take another, one of my favorites. A friend in need is a friend indeed. I heard this a lot when I was a child. My grandfather often said it.

A friend in need is a friend indeed. The message is clear. False friends will disappoint you. They will not help you when you need them most. True friends will help you when you need them most. And if a friend of yours needs help, be a true friend and help.

A friend in need is a friend indeed. What is it about the language of this statement that makes it so effective?

Define what a proverb is, and use the examples from the talk to explain the effectiveness of proverbs.

Album 1, Track 10

PRE–TEST — SPEAKING QUESTION 5 (p. 23)

Listen to a conversation between two students.

M: Hi, Jenna! Are you coming to the retirement party for Professor Lemay?

W: Uh … I don't know. I didn't know about the party. When is it?

M: Tomorrow, at three o'clock, in the reception room at the University Center. Everyone—I mean, most of the people we know will be there. I hope you can come.

W: I'd really like to! Professor Lemay was one of my favorite teachers. But, wouldn't you know, I just agreed to take the afternoon shift in the lab tomorrow. I have to be there all afternoon to monitor the cultures for Dr. Young's research.

M: Oh, that's too bad. Do you have to do it? I mean, can't you ask someone else to do it for you?

W: I don't know. It might be hard for me to find someone else with such short notice.

M: You should try anyway. You should be at this party for Professor Lemay. It's your chance to say good–bye.

W: I'd like to see him before he leaves. Maybe there's another time I can visit him before he goes. Maybe I can find him in his office later this week. I could

stop by his office on Friday. Maybe he'll still be there. Do you know when he's leaving campus?

M: I'm not sure.

W: I hope I get a chance to say good–bye. I'd like to thank him for all the help he gave me.

The students discuss two possible solutions to the woman's problem. Briefly describe the problem. Then state which solution you prefer and explain why.

Album 1, Track 11

PRE–TEST — SPEAKING QUESTION 6 (p. 23)

Listen to part of a lecture in a communications class.

As image makers, advertisers send powerful messages about what the future may be like. When researchers examined several hundred ads, they identified three general characteristics in images of the future.

First, the colors are bright, and the lines are strong. The future is depicted in bold, vivid colors, mainly hues of red and blue. Colors attract us to a particular web page, or a page in a magazine, or a television screen. We see the company of the future bathed in a golden sunset or a shimmering rainbow of colors. Strong lines direct our attention forward. Triangles, arrows, and tall buildings jut into the sky, leading our imagination into the future.

Second, many ads show the future as a kinetic force, something moving at a very high speed. There are images of fast–paced cars and computer technology rushing us to the forefront of a global race. The kinetic force may be a person leaping across a deep, wide, or empty space—all the way into the future. The image rushes us to a world beyond our horizon—beyond the dynamic city, the high–speed train, the kinetic force.

Third, the future is portrayed as something positive: brighter, promising, full of potential. The future is also something we can control. Ads show us that we can prepare and plan for the future. If we want a secure future, ads tell us we can invest in universities, financial securities, or insurance. And to ensure that there will be a future at all, we are asked to teach our children, save energy, and protect the environment.

Using points and examples from the lecture, explain how the future is portrayed in advertising.

Album 1, Track 12

PRE–TEST — WRITING SECTION DIRECTIONS (p. 24)

The Writing section measures your ability to use writing to communicate in an academic environment. There are two questions.

Question 1 is a writing task based on reading and listening. You will read a passage, listen to a lecture, and then write a response to a question about the relationship between the lecture and the reading. You have 20 minutes to plan and write your response.

Question 2 is writing based on knowledge and experience. You will write an essay in response to a question that asks you to state, explain, and support an opinion on an issue. You have 30 minutes to plan and write your essay.

Album 1, Track 13

PRE–TEST — WRITING QUESTION 1 (p. 25)

Now listen to part of a lecture on the topic you just read about.

Now we'll turn our attention to another class of freshwater ecosystem: standing bodies of fresh water—such as lakes, ponds, and marshes. These are called lentic ecosystems, and they differ from lotic ecosystems in a number of ways.

First, in lentic ecosystems, the water does not flow as it does in rivers and streams. While the water of lakes is subject to the movement of wind and waves, as well as some current, it is essentially a stationary body of water, not one that flows over the earth from one point to another.

Second, in lentic ecosystems the oxygen content of the water is not the same throughout the entire body of water. The oxygen content varies according to the depth of the water. Oxygen is produced during photosynthesis, which occurs only in the upper levels of a lake, where algae and other microscopic plants live. The deepest parts of a lake are often depleted of oxygen. This is because the depths of a lake are where the decomposition of organic matter occurs, and decomposition actually decreases the oxygen supply.

Third, in contrast to lotic ecosystems, a much greater share of organic production in lentic ecosystems occurs in the body of water itself. Most of the organic matter is produced by algae floating near the surface. Shallow, warm lakes are nutrient–rich and highly productive, while deep, cold lakes are less so. Microscopic plankton thrive in warmer water near the surface. Rooted and floating aquatic plants flourish in the shallow water close to shore.

The lecture discusses lentic ecosystems. Summarize the points made in the lecture, and explain how they contrast with specific points made in the reading passage.

ALBUM 2 — LISTENING

Album 2, Track 1

2.1   IDENTIFYING THE TOPIC AND MAIN IDEA

Focus (p. 217)

Listen to a conversation in a university office.

W: Good afternoon. May I help you?
M: Hello. I'm thinking of taking Dr. Perry's class this summer—Intro to Political Science. And I was wondering … uh … is there a … do you happen to have a book list for that class?
W: I can check the computer to see if she submitted it yet.
M: Thanks. I'd appreciate it.
W: Did you say Introduction to Political Science?
M: Yes. For summer session.
W: Here it is, I found it. Oh … and it sure looks like a substantial amount of reading!
M: Really? Is it long?
W: Would you like me to print out a copy for you?
M: Yeah, that would be great!
W: All right. This will only take a few minutes.
M: Thank you. I really appreciate it.

What is the subject of the conversation?

Album 2, Track 2

Exercise 2.1.A (p. 219)

Question 1. Listen to a conversation between two students.

M: Hi, Kelsey! How's it going?
W: Well, I don't know. I just got my history paper back, and my professor didn't grade it. He just wrote on it, "Come and talk to me about this."
M: Really? Is that all he said? Didn't he make any other comments?
W: No. So I'm really confused. This is the first time I ever got a paper back with no grade on it.
M: That is strange, isn't it?
W: Sure is. I did everything I was supposed to. I mean, I followed the instructions of the assignment.
M: You'd better go talk to him. You need to find out what he's thinking.
W: Yeah, I will. I hope he doesn't ask me to rewrite the paper.

What is the woman's problem?

Question 2. Listen to a conversation between two students.

W: I don't know about you, but I sure am ready for spring break!
M: Are you doing anything special?
W: I'm going to Mexico to hang out on the beach! Four of us will be staying at a resort owned by Maria's family. How about you?

M: I wish I could do the same. Unfortunately, I told my brother I would help him move. But, I don't mind. It's my turn. He's done so much for me in the past.

W: Well, I'll be thinking of you as I bask in the sun.

M: Gee, thanks. I'll repay the favor some day!

What is the conversation mainly about?

Question 3. Listen to a conversation between two students.

M: What courses will you be taking next semester?

W: I won't be taking any courses. I'll be doing an internship instead.

M: Oh, really? Where?

W: At the Children's Union. It's a nonprofit agency that works on children's issues, like education, nutrition, crime, family issues—even music and the arts.

M: That sounds like a great experience because you want to work in that area.

W: Yes, I do, and I'm really excited. The position is actually very political. I'll be traveling all over the state, helping to organize events in a lot of different places. I may even get to spend some time in the state capital.

M: Excellent! I'm sure you'll learn a lot. Good luck!

W: Thanks. I hope this will lead to a job after graduation.

What is the woman mainly discussing?

Questions 4 through 5. Listen to part of a discussion between two students.

W: Are you ready for our first quiz in botany?

M: I guess so, if only I could remember the difference between xylem and phloem. I can't seem to get it straight on which one goes up and which one goes down.

W: I always think of a tree and imagine a "P" at the top, up in the branches, and an "X" at the bottom, down in the roots. "P" is above "X" in the tree, just as "P" comes before "X" in alphabetical order.

M: Okay. Now what?

W: Well, if "P" is up in the branches, it has to go down.

M: Okay. Then it's phloem that goes down.

W: Right. And "X" is down in the roots, so it has to go up.

M: Xylem is down, so it must go up. Xylem up, phloem down.

W: Right! Now just imagine your tree tomorrow during the quiz!

4. What problem does the man have?
5. How does the woman help the man?

Album 2, Track 3

Exercise 2.1.B (p. 220)

Question 1. Listen to part of a talk given to first–year university students.

The place to go for parking permits is the Safety and Security Office on the first floor of the University Services Building. Parking permits are required for all on–campus parking. Special permits are available for students who carpool. You can also get passes for the Fourth Avenue Garage, bus passes, and maps there. The hours are 8:00 a.m. to 7:00 p.m. Monday to Thursday, and 8:00 to 4:00 on Fridays.

Safety and Security also provides special services 24 hours a day. These include escort service to and from your car, criminal incident reporting and investigation, lost and found, and battery jumper service.

What is the talk mainly about?

Question 2. Listen to part of a talk in a history class.

In the Nile Valley ten thousand years ago, the people used stones to crush grain into coarse flour. Then they turned the flour into primitive forms of bread. Primitive bread wasn't like the bread we know today; it was simply flour dough dried on heated stones. The invention of ovens came later. Leavened breads and cakes, which are made to rise by the action of yeast, were also a discovery of the ancient Egyptians. The Egyptians were the first people to master the art of baking. News of this new wonder food spread to other places in the Middle East. Soon other people were collecting seed, cultivating land, and inventing ways to turn grain into flour.

What does the professor mainly discuss?

Question 3. Listen to part of a lecture in an agriculture class.

One thing that really concerns water resource analysts is how much water agriculture uses—much more than all other water–using sectors of society. One of our greatest concerns is the very high use of water by irrigation. Of course, some forms of irrigation use water more efficiently than others do. The efficiency of water use varies by region, crop, agricultural practice, and irrigation technology. The least efficient types of irrigation are the traditional surface methods, such as field flooding. It takes a lot of water to flood a field. The water collects into ponds or basins, but then most of it either evaporates into the air or passes down through the soil into groundwater. This means that less than half of all the water applied to the field is actually used by the crop. The rest is lost to evaporation or to groundwater.

What is the lecture mainly about?

Question 4. Listen to part of a lecture in a geography class.

The dunes called Spirit Sands make up the Manitoba Desert—Canada's only desert. These five kilometers of dunes were formed 10,000 years ago, when an ancient river dumped billions of tons of sand and gravel at the edge of a glacial lake.

The dunes of Spirit Sands are constantly changing.... they are truly "rolling" dunes. Here's how it works. The sand in each dune becomes progressively finer toward the top. The heavier particles tend to settle at the base on the windward side. The wind blows the finer particles up the slope, and eventually they kind of trickle down the other side. Thus, the dune sort of walks downwind. It will reverse direction when the wind changes. Each dune is covered with tiny, rolling waves, and each wave itself is a tiny dune.

What is the lecture mainly about?

Question 5. Listen to part of a lecture in a biochemistry class.

There've been several influential studies in pain management. Some of the most interesting of these study endorphins, the body's own natural painkillers. For example, we now know that exercise stimulates the production of endorphins. Lack of exercise, on the other hand, not only shuts down endorphin production, but can also lead to muscle deterioration. This is why you see a lot of pain specialists prescribing exercise for patients with chronic pain.

Another interesting area involves the power of the placebo effect. We've known for some time that a sugar pill or other inactive placebo can sometimes make a sick person feel better. Somehow, the power of suggestion … or faith in the doctor, or the drug … will start a process of healing. We now think a neurochemical component—what may actually happen is the placebo effect allows some people to sort of tap into the supply of endorphins in their own brains.

What is the lecture mainly about?

Album 2, Track 4
Exercise 2.1.C (p. 221)

Question 1. Listen to part of a lecture in a psychology class.

One study on aging suggests that the key to a longer life might be the way you think about yourself as you get older, that is, how you see your own aging. The researchers found that people who view aging positively live longer than people who view it negatively.

This study began 26 years ago and took place in a small town in the Midwest. The participants were 640 men and women who were 50 to 90 years old at the time. The subjects were asked to agree or disagree with statements about aging … for example, statements like "As you get older, you become less useful" and "Older people can't learn new skills." The data showed that respondents with the most positive attitudes survived a median of 22 years after their initial interview, while those with negative views lived just 15 years—a difference of seven years.

What is the speaker's main point?

Questions 2 through 3. Listen to part of a talk in a business management class.

An increasing number of newcomers to the American workforce come from populations that have been underserved in the past because of racial, ethnic, gender, or cultural differences. The increase in minority populations brings about "market place" demands. There is a growing economic need to respond to diversity, as organizations must manage and train this increasingly diverse workforce.

The primary goal of all training and development programs is to provide workers at all levels of an organization with the knowledge and skills to perform their jobs and help the organization meet its business goals. For most organizations,

the decision to provide diversity training is a business rather than a moral decision. Good management depends on working effectively with other people by understanding and appreciating differences in perspective. Organizations that do not respond to diversity experience lawsuits, high turnover, low morale and productivity, loss of talent to competitors, additional recruitment and training costs, and negative publicity.

2. What is the topic of the talk?
3. What is the speaker's main point?

Questions 4 through 5. Listen to part of a lecture in a biology class.

A marsh is a wetland where the soil is regularly or permanently saturated with water. Because of the water, marsh vegetation is usually soft-stemmed or herbaceous—grasses, sedges, and mosses. Marshes are among the richest of all biomes. Animal life is highly diverse and includes an array of insects, amphibians, reptiles, and birds. Because marshes are so biologically productive, an abundance of energy-rich organic matter enters the food web each year. Much of this energy-rich biomass comes from dead plant and animal material that is broken down by bacteria and water fungi. The water in marshes may become tea-colored or dark brown because of the organic acids from the decaying vegetation. In the past, people viewed marshes—and most wetlands—as the source of mosquitoes, bad odors, and disease. As a result, many wetlands were destroyed to make way for agricultural development. Now, however, we recognize the ecological importance of marshes and we're putting a lot of research into figuring out how they can be restored.

4. What is the lecture mainly about?
5. What is the professor's main point?

Questions 6 through 8. Listen to part of a discussion in a food science class.

W: The primary ingredient of chocolate is cocoa, which comes from the beans of the cacao, or cocoa tree, which is native to the tropical forests of the Americas and now grown on plantations in Asia and Africa. The tree's fruit is a pod, about 10 to 30 centimeters long, with several beans inside each pod. Certain key factors govern the production of high quality cocoa. For example, the pods ripen continually throughout the year, but only about half of them are mature at any given time, and only the mature pods can be harvested because only they will produce top quality ingredients.

M: Could you say more about how the beans are processed?

W: Sure. Workers cut the pods from the tree with machetes or knives mounted on poles. They cut open the mature pods and remove the seeds by hand. At first, the seeds—the beans—are still covered with pulp from the pods. They are are piled on the ground and allowed to dry in the sun for several days.

M: And this is all done right there on the plantation?

W: Yes, and this air-drying is another important step in the process. This is when enzymes from the pulp combine with natural, airborne yeasts to cause a small amount of fermentation, and this fermentation is what makes the final product even more delicious. During fermentation, the beans reach a temperature of about 51 degrees Celsius, which kills the seed embryos and prevents the beans from sprouting while in transit. After the beans have fermented enough, they're stripped of the remaining pulp. At this point, the beans are sent to the processing plant to be roasted—first on screens and then in revolving cylinders with heated air blowing through. The roasting process causes a browning reaction, when more than 300 different chemicals in the beans interact. And this is the magic moment. This is when the beans start to acquire the rich flavor we associate with chocolate.

6. What is the main topic of the discussion?
7. What aspect of the cocoa tree does the professor mainly discuss?
8. What main point does the professor make?

Album 2, Track 5

2.2   LISTENING FOR DETAILS

Focus (p. 223)

Listen to a professor talk about hearing loss.

Long–term exposure to noise can lead to loss of hearing. The relative loudness of sounds is measured in decibels. Just to give you an idea of what this means, the sound of a whisper is 30 decibels, while a normal conversation is 60 decibels. The noise a vacuum cleaner makes is around 85 decibels.

The danger zone—the risk of injury—begins at around 90. Continual exposure to sounds above 90 decibels can damage your hearing. Loud noises—especially when they come at you every day—all this noise can damage the delicate hair cells in your inner ear. Lots of everyday noises are bad for us in the long run. For example, a car horn sounds at around 100 decibels. A rock band at close range is 125 decibels. A jet engine at close range is one of the worst culprits at an ear–busting 140 decibels.

The first thing to go is your high–frequency hearing, where you detect the consonant sounds in words. That's why a person with hearing loss can hear voices, but has trouble understanding what's being said.

Now choose the best answer to each question.

1. At what decibel level does the risk of hearing loss begin?
2. Which sounds could contribute to hearing loss?

Album 2, Track 6

Exercise 2.2.A (p. 226)

Questions 1 through 2. Listen to a conversation between two students.

M: I had a lot of expenses this quarter, and the money my parents sent didn't last very long. I may have to get some kind of job.
W: You can probably find something right here on campus. You should check out the job board in the student center.
M: Where is that exactly?
W: In the student center, on the first floor, next to

counseling. In fact, I think it's part of the counseling center. You can ask one of the counselors if you want more information about any of the jobs listed.
M: My problem is that I need the money but I don't have a lot of spare time. I'd like a quiet job that would allow me to get some reading done.
W: Then go on over there. Maybe there's an opening for night watchman.

1. What does the woman suggest the man do?
2. What type of job does the man want?

Questions 3 through 5. Listen to a conversation on a college campus.

M: Hey, Lorrie, are you doing anything on Wednesday afternoon?
W: I usually either go to the computer lab or go home after I get out of class. Why?
M: Well, we're having our annual book sale at the library, and we need extra cashiers.
W: When is the sale?
M: All day Wednesday, from ten until six. The busiest time will be from around noon to three. If you're free in the afternoon, why not volunteer to help us out? The library will give you ten dollars in book credit for every hour you work. You have to use the credit at this sale, but that will get you a lot of books. Most are priced around one or two dollars.
W: Why are you selling books from the library?
M: The sale includes mostly books people have donated to the library. There are a lot of paperbacks and things like encyclopedias.
W: Oh, I see. I guess I could spare a few hours.
M: Great! I can put your name down then?
W: Sure. I'll be there around noon.
M: Thanks, Lorrie!

3. What does the woman agree to do?
4. How are book sale workers compensated?
5. When will the woman arrive at the book sale?

Questions 6 through 7. Listen to a conversation between two students.

M: How do you like your classes this term?
W: All of my classes are really good. I especially like political science with Professor Hahn.
M: Oh, I had Professor Hahn for American history. We had to write a lot of papers. But one time we had a debate, and I'll never forget that.
W: Her assignments are challenging but useful. And she has the most interesting stories to illustrate her lectures. She really makes us think.
M: And she really makes you work in her class!
W: I know. But I'm starting to figure things out as a result of this class.
M: Great!

6. Why does the woman like her class with Professor Hahn?
7. What does the man say about Professor Hahn?

Questions 8 through 10. Listen to a conversation between a student and a professor.

W: Professor Abraham, did you want to see me?
M: Yes, please come in Nina, I have a job here that I

hope you can help me with.
W: I'd like to, if I can.
M: Well, see this stack of paper? These are all journal articles that I need to go through for my research. It would really help if they were arranged more logically. Can you help me? I imagine it will take a few hours of your time.
W: Yes, of course I can. How do you want them organized?
M: Well, primarily by subject, and then by date. There are articles from the past four or five years. Most are about primate behavior, but a few deal with other mammals or birds, or with behavioral psychology in general.
W: This will be interesting. I have some free time tomorrow afternoon. Would that be all right?
M: That sounds perfect.

8. What does the professor want the woman to do?
9. What is the subject of the professor's research?
10. When will the woman do the work?

Album 2, Track 7

Exercise 2.2.B (p. 227)

Questions 1 through 4. Listen to part of a discussion in an anthropology class.

M: The men of the northwoods tribes were the hunters. The hunting season began in the fall and continued until midwinter. These expeditions frequently took the hunters away from the village for long periods of time. Moose, deer, beaver, bear, and elk were the animals sought. Large deer drives were common, and small animals were taken with snares or the bow and arrow.
W: Did the women ever go hunting with the men?
M: The women often accompanied their husbands on hunting parties. Their job was to take charge of the camps.
W: Do you mean they just cooked for the men? I thought the Native Americans had more of a system of equality.
M: Overall, men and women shared the labor. On hunting expeditions, women basically supported the men, whose job was to procure the game. On the other hand, women controlled other realms of life. For example, women managed all of the agricultural operations. Also, a woman headed each clan, and these women were respected for their role as keepers of the clan.

1. When did the hunting season take place?
2. What animals did the northwoods tribes hunt?
3. According to the man, how did women participate in hunting?
4. Which activities did women control?

Questions 5 through 7. Listen to part of a talk in an introductory art class. The professor is talking about choosing a career in the arts.

M: Before you undertake a career in the arts, there are a number of factors to consider. Whether your goal is to be an actor or an animator, a saxophonist or a

sculptor, talent is an essential consideration. But talent alone won't guarantee a successful career in the arts; you also need training, experience, and self-discipline. Most importantly, however, you should realize that a career in the arts requires a personal sense of commitment—a calling—because art does have a history of insecure employment. A lot of artists find it difficult—even impossible—to live on the money they make from their art. Most have to supplement their income by teaching, or by working behind the scenes, or by doing other work not related to the arts.
W: In your opinion, what's the best way for us to know if we really have a calling to art?
M: Well … those of you who are interested in art as a career should talk with arts professionals, or work in the arts yourselves. Professionals can give good firsthand advice, but experience is the best way to get a feel for the field.
W: What kind of experience? I mean … how do we get started?
M: Experience doesn't have to be formal. It can be part-time or volunteer work. For example, if you want to be a photographer or graphic designer, you could work for your school newspaper. Or if your interest is acting, you could start out in community theater. The important thing is getting started—spending time doing something in your chosen medium.

5. According to the professor, what factors are important in choosing a career in the arts?
6. According to the professor, why does a career in the arts require a special calling?
7. How does the professor suggest one get started in a career in the arts?

Questions 8 through 10. Listen to a discussion in a speech communications class.

W: For your speaking assignment, you will want to follow a logical series of steps in preparing for your speech. The first step, of course, is to realize the importance of the speech to you.
M1: But isn't that always the same in this class? After all, you give us an assignment and we want to get a good grade for it.
W: Yes, that's true, but the grade isn't the only thing that's important.
M2: Yeah, Paul, think of us, your listeners! We want you to believe in what you're saying!
W: Next, of course, you select your subject. Then, decide on your purpose. Do you simply want to inform us about your subject? Or do you want to influence us in some way? Write down a statement of exactly what you wish to accomplish in the speech. This is the first step in organizing your thoughts.
M1: Is entertainment a purpose?
W: It could be, yes. Your purpose could be to make your audience laugh.
M2: I expect you to be really funny, Paul!
W: After you decide on your purpose and organize your ideas, you are ready to develop your ideas interestingly and soundly. Why don't you all just take the next few minutes to start brainstorming? Jot down ideas that come to mind—things that matter to you, things you feel strongly about.

8. According to the instructor, what is the first step in preparing a speech?
9. What examples of purpose are mentioned in the discussion?
10. What does the instructor want the students to do next?

Album 2, Track 8

Exercise 2.2.C (p. 228)

Questions 1 through 5. Listen to a talk in an art class. The instructor is talking about pigments.

Whether you're working with oil, tempera, or watercolor, it's the pigment that gives the paint its color. A pigment can either be mixed with another material or applied over its surface in a thin layer. When a pigment is mixed or ground in a liquid vehicle to form paint, it does not dissolve but remains suspended in the liquid.

A paint pigment should be a smooth, finely divided powder. It should withstand the action of sunlight without changing color. A pigment should not exert a harmful chemical reaction upon the medium, or upon other color pigments it is mixed with.

Generally, pigments are classified according to their origin, either natural or synthetic. Natural inorganic pigments, also known as mineral pigments, include the native "earths" such as ochre—yellow iron oxide—and raw umber—brown iron oxide. Natural organic pigments come from vegetable and animal sources. Some examples are indigo, from the indigo plant, and Tyrian purple, the imperial purple the Romans prepared from a shellfish native to the Mediterranean.

Today, many pigments are synthetic varieties of traditional inorganic and organic pigments. Synthetic organic pigments provide colors of unmatched intensity and tinting strength. The synthetic counterparts of the yellow and red earths are more brilliant and, if well prepared, are superior in all other respects to the native products. Inorganic synthetic colors made with the aid of strong heat are generally the most permanent for all uses. In contrast, pigments from natural sources are less permanent than the average synthetic color.

1. What is a pigment?
2. According to the instructor, what characteristic should a pigment have?
3. How are pigments generally classified?
4. Which natural pigment did the Romans obtain from a shellfish?
5. According to the instructor, why are synthetic pigments superior to natural pigments?

Questions 6 through 10. Listen to part of a lecture in a sociology class.

So... when children grab for their favorite toys, what's guiding them? Is it social conditioning, or is it nature? Research shows that two–year–old boys like to play with dolls and kitchen sets as much as little girls do. Still, by age five or so, most will tell you those toys are for girls. The older they get, the more children will say that a certain toy is either for girls or for boys. How do they learn this?

I believe—and research supports this—that a child's choice of toys is a natural occurrence, not a sexist plot by society. Studies show that monkeys, like children, pick their toys based on gender. When male and female monkeys were given a wide choice of toys to play with, male monkeys spent more time playing with cars and balls, and females spent more time with dolls and pots.

In one study of human children, researchers observed children playing with toys in a preschool class. There were eight boys and three girls in the class. During the hour for free play, two of the girls usually went straight to the kitchen area and stayed there most of the hour. One girl usually sat at the table, coloring and drawing pictures. The boys usually spent most of the hour with blocks—building towers and then knocking them down.

I'll briefly summarize the rest of their findings. First, they observed that younger children of both sexes play with both dolls and trucks, with no apparent thought of being a boy or girl. But around age five, the boys start moving away from kitchen play, and the girls start ignoring cars and trucks. Older kids of both sexes like blocks. And ... sometimes kids will hear that they shouldn't play with something because it's a boy or girl toy. Sometimes an older kid tells them; sometimes it's a parent.

So, it seems that parents and older children do reinforce the gender stereotypes to some extent. But still, despite some minor evidence of social conditioning, the research supports the idea that most boys and girls are naturally drawn to different types of toys, and it doesn't matter what their parents and society teach them.

6. What is the lecture mainly about?
7. According to the professor, what does research reveal about toy choices in the youngest children?
8. According to research mentioned by the professor, what types of toys do male monkeys prefer?
9. At what age do children start showing gender differences in their choice of toys?
10. What is the main point made in the lecture?

Album 2, Track 9

Exercise 2.2.D (p. 229)

Questions 1 through 2. Listen to a discussion between two students.

M: That was a pretty good history lecture, don't you think?
W: Well, to be honest, I didn't understand what Dr. Marquez meant by "partible inheritance," and it seems like that's an important thing to know.
M: Partible inheritance means that a man's property would be divided equally among all his children. After the man died, that is.
W: Oh. Then what's "primogeniture"?
M: That's when all the property goes to the eldest son. Just think about the word "primogeniture." "Primo" means "one" or "first," right?
W: Right. Oh, I get it! "Primogeniture" is when the first son gets everything.
M: That's right.
W: Now it's starting to make sense.

1. What are the students discussing?
2. What does "primogeniture" mean?

Questions 3 through 5. Listen to part of a discussion in a business class. The professor is talking about small businesses.

W: Small business owners usually consider themselves successful when they can support themselves solely from the profits of their business. So, why do so many small businesses fail each year? Well, for one thing, they usually face stiff competition from larger, more established companies. Large companies generally have cash reserves that enable them to absorb losses more easily than small firms can. Still, with the right combination of factors, a small business can do quite well.

M: My friend has a bicycle shop, and he runs the entire operation by himself. He buys the inventory, repairs bicycles, and sells to customers. He also builds the displays and cleans the shop—he does everything! And he manages to stay in business!

W: It is possible to make it—with hard work, good management, and a product or service for which there's a demand. A small business owner performs a lot of different tasks. It's absolutely essential to be a competent manager, as I'm sure your friend is. You also need to have a thorough knowledge of your field—a combination of formal education and practical training suited to your kind of business. To run a store, for example, you need to know how to keep track of your inventory—what you have to sell—and your accounts, so you need courses in accounting and business. Experience in retailing is helpful, too. Your primary responsibilities center on planning, management, and marketing, so organizational skills are a must. To keep your store in business, you have to adapt to changing market conditions. This means improving services or promoting your products in innovative ways.

3. According to the professor, why do many small businesses fail?
4. According to the professor, what is essential for success as a small business owner?
5. What are two responsibilities of a store owner?

Questions 6 through 10. Listen to a discussion between a student and a biology teaching assistant.

W: Hi, Gordon.
M: Hello, Julie. How are you?
W: Fine. I wonder if I could ask you a few questions.
M: Sure. What's on your mind?
W: Well, something happened—I mean I saw something happen—on a hike I did last weekend, and I was wondering if it sort of fit what we learned about muscle cells.
M: This sounds like it might be interesting. What did you see?
W: Well, I was hiking with my friend—on the desert canyon trail—and we ran into these two guys sitting by the side of the trail. It turns out they were part of a high school group. My friend and I stopped to talk to them, and it turns out that one of them was sort of having trouble. He said he'd been having leg cramps for about five hours.
M: Oh. That's not good on the canyon trail.
W: I know. We asked if they had water and food, and they said a little, but their teacher went back to get some more. The guy with the cramps said he didn't feel like eating. So, we gave them one of our water bottles, and we just went on. Later on, on the way back, we ran into them again. This time the teacher

and the ranger were there. The guy was eating saltine crackers. It turns out he'd skipped breakfast that day.
M: Well that was a dumb thing to do! A strenuous hike in the desert is not the time to diet.
W: So, I wondered if his muscle cramps were because of what we talked about in class, because lactic acid ferments when the cell has no oxygen.
M: I'd say that's what happened with this young man. Do you remember why it happens?
W: Well, I know that human muscle cells make ATP by lactic acid fermentation when oxygen is scarce. It's what happens when … during exercise, when ATP production needs more oxygen than the muscles can supply. The cells then have to switch from aerobic respiration to fermentation. This means lactate collects in the muscle as a waste product, and that causes muscle pain.
M: That's absolutely correct. And the young man made his problem worse by not eating after he first experienced cramps. He was simply out of fuel. His teacher did the right thing by getting him to eat something salty.
W: I guess it's important to balance food and water intake.
M: That's right. Well, Julie, it looks like you saw biology in action!
W: Yeah! It's cool. I can really understand what happened.

6. What does the woman want to discuss with the teaching assistant?
7. Where did the woman meet the young man who had a problem?
8. What help did the young man receive?
9. Why did the young man experience muscle cramps?
10. What point does the teaching assistant make about what the woman saw?

Album 2, Track 10

QUIZ 1 — QUESTIONS 1–5 (p. 232)

Listen to a discussion in a business class.

M1: The computerized workplace can be hazardous to your health if you don't take preventative measures. Today we'll go over what some of these hazards are, and more importantly, what can be done about them. One major complaint—maybe the biggest complaint—of people who spend time at the computer is eyestrain. To help ease the strain on the eyes, the computer screen should be about two feet from your eyes. The entire screen should be in focus. The brightness and contrast should be adjusted for best readability. A good way to relieve eyestrain is to look away from the screen frequently. Focus your eyes on objects that are far away, like something outside—the building across the street or the tree in the parking lot.
W: But what if your office doesn't have a window? I mean, I've worked in lots of places where there's no window.
M1: Then in that case, you need to get up and walk around. You should never sit for more than 30 minutes at a time anyway. This is important for the rest of your body as well, namely your back. Neck

and back pain are a big problem for computer people. Always make sure your screen, keyboard, and chair are at the right height for you.

M2: I think it's important to have a comfortable chair, one that sort of shifts your weight a little bit forward. I put a cushion on my chair, and that really helps my lower back.

M1: That's not a bad idea. The right chair is a must, the right posture as well. Remember what your mother told you—sit up straight, with your feet on the floor. Another thing I wanted to talk about is air pollution in the workplace—sorry, did you have a question, Martha?

W: I've heard that copy machines are bad for you. Is there anything to this?

M1: Photocopy machines aren't a health hazard for people who use them only occasionally. But for people who use them a lot, there can be bad effects. For example, people who handle the toners can get skin rashes. If you handle the toner, you should pour it in slowly, to avoid spreading the dust, and always wash your hands afterward. Another problem—if the machines are in an area that's not well ventilated—is ozone.

W: Ozone! No kidding!

M1: It's true. Almost all photocopiers give off some ozone. However, the amount is usually less than what's considered hazardous. Most machines have an ozone filter, but this can still leak if the machine's not properly maintained. If you can smell a sort of electrical odor coming from the machine, it's a sign that it's giving off too much ozone.

1. What is the discussion mainly about?
2. What does the instructor recommend for relieving eyestrain?
3. According to the discussion, why is it important to have the right chair?
4. According to the instructor, what health problem is associated with copy machines?
5. Where in the workplace might ozone be a problem?

Album 2, Track 11

Quiz 1 — Questions 6–10 (p. 233)

Listen to a lecture given to students in a tourism program.

Why do people travel to distant lands? Many centuries ago, the reasons for travel were primarily economic or political. The idea of traveling for personal enrichment is fairly modern, only a few centuries old, and traveling just for adventure is even newer.

Humans have always traveled across the earth. Early hunting–gathering people migrated in search of resources to sustain themselves. Later, after the spread of civilization, traders journeyed throughout Europe, North Africa, and the Middle East in search of perfumes, spices and other goods. Vikings traveled across the seas in search of fish, timber, and other natural resources. Europeans explored Africa and the Americas, conquering other civilizations and establishing colonies. These activities—the search for resources, the growth of trade, conquest and colonization—all stimulated the growth of tourism.

While the earliest tourists traveled in search of resources, later tourists took trips for cultural, educational, and scientific purposes. During the seventeenth century, the young members of Europe's wealthy classes took "grand tours" through Europe to learn about languages, theater, music, and art. Beginning in the nineteenth century, naturalists like Charles Darwin studied animal and plant species in exotic places. Darwin's travels created interest in traveling for scientific advancement. In the early twentieth century, John Muir began to write about his wanderings through the southern United States, Alaska, and India, and his writings inspired people to preserve the natural world. Other travel heroes, such as Ernest Hemingway, wrote of their African safaris to hunt big game, and this exposed people to the possibilities of journeying to faraway places for adventure.

The tourists of today take trips purely for pleasure, recreation, adventure, and, of course, personal growth. Many travelers now seek out the most distant places and the most unusual cultures. We can see this in ethnic tourism, a contemporary version of cultural tourism that includes visits to traditional villages and people's homes to observe social customs, see native arts and crafts, and watch local ceremonies, and so on. Ethnic tourism helps preserve aboriginal cultures that might otherwise be endangered by assimilation into the larger society. In fact, ethnic tourism allows us to enjoy folk dances and songs and ceremonies that might otherwise be lost.

Another growing area of tourism is environmental tourism, which is related to ethnic tourism. Environmental tourists travel to pristine wilderness areas where few people have gone before. Their goal is to observe and learn about nature. The African safaris of today are environmental tourism. Their purpose is to observe and photograph wildlife rather than kill it.

6. What is the main topic of the lecture?
7. According to the professor, what is the main reason that people traveled many centuries ago?
8. According to the professor, which of the following originated in the past two centuries?
9. What does the professor say about ethnic tourism?
10. What is the main point made in the lecture?

ALBUM 3 — LISTENING

Album 3, Track 1

2.3   Determining Attitude and Purpose

Focus (p. 234)

Listen to part of a conversation between a student and an academic adviser.

W: Hi, Greg. Um…do you have a minute?

M: Nicole. Hello. I have … uh … about twenty minutes. Come in and sit down.

W: Thanks. I wanted to talk about the school psychology program. I've been thinking about this for a while, and I've decided to change my major to counseling.

M: Really? It's quite a change from being an accountant to being a counselor!

W: I know. It's funny, isn't it? All my life I thought I wanted to run my own business someday. But this year I've been working as a volunteer tutor—at Garfield Elementary—and I'm just so impressed with what the counselors are doing there.

M: Did you say Garfield?

W: Yes, where those kids in the accident went to school.

That was terrible, that accident. It was such a shock to the whole school. But it was eye opening for me. I had a chance to observe some of the counselors talking to the kids, helping them deal with the tragedy. They—the counselors, that is—they were so, so … they were really amazing. It really got me thinking about … about how to make … how to help people heal. I started thinking, "This is something I'd like to do."

Now choose the best answer to each question.

1. Why does the student go to see her adviser?
2. What is the student's attitude toward the school counselors that she observed?

Album 3, Track 2

Exercise 2.3.A (p. 237)

Questions 1 through 2. Listen to a conversation between a student and a professor.

M: Professor Park?
W: Hello, Tony. How can I help you?
M: Professor Park, I have a problem. My father had to have surgery, and I have to go to Oklahoma. I don't know how long I'll be gone. I was wondering if I could take an Incomplete for your class.
W: I'm so sorry to hear about your father. Of course you can take a grade of Incomplete. It means you would have six weeks to make up the term paper and the final exam. There is also a form that you need to fill out that I have to sign.
M: I've got the form right here.
W: Oh, then why don't we take care of it right now?

1. Why does the student go to see his professor?
2. What is required for an Incomplete?

Questions 3 through 5. Listen to part of a conversation that takes place in the student services office of a university.

M: Excuse me, I'm looking for Janice.
W: I'm Janice. What can I do for you?
M: The cashier in the cafeteria sent me here. I'd like to change my meal plan.
W: What plan do you have now?
M: Two meals a day, breakfast and dinner. But I have an early morning class three days a week, and I don't have time to eat breakfast in the cafeteria.
W: What, no breakfast? That's not good!
M: Oh, I still eat! We take turns bringing doughnuts or bagels to have at the break.
W: Glad to hear it. So … uh … what you have now is Plan B. And what did you want to do?
M: Well, I was thinking of switching to dinner only, if I can do that, and get a refund for the breakfast I don't eat.
W: Do you know about Plan C?
M: Plan C?
W: It's for lunch and dinner, and costs only $20 more than Plan B.
M: Oh, really? Hmm. That sounds like a good deal.

3. What is the purpose of the conversation?

4. Why does the woman say this:
   "What, no breakfast? That's not good!"
5. Why does the woman tell the man about Plan C?

Questions 6 through 7. Listen to a conversation between a student and a professor.

W: Professor Curtis, may I ask you something?
M: Of course.
W: My daughter was sick yesterday, and I had to stay home with her. I was wondering—could I make up the quiz?
M: I usually don't do that for quizzes, only for tests.
W: But I'm concerned this will affect my grade. I need to do well in this class.
M: Then I've got an idea. If you want to show me what you've learned, give me a one–page report, summarizing the most important thing you got out of the chapter.
W: Oh, I can do that. That's even better than a quiz. Thank you, Professor Curtis.

6. Why does the student speak to the professor?
7. What does the professor suggest the student do?

Questions 8 through 10. Listen to a telephone conversation between two graduate students.

W: Hello.
M: Leona? This is Jaspar.
W: Hi! I've been waiting for you to call. Could you get Dr. Bryant for next week?
M: Dr. Bryant is on sabbatical, but Professor Slocum says he'd be happy to visit our class.
W: I don't know Professor Slocum.
M: He's an expert on the natural history of the region and has written several books on the topic. I think he'll be an excellent addition to our seminar.
W: Good work, Jaspar! This assignment to invite a guest speaker has turned out to be harder than I thought.
M: But it's a great assignment, and besides, everyone has to do it. Look at all the professional contacts we're making!
W: You're right, it's very useful. Thanks, again, and I'll see you tomorrow!

8. What are the speakers mainly discussing?
9. Why does the man say this:
   "He's an expert on the natural history of the region and has written several books on the topic. I think he'll be an excellent addition to our seminar."
10. What is the man's opinion of the assignment?

Album 3, Track 3

Exercise 2.3.B (p. 238)

Questions 1 through 2. Listen to part of a discussion in a writing class.

M: You probably noticed in your reading for this week that all the stories involved cases of miscommunication between people. You probably also noticed that a lot of this miscommunication was due to cultural differences. This is all good stuff, and so I thought it would be a good idea if this week's journal theme were along the same lines. What I'd like you to do is think and write about a time when you—or someone you know—experienced some type of miscommunication. It could be any kind of problem in conveying or in understanding a … Yes?

W: But isn't this the same topic as last week? I mean, I feel I've already written a lot about it. I had to do something like this in two of my other classes too. Can't we write about something else for a change?

M: What did you have in mind?

W: I mean, I'm getting tired of writing about my life. And I don't feel qualified to write about any of my friends' problems.

M: Then why not focus on someone you don't know personally? For example, a scene in a movie or a television show.

W: Oh. I can do that?

M: Of course. What's important is your awareness of—that you can recognize instances of miscommunication.

1. What is the main purpose of the discussion?
2. What is the woman's attitude toward the assignment?

Questions 3 through 6. Listen to part of a talk in a United States history class. The professor is talking about economics in colonial New England.

W: We know that in colonial New England, the Native Americans—compared to the European colonists—had a far greater knowledge of what resources in the environment could be eaten or made useful. Native Americans used a wide range of resources for economic subsistence, and these resources were simply used by the family that acquired them. Only a few resources were accumulated for the purpose of showing a person's social status—for example, shells, furs, and ornaments of the hunt.

M: Excuse me, Dr. Singer, but did they … um … did the Native Americans have a concept of wealth?

W: The Native Americans believed a person's status came more from kinship and personal alliances than from stores of wealth. Their definition of "need" was what they needed to survive. So if they had food, clothing, and shelter, they considered themselves wealthy. For the European colonists, on the other hand, resources in the environment were seen more as commodities, as goods that could be exchanged in markets. European economies measured commodities in terms of money values—abstract equivalencies that could be accumulated and could function as indicators of wealth and social status. So, for the colonists, "need" was defined by the markets that bought New England goods. So the Europeans perceived few resources in New England ecosystems, but they saw many commodities—fur, fish, timber—which could be sold in the marketplace for profit.

3. What is the main purpose of the talk?
4. What does the professor say about the Native Americans' use of resources?
5. Listen again to part of the discussion. Then answer the question.
   "Excuse me, Dr. Singer, but did they … um … did the Native Americans have a concept of wealth?"
   "The Native Americans believed a person's status came more from kinship and personal alliances than from stores

of wealth. Their definition of "need" was what they needed to survive. So if they had food, clothing, and shelter, they considered themselves wealthy."
Why does the professor say this:
"So if they had food, clothing, and shelter, they considered themselves wealthy."

6. Why does the professor say this:
"So the Europeans perceived few resources in New England ecosystems, but they saw many commodities—fur, fish, timber—which could be sold in the marketplace for profit."

Questions 7 through 10. Listen to part of a talk in an anthropology class. The professor is discussing culture.

M: What would human life be without culture? It's impossible for us to imagine what we'd be like without language, without art or religion or technology. Over hundreds of thousands of years of evolution, these aspects of our cultures have become as much a part of us as our anatomy and physiology. We have a lot in common with the people around us. In fact, the number of ideas we have in common with nearby people is very large. A complete list of shared ideas—for example, ideas we share with our own—the people around us—this list would include our ideas about what's right and wrong, what's beautiful and ugly, and so on … also our ideas about food, work, love, marriage—every aspect of our lives—even our rules about how to behave toward strangers, friends, animals, and the earth. Think of a particular group of people—any group—say, for example, college students. If you could take all the ideas and behaviors, all the tools and technology, all the things that college students share as a result of being in contact with each other, you'd have what anthropologists call student culture.

W: So, what you're saying is culture is sort of like a club. College students are a club. It's because our experience is … like, we go to class, we do homework, we have our computers and cell phones, we hang out with other students. Sometimes we forget what the outside world is like. This is why—that's what we have in common with other students—it's why our culture makes us feel like part of a club, right?

M: Hmmm. In a way a culture is like a club—neighboring cultures might share the same ideas and rules, like neighboring clubs do. But the comparison doesn't completely cut it. Think about it. A club has borders that we can define—but we run into trouble if we try to draw borders around a culture. Culture isn't a thing. It's an idea. Still—even though the idea of culture is problematic—some of us believe that by continuing to study cultures, we will eventually be able to explain the similarities and differences among us.

7. What is the purpose of the talk?
8. Why does the professor mention student culture?
9. What is the woman's attitude toward student culture?
10. What does the professor think of comparing a culture to a club?

Exercise 2.3.C (p. 239)

Questions 1 through 2. Listen to part of a talk in a business management class.

Management requires a great deal of energy and effort—more than most people care to make. One factor that affects managers and inhibits their capacity to provide leadership is stress. Stress has lots of causes—work overload, criticism from workers—and can have negative health effects, including loss of sleep.

It's a fact: managers have to deal with stress. Some handle it by making time to be by themselves. Most have some favorite place or pastime—a beach to walk on, maybe a stream to fish in, or a game to play with the kids. It's important to have some form of rest and relaxation—creating art, working with your hands, gardening, playing sports—the list goes on. Rest doesn't always mean inactivity. For some people, exercise is rest.

1. What is the main purpose of the talk?
2. What is the professor's opinion of rest?

Questions 3 through 6. Listen to part of a lecture in a psychology class. The professor is talking about clinical psychology.

In order to know how behavior patterns can be changed, the clinical psychologist has to know what causes the client to behave the way he or she does. Identifying the cause is called diagnosis. In diagnosis a psychologist uses two basic tools: interviews and psychological tests. Through interviews and tests, the psychologist tries to classify the problem to see if it falls into any known categories.

A psychologist may also attempt to describe the client's personality in terms of how he or she deals with life. For example, some people like to lead, and some prefer to follow the lead of others. Some people are active and outgoing, while others are quiet and reflective.

In a diagnostic interview, the psychologist takes the client's case history. This means learning how the client got along with parents, teachers, and friends, as well as how the person handled difficult situations in the past.

Psychological testing is the other way that a psychologist tries to diagnose the client's problems. Clinical psychologists have developed tests that can help them learn about a person's intelligence and personality, as well as tests that show whether a person's behavior or perception is influenced by emotions, disabilities, or other factors.

Personality testing is useful in discovering how the client tries to adjust to life. Personality tests can reveal unconscious feelings the person is unable to talk about. This information can be important and could help shorten the length of treatment required.

3. What is the purpose of the lecture?
4. How do clinical psychologists diagnose a client's problems?
5. Why does the professor discuss taking a client's case history?
6. According to the professor, why are personality tests useful?

Questions 7 through 10. A public health officer has been invited to speak to a biology class. She will be discussing bats.

Listen to the beginning of the talk.

Now that the warmer weather and longer days are here, we aren't the only ones spending more time outdoors. This is an active time for bats as well. Migratory bats are now returning to the area, and young bats are starting to explore their environment. Young bats go off course, and this is when most people come into contact with them.

Bats are a normal part of our environment and can even be a good thing. Bats help keep down the insect population, especially mosquitoes. Normal bat activity includes sleeping during the daytime and becoming active and flying around in search of food at night, starting at dusk. It's unusual to see a bat during the day. Normal bats don't fly around in the daytime, or lie or crawl on the ground, so if you encounter a bat like that, you should call the health department immediately.

If you have bats in your attic or house, contact a pest control agency. They do not kill the bats, but make recommendations on how to get the bats out of your home. You'll want to create a one–way valve from your house to outside so they can get out but can't come in. To avoid having bats in your house altogether, find all possible entry points into the house and close them by caulking or screening the gap. Bats can squeeze through a gap of one–half inch.

Bats are the most likely carriers of rabies in our area, and almost one hundred percent of rabies cases are fatal. Make sure your dogs and cats are vaccinated against rabies. If you should come in physical contact with a bat, it's important to get in touch with the health department or a doctor immediately. If possible, catch the bat so it can be tested for rabies.

7. What is the main purpose of the talk?
8. Why does the speaker say this:
   "Bats help keep down the insect population, especially mosquitoes."
9. How can you prevent bats from entering your house?
10. Why does the speaker recommend getting medical advice if you come in physical contact with a bat?

Exercise 2.3.D (p. 240)

Questions 1 through 5. Listen to part of a lecture in an anthropology class. The professor is discussing humor and laughter.

Being amused is a condition we're all familiar with, but what exactly is a sense of humor? Well, it's something very personal, and yet we communicate it to others by laughing. Laughter is a universal human expression. All normal human beings can laugh. Children as young as one month old will laugh. People often laugh together, and people laugh louder and more frequently when other people around them are also laughing. Every comedian knows this, and research has confirmed it.

Physically, laughter is an involuntary tensing of the chest muscles, followed by a rapid inhalation and exhalation of breath—a mechanism that releases tension. For most people, a good laugh is welcome—and worth looking for—because it brings pleasure and relief.

Human adults everywhere in the world enjoy making their children laugh. Adults make playful attacks on their children, tickling, teasing, and even pretending to bite them. Adults will throw small children up in the air and catch them again. This causes the child to experience mild stress, but in a secure setting because the stress is carefully controlled by the parent. And when the child laughs, it's a signal that he or she has successfully dealt with mild feelings of insecurity. This teaches the child about the shocks and fears that are part of human life, and which every human eventually has to deal with. This element of shock in an otherwise safe situation is a universal characteristic of situations where people laugh.

Our sense of humor allows us to tell stories about situations we haven't experienced firsthand. We call these little stories "jokes." We tell jokes to show our frustration with the society we live in, especially its … well, its rules. Social rules and conventions provide us with a range of situations that we can turn into humor. And the things we joke about—the conventions and rules we live by—are sort of tense areas in our society, they're areas where we can see the need for change. Humor gives us the power to think about changing the rules. Making jokes and laughing are safe ways to change our social rules and conventions. Therefore, comedians—whether they know it or not—are agents of social change.

The ability to laugh is a vital part of being human. People who laugh together—or laugh at each other's jokes—feel close to each other. Laughter creates a sense of connection. Humor can also help us deal with anxieties that we can't escape. Failure, fear, pain, and death—they're all real to us, as they are to no other animal on Earth. And without a sense of humor, it would be difficult for us to live with everything we that know about the world.

1. According to the professor, why do most people welcome laughter?
2. Why does the professor say this:
   "Adults make playful attacks on their children, tickling, teasing, and even pretending to bite them. Adults will throw small children up in the air and catch them again."
3. Which of the following is a universal characteristic of situations where people laugh?
4. Why does the professor talk about social rules and conventions?
5. Listen again to part of the lecture. Then answer the question.
   "The ability to laugh is a vital part of being human. People who laugh together—or laugh at each other's jokes—feel close to each other. Laughter creates a sense of connection. Humor can also help us deal with anxieties that we can't escape. Failure, fear, pain, and death— they're all real to us, as they are to no other animal on Earth. And without a sense of humor, it would be difficult for us to live with everything that we know about the world."
   Why does the professor say this:
   "And without a sense of humor, it would be difficult for us to live with everything that we know about the world."

Album 3, Track 6

Exercise 2.3.E (p. 241)

Questions 1 through 5. Listen to a talk in a geology class.

Now that you know how sedimentary rocks are formed, the next step is to look at various shapes and learn to read them. On our next field trip, we'll see several of the formations called mesas. This landform gets its name from its flat top. "Mesa" means "table" in Spanish. The Spanish people who explored the area thought these flat–topped hills looked sort of like tables. A mesa is wider than it is high—kind of like a large table. We'll also see a variety of other formations, such as buttes, spires, and pillars. All of these spectacular forms are the result of the erosion of rocks of differing hardness. Water erodes rocks both mechanically and chemically. The fast–moving water of rivers carries silt, gravel, and rock debris, and this scours the rock underneath. Slow–moving standing water also erodes when it enters tiny rock pores and dissolves the cements holding the rock together.

On a mesa, conditions are optimal for erosion. With enough time, even the durable top of a mesa will decrease in size. The sides of a mesa are often made of shale or softer sandstone. The slope of the sides will increase the water's speed and force as it runs down. Freezing and thawing loosen the surface rock. Debris carried by the running water cuts away the softer surface rock. As the softer base of the mesa recedes, the edge of the top is weakened, and it eventually cracks, splits, and falls.

As a mesa is shrunk in size by water, it may be cut into smaller landforms. If these smaller remnants are at least as high as they are wide, they are called buttes. The great buttes we'll see were all created by water rather than wind erosion. Further erosion can change a butte into a tower or spire. This is because the shaft of the spire is usually harder than the base on which it stands, and like a mesa or butte, it's capped with a rim of even harder rock. The spires you'll see were left standing after the sandstone around them eroded away. You can see why they're also called chimneys. I mean, they sort of jut up from the sandstone floor.

Further erosion of the softer rock may reduce the spire to some interesting and really weird forms. We'll see some hourglass–shaped rocks, mushroom–shaped rocks, and a sort of strangely eroded pillar. Over time, erosion finally topples these rocks to the ground. They might remain there as boulders, or they might undergo further erosion that completely demolishes them so they disintegrate into pebbles. Finally, these pebbles end up as the sand we walk on as we explore the surface of the plateau.

1. What is the main purpose of the talk?
2. Why does the professor say this:
   "A mesa is wider than it is high—kind of like a large table. We'll also see a variety of other formations, such as buttes, spires, and pillars."
3. What reasons are given for the erosion of a mesa?
4. Listen again to part of the talk. Then answer the question.
   "The spires you'll see were left standing after the sandstone around them eroded away. You can see why they're also called chimneys. I mean, they sort of jut up from the sandstone floor."
   Why does the professor say this:
   "I mean, they sort of jut up from the sandstone floor."
5. Listen again to part of the talk. Then answer the question.
   "Further erosion of the softer rock may reduce the spire to some interesting and really weird forms. We'll see some hourglass–shaped rocks, mushroom–shaped rocks, and a sort of strangely eroded pillar. Over time, erosion finally topples these rocks to the ground. They might remain there as boulders, or they might undergo further erosion that completely demolishes them so they disintegrate into pebbles."
   Why does the professor say this:
   "They might remain there as boulders, or they might undergo further erosion that completely demolishes them so they disintegrate into pebbles."

Album 3, Track 7

QUIZ 2 — QUESTIONS 1–5 (p. 246)

Listen to a conversation between a student and a professor.

M: Professor Vincent, could I ask you something?

W: Certainly.

M: There's a lot we have to remember for the test on Monday. I mean, there are a lot of details about all the different styles—Art Nouveau, and Art Deco, and Art Moderne—I have a hard time keeping them all straight.

W: Hmm. Well… how can I help?

M: It just seems to me that Art Deco and Art Moderne are the same thing.

W: They're not the same, although there is some historical overlap. They were both popular in the 1930s, although Art Deco appeared a little earlier, in 1925.

M: Okay, so they were popular at about the same time. That's getting confusing. They look so similar it's hard to see why they're considered different styles.

W: Well, as I said in my lecture, Art Deco has more decoration than Art Moderne. Art Deco is the style you see in a lot of movie theaters and hotels that were built in the twenties and thirties. Art Deco has facades with geometric designs … and uh … windows with decorative spandrels. Deco buildings have straight lines and slender forms. "Sleekness" is the word. At the time, in the 1930s, sleek was "modernistic."

M: But that's what's getting confusing! Doesn't "modernistic" also apply to Art Moderne? I mean, look at the name.

W: Both styles are what we call modernistic, but Art Moderne is simpler than Art Deco. It has things like more rounded corners, flat roofs, and the walls are smooth and don't have any decoration. Moderne is more streamlined than Deco. The walls are smooth, and the trim is usually stainless steel. A lot of the windows are round, kind of like the portholes on a boat.

M: Oh … I know a building like that. It's downtown, on Second Avenue. It has a rounded corner and round windows. Maybe it's Art Moderne. It used to be a gas station, but now it's a restaurant.

W: Yes, I know that building, and yes, you're correct. It is an example of Art Moderne!

M: Oh, really? That's great. There's another building I like—the Maritime Building—it's also downtown, on Washington Street. It was built in 1927. I know that from the cornerstone. You should see the lobby. It's just beautiful. There's a geometric pattern in the tile on the floor—kind of a big circle with lots of triangles. And you should see the elevator doors—all these swirly decorations—they're really amazing!

W: The Maritime Building is a structure of historical significance. And you know what style it is. You just described it perfectly.

M: Oh, of course! It's Art Deco!

W: A near–perfect example.

M: You know what? I think I'll go downtown and look at both of those buildings before the test. It would help me remember the differences.

W: That's a good idea.

M: Thanks, Professor Vincent. This has been a big help!

W: My pleasure.

1. Why does the student speak to the professor?
2. What is the main topic of the conversation?
3. According to the professor, which of the following are characteristics of Art Deco?
4. According to the professor, how is Art Moderne different from Art Deco?
5. Listen again to part of the conversation. Then answer the question.
   "The Maritime Building is a structure of historical significance. And you know what style it is. You just described it perfectly."
   "Oh, of course! It's Art Deco!"
   "A near–perfect example."
   Why does the professor say this:
   "A near–perfect example."

Album 3, Track 8

QUIZ 2 — QUESTIONS 6–10 (p. 247)

Listen to part of a talk in an economics class.

One very important institution in our economy is the bank. Banks manage money for individual people, corporations, and the government. Banks provide a number of important services for you and your family. Most importantly, they're a safe place to store your money. They also provide an easy way for you to transfer money from one place to another. When you write a personal check, the check authorizes the bank to give your money to the person or business whose name is on the check.

Of course, banks also lend money. Ordinary people take out bank loans for a number of reasons—to pay for college, to buy or remodel a home, to start or expand a business, and so forth. Banks provide these services to individuals; however, their main function is to lend large sums of money, for example, to corporations. When people or corporations borrow money from a bank, they must, of course, pay interest—a percentage of the money they borrowed.

Banks pay interest on the money they hold, and charge interest on the money they lend. For a bank to make a profit, it has to collect more interest than it pays out.

Sometimes banks invest money as well as lend it. To invest money means to put it into a corporation or some other project—for example, building a housing complex or doing medical research—in exchange for a share of the profits. Most businesses need loans and investments at some time, and banks are an important source of both.

You might wonder what would happen if all the people with money in a bank wanted to take their money out at the same time. I mean, how would the bank be able to give everyone their money, if it had lent out or invested most of it? In fact, this can be a serious problem for banks. They count on the fact that most people won't want their money for a long time once it's deposited. That leaves the bank free to lend or invest the money. If every person—or even lots of people—tried to withdraw their money at the same time, the bank might not be able to honor all of its deposits. This causes some banks to fail, or go bankrupt.

Bank failures used to be common during times of recession or depression. They were especially common during the Great Depression of the 1930s. When Franklin Roosevelt became president in 1933, one of the first things he did was close all the banks, so depositors wouldn't panic and try to take all their money out.

6. What is the main purpose of the talk?

7. For what reasons do individuals take out bank loans?
8. How do banks make a profit?
9. Why does the professor say this:
"If every person—or even lots of people—tried to withdraw their money at the same time, the bank might not be able to honor all of its deposits."
10. Why were banks closed during the Great Depression of the 1930s?

Album 3, Track 9

QUIZ 3 — QUESTIONS 1–5 (p. 248)

Listen to part of a lecture in a natural history class.

W: Coal is a substance of plant origin. It's composed mostly of carbon with varying amounts of mineral matter. Coal has been accumulating on Earth for millions of years, but only since the nineteenth century has it been used so much, mainly as a fuel. Coal has formed only since land plants evolved on Earth. Large amounts were formed in the Carboniferous period and during the more recent— yes, Tim?

M: Excuse me, Doctor Lopez. The Carboniferous period—when was that?

W: The Carboniferous period was a time in Earth's history that lasted from 350 million years ago to about 280 million years ago. And, by the way, what does that name tell you?

M: There was a lot of carbon.

W: That's right—carbon, the main ingredient of coal. During the Carboniferous period, there were a lot of plants on Earth, and these plants contained carbon that later hardened into coal. Coal started to form when huge quantities of vegetable matter collected and decomposed in swamps. Over time, layers of decaying vegetation piled up, one layer on top of another. The top layers compressed and squeezed the bottom layers, and the bottom layers turned into a thick material called peat. Bacteria digested the organic plant remains, breaking or cracking the large molecules into smaller units of hydrocarbons. Eventually, layers of sand, rock, and other mineral sediments accumulated on top of the peat beds. After millions of years, the sediment was buried and heated by compression. And what happened to the peat on the bottom?

M: It turned into coal.

W: Yes. That's right. This was because the pressure and heat of the sediment forced out much of the volatile matter in the peat. The pressure and heat were essential, and the result was compact layers of coal. Today in the Mississippi Delta, plant debris and sand are building up at such a rate that the delta is sinking under the weight. This is carrying the debris down to depths where it will experience compression and high temperature. And that's how it's happened all over. Coal deposits can be found on every continent on Earth. But even though coal is very plentiful and affordable, its widespread use is our number one environmental concern. The burning of coal for energy sends soot and smoke into the air, releasing harmful greenhouse gases that contribute to global warming. A lot of us in the scientific community feel that the use of coal as a fuel should be discouraged.

We feel that in place of coal, we should be exploring cleaner, renewable sources of energy.

1. What is the lecture mainly about?
2. According to the professor, when did coal begin to form on Earth?
3. According to the lecture, which of the following are stages in coal formation?
4. Why does the professor say this:
"The pressure and heat were essential, and the result was compact layers of coal. Today in the Mississippi Delta, plant debris and sand are building up at such a rate that the delta is sinking under the weight. This is carrying the debris down to depths where it will experience compression and high temperature."
5. Why does the professor say this:
"But even though coal is very plentiful and affordable, its widespread use is our number one environmental concern."

Album 3, Track 10

QUIZ 3 — QUESTIONS 6–10 (p. 249)

Listen to part of a lecture in a communications class.

Researchers study television to understand its effects on viewers and to measure its effectiveness in selling products. Much of the research on TV audiences is market research, paid for by corporations with something to sell. Let me repeat: research on television is funded largely by advertisers.

The television industry depends on advertising money to survive, and this relationship influences what television offers viewers. Advertisers aim to reach mass audiences and specific social groups. In turn, the television industry tries to meet the needs of advertisers, because pleasing the advertisers is nearly as important as pleasing the public. This means advertisers have a lot of control over what programs are made and when they are shown.

The American television industry is controlled by people who are more interested in the culture of consumerism than in preserving cultures or natural resources. I mean, for the first time in history, most of the stories children learn don't come from their parents or schools; they come from a small number of large corporations with something to sell. And this culture of consumerism is exported to other countries.

Television is the most effective marketing tool ever created. Many advertisements apply basic psychology by sort of appealing to our insecurities and desires. Ads convince us that the things we once thought were luxuries are now necessities. Television is highly skilled at creating images of affluence, not just in the ads, but in the programs as well. Using sophisticated market research, programmers and advertisers sort of paint a picture of life centered on material possessions. This kind of life may look glamorous and desirable, but it's all at the expense of personal relationships.

As you probably can tell, I tend to agree with critics of the media. Advertising does create false needs, and products we really need don't require advertising. Television promotes consumerism. It shows us things, things, and more things. It encourages greed and envy. Television helps create a wasteful society, where things are thrown out long before they are worn out.

6. What is the main idea of the lecture?
7. According to the professor, why do researchers study

8. According to the professor, why do advertisers have control over television programming?
9. Listen again to part of the lecture. Then answer the question.
"Television is highly skilled at creating images of affluence, not just in the ads, but in the programs as well. Using sophisticated market research, programmers and advertisers sort of paint a picture of life centered on material possessions. This kind of life may look glamorous and desirable, but it's all at the expense of personal relationships."
Why does the professor say this:
"This kind of life may look glamorous and desirable, but it's all at the expense of personal relationships."
10. What is the professor's opinion of television?

ALBUM 4 — LISTENING

Album 4, Track 1

2.4   MAKING INFERENCES AND PREDICTIONS

Focus (p. 250)

Listen to a conversation between a student and a professor.

W: Professor Elliott, did you read the draft of my paper yet?
M: Well hello, Amy. Uh, yes, I did read it. As a matter of fact, I wanted to talk to you about it. I'm glad you stopped by. I think I have your paper … here we go, I have it right here.
W: Is there something wrong with it?
M: No, not terribly, but … I can't tell where you're going with it.
W: Oh. I'm not sure I understand.
M: Let me put it like this. You start out strong. In fact, your introduction is done quite well. You really get your teacher interested in technology and society and how they're related and all. The middle part, too— where you interview the engineer—that, that's very engaging. Lots of good and original ideas. But after that … well, I'm lost. What does it all mean? It just gets a little vague.
W: Oh, I think I see what you mean. Do you mean my conclusion's not clear?
M: Well, it's a little too open. You need to tie it all together … leave your reader with one clear thought, one new way of thinking about technology.
W: Oh well, I see. Um … maybe I'd better work on that part some more. I really appreciate your comments. This helps me a lot. Thanks, Professor Elliott.
M: My pleasure. Any time.

Now choose the best answer to each question.

1. What does the professor imply about the student's paper?
2. What will the student probably do?

Album 4, Track 2

Exercise 2.4.A (p. 254)

Questions 1 through 2. Listen to a conversation between a student and his adviser.

M: Excuse me, Mrs. Lyons, do you have a minute?
W: Yes, how are you, Bruce?
M: Fine, I guess. But I'm having a hard time keeping up in geometry. I think I'd better get out of the class and try again next quarter.
W: Let's have a look at the preliminary list for next quarter. Hmm. I'm afraid geometry won't be offered again in the spring.
M: Oh, no.
W: If you feel your workload is too heavy now, why not drop your history class? You could easily get that course again. It's offered every quarter.
M: Oh, all right. If I drop history, maybe then I'll be able to catch up in geometry. Thanks, Mrs. Lyons.
W: You're welcome, Bruce. Good luck!

1. Why does the student go to see his adviser?
2. What will the student probably do?

Questions 3 through 4. Listen to a conversation between two students.

M: I ran into a problem when I tried to register by telephone. I got a message that said I had an outstanding charge on my account that needed to be paid before I could complete my registration.
W: What does that mean?
M: I'm not sure. A recorded voice just said I had to go to the Student Accounts Office.
W: Do you have any idea what it could be about?
M: The only thing I can think of is last quarter my roommate broke the shower door in our suite, and maybe they billed me by mistake.
W: Oh, I'll bet that's expensive. You'd better go to the accounting office and try to clear it up.
M: Yeah, and I'd better make sure my roommate pays for the damage. I do need to register for next quarter.

3. What is the man's problem?
4. What will the man probably do?

Questions 5 through 7. Listen to a conversation between a student and a professor.

W: Professor Pollard?
M: Yes?
W: I've … um … I registered for your psychology course for summer session. But I have to go to Vancouver and won't be back until June 25.
M: Oh. That means you'll miss the first week.
W: I know. Could I … um … make up the work when I get back?
M: That would be kind of a problem. It's like this … we'll cover the important basics during the first week. And you'll be forming study groups and starting to plan your research projects. The first group report is due on the 25th.
W: Would I still be able to join a group?
M: I don't think that would be fair to the others in your group. Summer session is only six weeks, and you

can't afford to get a late start.

W: That's OK. I understand. Will you teach this course again in the fall?

M: Yes. In fact, in fall semester there'll be two, maybe three sections.

5. Why does the student go to see her professor?
6. What does the professor imply?
7. What will the student probably do?

Questions 8 through 10. Listen to a conversation between two students.

M: I haven't seen you around lately. Where have you been hiding yourself?

W: I live off campus now, in Forest Glen.

M: Oh, those are the apartments in Glenwood that the university owns, right?

W: Right, and would you believe they don't cost much more than the dormitories?

M: I didn't realize that. But how did you manage to get in Forest Glen? I thought it was just for married students.

W: Three of the buildings are for married people only, but anyone can live in the rest. And the best part of it is I can ride the city bus for free! All I had to do was show my rent receipt to the transit company, and they gave me a bus pass that's good for the whole semester!

M: Maybe I'll look into that. I might save some money on parking.

W: Why not? The apartments are nice and spacious, and you wouldn't even need your car.

8. What are the students mainly discussing?
9. What can be inferred about the woman?
10. What will the man probably do?

Album 4, Track 3

Exercise 2.4.B (p. 255)

Questions 1 through 2. Listen to an art instructor talk about composition.

Composition is the organization of shapes and forms into a whole—an expressive whole. The elements of composition—line, shape, tone, and color—need to be well arranged, need to be ordered. They need to be coherent … just like the words and phrases and sentences in a piece of writing.

All paintings have a compositional element. Successful paintings sort of suggest the third dimension, the sense that the design goes beyond the picture frame. A picture's unity—which includes the shapes, tones and colors—is linked to what the artist has to say. The artist's message is strongest when it's clear. A composition is better if it says one thing strongly than if it tries to say too many things. A crowded composition is sort of fussy and splintered and lacks unity. Even a painting of a single object needs thoughtful composition so the character of the object is present in every shape.

1. What does the instructor imply about composition?
2. With which statement would the instructor most likely agree?

Questions 3 through 6. Listen to part of a talk in a biology class.

Biology is considered one of the natural sciences. It is the science of life and life's processes. And like life, science is better understood by observing it than by trying to create a precise definition. Over the next fifteen weeks, we will be observing the science of biology.

In many ways, biology is the most demanding of all sciences. This is partly because living systems are so complex. Biology is also a multidisciplinary science. It requires knowledge of chemistry, physics, and mathematics. And of all the sciences, biology is the most linked to the social sciences and humanities.

The word "science" comes from a Latin verb meaning "to know." Science is a way of knowing. It emerges from our curiosity about ourselves and our world. Striving to understand is one of our basic drives.

Who are scientists? Scientists are people who ask questions about nature and who believe that these questions can be answered. Scientists are explorers who are passionate about discovery.

This course has something for all of you to discover. If you're a biology major or a pre–medical student, you'll discover ways to become a better scientist. If you're a physical science or engineering major, you'll discover in biology many applications for what you've learned in your other science courses. And if you're a non–science major, you've chosen a course in which you can sample many disciplines of discovery.

3. What is the main purpose of the talk?
4. According to the professor, why is biology the most demanding of all sciences?
5. What does the professor imply about scientists?
6. What is probably true about the students in this course?

Questions 7 through 10. Listen to a lecture in a botany class. The professor is talking about plant hormones.

The word "hormone" is derived from a Greek verb that means "to excite." Hormones are found in all multi–cellular organisms and function to coordinate the parts of the organism. A hormone is a chemical signal. It's produced by one part of the body and is then transported to other parts of the body, where it triggers responses in cells and tissues.

The concept of chemical messengers in plants first emerged from a series of classic experiments on how plant stems respond to light. Think about this. A houseplant on a windowsill grows toward light. If you rotate the plant, it will soon reorient its growth until its leaves again face the window. The growth of a plant toward light is called phototropism. In a forest or other natural ecosystem where plants may be crowded, phototropism directs growing seedlings toward the sunlight that powers photosynthesis.

Some of the earliest experiments on phototropism were conducted in the late nineteenth century by Charles Darwin and his son, Francis. The Darwins observed that a grass seedling could bend toward light only if the tip of the shoot was present. If the tip was removed, the shoot would not curve toward light. The seedling would also fail to grow toward light if the tip was covered with an opaque cap.

The Darwins proposed the hypothesis that some signal was transmitted downward from the tip into the part of the stem that controlled growth. Later experiments by other scientists studying phototropism led to the discovery of chemical messengers that stimulated growth in the stem. These chemical messengers were hormones.

7. What do plant hormones do?
8. What can be inferred about phototropism in plants?
9. Which grass seedlings would probably NOT bend toward light?
10. What can be inferred about the tip of a plant's stem?

Album 4, Track 4

Exercise 2.4.C (p. 256)

Questions 1 through 2. Listen to a conversation between two students.

W: Have you finished your paper for anthropology yet?
M: No, I haven't even started. I'm having trouble coming up with a good idea. We're supposed to describe the cultural characteristics of a group, but any group I can think of would seem too artificial. I don't know much about any one cultural group.
W: Of course you do. Write about your own culture!
M: But that's my problem. I don't really have a culture.
W: That's ridiculous! Everyone has a culture. What about the culture of your family? Or your high school? Or your hometown?
M: I grew up in a small town where almost everyone works in the orchards.
W: Bingo! Write about the culture of the orchard community.
M: I never thought of that. Well, why not? It's something I know a lot about.

1. What is the man's problem?
2. What will the man probably do?

Questions 3 through 4. Listen to a conversation between a student and a professor.

M: Professor Martin, I will have to miss class tomorrow. My great aunt passed away and her funeral is tomorrow.
W: Oh, let me offer my condolences to you and your family.
M: Thank you. My aunt was a wonderful lady. Ah, so would it be possible for me to take the test next week?
W: Of course. Eric handles all make–ups. He's the instructional aide for our department. Can you stop by the office today and make an appointment with him?
M: Sure. Would he be there now?
W: He should be. He works every day.
M: Then I'll do it right now. Thank you, Professor Martin.
W: You're welcome, Jerry. Take care.

3. Why does the professor say this:
"Oh, let me offer my condolences to you and your family."
4. What will the student probably do next?

Questions 5 through 7. Listen to a conversation between two students.

M: I can't believe how much my books cost this semester! I just spent over one hundred dollars in the university bookstore, for only four books! And I still need the book for chemistry. That one costs fifty–five

dollars! It's a little more than my budget can handle at the moment.
W: Science books are always out of sight. But did you know there's another bookstore in the Pioneer District? They carry used copies of most of the textbooks for the university.
M: I wonder if they'd have my chemistry book. I need the third edition.
W: I found all of my books there. You can sell any kind of book, too, not just textbooks.
M: That's not a bad idea. Where did you say that was again?

5. What is the man's problem?
6. What can be inferred about the man?
7. What will the man probably do?

Questions 8 through 10. Listen to a conversation in a campus pharmacy.

W: Hello. I'm here for an allergy medication. The nurse sent me—I think her name was Margaret—in the student clinic. She said I didn't need a prescription, and that you would know the right medication. It's for allergies, for my itchy nose and burning eyes. I've been having sneezing fits, and it's driving me crazy.
M: All right. I think she means the new product, the really strong one.
W: Maybe that's the one. She says it really works for allergies.
M: All right. We have—you have a choice actually of capsules or tablets. There's no difference in price.
W: It doesn't matter. Hmm … capsules, I guess.
M: All right. Now, this is a powerful drug, so you need only—no more than two capsules every six hours. And you shouldn't drink alcohol, drive a car, or operate machinery.
W: Uh oh! I have a big test tomorrow! I don't know … if this is going to make me drowsy … Do you have anything else that's effective but won't knock me out?
M: Nothing that will relieve your symptoms like this drug. Why don't you—you could take two capsules three or four hours before your test. That way, the drug's still working, but the drowsiness has mostly worn off when you take your test.
W: Okay. Well, I guess I have no choice. I can't start sneezing during the test.

8. What does the man imply about the medication?
9. Listen again to part of the conversation. Then answer the question.
"Uh oh! I have a big test tomorrow! I don't know … if this is going to make me drowsy … Do you have anything else that's effective but won't knock me out?"
What can be inferred about the woman?
10. What will the woman probably do?

Album 4, Track 5

Exercise 2.4.D (p. 258)

Questions 1 through 6. A historian has been invited to speak to an urban studies class. Listen to part of the lecture.

The agricultural revolution of ten thousand years ago started the great shift from rural to urban living. As human settlements evolved from simple groups of huts to larger villages, and then to towns and cities, their basic pattern changed.

The early rural villages grew naturally—sort of organically—as if they were plants or bushes, and buildings were clustered near water sources, and around village gardens, with trees for shade and pastures for animals.

A lot of us yearn to escape to these simpler, more romantic settlements of the past. But there are probably more of us who have a powerful urge to explore new ideas and to build bigger and better structures. We now have super-settlements called cities. Our city planners and architects have converted the organic pattern of the village into a geometrically perfect grid. Our natural habitat has been transformed into an expanse of hard, straight surfaces, with stone and metal and concrete and glass.

Of course, the city is still a wonderful place for stimulation, for opportunity, and for cultural interaction. In fact, you could say the city is our most spectacular creation. And, believe it or not, it still has elements of the rural past.

In the average North American city, about one-third of the surface is given to streets and buildings. The rest is covered by trees and grass—foresters call it the urban forest—meaning all the trees in city parks, the trees planted along streets and highways, and the trees in people's yards. The extent of this forest is sort of amazing—two-thirds of our urban space.

The concept of a tree-lined village green has a long history, but one of North America's first public parks—that was sort of created as a unified project—was Central Park in New York City. Central Park was designed by landscape architects Olmsted and Vaux in the late nineteenth century. They took their inspiration from the gardens of European estates and the romantic landscape paintings from that period.

Central Park was set in a rectangular site covering over 800 acres in the middle of Manhattan Island. By the nineteenth century, the original forest was long gone. The area had been used as a common pasture for farm animals, but eventually it deteriorated into a kind of urban wasteland, dotted with garbage dumps.

Olmsted and Vaux transformed this wasteland into something like its original appearance, with rolling hills, grassy meadows, and woody thickets with thousands of trees. The result is sort of an oasis in the middle of steel and stone. Central Park has been called "the city's lung" because of its purifying effect on the air, not to mention its effect on the human psyche. It remains one of the best examples of what we can do with the open spaces of our cities.

When you look at how far we've come as humans, when you consider that we've developed something called civilization, you come to realize that the finest evidence of our civilization is the city. The city is a symbol of experimentation and creation, a place where we can come together for work and entertainment, for art and culture, for wonder and opportunity. And, like the rural villages of the past, the city is where we come together to share cultural experiences with other humans—indeed, to define what it is to be human.

1. What topics does the speaker discuss?
2. How did early rural villages differ from the cities of today?
3. What is the urban forest?
4. Why does the speaker talk about New York City?
5. Listen again to part of the lecture. Then answer the question.
   "Olmsted and Vaux transformed this wasteland into something like its original appearance, with rolling hills, grassy meadows, and woody thickets with thousands of

trees. The result is sort of an oasis in the middle of steel and stone. Central Park has been called 'the city's lung' because of its purifying effect on the air, not to mention its effect on the human psyche. It remains one of the best examples of what we can do with the open spaces of our cities."
   What does the speaker imply about New York's Central Park?
6. What is the speaker's opinion of the city?

Album 4, Track 6

Exercise 2.4.E (p. 259)

Questions 1 through 6. Listen to a discussion in a biology class.

W1: Various species of Pacific salmon make a round trip from the small streams where they hatch, to the sea, and then back to the stream of their origin, where they spawn and die. This round trip is known as the salmon's run. The end of the salmon's run is the beginning of the next generation. Pacific salmon hatch in the headwaters of a stream. As fry, the fish then migrate downstream via rivers, and eventually to the ocean, where they require several years to mature. While in the sea, salmon from many river systems school and feed together. When mature, the salmon form into groups of common geographic origin and migrate back toward the river they emerged from as juveniles.

M: Is it true that they find their way home by their sense of smell?

W1: During the first stage of their return, they navigate by the position of the sun. But later, when they reach the river leading to their home stream, their keen sense of smell takes over.

M: Just what is it that they can smell? The other fish?

W1: The water flowing from each stream carries a unique scent. This scent comes from the types of plants, soil, and other components of that stream. This scent is apparently imprinted in the memory of a salmon fry before it migrates to the sea.

W2: I had a real shock when I was hiking once. I was looking at a waterfall, and I saw a salmon jump up, about ten feet! At first, I couldn't believe my eyes. But then I saw another one do it! And then several more! It was an awesome sight.

M: They must have an incredibly powerful instinct.

W1: The survival of their species depends on their ability to get home and reproduce. And, of course, other species depend on the survival of the salmon. Salmon provide an important link in the food web. They spend 90 percent of their lives in the ocean, where they feed on plankton, shrimp, and small fish. When they make their return journey, they carry nutrients from the ocean back to the rivers and streams.

M: I used to live near a river, and the eagles would gather for the salmon run every year. They'd gorge themselves on all the salmon that had just spawned.

W1: Nothing is wasted in nature. After the salmon spawn, their carcasses feed birds, mammals, and vegetation—and even their own newly hatched offspring.

1. What is the discussion mainly about?
2. What does the professor mean when she says this:

"This round trip is known as the salmon's run. The end of the salmon's run is the beginning of the next generation."

3. According to the discussion, how do salmon find their way to their home stream?
4. Listen again to part of the discussion. Then answer the question.
"I had a real shock when I was hiking once. I was looking at a waterfall, and I saw a salmon jump up, about ten feet! At first, I couldn't believe my eyes. But then I saw another one do it! And then several more! It was an awesome sight."
Why does the student say this:
"At first, I couldn't believe my eyes."
5. According to the discussion, why are salmon an important link in the food chain?
6. What can be concluded from this statement:
"Nothing is wasted in nature. After the salmon spawn, their carcasses feed birds, mammals, and vegetation—and even their own newly hatched offspring."

Album 4, Track 7

QUIZ 4 — QUESTIONS 1–5 (p. 262)

Listen to a conversation in a university office.

M: Jackie, I wonder if I could talk to you about something.
W: Sure. What's on your mind?
M: There's an opening at channel 12 that kind of interests me—an internship. I was kind of thinking of applying for it.
W: You mean the television station? What sort of job? Oh, I hope that doesn't mean you'll have to leave us!
M: No, no, I wouldn't quit my job. It's a part–time internship for production assistant. Production work, general stuff … probably mostly I'd be a gofer.
W: I see.
M: Anyway, it'd be a way in the door. Unfortunately, it's not a paid internship, but that doesn't matter. It's the experience—the chance to work in television—that's more important to me right now. Some day I'd like to write, or produce. I probably don't stand much of a chance, though. I'm sure there'll be lots of other people who apply, with more qualifications than me.
W: Don't be so sure about that. You never know. Sometimes it's not the credentials but the person who matters. My friend got a really good job in the mayor's office—public relations, a power position— and before that the only work she'd done was emergency rescue—evacuating people in helicopters! Flood victims, accidents and the like. And then she goes and lands this glamour job in the mayor's office, with no experience in politics whatsoever!
M: Wow!
W: Yeah. So you can never tell.
M: Still, I'm going to need all the help I can get. If I could only … uh … convince them of how much—I need them to know how much this would mean to me. I was wondering, Jackie, if you….
W: You want a recommendation?
M: Uh, yeah, like I said, I need all the help I can get.
W: I'd be happy to do what I can. I feel I know your work pretty well. Here in the lab you've always been good at troubleshooting, and helping people figure out their e–mail. I can emphasize that in the letter.

When do you need this?
M: Um … by the end of the week? The application is due next Tuesday.
W: All right, Alex. I hope this will work out for you.
M: If not this, then something else.
W: There you go. That's the spirit!

1. What is the conversation mainly about?
2. Why does the man want to get the internship?
3. What does the man imply when he says this:
"I probably don't stand much of a chance, though. I'm sure there'll be lots of other people who apply, with more qualifications than me."
4. Why does the woman tell a story about her friend?
5. What does the man want the woman to do?

Album 4, Track 8

QUIZ 4 — QUESTIONS 6–10 (p. 263)

A naturalist has been invited to speak to the members of a college hiking club. Listen to part of the discussion.

W1: Because of their protected status, a lot of bears have lost their fear of people. This may make them appear tame, but they're still potentially very dangerous. Bears are wild animals. One or two bear attacks occur each year in Glacier Park. The majority of attacks occur because people have surprised the bear.
M: What should we do if we surprise a bear?
W1: You should try to avoid encounters in the first place by being alert. And make noise. Talk loud. Holler. Bears will usually move out of the way if they hear people approaching.
W2: Some people say to carry bells, or put bells on your pack.
W1: Most bells—even the so–called bear bells—are not loud enough. Calling out or clapping hands at regular intervals are better ways to make your presence known.
M: But isn't it kind of rude to make a lot of noise in the woods? I mean, people go there for peace and quiet.
W1: In bear country, noise is good for you. Hiking quietly endangers you, the bear, and other hikers. People sometimes assume they don't have to make noise while hiking on a well–used trail. Some of the most frequently used trails in Glacier Park are surrounded by excellent bear habitat. You can't predict when and where bears might appear along a trail.
M: That's for sure. I remember my surprise when a black bear charged me. It must have been running away from hikers who surprised it on the trail ahead of me.
W1: Don't assume a bear's hearing is any better than your own. Some trail conditions make it hard for bears to see, hear, or smell approaching hikers. You should be especially careful near streams, against the wind, or in dense vegetation. Stay with your group and, if possible, avoid hiking early in the morning, late in the day, or after dark, when bears are more likely to be active. Bears spend a lot of time eating, so avoid hiking in areas like berry patches or fields of glacier lilies.
W2: How will the bear act if we surprise it?
W1: Bears react differently to each situation. They may appear to tolerate you, and then attack without warning. The most important advice I can give you is

---

never to approach a bear intentionally. Each bear will react differently, and its behavior can't be predicted. All bears are dangerous and should be respected equally.

6. What is the discussion mainly about?
7. What does the naturalist think of bear bells?
8. Listen again to part of the discussion. Then answer the question.
   "Don't assume a bear's hearing is any better than your own. Some trail conditions make it hard for bears to see, hear, or smell approaching hikers. You should be especially careful near streams, against the wind, or in dense vegetation."
   Why does the naturalist say this:
   "You should be especially careful near streams, against the wind, or in dense vegetation."
9. What can be inferred about the behavior of bears?
10. Which situations should hikers avoid?

Album 4, Track 9

QUIZ 5 — QUESTIONS 1–5 (p. 264)

Listen to a talk in a business management class.

What do we mean when we talk about leadership? First, it's important not to confuse leadership with power. It's true that— by definition—leaders always have some degree of power. Leaders have power because of their ability to influence other people. However, many power holders do not have the qualities of leadership. Consider the headwaiter in your favorite restaurant. The headwaiter has power to some degree—for example, the power to seat you at the best table by the window—but he doesn't necessarily have the qualities we associate with leadership.

We have to distinguish between leaders and power holders. There are a lot of powerful people who lack leadership skills. A military dictator has power. So does the robber who sticks a gun in your face and demands your wallet. Leadership is something else.

Leadership and power are not the same thing, although they are similar in this one way. Both leadership and power involve the ability to … bring about the results you want, and to … prevent the results that you don't want to happen.

Here's another way to think of it. In sociological terms, … uh … power is simply the ability to bring about certain behavior in other people. For example, parents have power over their children, and they use it to get their children to behave in acceptable ways. Teachers have power, and so do mid–level managers—all as a result of their position.

Where does power come from? The sources are varied. Probably the oldest source of power is the ability to use physical force—a source available to both the military and the biggest kid on the playground. The power that comes from physical might is not the same as leadership. Just think of the military dictator … or the school bully. We don't usually think of these power holders as leaders—despite the brute force they use to control others.

Wealth, position, the ability to motivate—all of these are sources of power. Being close to others with power is a source of power. That's why people gravitate toward political leaders. Some power comes from qualities people were born with—like physical beauty, or the ability to influence friends. Science and technology are also sources of power. Corporations understand this and spend huge amounts of money on research,

information systems, and consultants.

Although leadership and power are different things, they're related in important ways. Consider, for example, a chief executive officer who has the ability to motivate people, a CEO with vision, who can lift the spirit of his or her employees and bring about a rise in productivity—that is leadership. But consider this scenario. The company realizes they're sort of falling behind in the technology race, so the CEO responds by increasing the amount of money available to the company's research division. That is the exercise of power. Authorizing a spending increase could have been made only by a chief executive with the power to do so. Remember, both leadership and power involve the ability to accomplish the results you want, and successful managers understand how the two work together to make this happen.

1. What is the talk mainly about?
2. Why does the professor talk about the headwaiter in a restaurant?
3. Why does the professor say this:
   "A military dictator has power. So does the robber who sticks a gun in your face and demands your wallet. Leadership is something else."
4. According to the professor, how are leadership and power similar?
5. Listen again to part of the talk. Then answer the question.
   "Authorizing a spending increase could have been made only by a chief executive with the power to do so. Remember, both leadership and power involve the ability to accomplish the results you want, and successful managers understand how the two work together to make this happen."
   What does the professor imply about successful managers?

Album 4, Track 10

QUIZ 5 — QUESTIONS 6–10 (p. 265)

A forester has been invited to speak to a group of students. Listen to part of the talk.

M1: No matter whether we live in the country, the suburbs, or the city, we come in contact with forests every day. A combination of trees, other plants, insects, wildlife, soil, water, air, and people is a forest. I'm a professional forester. That means I've been trained in the management of forests. Managing a forest is both a science and an art, which is why my education included courses in the biological, physical, and social sciences, as well as the humanities.

W: Doesn't being a forester mean you always work in the woods?

M1: Foresters, of course, do work in the woods. More and more, however, they also work in laboratories, classrooms, planning agencies, corporate offices, and so forth. In fact, our professional organization, the Society of American Foresters, lists over 700 job categories.

M2: I've always been confused about the difference between a national park and a national forest. In a lot of ways they're similar. For example, we can camp and hike in both.

M1: There is a difference between them. National parks, such as Yellowstone, are set aside and preserved in a near–natural state, mainly for the recreational enjoyment of the public. Our parks are administered by the Department of the Interior. National forests, on the other hand, are administered by the Department of Agriculture. Our forests are managed for their many benefits, including recreation, wood products, wildlife, and water.

M2: That means there's a difference between a forester and a park ranger, right?

M1: Yes, there are differences. A forester manages an area of forest for forest products, water quality, wildlife, recreation, and so on. A park ranger, on the other hand, manages an area in a national or state park, mainly for recreation. Another difference is who owns the land. A forester can work on federal, state, or private land, while a park ranger is almost always a government employee.

W: My major is biology, but I'd like to work in the woods in the area of wildlife preservation. Would that make me a forester or a biologist?

M1: Some foresters are primarily biologists. But most foresters majored in forestry management. Foresters and wildlife biologists often work together as a team. Both foresters and biologists want to see that various types of habitat flourish. Deer, for example, require a different habitat than wolves—yet the forest can accommodate them both.

6. What is the talk mainly about?
7. What can be inferred about the profession of forestry?
8. Why does the student say this:
"I've always been confused about the difference between a national park and a national forest. In a lot of ways they're similar. For example, we can camp and hike in both."
9. Listen again to part of the talk. Then answer the question.
"National parks, such as Yellowstone, are set aside and preserved in a near–natural state, mainly for the recreational enjoyment of the public. Our parks are administered by the Department of the Interior. National forests, on the other hand, are administered by the Department of Agriculture. Our forests are managed for their many benefits, including recreation, wood products, wildlife, and water."
What can be inferred about national parks?
10. Listen again to part of the talk. Then answer the question.
"My major is biology, but I'd like to work in the woods in the area of wildlife preservation. Would that make me a forester or a biologist?"
"Some foresters are primarily biologists. But most foresters majored in forestry management. Foresters and wildlife biologists often work together as a team. Both foresters and biologists want to see that various types of habitat flourish."
Why does the forester say this:
"Both foresters and biologists want to see that various types of habitat flourish."

ALBUM 5 — LISTENING

Album 5, Track 1

2.5 UNDERSTANDING FUNCTION

Focus (p. 266)

Listen to a conversation between a student and a professor.

M: Professor Engel, I need to ask you something about my project.
W: All right.
M: Could I … uh … I'm having trouble finding enough information to support my thesis. I mean, I found a couple of articles, but they're kind of old. There don't seem to be any studies more recent than five years ago.
W: Did you check the list of abstracts in the database I talked about in class?
M: Yes, but I still couldn't find much.
W: Maybe you need to refine your search.
M: Maybe … uh … all right. I guess I can keep trying. I'll also go through the articles I found more carefully. There's probably something in there I can use.
W: Is that all? I have a faculty meeting in five minutes.
M: Uh… There is something else I wanted to talk about, another idea I have. I'll come back tomorrow during your office hours.
W: All right, Dylan. See you then.

Why does the professor say this:
"Is that all? I have a faculty meeting in five minutes."

Album 5, Track 2

Exercise 2.5 A (p. 269)

Questions 1 through 3. Listen to part of a conversation in a university office.

W: Hello. Is this where I can get a scholarship application?
M: Yes. Which scholarship are you applying for?
W: Oh … um, there are three that I'm interested in.
M: Okay. Each scholarship has its own requirements. For every one, there's a form to fill out. Some of them require recommendations from faculty or a list of references—
W: Uh–huh.
M: —and some require an essay.
W: Oh, great … my favorite thing.
M: Sorry?
W: Oh, nothing. Well, here's the list of the scholarships I'm applying for.
M: Okay. Let me get you those packets.
W: Thanks. What kind of essay do they want?
M: Oh, usually it's a general statement about what your goals are, you know, and how your program of study will help you achieve those goals. That lets the scholarship committee understand more about you.
W: That sounds easy enough.
M: There's nothing hard about it. You don't even have to write a different essay for each application.

W: But didn't you just say that each one has different requirements?

M: They do, but they're all pretty similar. All of them want to know the same things about you. You can write a basic statement about your goals and then vary it a little for each individual application.

W: Do you think that would be enough?

M: Oh, sure. One thing I would say, though, is you should get your applications in early. You'll go crazy if you wait until the last minute. If an essay isn't required, write one anyway and attach it to your application.

W: Really? Do you think I should?

M: It can't hurt.

1. Listen again to part of the conversation. Then answer the question.
"Okay. Each scholarship has its own requirements. For every one, there's a form to fill out. Some of them require recommendations from faculty or a list of references—"
"Uh–huh."
"—and some require an essay."
"Oh, great ... my favorite thing."
What can be inferred about the woman?

2. Listen again to part of the conversation. Then answer the question.
"There's nothing hard about it. You don't even have to write a different essay for each application."
"But didn't you just say that each one has different requirements?"
What does the woman mean?

3. Listen again to part of the conversation. Then answer the question.
"If an essay isn't required, write one anyway and attach it to your application."
"Really? Do you think I should?"
"It can't hurt."
What does the man imply?

Questions 4 through 6. Listen to a conversation between a student and a professor.

M: Excuse me, Dr. Kline. Do you have a minute?

W: Hello, Daniel. Come on in. What can I do for you?

M: It's about my midterm grade. I ... I'm surprised it's so low. I work hard. I, uh, spend a lot of time studying.

W: Oh. Well, let's have a look at your assignments ... here we go. Okay, I've pulled up your record. Hmm ... you had a "C" on the midterm exam and a "B" on your first paper. But unfortunately, I don't have anything here for the second and third papers.

M: I know ... I've been sort of busy. My younger brother's starting classes here in January, and I have to show him around and help him find a place to live. He's staying with me for now, but he doesn't have a car, so I have to drive him everywhere.

W: Does your brother know about the bus system?

M: Uh, it's kind of a problem. My parents want me to help him get settled.

W: I see. That does make it tough for you.

M: Would it be all right if I made up those two assignments? I started one of them, but I didn't have time to finish typing it.

W: Yes, of course you can make up the work, but you need to do that as soon as possible. Remember, these short papers, together with the term paper, count for

50 percent of your final grade.

M: I know. Don't worry. I'll get it together.

W: Okay then.

M: Thanks, Dr. Kline. I appreciate your time.

4. Why does the student speak to his professor?

5. Listen again to part of the conversation. Then answer the question.
"I know … I've been sort of busy. My younger brother's starting classes here in January, and I have to show him around and help him find a place to live. He's staying with me for now, but he doesn't have a car, so I have to drive him everywhere."
"Does your brother know about the bus system?"
What does the professor imply when she says this:
"Does your brother know about the bus system?"

6. Why does the student say this:
"Don't worry. I'll get it together."

Album 5, Track 3

Exercise 2.5.B (p. 270)

Questions 1 through 3. Listen to part of a lecture in a botany class.

W1: There are many variations in the size, shape, and color of flowers. Before we go on, let's quickly go over the parts of a flower. In a perfect, idealized flower, its four organs are arranged in four whorls, all attached to the receptacle at the end of the stem. Closest to the stem are the sepals, which look like leaves because they're usually green. Next are the petals, the colorful layers of the flower, which make the flower attractive to insects and birds. And then, inside the petals, we have the stamens and the sepals, the flower's reproductive parts. So, to sum up— uh ... yes?

W2: Excuse me, Professor Dryden, but ... uh ... is that ... uh ... are you sure about that?

W1: Sure about ...?

W2: I thought you said that the sepals were outside the petals, not inside.

W1: Yes, they are. Oh, sorry, I believe I misspoke. Thank you for noticing. Yes, the sepals are outside the petals. Inside, it's the stamens and the carpels. Okay. To sum up, the four parts of a flower are the sepals, the petals, the stamens, and the carpels. All right now, moving on ... during the millions of years in the history of flowering plants, numerous variations evolved. One important element in plant classification is the arrangement of flowers on their stalks. For example, members of the composite family, which includes sunflowers, have flower heads that form a central disk made up of hundreds of tiny, complete flowers, and the so–called petals surrounding the disk are actually imperfect flowers called ray flowers.

M: Professor Dryden?

W1: Yes, Matthew?

M: So what you're saying is ... a single sunflower is really a lot of little flowers put together?

W1: The flower head consists of hundreds of tiny, tightly packed complete flowers that stand upright on a flat disk. The petals—what look like petals—are actually larger flowers called rays that extend out from the rim. Does that help?

M: Uh, I guess so.

W1: This will make more sense in the lab this afternoon.

1. Listen again to part of the discussion. Then answer the question.
"And then, inside the petals, we have the stamens and the sepals, the flower's reproductive parts. So, to sum up— uh ... yes?"
"Excuse me, Professor Dryden, but ... uh ... is that ... uh ... are you sure about that?"
"Sure about ...?"
Why does the student say this:
"...are you sure about that?"

2. Why does the professor say this:
"Okay. To sum up, the four parts of a flower are the sepals, the petals, the stamens, and the carpels. All right now, moving on ..."

3. Listen again to part of the discussion. Then answer the question.
"The flower head consists of hundreds of tiny, tightly packed complete flowers that stand upright on a flat disk. The petals—what look like petals—are actually larger flowers called rays that extend out from the rim. Does that help?"
"Uh, I guess so."
"This will make more sense in the lab this afternoon."
What does the professor imply when she says this:
"This will make more sense in the lab this afternoon."

Questions 4 through 6. Listen to part of a talk in a sociology class.

M1: Culture consists of the beliefs, values, rituals, symbols, and norms of a society. Norms are the "rules" that maintain social order. Some norms tell us how to behave—for example, that we should obey authority and treat others with respect. Some norms are traditions or customs, such as clothing styles. Speaking of clothing … that reminds me of a place where I used to work. It was my first job after college. It was a big corporation, an investment bank, and the uniform was the traditional dark suit, white shirt, and striped tie. Anyway, that dress code is a good example of a cultural norm. In this case, the dark suit and striped tie symbolized the culture of the organization. Yes, Kayla?

W: What were some other things that identified the culture? I mean, besides the suit and tie.

M1: Good question! In the bank, there were definite norms of behavior. Office conduct was formal. Business hours were standard. Generally speaking, it was a well–established company with a traditional corporate culture. A person's rank was signified by the suit he wore and the size and location of his office. A corner office was a sign of a higher status. There were also rituals, like the executive fishing trip, which brought people together to celebrate corporate unity.

M2: The place where my mother works has a company song, and everyone has to learn it. They sing it at parties and award ceremonies. They also have company colors that everyone wears at these parties, so this means my mother has a lot of blue and gold outfits.

W: You're kidding! Really?

M2: It's a good thing my mother likes those colors.

M1: The company colors are like the flag of any nation, and the company song is a good example of a corporate text. As in any society, these things define the whole group.

W: My brother works for a technology company, and the culture there is very laid–back. Everyone goes to work in blue jeans. They come and go as they please. They even bring their pets to work. My brother brings his dog to work.

M1: That's a good example of an informal workplace culture where there are no fixed traditions to follow. I'm sure you can all think of other examples that you know.

4. Why does the professor say this:
"Some norms are traditions or customs, such as clothing styles. Speaking of clothing … that reminds me of a place where I used to work. It was my first job after college."

5. Listen again to part of the discussion. Then answer the question.
"They also have company colors that everyone wears at these parties, so this means my mother has a lot of blue and gold outfits."
"You're kidding! Really?"
"It's a good thing my mother likes those colors."
Why does the woman say this:
"You're kidding! Really?"

6. Listen again to part of the discussion. Then answer the question.
"My brother works for a technology company, and the culture there is very laid–back. Everyone goes to work in blue jeans. They come and go as they please. They even bring their pets to work. My brother brings his dog to work."
"That's a good example of an informal workplace culture where there are no fixed traditions to follow."
Why does the professor say this:
"That's a good example of an informal workplace culture where there are no fixed traditions to follow."

Album 5, Track 4

2.6 LISTENING FOR ORGANIZATION

Focus (p. 272)

Listen to part of a lecture in a botany class.

All leaves carry out photosynthesis in basically the same way. When carbon dioxide and water are present, photosynthesis can begin. Water enters the leaf through the stem. The chemical reactions of photosynthesis take place in two stages: the light–dependent reactions and the light–independent reactions. First, when sunlight shines on a leaf during the light–dependent stage, light energy is absorbed by the leaf's chlorophyll molecules. This energy is used to split the hydrogen and oxygen in the water in the leaf. Then, during the light–independent stage, hydrogen from the water combines with carbon dioxide, forming carbohydrates, including the sugar glucose and other molecules that are rich in food energy for the plant. In the process, excess oxygen is released to the outside air through the leaf's pores. Finally, the plant transports the products of photosynthesis. Microscopic veins in the leaf carry the food out through the stem and into the cells of the plant. Photosynthesis continues all throughout the growing season, that is, as long as the leaves remain green.

Which of the following best describes the organization of the lecture?

Album 5, Track 5

Exercise 2.6 A (p. 274)

Question 1. Listen to part of a talk in a business class.

Each kind of insurance protects its policyholder against possible financial loss. Life insurance pays your family a certain sum upon your death. The purpose of life insurance is to provide your family with financial security, an immediate estate that will allow them to maintain the household after you die. Health insurance protects you against large medical expenses. When you pay premiums to your insurance company, you can ensure payment of your medical bills. Another kind, property–liability insurance, is sometimes called casualty insurance because it covers the cost of accidents—like automobile accidents, fire, and theft. If you're like most people, your home is the largest single investment you make in your life. This is why most homeowners have some type of property–liability insurance.

1. Which of the following best describes the organization of the talk?

Questions 2 through 3. Listen to part of a talk given by an academic adviser.

A bachelor's degree in engineering is the generally accepted educational requirement for most entry–level engineering jobs. In a typical four–year engineering program, the first two years are spent studying basic sciences— mathematics, physics, chemistry, and introductory engineering—and the humanities, social sciences, and English. The last two years are devoted to specialized engineering courses. Some programs offer a general engineering curriculum, letting students choose a specialty in graduate school or to acquire one later on the job.

Several engineering schools have formal arrangements with liberal arts colleges … programs, for example, where a student spends three years in a liberal arts college studying a pre–engineering subject and a couple years in an engineering school, and then … well then receives a bachelor's degree from each school.

Now most engineers have some training beyond the bachelor's degree. An advanced degree is desirable for promotion, or is necessary to keep up with new technology. Graduate training is essential for most teaching and research positions.

Now a number of colleges and universities offer five–year master's degree programs offering an accelerated, intensive program of study. Some schools—particularly the state technical schools—have five– or six–year cooperative programs where students coordinate classroom study with practical work experience. These programs are popular because, in addition to gaining useful job experience, students can finance part of their education.

2. What is the speaker mainly discussing?
3. How does the speaker organize the information that he presents?

Questions 4 through 5. Listen to part of a talk in a health class.

W: RSI—repetitive strain injury—is probably the fastest–growing job–related illness. We hear about RSI so much today because of high–speed keyboard technology. Repetitive strain injury—also called repetitive motion syndrome—is a real problem for people who sit at the computer all day. RSI is brought on by doing the same movements with the arms and hands over and over again, all day long. This type of injury … RSI … it's … uh … been a problem for a long time for violinists, typists, mechanics, construction workers—anyone whose job involves repeated wrist movements.

M: My mother used to work in the lab at St. Peter's, and she got something like that. She worked there for around fifteen years—and it got to the point where she couldn't handle the instruments anymore. You could hear her fingers crack and pop when she moved them.

W: Hmm. Your mother may have had RSI—a serious case, from the sound of it. RSI affects different people differently. Some people get an inflammation of the sheathing around the tendons in the hand called tendonitis. The inflammation makes your fingers painful and hard to straighten. It's possible your mother's problem was tendonitis. A more serious condition that a lot of workers develop is carpal tunnel syndrome. That's when the nerves that go through the wrist to the hand are pinched by swollen tissue. The swelling causes a numbness or tingling sensation in the hand, and pain shoots up from the wrist—either up the arm or down into the hand. The pain can be so bad at night it wakes you up.

4. What aspect of RSI does the instructor mainly discuss?
5. How does the instructor develop the topic of RSI?

Questions 6 through 8. Listen to part of a lecture in a geography class.

Avalanches are a constant threat on mountain highways. The Rogers Pass stretch of the Trans–Canada is at risk of being buried in snow from November to April every year. This is why the highway now has a sophisticated defense system. The best way … it's important to control an avalanche when it's small … so a slide is set off while it's still small, before it builds up into a serious danger.

A team of snow technicians monitors the snowpack. They sort of "read" the snow and try to predict when it's likely to slide. They study data from the weather stations in the mountains. As the danger increases, they drop explosives onto test slopes to see if the snow can be made to slide.

It's kind of tricky trying to decide just when the snow will slide. The weight of the snow, together with the force of gravity, is what starts an avalanche. The technicians don't want to wait till it's too late, but if they're too early, before conditions are just right, the snow won't release.

When the time is right, they close the road and remove all traffic from the pass. Most closures last two to four hours. Then the army comes in. A ten–man artillery crew operates a mobile 105 mm howitzer, firing shells into the slopes. This sends out shock waves that trigger the avalanches. Slides are set off, one by one. The technicians direct the action, telling the troops where to aim the gun. Visibility can be awful. Then they have to check and see if the avalanche has released well enough. Sometimes they drive their trucks below the slide path—kind of dangerous work—and they listen to the snow come down. Sometimes, if the slide is bigger than they expected, they might have to make a speedy getaway.

6. What is the lecture mainly about?
7. Which of the following best describes the organization of the lecture?
8. According to the lecture, which of the following statements describe steps in achieving a controlled avalanche?

Album 5, Track 6
Exercise 2.6.B (p. 275)

Question 1. Listen to part of a talk in an art class.

If you are unsure of drawing directly in pen and ink, start off with a light pencil sketch. This will allow you to make sure that your proportions are correct and that you are happy with the composition. Take a few minutes to study your subject— this chair and violin. Notice how the straight lines of the chair differ from the curves of the violin. Once you are ready to begin drawing, define the shape of the chair with clean straight lines. Then add contrast by drawing the outline of the violin with gently curved lines. You may have to apply more pressure to the nib when drawing curved lines to allow the ink to flow easily. When you have drawn the outlines of both objects, add in the finer details, such as the seat of the chair and the violin strings. Suggest the texture of the woven seat by using light and dark strokes of the pen.

1. Which of the following best describes the organization of the talk?

Question 2. Listen to part of a talk in a music class.

Drums can be divided according to shape. Some of the types are tubular, vessel, and frame drums.

One of the most common tubular drums is the long drum. A lot of long drums are cylindrical—they have the same diameter from top to bottom—like this Polynesian drum. This drum was carved from a length of tree trunk and has a single– skin head.

For vessel drums, we have the kettledrum. Kettledrums have a single membrane stretched over a pot or vessel body. Vessel drums come in a variety of sizes, from the very large drums of Africa to the very compact and portable drums like this one from Hawaii.

The third type I want you to see is the frame drum. A frame drum consists of one or two membranes stretched over a simple frame, which is usually made of thin wood. The frame is shallow, which adds little resonance when the skin is beaten. A lot of frame drums—like this Turkish tar—have metal jingles attached to the rim.

2. How does the speaker develop the topic of drums?

Questions 3 through 4. Listen to part of a talk in a film class.

The part of filmmaking that most people know about is the production phase—when the film is actually being shot. But a lot of the real work is done before and after the filming. The film's producers are in charge of the whole project. The producer hires a director to make the creative decisions. The producer and the director work together to plan the film. They hire writers to develop a script for the film. Then, from the script comes the storyboard, an important step in the planning. The storyboard is like a picture book, with a small picture for each camera shot. Under each picture, there's a summary of the action and sometimes a bit of dialogue.

Then comes the production, when the filming takes place. During production, the director and crew concentrate on getting the perfect camera shot. The director may ask for several takes of the same shot, sometimes changing the script for each take.

After the filming is done, there's still a lot to do. This is the post–production phase and includes editing the film. The editor's job is to cut up the various film sequences and then put them together in the right order so the story is told in the best way. The editor works closely with the director, as well as various artists and technicians. This is when the sound and special effects are added—the final result being the finished movie you see in the theater.

3. What is the talk mainly about?
4. How does the professor organize the information that he presents?

Questions 5 through 7. Listen to part of a talk in a botany class.

There are several common leaf arrangements in wildflowers. In the usual arrangement, the one called alternate, each leaf is attached at a different level on the stem. This poppy is a good example. See how … uh … there's a leaf here, on the right side, and above that a leaf on the left here, and above that, one on the right again … and so on, alternating right and left, all the way up the stem.

Another type is the opposite arrangement. Notice the difference between the alternate leaves on the poppy and the opposite leaves on this bee plant. The bee plant's leaves are paired on opposite sides of the stem. See how they're attached at the same level of the stem, but on opposite sides.

And here we have yet another kind. This one's called basal, and our example is the amaryllis. Notice how all the leaves are at ground level, at the stem's base. The amaryllis … this particular plant, and all other members of the amaryllis family … uh … it has narrow basal leaves and a long, leafless stalk.

I have some lovely samples to share with you today. I'd like you all to come up and examine the contents of … uh … these two tables. Many of them are specimens of the sunflower family, which includes several species with alternate and opposite leaves. Take a good look and see if you can identify the three types of arrangements. It's okay to handle … but let me ask you to please handle with care, as some of them are quite delicate.

5. How does the instructor organize the information that she presents?
6. Based on the information in the talk, indicate whether each sentence below describes the alternate, opposite, or basal leaf arrangement.
7. What will the students probably do next?

Album 5, Track 7

QUIZ 6 — QUESTIONS 1–5 (p. 277)

Listen to a conversation in a university office.

M: Hi.

W: Hello. Can I help you?

M: Uh ... yeah ... I hope so. I left my jacket in the cafeteria, and I was wondering if anyone had turned it in.

W: When did you lose it?

M: Yesterday, after lunch, probably ... uh ... between one and two o'clock.

W: Well, no one here in the cafeteria reported finding it. Did you check Lost and Found?

M: Uh ... no. Where's Lost and Found?

W: Upstairs, in the security office. The Lost and Found desk is on the right as you go in. If anyone turned in your jacket, they would probably have it there. You can also report it missing.

M: Oh, okay. Thanks. I'll give it a try. I'd really like to have that jacket back.

W: I hope you do. Good luck with it.

M: Oh ... and another thing.

W: Yes?

M: I was ... uh ... Are you the person who decides what's on the menu in the cafeteria?

W: I'm the food services manager, yes.

M: Well, I wondered if ... uh ... you ever thought about healthy food choices. I mean, uh ...

W: Yes?

M: There's a lot of fried food and some pretty unhealthy things, like onion rings and some pretty greasy pizza.

W: Those are the things that most people want. We try to serve what people want. We sell a lot of onion rings and pizza! And it's not all greasy. We have a salad bar and plenty of nutritious and low–fat options. We have a vegetarian pizza on the menu.

M: Well, you never have veggie pizza when I'm here. I know it's on the menu, but you're always out of it.

W: Hmmm. Really? We can fix that. I'll talk to the chef.

M: I think I had it only one time. It's pretty good, actually. In fact, I wish you had more vegetarian options. I mean, I'm not a vegetarian or anything, but a lot of my friends are. I eat meat, but I'd still like to see more healthy options. Like the salad bar could be better. How about adding more fresh vegetables, like organic tomatoes from the farm here on campus?

W: We do use produce from the organic farm ... when it's in season ... or at least we try to.

M: What about sushi? It would be great if you had sushi.

W: Hmmm. Well, you do have a lot of ideas, but some of these things would be a challenge for our kitchen. We can't serve everything that every student would possibly want. But we can do a better job with what we have—more fresh vegetables, for instance. I work closely with the manager of the organic farm, and· I'm sure we can get fresh produce during most of the year.

M: That would be great.

W: There's only so much I can do with the budget I have. But I do appreciate your suggestions, and I'll check into the pizza situation.

M: Thanks.

1. What topics do the speakers mainly discuss?

2. Why does the man say this:
    "Well, I wondered if ... uh ... you ever thought about healthy food choices. I mean, uh ..."
3. What is the man's opinion of the food in the cafeteria?
4. How does the woman respond to the man's comments?
5. What does the woman imply when she says this:
    "There's only so much I can do with the budget I have."

Album 5, Track 8

QUIZ 6 — QUESTIONS 6–10 (p. 278)

An epidemiologist has been invited to speak to a public health class. Listen to part of the talk.

Epidemiology is the field of medicine that deals with epidemics—outbreaks of disease that affect large numbers of people. As an epidemiologist, I look at factors involved in the distribution and frequency of disease in human populations. For example, what is it about what we do, or what we eat, or what our environment is, that leads one group of people to be more likely—or less likely—to develop a disease than another group of people? It's these factors that we try to identify.

We gather data in a variety of ways. One way is through what we call descriptive epidemiology, or looking at the trends of diseases over time, as well as ... uh ... trends of diseases in one population relative to another. Statistics are important in descriptive epidemiology, because numbers are a useful way to simplify information.

A second approach is observational epidemiology, where we observe what people do. We take a group of people who have a disease and a group of people who don't have a disease. We look at their patterns of eating or drinking and their medical history. We also take a group of people who've been exposed to something—for example, smoking—and a group of people who haven't, and then observe them over time to see whether they develop a disease or not. In observational epidemiology, we don't interfere in the process. We just observe it.

A third approach is experimental epidemiology, sometimes called an intervention study. Experimental research is the best way to establish cause–and–effect relationships between variables. A typical experiment studies two groups of subjects. One group receives a treatment, and the other group—the control group—does not. Thus, the effectiveness of the treatment can be determined. Experimental research is the only type of research that directly attempts to influence a particular variable—called the treatment variable—as a way to test a hypothesis about cause and effect. Some examples of treatments that can be varied include the amount of iron or potassium in the diet, the amount or type of exercise one engages in per week, and the minutes of sunlight one is exposed to per day.

The Health Research Institute, of which I am the director, is mostly involved in experimental studies—I say mostly because we study treatment and non–treatment groups and then compare the outcomes. However, we do collect and study various types of data in any given year. From these different approaches—descriptive, observational, and experimental—we can judge whether a particular factor causes or prevents the disease that we're looking at.

6. What is the talk mainly about?
7. How does the speaker develop the topic?
8. According to the talk, why do some epidemiologists observe two groups of people?

9. Which of the following statements describes experimental epidemiology?

10. Listen again to part of the talk. Then answer the question.
"The Health Research Institute, of which I am the director, is mostly involved in experimental studies—I say mostly because we study treatment and non–treatment groups and then compare the outcomes. However, we do collect and study various types of data in any given year. From these different approaches—descriptive, observational, and experimental—we can judge whether a particular factor causes or prevents the disease that we're looking at."
Why does the speaker talk about her own work?

Album 5, Track 9

QUIZ 7 — QUESTIONS 1–5 (p. 279)

Listen to part of a conversation between a student and a professor.

W: Hey, Professor Woodson, do you have a minute?

M: Sure, Brooke. What's on your mind?

W: Well, I have a question about the group project.

M: Okay.

W: I'm ... uh ... I wanted to ask you if it has to be with a group. I mean, can we do it alone instead?

M: Well, the assignment is to form into teams, and design and carry out a project together.

W: Yeah, I know that's what you said, but I'd rather do mine solo.

M: Oh? ... Why?

W: Well ... actually, I don't feel good about it being a group grade. Um ... I ... to be honest, it doesn't seem like a good idea. I mean, some people work harder than others. There's always someone who just goes along for the ride—

M: Hmm.

W: —and they end up with the same grade as the people who have all the ideas and do most of the work. That just doesn't seem fair.

M: Well, I understand your concerns. It's not unreasonable to feel the way you do. But I believe it's possible for everyone to benefit from an arrangement like this. In life, in the workplace—whatever your job is—you will have to work in a team. This is true in business, technology, government, human services, education, research—whatever you end up doing, you'll have to work on projects with other people. So this assignment is experience for life.

W: Yeah, I know what you're saying, but I can't say that I like it. There are also times when you're on our own, and it's sink or swim. That's been my experience, anyway.

M: Hmm. Well, this is an opportunity to form another experience.

W: Ugh ... I thought you might say something like that.

M: Why don't you talk to a few of your classmates? Find out what kind of project they're thinking about. You might be surprised. They might be way ahead of you on this, but you'll never know unless you ask.

W: I've already started thinking about what I want to do. It's field research in something that interests me—systems design—and I've already talked to a guy who can help me set up some observations with his company.

M: That's good. But you still need to set up something

with a project partner. Someone might have ideas that would combine with yours in an interesting way. You don't have to do exactly the same thing as your partner. Maybe you approach systems design in a different way, or maybe your partner is interested in a different kind of system.

W: Yeah ... I don't know.

M: In fact, instead of having a lecture tomorrow, it's free time for project planning. I recommend you meet with some classmates in the coffee shop. You can email me if you have questions.

W: Well, maybe ... okay. I like the idea of a free day for planning.

1. Why does the student speak to the professor?

2. What does the student mean when she says this:
"Yeah, I know that's what you said, but I'd rather do mine solo."

3. What reason does the professor give for doing the project as assigned?

4. What does the professor suggest the student do?

5. Listen again to part of the conversation. Then answer the question.
"Someone might have ideas that would combine with yours in an interesting way. You don't have to do exactly the same thing as your partner. Maybe you approach systems design in a different way, or maybe your partner is interested in a different kind of system."
"Yeah ... I don't know."
Why does the student say this:
"Yeah ... I don't know."

Album 5, Track 10

QUIZ 7 — QUESTIONS 6–11 (p. 280)

A professor of education is giving a lecture about child development. Listen to part of the lecture.

In some ways, mental development is related to social development in school–aged children. Between the ages of six and twelve, children move from being able to think only on a concrete level—that is, about real objects they can touch—to being capable of abstract thought. In their social development, children gradually acquire interpersonal reasoning skills. They learn to understand the feelings of other people, and also learn that a person's actions or words don't always reflect their inner feelings.

When children first start school, at around four to six years old, they can focus on only one thought at a time. Socially, they can understand only their own perspective, and don't yet understand that other people may see the same event differently from the way they see it. They don't reflect on the thoughts of others. What I mean is, children at this age are self–centered, and for this reason it's known as the egocentric stage of social development.

Children six to ten years old solve problems by sort of generalizing from their own experiences. What I mean is, they can understand only what they've experienced for themselves. They can't think theoretically or abstractly. They have to handle real objects in order to solve problems. But socially, children are learning to distinguish between the way they understand social interactions and how other people interpret them.

From ten to twelve years old, children's mental processes are still sort of tied to direct experience. But on a social level, children can now understand actions as an outsider might see them. This permits children to understand the expectations people have of them in a variety of situations. Children can now manage various social roles—for example, son or daughter, older or younger brother or sister, fifth grader, classmate, friend, teammate, and so on. Because they can play multiple roles, this stage is known as the multiple role–taking stage.

Beginning around age twelve, children can start dealing with abstractions. What I mean is, they can form hypotheses, solve problems systematically, and not have to handle real objects. And the social perspective is also expanding, because in this stage children can now take a more analytical view of their own behavior, as well as the behavior of other people. Sometime between twelve and fifteen years old, a societal perspective begins to develop. I mean, the young teenager is now able to judge actions by how they might influence all individuals, not just the people who are immediately concerned.

6. What is the main idea of the lecture?
7. At what age is a child least able to recognize the thoughts of other people?
8. Listen again to part of the lecture. Then answer the question.
    "Children six to ten years old solve problems by sort of generalizing from their own experiences. What I mean is, they can understand only what they've experienced for themselves. They can't think theoretically or abstractly. They have to handle real objects in order to solve problems."
    Why does the professor say this:
    "They have to handle real objects in order to solve problems."
9. What can be inferred about children in the multiple role–taking stage?
10. According to the professor, which of the following statements describe stages in the social development of children?
11. With which statement would the professor most likely agree?

Album 5, Track 11

QUIZ 7 — QUESTIONS 12–17 (p. 281)

Listen to a discussion in a music history class.

M1: Every jazz player knows what he or she means by improvisation. And all writers know what they mean by improvisation. The result, of course, is a lot of confusion and disagreement about what improvisation really is. We hear about the different types of improvisation—free improvisation and controlled improvisation and collective improvisation. What does it all mean? Yes, Mary?

W: My dictionary says improvise means "to compose or recite without preparation."

M1: That's true, but it tells us only part of the story. As we know, musicians learn how to play their instruments before they can improvise. So they do have some preparation.

M2: Maybe a better definition is "composing and performing at the same time."

M1: That tells us another part of the story. Let's try to understand it more by looking at history. Improvisation is as old as music itself. In the beginning, music was largely improvisational,

supplied on the spur of the moment by prehistoric people who "made" music for work, play, war, love, worship, and so on. Music was not separate from everyday life. Rather, music was a force that communicated the relationship of people to nature, and people to each other. Two thousand years ago, the practice of improvisation was widespread among the ancient Greeks. The Greeks based their improvisations on what we might call stock melodies—a collection of tunes known by all musicians. In sixteenth–century Italy, organists had contests for improvising. The ability to improvise in a fugal style—several melodies going at the same time—was a standard requirement for all appointments to organ positions. So, these "cutting" contests were like job interviews.

M2: Did some of the early jazz musicians also have that kind of contest?

M1: Yes, some of them did. With jazz, improvisation has always been important. Actually, the early jazz musicians were very similar to the ancient Greeks in the ways they were making a music that was partly their own and partly derived from the stock melodies in their environment. In most cases, African–American jazz musicians improvised on the European melodies they heard popular white bands playing.

W: Were they really just creating music, without any preparation except hearing other musicians?

M1: I'm glad you asked that. There were a number of jazz musicians who had played in army bands, and they had training of one kind or another. It was these trained military bandsmen who were responsible for the rise of jazz improvisation.

12. What is the discussion mainly about?
13. According to the discussion, why is improvisation difficult to define?
14. How does the professor develop the topic of improvisation?
15. Why does the professor say this:
    "The Greeks based their improvisations on what we might call stock melodies—a collection of tunes known by all musicians. In sixteenth–century Italy, organists had contests for improvising."
16. Based on the information in the discussion, indicate whether each phrase below describes prehistoric people or jazz musicians.
17. What point does the professor make about early jazz improvisation?

Album 5, Track 12

QUIZ 8 — QUESTIONS 1–5 (p. 282)

Listen to a conversation between a student and a professor.

W: Dr. Zarelli?
M: Hello, Karen. How are you?
W: Pretty good, thanks. I was hoping ... um ... we could talk about the project that's due at the end of May.
M: Of course. What can I do for you?
W: Well ... the project plan ... that part's due next week, right?
M: Uh ... I believe that's right. Let me look at the syllabus. I tend to forget dates unless I have them right in front of me! Uh ... yes, that's right, the first

due date—the project plan—is due next week, on Monday, May 3.

W: I'm a little—I'm not sure about what you want. Do you just … uh … what exactly should the plan look like?

M: Well, a description—a summary of your project. A short description of the topic and a summary of your materials and methods and what you hope to accomplish.

W: I have an idea … um … it's something that interests me. But I'm not sure if—I don't know whether it fits the assignment. It's not about marketing as much as—it has more to do with social change.

M: Let's try it on for size. Tell me your idea.

W: Well, my boss—I work part–time at a credit union—and my boss is a person who's done a lot of different things. She used to be the president of an organization that helped set up cooperatives for women artisans in India. They make clothes mostly, and things like tablecloths and toys. She's really interesting—my boss, I mean—and so are the stories about her work. I guess you could say she works for economic development, but also for social change because it's work that affects women and their role in society.

M: Can you tell me more about the organization?

W: Sure. They're called Hearts and Hands. I looked at their Web site. They have a motto, "Changing views, changing lives," and their mission statement is "To empower artisans by providing economic opportunities and exposure to new ideas." My boss was the president for five years, and she's still on their board of directors.

M: Hmm. And what would you like to do with all this?

W: Well, I'd like to interview my boss—a more formal interview—and write about her work with Hearts and Hands.

M: OK, and …?

W: I could do a case study about a group that works for both economic and social change. I could combine the interview data with information from their Web site.

M: It would also be a good idea to link some of your findings with the theories and models we've discussed in class.

W: Oh, like, for example, their product catalog? They have a printed catalog, and it's also online.

M: Great idea! You could include an analysis and evaluation of their catalog. I have to say, Karen, you've got a fairly solid plan here. Your idea of a case study of an economic development organization is a good one, and it fits right in with our course content. All you need to do now is put down your plan on paper.

W: Really? I'm so glad to hear you say that! I'll do it then. I'll write it up for next week. Thank you, Dr. Zarelli. You've been a great help!

M: It's my pleasure. Glad you stopped by.

1. Why does the woman go see her professor?
2. When is the project plan due?
3. Listen again to part of the conversation. Then answer the question.
   "I'm a little—I'm not sure about what you want. Do you just … uh … what exactly should the plan look like?"
   Select the sentence that best expresses how the woman probably feels.

4. What topics will the woman write about?
5. What information will the woman include in her project?

Album 5, Track 13

Quiz 8 — Questions 6–11 (p. 283)

Listen to part of a discussion in an anthropology class.

W1: Anthropology is the quest to fit together the pieces of the human puzzle. The science of anthropology has two major divisions: physical and cultural. Physical anthropology studies human evolution and variation and uses methods of physiology, genetics, and ecology. It's concerned with human biology and tries to solve the mystery of how humans came to be human. Researchers ask questions about the events that led a tree–dwelling population of animals to evolve into two–legged beings with the power to learn—a power that we call intelligence. They ask questions—and I see a question now. Yes?

M: Excuse me, Professor Monroe, but I thought this was a course in anthropology. I didn't know it would be all about science and biology.

W1: This is a course in anthropology, and it is about all those things. It's a two–part introductory course. We start with physical anthropology this quarter, and next quarter we move on to cultural anthropology.

M: Oh … The course description implied something else. I thought it would be about different cultures … about people, humanity.

W1: Anthropology is about those things too. Just hear me out. All anthropologists study humanity. They try to discover how humanity was first achieved, what made humanity branch out in different directions and why separate societies behave similarly in some ways but quite differently in other ways. Physical anthropologists study the fossils and organic remains of once–living primates. They study the connections between humans and other living primates. In the lab, they use the methods of physiology and genetics to study blood chemistry for clues to the relationship of humans to various primates. … Yes?

W2: Our reading list includes a book by Richard Leakey. Is he the guy who did all the research in Africa?

W1: Yes, Richard Leakey is the son of Louis and Mary Leakey. The Leakeys are a well–known family of physical anthropologists. Their research, starting in the 1930s, showed us that human evolution centered there, in East Africa, rather than in Asia. They discovered stone tools and other hominid evidence that pushed back the dates of the earliest humans to nearly four million years ago.

W2: Cool. I saw something about that on television, but it was a long time ago.

W1: Okay now. All right … I want to return to the topic of cultural anthropology because that will be our focus next quarter. Okay. Cultural anthropology studies human culture in different ways … through archaeology … social anthropology … linguistics. Like physical anthropologists, cultural anthropologists study clues about human life in the distant past. However, cultural anthropologists also look at similarities and differences among human communities today. Some of them do research in the field. They live and work among people in societies that are different from their own. Anthropologists who do fieldwork often produce an ethnography, a written description of the daily activities of the people which tells the story of their community life as a whole. One of the most famous field anthropologists was Margaret Mead. In the 1920s, Margaret Mead went to Samoa to pursue her first field assignment—a study that eventually led to her book *Coming of Age in Samoa*. Mead was a pioneer in the field. During her long life, she wrote several major works—on a broad range of topics—from child rearing in the Pacific to the nature of cultural change.

M: I read one of her books in high school, and that's what turned me on to anthropology.

W1: Next quarter's reading list includes a number of Mead's writings, so I hope you will all stay and enjoy the ride.

M: I will. I didn't realize anthropology included so many different things.

6. How does the professor mainly organize the information that she presents?

7. Listen again to part of the discussion. Then answer the question.
"Oh ... The course description implied something else. I thought it would be about different cultures ... about people, humanity."
"Anthropology is about those things too. Just hear me out."
Why does the professor say this:
"Just hear me out."

8. What does the professor say about the Leakey family?

9. According to the professor, which of the following would most likely be done by a physical anthropologist?

10. Listen again to part of the discussion. Then answer the question.
"Like physical anthropologists, cultural anthropologists study clues about human life in the distant past. However, cultural anthropologists also look at similarities and differences among human communities today. Some of them do research in the field. They live and work among people in societies that are different from their own."
What can be inferred about cultural anthropology?

11. Why does the professor say this:
"Next quarter's reading list includes a number of Mead's writings, so I hope you will all stay and enjoy the ride."

Album 5, Track 14

QUIZ 8 — QUESTIONS 12–17 (p. 284)

Listen to part of a lecture in a geology class.

Mount St. Helens is in the Cascade Range, a chain of volcanoes running from southern Canada to northern California. Most of the peaks are dormant—what I mean is, they're sleeping now, but are potentially active. Mount St. Helens has a long history of volcanic activity, so the eruptions of 1980 weren't a surprise to geologists. The geologists who were familiar with the mountain had predicted she would erupt.

The eruption cycle had sort of a harmless beginning. In March of 1980, seismologists picked up signs of earthquake activity below the mountain. And during the next week, the earthquakes increased rapidly, causing several avalanches. These tremors and quakes were signs that large amounts of

magma were moving deep within the mountain. Then, suddenly one day there was a loud boom, a small crater opened on the summit. St. Helens was waking up.

The vibrations and tremors continued. All during April there were occasional eruptions of steam and ash. This attracted tourists and hikers to come and watch the show. It also attracted seismologists, geologists, and—of course—the news media.

By early May, the north side of the mountain had swelled out into a huge and growing bulge. The steam and ash eruptions became even more frequent. Scientists could see that the top of the volcano was sort of coming apart. Then there were a few days of quiet, but it didn't last long. It was the quiet before the storm.

On the morning of May 18—a Sunday—at around eight o'clock, a large earthquake broke loose the bulge that had developed on the north face of the mountain. The earthquake triggered a massive landslide that carried away huge quantities of rock. Much of the north face sort of swept down the mountain. The landslide released a tremendous sideways blast. Super–heated water in the magma chamber exploded, and a jet of steam and gas blew out of the mountain's side with tremendous force. Then came the magma, sending up a cloud of super–heated ash. In only 25 seconds, the north side of the mountain was blown away. Then, the top of the mountain went too, pouring out more ash, steam, and magma. The ash cloud went up over 60,000 feet in the air, blocking the sunlight.

Altogether, the eruptions blew away three cubic kilometers of the mountain and devastated more than 500 kilometers of land. The energy of the blast was equivalent to a hydrogen bomb of about 25 megatons. It leveled all trees directly to the northeast and blew all the water out of some lakes. The blast killed the mountain's goats, millions of fish and birds, thousands of deer and elk—and around sixty people. The ash cloud drifted around the world, disrupting global weather patterns.

For over twenty years now, Mount St. Helens has been dormant. However, geologists who've studied the mountain believe she won't stay asleep forever. The Cascade Range is volcanically active. Future eruptions are certain and—unfortunately—we can't prevent them.

12. What is the lecture mainly about?

13. According to the professor, how did the cycle of volcanic eruptions begin?

14. Why does the professor say this:
"This attracted tourists and hikers to come and watch the show. It also attracted seismologists, geologists, and—of course—the news media."

15. Listen again to part of the lecture. Then answer the question.
"By early May, the north side of the mountain had swelled out into a huge and growing bulge. The steam and ash eruptions became even more frequent. Scientists could see that the top of the volcano was sort of coming apart. Then there were a few days of quiet, but it didn't last long. It was the quiet before the storm."
What does the professor mean when he says this:
"Then there were a few days of quiet, but it didn't last long."

16. What were some effects of the eruption?

17. What can be concluded about Mount St. Helens?

ALBUM 6 — SPEAKING

Album 6, Track 1

Exercise 3.4.A (p. 304)

Talk about a new skill that you would like to learn. Use details and examples to explain your answer.

Now listen to a sample response.

I would like to learn how to play the guitar. Right now I can't play any musical instruments, so that would be a new skill for me. It would be a good skill to have because I could take my guitar to parties and play music for my friends. Also, I could join a band and play songs with other musicians. Maybe I could make money, but I don't care about that. The most important reason is because I enjoy music, and I would like to understand it better.

Album 6, Track 2

Quiz 1 — Question 1 (p. 305)

What is the most interesting class you have ever taken? Explain the aspects of the class that made it interesting. Include details and examples in your explanation.

Album 6, Track 3

Quiz 1 — Question 2 (p. 305)

Some people like to read classic works of literature. Others prefer watching film versions of the same stories. Which do you prefer and why? Include details and examples in your explanation.

Album 6, Track 4

Quiz 2 — Question 1 (p. 306)

Describe a city or town where you have lived. Explain why this place is either a good place or not a good place to live. Include details and examples in your explanation.

Album 6, Track 5

Quiz 2 — Question 2 (p. 306)

Some students take one long examination at the end of a course. Others have several shorter tests throughout the course. Which situation do you think is better for students, and why? Include details and examples in your explanation.

Album 6, Track 6

Quiz 3 — Question 1 (p. 307)

Describe your idea of the perfect job. Explain why this job would be appealing to you. Include details and examples in your explanation.

Album 6, Track 7

Quiz 3 — Question 2 (p. 307)

Some people like taking their vacation in a city. Others prefer spending their vacation in the countryside. Which do you prefer and why? Include details and examples in your explanation.

3.5 INTEGRATED SPEAKING: CONNECTING INFORMATION

Album 6, Track 8

Study (p. 310)

Now listen to two students as they discuss the campus food service.

W: Have you voted on the food service yet?
M: No, but I intend to. I'm going to vote for the second option.
W: That's the one that closes the main cafeteria, isn't it?
M: Right.
W: But the main cafeteria is in the Student Center. That's where everyone goes at lunchtime. Doesn't it make sense to have food there?
M: But it's always so crowded in there at lunchtime. You have to wait a long time in the food line. And there are never enough places to sit.
W: That's true, but they say they'll add more tables.
M: There aren't enough bike racks outside either. I have no place to put my bike. Most of the time I eat at one of the snack bars. Besides, I like the idea of having several smaller eating places all over campus. That seems a lot more convenient, since we have classes all over campus anyway. It also means less crowding, and you don't have to wait as long to get your food. More food choices, too—I kind of like the idea of barbecue on campus.
W: Yeah, that does sound good, doesn't it?

The man expresses his opinion about the campus food service. State his opinion and explain the reasons he gives for holding that opinion.

Album 6, Track 9

Exercise 3.5.A (p. 311)

Now listen to two students as they discuss the course for tutors.

W: Hey, Gavin, you should enroll in this course for tutors.
M: Me? I'm not a tutor.
W: But you want to go to graduate school, right?
M: Right.
W: And in graduate school you'll be a teaching assistant, right?
M: Probably.
W: Then this training course is just what you need. It will give you a head start on learning how to teach. Some of the universities don't give their TAs much training. They just expect you to know how to do it, so this course might be really useful for the future.
M: Maybe. I could at least get a job as a math tutor.

W: And you'd learn how to do it right. You'd learn some practical theories about teaching and learning.
M: True.
W: Anyway, it might give you skills that could be useful later—no matter what kind of work you end up doing.

The woman expresses her opinion about the training course for tutors. State her opinion and explain the reasons she gives for holding that opinion.

Album 6, Track 10
Exercise 3.5.B (p. 312)

Now listen to two students as they discuss the proposal.

W: I just heard the college is increasing the phys. ed. requirement to two courses.
M: Well, that's what they want to do, but I don't think it will happen. Everybody I know hates the idea.
W: Why? Phys. ed. is good for us! Most students need to get more exercise. That's why we have a new phys. ed. building.
M: But it's not up to the college to require us to get more exercise. We have a responsibility to make that choice on our own. I don't think there should be any phys. ed. requirement in college—high school, yes, but not college. Our main job in college is to study. We need to exercise our brains, not our bodies. Besides, I already get a lot of exercise. I'm on my neighborhood basketball team and I also go hiking and rock climbing.
W: Well, obviously you don't need physical education, but other people do.

The man expresses his opinion about the physical education requirement. State his opinion and explain the reasons he gives for holding that opinion.

Album 6, Track 11
Exercise 3.5.C (p. 313)

Now listen to a student as she speaks to other students who are parents.

My two sons have been enrolled at the campus childcare for a semester now. However, I have to say our experience has been less than satisfactory. For one thing, there really isn't enough space there. There's room for only 20 children at a time, which means a lot of people can't get their children in. My children were on the waiting list for three months before getting in. This is a real problem because it prevents a lot of parents from going to college. The college really needs to find a bigger space so there'll be more room for children, don't you think?

Another thing is, they need to extend the evening hours past nine o'clock because some of the classes don't end until 9:30. So if you have a class that lasts till 9:30, you have to leave early to pick up your children. This isn't fair to the parents who need those night classes because they miss important information in class.

The woman expresses her opinion on the on–campus childcare. State her opinion and explain the reasons she gives for holding that opinion.

3.6 INTEGRATED SPEAKING: TAKING NOTES

Album 6, Track 12
Focus (p. 314), Study (p. 317)

Now listen to part of a lecture in a design class.

The warm colors cause feelings ranging from comfort and love to anger and hostility. Red is the color that we pay the most attention to. It is the warmest and most energetic color. Red can raise the blood pressure and make the heart beat faster. Red can add excitement to a room, but it would not be the color of choice for a hospital or a prison. Orange is a warm color, with an effect like red, but to a lesser extent. Orange expresses energy and enthusiasm, which is why we see a lot of orange in shopping malls and restaurants.

And then we have the cool colors. These generally have a calming effect. Blue represents peace, harmony, unity, and security. Blue is the color of water and the sky. Blue causes the body to produce calming chemicals, so it's often used in bedrooms and in the doctor's waiting room. Another cool color, green, is one of the most–cited favorite colors and currently the most popular decorating color. Green refreshes the body and mind. Green symbolizes nature. It evokes a sense of health, youth, and renewal. Green is the easiest color on the eye and can actually improve vision, so it's a good choice for the office or workroom.

Use the examples from the lecture to explain the effects of color.

Album 6, Track 13
Exercise 3.6.A (p. 318)

Now listen to part of a lecture in a psychology class.

In a recent study on emotional intelligence, the researcher interviewed gifted students from 12 to 17 years old. All of the subjects were extremely enthusiastic young people with high intellectual and artistic abilities. Many were active in the performing arts, such as theater and music, which involve working cooperatively with others. Many were active in student government or various community service clubs, where their leadership and social skills could be engaged.

Most of the subjects experienced emotional highs and lows that caused intense happiness, but also conflict, pain, and a tendency to get overexcited. For example, one 16–year–old, a gifted musician, said, "People think that my life is easy because I am talented, but I have a lot of problems just because of these talents. I am a very sensitive and emotional person. I get angered or saddened very easily." What that student said shows us that people with emotional intelligence understand their feelings.

Almost half of the subjects reported sometimes feeling embarrassed and guilty for being "different" from everyone else. However, all of them said they had at least one close friend and a "good" or "very good" relationship with their parents.

Explain emotional intelligence and how the examples given by the professor illustrate the concept.

Album 6, Track 14
Exercise 3.6.B (p. 319)

Now listen to part of a lecture in a sociology class.

Each of us plays more than one social role, so conflict among our various roles is a fact of life. When we experience stress and confusion, it's often because our different roles have different scripts for how we should behave.

For example, the role of student requires you to study, earn good grades, and ultimately complete a degree. As a college student, you've probably noticed that your parents and your friends—both role partners to you—often expect different behavior from you. Your parents want you to stay home and study hard, while your friends say, "You've studied enough; let's go out and party." In this case, you feel the stress of the conflict between your role as a child and your role as a friend.

You might also feel stress over choosing an academic major. Your parents may want you to study medicine or business, but you play guitar and write songs, and all of your friends are musicians. You dream about playing in a band with your friends. In this case, you feel the pressure of your parents' expectation, but you also feel drawn to your friends, your role partners in the music world.

Explain role conflict and how the examples given by the professor illustrate the concept.

Album 6, Track 15
Exercise 3.6.C (p. 320)

Now listen to part of a lecture in a biology class.

Birds spend most of their day in search of food. A few species will store food in hiding places for later use. These birds appear to have highly developed memories. For example, nutcrackers bury food and are able to remember the locations of the hiding places with great accuracy. They use landscape features—like distinctive rocks, logs, and other landmarks—as spatial cues that signal where their food is buried. Recognition of these landmarks allows the birds to return later and dig up the food.

And here's the interesting part. In one study of nutcrackers, after the birds had buried their food, the researchers went to the area where the food was buried and moved a log or a rock. When the birds returned to that area, they were observed digging for the food. But in the places where a log or rock had been moved, the birds appeared to search in a particular spatial relationship to the object. For example, if food had been buried three meters to the west of a large flat rock, and the rock was moved two meters to the north, the birds would dig three meters to the west of the rock in its new location.

The professor describes the behavior of a species of bird. Explain how the birds' behavior illustrates the concept of spatial memory.

3.7 INTEGRATED SPEAKING: DELIVERING YOUR RESPONSE

Album 6, Track 16
Focus (p. 322), Study (p. 325)

Now listen to part of a lecture in a design class.

The warm colors cause feelings ranging from comfort and love to anger and hostility. Red is the color that we pay the most attention to. It is the warmest and most energetic color. Red can raise the blood pressure and make the heart beat faster. Red can add excitement to a room, but it would not be the color of choice for a hospital or a prison. Orange is a warm color, with an effect like red, but to a lesser extent. Orange expresses energy and enthusiasm, which is why we see a lot of orange in shopping malls and restaurants.

And then we have the cool colors. These generally have a calming effect. Blue represents peace, harmony, unity, and security. Blue is the color of water and the sky. Blue causes the body to produce calming chemicals, so it's often used in bedrooms and in the doctor's waiting room. Another cool color, green, is one of the most-cited favorite colors and currently the most popular decorating color. Green refreshes the body and mind. Green symbolizes nature. It evokes a sense of health, youth, and renewal. Green is the easiest color on the eye and can actually improve vision, so it's a good choice for the office or workroom.

Use the examples from the lecture to explain the effects of color.

Album 6, Track 17
Exercise 3.7.A (p. 326)

Now listen to a student and her adviser as they discuss campus housing.

W: Next semester, I'd like to live on campus. My best friend from high school will also start school here, and the two of us want to share a room in the dormitory.

M: Okay, but are you sure you want to room with your friend from high school?

W: Of course. We were best friends last year.

M: You know, this might sound strange, but generally we don't recommend that you share a room with your best friend.

W: Really?

M: It could work out, but a lot of times it can destroy a friendship. The reason is that knowing someone—even being best friends—isn't the same as living together. A better idea might be to live on the same floor as your friend—in the same "neighborhood," so to speak—but have someone else for a roommate. This way, you'll preserve your friendship and also get to know new and interesting people.

W: That does sort of make sense.

M: Or you could live in a dorm with others of your academic major. You'll meet people with similar interests and develop relationships that can benefit you later, in your professional life.

W: I need to think about this. Thank you for your advice.

The man expresses his opinion about the woman's desire to live on campus. State his opinion and explain the reasons he gives for holding that opinion.

Album 6, Track 18

Exercise 3.7.B (p. 327)

Now listen to part of a lecture in a health class.

How many of you get the winter blues? You know what I mean. It's when you feel sleepy or sad, or you don't have any energy on these short winter days. Well, if you experience the winter blues, it's not just in your imagination. The condition known as seasonal affective disorder—or SAD—is linked to changes in the amount of daylight at different times of the year. People with SAD have repeated bouts of depression during the fall or winter, when the periods of daylight are shorter.

Research suggests that SAD is related to the body's biological clock and to changes in body temperature and hormone levels. So, when your body doesn't get enough sunshine, the result is symptoms that are similar to those of a major depression, but usually not as severe. Typically, you have no energy and just want to sleep more, or you eat more carbohydrates and gain weight.

The symptoms usually disappear when the hours of daylight increase again in the spring. That is, the symptoms go away when the underlying problem—the lack of sunlight—goes away. There's also a treatment for SAD that uses a special light that will fool your body into thinking it's getting sunlight.

The professor describes seasonal affective disorder—SAD. Explain how SAD is an example of depression.

Album 6, Track 19

Exercise 3.7.C (p. 328)

Now listen to two students as they discuss seminars.

W: I just transferred here from another college, and we didn't have seminars there. I don't think I'll like seminars.

M: How do you know you won't like seminars, if you've never had one before?

W: Well, the program seminar reminds me of the class discussions we had in high school. I didn't like those discussions because two or three students always did all the talking. Everyone else in the class had to listen to what the big talkers had to say. There was never a chance for the shy or quiet people to speak up and say what they were thinking. So, most of the discussions were pretty boring.

M: But the seminars at this school aren't like that. Sometimes one or two students lead the discussion, but usually everyone participates.

W: I'd rather listen to what the professor has to say. After all, it's the professor who has the knowledge. It's the professor who's supposed to teach us, not the students.

M: I think you'll change your mind about seminars after you see what they're really like.

The woman expresses her opinion about seminars. State her opinion and explain the reasons she gives for holding that opinion.

Album 6, Track 20

Exercise 3.7.D (p. 329)

Now listen to part of a lecture in a history class.

Cesar Chavez was a labor union organizer who used nonviolent action to achieve the goals of fair pay and better working conditions for farm workers.

When Chavez organized a union of grape pickers in California, some of the farm owners refused to accept the union. This led Chavez to organize a nationwide boycott of grapes. Workers stopped picking grapes, and the grapes started to rot on the vines. The boycott got a lot of attention. People from all over the country—public officials, religious leaders, and ordinary citizens—all went to California to march in support of the farm workers. As a result of the boycott, some grape growers signed agreements allowing their workers to join the union, and the workers began to pick grapes again.

On another occasion, Chavez called for a boycott of lettuce produced by growers without labor unions. People from all parts of the country refused to buy lettuce. Some even protested in front of supermarkets.

These boycotts hurt the grape and lettuce growers economically when people stopped buying their products. But even more importantly, the boycotts hurt the reputation of the growers. The boycotts forced the growers to accept labor unions and to improve conditions for farm workers.

Explain boycotts and how the examples given by the professor illustrate the concept.

Album 6, Track 21

Exercise 3.7.E (p. 330)

Now listen to two students as they discuss the theater course.

M: This course isn't open to students! That means we can't take it. Don't you think that's strange?

W: Not really. This course is for people who live in town, people who don't go to college.

M: I don't think that's right. We pay tuition and fees, so we should be able to take any course we want at this school.

W: But this is a chance for other people to learn about theater. It's a community class.

M: But it's not fair. What if I want to learn about theater, too? I'm a full-time student. I'm not in the Theater Arts program, but I'd love the chance to work on a play. The instructor is the director of the theater program. I would enjoy taking this course just for fun. But I can't because I'm a student! It doesn't make sense!

W: Hmm. Maybe you should go talk to the dean.

M: I think I will. Maybe I can convince him that this rule discriminates against students.

The man expresses his opinion about the theater course. State his opinion and explain the reasons he gives for holding that opinion.

Album 6, Track 22
Exercise 3.7.F (p. 331)

Now listen to part of a lecture in a psychology class.

We have new evidence that sleep improves our ability to learn language. Researchers have found that sleep improves the ability of students to retain knowledge about computer speech—even when the students forget part of what they've learned.

The researchers tested college students' understanding of a series of common words produced by a computer that made the words difficult to understand. They first measured the students' ability to recognize the words. After that, they trained the students to recognize the words and then tested them again to measure the effectiveness of the training.

One group of students was trained in the morning and tested twelve hours later, at night. During that 12–hour period, the students had lost much of their learning. The students were then allowed a night's sleep, and were retested the next morning. When they were tested again in the morning, their scores had improved significantly from the night before.

The researchers were amazed by the loss of learning the students experienced during the day and then recovered after sleeping. The students forgot what they learned during the day because they listened to other speech or thought about other things. The results of the study are fairly clear: a good night's sleep is good for learning. Even if information is forgotten, sleep helps restore a memory.

Explain the impact of sleep on learning and how the example given by the professor supports this idea.

3.8   INTEGRATED SPEAKING: SUMMARIZING A PROBLEM

Album 6, Track 23
Focus (p. 333), Study (p. 336)

Listen to part of a conversation between two students.

M: The college newspaper is so much better now that you're the editor.
W: Thanks!
M: And you want to go to graduate school for journalism, so being editor is valuable experience.
W: Yes, I know. But, unfortunately, I might have to quit soon.
M: Quit? Why?
W: The paper takes a lot of time. There are so many meetings, and so much to do. I stay up late every night, and I have swimming practice early in the morning.
M: You can't quit the paper! You need to stay on as editor. The experience will help you get into graduate school.

W: I know. I'd like to stay at the paper, but if I quit, I'll have more time for swimming practice. My coach just recommended me for the sport scholarship, and he thinks I have a really good chance at winning this scholarship, if I just train a little harder. I'd have to get up earlier, but with my late nights at the newspaper … well … it's a conflict. I just don't see how I can do both.
M: Well, in that case, maybe you should leave the newspaper. Maybe the sports scholarship is more important.
W: The newspaper is important to me too, but it leaves me less time for swimming.

The students discuss possible solutions to the woman's problem. Briefly describe the problem. Then state which solution you prefer and explain why.

Album 6, Track 24
Exercise 3.8.A (p. 337)

Listen to a conversation between two students.

W: Is something wrong with your arm?
M: Not really, it's just that my elbow is bothering me. It's been sore lately. I think I hurt it.
W: That's too bad. Why don't you go to the clinic and have someone look at it?
M: Oh, it's not that bad. It's just a little sore.
W: But you're holding your arm in a funny way. You should have a doctor check it. You could do it now. We're heading toward the clinic right now.
M: I don't have the time to go to the clinic right now. I have baseball practice at three o'clock.
W: Baseball practice! You shouldn't play baseball if your elbow hurts!
M: I can't afford to miss any more practices. I've missed too much already, and my coach will be angry. He said he'd put me off the team if I miss another practice. I don't want that to happen. Baseball is important to me. I can't let the team down. ·
W: Then you'd better go to practice, but be sure to tell your coach about your elbow. Tell him you hurt it. You need to give it a rest. You could make it a lot worse if you're not careful.

Briefly summarize the problem the speakers are discussing. Then state which solution you would recommend. Explain the reasons for your recommendation.

Album 6, Track 25
Exercise 3.8.B (p. 338)

Listen to part of a conversation between a student and her academic adviser.

W: I need help with my registration for Winter Quarter.
M: Okay. What kind of help?
W: I still need to fill my social science requirement, so I need another course, but it doesn't look like anything will fit into my schedule for winter.

M: Hmm. I see what you mean. You've already got a full schedule. But I'm sure we can figure something out. Aaaah … well … you could take an evening course. There are lots of evening classes in social sciences for Winter Quarter.

W: An evening course … ugh … I don't like going to class at night. It makes the day so long.

M: Well, with your schedule, this may be your best choice for Winter Quarter. Another possibility, of course, is to wait until next quarter and fulfill the social science requirement then. Can you do that—wait until Spring Quarter?

W: I'm doing an internship at the nursing home in the spring. That will be full–time, and I'm not sure I can handle another course on top of that. I expect the internship will be very demanding. And then I hope to graduate in June. So this is kind of a problem for me.

Briefly summarize the problem the speakers are discussing. Then state which solution you would recommend. Explain the reasons for your recommendation.

Album 6, Track 26

Exercise 3.8.C (p. 338)

Listen to a conversation between two students.

W: How are your classes going?

M: All right mostly, well, that is, except for environmental science. The class is fine, but my learning partner—the guy I'm supposed to do my project with—well, to be honest, he's lazy. I've done all the work so far, but we're being graded together.

W: That's not good. You need to have a serious talk with your partner. You can't let him ruin your grade. You need to lay out a plan for who does what and when. He has to take responsibility for his part of the project.

M: That's for sure. He's hard to get a hold of, too. I've left several messages on his answering machine.

W: You'd better let your professor know about this. Maybe he'll let you do the project with someone else.

M: It's kind of late for that. Besides, I've already started working on it, and so has everyone else.

W: You never know. Maybe you could sort of look around for another group to join. But I would see what your professor says first.

The students discuss a problem that the man has. Briefly summarize the problem. Then state what you think the man should do, and explain why.

Album 6, Track 27

Exercise 3.8.D (p. 339)

Listen to a conversation between two students.

M: Hi, Nicole. How's it going?

W: My classes are going well. I wish I could say the same for my car.

M: What's wrong with your car?

W: I'm not sure, exactly. It just won't start up sometimes. It gave me a lot of trouble this morning. It took me ten minutes to get it running, and then I was late for class. I need to have it checked out, but my regular mechanic is expensive, and I still have to pay my tuition.

M: You could take your car to the community college. They have a program in automotive technology, and they fix students' cars for less than a regular mechanic would charge.

W: But I'm not a student at the community college.

M: Check it out anyway. Maybe you don't have to be a student at that school. Just tell them you're a student.

W: Well, maybe.

M: Another place you could try is the bulletin board in the Student Center. People sometimes advertise services like this. Maybe you can find a mechanic that's not too expensive.

W: Hmm. Maybe. Thanks for the tips.

M: No problem. Good luck.

The students discuss possible solutions to the woman's problem. Briefly describe the problem. Then state which solution you prefer and explain why.

Album 6, Track 28

Exercise 3.8.E (p. 339)

Listen to a conversation between a student and a professor.

M: Professor Fisher, I'm not going to be in class on Monday, so I'll miss the test. I was wondering if I could make it up later.

W: Well, you know my policy is not to give make–up tests. If you miss one test, then you can try to earn extra points on the other tests. But … haven't you already missed a test?

M: Um … yeah, I missed one a few weeks ago.

W: Then try not to miss this test, and try to do well on it too. Your test scores so far have not been strong. You could be in danger of not receiving credit for the course.

M: Do you mean I might fail?

W: At this point, you need to do something to raise your grade. Why don't you get a tutor to help you, or get a classmate to be your study partner?

M: Well, I guess I could. But, to tell the truth, I don't have the extra time for a tutor or a study partner.

W: Then, in that case, you need to think about whether or not you should stay enrolled in this course. If you're too busy to study and come to class, you should consider dropping it.

The speakers discuss a problem that the man has. Briefly summarize the problem. Then state what you think the man should do, and explain why.

3.9 INTEGRATED SPEAKING: SUMMARIZING INFORMATION

Album 6, Track 29
Study (p. 346)

Listen to part of a lecture in a world history class. The professor is talking about mass migrations of people.

In the nineteenth century, there were several periods when large numbers of people moved from one place to another around the world. In many cases, people moved to another continent. These mass migrations were on a much larger scale than any previous migrations in history. One major movement was from Europe to the Americas, Australia, and Africa. This migration of Europeans involved around 60 million people over one hundred years. Another mass migration was from Russia to Siberia and Central Asia. Another was from China, India, and Japan to Southeast Asia.

These large movements of people were made possible by the new cheap and fast means of transportation, specifically railroads and steamships. Another important factor was the rapid growth in banking and capital, by which large investors financed a lot of the settlement. In some places, immigrants were given free land and other benefits if they settled there. This is what encouraged a lot of people—both immigrant and native–born—to move westward in the United States and Canada. Thus, most regions of the U.S. and Canada were populated by the end of the nineteenth century.

The majority of the people in these mass migrations came from the lower social and economic classes of society. The immigrants were motivated mainly by the hope of a better life for themselves and their children. Since most of the immigrants were unskilled workers, their main contribution to their new countries was the labor they supplied. It was the hard work and high hopes of the immigrants that contributed to the economic growth of their new countries.

Using points and examples from the lecture, describe the mass migrations of people in the nineteenth century, and explain why these migrations occurred.

Album 6, Track 30
Exercise 3.9.A (p. 347)

Listen to part of a talk in a hotel management class.

Hotel managers are responsible for the overall operation of their establishment. They see that guests receive good service so they will come back to that hotel. Managers are also in charge of finances and see that the hotel earns a profit without sacrificing service.

The top executive in a hotel is the general manager. In a small hotel the general manager may also be the owner. In large establishments with many facilities, the general manager directs the work of department managers such as executive housekeepers, personnel managers, and food and beverage managers. General managers need to be skilled in areas of leadership and financial decision making. They must be able to judge when to make budget cuts and when to spend money for advertising or remodeling in order to earn profits in the future.

Another type of manager is the controller. Hotel controllers usually work in large hotels, where they are responsible for the

management of money. They manage the accounting and payroll departments and find ways to improve efficiency. The controller is an expert at interpreting financial statements, so the general manager and other top managers in the hotel consult with the controller on all financial matters.

Large hotels rely heavily on advertising and public relations to sell their services. Such hotels have sales managers to market the services of the hotel. Sales managers have constant contact with customers and know what selling points appeal to the public. Sales managers need courses in business, marketing, and advertising in addition to hotel management.

Using points and examples from the talk, describe the duties of different types of managers in large hotels.

Album 6, Track 31
Exercise 3.9.B (p. 348)

Listen to part of a lecture in a meteorology class. The professor is discussing climate.

Several features on the earth's surface influence climate. Two of these features are ocean currents and landforms.

Ocean currents are formed when the earth's rotation and prevailing winds work together. The prevailing winds push the ocean waters westward in the Atlantic, Pacific, and Indian oceans until these waters bounce off the nearest continent. This causes two large, circular ocean currents, one in each hemisphere. The current in the Northern Hemisphere turns clockwise, and the one in the Southern Hemisphere turns counterclockwise. These currents move warm water from the equator to the north and south.

Warm and cold currents in the world's oceans affect the climates of nearby coastal areas. For example, the warm Gulf Stream in the Atlantic Ocean warms the coast of northwestern Europe. Without the Gulf Stream, the climate of northwestern Europe would be more like that of the cold sub–Arctic.

Landforms such as mountains also affect climate. Because of their higher elevation, mountains tend to be cooler, windier, and wetter than valleys. For example, even though Mount Kilimanjaro, Africa's highest peak, stands near the equator, its summit is always covered with snow. Another thing mountains do is interrupt the flow of winds and storms. When moist winds blow from the ocean toward land, then hit a mountain range, the moist air becomes cooler as it's forced to rise. This causes the air to lose its moisture as rain and snow on mountain slopes that face the wind. The air on the other side of the mountain will be warmer and drier.

Using points and examples from the lecture, explain how two features of the earth's surface influence climate.

Album 6, Track 32
Exercise 3.9.C (p. 348)

Listen to part of a lecture in a sociology class.

A crowd is a temporary gathering of people who share a common focus. One interesting aspect of crowd behavior is that how the crowd ends up isn't always clear at the beginning. Crowds can be unpredictable. They have the potential for several different outcomes. For example, the crowd could just break up, or it could turn angry, or the police could break it up, or it could become a riot.

Crowds have an expressive quality. They show strong emotions, and these feelings can be either positive or negative. You've probably been at events, for example, when the musicians at a concert were drowned in cheers, or, on the other hand, maybe they were booed off the stage. Maybe you've even been in crowds where emotions got out of hand, and everyone stormed the stage or tore down the goalposts. When this happens, the crowd becomes out of control.

But not all expressive crowds are out of control. Some are organized into demonstrations for or against a specific goal. Demonstrations usually have their own rules for behavior—such as marching and chanting—but they, too, can be unpredictable. The mood can change quickly, from peaceful to angry to destructive.

In some crowds, there's a feeling that something should be done, but a lack of certainty about what to do. This leads to a particular mood based on that uncertainty, and finally, to a breaking of the rules.

Using points and examples from the lecture, explain how crowd behavior can be unpredictable.

Album 6, Track 33
Exercise 3.9.D (p. 349)

Listen to part of a lecture in an architecture class.

In the late nineteenth century, New York's early "skyscrapers" were steel–framed stone buildings that were only eight or nine stories tall. Then, in 1902, the city got its first true skyscraper. It was called the Flatiron Building, and it was the first structure to come close to being the ideal skyscraper—that is, an office tower that stood apart, forever free on all sides.

The Flatiron Building is twenty–two stories tall. It has a steel frame that's covered on the outside with stone. The first three stories give a sense of heaviness to the lower part of the building. The next thirteen stories have windows grouped in pairs, with carved geometric patterns between them. The top stories are even more decorated with columns and arches, and the top is a heavy crown of carved stone.

The Flatiron Building is different from most other skyscrapers because of the shape of the site it's built on. The irregular, triangle–shaped site was the result of three streets coming together. Because the site is surrounded by streets, the Flatiron Building will always stand alone, separate from other buildings on all three sides.

The building's name—actually its nickname—was a joke about its flatiron shape. At that time, electric irons hadn't been invented, so clothing was pressed with a flatiron, a heavy triangle–shaped piece of iron that was heated on top of a stove. People joked that the building looked like a flatiron, and the name stuck.

Because the Flatiron Building was so narrow, a famous photographer said it looked like the front end of a huge steamship. We can honestly say that this bold design, this strange, tall, thin building, changed the design of the office building forever.

Using points and details from the lecture, describe the Flatiron Building and explain how it got its name.

Album 6, Track 34
Exercise 3.9.E (p. 349)

Listen to part of a talk in a biology class. The professor is discussing animal life in water and on land.

Animal life began in water. When some animals moved from water to land, it was a dramatic event in animal evolution because land is an environment that is very different from water. There were several important physical differences that animals had to adapt to.

The first difference between water and land is the oxygen content. Oxygen is at least 20 times more abundant in air than in water, and it spreads much more quickly through air than through water. Consequently, land animals can get oxygen much more easily than water animals can—that is, once land animals evolved the appropriate organs, such as lungs.

A second difference is in the density of water and air. Air is much less dense than water, and because of this, air provides less support against gravity than water does. This means that land animals had to develop strong legs to support themselves. They also needed a stronger skeleton with better structural support—a skeleton and bones designed for standing and moving in air rather than in water.

And a third difference between life in water and on land is, on land, the temperature of the air changes more easily than it does in water. This means that land environments experience severe and sometimes unpredictable cycles of freezing, thawing, drying, and flooding. Therefore, land animals need to protect themselves from temperature extremes. Land animals had to develop behavioral and physiological strategies to survive in warm and cold temperatures. And one important strategy is being able to maintain a constant body temperature—a physiological strategy that birds and mammals possess.

Using points and details from the talk, describe the physical differences that animals had to adapt to when they moved from water to land.

3.10 Evaluating Integrated Speaking

Album 6, Track 35
Exercise 3.10.A (p. 354)

Now listen to part of a lecture in a sociology class.

Your first agents of socialization are your parents or the other adults who take care of you when you're a baby. Your parents give you the first important lesson in how to behave in society. They teach you a world of meaning—what to believe, how to look at the world, and how to relate to others around you, especially your family. Your parents teach you what is and isn't proper behavior. Your parents serve as role models for adulthood—a social role you will eventually occupy. As you get older, they may prepare you for adulthood by giving you more responsibility or more freedom to make your own choices.

When you're a teenager, your peers—your friends and classmates—are important agents of socialization. Your peers support you and help you grow up and out of your family's nest. Through interactions with your peers, you learn the social role of friend.

Your parents and your peers are important agents of socialization, but in different ways. Your parents give you guidance on long–term goals, like career choice, but your peers are more likely to influence your immediate lifestyle choices, like how you dress and what you do for fun.

Explain agents of socialization and how the examples given by the professor illustrate the concept.

Now listen to a sample response.

Agents of socialization are the people who teach us important lessons about life. They teach us about our social roles. For example, the professor talks about parents. Parents are the first agents of socialization because they teach us how to behave. They teach us how to see the world and how to treat our family. Parents are role models for how to be an adult. Another example is peers. They are friends and classmates. They teach us the social role of friend. Also, they teach us how to have fun. Parents and peers are different, but both influence our goals. Both parents and peers are important agents of socialization.

Album 6, Track 36

Exercise 3.10.B (p. 355)

Listen to a conversation between two students.

M: How do you like your apartment?
W: Well … it's okay. I mean, I like the apartment, and I don't mind living off campus, but it's kind of far away. There's a bus, but the schedule doesn't work out very well for my early morning class.
M: How so?
W: I have a seven o'clock class, three days a week, but the bus I need to catch leaves at six—there's only one bus an hour—and that's just way too early for me. Then I get to campus forty minutes earlier than I need to.
M: Well, you could always use the extra time to eat breakfast on campus. The food's pretty good in the Corner Café. I eat there sometimes. It's never busy before seven o'clock.
W: Yeah, maybe.
M: Do you have a bicycle?
W: No, but I'm seriously thinking about getting one. If I had a bicycle, I could leave home whenever I wanted to. I wouldn't have to leave so early. There's a bike path along the river, so I wouldn't have to ride on the streets, except for the few blocks near my apartment.
M: You wouldn't even have to buy a bike because you can rent one at the bike shop.
W: Hmm. I didn't know that.

Briefly summarize the problem the speakers are discussing. Then state which solution you would recommend. Explain the reasons for your recommendation.

Now listen to a sample response.

The woman has a problem. She lives in an apartment off campus. She rides the bus to school, but the bus schedule doesn't work well for her. Her class starts at seven o'clock, but the bus leaves at six o'clock. She arrives at campus too early for her class. The speakers discuss possible solutions to the problem. One solution is a bicycle. If the woman had a bicycle, she could leave her apartment later because she would not have to get up early to take the bus. I recommend that she gets a bicycle. I prefer this solution because she could arrive at campus at a better time. Also, she could ride her bicycle on a path by the river, which would be safe and pleasant.

Album 6, Track 37

Exercise 3.10.C (p. 356)

Now listen as two students discuss the plan for a new classroom building.

M: It's good to know the administration is finally doing something about the crowding on campus. That new building sounds great.
W: Well, I don't think so. I don't see why they have to put the building there.
M: Why not? They have to put it somewhere, and that space isn't being used for anything.
W: That's not true! That site is a natural wooded area. It has a beautiful footpath, and lots of people go there to enjoy nature. I go there for peace and quiet. I go there to sketch and draw, and so do a lot of the art students. The film students like to work there. It's a beautiful place, and we don't want to lose it.
M: Yeah, but the whole school needs more classrooms, and more space for parking.
W: But this project will destroy an existing green space! For a building and a parking lot? We need green space too! Besides, adding more parking just encourages more cars. More people will drive to campus when they could take the bus. The university should promote green technology, not destroy what little green space is left.
M: Well, they have to do something about the crowding on campus.
W: True, but do they have to put the building there?

The woman expresses her opinion about the plan for a new building. State her opinion and explain the reasons she gives for holding that opinion.

Album 6, Track 38

Exercise 3.10.D (p. 357)

Listen to part of a lecture in a biology class. The professor is talking about spider webs.

Spider webs are flexible yet strong, and they can span great distances. Spider webs are made of silk produced by glands in the spider's abdomen. Spider silk is a protein composition that is stronger than steel of equal weight. A strand of silk can be stretched to almost twice its length without breaking.

Spider webs perform a variety of functions. The most obvious function is gathering food. Spider webs are very efficient at catching prey—up to 95 percent of the insects that touch the web—and this saves the spider from having to expend energy by chasing prey. Spider webs must be rebuilt almost daily, but that's no problem because spiders can build a new web very quickly. Also, they eat the old web, which replaces some of the energy used in building, so the silk's protein content is recycled.

Another function of the web is providing a home for the spider. Many spiders live on their webs. Some spiders mate and lay their eggs there. They also drink the dew that collects on the web. They store food there for later use, skillfully wrapped in spider silk.

Yet another function of the web is its performance as a communication medium. For many species, the web conveys vibrations during courtship and territorial disputes. Most spiders have poor vision, so they monitor what's going on around them by decoding vibrations that are received and transmitted by their webs. This communication system is so precise that the spider can immediately determine the identity, size, and movements of anything that touches the web, and then respond accordingly.

Using points and examples from the lecture, explain some of the properties and functions of spider webs.

ALBUM 7 — SPEAKING

Album 7, Track 1

QUIZ 4 — QUESTION 1 (p. 358)

Now listen to two students as they discuss the career workshop.

M: Are you going to the career workshop on Saturday?
W: Um. I don't know. I don't think so. I have a lot of studying to do this weekend.
M: You should go. It's supposed to be really good.
W: Oh, yeah? How?
M: My professor recommended it. He owns a small business downtown, and he'll be there. He says that talking to the business people who'll be there is one of the best ways to find out what's happening.
W: But my major isn't business; it's nursing.
M: Oh. But you should go anyway. There'll be a lot of people to talk to, people in health services. You should talk to people working in the field to find out more about what it's like. Some of them are graduates of this university.
W: But I have a test on Monday. I really need to study all day.
M: Study on Sunday instead. This is more important. The university has only one of these workshops each year. You shouldn't miss it. It's a good way to start looking for a job after graduation.
W: Hmm. Maybe you're right.

The man expresses his opinion about the career workshop. State his opinion and explain the reasons he gives for holding that opinion.

Album 7, Track 2

QUIZ 4 — QUESTION 2 (p. 359)

Now listen to part of a lecture in a psychology class.

All social contracts involve the concept of reciprocity, even those in our daily lives. For example, reciprocity is a key feature of friendship. Strong, intimate friendships are always reciprocal.

Sharing is important. In fact, an essential ingredient in the shift from acquaintance to friendship is the willingness of each person to share his or her feelings. The sharing of emotions establishes a personal, reciprocal relationship. Reciprocal friendship is the most intimate form of friendship, with long–term bonds of affection and mutual feelings of trust. Such friends seek each other out because they desire and enjoy each other's company.

Reciprocal friendships are balanced. If we receive more than we give, or give more than we receive, we're likely to be less satisfied with a friendship. And when a friendship changes from being reciprocal to being less so, we're generally less satisfied, less emotionally supported by the friendship. This is because the friendship is out of balance. It's one–sided because one person puts more into it than the other does. Of course, with our most intimate friends, we don't always "keep score" of who owes whom a favor. With our very close friends, reciprocity is spread out over time.

Use the examples from the lecture to explain the concept of reciprocity.

Album 7, Track 3

QUIZ 4 — QUESTION 3 (p. 360)

Listen to a conversation between two students.

W: This weekend is going to be crazy! I have two midterm exams on Monday, and I should study all weekend, but my parents are coming to visit. They'll want to spend time with me and want me show them around town. I look forward to seeing them, but I don't know when I'll have the time to study for my exams!
M: Why don't you join our biology group tonight? There are three of us so far. We're reviewing for the midterm, starting at six o'clock.
W: Tonight? Uh … I'd have to get the night off from work.
M: Well, if you can make it, then please come. We meet at Mark's house at six o'clock.
W: Uh … Okay, but I'll have to talk to my boss.
M: Another thing you could do is just explain to your parents that you have to study for examinations. I'm sure they'll understand. You don't have to spend the entire weekend with them. Just give them a list of places to go during the afternoon and then spend the evening with them.
W: Hmm. I could at least try that. I've got to do something to get ready for exams.

Briefly summarize the problem the students are discussing. Then state which solution you would recommend. Explain the reasons for your recommendation.

Album 7, Track 4

Quiz 4 — Question 4 (p. 360)

Now listen to part of a talk in a communications class.

Communicating with other human beings relies heavily on what is called body language—all the nonverbal signals that people send to each other. Humans have more than one hundred separate gestures and facial expressions. This makes us the biggest communicators in the animal world, even without our spoken language.

Body language communicates a great deal about how people perceive a social situation. When strangers first meet in a social situation, such as a meeting or a party, they often will lift their eyebrows to communicate friendly feelings. Also, they may make some hand or arm gesture, such as a salute or a handshake, to signal involvement.

The human face is extremely expressive. Eye movement, for example, has an important role in regulating the rhythm of conversation. In Western society, eye contact is usually held between people about one third of the time they are talking together. The closer and more friendly they are, the more often they look at each other. Often a speaker will signal his intention to speak by looking away from the other person and then continuing to look away while speaking. The listener signals his interest and attention by looking at the speaker and nodding his head slightly.

Most important is the smile, the very human gesture that recognizes the other person as a fellow social being. Even though a lot of body language varies in meaning across cultures, the meaning of the smile is the same in every culture. The smile has a tremendous power to generate friendly feelings. The smile is first seen in human babies as early as four or five weeks old, and a baby can be made to smile by any smiling human face, or even by any stimulus that resembles a face, such as a simple drawing.

Using points and examples from the talk, describe the uses of gestures and facial expressions in human communication.

Album 7, Track 5

Quiz 5 — Question 1 (p. 361)

Now listen to a student and a professor as they discuss the writing course.

M: Professor Olson, I'll be in your writing course next session, and I … uh … I was wondering if I could skip the peer feedback group and just come to the lecture and writing workshop.

W: Oh?

M: It's like this … I … uh … you see, I was in a student writing group before, but it didn't help at all with my writing. The other students were not good writers, so it was a waste of time. I can't learn from other students if they don't know how to write.

W: Learning how to write with other students, responding to the writing of others, expressing yourself in a small group—these are important steps in the learning process.

M: But I can learn better from a teacher because a teacher has more education and experience. The other students don't know how to teach writing. Isn't that the teacher's job?

W: I promise that you'll learn from the teacher, but you'll also learn more than you think from your peers.

The man expresses his opinion about the peer feedback group. State his opinion and explain the reasons he gives for holding that opinion.

Album 7, Track 6

Quiz 5 — Question 2 (p. 362)

Now listen to part of a lecture in a sociology class.

If we look at times of major social change, such as the Great Depression of the 1930s, we can see how variations in experience affected different cohorts. Everyone who was alive during that period was affected in some way by economic conditions, but because these circumstances hit each cohort at a different age, the effects were different for each.

For example, one study showed that people who were young children during the 1930s showed more long-term effects than did people who were teenagers at the time. The younger cohort spent a greater portion of their childhood under conditions of economic hardship, and that affected their family life and their educational opportunities. The negative effects of the Depression on the children's personalities could still be seen in adulthood.

In contrast, people who were teenagers during the Depression didn't show negative effects later in life. In fact, some of them showed more independence and initiative. Many teenagers had to work to help their families, and this early responsibility had a positive influence on their development. So, you can see how two cohorts that were close in age experienced the same circumstances differently because they were different ages at the time.

Explain the concept of cohort and how the examples given by the professor illustrate the concept.

Album 7, Track 7

Quiz 5 — Question 3 (p. 363)

Listen to a conversation between a student and a university officer.

W: How much does it cost for a permit to park my car on campus?

M: A parking permit is $45 for the quarter. But I'm required to tell you that a parking permit does not guarantee a parking space on campus.

W: What? It takes me an hour to drive here, and I have to park my car somewhere.

M: We know it's a problem. Our parking lots just aren't big enough for all the students we have this year. That's why I'm required to warn you about the situation.

W: What am I supposed to do? I have to drive to school.

M: One thing you can do, if possible, is register for classes that meet in the afternoon. The parking lots are usually full in the morning, but less full in the afternoon.

W: Okay.

M: Another thing you can do is park in our park–and–ride lot on Western Avenue, a mile from here. Your parking permit is good there, and you can usually find a parking space. You catch a free shuttle bus to campus from there. They run every 20 minutes.

W: Okay, thanks. I appreciate your advice.

The speakers discuss two possible solutions to the woman's problem. Briefly describe the problem. Then state which solution you prefer and explain why.

Album 7, Track 8

QUIZ 5 — QUESTION 4 (p. 363)

Listen to part of a lecture in a business management class.

No matter what size a business is, its organizational chart shows who is in charge of what, and who reports to whom. Organizational charts direct the flow of information so people can communicate in an orderly way.

Many companies have an organizational chart in the shape of a pyramid. In the pyramid chart, the labor force is on the bottom, supporting the whole structure. In the middle are the various layers of management, one on top of the other, all the way up to the chief executive officer at the top. The pyramid structure defines a formal chain of command. Information flows up the chain, and orders flow down. The pyramid is logical and orderly. Everyone knows his or her place in the hierarchy. However, with the pyramid, decision–making can take a long time because everything has to work its way up and down the chain of command.

Other companies have an organizational chart that looks more like a bicycle wheel. The wheel chart reveals a more integrated organization. Management is the hub, and all the departments are the spokes giving the wheel its shape. The labor force is the rim. Information flows around the rim in both directions, and up and down the spokes. The wheel chart implies a policy of open communication throughout the organization. This means that any staff member can go anywhere in the company to ask questions and get answers.

Using points and details from the lecture, explain what the pyramid chart and the wheel chart reveal about a company.

Album 7, Track 9

QUIZ 6 — QUESTION 1 (p. 364)

Now listen to two students as they discuss the request for volunteers.

W: What do you think? Are you going to volunteer for the conference?

M: Oh, I don't know. It's difficult for me to plan that far ahead. It's over a month away.

W: I know, but this conference is going to be great. There'll be a lot of prominent speakers from this country and all over the world, including a couple of scientists who won the Nobel Prize.

M: Really?

W: Yeah, and if we work for just two hours, we get to go to the reception and meet lots of experts on global warming. It's a great opportunity—kind of exciting for our school, isn't it? I mean, this conference is a really big event for us, and volunteering is a way to be a part of it.

M: That's true. But you have to work! Isn't it better to just attend the conference?

W: Ah, but this is one way to learn how a conference is organized. I'm really interested in knowing how to do this sort of thing since I plan to be involved in environmental issues.

M: And you want the free T–shirt.

W: Right!

The woman expresses her opinion about volunteering for the conference. State her opinion and explain the reasons she gives for holding that opinion.

Album 7, Track 10

QUIZ 6 — QUESTION 2 (p. 365)

Now listen to part of a lecture in a film history class.

There were lots of variations on the chase film. One of the most popular chase films was a comedy called *Personal*. This movie told the story of a wealthy man who is looking for a wife, so he advertises in a personal ad in the newspaper. His ad says that he will meet any potential wives at a famous landmark on a certain day. But when he goes to the place, he finds a crowd of eager women, who then chase him through the streets. This variation was such a hit that other filmmakers quickly copied it.

Another variation was the slapstick police chase made famous by the Keystone Kops. The Keystone Kops were the kings of early silent comedy. They were seven clownish policemen who created confusion and silliness as they chased villains and bank robbers. They dashed off to the chase on foot or hung onto a speeding car. The motion of the film was fast and jerky. A lot of the stunts involved fast–moving cars, tall buildings, and of course, somebody getting a cream pie in the face. All these variations on the chase film had fast action, excitement, and comedy.

Define the chase film, and explain how the examples given in the lecture illustrate the definition.

Album 7, Track 11

QUIZ 6 — QUESTION 3 (p. 366)

Listen to a conversation between two students.

M: Are you still going to transfer to the university in the fall?

W: I want to, but I've got a problem. I just talked to my adviser, and it seems I still need one more course to complete my basic requirements.

M: You do?

W: Yeah. I dropped a course a while back and never made it up. My adviser says I have to make up the course this summer, or I won't be able to transfer to the U.

M: I thought you were sailing to Hawaii this summer.

W: That's what I was planning to do. I promised my friend I'd go on the sailboat trip, and we've already paid a deposit. We were looking forward to it.
M: The sailboat trip sounds great.
W: I know! I really want to go!
M: You can delay going to the university, can't you? I mean, you don't have to transfer in the fall. You could start there next spring, right?
W: I'm not sure.
M: Oh, hmm. I don't know. Sailing sounds great, but the university is important too. Maybe you should cancel your trip and take the course you need. You can probably get a refund for the deposit you paid on the sailboat.
W: Maybe.
M: You just have to decide what's more important to you: going sailing or going to the university.
W: Right.
M: Well, good luck with that.
W: Thanks.

Briefly summarize the problem the students are discussing. Then state which solution you would recommend. Explain the reasons for your recommendation.

Album 7, Track 12

Quiz 6 — Question 4 (p. 366)

Listen to part of a lecture in a health class.

Many people experience insomnia, difficulty falling asleep or staying asleep. There is no single cause of insomnia, as several different factors—emotional, physical, and environmental—can interfere with sleep.

A common cause is emotional distress. This can be related to a single specific event. For example, there might be significant stress caused by a job loss or change, the death of a loved one, or moving to a different place. Insomnia caused by a single event is usually short–term, lasting from days to weeks. Long–term insomnia, on the other hand, is a recurring problem and may be caused by chronic stress, depression, or other health issues.

Insomnia can have physical causes, such as discomfort or pain due to illness or injury. Chronic back pain is a common cause. Also, what you consume can interfere with your sleep— drinking too much coffee, for example, or drinking it too late in the day. Alcohol can affect your sleep patterns. At first, alcohol might make you feel sleepy, but after its effects wear off, it may actually cause you to wake up during the night and have trouble getting back to sleep.

Finally, insomnia can be related to environmental factors such as noise, light, or extreme temperatures. Many people can't sleep during hot, humid summer weather. Other factors that throw off your normal sleep schedule are jet lag or switching from the day shift to the night shift at work.

Using points and examples from the lecture, explain some of the common causes of insomnia.

Album 7, Track 13

Quiz 7 — Question 1 (p. 367)

What book have you read that you would recommend to others? Explain why you think other people should read this book. Include details and examples to support your explanation.

Album 7, Track 14

Quiz 7 — Question 2 (p. 367)

Some people have a few favorite foods that they eat most of the time. Others are always trying new dishes and styles of cooking. Which do you prefer and why? Include details and examples in your explanation.

Album 7, Track 15

Quiz 7 — Question 3 (p. 368)

Now listen to two students as they discuss the proposal.

W: Have you heard about the proposal to limit our course load?
M: Yeah. But I don't really see why it's necessary.
W: I don't either. So what if people want to take more than 20 credits? I've done it twice already, and I never had any problem finishing the work. It's hard, I mean you're working all the time, but if you manage your time well, you can do it.
M: It's not something I'd want to do, but I can see your point.
W: Actually, this proposal is kind of a problem for me because I need only 21 more credits to graduate. I was hoping to graduate this spring. If I'm only allowed to take 20 credits, that makes it impossible for me to graduate. I'd have to go to summer school.
M: Oh, that's too bad.
W: And if I take a class this summer, that's more tuition I have to pay. I don't want to ask my family for any more money. So this new policy causes a financial problem for me. I think I'll go hear the dean speak, but I also have some tough questions to ask her.

The woman expresses her opinion about the proposal. State her opinion and explain the reasons she gives for holding that opinion.

Album 7, Track 16

Quiz 7 — Question 4 (p. 369)

Now listen to part of a lecture in a biology class.

Coevolution can be seen in the interaction between insects and flowering plants. Certain insects pollinate certain flowers, and both species benefit. The insect gets food, and the plant gets pollinated. In turn, the flower evolves features to attract that insect, and the insect evolves features to best fit that flower. It's a beautiful arrangement.

Some flowers evolve a particular shape in order to benefit a particular pollinator. Flowers that are pollinated by moths often have spurs or tubes the exact length of a certain moth's "tongue." One example is the yucca flower. These flowers have evolved a certain shape so that only the tiny yucca moth can pollinate them. The moth lays its eggs in the yucca flower, and the moth larvae live inside the developing flower, where they eat the yucca seeds.

Another example is the common snapdragon that many people plant in their gardens. The snapdragon evolved along with a particular bee. The flower has an irregular shape with a landing platform. Only a bumblebee of just the right size and weight can land on the platform and cause the flower to open, so only this bee gets the nectar. The flower won't open for other bee species or other insects that are too small or too large.

Use the examples from the lecture to explain the concept of coevolution.

Album 7, Track 17

QUIZ 7 — QUESTION 5 (p. 370)

Listen to a conversation between a student and a professor.

M: Hi, Professor Hogan, do you have a minute?
W: Of course, Dustin. What can I do for you?
M: I have trouble remembering the material from class. When I listen to your lectures, I understand everything, but then I always forget it during the tests.
W: Do you take notes in class?
M: Yes, but sometimes I can't understand my notes when I look at them later.
W: Hmm. I can suggest a couple of things. First, you should review your lecture notes as soon as possible after class, when the material is still fresh in your mind. Our class ends at noon. If you can, look over your notes while you're eating lunch. That's a good time to underline things, and make notes to yourself about things to look up later or ask about in class.
M: Okay.
W: And the other thing is to get enough sleep. Take a short nap, not in class, but after you've been studying for a few hours.
M: But won't I forget what I just studied?
W: Believe it or not, sleeping helps you remember what you just studied. So, it's a good idea to study in the evening and then get a good night's sleep.

The speakers discuss possible solutions to the man's problem. Briefly describe the problem. Then state which solution you prefer and explain why.

Album 7, Track 18

QUIZ 7 — QUESTION 6 (p. 370)

Now listen to part of a lecture in a marketing class.

Manufacturers choose different ways to present their goods for sale. The three main ways of selling goods are direct sales, retail sales, and wholesaling.

Direct sales take place away from a store. Direct sales usually take place in the customer's home, although sometimes it's in a business setting. Direct sales include the activities of door-to-door salespeople and real estate agents. Other examples are catalog shopping, telemarketing, and at-home Internet shopping.

The second type of sales—retail sales—take place in stores. Department stores, discount chains, supermarkets, hardware stores, car dealerships, drugstores, convenience stores—all of these are retail stores, where consumers directly purchase small quantities of goods. Most manufacturers choose to sell their products through retail stores because they're a convenient way for consumers to buy. Consumers can inspect merchandise and take their purchases with them. They can exchange or return things easily. They can ask sales clerks for advice about products, or about how something works.

The third type of sales is wholesaling—where goods are sold below the retail or direct-sale price. Wholesale prices are lower because customers are buying in large quantities or in a low overhead setting. Wholesalers operate in a variety of ways. Some have their own outlet stores where they sell directly to consumers. Others send sales representatives to retail stores that buy goods at wholesale prices and then mark them up for resale. Because it's difficult for a manufacturer to contact every buyer directly, wholesaling is the most practical method for the widespread distribution of goods.

Using points and examples from the lecture, explain the three main ways that manufacturers sell goods to consumers.

Album 7, Track 19

QUIZ 8 — QUESTION 1 (p. 371)

What is the best gift you have ever received? Describe this gift and explain its importance to you. Include details and examples in your explanation.

Album 7, Track 20

QUIZ 8 — QUESTION 2 (p. 371)

Some students like to study for a long period of hours at a time. Others divide their study time into many shorter sessions. Which method do you think is better for studying and why? Include details and examples in your explanation.

Album 7, Track 21

QUIZ 8 — QUESTION 3 (p. 372)

Now listen to two students as they discuss scholarships.

M: So… are you applying for any scholarships?
W: Oh, I don't know.
M: You should! You've got what it takes to get a scholarship.
W: I don't know… my grades aren't that great.
M: But it's not just grades that matter. You have leadership skills. You've done all that volunteer work at the senior center, setting up activities for the old folks. That's exactly the sort of thing that impresses the scholarship committee.
W: The senior center is just something I like to do. I enjoy the people there.
M: If I were you, I'd apply for every scholarship available. And in the application, describe your volunteer work with the elderly. That's exactly the sort of "distinguished contribution to your

community" that can help you.

W: Do you think so?

M: Trust me. You deserve a scholarship, and I think you have a good chance of getting one. You should definitely apply. Even if you don't get one this year, it's good experience to fill out an application. It makes you think about your own accomplishments, and it's good practice for job hunting later.

W: Maybe you're right. Thanks for the suggestion.

The man expresses his opinion on applying for scholarships. State his opinion and explain the reasons he gives for holding that opinion.

Album 7, Track 22

QUIZ 8 — QUESTION 4 (p. 373)

Now listen to part of a lecture in a psychology class.

The people most likely to be part of our convoy are parents and siblings, spouse or partner, and friends. Even pets can be important members.

Over the years, our convoy changes in size and makeup. Friends are gained or lost, we lose our parents to death, and we gain or lose partners through marriage or divorce. However, most of us have some members who stay with us for most of our life.

In our late teens and twenties, we start building our convoy. Friends are probably the biggest percentage of our convoy at this time. Later, in our thirties, our convoy is still there, but we may not spend as much energy on expanding it. Some of our friends go off in different directions. We lose touch.

In middle age, we still add or lose friends, but we seem to focus more on maintaining the relationships with core members—our spouse, close friends and family. After we retire from working, our convoy shrinks in size, but it's very important to us. Spouses and partners remain central. Close friends and siblings increase in importance. In old age, our convoy shrinks again, as spouses and friends die. This makes the remaining members, including friends and pets, much more important to us.

Explain the convoy and how the examples given by the professor illustrate the concept.

Album 7, Track 23

QUIZ 8 — QUESTION 5 (p. 374)

Listen to a conversation between two graduate student teaching assistants.

M: Hi, Molly. How are you?

W: I was afraid you'd ask. Things couldn't be much worse. Dr. Carter just gave me over forty student papers to grade, and she wants them all done by the end of the week! And I have to write a research paper for genetics, plus I have a big test coming up in another class. I don't see how I can get it all done. If I grade all these papers, I'll never have time for my own coursework.

M: Wow. Why don't you ask Dr. Carter for more time to grade the papers?

W: I could, I suppose, but she really needs them done

because the students want them back.

M: Dr. Carter doesn't realize how overworked we are unless we tell her. It might help to mention it.

W: She expects a lot from us. Ugh. I've got way too many things to do.

M: Well, here's something else you could do. You could set a strict time limit for grading the papers. Since they need to be done by the end of the week, I'd do that first, before all of your other work, but set a time limit for each paper—oh, I don't know, say 15 minutes apiece—and then don't spend any more time than that on any paper. That's the only way you'll get them all done.

Briefly summarize the problem the speakers are discussing. Then state which solution you would recommend. Explain the reasons for your recommendation.

Album 7, Track 24

QUIZ 8 — QUESTION 6 (p. 374)

Listen to part of a lecture in an ecology class. The professor is discussing abiotic factors in ecosystems.

Ecosystems are made up of both living and nonliving components. The nonliving—or abiotic—components of ecosystems include physical factors such as sunlight, rainfall, temperature, and wind.

The abiotic factor of sunlight provides the energy that drives ecosystems. Almost all forms of life get their energy from sunlight. Plants use sunlight to manufacture their food. Sunlight is important to the development and behavior of many plants and animals that are sensitive to the relative lengths of day and night. The amount of daylight is a signal for seasonal events, such as the flowering of plants and the migration of birds.

Rainfall and temperature are abiotic factors that affect habitats and food supplies in several ways. Climate greatly influences the plant community, which then determines the availability of food, nest sites, and shelter for animals. Air temperature is an important factor because of its effect on biological processes. Air temperature affects the ability of organisms to regulate their body temperature. Not all plants and animals can maintain an active metabolism at very low or very high temperatures.

The abiotic factor of wind increases the effects of air temperature—what we call the wind chill factor, the combined effect of wind speed and air temperature. Wind chill increases heat loss in organisms. Wind also causes water loss in organisms by increasing the rate of evaporation in animals and the rate of transpiration in plants.

Using points and examples from the lecture, explain how various abiotic factors in ecosystems affect plants and animals.

ALBUM 8 — WRITING

4.1 INTEGRATED WRITING: CONNECTING INFORMATION

Album 8, Track 1

Study (p. 383), Study (p. 390)

Now listen to part of a lecture on the topic you just read about.

The plow is responsible for larger crop yields, but there are also some problems with it. For one thing, simply producing large amounts of food is not enough. Food has to be produced in a sustainable way so natural resources are conserved for future generations. No–till agriculture—farming without the plow—has the potential to help develop a more sustainable agriculture.

Another problem is that overuse of the plow is a major cause of damage to the land. Plowing leaves the soil vulnerable to erosion by wind and water. An example is the Dust Bowl disaster, when extensive plowing, combined with long periods of no rain, caused the dry topsoil to be blown away in dust storms. Plowing also increases erosion by water, and the channels in fields promote the runoff of soil and fertilizers into lakes, rivers, and oceans.

In contrast, no–till farming minimizes soil damage. Instead of plowing under the remains of last year's crop—stalks and other litter—farmers leave it on the fields, where it acts as mulch to conserve water and protect the soil from erosion. Leaving crop residue in place increases levels of organic matter and improves soil productivity.

Finally, overuse of the plow is a threat to rural livelihoods, particularly in the developing world. No–till farming has economic advantages. For example, the number of passes over a field needed to grow and harvest a crop decreases from seven or more to about four, thereby saving fuel and labor costs. In fact, no–till farming uses 50 percent less fuel, and 30 to 50 percent less labor than plow–based farming. This means a significantly lower production cost per acre.

Summarize the points made in the lecture, being sure to explain how they challenge specific points made in the reading passage.

Album 8, Track 2

Exercise 4.1.A (p. 385)

Now listen to part of a lecture on the topic you just read about.

Pruning needs to be done wisely because trees that are badly pruned can become a hazard. A good example is the silver maple belonging to one of my clients. This once–beautiful hardwood was the innocent victim of tree topping—a pruning practice that simply cuts off the tops of major branches. Because of the poor pruning it received, this tree is now dangerous and has to be removed.

Tree topping causes several problems. First, it won't keep a tree small. On the contrary, cutting back the tip of a branch will force the development of side branches. The growth rate of a tree speeds up, and within a few years, the tree is close to its original size. My client's tree now has seven long 300–pound branches stretching out over the house and driveway. Any one of these could crush a car.

Second, topping is very stressful for trees. Such heavy pruning removes too many leaves, the tree's food factories, and so the tree may starve. The shoots that grow back after topping are weak, and they break off easily in the wind. My client's maple tree has several small branches that are dead or dying, and there's evidence of insect damage.

Finally, topping destroys a tree's natural shape. It turns a beautiful branching tree into an ugly eyesore—not to mention a safety hazard. The silver maple should have one main trunk with three or four sturdy lateral branches. Instead, it has seven weak branches. Topping destroyed its natural shape and gave it a weak branch structure. The tree should have had an occasional light pruning instead of the chainsaw butchering it got.

Summarize the points made in the lecture, being sure to explain how they contrast with specific points made in the reading passage.

Album 8, Track 3

Exercise 4.1.B (p. 386)

Now listen to part of a lecture on the topic you just read about.

The importance of visual–spatial intelligence can be seen in the game of chess. First of all, chess masters have an amazing ability to draw a picture of a chessboard they've seen for just a few seconds—if the pieces on the board are set in meaningful positions, as they are in the middle of a real game. But if the chess pieces are randomly located, in no meaningful pattern, the chess master may not be able to reconstruct the board.

Second, the chess player has to remember the movements of the chess pieces. In a form of chess called blindfold chess, a person plays several games at the same time. For example, a blindfolded chess player might be playing ten games against ten different opponents, going from table to table. His opponents can see the chessboard, but the blindfolded player can't. The blindfolded player's only information about the chessboard is from someone announcing his opponent's last move. He has to hold a picture of the chessboard in his mind.

Furthermore, chess players have strong visual memories of important games they've played in the past. This memory isn't just simple recall. Rather, it's the ability to remember a game's patterns of reasoning. The chess player remembers plans and strategies—not just a rote list of moves. For most chess players, each game has its own character and shape. As the player recalls a given position, he remembers his reasoning at an earlier time. He remembers a specific move—not all by itself—but as part of a strategy. He recalls why that move was necessary. Thus, he is able to predict what will happen next in the game.

Summarize the points made in the lecture, being sure to explain how they illustrate specific points made in the reading passage.

4.2 INTEGRATED WRITING: TAKING AND USING NOTES

Album 8, Track 4

Focus (p. 388)

Another problem is that overuse of the plow is a major cause of damage to the land. Plowing leaves the soil vulnerable to erosion by wind and water. An example is the Dust Bowl disaster, when extensive plowing, combined with long periods of no rain, caused the dry topsoil to be blown away in dust storms. Plowing also increases erosion by water, and the channels in fields promote the runoff of soil and fertilizers into lakes, rivers, and oceans.

Album 8, Track 5

Exercise 4.2.A (p. 393)

Now listen to part of a lecture on the topic you just read about.

You all know about the city planners' proposal to develop the land between the lake and the bay. Well, I'm part of a citizens group that's organizing to protest the proposal. There are a number of reasons to oppose the plan. One reason is that the development would destroy the view from across the lake to the bay. We propose an alternative plan that calls for converting the land into a park and common space for the entire community to enjoy. We believe the land belongs to everyone, not just the developers, and a park will preserve the area's natural beauty, which is our most valuable resource for attracting people downtown.

Another reason to oppose this development is, the proposed housing is all upscale condominiums and apartments, which would be too expensive for most people. None of the housing is geared toward middle– and low–income people. It's just crazy—not to mention unfair—that most of the workers in the new shops and restaurants won't be able to afford to live in the neighborhood.

Finally, it's important to know that the plan is heavily backed by the construction industry. Building contractors, developers, and real estate companies would make a lot of money, but what about everyone else? More importantly, at what expense to the environment? The land in question borders the lake. The economic success of a few people should not be balanced against the environment. Development would mean that all the trees near the lake would be cut, meaning the loss of habitat for urban wildlife. And most of us agree that the city needs more green space, not less.

Summarize the points made in the lecture, being sure to explain how they oppose specific points made in the reading passage.

Album 8, Track 6

Exercise 4.2.B (p. 394)

Now listen to part of a lecture on the topic you just read about.

Psychology is a social science. How do we know this? Well, first of all, psychology studies the relationship between the human mind and social behavior. Psychology studies the overall processes of mental activity—not just the physiological processes but how these processes influence human behavior and society. Psychology assumes that any given behavior or mental process affects and is affected by interrelated biological, psychological, and social factors. Psychologists seek to understand how humans come to perceive, understand, and interact with their environment. They work to develop generalizations about human consciousness and social interaction.

Second, as a social science, psychology is based on the subjective interpretation of phenomena and on knowledge by description. Everything is subject to interpretation, so it's impossible for psychologists to derive objective facts about the human mind. Psychologists use both quantitative and qualitative methods, as well as both inductive and deductive reasoning in describing human behavior. They structure experiments to gather data and then examine this data for patterns that lead them to develop new theories.

Third, all subfields of psychology study the interaction of mental processes and social behavior. Some subfields are purely social science, such as social psychology and organizational psychology. Other subfields, such as cognitive psychology and developmental psychology, have a natural science base and a social science application. The common thread in all of these subfields is the integration of mental processes and human behavior.

Summarize the points made in the lecture, being sure to explain how they contrast with specific points made in the reading passage.

4.3 INTEGRATED WRITING: DEVELOPING YOUR RESPONSE

Album 8, Track 7

Study (p. 399)

Now listen to part of a lecture on the topic you just read about.

The plow is responsible for larger crop yields, but there are also some problems with it. For one thing, simply producing large amounts of food is not enough. Food has to be produced in a sustainable way so natural resources are conserved for future generations. No–till agriculture—farming without the plow—has the potential to help develop a more sustainable agriculture.

Another problem is that overuse of the plow is a major cause of damage to the land. Plowing leaves the soil vulnerable to erosion by wind and water. An example is the Dust Bowl disaster, when extensive plowing, combined with long periods of no rain, caused the dry topsoil to be blown away in dust storms. Plowing also increases erosion by water, and the channels in fields promote the runoff of soil and fertilizers into lakes, rivers, and oceans.

In contrast, no–till farming minimizes soil damage. Instead of plowing under the remains of last year's crop—stalks and other litter—farmers leave it on the fields, where it acts as mulch to conserve water and protect the soil from erosion. Leaving crop residue in place increases levels of organic matter and improves soil productivity.

Finally, overuse of the plow is a threat to rural livelihoods, particularly in the developing world. No–till farming has economic advantages. For example, the number of passes over a field needed to grow and harvest a crop decreases from seven or more to about four, thereby saving fuel and labor costs. In fact, no–till farming uses 50 percent less fuel, and 30 to 50 percent less labor than plow–based farming. This means a significantly lower production cost per acre.

Summarize the points made in the lecture, being sure to explain how they challenge specific points made in the reading passage.

Album 8, Track 8

Exercise 4.3.A (p. 401)

Now listen to part of a lecture on the topic you just read about.

Okay, you've all read about how Pluto is no longer a planet. Well, let me offer another view. First of all, you should know that the decision by the International Astronomical Union was not unanimous. In fact, the vote was controversial, and there is a lot of scientific disagreement about the decision to change Pluto's status. Several scientists maintain that Pluto is indeed a planet. Pluto orbits the sun, has enough gravity to pull itself into a ball, and has its own satellites—moons. While its orbit isn't completely clear of debris, Pluto is still the biggest body in its neighborhood.

Second, about the new definition of planet, well, critics don't find it to be adequate or realistic. They believe that, instead of narrowing the definition, it should have been widened to include Pluto and similar bodies. Our solar system is complex. It contains countless objects of all sizes. The definition of planet should include any large body that revolves around the sun and is not itself a satellite of another planet. This broader definition would make full–fledged planets of 50 or more additional objects in the solar system.

Finally, calling Pluto a "dwarf planet" causes controversy and confusion. Why is a dwarf planet not a real planet? The astronomer's union did not consider the historical and cultural role that Pluto has played. For 80 years, children have learned about the nine planets in our solar system. Saying that Pluto is not a real planet confuses both teachers and students. It has forced us to go back and rewrite textbooks, redraw charts, and rebuild museum exhibits.

Summarize the points made in the lecture, being sure to explain how they contradict specific points made in the reading passage.

Album 8, Track 9

Exercise 4.3.B (p. 402)

Now listen to part of a lecture on the topic you just read about.

Companies organized around the concept of the small work group generally have high levels of worker satisfaction. There are several reasons for the success of the small work group.

First, the group fills important social and emotional needs of workers. By small work group, I mean a group of usually around three to fifteen people with one lead person. The work group is the basic unit of a company's social organization. What takes place day to day within that group affects worker attitudes, motivation, and productivity—and ultimately, the quality of the company's product or service.

Second, the work group improves worker motivation because it promotes an atmosphere of security. When workers are members of a team, they know their performance matters to the success of the group. Knowing that their skills contribute to the team gives workers a sense of ownership and accomplishment. Ultimately, when workers have a sense of team pride and personal fulfillment, they are more valuable to the organization.

Third, the small work group gives individuals a sense of autonomy. Workers need to feel in control of what happens during the workday. They feel alienated when they have no voice. If workers have their say—especially within the work group—they feel a greater sense of pride in their work. Managers have to accept that workers deserve to have a voice in the decisions that affect them. Workers should be able to participate in the setting of goals and the evaluation of results. Managers have to face this reality if they want to have a highly motivated workforce.

Summarize the points made in the lecture, being sure to explain how they support specific points made in the reading passage.

Album 8, Track 10

Exercise 4.3.C (p. 403)

Now listen to part of a lecture on the topic you just read about.

Now I'd like to offer a different view of alternative medicine. First, health–care practices should be based solely on scientific evidence. Conventional medicine is based on science. It applies health science, biomedical research, and medical technology to diagnose and treat injury and disease. Alternative medicine, on the other hand, is not based on science. This means that alternative practices can not be tested, refuse to be tested, or consistently fail tests. Because alternative therapies are not based on scientific evidence, they can not be proven effective.

Second, people turn to alternative therapies because they are misinformed or misled. There are 40 million websites advertising alternative therapies, and most of them are unproven. Many people believe in these treatments because they want something to believe in. There's also been an increase in conspiracy theories towards conventional medicine, such as the belief that medicine makes patients dependent on drugs. These beliefs reflect the low level of scientific literacy among the public and an increase in anti–scientific attitudes.

Most importantly, with alternative medicine, there's no guarantee that a practitioner has any formal training or professional credentials. Conventional medicine, on the other hand, requires a degree from a university medical school, followed by a period of supervised practice or internship, residency, postgraduate training, and in most countries, a legal requirement for doctors to be licensed or registered by a national medical organization. With alternative medicine, anyone can set up a practice as a "healer," with no oversight, no peer review, and no scientific evidence that the treatments are safe or effective.

Summarize the points made in the lecture, being sure to explain how they challenge specific points made in the reading passage.

4.5 EVALUATING INTEGRATED WRITING

Album 8, Track 11

Exercise 4.5.A (p. 411)

Now listen to part of a lecture on the topic you just read about.

Several facts refute the idea that antibiotics are wonder drugs. First, as soon as we developed antibiotics, new strains of bacteria appeared that were resistant to some or all of the drugs. For example, hospitals started using antibiotics in the 1950s, but today many drug–resistant hospital infections make it safer for some people to stay home than go to the hospital. The rise in dangerous hospital infections is clear evidence that antibiotics are not the wonder drugs they used to be.

Second, bacteria can create very effective weapons against antibiotics. It happens like this. If you douse a colony of bacteria with an antibiotic, the colony will be killed—that is, all except for a few cells that carry a resistance gene for that particular antibiotic. The surviving cells quickly multiply, and soon you have a new strain of bacteria that's resistant to that drug. Some bacteria develop enzymes to counteract every antibiotic we throw at them. So, no matter what antibiotic we use, the bacteria will come up with a way to make it useless.

Third, antibiotics are no longer effective cures for some infections. For example, today you could treat a pneumonia patient with 24 million units of penicillin a day, but the patient might still die. This is because several strains of bacteria are now completely resistant to penicillin. Another consequence is the reappearance of tuberculosis as a major illness. Twenty years ago, doctors thought tuberculosis was a defeated disease. Since then, however, new cases of tuberculosis have increased by 20 percent, and several strains of the disease are resistant to any drug we attack them with.

Summarize the points made in the lecture, being sure to explain how they cast doubt on specific points made in the reading passage.

Album 8, Track 12

QUIZ 1 (p. 415)

Now listen to part of a lecture on the topic you just read about.

As we interpret the results of these experiments with chimpanzees, we can see there are several problems. First, the "mark test" was repeated many times, but some of the results were inconsistent. For example, one study with eleven chimpanzees found that only one of the chimps touched the mark during the test. Why were those results so different from the results of other tests, which showed a high rate of chimps touching the mark? This inconsistency is troubling.

Second, chimpanzees perform these very same behaviors routinely, whether or not there's a mirror. All chimpanzees touch their heads and faces a lot, with or without a mirror. In an experiment with eleven chimpanzees, one chimp rubbed his head while coming out of the sleeping drug. He rubbed the mark off even before he had the chance to see it in the mirror—thus confounding the test results and making it impossible to conclude anything.

Third, some of the behaviors we call self–aware are also social responses that chimpanzees usually show in the presence of other chimps. Self–grooming in chimpanzees is a social behavior. When chimps are put in a cage with a mirror along one wall, they show an increase in the amount of self–grooming. So do chimps that can see other chimps in the cage next to them. All of this grooming is normal social behavior. It's part of fitting in with the group. So we can't always tell from a chimp's behavior whether the chimp is reacting in a "self–aware" manner to a mirror image, or whether it's reacting "socially" to the image as that of another chimp.

Summarize the points made in the lecture, being sure to explain how they cast doubt on specific points made in the reading passage.

Album 8, Track 13

QUIZ 2 (p. 416)

Now listen to part of a lecture on the topic you just read about.

While it's true that wind power is a promising source of energy, there are some drawbacks. One is that the amount of energy produced is unpredictable. The strength of the wind can vary from none at all to storm force. Consequently, wind turbines don't generate the same amount of electricity all the time. Also, wind is very spread out. This means it would take a large number of wind generators—and large amounts of land—to produce electricity in useful amounts. We can't build wind turbines everywhere, simply because lots of spaces aren't windy enough to generate power.

Another drawback is the cost. Wind energy is expensive to develop. Even though the cost has decreased in the past few decades, the technology for wind requires a higher initial investment than it does for fossil fuel generators. And ideal locations for wind farms can be very expensive to buy. Good sites are often located in remote areas, far from the cities where the electricity is needed. This means that transmission lines have to be built to bring the electricity from the wind farm to the city.

Furthermore, wind power plants do have some negative impacts on the environment. For example, there's concern about the noise produced by the blades. One wind generator makes a low, swooshing sound, so you can imagine the amount of noise several dozen of these generators will make. Another problem is the high number of birds killed by flying into the blades. Migrating birds like strong winds, and it's common for them to fly into wind turbines. In one case, researchers found two hundred dead birds on a wind farm in California.

Summarize the points made in the lecture, being sure to explain how they challenge specific points made in the reading passage.

Album 8, Track 14

QUIZ 3 (p. 417)

Now listen to part of a lecture on the topic you just read about.

One of the leading artists of Abstract Expressionism was the painter Jackson Pollock. Like other artists of the movement, Pollock painted as a form of self–expression. Several qualities distinguish Pollock as one of the greatest American artists.

First, he was influential not just for his art but for the process of creating it. His devotion to the act of painting led to the term "action painting." He painted his huge canvases on the floor. This was so he could work around and over the big canvas. Pollock felt more at ease on the floor. He could walk around the painting, work from all four sides, and literally be in the painting. His technique was sort of a dance with the canvas. As he danced around the borders of the canvas, he spattered the canvas with sprays and drips of paint.

Second, Pollock controlled the drip to give his paintings a special character. His technique was to hold the brush a foot above the canvas and then throw lines of paint in the air so the paint would fall on the canvas. He performed this gesture skillfully, and each painting would literally grow from this controlled drip. Pollock's trademark drip made his paintings immediately identifiable as his work.

Third, a lot of Pollock's paintings were called "all–over" paintings because the paint fills the entire canvas. In these paintings, the enormous canvas is filled with a series of lines, curves, and loops—twisting forms of color that suggest movement—an effect created entirely by the skillful gestures of the artist's brush.

The lecture discusses the painter Jackson Pollock. Summarize the points made in the lecture, being sure to explain how they illustrate specific points made in the reading passage.

Album 8, Track 15

QUIZ 7 — QUESTION 1 (p. 450)

Now listen to part of a lecture on the topic you just read about.

For three–quarters of a century, there's been a lot of research on the "fight or flight" response. However, one problem with the research is that 90 percent of it has been done on men. More recent studies suggest that men and women deal with stressful situations differently. While men are likely to have a "fight or flight" reaction, women react in a way that's more accurately described as "tend and befriend."

This "tend and befriend" response was discovered when two women scientists were talking in the lab one day. One of them made a joke that when the women who worked there were under stress, they came in, cleaned the lab, made coffee, and sat down and talked with their female colleagues. But when the men were stressed, they would argue with someone, or they'd go off somewhere on their own. The point is, while the men would verbally attack another person, the women would attack a problem—they would tend to the mess in the lab. The women didn't fight with another person. They sat down and talked with other women.

Recent studies show that when women are stressed, there's a release of hormones that actually weaken the fight or flight response. So, rather than fighting, women are likely to try and defuse the situation, to avoid a fight, to make the threat less threatening. And rather than fleeing, they turn to other people for help. They call a girlfriend, go out to lunch together, go shopping or go jogging together. Instead of escaping in solitary activities, women look for advice and support from friends.

Summarize the points made in the lecture, being sure to explain how they differ from specific points made in the reading passage.

Album 8, Track 16

QUIZ 8 — QUESTION 1 (p. 452)

Now listen to part of a lecture on the topic you just read about.

There are several problems with method acting. First, when a playwright creates a plot and characters, he or she determines what the action of the story should be. It's not the actor's job to look for deeper meaning in the so–called "subtext." The actor's responsibility is to recite the dialogue as the writer intended. It's not necessary for actors to search for conflicting emotions. What is necessary is for actors to convey the message that the writer intended.

Second, in method acting, the actors depend on their own emotions and experiences to play a character. Well, this is unrealistic because, well, what if you've never done or felt the things your character did? What if your character is, say, a violent criminal… or a murderer? Are you supposed to think about killing someone? That could be very disturbing for an actor, and it's hardly necessary for successful acting.

Third, good acting requires skill training. Classically trained actors don't have to conjure up past emotions. They simply communicate these emotions through external means. They use their face, their body, and their voice to convey a character's emotions. Good acting doesn't require an actor to "live the part." All it takes is training in a wide range of skills, including speech clarity, voice projection, dialects, movement, dance, body language, and so on. It's ridiculous for an actor to try and "become" the character. For example, there was a well–known actor who once went without sleeping or bathing for two days in order to immerse himself in a role. That is just going too far!

Summarize the points made in the lecture, being sure to explain how they oppose specific points made in the reading passage.

ALBUM 9 — TEST 1

Album 9, Track 1

TEST 1 — LISTENING SECTION DIRECTIONS (p. 468)

The Listening section measures your ability to understand conversations and lectures in English. You will hear each conversation and lecture only one time. After each conversation or lecture, you will answer some questions about it. The questions typically ask about the main idea and supporting details. Some questions ask about a speaker's purpose or attitude. Answer the questions based on what the speakers state or imply.

You may take notes while you listen. You may use your notes to help you answer the questions. Your notes will not be scored.

In some questions, you will see this icon: 🎧. This means that you will hear, but not see, part of the question.

Some questions have special directions, which appear in a gray box. Most questions are worth one point. If a question is worth more than one point, the directions will indicate how many points you can receive.

You will now begin part 1 of the Listening section.

Album 9, Track 2

TEST 1 — LISTENING PART 1
QUESTIONS 1–5 (p. 469)

Listen to a conversation in a university office.

M: Good afternoon. May I help you?
W: Yes, I hope so. My name is Jennifer Taylor, and I'm in the communications program. Our class is doing a radio program, and we'll have interviews with a lot of people from all parts of campus life. We'd like to interview the new Dean of Students, if he's willing.
M: Hmm. That sounds interesting.
W: I hope Dean Evans will agree to meet with us, and let us tape the conversation for the radio. It would be a way for the whole community to get to know him, get to know his ideas and everything … like the kind of vision he has for the university.
M: How much time would you need?
W: Oh, probably about an hour, no more than that.
M: Hmm. I'm sure the dean would like to participate, but … uh … you know, his schedule is pretty tight.
W: Oh, I was afraid of that. Um …
M: He's all tied up this week. Everybody wants to, you know, get acquainted. But we can probably work something in. When would you like to do the interview?
W: The radio station can air the show on either the 16th or the 23rd, so we'd have to work around that.
M: Let me look at the dean's schedule … Let's see … it looks like he's got a lot of meetings this week, and, well, most of next week, too, but what about the week after that? He doesn't have anything scheduled on Tuesday or Wednesday afternoon. Would either of those days work for you?

W: Um, yeah, I think so. How about Tuesday afternoon?
M: On Tuesday, he's free from two o'clock till four–thirty.
W: Let's see. I'll be in class until two–thirty, so how about three?
M: All right. Three o'clock, Tuesday, April 15.
W: Okay, that will be great. Thank you so much. This will be a great way for everyone to learn about our new dean. We really appreciate the opportunity to do this.
M: You're really quite welcome. It's our pleasure. In fact, I've put it on the dean's calendar, and we will see you on the 15th.
W: The 15th. Okay. Thank you very much.

1. What is the purpose of the conversation?
2. Why does the man say this:
"I'm sure the dean would like to participate, but … uh … you know, his schedule is pretty tight."
3. Why does the woman want to meet with the dean?
4. What can be inferred about the dean?
5. When will the meeting with the dean take place?

Album 9, Track 3

TEST 1 — LISTENING PART 1
QUESTIONS 6–11 (p. 471)

Listen to a discussion in an economics study group. The students are studying for a test.

M: Okay … so what do we do next?
W: Why don't we go over the chapter on analysis of costs? That'll be on the test.
M: Okay.
W: Let's start with "opportunity cost." That part's still confusing to me. I understand fixed cost and variable cost, and marginal cost, the cost of producing one more unit of something. I'm sure there'll be a question about that on the test. But I don't get "opportunity cost."
M: Opportunity cost—that's when you have to consider the things you give up when you make a certain decision. You have an opportunity cost when you're forced to choose between different alternatives.
W: Okay. That sort of makes sense.
M: Say you want to have your own business, so you, so you open a restaurant. You put in 60 hours a week, but you don't pay yourself wages. At the end of the first year, your restaurant shows a profit of … um … say, 30 thousand dollars—looks pretty good for a small business. But is it really that good? An economist would say no, because you have to count your own labor as a cost, even if you don't get paid. You have to consider that you had alternative opportunities for work, and you have to count that lost opportunity as a cost. You could have taken a job at, say, an accounting firm and earned 50 thousand a year. This is the opportunity cost—the earnings you gave up—because you decided to open your own business instead.
W: Okay. So what that means is … um … if I lost 50 thousand dollars by not taking an accounting job, then … my restaurant's profit of 30 thousand isn't that great after all—at least in an economic sense. Maybe I had more enjoyment, though—I mean the enjoyment of being my own boss.

DELTA'S KEY TO THE TOEFL IBT®

M: Right. But your enjoyment comes with a cost. An economist would say the real profit of your restaurant isn't 30 thousand dollars. You'd have to subtract the 50 thousand opportunity cost of your own labor. When you subtract 50 thousand from 30 thousand, you find you have a net loss of 20 thousand dollars!

W: Wow! That means the enjoyment of having my own business cost me 20 thousand dollars!

M: Yeah. Something like that.

W: This is really different from what we learned about costs in my accounting class. I think an accountant would say my 30 thousand–dollar profit made me a viable business. But an economist—if I understand it correctly—an economist would say my business is a loser!

M: Right. And that's because an economist tries to look at all the factors, all the costs. An economist would count the opportunity cost.

W: An economist looks at the big picture.

M: Right. An economist's definition of costs is broader than an accountant's. Opportunity cost is actually a very broad concept. It takes into account the cost of the choices we make. When we choose one thing, we have to give up something else.

W: That's right. We chose to go to college, so that means we had to give up full–time employment, for the time being.

M: Right! So, how do you measure the true cost of a college education?

W: Well, it's more than what we pay for tuition and books! We have to subtract the income we lose by not working full time.

M: Yeah, and that's why college is really more expensive than it seems.

6. What are the students mainly discussing?
7. How does the man help the woman understand a concept that she finds difficult?
8. Listen again to part of the conversation. Then answer the question.
"Say you want to have your own business, so you, so you open a restaurant. You put in 60 hours a week, but you don't pay yourself wages. At the end of the first year, your restaurant shows a profit of … um … say, 30 thousand dollars—looks pretty good for a small business. But is it really that good?"
Why does the man ask this:
"But is it really that good?"
9. According to the man, how does an economist's view of costs differ from that of an accountant?
10. What can be inferred about the true cost of a college education?
11. Why does the man say this:
"When we choose one thing, we have to give up something else."

Album 9, Track 4

Test 1 — Listening Part 1
Questions 12–17 (p. 473)

Listen to a talk in a botany class.

When European explorers first approached the coast of North America, even before their ships landed, the first thing they noticed was the pungent aroma carried to the ships by the offshore breezes. Some sea captains thought this aroma was the scent of the valuable Oriental spices that had prompted their voyages of exploration. But in fact, the agreeable smells didn't come from spices; they came from the lush vegetation of the North American forests.

The fragrance came from the blossoms of numerous trees and from the volatile oils in pine sap. Pine sap is a resinous fluid that pine trees put out to heal wounds caused by wind, fire, and lightning, and also to protect the pine tree's seeds. Pine sap was a valuable commodity to the sailors who explored the coast. The smell of pine meant there was an abundant supply of what were known as naval stores—pitch and pine tar. Pitch and pine tar were thick, sticky, semi–solid substances that were made by distilling pinewood. Sailors used naval stores for caulking and waterproofing their wooden ships, which kept them seaworthy.

The Europeans found fragrant trees all along the Atlantic coast, from Massachusetts in the north to Florida in the south. Everywhere along the coast, the air was filled with the strong perfume of the flowering dogwood. The Native Americans already knew about the medicinal properties of the dogwood, and they used its bark and roots to treat malaria and other fevers. They brewed the aromatic bark into a bitter, astringent tea. European settlers also used the dogwood to relieve attacks of malaria. They soaked the dogwood bark in whiskey and drank the strong infusion. This was before they knew about quinine from South America, and before quinine became available.

In the south, probably the best–known aromatic tree was the sassafras. The sassafras is a fast–growing tree, a member of the laurel family. Like the other fragrant laurels—cinnamon, bay, and camphor—sassafras is noted for its aromatic bark, leaves, roots, flowers, and fruit. I have a sassafras twig with me here, which I'll pass around so you can all enjoy its smell. Just give it a small scrape with your thumbnail to release the scent. I think you'll find it strong but pleasant.

The Choctaw Indians used powdered sassafras leaves as a spice. Other Native American tribes used sassafras tonic as a cure for everything from fever to stomachache. News of this wonder tree reached Europe in the sixteenth century by way of the French and the Spanish, and sassafras was one of the first exports from North America to Europe. It sold for a high price on the London market, which sort of inspired other English explorers to … um … seek their fortunes in the North American colonies.

For centuries, sassafras enjoyed a fantastic reputation as a cure for almost every disease. Maybe you've heard of the medicinal spring tonic of the old days. Well, sassafras was a main ingredient in spring tonic—the stuff pioneer parents gave their kids. My grandmother had to take spring tonic that her grandmother made from sassafras.

Sassafras leaves, bark, and roots used to provide the flavoring for root beer and chewing gum. Sassafras was also used in soaps and perfumes. However, in the 1960s, the United States Food and Drug Administration found sassafras oil to be a potential carcinogen for humans because it caused cancer in rats. Since that time, sassafras has been banned for human consumption. No one really knows just how harmful it is to human beings, but some studies show that one cup of strong sassafras tea contains more than four times the amount of the volatile oil safrole that is hazardous to humans if consumed on a regular basis.

12. According to the speaker, what did European explorers notice as they sailed toward the shores of North America?
13. According to the speaker, why was pine sap a valuable commodity?

14. How was the flowering dogwood used?
15. Why does the speaker say this:
    "Just give it a small scrape with your thumbnail to release the scent. I think you'll find it strong but pleasant."
16. Why was sassafras once considered a wonder tree?
17. Listen again to part of the talk. Then answer the question.
    "However, in the 1960s, the United States Food and Drug Administration found sassafras oil to be a potential carcinogen for humans because it caused cancer in rats. Since that time, sassafras has been banned for human consumption. No one really knows just how harmful it is to human beings, but some studies show that one cup of strong sassafras tea contains more than four times the amount of the volatile oil safrole that is hazardous to humans if consumed on a regular basis."
    What does the speaker imply about sassafras?

Album 9, Track 5

TEST 1 — LISTENING PART 2
QUESTIONS 1–5 (p. 475)

Listen to a conversation between a student and a professor.

M: Professor Gibson, may I speak to you?
W: Sure, Jason. What can I do for you?
M: Well, I'm, uh, thinking about Spring Quarter registration—about what I'd like to do. I'd like to take your seminar—Organizational Development.
W: Good.
M: But I don't have the prerequisite that's listed in the college catalog, you know, Statistics 210.
W: Oh. That statistics course is necessary before you can take the seminar. The reading list for the seminar assumes you've got a solid understanding of numerical data.
M: That's what I wanted to talk to you about. You see, I, uh, thought I could take Statistics 210 at the same time as the seminar—that is, if that's all right with you.
W: Well, not really, no. You need the course before you begin the seminar. Unless you have a good grasp of advanced statistics, you'll find the quantitative analyses very difficult, if not impossible. There's a good reason for the prerequisite.
M: I already took Introduction to Statistics, and that covered the basics. Isn't that enough?
W: I'm afraid not. Sorry, you really need the advanced methods you'll get in Statistics 210.
M: I see. Well, then I guess I could wait till next fall to take your seminar.
W: I'm not going to be teaching next year. I'll be on sabbatical, so there will probably be a visiting professor teaching Organizational Development.
M: Oh, I didn't know you'd be on sabbatical. I was looking forward to being in your seminar. I've learned so much from you in every one of your classes.
W: That's very kind of you to say so.
M: I mean it. I really looked forward to being in your seminar. Next year's my last year here before I graduate, so … I guess … uh, is there any way I can still do this? I mean, what if I hired a tutor to help me cram the statistics. Spring break is coming up. I don't have anything else to do. I'm not going anywhere or anything. I could get hold of the

textbook and start studying the material.
W: Well, Jason, I don't know of any student who'd rather study over spring break than go to the beach and play!
M: Do you know a tutor who could help me?
W: Well, I don't know. I—uh—
M: What about one of your teaching assistants?
W: You seem very determined. I suppose I could ask some of my TAs what they're doing over spring break, but I'm not convinced it's the best way to study advanced statistics.
M: I'll work really hard. I promise!
W: All right. I'll tell you what. If you really want to do it this way, if you're determined to register for my seminar, then you'll also need to take Statistics 210 in the spring. I usually insist that students have the statistics course before the seminar rather than at the same time, but you seem serious about this. I'll consider making an exception in your case, that is, if you get a tutor and start early, and if you take Statistics 210 in the spring, and if you also join my TA's study group.
M: I didn't know your TA had a study group.
W: It's for students in the seminar. They meet for three hours each week during Spring Quarter. I strongly recommend—in fact, I require you to join the group because you'll need the extra help. Will you do that?
M: Sure, I can do it.
W: Good. Good. You've got a busy quarter ahead of you.
M: For sure! Hey, thanks so much, Professor Gibson.
W: You're welcome.

1. Why does the student go see his professor?
2. What is the professor's initial response to the student's request?
3. Why does the student say this:
   "Next year's my last year here before I graduate, so … I guess … uh, is there any way I can still do this?"
4. What does the professor mean when she says this:
   "You seem very determined. I suppose I could ask some of my TAs what they're doing over spring break, but I'm not convinced it's the best way to study advanced statistics."
5. What does the professor insist that the student do?

Album 9, Track 6

TEST 1 — LISTENING PART 2
QUESTIONS 6–11 (p. 477)

Listen to part of a discussion in a philosophy class. The class is studying Plato.

M1: Plato believed the only true reality consists of ideas. Thus, we often refer to his philosophy as "idealism." He didn't think people could create ideas; rather, we discovered them. For instance, the mathematical concept of two plus two equals four—this is an idea that's always existed. It's always been true that two plus two equals four—even before people discovered it. Plato's ideas were—and still are—valuable because they've stimulated a great deal of thinking about the meaning and purpose of humanity, society, and education. The ideas of Plato survive in our thinking today, and survive in our educational system. Another important principle—yes?

W: Excuse me, Dr. MacDonald, but could you … like … uh … say more about how Plato's ideas are in education today?

M1: Sure. Plato believed the state should take an active role in education—most governments today agree—and the state should create a curriculum that leads students from thinking about concrete information toward thinking about abstract ideas. Higher–level thinking would develop the individual student's character, and thus ultimately benefit the larger society. Plato believed our most important goal was the search for truth. The idealists of today generally agree that a major focus of education should be on the search for knowledge, but some feel it's not truth per se that's important as much as the search for truth. Idealists favor learning that's holistic over learning that's specialized. For instance, idealists consider subjects like chemistry and physics useful, but they're of real value only when they help us to see the whole picture of our universe. Idealists aren't concerned with turning out graduates with specific technical skills as much as giving students a broad understanding of the world they live in.

W: But isn't that kind of impractical? I mean, most of us go to college because we want knowledge about certain subjects, not the whole universe.

M1: Idealists believe that education should teach students to think—not what to think, but how to think. Thinking is the skill that develops character. If you develop the ability to think, you—and all of humanity—will become more noble and rational.

M2: The philosophy of idealism seems kind of conservative.

M1: Idealism is often criticized as being a conservative philosophy because so much of its emphasis is on character development and preserving traditions. Idealists care about ultimate truths, so their notion of education is largely a matter of passing on knowledge.

M2: But what's the ultimate truth? Who gets to decide what's true?

M1: Who gets to decide what's true? Excellent question … and it's questions like this that have led to a weakening of idealism today. Developments in science and technology have changed what we've thought of as true. Our contemporary emphasis on relevance, usefulness, and innovation—as opposed to lasting values—all of these trends have cut idealism down to size.

W: I think all the concern with character development is kind of old–fashioned. Doesn't that make people … uh … doesn't it just lead to conformity?

M1: Good point. Critics of idealism would agree with you that "character development" comes at the expense of creativity, and that too much emphasis on traditional values can be harmful—if it makes students stop questioning what they're being taught.

6. What aspect of Plato's philosophy does the professor mainly discuss?
7. Why does the professor mention the mathematical concept of 2 + 2 = 4?
8. What do idealists believe about higher–level thinking?

9. Listen again to part of the discussion. Then answer the question.
   "Idealists aren't concerned with turning out graduates with specific technical skills as much as giving students a broad understanding of the world they live in."
   "But isn't that kind of impractical? I mean, most of us go to college because we want knowledge about certain subjects, not the whole universe."
   What is the woman's attitude toward the idealist view of education?
10. Listen again to part of the discussion. Then answer the question.
    "Who gets to decide what's true? Excellent question … and it's questions like this that have led to a weakening of idealism today. Developments in science and technology have changed what we've thought of as true. Our contemporary emphasis on relevance, usefulness, and innovation—as opposed to lasting values—all of these trends have cut idealism down to size."
    What does the professor mean when he says this:
    "…all of these trends have cut idealism down to size."
11. According to the professor, what do critics say about idealism?

Album 9, Track 7

TEST 1 — LISTENING PART 2
QUESTIONS 12–17 (p. 479)

Listen to a lecture in a physics class. The professor is discussing energy and work.

In physics, energy is defined as the ability to do work. And in physics, work doesn't refer to what you do at your job. In physics, work means moving an object when there is some resistance to its movement. Every time we lift an object, push it, pull it, or carry it, we are doing work.

Two things are necessary for work to occur. First, force—or energy—must be applied to the object. If no energy is used, no work has been done. Second, the object must be moved a distance. If the object is pushed or pulled but it doesn't move, no work has been done.

When we move an object, there's always some resistance, or opposition to movement. Resistance is a force that tends to oppose or slow down movement. Whenever an object meets resistance, more energy is needed to do the work. A good example is what happens when a farmer's plow moves through the soil. The plow encounters resistance if it gets too deep into the soil, or if rocks and roots in the soil make the soil hard to turn. When this happens, the tractor's engine has to work harder. The engine strains under the load and uses more fuel.

Each time we do work, we use energy. If our muscles do the work, energy in the form of food is required. If a machine does the work, energy in the form of oil, gas, coal, electricity, or some other source is required. Without energy, no work can be done.

Energy comes in several different forms. It can take the form of heat, light, motion, electricity, chemical energy, nuclear energy, and so on. Energy can change forms, but it cannot be created or destroyed. Energy is always conserved—that is a law of nature. This law is known as the law of conservation of energy, or the first law of thermodynamics. The law states that energy can be converted from any form to any other form, but no matter what form it takes, it's still energy, and none of the energy disappears when it changes form.

Machines do work by converting one form of energy to another. For example, a car converts the chemical energy in gasoline to kinetic energy—to motion. A stove converts electrical energy or chemical energy into heat energy that cooks our food. The law of conservation of energy tells us that a machine needs to have a source of energy. And a machine can't supply more power than it gets from its energy source. When the fuel runs out, the machine stops. The same rule applies to living organisms: if the organism doesn't have food, it dies.

The law of conservation of energy tells us that the energy of any system—whether the system is a machine, a living organism, or an ecosystem—that the energy must balance out in the end. The amount of energy in the system is conserved, even though the energy changes forms.

The earth as a whole is a complex system that receives almost all its energy from the sun in the form of light. Some of the solar energy converts to heat, which warms the earth. Some of it evaporates water, forms clouds, and produces rain. Some energy is captured by plants, and is turned into chemical energy during photosynthesis. The first law of thermodynamics—conservation of energy—says the earth must end up with the same amount of energy it started out with. The energy changes forms, but no energy is lost or gained.

12. How does the field of physics define "work"?
13. Listen again to part of the lecture. Then answer the question.
    "Whenever an object meets resistance, more energy is needed to do the work. A good example is what happens when a farmer's plow moves through the soil. The plow encounters resistance if it gets too deep into the soil, or if rocks and roots in the soil make the soil hard to turn. When this happens, the tractor's engine has to work harder. The engine strains under the load and uses more fuel."
    Why does the professor talk about a plow?
14. Which statement best reflects the first law of thermodynamics?
15. Which two sentences illustrate the conversion of energy from one form to another?
16. Listen again to part of the lecture. Then answer the question.
    "The law of conservation of energy tells us that a machine needs to have a source of energy. And a machine can't supply more power than it gets from its energy source. When the fuel runs out, the machine stops. The same rule applies to living organisms: if the organism doesn't have food, it dies."
    Why does the professor say this:
    "The same rule applies to living organisms: if the organism doesn't have food, it dies."
17. What can be inferred about the energy in the earth as a whole system?

Album 9, Track 8

TEST 1 — SPEAKING SECTION DIRECTIONS (p. 481)

The Speaking section measures your ability to speak in English about a variety of topics. There are six questions in this section.

In questions 1 and 2, you will speak about familiar topics. Your responses will be scored on your ability to speak clearly and coherently about the topics.

In questions 3 and 4, you will first read a short text and then listen to a talk on the same topic. You will then be asked a question about what you have read and heard. You will need to combine appropriate information from the text and the talk to provide a complete answer to the question. Your responses will be scored on your ability to speak clearly and coherently and on your ability to accurately convey information about what you have read and heard.

In questions 5 and 6, you will listen to part of a conversation or lecture. You will then be asked a question about what you have heard. Your responses will be scored on your ability to speak clearly and coherently and on your ability to accurately convey information about what you have heard.

You may take notes while you read and while you listen to the conversations and lectures. You may use your notes to help prepare your responses.

Album 9, Track 9

TEST 1 — SPEAKING QUESTION 1 (p. 482)

What game do you enjoy playing? Describe the game, and explain why you like to play it. Include details and examples in your explanation.

Album 9, Track 10

TEST 1 — SPEAKING QUESTION 2 (p. 482)

Some people drive their own car to school or work. Others ride a bus, train, or other form of public transportation. Which do you think is better and why? Include details and examples in your explanation.

Album 9, Track 11

TEST 1 — SPEAKING QUESTION 3 (p. 483)

Now listen to a student as he discusses online courses with his academic adviser.

M: I want to take astronomy next quarter, and I was thinking of registering for the online course.
W: Have you ever taken an online course before?
M: No. But I have a computer, and it seems fairly easy to take a course this way.
W: Let me just point out a couple of things. First, you have to be able to learn on your own, mainly by reading. So you have to be self–motivated. There are a few online lectures, but mainly you have to read the information on a computer. You also have to keep up with a schedule, just as in any other class. So unless

you're self–motivated, online courses are generally not a good idea. In fact, there's a fairly high dropout rate for online courses.

M: Hmmm. I didn't know that. It seems like it would be so easy because you don't have to be in class at a specific time.

W: Believe it or not, the main reason that students drop out is they miss going to class. They miss the face–to–face contact with the professor. So, if interacting with the professor and other students is important to you, then you should consider taking a regular classroom course.

The adviser expresses her opinion about online courses. State her opinion and explain the reasons she gives for holding that opinion.

Album 9, Track 12

TEST 1 — SPEAKING QUESTION 4 (p. 484)

Now listen to part of a lecture in a zoology class.

One example of a homeostatic system is temperature control, by which some animals can maintain a constant internal body temperature. The large ears of a rabbit are an amazing device in homeostasis. The rabbit can regulate the amount of blood flowing through blood vessels of its big ears. This adjusts heat loss to the rabbit's surroundings and maintains the stability of the rabbit's body temperature.

The control center for body temperature is the brain, and nerve cells in the skin do much of the work. Here's what happens. When the rabbit's body temperature increases, because of exercise or hot surroundings, the rabbit's brain notices the change and it sets out to bring the temperature back to normal. So the brain turns on the body's cooling system. In the rabbit's ears, the blood vessels expand and fill with warm blood. Heat is then able to escape from the surface of the skin on the ears. This causes the rabbit's body temperature to drop, and the brain can then turn off the cooling system.

On the other hand, when the rabbit's body temperature decreases because of cold surroundings, the brain turns on the body's warming system. Blood vessels in the ears constrict and get narrow, and send blood from the skin to deeper parts of the rabbit's body. And this reduces heat loss from the ears.

The professor describes the large ears of a rabbit. Explain how the rabbit's ears are used in homeostasis.

Album 9, Track 13

TEST 1 — SPEAKING QUESTION 5 (p. 485)

Listen to a conversation between two students.

W: Hi, Jim. How's your quarter going?

M: Well, to be honest, not very well. I just got my geology test back and I'm afraid my grade was not very good. I was expecting it to be higher. I'm disappointed, too, because I like my professor, and I need to pass this course.

W: Oh. Would it help if you got a tutor? I can recommend someone, a graduate student who knows a lot about geology. He was my tutor last year, and it really helped. I learned how to study better. I can give

you his phone number.

M: I don't know. The main problem is I just don't have enough time to study. My other activities—mainly sports, and student government too—those things are taking up too much of my time. That means I have less time for geology.

W: Well, maybe this is a good time to cut down on some of your activities. Can you give up anything—any of your sports—the least important, at least for a while?

M: I don't know. That would be tough.

W: But you need more time to study. You'd only have to give up something temporarily, just until you can improve your grade.

M: Ugh. I need to do something fast because I can't fail the course.

The students discuss possible solutions to the man's problem. Describe the problem. Then state which solution you prefer and explain why.

Album 9, Track 14

TEST 1 — SPEAKING QUESTION 6 (p. 485)

Listen to part of a lecture in a linguistics class.

The communication between a baby and his mother has many of the same features as communication in music. One feature is timing. A mother and a child have a shared sense of timing, both before and after the child is born. The mother and child sort of "swing" together in a common rhythm.

By the time he's two months old, a baby can make sounds with a musical inflection when he's "talking" with his mother. Just as one musician will lead another in a performance, a child will often lead the earliest "conversations" with his mother. This interplay is musical in the way it connects two people in an exchange of sounds. It shows that a child has, from the very beginning, an ability to communicate with his mother. The child recognizes his mother's voice. He also learns very quickly how to use his own voice in various ways.

The communication between babies and mothers develops from the intense daily contact between them. The mother creates a special language for her child—baby talk—a very special, very musical language. Several studies show that babies understand the patterns of baby talk, and will respond appropriately—by using facial expressions, movements, and their voice.

Babies develop a large vocabulary of meaningful sounds long before any of those sounds become real words. The meaning lies in the music of the sounds—different meanings expressed by changes in intonation, rhythm, and timing—all characteristics of music.

Using points and examples from the lecture, explain how the communication between babies and mothers is musical in nature.

Album 9, Track 15

Test 1 — Writing Section Directions (p. 486)

The Writing section measures your ability to use writing to communicate in an academic environment. There are two writing questions.

Question 1 is a writing task based on reading and listening. You will read a passage, listen to a lecture, and then write a response to a question about the relationship between the lecture and the reading. You have 20 minutes to plan and write your response.

Question 2 is writing based on knowledge and experience. You will write an essay in response to a question that asks you to state, explain, and support an opinion on an issue. You have 30 minutes to plan and write your essay.

Album 9, Track 16

Test 1 — Writing Question 1 (p. 487)

Now listen to part of a lecture on the topic you just read about.

There's been some interesting research on the power of information. In one study, political scientists found that highly educated thinkers were even less open to new information than less educated people were. So we can't say that education alone is the solution to society's problems.

First, the researchers found that facts don't necessarily have the power to change people's minds. When misinformed people were given the corrected facts in news stories, they seldom changed their minds. In fact, they often became even more strongly set in their beliefs. The facts were not curing the misinformation. These results make it difficult to be optimistic about the effectiveness of fact checking.

Second, in reality, people often base their opinions on their beliefs rather than on facts. Their previous beliefs dictate which facts they choose to accept. People will twist the facts to fit their beliefs. Moreover, beliefs can lead people to accept bad information uncritically just because it strengthens their beliefs. Reinforcement of their beliefs makes people more certain they are right, which makes them less likely to listen to any new information that doesn't fit. So the new information has no effect on their opinions—even when the information is factually correct.

Finally, if people feel threatened or insecure, they will not listen to new information. This is why some politicians benefit from keeping people in a state of fear. The more threatened people feel, the less likely they are to listen to opposing opinions. When people are kept misinformed and afraid, they are easier to control.

Summarize the points made in the lecture, being sure to explain how they contradict specific points made in the reading passage.

ALBUM 10 — TEST 2

Album 10, Track 1

Test 2 — Listening Section Directions (p. 502)

The Listening section measures your ability to understand conversations and lectures in English. You will hear each conversation and lecture only one time. After each conversation or lecture, you will answer some questions about it. The questions typically ask about the main idea and supporting details. Some questions ask about a speaker's purpose or attitude. Answer the questions based on what the speakers state or imply.

You may take notes while you listen. You may use your notes to help you answer the questions. Your notes will not be scored.

In some questions, you will see this icon: 🎧. This means that you will hear, but not see, part of the question.

Some questions have special directions, which appear in a gray box. Most questions are worth one point. If a question is worth more than one point, the directions will indicate how many points you can receive.

You will now begin part 1 of the Listening section.

Album 10, Track 2

Test 2 — Listening Part 1
Questions 1–5 (p. 503)

Listen to a conversation between a student and her academic adviser.

M: Hello, Anna. How are you?
W: I'm busy. The quarter's going by really quickly.
M: Have you thought about what you're doing next quarter?
W: Literature, sociology, math, and I'm hoping to do something in the arts, maybe some sort of work experience or internship.
M: Really! What did you have in mind?
W: Well, there's this theater group I just found out about in Chester. I went to a couple of their plays. They're an interesting company. They perform a lot of new works, and they also do older plays that aren't very well known, and, well, I'm really impressed and would love to work with them in some way.
M: I didn't know you were into theater. Do you act?
W: Not really ... I took drama in high school, but I was awful on the stage. No, it's not acting that interests me as much as all the other stuff.
M: Like what? Directing? Lighting?
W: All of it, actually. This theater I told you about—they have the best sets! I'd like to build sets. Or make costumes, find props—I don't know, even work in the office. It's the whole atmosphere of the theater that I find exciting.
M: Then it sounds like an internship might be a good move for you.
W: But, as far as that goes, my problem is I don't know anything about setting it up.
M: Do you know anyone who works there?

DELTA'S KEY TO THE TOEFL IBT®

W: No, I only found out about it 'cause I went to a couple of plays.

M: What other experience do you have in the arts? You mentioned sets and costumes. Have you ever worked on anything like that before?

W: I took a drawing class last year, and I once had a summer job as a house painter.

M: Hmm. I see. Yes, both of those things could help you. Why don't you put together a portfolio of your drawings? Choose things that might be relevant—like … uh …

W: A lot of my drawings were of buildings.

M: Hmm. Sure, drawings of buildings might be relevant.

W: Okay.

M: You should also write a letter to the manager of the theater. Tell him or her about your interest in that particular theater and why you'd like to be an intern there. Describe any relevant experience you have— your job as a house painter—and anything else you can think of. Then, about a week after you send it, follow up with a phone call.

W: This all sounds like good advice. I'm glad I came to see you today. You make it sound so easy.

M: Come back and tell me how it goes.

W: Okay. Thanks.

1. What are the speakers mainly discussing?
2. What does the woman like about theater?
3. What is the woman's opinion of her own acting ability?
4. Why does the man say this:
   "Like what? Directing? Lighting?"
5. What does the man suggest the woman do?

Album 10, Track 3

TEST 2 — LISTENING PART 1
QUESTIONS 6–11 (p. 505)

Listen to a lecture in a biology class. The professor is discussing carbon.

Carbon is the basic chemical component of all organic compounds. The movement of carbon through an ecosystem parallels the movement of energy, as carbon is cycled through a number of life processes. For example, carbohydrates are produced during plant photosynthesis, and carbon dioxide is released along with energy during plant and animal respiration. In the carbon cycle, the processes of photosynthesis and respiration balance each other and provide a link between the atmosphere and the earth environments.

Plants acquire carbon from the atmosphere in the form of carbon dioxide. Through photosynthesis, plants take in carbon through their leaves and incorporate it into the organic matter of their own biomass. Some of the organic material from plants becomes the carbon source for plant–eating animals. So, when a deer eats the new leaves of a tree, it consumes some of the carbon from the tree.

Respiration by all organisms—plants and animals—returns carbon dioxide to the atmosphere. The cycling of carbon dioxide in the atmosphere is essentially global. What this means is, some of the carbon and oxygen atoms that a plant acquires from the air as carbon dioxide may have been released into the atmosphere by the respiration of a plant or animal in some distant location.

Carbon recycles through plants at a relatively fast rate because plants have a high demand for the gas. However, some carbon is diverted from the cycle for longer periods. This happens, for example, when carbon is collected in wood. When trees die, the decomposition of wood in the fallen logs eventually recycles this carbon to the atmosphere as carbon dioxide. Forest fires can oxidize wood into carbon dioxide much faster. Some processes, however, can divert carbon from short–term cycling for millions of years. For example, in some environments, plant matter accumulates much faster than it decomposes. Under certain conditions, these deposits of plant matter eventually form coal and petroleum that become locked away, buried in the earth, for millions of years.

The amount of carbon dioxide in the atmosphere varies slightly with the seasons. In the Northern Hemisphere, concentrations are lowest during the summer and highest during the winter. This is because in summer plants reach their highest level of photosynthetic activity, reducing the amount of carbon dioxide in the atmosphere. In contrast, during winter, the vegetation releases more carbon dioxide by respiration than it uses for photosynthesis, causing a global increase in the gas.

Another factor affecting atmospheric carbon levels is our burning of fuels. As I just stated, some carbon is stored underground in the form of coal and petroleum—fossil fuels. We're now digging up this carbon, which has been buried for a long time. We're burning it as fossil fuels and turning it into carbon dioxide. The combustion of wood, coal, and petroleum adds more carbon dioxide to the atmosphere. As a result, the amount of atmospheric carbon dioxide is steadily increasing.

This increase in carbon dioxide is disrupting the balance of carbon in the global cycle. The consequences of this are a cause of conflict between scientists and policy makers, and we'll explore some of them when we meet tomorrow.

6. What is the main purpose of the lecture?
7. What point does the professor make about the cycling of carbon dioxide in the atmosphere?
8. Listen again to part of the lecture. Then answer the question.
   "Some processes, however, can divert carbon from short–term cycling for millions of years. For example, in some environments, plant matter accumulates much faster than it decomposes. Under certain conditions, these deposits of plant matter eventually form coal and petroleum that become locked away, buried in the earth, for millions of years."
   Why does the professor say this:
   "Under certain conditions, these deposits of plant matter eventually form coal and petroleum that become locked away, buried in the earth, for millions of years."
9. According to the professor, what factors affect the amount of carbon dioxide in the atmosphere?
10. According to the professor, why is the level of atmospheric carbon dioxide lowest during the summer?
11. What does the professor mean when she says this:
    "This increase in carbon dioxide is disrupting the balance of carbon in the global cycle. The consequences of this are a cause of conflict between scientists and policy makers, and we'll explore some of them when we meet tomorrow."

Album 10, Track 4

TEST 2 — LISTENING PART 1
QUESTIONS 12–17 (p. 507)

Listen to part of a lecture in an anthropology class.

M: Every human society has developed some interest in activities that could be considered sports. The more complex the culture, the more various the range of sporting behavior. There are certain elements in all human sports that are clues to the common underlying structure of sports. Sports tell us a great deal about the kinds of behavior that our prehistoric ancestors evolved—activities that were basic survival skills. Now, let me ask you—what skills were most important to the survival of our ancestors? Yes, Lynne?

W: The ability to find food?

M: Yeah …. But what skills were necessary to find food?

W: Um … good eyesight?

M: Okay. What else?

W: Well, if they were hunters, they also had to be fast runners … and they had to have good eyes and a good arm—I mean a good aim—so they could kill game.

M: Yes! And isn't it interesting that you just used the word "game"? Our prehistoric ancestors were gamers—they hunted game animals to survive. Look at the number of sports that originated in hunting. First, hunting itself. But for some societies, the ancient pattern of killing prey is kept alive in the form of blood sports—these are sports that involve the killing of an animal. Even in places where the killing is no longer a matter of survival, it still survives as a sport. The animals—like ducks or pheasant, certain fish—are often eaten as luxury foods. It's the personal sense of mastery, the sort of delight in the skills of the hunter … these are more important than the food itself. For our prehistoric ancestors, the climax of the hunt was always a group celebration, with songs of praise for the hunters. As hunting sort of became more symbolic, spectators became more important. The ancient Romans brought the hunt to the people by confining it to an arena— the Coliseum. The Coliseum made the hunting field smaller, and this sort of intensified the activity for the entertainment of the spectators. The systematic killing of animals for sport still survives in parts of the world today—think of bullfights and cock fights. But animal sports are only part of the picture. Today, people find human competition more satisfying than competition involving just animals. Take track and field sports. These don't involve animals, but they did originate in hunting. The earliest sports meetings—or meets, as we call them—were probably ritualized competitions of important skills. Think of how many Olympic sports there are that involve aiming, throwing, and running—which are all hunting skills. The difference is that now the hunting has become totally symbolic. In some sports, there's still a strong symbolic element of the kill. Wrestling, boxing, fencing, martial arts—all these are examples of ritualized fighting. Even tennis is kind of a fight— of course, an abstract one. There are lots of direct references to fighting in the language of sports, too. For example, what do soccer and chess players do?

They "attack" or "defend."
Today, even the most violent fighting sports have strict rules that are designed to prevent serious injury. There's also some kind of referee to make sure that the rules are observed. In sports, the objective is victory, not the actual destruction of your opponent. Another objective is to impress and entertain the spectators—not to shock or offend them. Because sports contain such a powerful negative element, most have an ideal of acceptable behavior— something we call "sportsmanship." There's also a universal convention in sports where the winner honors the defeated opponent—with a handshake, with words of praise, or some token of respect.

12. What is the main idea of the lecture?
13. Listen again to part of the discussion. Then answer the question.
    "Now, let me ask you—what skills were most important to the survival of our ancestors? Yes, Lynne?"
    "The ability to find food?"
    "Yeah …. But what skills were necessary to find food?"
    Why does the professor say this:
    "Yeah …. But what skills were necessary to find food?"
14. According to the professor, why did the ancient Romans build the Coliseum?
15. What point does the professor make about track and field sports?
16. Which sports contain a symbolic element of the kill?
17. What does the professor imply about the negative element of sports?

Album 10, Track 5

TEST 2 — LISTENING PART 2
QUESTIONS 1–5 (p. 509)

Listen to a conversation between a student and a professor.

M: Hi, Professor Reynolds.

W: Oh, hi, Jeff. I just read your note. You wanted to talk about something?

M: Uh, yeah, just an idea I have. I've been thinking— um, I was reading about what's been going on with those houses on Fox Point.

W: You mean the slide?

M: Yeah, that's right. The paper said a few days ago there was only one house that was affected, but this morning there was another article saying there were lots more houses involved than they previously thought, maybe as many as fifteen or twenty homes. A couple of houses have big cracks in the foundation.

W: I read the article too. It seems like nothing but bad news for the homeowners.

M: Yeah. My old boss lives out there on Fox Point. I don't know if his house is one that's affected. Anyway … I was … um … I was sort of thinking I could write a paper on it. I remember how in your Intro to Geology course we studied gravity movements. I thought maybe … um … the slide on Fox Point was a case of subsidence … um … when the earth sinks 'cause there's a weakening of support. I was thinking this might be an example of settlement.

W: Settlement happens from the more or less gradual compacting of underlying material—for example, when wet soil at the surface dries and shrinks, and creates a depression. It can also happen when frozen ground melts.

M: In class you talked about the Leaning Tower of Pisa.

W: Yes. The settlement that's caused the Tower of Pisa to lean is due to the failure of a clay layer beneath it. Engineers have been working on it for decades, but still haven't been able to stop the process.

M: There was another kind of settlement you talked about … um … when groundwater's removed.

W: Yes, that's what happened in the San Joaquin Valley in California. Part of the valley floor sank 30 feet because of the removal of groundwater for irrigation. But the problem on Fox Point may not be subsidence at all. This probably has more to do with the slope, and with the amount of rain we've been having lately.

M: So … it's just a regular old mudslide, not like the Leaning Tower?

W: It's probably not like the Leaning Tower.

M: The article did say the houses were on a slope, but it's only slight, it's not steep at all.

W: Mudslides are most common on intermediate slopes—27 to 45 degrees—because these slopes are gentle enough for sediment to accumulate and steep enough for sliding. One suggestion I have is to take a look at the county's Web site. There's a page on the geology of the region. This area has a history of slides. There was one on Johnson Island about ten, twelve years ago.

M: Oh, really? I didn't know that. Maybe there's a connection.

W: Possibly. It's an idea to work on.

M: Well, this gives me a place to start. Thanks, Professor Reynolds. I appreciate your input.

1. Why does the student go to see the professor?
2. What topic is the man mainly interested in?
3. Why does the student say this:
   "In class you talked about the Leaning Tower of Pisa."
4. According to the professor, where are mudslides most common?
5. What will the man probably include in his research?

Album 10, Track 6

TEST 2 — LISTENING PART 2
QUESTIONS 6–11 (p. 511)

Listen to part of a discussion in an astronomy class.

W1: Since your next test is on Friday, I thought we would take the rest of today's class to review the chapter. Why don't we start with some of your questions? Is there anything in particular you'd like to go over before the test? Yes, Cody.

M: I'm not sure I understand everything we need to know about meteors and comets, like how they're different. They're sort of similar, aren't they?

W1: Not exactly. Meteors are tiny bits of mineral or rock that strike the atmosphere. Billions of them crash into the atmosphere every day, and they're vaporized, and they drop tons of cosmic dust on the earth. Comets, on the other hand, don't enter the atmosphere. They follow an orbit around a star, like our sun.

W2: The stuff from a meteor that falls to Earth—that's called a meteor shower, right?

W1: Right, and meteor showers are also called shooting stars. Meteor showers are named for the constellation we see them in—take the Leonid meteor shower, which is in the constellation Leo. A meteor shower appears to radiate from a single point in the sky. That's because all the particles are traveling in parallel paths, and at the same velocity. Meteors put on a spectacular show, but they never reach the ground intact. They're made up of ice and dust grains that are too small to survive passing through the atmosphere. And, uh, meteor showers happen at regular intervals every year because they're debris left over from periodic comets.

M: Excuse me, Professor Morgan, you just said meteor showers are debris left over from comets. So there's a connection between them? Meteors come from comets?

W1: That's right. They do. And it wouldn't be a bad idea to go back and reread that section of the chapter. You might see this again on Friday. Meteors are formed when a comet breaks up or leaves debris in its wake. So, meteors and comets often—well, they sort of travel together, on the same path around the sun.

M: That makes sense. Then it looks like meteors are a lot smaller than comets.

W1: Yes, that's usually true. Comets look different, too. Comets have a tail. Comets actually have three distinct components: the nucleus, consisting of rock and ice; the coma, consisting of gases and dust; and the tail, which is formed when gases and dust spread out from the nucleus or coma.

M: Okay. A comet has a nucleus, a coma, and a tail. Um … you were … uh … you said something about periodic comets?

W1: All comets are periodic because they complete their orbits in a certain interval of time. A comet has a short-term period if it completes its orbit in less than 200 years. Like Halley's Comet. Halley's Comet is periodic, and it's predictable too. It has a period of about 76 years.

W2: My parents saw Halley's Comet the last time it passed by Earth.

W1: I saw it too, in 1986. Hopefully, you'll be here to see it come again. You will all be watching it with your great-grandchildren.

W2: I hope so! That would be amazing.

6. What is the discussion mainly about?
7. What happens when a meteor strikes the atmosphere?
8. Why does the student say this:
   "Excuse me, Professor Morgan, you just said meteor showers are debris left over from comets. So there's a connection between them? Meteors come from comets?"
9. What does the professor imply when she says this:
   "And it wouldn't be a bad idea to go back and reread that section of the chapter. You might see this again on Friday."
10. What does the professor say about comets?
11. Listen again to part of the conversation. Then answer the question.
    "My parents saw Halley's Comet the last time it passed by Earth."
    "I saw it too, in 1986. Hopefully, you'll be here to see it come again. You will all be watching it with your great-grandchildren."
    "I hope so! That would be amazing."
    What can be inferred about Halley's Comet?

Album 10, Track 7

TEST 2 — LISTENING PART 2
QUESTIONS 12–17 (p. 513)

Listen to a talk in a music education class.

Learning to play a musical instrument is one of the best experiences that a young child can have. Learning to play music begins with listening to others play music. A child's first experience with playing an instrument should be by ear, without the distraction of printed music. Playing by ear is the natural beginning for children. The ability to play by ear will help them throughout their lives, and it also enriches the experience of music making. But children should eventually learn to read music. So, when is the right time? And what's the best way for a child to learn how to read music?

A lot of children start playing an instrument at the age of eight or nine. It's best for them to spend a couple of years playing by ear before the teacher introduces notation—printed music. Children should first be able to feel that their instrument is a part of them. Playing by ear is the best way for children to become comfortable with their instrument.

The teacher should introduce notation only when the child is ready. The right time is when the child feels a need for notation. This might be when the child has learned so many pieces it's sort of difficult to remember them all. Then the teacher can present the printed music as a memory aid, so learning to read music has a practical purpose and isn't just a meaningless task.

A good time to teach notation is when a group of children play together. The printed score is a way to help them sort of keep track of who plays what and when. The score will organize their cooperative effort in a way that makes sense to them.

Another good time is when the child wants to play music that's so complex it would be difficult to learn by ear. In this case, learning to read music is a natural step toward playing the music the child wants to play. The teacher should play the score for the child the first time through, and demonstrate how the notes on the page are transformed into music. The child listens as he or she looks at the printed notes. This way, the child can begin to see how the notes represent sound and a printed score becomes a piece of music. As the child listens—and maybe plays along—he or she begins to understand the shape of the new piece.

For students who play a chord–producing instrument—the guitar, for example—a natural first step toward reading music is playing by chord symbols. Chord symbols are found in a lot of different styles of music—like pop and jazz—and at various levels of difficulty. Chord symbols are a simple form of written music—they're kind of a halfway point between playing by ear and reading a standard musical score.

After children can play by ear, and then by chord symbols, the next step is to read standard music notation. Although that's the natural order for children to learn, it doesn't mean that each successive step is better than the one that came before. The three methods of playing music—playing by ear, playing chords, and playing by standard notation—are all valuable in their own way. Some children will always prefer to play by ear. Others will like chord playing and have no desire to learn another method. And still others will find their musical home in the tradition of note reading. It's the job of the music teacher to fit the method to the needs of the students.

12. What is playing by ear?
13. Listen again to part of the talk. Then answer the question.

"Playing by ear is the natural beginning for children. The ability to play by ear will help them throughout their lives, and it also enriches the experience of music making. But children should eventually learn to read music. So, when is the right time? And what's the best way for a child to learn how to read music?"
Why does the professor ask this:
"So, when is the right time? And what's the best way for a child to learn how to read music?"

14. According to the professor, when should children learn to read musical notation?
15. According to the professor, why should a music teacher play the score for a child the first time?
16. According to the professor, what is the natural order for children to learn music?
17. What does the professor imply about the three methods of playing music?

Album 10, Track 8

TEST 2 — SPEAKING SECTION DIRECTIONS (p. 515)

The Speaking section measures your ability to speak in English about a variety of topics. There are six questions in this section.

In questions 1 and 2, you will speak about familiar topics. Your responses will be scored on your ability to speak clearly and coherently about the topics.

In questions 3 and 4, you will first read a short text and then listen to a talk on the same topic. You will then be asked a question about what you have read and heard. You will need to combine appropriate information from the text and the talk to provide a complete answer to the question. Your responses will be scored on your ability to speak clearly and coherently and on your ability to accurately convey information about what you have read and heard.

In questions 5 and 6, you will listen to part of a conversation or lecture. You will then be asked a question about what you have heard. Your responses will be scored on your ability to speak clearly and coherently and on your ability to accurately convey information about what you have heard.

You may take notes while you read and while you listen to the conversations and lectures. You may use your notes to help prepare your responses.

Album 10, Track 9

TEST 2 — SPEAKING QUESTION 1 (p. 516)

Describe a person who has influenced you in an important way. Explain why this person has had an effect on your life. Include details and examples in your explanation.

Album 10, Track 10

TEST 2 — SPEAKING QUESTION 2 (p. 516)

Some people get most of their news from the radio or television. Others read news on the Internet. Which source of news do you think is better and why? Include details and examples in your explanation.

Album 10, Track 11

TEST 2 — SPEAKING QUESTION 3 (p. 517)

Now listen to two students as they discuss the attendance policy.

M: It looks like we're going to be in the same biology class. I'm going to miss the first day because I won't be back from vacation yet, so I'll ask you for the lecture notes.

W: But you can't miss the first day! Attendance is mandatory on the first day.

M: Oh, I don't agree with that. It will be all right. That policy is unfair anyway.

W: It's not unfair! The instructor has the right to set the attendance policy, and the right to kick you out of class if you don't follow it. The way I look at it, if the instructor has to be there every day, then so should the students. That seems fair to me.

M: Oh, but the students can read and study on their own. It's not important to go to class. The only thing that's important is the examinations.

W: I disagree. I think it's important to participate in class. That's an important part of learning.

M: But you can learn what you need to know by studying on your own!

W: But how do you know you won't miss something important? You can't always understand everything on your own. That's why you need to go to class. And that's why there's an attendance policy.

The woman expresses her opinion about the attendance policy. State her opinion and explain the reasons she gives for holding that opinion.

Album 10, Track 12

TEST 2 — SPEAKING QUESTION 4 (p. 518)

Now listen to part of a lecture in a linguistics class.

According to the gestural theory, human language first evolved as a gesture system before it became a vocal system. There's evidence to support this. Non–human primates also use gestures to communicate, and some of their gestures resemble those of humans. Chimpanzees use combinations of gestures and sounds to alert the group to the presence of danger or the availability of food.

New research supports the theory as well. In a study of dance, researchers measured brain activity in subjects as they performed various movement tasks while listening to music. The researchers found that, for every movement task, there was activity in the right half of the brain corresponding to the area in the left brain associated with speech. The researchers found that leg movement activates the brain in a way similar to speech production. This suggests that dance began as a form of communication. In other words, it strengthens the gestural theory of language evolution.

Dance can convey ideas clearly, so it probably functioned as an early form of language. Dance can communicate ideas and feelings. Dance is theatrical. It can tell stories. Early humans created dances to imitate animals and other humans, to tell stories about their lives, and to express emotions.

Explain the gestural theory of language and how the examples given by the professor support the theory.

Album 10, Track 13

TEST 2 — SPEAKING QUESTION 5 (p. 519)

Listen to a conversation between two students.

W: So, will you be doing the internship at the bank next semester?

M: Maybe. I still haven't decided. My parents want me to do it because they want me to go into banking. But Dr. Kim has asked me to be her intern.

W: Dr. Kim is your sociology professor, right?

M: That's right. She's doing a study of population growth, and she wants me to be her research assistant. It's an honor to be asked. I mean, there's only one internship, and several other students want it. I want it. But if I accept it, my parents will be disappointed.

W: Do you want your career to be in banking?

M: I used to think so, but now I'm not so sure. I'm more interested in working with statistics, you know, doing pure research.

W: Then you should do the internship with Dr. Kim. That way you'll know for sure if pure research is what you want to do.

M: My father won't be happy about it.

W: How do you know? Talk to him. Explain why the other internship excites you. Tell him it's a great opportunity to work with Dr. Kim, and quite an honor for the professor to ask you. That might actually please your father. In the end, you have to do what makes you happy.

The students discuss possible solutions to a problem that the man has. Describe the problem. Then state what you think the man should do, and explain why.

Album 10, Track 14

TEST 2 — SPEAKING QUESTION 6 (p. 519)

Listen to part of a talk in a biology class. The professor is discussing competition in bird populations.

Competition is the struggle over scarce resources. Whenever there's a limited supply of a resource—such as food, nesting sites, or mates—there will be competition. Competition can take place between birds of the same species or between birds of different species.

There are two forms of competition: direct and indirect. Direct competition is when a bird actively excludes others from getting resources. A common example is stealing. One bird may simply take food from another. Another example is establishing territories. Especially during the breeding season, birds maintain and defend some sort of territory. They form territories to defend resources like food, or to maintain access to good nesting sites, or to attract mates. Some birds compete directly by fighting, for example, when they compete for mates. Others fight over food. You can see this if you watch gulls feeding on the garbage at the local dump.

The second type of competition is indirect. Indirect competition is when birds simply use up a resource. When one species eats all the seeds or berries or grubs, this will prevent other species from using that resource. Indirect competition is less open than direct competition, but it can have just as great an influence on populations. For example, a flock of geese grazing in a field will gradually decrease the amount of food there. The larger the flock, the faster the food will be consumed, and this will reduce the amount of food available for other species.

Using points and examples from the lecture, explain direct and indirect competition in bird populations.

Album 10, Track 15

TEST 2 — WRITING SECTION DIRECTIONS (p. 520)

The Writing section measures your ability to use writing to communicate in an academic environment. There are two writing questions.

Question 1 is a writing task based on reading and listening. You will read a passage, listen to a lecture, and then write a response to a question about the relationship between the lecture and the reading. You have 20 minutes to plan and write your response.

Question 2 is writing based on knowledge and experience. You will write an essay in response to a question that asks you to state, explain, and support an opinion on an issue. You have 30 minutes to plan and write your essay.

Album 10, Track 16

TEST 2 — WRITING QUESTION 1 (p. 521)

Now listen to part of a lecture on the topic you just read about.

There's a well–known study that points to some of the negative aspects of same–age peer groups. This study looked at a group of 22 normal eleven–year–old boys at a summer camp. All of the boys came from similar backgrounds.

The first thing the researchers noticed was that when the boys were randomly divided into two groups, there was an increase in negative attitudes between the groups. Even though competition was discouraged, and there were joint activities with the two groups, they started to show signs of feeling competitive. For example, they named themselves the Eagles and the Rattlers, and they started to tease and belittle each other. A series of contests was then set up between the groups—baseball, skits, cabin inspections—with prizes for the winners. These contests only increased the teasing and insults between the groups.

The second important finding was that when the two groups were put back together again, and given a cooperative task, conflict was reduced. The boys were given important goals to reach together, such as fixing the broken water tank so they would all have clean drinking water. This cooperative project greatly reduced prejudice in just a few days. The boys forgot their differences and got the job done. After a week of working together, most of the conflict between the groups had disappeared.

The researchers concluded that when children of the same age are divided into groups, competition comes more naturally than cooperation. Moreover, the study suggests that without the supervision of adults and the structure of a cooperative task, the teasing, insults, and negative attitudes would probably have

become more extreme.

Summarize the points made in the lecture, being sure to explain how they challenge specific points made in the reading passage.

ALBUM 11 — TEST 3

Album 11, Track 1

TEST 3 — LISTENING SECTION DIRECTIONS (p. 536)

The Listening section measures your ability to understand conversations and lectures in English. You will hear each conversation and lecture only one time. After each conversation or lecture, you will answer some questions about it. The questions typically ask about the main idea and supporting details. Some questions ask about a speaker's purpose or attitude. Answer the questions based on what the speakers state or imply.

You may take notes while you listen. You may use your notes to help you answer the questions. Your notes will not be scored.

In some questions, you will see this icon: 🎧. This means that you will hear, but not see, part of the question.

Some questions have special directions, which appear in a gray box. Most questions are worth one point. If a question is worth more than one point, the directions will indicate how many points you can receive.

You will now begin part 1 of the Listening section.

Album 11, Track 2

TEST 3 — LISTENING PART 1
QUESTIONS 1–5 (p. 537)

Listen to a conversation between a student and a music professor.

M: Hi, Professor Casey. How are you?
W: Fine, thanks, Michael. I heard you got the scholarship for the summer program at Silverwood. Congratulations!
M: Thank you. I mean, thank you very much—I'm sure your recommendation helped me a lot.
W: I was happy to do it. So are you ready for summer?
M: I wish it was next week, but I … uh … still have a lot to do before exams. But I'm looking forward to it. I'll be studying oboe with Peter Stanley—he heads the woodwind ensemble there.
W: I know him. You couldn't ask for a better teacher. That's great. I'm really happy for you.
M: Thanks. I'm looking forward to it. He was on the panel for my interview. I'll be studying oboe with him, and also orchestra—Dr. Fine is the conductor—and I'm hoping to do the French horn, too, and maybe take up the krummhorn—it has such a cool sound. They're supposed to have an early music specialist there, but I forgot her name.
W: The krummhorn!
M: Yeah.
W: That's right. You did tell me of your interest in medieval and Renaissance music. I hope you get a chance to pursue that. There's been a revival of interest there. Well, Michael, it looks like you'll have a full plate this summer.
M: I know. I'm sure I'll be working hard! But it'll be great.

W: So what comes after that? What are your plans for next year? You'll be a sophomore, right?
M: Right. I'll be coming back here, so I'm sure I'll be seeing you. You'll still be teaching theory and composition, right?
W: Of course I will. And I look forward to having you in class.
M: What will you be doing this summer?
W: I'll be teaching Theory I and II, and coaching voice.
M: Uh–huh. You're also in a band, aren't you? I mean, outside of school?
W: Yes, I am—a jazz quintet. We do mostly standards. I play piano and sing. For me, that's fun and relaxation time.
M: My girlfriend said she heard you at the Back Alley.
W: Yes, we play there every Wednesday night. You should come hear us sometime.
M: I'd like that. I'll bring my girlfriend. She says you were really good.
W: Well then, I hope to see you some Wednesday night.
M: I'll be there. Well … I gotta go now. I'm supposed to meet my German teacher in fifteen minutes. And thanks again for the recommendation.
W: It's my pleasure, Michael. You'll make the most of it, I'm certain. Good luck!

1. What topics do the speakers mainly discuss?
2. What does the professor mean when she says this: "I know him. You couldn't ask for a better teacher."
3. Why does the professor say this: "Well, Michael, it looks like you'll have a full plate this summer."
4. What does the professor do for relaxation?
5. What can be inferred from the conversation?

Album 11, Track 3

TEST 3 — LISTENING PART 1
QUESTIONS 6–11 (p. 539)

Listen to part of a lecture in a geology class. The professor is talking about fossils.

Although the existence of fossils had been known for centuries, it wasn't until the early nineteenth century that their significance as geologic tools became evident. That was when a British engineer and canal builder made an interesting discovery. He noticed that each rock layer in the canals he worked on contained fossils that were unlike those in the rocks either above or below. Each layer held fossils of different types of ancient plants or animals. Furthermore, the engineer noticed that the characteristic fossil content of each layer could be used to determine the age of the rock. Rock layers from some areas could be matched to the layers in other areas.

The process of comparing sedimentary rocks at different locations to determine the relationship between them is known as correlation. Correlation involves comparing the rock types, the sequence of rock layers, and the fossils in different places. Correlation gives us a better understanding of geologic history. By correlating the rocks from one place to another, we've been able to develop a geologic time scale that applies to the whole planet.

This leads us to one of the most important principles in historical geology: the principle of fossil succession. The principle of fossil succession states that fossil organisms succeed one another in a definite order. Fossils show a definite succession, a progressive change from simple to complex. Thus, fossils document the evolution of life through time. Therefore, we can identify the time period of rock layers by the types of fossils we find there.

The principle of fossil succession tells us that different groups of fossils are found in different layers of rock. Fossils found at the base of a rock formation may extend part way up and then disappear. After a fossil has disappeared in a rock formation, it never reappears in a higher layer of that formation. The fossils at the bottom don't appear at the top, and those at the top don't appear at the bottom. This pattern means that fossil species existed for specific periods of the earth's history, and then they became extinct. Extinction is forever; thus, certain fossils disappeared from the record.

Fossils are the most useful means of correlating rocks of similar age in different regions. We pay particular attention to certain fossils called index fossils, such as trilobites and fishes, which point to various ages in the evolution of life. For example, we can see an Age of Trilobites—small sea creatures—quite early in the record. Then, in succession, we find an Age of Fishes, an Age of Reptiles, and an Age of Mammals. These "ages" refer to life forms that were especially plentiful during particular time periods. This same succession of organisms, always in the same order, is found in rock formations on every continent.

In addition to being important time indicators, fossils are important environmental indicators. We can learn a great deal of information about past environments by studying the fossil record. For example, when we find the fossils of certain shells, we can assume that the region was once covered by water. In the deserts of the American Southwest, fossils provide clues that the environment was much wetter in the past than it is today. We've found sandstone with ripple marks—delicate, wavy ridges that formed millions of years ago when mud and silt at the edge of a shallow sea were rippled by the action of the water. There are also numerous fossils of oyster shells and water–loving plants such as ferns.

6. What is the main idea of the lecture?
7. According to the lecture, what important contribution came from a nineteenth–century British canal builder?
8. According to the professor, how does the correlation of rocks in different places contribute to scientific understanding?
9. Why does the professor talk about the principle of fossil succession?
10. Listen again to part of the lecture. Then answer the question.
    "The fossils at the bottom don't appear at the top, and those at the top don't appear at the bottom. This pattern means that fossil species existed for specific periods of the earth's history, and then they became extinct. Extinction is forever; thus, certain fossils disappeared from the record."
    What does the professor mean by this statement: "Extinction is forever; thus, certain fossils disappeared from the record."
11. Why does the professor say this:
    "We've found sandstone with ripple marks—delicate, wavy ridges that formed millions of years ago when mud and silt at the edge of a shallow sea were rippled by the action of the water. There are also numerous fossils of oyster shells and water–loving plants such as ferns."

Album 11, Track 4

TEST 3 — LISTENING PART 1
QUESTIONS 12–17 (p. 541)

Listen to part of a talk in a biology class.

M: Until recently, we knew almost nothing about how important bees are in maintaining natural diversity. Now we know more about them. We know, for example, that honeybees are the dominant pollinators because they play a role in pollinating four out of five food crops in North America. We also know that honeybees—along with the other insects, bats, and birds that transfer pollen between flowers—all together they contribute more than ten billion dollars a year to fruit and seed production on North American farms. Pollination is one of nature's services to farmers. So think about this: if you eliminated the pollinators, it would take the food right out of our mouths. We biologists never imagined we'd see the day when wild plants or crops suffered from pollinator scarcity. But, unfortunately, that day has come. In fact, farmers in Mexico and the U.S. are suffering the worst pollinator crisis in history. So … what happened? Any ideas? Alicia?

W: Is it … um … because of natural enemies? I read something about a kind of parasite that's killed lots of bees.

M: It's true. An outbreak of parasitic mites has caused a steep decline in North American populations of honeybees. But parasites aren't the only factor.

W: What about the pesticides used on farms? All those chemicals must have an effect.

M: Most definitely, yes. Pesticides are a major factor. Both wild and domesticated bees are in serious trouble because of pesticides. In California, farm chemicals are killing around ten percent of all the honeybee colonies. Agriculture in general is part of the problem. Think about this for a minute: the North American continent is a vast collection of "nectar corridors" made up of flowering plants. These corridors stretch for thousands of miles, from Mexico to as far north as Alaska. And every year, there's an array of migratory pollinators flying north and south with the seasons, following the flowers. The migratory corridors—the flyways—are like … uh … something like a path of stepping–stones for the pollinators, with each "stone" being a collection of flowering plants. But our system of large–scale agriculture has interfered. During the past fifty years, millions of acres of desert in western Mexico and the southwestern United States have been turned into chemically intensive farms, planted with exotic grasses, creating huge stretches of flyway that are devoid of nectar–producing plants for migratory pollinators. What we have now are huge gaps between the stepping–stones—patches of plants here and there. A couple of migratory pollinators are worth noting. One is the lesser long–nosed bat, and another is the most famous pollinator—what is our most famous pollinator? Or I should say our most beautiful pollinator.

W: Oh, I know. It's the monarch butterfly!

M: The monarch butterfly—yes. Millions of monarchs from all over the U.S. and southern Canada fly south every year in late summer. The monarch is the only butterfly that returns to a specific site year after year. Unfortunately, the herbicides used on the milkweed in the Great Plains are taking a toll on monarchs, and fewer of them are reaching their winter grounds in Mexico. Another important pollinator is the long–nosed bat. These amazing animals feed on cactus flowers. What they do is, they lap up the nectar at the bottom of the flower, and then when the bat flies off to another cactus, the pollen stuck to its head is transferred to that plant's flower. But the long–nosed bat is having a tough time, too. Some desert ranchers mistake them for vampire bats, and they've tried to poison them, or dynamite the caves where they roost.

12. What is the talk mainly about?
13. According to the professor, what factors have affected pollinator populations?
14. Listen again to part of the talk. Then answer the question.
    "But our system of large–scale agriculture has interfered. During the past fifty years, millions of acres of desert in western Mexico and the southwestern United States have been turned into chemically intensive farms, planted with exotic grasses, creating huge stretches of flyway that are devoid of nectar–producing plants for migratory pollinators. What we have now are huge gaps between the stepping–stones—patches of plants here and there."
    Why does the professor say this:
    "What we have now are huge gaps between the stepping–stones—patches of plants here and there."
15. Listen again to part of the talk. Then answer the question.
    "Millions of monarchs from all over the U.S. and southern Canada fly south every year in late summer. The monarch is the only butterfly that returns to a specific site year after year. Unfortunately, the herbicides used on the milkweed in the Great Plains are taking a toll on monarchs, and fewer of them are reaching their winter grounds in Mexico."
    What can be inferred about monarch butterflies?
16. According to the professor, which pollinator feeds on the nectar of cactus flowers?
17. How does the professor support his main point about the pollinator crisis?

Album 11, Track 5

TEST 3 — LISTENING PART 2
QUESTIONS 1–5 (p. 543)

Listen to a conversation in a university bookstore.

M: Is there something I can help you with?
W: Uh, yes, as a matter of fact. I'm trying to decide what to do. I'm taking a physics class, at least I'd like to take the class, but I was put on the waiting list because it was overenrolled.
M: Okay, so you—
W: I don't know if I'll actually end up in the class, so I don't know if I should buy the book yet.
M: If you do get in the class, the registrar's office will let you know right away. As soon as there's an opening in the class, if someone drops out, then whoever's next on the waiting list gets in automatically. They'll let you know as soon as that happens. They'll send you a message by e–mail.
W: Right. That's what they told me. Anyway, I … um …

I heard this course is kind of demanding. I talked to the professor, and he said it's important to keep up with the reading, and that a lot of important concepts are covered in the first two weeks. So, to make a long story short, I think I want to buy the textbook now—assuming I will get into the class—so I can get started on the reading.
M: Okay.
W: But I … um … in case I don't get in … um … would I be able to return the book and get my money back?
M: Sure. That is, if you haven't written anything in it. We give a full refund if you return it by the end of the first week of the quarter. In the second and third weeks, we refund half of your money.
W: Really? Is that all? That seems kind of stiff. I mean, this book costs ninety dollars!
M: I know, I know. But unfortunately, that's the bookstore's policy. I know … it's kind of unfair in your situation. Sorry.
W: Only half your money back. Wow. That does make it more complicated. Now I don't know what to do. If I don't start reading the book, and then get in this class, I'm afraid I'll fall behind. But I can't afford to buy a book I don't need.
M: But if you do get in the class, you usually know that by the end of the first week … sometimes by the second week.
W: Well, then maybe I should just buy the book anyway. There are only a few copies of it left on the shelf.
M: Is that right? Thanks for letting me know. I'd better check it in back and see if we have any more. This must be a popular course.
W: It is. It's required for pre–engineering students.
M: Oh, so you want to be an engineer?
W: Yeah.
M: That's great! My brother's in engineering school. He's a teaching assistant for Doctor Kelly.
W: Really! Doctor Kelly teaches the class I want to get into! He's the best professor in the whole department.
M: It's true. I've heard other people say that too.
W: If I don't get his class this quarter, maybe next quarter I will.
M: And you'll have gotten an early start on reading the book, that is, if you buy it today.
W: Right. You talked me into it. Thanks for your help.
M: No problem. Good luck getting into the class!

1. What is the woman's problem?
2. What does the man say about students who are put on the waiting list for a class?
3. Why does the woman say this:
   "Really? Is that all? That seems kind of stiff. I mean, this book costs ninety dollars!"
4. On which two points do the speakers probably agree?
5. What will the woman probably do?

Album 11, Track 6

TEST 3 — LISTENING PART 2
QUESTIONS 6–11 (p. 545)

Listen to a discussion in an art class.

M1: Today I want to talk about the act of painting, I mean, controlling and manipulating the paint as you apply it. There are several elements that contribute to the ease or difficulty you have in controlling paint as you're brushing it on paper or canvas. One factor is the quality of the liquid material in the paint itself. Another is the nature of the surface to which it's applied. Now, think about the painting surface—the paper or canvas. When you're selecting the right surface to paint on, what should you be considering? Lisa?

W: I think you'd want to think about—if you're painting on paper—it seems the type of paper would matter. Is your paper smooth or is it coarse? That would make a difference in how well the paint would stick.

M1: Yes, that's a good point. The coarseness of the surface—and this is true for both paper and canvas—the coarseness is related to how the paint is absorbed. Liquid paints are literally taken from the brush by the coarseness of the surface. On very smooth paper, the low absorbency of the surface causes the paint to flow easily across the surface because the paper doesn't absorb it readily. On coarse papers, on the other hand, your brush drags more because the paper takes the paint thirstily from the brush. The coarse paper literally drinks up all the liquid paint. Each type of paper and each technique of painting has its own special requirements that will ease your control of the paint. Yes, Tom?

M2: I just thought of something else. Another important thing is the quality of the brush you use. I found that out the hard way because I used to always use cheap brushes. Then I realized that cheaper brushes just don't apply the paint very well. Some of my brushes would just plop down all the paint at once and leave a big blob in one place. Now I have better brushes. They're expensive, but it's worth it.

M1: Tom, you learned a lesson that all artists learn sooner or later. A good brush makes all the difference in the world. All painters—I mean you should all have a supply of the highest–grade brushes you can find. Brushes are one part of your equipment where you shouldn't skimp because poor–quality brushes are a severe handicap to good painting.

W: The brushes sold in the university bookstore, are they, uh, in your opinion, are they high quality?

M1: Yes. All the brushes in our bookstore are very good.

W: But how can you tell that? Can you tell a brush is good by looking? Or is it the price that tells you?

M1: You can tell by the brush's appearance. A high–quality oil painting brush is made from the best grades of bleached animal hair: hogs' bristles. You can tell if a brush is good by looking closely at the tips of the hairs. Of course, the quality of the brush will also be reflected in the price. The tip of a high–quality paintbrush is made up of the natural split ends of the hair or bristle of a hog. The tips are never cut or trimmed. All shaping and trimming is done at the root end, where the bristles are attached to the handle. Hog–bristle brushes hold the paint in the hair's split ends. Poor quality brushes lose their hair, or they don't apply paint properly, as Tom pointed out. Sometimes brush companies trim the bristles excessively so the brush looks good, but without split ends, the brush won't pick up and place paint properly. Bristle brushes come in three major shapes: rounds, flats, and brights. The shape, of course, refers to the shape of the bristles—whether the bristles are round—arranged in a circle—or flat—arranged in a flat line. Flat brushes are more versatile than round ones, so the flats are much more popular. The third type of brush, the bright, is sometimes confused with the flat brush because the bristles are actually flat, but much shorter. A bright is essentially a shorter version of a flat, with the bristles arranged in a flat line. The brights are designed to give you a little more control, especially with thicker paints. They're the most effective brushes for applying oil paints that have a consistency like butter.

6. What is the discussion mainly about?
7. According to the discussion, what factors affect an artist's ability to control the paint?
8. Listen again to part of the discussion. Then answer the question.
   "On very smooth paper, the low absorbency of the surface causes the paint to flow easily across the surface because the paper doesn't absorb it readily. On coarse papers, on the other hand, your brush drags more because the paper takes the paint thirstily from the brush. The coarse paper literally drinks up all the liquid paint."
   What does the professor imply about the paper on which paint is applied?
9. Why does one of the students say this:
   "Some of my brushes would just plop down all the paint at once and leave a big blob in one place. Now I have better brushes. They're expensive, but it's worth it."
10. According to the professor, what is one sign of a high–quality brush for oil painting?
11. In discussing the three types of brushes, how does the professor distinguish them?

Album 11, Track 7

TEST 3 — LISTENING PART 2
QUESTIONS 12–17 (p. 547)

Listen to a lecture in a United States history class.

The battle at Antietam Creek in 1862 was the bloodiest twenty–four hours of the Civil War. Nearly 8,000 men lost their lives and another 15,000 were severely wounded. No single day in American history has been as tragic. Antietam was memorable in another way, too—it saw the advent of the war photographer.

The best known pictorial records of the Civil War are the photographs commissioned by Mathew Brady, a leading portrait photographer of the time. Brady owned studios in New York and in Washington, and was known for his portraits of political leaders and celebrities. At the outbreak of the Civil War, he turned his attention to the conflict. He wanted to document the war on a grand scale, so he hired twenty photographers and sent them into the field with the troops. The battlefield carried dangers and financial risks, but Brady was persistent.

Brady himself did not actually shoot many of the photographs that bore his name. His company of photographers took the vast majority of the pictures—images of camp life, artillery, fortifications, railroads, bridges, battlefields, officers, and ordinary soldiers. Brady was more of a project manager. He spent his time supervising his photographers, preserving their negatives, and buying negatives from other photographers.

Two days after the battle at Antietam, two photographers from Brady's New York gallery took a series of photographs that ushered in a new era in the visual documentation of war. This was the first time that cameras had been allowed near the action before the fallen bodies of the dead were removed. Within a month of the battle, the images of battlefield corpses from Antietam were on display at Brady's gallery in New York. A sign on the door said simply, "The Dead of Antietam." America was shocked. The exhibition marked the first time most people had ever seen the carnage of the war. The photographs had a sensational impact, opening people's eyes as no woodcuts or lithographs had ever done.

The New York Times wrote, "If Mr. Brady has not brought bodies and laid them in our door–yards, he has done something very like it." Thousands of people, especially mothers and wives of men serving in the Union forces, flocked to look at these first dramatic images of death and destruction. Suddenly the battlefield was no longer comfortably distant—the camera was bringing it closer, erasing romantic notions about war.

Mathew Brady's work was the first instance of the comprehensive photo–documentation of a war—the Civil War—which as a result became the first media war. Photography had come of age, although it was still a relatively new technology with several limitations. For example, the exposure time of the camera was slow, and negatives had to be prepared minutes before a shot and developed immediately afterwards. This meant that it was not possible for photographers to take action pictures. They were limited to taking pictures of the battlefield after the fighting was over. Another limitation was that newspapers couldn't yet reproduce photographs. They could print only artists' drawings of the scene. Nevertheless, photography made a huge impact, and media coverage of war—and public opinion about war—would never be the same again.

12. What is the main idea of the lecture?
13. Listen again to part of the lecture. Then answer the question.
    "The battle at Antietam Creek in 1862 was the bloodiest twenty–four hours of the Civil War. Nearly 8,000 men lost their lives and another 15,000 were severely wounded. No single day in American history has been as tragic."
    What does the professor mean by this statement:
    "No single day in American history has been as tragic."
14. Who was Mathew Brady?
15. Listen again to part of the lecture. Then answer the question.
    "Within a month of the battle, the images of battlefield corpses from Antietam were on display at Brady's gallery in New York. A sign on the door said simply, 'The Dead of Antietam.' America was shocked. The exhibition marked the first time most people had ever seen the carnage of the war. The photographs had a sensational impact, opening people's eyes as no woodcuts or lithographs had ever done."
    Why does the professor say this:
    "The photographs had a sensational impact, opening people's eyes as no woodcuts or lithographs had ever done."
16. What were some of the limitations of photography during the Civil War?
17. What does the professor imply about Mathew Brady?

Album 11, Track 8

TEST 3 — SPEAKING SECTION DIRECTIONS (p. 549)

The Speaking section measures your ability to speak in English about a variety of topics. There are six questions in this section.

In questions 1 and 2, you will speak about familiar topics. Your responses will be scored on your ability to speak clearly and coherently about the topics.

In questions 3 and 4, you will first read a short text and then listen to a talk on the same topic. You will then be asked a question about what you have read and heard. You will need to combine appropriate information from the text and the talk to provide a complete answer to the question. Your responses will be scored on your ability to speak clearly and coherently and on your ability to accurately convey information about what you have read and heard.

In questions 5 and 6, you will listen to part of a conversation or lecture. You will then be asked a question about what you have heard. Your responses will be scored on your ability to speak clearly and coherently and on your ability to accurately convey information about what you have heard.

You may take notes while you read and while you listen to the conversations and lectures. You may use your notes to help prepare your responses.

Album 11, Track 9

TEST 3 — SPEAKING QUESTION 1 (p. 550)

Describe an event such as a holiday or other occasion that you enjoy celebrating. Explain why the event is significant to you. Include details and examples to support your explanation.

Album 11, Track 10

TEST 3 — SPEAKING QUESTION 2 (p. 550)

Some people keep in touch with friends and family by letter or e–mail. Others keep in touch by telephone. Which method do you prefer to use, and why? Include details and examples in your explanation.

Album 11, Track 11

TEST 3 — SPEAKING QUESTION 3 (p. 551)

Now listen to two students as they talk about the required discussion section.

W: What do you think of the new requirement? Starting next quarter, we need a discussion section for every lecture course we take.
M: It sounds like something I'm okay with.
W: Oh, I think it's just a bother. We already have three hours of lecture every week.
M: But that's not enough. The professor never covers everything we need to know for the examination. And there's hardly any time to ask questions.
W: Oh, but you can ask the professor questions during office hours.

M: Have you ever actually tried to do that? Some professors are never in their office, and the ones who are, well … they're usually too busy to talk to students. I like the idea of a discussion section. It gives us more of a chance to talk to the teacher, and other students too. Lecture classes are so big that you never get to know your classmates. Discussion classes have only around 20 or 25 people, and that's really nice. It's a lot more personal and informal, and you can learn so much more. Besides, it's easy to get a high grade in the discussion section.

The man expresses his opinion about the required discussion section. State his opinion and explain the reasons he gives for holding that opinion.

Album 11, Track 12

TEST 3 — SPEAKING QUESTION 4 (p. 552)

Now listen to part of a talk in a health class.

When too much water is lost from the body and not replaced, dehydration develops. This can happen more easily than you think. It happened to a patient in the clinic yesterday.

When the body loses fluid, we feel thirsty. If we don't drink fluid or, as in the case of many elderly people, we fail to perceive the thirst message, the symptoms of dehydration can move quickly from thirst to weakness and exhaustion. This is what happened to our patient yesterday, and she wasn't even elderly. She was a busy professional woman in her thirties. She was having a very hectic day and simply forgot to drink. She was too distracted by all her responsibilities to notice that she was thirsty. And then she skipped lunch. Late in the afternoon, she became aware that she didn't feel well, but she ignored the symptom and kept going.

By the time a co–worker brought her into the clinic, the woman felt weak and confused. She had difficulty walking without assistance. Her heart rate was fast and her blood pressure low. She was in serious trouble. But once we put her on intravenous fluids, her condition quickly improved. We found no other serious problem, so she was able to go home after a few hours.

Explain dehydration and how the example given by the professor illustrates the condition.

Album 11, Track 13

TEST 3 — SPEAKING QUESTION 5 (p. 553)

Listen to a conversation between a student and a college officer.

M: May I help you?
W: I hope so. I need to get an official copy of my transcript, but it seems I can't do that because there's an unpaid charge in my student account. The charge is a mistake—it's for a window my roommate broke in our dormitory room. Somehow the charge ended up on my account instead of hers. The problem is, I need my transcript right away because I'm applying for a scholarship.
M: I see. Well, the fastest thing would be for you to just pay the charge to clear your account, and then

your roommate pay you back. Or you could send your roommate in to pay it.
W: Can't you just remove the charge from my account? After all, it's the university's mistake.
M: I can't do that until I get approval from the Housing Office, and that could take a while. But here's what you can do. Go down the hall right now and talk to the dean's secretary. Tell her what you've told me. She might let us release your transcript now, and then we can worry about the problem on your account later.

Briefly summarize the problem the speakers are discussing. Then state which solution you would recommend. Explain the reasons for your recommendation.

Album 11, Track 14

TEST 3 — SPEAKING QUESTION 6 (p. 553)

Listen to part of a lecture in a theater class.

There are three characteristics of theater that define it as a separate art. First, unlike other arts, which can deal with any subject you can imagine, the subject of theater is always human beings. This is true even when the performers play animals or objects. The focus of drama is on human experiences, such as love, war, friendship, power, madness, and death. Different plays emphasize different themes, but the concerns are always human.

Second, theater is universal. By that, I mean there's an impulse toward creating theater in every society. This isn't surprising, considering the human–centered quality of theater. In every culture, we find rituals, ceremonies, and celebrations that include elements of theater. At different times in different places, these ceremonies developed into a separate art of theater. And everywhere there is theater, it has certain essential qualities: a story is presented by performers to an audience.

The third characteristic of theater is its transitory nature. A performance changes from moment to moment, but it's always in the present tense, and each moment is a direct, immediate adventure for the audience. Theater's transitory nature is a quality it shares with music and dance, and sets it apart from literature and the visual arts. A novel or a painting is a fixed object; it exists as a finished product. Theater, on the other hand, is not an object but an event. Theater is an experience created by a series of sights, sounds, and impressions.

Using points and details from the lecture, explain the characteristics of theater that define it as a separate art.

Album 11, Track 15

TEST 3 — WRITING SECTION DIRECTIONS (p. 554)

The Writing section measures your ability to use writing to communicate in an academic environment. There are two writing questions.

Question 1 is a writing task based on reading and listening. You will read a passage, listen to a lecture, and then write a response to a question about the relationship between the lecture and the reading. You have 20 minutes to plan and write your response.

Question 2 is writing based on knowledge and experience. You will write an essay in response to a question that asks you to state, explain, and support an opinion on an issue. You have 30 minutes to plan and write your essay.

Album 11, Track 16

TEST 3 — WRITING QUESTION 1 (p. 555)

Now listen to part of a lecture on the topic you just read about.

Unfortunately, a big problem in the dog industry is that too many breeders lack both an understanding of science and a sense of ethics. These so–called "backyard breeders" think they can just raise dogs in their backyard and make a little money. Too often, these unqualified breeders sell puppies to unsuspecting people, who then end up with a problem dog. Backyard breeders are more concerned with profit than with animal welfare. In short, they exploit animals for profit.

Another problem is that the focus on breed purity leads to inbreeding. In fact, it's the breed registries that encourage inbreeding, thereby contributing to the spread of genetic disorders. Inbreeding is the overuse of one male dog with desirable traits, in an attempt to improve the breed. However, the dog may carry the gene for a harmful trait. Because inbreeding limits the gene pool, the harmful genes become widespread. This is why purebred dogs have so many genetic disorders, such as hip and bone problems, heart conditions, deafness, and so on.

Still another problem with the culture of dog breeding is the proliferation of "puppy mills"—businesses that mass–produce the more popular breeds. Puppy mills produce an overpopulation of dogs, many of them raised in conditions that cause health and behavior problems. This means more unwanted dogs. Kennel clubs and registries add to the problem by encouraging the breeding of purebred dogs, when millions of mixed–breed dogs are killed every year in animal shelters. Popular culture plays a role too. For example, after the film *101 Dalmatians*, hundreds of dalmatians were dumped in shelters, once the owners realized the dogs were not like the cute little puppies in the movie.

Summarize the points made in the lecture, being sure to explain how they contradict specific points made in the reading passage.

ALBUM 12 — TEST 4

Album 12, Track 1

TEST 4 — LISTENING SECTION DIRECTIONS (p. 570)

The Listening section measures your ability to understand conversations and lectures in English. You will hear each conversation and lecture only one time. After each conversation or lecture, you will answer some questions about it. The questions typically ask about the main idea and supporting details. Some questions ask about a speaker's purpose or attitude. Answer the questions based on what the speakers state or imply.

You may take notes while you listen. You may use your notes to help you answer the questions. Your notes will not be scored.

In some questions, you will see this icon: 🎧. This means that you will hear, but not see, part of the question.

Some questions have special directions, which appear in a gray box. Most questions are worth one point. If a question is worth more than one point, the directions will indicate how many points you can receive.

You will now begin part 1 of the Listening section.

Album 12, Track 2

TEST 4 — LISTENING PART 1
QUESTIONS 1–5 (p. 571)

Listen to a conversation in a university housing office.

M: Hi. Um … I live in Tower One … and I was … um … I'd kind of like to live in a smaller building. I'm thinking of moving next semester.

W: Do you know about the villages? They're on the other side of campus from the towers.

M: Uh huh. I've seen them—I mean, from the outside. What's the rent like? I mean, compared to the towers.

W: The rent depends on the situation, like how many people are in the suite.

M: Suite? What's that?

W: It's a unit for either four, six, or eight people. They're like apartments.

M: Oh. Aren't there any private rooms?

W: No, not in the villages. It's all suites. The bedrooms are for two people—that part's kind of like in the dormitories. You have to share a bedroom with another student. The suites have two to four bedrooms, one or two bathrooms, and a kitchen with a stove and a microwave, and a full refrigerator. Some of them also have a big living room.

M: Oh, that sounds kind of nice. So … what's the rent like?

W: I've just been checking in the computer. It looks like there's going to be a couple of openings next semester, but there's also a waiting list with about twenty–something people on it.

M: Oh.

W: Yeah. A lot of people want to live in the villages. I lived there for two years myself, before I moved to a house off campus.

M: Uh huh. So what is the rent?

W: Oh, sorry. Um … Okay, the buildings in Swanson Village all have four–person suites. Those are 900 dollars a semester.

W: Wow.

M: And the other villages … let me see … they're anywhere from eight–fifty to a thousand. It depends. The six– and eight–person units are usually a little less. The ones with living rooms are a little more.

M: Wow. That's more than I expected.

W: The cheaper ones are less than the dorms in the towers.

M: Yeah, but I was hoping it'd be a lot less. But still … I'd kind of like to get out of the towers. Um … how do I get on the waiting list?

W: I can add your name now, if you like.

M: Okay. It's Ian Jacobs.

W: Ian Jacobs. Okay, Ian, I've added you to the waiting list. What we'll do is send you a notice by e–mail if something opens up in the villages. Your name is uh … number twenty–seven on the list.

M: Number twenty–seven … oh … wow.

W: You'd be surprised. Sometimes people change their minds, so people further down the list get a chance. You'll get in the villages eventually, maybe next semester.

M: Okay. Thanks for your help.

W: No problem. Have a nice day!

1. What is the purpose of the conversation?
2. What are some features of the suites in the villages?
3. Listen again to part of the conversation. Then answer the question.
   "Oh, that sounds kind of nice. So … what's the rent like?"
   "I've just been checking in the computer. It looks like there's going to be a couple of openings next semester, but there's also a waiting list with about twenty–something people on it."
   "Oh."
   "Yeah. A lot of people want to live in the villages. I lived there for two years myself, before I moved to a house off campus."
   "Uh huh. So what is the rent?"
   "Oh, sorry."
   Why does the woman say this:
   "Oh, sorry."
4. What does the man think of the cost of rent in the villages?
5. Listen again to part of the conversation. Then answer the question.
   "Ian Jacobs. Okay, Ian, I've added you to the waiting list. What we'll do is send you a notice by e–mail if something opens up in the villages. Your name is uh … number twenty–seven on the list."
   "Number twenty–seven … oh … wow."
   Select the sentence that best expresses how the man probably feels.

Album 12, Track 3

TEST 4 — LISTENING PART 1
QUESTIONS 6–11 (p. 573)

Listen to a lecture in a world history class.

For thousands of years, early peoples found their food in nature. They hunted and fished, and ate plants and fruits that grew wild. What led these people to invent agriculture, a completely different way of life?

We know that ancient people changed from hunters and gatherers to farmers when they began to domesticate wild plants and animals. The first farmers on each continent did not have other farmers to observe, so they could not have chosen farming consciously. However, once agriculture had started in one part of a continent, neighboring people could see the result and make the conscious decision to farm.

We have no written records about prehistoric agriculture in the Americas, and very few artifacts or physical clues. We do have evidence that early people used sharp sticks to dig furrows for planting seeds. Those sticks were probably the first agricultural tools. We think the first Americans began to grow crops around ten thousand years ago. The evidence comes from a cave in Mexico, where cultivated squash seeds have been found. These seeds are evidence of the early domestication of plants.

Hunting–gathering people selected wild plants for domestication for various reasons. Some plants had tasty fruit, some had fleshy or seedless fruit, and some had fruit with oily or tasty seeds. In a certain part of prehistoric Mexico, there was a kind of squash that grew in abundance on hillsides. The flesh of this squash was bitter, so the people didn't eat it, but the seeds were tasty and nourishing, and the people liked to gather them. The people brought the squash seeds back to their camp. As they ate the seeds, some seeds fell to the ground all around the camp. Later, some of these seeds germinated and produced new plants. Thus, the hunter–gatherers became farmers sort of by accident. It was probably not a conscious decision to plant squash in their camp, yet that was the result.

Now the people had a wild garden of squash plants at their campsite. This was fortunate, so they started to take more of an interest in the plants. They tried to protect the plants in practical ways. They cut back and cleared out the less healthy–looking plants. They pulled up other types of plants that were weeds. They gave the plants water during long dry spells. Eventually, the people realized that seeds grew better when they were planted in earth that was turned over. So they began to scratch the earth with a digging stick and to plant seeds systematically in rows. They realized that a tilled, watered, weeded garden provided larger, better, more numerous squash plants than those that grew naturally on a dry hillside. Thus, with a series of conscious decisions, the people started cultivating a new breed of squash plants. Because of their success with squash, they started to experiment with other kinds of plants. In time, they built a fence around the garden to protect it from animals. At this point, agriculture was firmly established in their culture.

Of course, all of this didn't happen overnight. The process probably took thousands of years. Different peoples acquired agriculture at different times in prehistory. In some areas, crops and agricultural technology spread as ancient peoples conquered and traded with one another. In other places, agricultural technology developed in isolation. Even so, it's very likely that the change from a hunting–gathering society to an agricultural society followed a similar pattern in different regions of the world.

6. What is the main purpose of the lecture?
7. What is probably true about the origins of agriculture?
8. According to the professor, which of the following occurred as plants were first being domesticated?
9. Why did the people begin to use digging sticks?
10. Listen again to part of the lecture. Then answer the question.
    "Because of their success with squash, they started to experiment with other kinds of plants. In time, they built a fence around the garden to protect it from animals. At this point, agriculture was firmly established in their culture. Of course, all of this didn't happen overnight."
    Why does the professor say this:
    "Of course, all of this didn't happen overnight."
11. What point does the professor make about the transition from hunting–gathering to agriculture?

Album 12, Track 4

TEST 4 — LISTENING PART 1
QUESTIONS 12–17 (p. 575)

Listen to a discussion in a biology class.

W1: In our last meeting we discussed how science is a process. Science involves formation of a hypothesis and the testing of that hypothesis through observation and experimentation. We use this process to answer our questions about nature. Today we'll focus on science and technology. Technology, especially in the form of new instruments, can extend our ability to observe and measure natural phenomena. Technology enables us to work on questions that were previously unapproachable. In turn, technology often applies the discoveries of science. Can anyone think of an example of technology that applies scientific knowledge? Yes, Rosa?

W2: The electron microscope. The people who invented the electron microscope used electromagnetic theory from physics.

W1: Yes. The electron microscope is an excellent example of applied science. What else is there?

M1: Well, there are all sorts of computer models, and there's DNA technology, which is used in forensic science, and there's genetic engineering used in agriculture. Computer models and genetic engineering are applied science.

W1: Yes, those are all good examples of technology that applies scientific knowledge. A lot of technology was developed as a direct result of the scientific process. On the other hand, not all technology can be described as applied science. In fact, technology came before science in human prehistory. In prehistoric times, technology was driven by inventive humans who built tools, made pottery, designed musical instruments, and so on, all without science— that is, without people necessarily understanding why their inventions worked.

M2: Technology might not be scientific, but I think technology mostly helps us. It helps us cure diseases so people can live longer. It lets us produce more food than ever before. We can go places and build in places where we never could before.

W1: But look at the environmental consequences, like acid rain and pollution.

M1: Not to mention nuclear accidents, toxic waste, global warming, and extinction of species—technology can't save us from ourselves.

W1: You're all raising some very important issues. Technology has improved our standard of living in many ways. It's kept us healthier and enabled us to live longer lives. It's enabled the human population to grow by a factor of ten in just a few centuries. But technology is a double–edged sword. You've just mentioned some of the environmental repercussions. Technology does have to be watched closely, monitored, and even criticized. Science and technology are partners. Science can help us identify problems and provide insight about what course of action may prevent further damage. But solutions to these problems have as much to do with politics, economics, and culture as they do with science and technology.

M1: I think scientists have a responsibility to educate politicians and the public about the consequences of certain technologies—such as genetic engineering. This is why I'm a science major now, but I've decided to get a master's degree in public policy.

W1: And a decision like that is important. Scientists should try to influence how technology applies the discoveries of science. The relationship between science and technology is very important. It's a relationship that is crucial to our study of life.

12. What is the discussion mainly about?
13. What does the electron microscope provide an example of?
14. Why does the professor mention tools, pottery, and musical instruments?
15. Why does one of the students say this:
    "Not to mention nuclear accidents, toxic waste, global warming, and extinction of species—technology can't save us from ourselves."
16. What does the professor mean by this statement:
    "But technology is a double–edged sword."
17. Why does one of the students plan to get a master's degree in public policy?

Album 12, Track 5

TEST 4 — LISTENING PART 2
QUESTIONS 1–5 (p. 577)

Listen to a conversation between a student and a professor.

W: Professor Ellsbury? There's something I need to talk to you about.

M: Why, hello, Sophie. Come in. How can I help you?

W: I'm, uh, I have to go back home and stay with my parents for a few weeks or maybe longer.

M: Oh?

W: Yeah, my mother is having surgery next week, and it will be a long recovery. It might take several weeks for her to recover enough to help my father with his business. So I have to help my mom and also do the accounting for my dad's business.

M: I see. Oh, this does make it tough for you. How do you plan to get your coursework done?

W: Uh, that's what I need to talk to you about. My folks really need me at home for about a month. I, uh, I really want to be there to help out.

M: Of course. I understand. Your family needs you. But you're going to miss several lectures.

W: I'll watch the online versions of your lectures. I want to finish the course and get credit. So I need to ask you for an extension on my project.

M: Well, I know you've already put a lot of work into your project, but won't you be spending all your time with your parents?

W: Yes, but I know I can finish my research while I'm there. And since you've already approved my project plan, couldn't I just get an extension on the due date?

M: Hmm. Okay. Here's what we can do. There are only three weeks left in the quarter. I suggest that you take a grade of Incomplete. That would give you two months after the end of the quarter to complete your project. That would give you until… let's see, ah, it would be… you would have until the middle of February. Then, if everything is satisfactory, you would receive a final grade for the course. However, your grade won't show up in your record until the end of winter quarter.

W: That would be great. I'm sure I could finish my project by February. But I might need to email you sometimes, if I have questions or need help. Would that be all right?

M: Of course. Please do. I'll want to know how you're doing.

W: Okay.

M: When do you leave for home?

W: Not till Sunday. I'll be in class for the rest of the week, and I've got to take a test for another class on Saturday.

M: Well, Sophie, we'll miss having you in class. But you're a good student, and I have confidence in you.

W: Thank you. I wish I didn't have to leave, but I have no choice.

M: Sure. I understand. I hope everything goes well with your mother.

W: I hope so too. And thanks, professor.

M: No problem. See you this afternoon, right?

W: Right. See you in class.

1. Why does the student go to see the professor?
2. Why does the professor say this:
   "I see. Oh, this does make it tough for you. How do you plan to get your coursework done?"
3. What does the student say she will do to complete the course?
4. What does the professor suggest the student do?
5. What does the professor imply when he says this:
   "Well, Sophie, we'll miss having you in class. But you're a good student, and I have confidence in you."

Album 12, Track 6

Test 4 — Listening Part 2
Questions 6–11 (p. 579)

Listen to a lecture in a Canadian studies class. The professor is talking about art.

The painter Arthur Lismer wrote, "Most creative people, whether in painting, writing or music, began to have a guilty feeling that Canada was as yet unwritten, unpainted, unsung." According to Lismer, there was a job to be done, and so a generation of artists set out to create a school of painting that would record the Canadian scene and reinforce a distinctive Canadian identity. Calling themselves the Group of Seven, they proclaimed that—quote, "Art must grow and flower in the land before the country will be a real home for its people."

The Group's origins date back to the 1911 showing in Toronto of the painting "At the Edge of the Maple Wood" by A.Y. Jackson of Montreal. This painting's vibrant color and texture made a deep impression on local artists. They persuaded Jackson to come to Toronto and share a studio with them. Jackson began to accompany another painter, Tom Thomson, on sketching trips to Algonquin Park, north of the city.

Several of the artists worked at the same Toronto commercial design firm, and it was here that they met and discovered their common artistic interests. After work, they socialized together at the Arts and Letters Club. They talked about finding a new direction for Canadian art, a distinctly Canadian style of painting. It was a romantic quest—mainly fueled by the restless spirit of Tom Thomson, who led the others to the Canadian wilderness to sketch and paint.

A patron gave the artists the famous Studio Building in Toronto. It was here that Thomson did some of his finest paintings from sketches made in the wild. Among them was "The Jack Pine," one of the nation's best-loved pictures. But then, suddenly and tragically, Thomson died in 1917—drowning in a canoe accident—shocking his fellow painters and Canadian art lovers.

The other artists continued their sketching trips to the vast wilderness of northern Ontario. It was there that they found inspiration for some of their greatest paintings. Each artist had his own vision and his own technique, but they all captured the essence of wilderness Canada—a bleak, somber, incredibly beautiful landscape of rock outcroppings, storm-driven lakes, and jack pine trees—a land totally uninhabited by people.

After a 1919 trip to the wilderness, the artists decided to organize an exhibition and to formally call themselves the Group of Seven. The seven founding artists were Jackson, Lismer, Harris, MacDonald, Varley, Johnston, and Carmichael.

Their 1920 exhibition was an important moment in Canadian art. It proclaimed that Canadian art must be inspired by Canada itself. However, the initial response was less than favorable. Several major art critics ignored the show, while others called the paintings crude and barbaric. Yet, when British critics praised the Group's distinctly Canadian vision, the Canadian public took another look. Later exhibitions drew increasing acceptance for the Group's work, establishing them as the "national school." Before long, they were the most influential painters in the country, and several of their paintings have become icons of Canada.

A.Y. Jackson was influential for his analysis of light and shadow. Arthur Lismer's work has an intensity all its own—particularly his painting of the "Canadian Jungle," the violently colored forest in the fall. Lawren Harris went further than the rest in simplifying the forms of nature into sculptural shapes, organizing an entire scene into a single, unified image, and eventually into abstraction.

6. Which of the following best describes the organization of the lecture?
7. What is the professor's point of view concerning the Group of Seven?
8. Listen again to part of the lecture. Then answer the question.
   "After work, they socialized together at the Arts and Letters Club. They talked about finding a new direction for Canadian art, a distinctly Canadian style of painting. It was a romantic quest—mainly fueled by the restless

spirit of Tom Thomson, who led the others to the Canadian wilderness to sketch and paint."

Why does the professor say this:

"It was a romantic quest—mainly fueled by the restless spirit of Tom Thomson, who led the others to the Canadian wilderness to sketch and paint."

9. What subjects did the Group of Seven paint?

10. What does the professor mean by this statement:
"Before long, they were the most influential painters in the country, and several of their paintings have become icons of Canada."

11. Listen again to part of the lecture. Then answer the question.
"A.Y. Jackson was influential for his analysis of light and shadow. Arthur Lismer's work has an intensity all its own—particularly his painting of the "Canadian Jungle," the violently colored forest in the fall. Lawren Harris went further than the rest in simplifying the forms of nature into sculptural shapes, organizing an entire scene into a single, unified image, and eventually into abstraction."

What can be concluded about the Group of Seven's style of painting?

Album 12, Track 7

TEST 4 — LISTENING PART 2
QUESTIONS 12–17 (p. 581)

Listen to a discussion in an ecology class. The class is studying the hydrologic cycle.

W1: Water is essential for life, and in parts of the world, it's a precious commodity. Water continuously circulates from the ocean to the atmosphere, to the land, and back to the ocean, providing us with a renewable supply of purified water. This complex cycle—known as the hydrologic cycle—balances the amount of water in the ocean, in the atmosphere, and on the land. We get our understanding of how the cycle operates from research in climatology and hydrology. So … who can tell me what climatology is?

M: It's the study of climate … and … uh … the causes and effects of different climates.

W1: That right. And what is hydrology? Sarah?

W2: Well, "hydro" means "water," so it's something to do with water … like the study of water.

W1: Yes, the prefix "hydro" does refer to water. The hydrologic cycle is the water cycle. And hydrology is the study of the water—the distribution and effect of the water—on the earth's surface and in the soil and layers of rock. Think of climatology as the atmospheric phase, and hydrology as the land phase of the water cycle. Climatologists study the role of solar energy in the cycle. They're mainly concerned with the atmospheric phase of the cycle—how solar energy drives the cycle through the … uh … processes of evaporation, atmospheric circulation, and precipitation. Water is continuously absorbed into the atmosphere as vapor—evaporation—and returned to the earth as rain, hail, or snow—precipitation. The amount of water evaporating from oceans exceeds precipitation over oceans, and the excess water vapor is moved by wind to the land.
The land phase of the cycle is the concern of hydrologists. Hydrologists study the vast quantities of water in the land phase of the cycle, how water moves over and through the land, and how it's stored on or within the earth. Over land surfaces—of the precipitation that falls over land, small amounts evaporate while still in the air and … uh … reenter the atmosphere directly. The rest of it reaches the surface of the land. The water that falls to earth is stored on the surface in lakes, or it penetrates the surface, or it runs off over the surface and flows in rivers to the ocean. Some of the water is stored temporarily in the upper soil layers and used later by trees and plants. When it rains—yes?

M: I was … um … I wondered if that makes trees and plants part of the hydrologic cycle. I mean, they take in water, and the water moves through them, and then later on … um … the water evaporates from their leaves.

W1: I'm glad you mentioned that, Justin. Plants do play an important role in the land phase of the cycle and are therefore part of the cycle. Trees and plants circulate and store water—they draw it up through their roots and return it to the atmosphere through their leaves during evapotranspiration.
When it rains, if the soil is already saturated, water will seep downward through the upper soil layers, and possibly reach the water table. When it reaches the water table, it passes into groundwater storage. Most of the groundwater later returns to the surface, either as springs or as stream flow, supplying water to plants. Eventually, all of the water falling on land makes its way back to the ocean. The movement of water from land to the ocean is called runoff. Runoff and groundwater together balance the amount of water that moves from the ocean to the land. Every molecule of water in the natural system eventually circulates through the hydrologic cycle. Tremendous quantities of water are cycled annually. And, as Justin pointed out, living organisms—plants, and animals as well—are also part of the cycle, since water is a large part of the mass of most organisms. Living organisms store and use water, since water is the solvent for most biological reactions.

12. What is the hydrologic cycle?
13. Which of the following statements describes climatology?
14. What do hydrologists mainly study?
15. What happens to water that falls to the earth as precipitation?
16. Why does the professor say this:
"Eventually, all of the water falling on land makes its way back to the ocean. The movement of water from land to the ocean is called runoff. Runoff and groundwater together balance the amount of water that moves from the ocean to the land."
17. What can be inferred about plants in the hydrologic cycle?

AUDIO SCRIPTS

Album 12, Track 8

Test 4 — Speaking Section Directions (p. 583)

The Speaking section measures your ability to speak in English about a variety of topics. There are six questions in this section.

In questions 1 and 2, you will speak about familiar topics. Your responses will be scored on your ability to speak clearly and coherently about the topics.

In questions 3 and 4, you will first read a short text and then listen to a talk on the same topic. You will then be asked a question about what you have read and heard. You will need to combine appropriate information from the text and the talk to provide a complete answer to the question. Your responses will be scored on your ability to speak clearly and coherently and on your ability to accurately convey information about what you have read and heard.

In questions 5 and 6, you will listen to part of a conversation or lecture. You will then be asked a question about what you have heard. Your responses will be scored on your ability to speak clearly and coherently and on your ability to accurately convey information about what you have heard.

You may take notes while you read and while you listen to the conversations and lectures. You may use your notes to help prepare your responses.

Album 12, Track 9

Test 4 — Speaking Question 1 (p. 584)

What foreign country would you like to visit? Choose a country and explain why you would like to go there. Include details and examples to support your explanation.

Album 12, Track 10

Test 4 — Speaking Question 2 (p. 584)

In some schools, teachers decide what classes students must take. Other schools allow students to select their own classes. Which system do you think is better and why? Include details and examples in your explanation.

Album 12, Track 11

Test 4 — Speaking Question 3 (p. 585)

Listen to two students as they discuss the swimming pool hours.

M: What do you think about the new pool hours?
W: It doesn't affect me much, since I only swim on weekends, and those times aren't changing. What about you?
M: Well, it's kind of a big change to the pool schedule. They're completely eliminating times in the late afternoon, after three o'clock. That's when I like to swim—right after my last class.
W: It looks like they're adding more swimming classes in the afternoon and evening.
M: Yeah, but I don't see why they have to close the pool to everyone else. A class doesn't usually take up the whole pool. I don't see why they can't leave half of the pool open for people who just want to swim laps. It's not fair to just take away our pool time like this. The least they could do is extend the morning hours. They should open the pool at seven instead of nine in the morning. That would make up for the time they cut in the afternoon.
W: You would go swimming at seven o'clock in the morning?
M: Sure. I'm a morning person—and what a way to start the day!

The man expresses his opinion about the change in swimming pool hours. State his opinion and explain the reasons he gives for holding that opinion.

Album 12, Track 12

Test 4 — Speaking Question 4 (p. 586)

Now listen to part of a lecture in a sociology class.

Let me tell you about an interesting study that took place in hotels. If you've stayed in a hotel recently, you've probably noticed a sign in the bathroom asking you to help save the environment by reusing your towels. You see, when towels are washed every day, a large hotel uses a lot of water and energy. So, many hotels are trying to reduce their costs and also help the environment.

In the study, researchers created two different signs for the bathrooms. Some rooms got a sign with a standard "green" message about saving the environment. Other rooms got a sign telling guests that most of their fellow guests had reused their towels.

And what do you think happened?

Well, the results confirmed what experts in persuasion had long believed. For towel reuse in hotels, social pressure beats "green" values. The social–norm message was about 25 percent more effective than the environmental message.

The results were even more remarkable in a follow–up study that tested different variations on the social–norm message. Telling guests that others who had stayed in the same room had reused their towels worked better than saying that other guests at the same hotel had done so, even though all the rooms were alike.

Use the examples from the lecture to explain how social norms influence human behavior.

Album 12, Track 13

Test 4 — Speaking Question 5 (p. 587)

Listen to a conversation between two students.

M: So, have you registered for next semester yet?
W: Not yet. I'm still thinking about what math class I should take. I'd like statistics, but the class is already full. So it looks like I'll have to take a different math course, like maybe calculus. But statistics would be more useful for what I want to do in graduate school.
M: If you really want the statistics class, why don't you

register for it and get on the waiting list? Then if someone drops it, you might get in.

W: Do you think so?

M: Sometimes you get in a class from the waiting list. You could register for both statistics and calculus. You'd be put on the waiting list for statistics, but if you also register for calculus, you'll be sure to get into one of the classes. Then, if an opening comes up in statistics, you can drop calculus. If it doesn't, then at least you have calculus for backup.

W: I guess I could do that. Another thing I could do is … I might go and talk to the instructor of the statistics class. Sometimes instructors make exceptions to the rule. If I can convince him that I really want the class, and I need it for graduate school, maybe he'll let me in, even though the class is full.

M: It's worth a try. Whatever you do, good luck!

W: Thanks.

Briefly summarize the problem the speakers are discussing. Then state which solution you would recommend. Explain the reasons for your recommendation.

Album 12, Track 14

TEST 4 — SPEAKING QUESTION 6 (p. 587)

Now listen to part of a lecture in a psychology class. The professor is discussing children's fears.

All children experience periods of fear. Fears are normal, and they help children solve issues of change and development. Fears also call parents' attention to a child's situation so the parent will provide extra support when the child needs it.

The fear of falling is built into each newborn baby in the form of a clasping motion. A baby will make this motion when he is uncovered or surprised, or when he is dropped suddenly. His arms shoot out sideways and then come together as if to grab anything or anyone nearby. The baby usually cries out when he makes this motion. The startled cry attracts a parent's attention. Thus, even from birth, a baby is able to use this natural fear of falling to get help.

Another fear that babies have is the fear of strangers, a natural fear that alerts the child to a new situation. Anxiety around strangers is one of the earliest signs of fear in babies. In studies that filmed babies as they played with adults, it was shown that even at one month old, the babies could distinguish between their mother, father, and strangers, and they showed this with clear differences in their own responses.

Fears appear during periods of new and rapid learning. At one year old, and all through the second year, a whole new world opens up when children learn to walk. They will both value and fear their new independence. At the same time they learn to run away from their parents, children also find new things to be afraid of—dogs, loud noises, strange people and places. Fears help children adjust to their new independence. By overcoming their fears, children acquire confidence in their own new abilities.

Using points and examples from the lecture, describe fears that young children experience, and explain how these fears help children.

Album 12, Track 15

TEST 4 — WRITING SECTION DIRECTIONS (p. 588)

The Writing section measures your ability to use writing to communicate in an academic environment. There are two writing questions.

Question 1 is a writing task based on reading and listening. You will read a passage, listen to a lecture, and then write a response to a question about the relationship between the lecture and the reading. You have 20 minutes to plan and write your response.

Question 2 is writing based on knowledge and experience. You will write an essay in response to a question that asks you to state, explain, and support an opinion on an issue. You have 30 minutes to plan and write your essay.

Album 12, Track 16

TEST 4 — WRITING QUESTION 1 (p. 589)

Now listen to part of a lecture on the topic you just read about.

We used to think earthworms were helpful, but now we know otherwise. One problem is that earthworms are causing significant damage to some forests by destroying the soil cover. I know a forest ecologist who's studying the soil near a popular fishing lake. She noticed the forest floor was changing rapidly near the shoreline, right where fishermen dump their unused bait worms. Right there, a thick layer of spongy duff was disappearing. When she took a shovel and looked at the soil, she found large numbers of earthworms. It was the worms that were destroying the soil cover.

Another problem is the threat earthworms pose to wildflowers. The worms are taking organic matter from the surface—duff—and moving it down deeper into the soil. The worms are cleaning the forest floor so well that the duff disappears in just a few weeks. And wherever the duff disappears, so do the wildflowers. Duff contains nutrients that are slowly released into the soil—the nutrients that plants need to sprout. But earthworms are literally eating the forest floor right out from under the plants. This has a devastating effect on the wildflowers that once adorned the lakeshore and attracted photographers.

A third problem is that the disappearance of the duff hurts animals too. The duff is the habitat for a lot of different animals—salamanders, insects, and spiders, to name a few—so when the duff disappears, so do these animals, and in turn, the other animals that feed on them. So, the negative effect of the earthworms is being felt across the whole forest ecosystem.

Summarize the points made in the lecture, being sure to explain how they refute specific points made in the reading passage.

ALBUM 13 — TEST 5

Album 13, Track 1

TEST 5 — LISTENING SECTION DIRECTIONS (p. 604)

The Listening section measures your ability to understand conversations and lectures in English. You will hear each conversation and lecture only one time. After each conversation or lecture, you will answer some questions about it. The questions typically ask about the main idea and supporting details. Some questions ask about a speaker's purpose or attitude. Answer the questions based on what the speakers state or imply.

You may take notes while you listen. You may use your notes to help you answer the questions. Your notes will not be scored.

In some questions, you will see this icon: 🎧. This means that you will hear, but not see, part of the question.

Some questions have special directions, which appear in a gray box. Most questions are worth one point. If a question is worth more than one point, the directions will indicate how many points you can receive.

You will now begin part 1 of the Listening section.

Album 13, Track 2

TEST 5 — LISTENING PART 1
QUESTIONS 1–5 (p. 605)

Listen to a conversation in a university library.

M: Hi. May I help you?
W: Yes. I placed a book on hold, and I got an e–mail saying that the book was here at the reference desk.
M: Oh, yes. I think I sent that e–mail. Ah ... are you Miranda?
W: Yes, that's right.
M: Okay, good. Sorry it took a while to get this book. It had to be shipped from another library. And ... here it is.
W: Thanks!
M: Now, as you know, this book is rare, so there are conditions for using it.
W: Yes, you said something about that in your e–mail. Can I ... uh ... how long will I be able to check it out for?
M: Well, see, that's the thing. Because it's a rare book, you can't check it out. You have to use it here in the library. It's here for a month, and if you need it any longer, you can renew it.
W: I have to use it here? I didn't realize.
M: Sorry. Yeah, that's the rule for rare books.
W: I didn't know it was rare. It's in great shape. It looks old.
M: We don't get a lot of requests for books like this. Most of these old works have been scanned, and so they're available online.
W: Not this one, apparently. But I like old books anyway, so it's a real treat to get to use this one. Oh, wow, it looks like it has writing in it, like someone in the past wrote notes in the margins.

M: Huh. Interesting.
W: So, then what are the rules? If I have to use the book here in the library, what do I do when I leave? Do you keep it for me?
M: Yes, we keep it here. You can use the book anywhere in the library, but then when you leave, you just have to give it back to me or anyone at this desk until the next day, or whenever you need it again. We keep it here, with your name on it—oh, I just need to scan your student I.D. card—and ... uh ... we keep it here for a month.
W: Am I allowed to photocopy pages?
M: Sure, if it's for your own research. The rules are like for any other book. But if you do make copies— because the book is so old, you need to be careful with the binding. You don't want to crack it.
W: Yikes.
M: Or you could ask one of the people in Copy Services to do it for you.
W: Hmm. I might. But ... maybe ... uh ... could I take pictures with my own camera? That might be safer than putting it on the copy machine.
M: It might. Sure, that would be okay.
W: I'm not even sure the images would be clear enough. I'll have to experiment.
M: Yeah.
W: Right now, I'm eager to take a look at this book.
M: Okay, good. I just need to scan your I.D.
W: Oh, okay. Sure.

1. What are the speakers mainly discussing?
2. What does the man say about the book?
3. According to the man, what is one rule for using the book?
4. Listen again to part of the conversation. Then answer the question.
   "Am I allowed to photocopy pages?"
   "Sure, if it's for your own research. The rules are like for any other book. But if you do make copies—because the book is so old, you need to be careful with the binding. You don't want to crack it."
   "Yikes."
   "Or you could ask one of the people in Copy Services to do it for you."
   What can be inferred from the conversation?
5. What will the student probably do?

Album 13, Track 3

TEST 5 — LISTENING PART 1
QUESTIONS 6–11 (p. 607)

Listen to part of a discussion in a biology class.

W1: To a scientist, a "fact" is simply a statement of our current understanding. The facts of science are really just attempts to state our best understanding of the natural world. Facts are based on observations we make and experiments we do. And a fact is only valid until it's revised or replaced by a new understanding. Even the facts presented in your biology textbook are subject to change. Uh ... yes, Andrew?
M: Uh, yeah. If a fact ... if a fact is something that's true, how can it be replaced? Does that mean, even in science, I mean ... how can a fact change?
W1: Uh–huh. Okay. All right ... let's take, for example, cell biology. The field of cell biology is full of "facts" that

were once widely held as true, but were later revised when biologists acquired a better understanding of cells. For example, it was once widely held as fact that living matter was made of substances that were very different from the substances in nonliving matter. According to this view—called vitalism—the chemical reactions in living matter did not follow the known laws of chemistry and physics, but were instead directed by some type of "vital force." Vitalism was thought to be based on facts, that is, until Friedrich Wohler showed that the biological compound urea could be synthesized in the laboratory from an inorganic compound. Wohler's work undermined the previously held "facts" of vitalism. He proved that the chemical reactions of organic matter follow all the laws of chemistry and physics.

M: So he gave us new facts to work with.

W1: Yes, that's right. He did. To scientists, facts are not hard and fast truths. So, how does new information change our understanding? Well, scientists usually follow a systematic approach to new information. And what do we call this systematic approach? Jodie?

W2: Are you talking about the scientific method?

W1: Yes, absolutely. The scientific method: how scientists deal with new information. The scientific method begins as a researcher makes observations, either in the field or in a research laboratory, and then formulates a hypothesis. And a hypothesis is simply a statement or explanation that's consistent with the available evidence. Sometimes a hypothesis takes the form of a model that appears to provide a reasonable explanation for a phenomenon. And to be useful, a hypothesis must be testable.

W2: Excuse me, professor, but could you say that a hypothesis is kind of a yes–no question? Like, is this model true? Is it a true explanation for something we observe ... yes or no?

W1: You could put it that way, yes. Is this hypothesis correct? Is it supported by data? And this is where the scientific method gets very systematic. The hypothesis must be testable, so the experiment must be designed so it either confirms or discredits the hypothesis. And when a hypothesis has been tested critically, under many different conditions, by many different researchers, using a variety of approaches, and the hypothesis is consistently supported by the evidence, it gradually acquires the status of a theory. And by the time an explanation or model is regarded as a theory, it's widely accepted by most scientists in the field. For example, there's little or no disagreement about the three tenets of cell biology: first, that all organisms consist of one or more cells; second, the cell is the basic unit of structure for all organisms; and third, all cells arise only from preexisting cells. In other words, biologists agree that the cell is the basic unit of life.

M: So that's a fact?

W1: The three tenets of cell biology are facts until we know otherwise.

6. What is the main topic of the discussion?
7. Why does the professor discuss the concept of vitalism?
8. What does the professor imply when she says this:
    "To scientists, facts are not hard and fast truths."
9. According to the discussion, how do scientists deal with new information?
10. What two statements about a hypothesis do the speakers make in the discussion?

11. Listen again to part of the discussion. Then answer the question.
    "And when a hypothesis has been tested critically, under many different conditions, by many different researchers, using a variety of approaches, and the hypothesis is consistently supported by the evidence, it gradually acquires the status of a theory. And by the time an explanation or model is regarded as a theory, it's widely accepted by most scientists in the field. For example, there's little or no disagreement about the three tenets of cell biology: first, that all organisms consist of one or more cells; second, the cell is the basic unit of structure for all organisms; and third, all cells arise only from preexisting cells. In other words, biologists agree that the cell is the basic unit of life."
    What can be inferred about the three tenets of cell biology?

Album 13, Track 4

TEST 5 — LISTENING PART 1
QUESTIONS 12–17 (p. 609)

Listen to part of a lecture in a history class. The professor is talking about aboriginal Canadians.

At the time of the first European settlement in North America, as many as half a million Native people were already living in what would later become Canada. Aboriginal peoples inhabited all areas of present–day Canada, but they were unevenly scattered across the land. The majority lived along the Pacific Coast, in the area of the Great Lakes, and in the southeast. The vast interior of the country was thinly populated.

Aboriginal Canadians lived in a close relationship with nature. Wherever they lived, the people were well adapted to their environment. Their economies were organized around the food supply. Most of the people were hunters and gatherers, living in mobile bands and following the seasonal rhythms of the food supply—the fish and game they depended on.

All right. Let's take a look at some of the cultural characteristics of the aboriginal peoples. Generally, we can divide aboriginal Canadians into five major groups, based on geography.

First, across most of Canada, from the Yukon to the Atlantic, were the various forest tribes who shared the hunting–gathering lifestyle. Despite their different languages and belief systems, all of the hunter–gatherers faced similar environmental challenges, so they shared many aspects of everyday life. They lived in small bands that migrated frequently. They used technology such as the birch–bark canoe. They made tools, weapons, clothing, and ceremonial objects from materials that were available locally. They were skilled in trapping fur–bearing animals and in curing animal skins, which gave Canada its first staple industry.

Second, to the north, were the Inuit. These were people well adapted to life in the Arctic, a region of cold, dark winters and short summers. The Inuit were completely dependent on fish and animal life. At sea they traveled in the kayak, and on land, the dog–sled. In the winter they lived in snow huts called igloos, and in the summer they lived in skin tents. They made clothing from caribou hides. They were skilled at making tools from animal bones and ivory.

The third major group lived to the south, in the area around the Great Lakes. Many of these people lived year round in permanent villages. They were the only group who pursued agriculture. The main crops were corn, beans, squash, and tobacco. Agriculture enabled thousands of people to live together in societies and develop complex political systems. The largest of these societies formed separate nations, and these nations dealt with each other through networks of kinship, trade, and sometimes war. They had well established trade routes and methods of trade. They exchanged goods and information long before the Europeans arrived.

The fourth group of aboriginal Canadians lived on the western plains. These were the tribes with the organization to hunt the large herds of prairie bison. The Plains people were excellent hunters. They developed efficient methods for hunting the bison that gathered in the same winter and summer ranges every year, moving back and forth along well–established pathways. The Plains people also hunted other animals, but the bison remained the basis of their economy, not to mention their ability to endure the long prairie winters.

Finally, in the far west, were the people adapted to a life of fishing. Food was abundant in this region of many rivers. The West Coast tribes were the great traders of aboriginal Canada. Both food and trade centered on salmon. The rich resource base of salmon and cedar enabled the coastal tribes to accumulate considerable amounts of wealth.

12. How does the professor organize the information that he presents?
13. What does the professor say about the economies of aboriginal Canadians?
14. Which of the following were characteristics of the hunting–gathering tribes of the forests?
15. Listen again to part of the lecture. Then answer the question.
    "Many of these people lived year round in permanent villages. They were the only group who pursued agriculture. The main crops were corn, beans, squash, and tobacco. Agriculture enabled thousands of people to live together in societies and develop complex political systems. The largest of these societies formed separate nations, and these nations dealt with each other through networks of kinship, trade, and sometimes war."
    What can be inferred about the societies the professor is describing?
16. What does the professor mean when he says this:
    "The Plains people also hunted other animals, but the bison remained the basis of their economy, not to mention their ability to endure the long prairie winters."
17. According to the professor, what cultural characteristic was shared by the aboriginal peoples all over Canada?

Album 13, Track 5

TEST 5 — LISTENING PART 2
QUESTIONS 1–5 (p. 611)

Listen to a discussion between a student and her tutor.

W: I want to go over a few things before the midterm exam. Okay?
M: Okay.
W: Dr. Peters said galaxies would be on the exam. So ... uh ... especially I wanted to ... uh ... talk about galaxies.
M: Okay. Cool.
W: Like how ... um ... I know that some galaxies are relatively close to one another. In the lecture she said galaxies don't act alone. They can influence each other and even collide with other galaxies.
M: Uh–huh.

W: She said that small galaxies can be pulled together by gravity, and then they can blend to form more massive galaxies ... except ... uh ... let me ask you this ... about galaxies colliding. If two galaxies collide, then don't the stars run into each other? I mean, if stars collide, then why don't they just blow up or make bigger stars, or is it they just combine into bigger galaxies?
M: Well, you see, when galaxies collide, they actually pass through one another.
W: They do?
M: Yeah.
W: How?
M: Let's back up a bit ... uh ... okay. So ... yeah, galaxies can be pulled together by their mutual gravitational attraction. But the individual stars don't actually bump into each other. That's because of the huge distances between stars. I mean, interstellar distances are really enormous.
W: Astronomical.
M: Yeah, astronomical distances between stars. I mean, the distances between galaxies are very large, but compared to stars, galaxies are relatively close to one another. And when gravity pulls two galaxies together, they sort of collide, but the stars just pass by each other, and what really happens is, the galaxies don't actually crash. But these so–called collisions do tend to distort a galaxy's shape. Eventually, two smaller galaxies become a large elliptical galaxy. So, we can say that the interaction between the galaxies has the effect of—it sort of plays a role in their evolution. The evolution of galaxies—the process of formation—is always going on.
W: Yeah, that's what Dr. Peters said. And she said we know this from computer models.
M: Yeah, that's right. The models suggest that collisions between spiral galaxies tend to make elliptical ones. The Milky Way is expected to collide with the Andromeda Galaxy in the next few billion years, and this will create an even huger elliptical galaxy.
W: So, then a spiral galaxy like the Milky Way probably never collided with any others?
M: Well ... hmm ... we're always learning new things about galaxies. Astronomers argue and speculate about this stuff all the time. They don't know everything about the evolution of galaxies. But they do have some idea about their origins.
W: You mean the Big Bang.
M: Yup. The Big Bang.
W: The Big Bang—that'll be on the exam. Why don't we go over that too?
M: Sure. We can do that.

1. What do the speakers mainly discuss?
2. According to the discussion, what can happen when two galaxies collide?
3. According to the discussion, what have astronomers concluded from computer models?
4. Listen again to part of the discussion. Then answer the question.
    "So, then a spiral galaxy like the Milky Way probably never collided with any others?"
    "Well ... hmm ... we're always learning new things about galaxies. Astronomers argue and speculate about this stuff all the time. They don't know everything about the evolution of galaxies."
    What does the tutor imply?
5. Why does the student say this:

"The Big Bang—that'll be on the exam. Why don't we go over that too?"

Album 13, Track 6

TEST 5 — LISTENING PART 2
QUESTIONS 6–11 (p. 613)

Listen to part of a discussion in a communications class.

M1: Most consumers believe they are immune to advertising. They believe they buy things based purely on the value of the product. They think advertising plays little or no role. But advertisers know better. Surveys and sales figures show that advertising can be very effective. This is because advertising works below the level of our awareness. It works even on people who think they're immune to its message. In fact, ads are designed to have an effect while being laughed at, criticized, mocked ... anything except being ignored. To understand how ads work, we need to analyze the language used in the advertising claim. The claim is the spoken or text part of an ad that makes a statement about the superiority of the product. If you study advertising claims, you should be able to recognize ads that are misleading. Some claims are complete lies. Some are honest statements about a truly superior product. But most claims fall somewhere in between. They're not exactly lies, nor are they helpful information. They fall on the narrow line between true and false ... through a careful choice of words. Many claims fall into this category because they're applied to "parity products." And what do I mean by parity product? Uh ... Jessica?

W: A parity product is something just like everything else. I mean, there are lots of different brands for the same product—like cereal or ... shampoo or ... something—and they're all basically the same.

M1: Yes, that's correct. And because no single product is truly better than others, the ad has to create the illusion of superiority. In fact, the largest advertising budgets are those that promote parity products—such as cereal and shampoo—also soft drinks, beer, detergents, and headache remedies—all parity products, with several brands that are all similar in quality. If any product is truly better than others, the ad will provide solid evidence of its superiority. But for a product that's merely the same quality as others, the advertising has to create the illusion of being superior. To create this illusion, advertisers depend on a handful of basic techniques. One technique is to compliment the consumer. This is when the claim says that the consumer is special or has good taste. The ad flatters the consumer by using some sort of praise to make him or her feel good. Another technique ... another type of claim ... is the celebrity endorsement. You've all seen this one. Somebody famous or someone with authority appears in the ad to give his or her endorsement to the product.

M2: Like when a basketball player endorses sneakers.

W: Right! Or when an actor or an actress sells clothing or makeup—

M2: Or cars.

W: They even endorse pizza. Or how about when a— when someone who used to be in politics sells vitamins or painkillers? That always seems funny to me.

M1: And remember, one way ads work is by seeming funny or amusing. If something is funny to you, it's having an effect on you. Okay then. I think you all know how the celebrity endorsement works. Another advertising technique is the scientific or statistical claim. This kind of ad uses some sort of scientific proof or experiment, very specific numbers, or an impressive–sounding mystery ingredient.

M2: Like when they say their toothpaste causes 50% fewer cavities.

W: Or their breakfast cereal has all 25 of the essential vitamins and minerals, or 50% more nutrition. Or whatever.

M1: Whatever is exactly it! The claim will be some number that may not be true, but it sure does sound impressive. You see, advertisers make any outrageous claim because it sounds good and because they know that few people will think about it critically. After all, smart consumers aren't influenced by ads ... are they?

6. What is the discussion mainly about?
7. Why does the professor say this:
   "Some claims are complete lies. Some are honest statements about a truly superior product. But most claims fall somewhere in between. They're not exactly lies, nor are they helpful information. They fall on the narrow line between true and false ... through a careful choice of words."
8. Which statement accurately describes parity products?
9. According to the professor, how do advertisers promote parity products?
10. Which advertising techniques do the speakers discuss?
11. Listen again to part of the discussion. Then answer the question.
    "The claim will be some number that may not be true, but it sure does sound impressive. You see, advertisers make any outrageous claim because it sounds good and because they know that few people will think about it critically. After all, smart consumers aren't influenced by ads ... are they?"
    What does the professor imply when he says this:
    "After all, smart consumers aren't influenced by ads ... are they?"

Album 13, Track 7

TEST 5 — LISTENING PART 2
QUESTIONS 12–17 (p. 615)

Listen to part of a lecture in a geology class. The professor is talking about streams.

Streams are the most dynamic agents of geological change on the surface of the planet. The force of moving water has the ability to erode, carry, and deposit sediment. A stream can cut down through uplifted land toward its base level, the lowest level its channel can erode to, which for most streams is sea level.

Streams respond immediately to changes in their environment. For example, when a heavy storm drops 25 centimeters of rain on a drainage basin, the streams in that region will rise quickly and flow more rapidly. The increase in stream flow will erode greater volumes of sediment. The sediment is later deposited downstream in places where the flow becomes blocked or slowed by debris.

A stream's environment is always changing. A stream's gradient—that is, the slope of the stream bed—must constantly adjust to maintain a balance between erosion and deposition—deposition being the deposit of sediment in the stream bed. A stream in a state of dynamic equilibrium is called a graded stream. The equilibrium of any graded stream is only temporary. It lasts only until the next change in the environment. For instance, there may be a sudden increase in sediment load—say, from a volcanic mudflow or the collapse of a stream bank—and this increase in sediment will upset the stream's equilibrium. Any change in sediment load will force the stream to adjust. Anything that disturbs the stream's equilibrium will cause a response.

Streams also respond to tectonic events. For instance, if normal faulting occurs across a stream channel, and the downstream section drops during an earthquake, a waterfall will form immediately. The stream then uses its increased energy to erode the edge of the newly uplifted portion. The stream always responds in a way that reduces the effects of the change and establishes a new graded state.

Waterfalls and rapids occur at sudden drops in the ground level along a stream's course. Usually they occur where erosion removes softer sections of rock, leaving harder rock as a "step" in the stream's profile. They also occur where faulting lowers or raises a portion of the stream bed. A waterfall exists only as long as the conditions that created it. A waterfall's plunging water cuts a deep pool at the base of the falls, called a plunge pool. The plunge pool undermines the step where the water falls off. As the falling water erodes the step away, the waterfall migrates upstream. Sometimes a waterfall gradually wears down to rapids, which over time completely erode, eventually returning the stream to its original graded state.

The best known waterfall in North America is Niagara Falls. Niagara Falls is roughly 55 meters high and 670 meters wide. It was created about 12,000 years ago, when the last great ice sheet retreated. The withdrawal of the ice uncovered a ridge of dolostone, which is resistant to erosion. Since then, the falls has migrated southward 11 kilometers from its point of origin. Billions of liters of water flow over the falls every year. The plunging water erodes the shale bed below the resistant cap of dolostone, and this continues to undercut the falls. In the past, the falls retreated at a rate of approximately one meter per year. However, today the United States and Canada divert approximately 75 percent of the river's discharge to generate hydroelectric power, and this diversion of water has greatly slowed the retreat of the falls.

12. What is the main point the professor makes in the lecture?
13. According to the professor, which environmental factors cause streams to respond?
14. Why does the professor say this:
"A stream in a state of dynamic equilibrium is called a graded stream. The equilibrium of any graded stream is only temporary. It lasts only until the next change in the environment."
15. What happens when faulting lowers or raises part of a stream bed?
16. Listen again to part of the lecture. Then answer the question.
"A waterfall's plunging water cuts a deep pool at the base of the falls, called a plunge pool. The plunge pool undermines the step where the water falls off. As the falling water erodes the step away, the waterfall migrates upstream. Sometimes a waterfall gradually wears down to rapids, which over time completely erode, eventually returning the stream to its original graded state."
What point does the professor illustrate?

17. According to the professor, what factor contributes to the retreat of Niagara Falls?

Album 13, Track 8
TEST 5 — LISTENING PART 3
QUESTIONS 1–5 (p. 617)

Listen to a conversation between a student and a professor.

M: Hi, Professor Campbell. I'm glad I caught you.
W: How are you, Tyler?
M: I'm doing great, looking forward to summer ... and I wanted to thank you again for your recommendation ... you know, the camp counselor position.
W: Oh, no problem. I was happy to do it. So, have you heard?
M: Yeah! I got the job!
W: Oh, that's great news! Congratulations!
M: Thanks. Yeah, I just found out this morning. Next week I go in to meet the rest of the team, I mean the other counselors ... and the director of the youth program. Some of them—the director, of course—I already met during the interview.
W: That's wonderful, Tyler! I know you'll do a great job, and this is an excellent way to get started in environmental education. I know the director very well. The summer youth program is one of the best in the country.
M: It's a big deal. I know! I'm really excited about it.
W: You'll have to let me know how it goes.
M: I will! Actually, in the interview the director asked if I'd write for their blog, and I said, of course, that's something I had hoped to do. They have a great website, and I look forward to contributing.
W: It's good exposure. Will you post some of your photographs?
M: Sure, of course. I'm sure to get lots of good pictures. Mainly I'll be working with the kids, supervising hikes ... teaching ecology ... but also have to document our trips in words and photos. We'll also have journal writing and photography workshops for the kids.
W: This job is perfect for you.
M: Yeah, I think so, and I'm sure your recommendation helped. Oh, another thing ... did you see my photograph in the new brochure ... the one for environmental studies?
W: I probably did. I've seen some of the new brochures. Which photo was yours?
M: The one of students fishing.
W: Oh, yes! With the boats?
M: Yeah, that's the one. They were catching fish for tagging.
W: Then I did see it. Good job!
M: I submitted five images, and that was the one the editor picked. They put it on the website too.
W: Good, good. Well, I look forward to your blog posts and seeing more of your photos.
M: I start right after finals. In fact, I only get three days off after my last exam, and then we have orientation with the kids. My first blog post will be about the orientation.
W: You'll be busy this summer.
M: Yeah, I will, but in a good way.
W: Mm–hmm. Well, I'm glad you dropped in. I have a

lecture in five minutes, so I ... uh ...

M: Okay. I just wanted to let you know I got the job. And thanks again. I really mean that.

W: It's my pleasure, Tyler. Stay in touch!

1. Why does the student speak to the professor?
2. What does the professor say about the student's news?
3. What will the student's summer job include?
4. Listen again to part of the conversation. Then answer the question.
   "Oh, another thing ... did you see my photograph in the new brochure ... the one for environmental studies?"
   "I probably did. I've seen some of the new brochures. Which photo was yours?"
   "The one of students fishing."
   "Oh, yes! With the boats?"
   "Yeah, that's the one. They were catching fish for tagging."
   "Then I did see it. Good job!"
   "I submitted five images, and that was the one the editor picked. They put it on the website too."
   What can be inferred about the student?
5. Why does the professor say this:
   "Well, I'm glad you dropped in. I have a lecture in five minutes, so I ... uh ..."

Album 13, Track 9

TEST 5 — LISTENING PART 3
QUESTIONS 6–11 (p. 619)

Listen to part of a discussion in a psychology class.

M1: Where in your body is this entity known as the "self"? Where is this you that perceives? Well, a few researchers have been asking this question. They've used various methods to find out where people believe their selves to be, and basically, the responses divide into two groups, two regions of the body. Where do you think the self is?

W: I'd say somewhere in the chest ... like in the heart ... or somewhere around the heart.

M2: I'm guessing it's in the brain because it's where our thinking goes on.

M1: Those are both good answers. That's exactly it. The research shows that the vast majority of people say their self is located either in their heart or their head. Some researchers probed further. They tried to find out whether more people chose the heart or the head. At first, the head seemed to be ahead. For example, one study used structured interviews to probe the location of the self.

W: How did they define the self? I mean, doesn't the word mean different things to different people?

M1: Good question. This particular study defined the self as "the I that perceives."

W: Where perception is. Consciousness.

M1: That's right. And the results were that 83 percent of the subjects said their self was a point between and behind their eyes ... in other words, in the center of their head.

M2: Interesting. So, this supports the position that the brain is the center of consciousness. That makes sense to me.

M1: Other studies used a different approach to the question. In another study, the researchers showed 87 online volunteers an outline of a human form and asked them to place an X on the spot where they felt their self was. Two general groups of responses emerged. The larger of these groups indicated that the self was near the brain, and a smaller group said near the heart.

M2: The same two responses as the other study.

W: But don't these different responses suggest that some studies are better than others at getting people to locate their true selves?

M1: That's another good question. Methodology is key. So, let's look at another study and another method. This time, the researchers used physical pointers to probe the location of the self. The pointer was a short metal stick clamped to a longer pole. The researchers slowly moved this pointer up and down people's bodies, telling them to call out when the stick pointed directly at them ... at the "I" spot, the self. Their results were interesting and significant. They found that if they started from the top, subjects were more likely to respond when the pointer hit the upper face. However, when they started from the bottom, at the person's feet, the same subjects were more likely to call out when the pointer reached the upper torso, the chest. So, depending on the direction the pointer moved, the subjects said that both locations—the head and the chest—felt right.

M2: Wow. So, the "I" spot can change, depending on the context?

M1: Uh–huh ... according to this study anyway.

M2: I guess that makes sense ... sort of ... well ... considering there are different things we could mean when we talk about the self.

W: Maybe there just isn't one right answer to the question. What if the self really does exist in different places for different people? For some people, maybe the self is where thinking takes place. For others, maybe the self is their emotional center.

M1: However we define the self, these three studies suggest that people lean toward the idea of a specific place where their self resides. One place is in the head. Another is in the heart. And for some people, both places are true in different contexts.

6. What is the discussion mainly about?
7. What issues and questions do the students raise in the discussion?
8. Which statement best states the main finding of the research described by the professor?
9. Listen again to part of the discussion. Then answer the question.
   "But don't these different responses suggest that some studies are better than others at getting people to locate their true selves?"
   "That's another good question. Methodology is key. So, let's look at another study and another method."
   What does the professor mean when he says this:
   "Methodology is key."
10. According to the professor, what was significant about the results of the study that used a physical pointer?
11. Why does the professor say this:
    "However we define the self, these three studies suggest that people lean toward the idea of a specific place where their self resides."

Album 13, Track 10

TEST 5 — LISTENING PART 3
QUESTIONS 12–17 (p. 621)

Listen to part of a lecture in a music appreciation class.

In Western classical music, singing voices are classified for male and female singers. The various male and female voices describe performers who sing in different ranges of high and low sound frequency. The high and low female voices are the soprano and the alto, with the mezzo–soprano as an intermediate class. The high and low male voices are the tenor and the bass, with baritone as an intermediate class. Today, we'll be listening to recordings of some of the more significant male roles in opera, so I'll talk more about the male voices: the tenor, the baritone, and the bass. Tomorrow we'll focus on the female voices.

In general, men have deeper voices than women do. This is because men have longer and thicker vocal cords. The average man's voice has a peak sound frequency of about 125 hertz, while that of an average woman's voice is about 250 hertz.

For the male voice, the high range is the tenor. The name "tenor" comes from the Latin word meaning "to hold." In early choral music, the tenor was the middle voice that held all of the other voices together. Beneath the tenor—voices lower in sound frequency—are the baritones and the basses, and above the tenor—voices higher in frequency—are the altos. The earliest surviving opera that's still widely performed is Monteverdi's *Orfeo*. The title role of the character Orfeo was written for the tenor. The role of Orfeo set the standard for leading male roles to be taken by the tenor voice.

There are several types of tenors, including the lyric tenor, which is the graceful tenor found in several of Mozart's operas. Another is the heldentenor, the most heroic male voice, a voice typical for the heroes in Wagner's operas. In fact, some of Wagner's roles are the most demanding ever for the tenor voice. Italian opera, too, has a multitude of heroic roles for a tenor voice that can accomplish high, trumpet–like tones. In a few minutes, we'll listen to some examples of these different tenors, but I just want to give you a brief introduction now.

Okay. The middle range of the male voice is the baritone. In general, German opera demands an especially strong middle–range baritone. The baritone voice is the so–called "normal" range of the male voice. The majority of male concert singers and singing actors in musical theater are baritones. This is because a man singing in his natural range can articulate words more clearly than a singer who is in some way extending his voice—either upward or downward—an effort that increases the risk of straining the voice.

Finally, we have the lowest range of the male voice: the bass. Throughout the history of opera, the bass voice has been used to portray father figures and elder statesmen, as well as the darkest villains. The first internationally successful Russian opera gave the main role to a bass singer. Since then, leading roles for the deep and powerful bass have become especially prized by performers and opera lovers everywhere. There are several variations on the bass voice. One is the lighter bass–baritone, which Mozart favored for many of his characters. Another is the basso profundo, the lowest male voice and the rarest of all singing voices. Because performers who can sing basso profundo are so rare, composers seldom write roles for it.

12. Which of the following best describes the organization of the lecture?
13. What accounts for the generally lower singing voices of men compared to women?

14. According to the professor, how did the tenor become the standard voice for leading male roles in opera?
15. Which two statements describe the tenor voice?
16. Listen again to part of the lecture. Then answer the question.
   "The baritone voice is the so–called 'normal' range of the male voice. The majority of male concert singers and singing actors in musical theater are baritones. This is because a man singing in his natural range can articulate words more clearly than a singer who is in some way extending his voice—either upward or downward—an effort that increases the risk of straining the voice."
   What does the professor imply?
17. Listen again to part of the lecture. Then answer the question.
   "Throughout the history of opera, the bass voice has been used to portray father figures and elder statesmen, as well as the darkest villains. The first internationally successful Russian opera gave the main role to a bass singer. Since then, leading roles for the deep and powerful bass have become especially prized by performers and opera lovers everywhere."
   What can be inferred about the bass voice?

Album 13, Track 11

TEST 5 — SPEAKING SECTION DIRECTIONS (p. 623)

The Speaking section measures your ability to speak in English about a variety of topics. There are six questions in this section.

In questions 1 and 2, you will speak about familiar topics. Your responses will be scored on your ability to speak clearly and coherently about the topics.

In questions 3 and 4, you will first read a short text and then listen to a talk on the same topic. You will then be asked a question about what you have read and heard. You will need to combine appropriate information from the text and the talk to provide a complete answer to the question. Your responses will be scored on your ability to speak clearly and coherently and on your ability to accurately convey information about what you have read and heard.

In questions 5 and 6, you will listen to part of a conversation or lecture. You will then be asked a question about what you have heard. Your responses will be scored on your ability to speak clearly and coherently and on your ability to accurately convey information about what you have heard.

You may take notes while you read and while you listen to the conversations and lectures. You may use your notes to help prepare your responses.

Album 13, Track 12

TEST 5 — SPEAKING QUESTION 1 (p. 624)

Describe a product or crop that is important to your country or region. Explain why this product is important. Include details and examples to support your explanation.

DELTA'S KEY TO THE TOEFL IBT®

Album 13, Track 13

TEST 5 — SPEAKING QUESTION 2 (p. 624)

Some students learn better when they attend a class in a room with a teacher. Other students learn more from online courses. Which system of learning do you think is better for students, and why? Include details and examples to support your explanation.

Album 13, Track 14

TEST 5 — SPEAKING QUESTION 3 (p. 625)

Now listen to two students as they discuss the new fee.

M: Did you read the e–mail about the new fee?
W: Uh ... I'm not sure. What new fee?
M: Next fall we have to pay an extra fifty dollars for the computer lab!
W: Really? Well, they are remodeling the building. They have to pass some of the cost on to us.
M: Yeah, but the fee applies to everyone—to all students—whether or not we actually use the lab. Why should everyone have to pay? What if you never use the lab? I don't go there. A lot of people don't. Everyone has their own laptops or tablets, or a phone with Internet.
W: Not everyone. I use the computers in the lab. I need the big screen for the work I do.
M: But it's not fair to charge everyone the lab fee. They should charge just the people who use the computers there.
W: Well, we have to pay for lots of things here that we never use.
M: That's the truth. There are already too many fees. Our tuition just increased by twenty percent. I hear the parking fees are going up too, and who knows what else. This school is getting too expensive. You should see the complaints on the website.
W: Yeah, I can imagine.

The man expresses his opinion about the new fee. State his opinion and explain the reasons he gives for holding that opinion.

Album 13, Track 15

TEST 5 — SPEAKING QUESTION 4 (p. 626)

Now listen to part of a lecture in a biology class.

Many animals have to cope with hot, dry conditions. Land snails, for example, have various ways to cope. Some snails simply move into the shade or crawl under piles of debris. Others climb up tall plants—bushes or trees—and some will even cling to man–made structures like fence posts or brick walls. The snails remain inactive until moisture returns.

Some animals deal with desert habitats or seasonal droughts. One example is the burrowing frog of Australia. During periods of hot, dry weather, this frog buries itself in the sandy ground and enters a state of dormancy. Some burrowing frogs cover their skin with a waterproof mucus, which prevents water loss. Some frogs store water in their bladder, which enables them to survive until the next rainy season.

Another example is a desert lizard of North America called the chuckwalla. This lizard is well adapted to desert conditions. During the hottest parts of the day, it escapes the heat by moving to an underground burrow—usually a crevice under the rocks—where it can stay cool. The lizard can remain inactive in its burrow, conserving energy, for weeks or months at a time, when food and water are scarce. It doesn't eat or drink until moisture and food return.

Explain aestivation and how the examples given by the professor illustrate the concept.

Album 13, Track 16

TEST 5 — SPEAKING QUESTION 5 (p. 627)

Listen to a conversation between two students.

W: So, what are your plans for next year?
M: Well, for one thing, I'm changing my major. I'm thinking of it anyway. I'd like to study communications.
W: Really? I thought you liked political science!
M: Not as much as I thought I did. My project last quarter made me think communications is a better fit for me. But the only problem is, this school doesn't have a communications department, so I'd have to transfer to another school.
W: Oh.
M: But ... I like this city—and this area—and I don't want to move.
W: Have you ever thought of designing your own program here? You could do independent study—an independent learning contract—here, at this school, where you develop your own program, with a faculty adviser. You would design projects around your area of interest—in your case, communications. You have to find the right adviser, though, someone who will agree to do it.
M: Huh. I've never done independent study before.
W: You know, another thing, there's a communications program at the art college in Newton. It's only forty miles from here, just a short commute by train. My friend goes to school there. She's a communications major. Some of their courses are online. You should go to their website and check it out.
M: I didn't even know Newton had an art college.
W: Media, design, writing—all of that. Good school, I hear.
M: Well, I need to do some research.

Briefly summarize the man's problem. Then state which solution you would recommend. Explain the reasons for your recommendation.

Album 13, Track 17

TEST 5 — SPEAKING QUESTION 6 (p. 627)

Listen to part of a lecture in an education class.

Many educators believe that engineering should be included in the basic education of every child. There are several good reasons for this.

First, engineering is based on a problem–solving perspective that matches how children naturally learn. Engineering is essentially problem solving, and if you watch young children at play, you will see a natural process of problem solving. Children make things. They build bridges and dams and towers. They test them by they knocking them down. They take things apart to understand how they work. If you watch young children interact with the world around them, you will see that children are natural engineers. Engineers identify problems and design solutions. Engineers build and test prototypes. They evaluate the performance and design of their solutions. Children do all of these things naturally, and this is why education should be structured around the design process.

Second, another reason for engineering education is that problem–solving skills are necessary for the twenty–first century. Young students need experiences with engineering and technology if they are going to succeed in the world they live in. Society depends on engineers to design the things that affect our daily lives. Engineers design where we live, how we communicate, how we travel, and even what we eat. All students—whether or not they go on to university, or go on to become engineers—everyone needs to know something about how things are made and how everything works. Students will be better prepared for their careers—and for life in general—if they can apply the design process to understand and solve the problems of the twenty–first century.

Using points and examples from the lecture, explain some of the reasons for including engineering in the basic education of children.

Album 13, Track 18

Test 5 — Writing Section Directions (p. 628)

The Writing section measures your ability to use writing to communicate in an academic environment. There are two writing questions.

Question 1 is a writing task based on reading and listening. You will read a passage, listen to a lecture, and then write a response to a question about the relationship between the lecture and the reading. You have 20 minutes to plan and write your response.

Question 2 is writing based on knowledge and experience. You will write an essay in response to a question that asks you to state, explain, and support an opinion on an issue. You have 30 minutes to plan and write your essay.

Album 13, Track 19

Test 5 — Writing Question 1 (p. 629)

Now listen to part of a lecture on the topic you just read about.

Let's look at how researchers for one company increased the productivity of their workers.

First, the researchers found that when workers share breaks with others on their teams, they are happier and more productive. The company tried scheduling staggered breaks for some groups and coordinated—or shared—breaks for others. The groups with staggered breaks had little opportunity to share tips or vent about angry customers with their teammates. In contrast, the teams with coordinated breaks allowed co–workers to complain and joke as much as they wanted. The teams that took breaks together were more satisfied with their jobs and

more efficient at serving customers.

Second, there should be no barriers to interaction within groups. The researchers found that the best place for the coffee pot is in the middle of a group, and it works better when each group has its own place for coffee. Workers who belong to a small team who speak frequently with each other are happier in their jobs than workers who do not. Even a single flight of stairs is a psychological barrier. People who work on different floors of a building almost never talk to each other.

Third, the company tried and rejected an open seating plan because it had a negative effect on how information was shared. When workers decided where to sit each day, researchers noticed a problem. A few socially important workers controlled the flow of information. Most of the important interactions happened at the desks of those few people, but the other people were left out. The company found that by assigning desks they could improve the flow of information so that everyone would be included.

Summarize the points made in the lecture, being sure to explain how they contradict specific points made in the reading passage.

INDEX

Y

PROGRESS CHARTS

Record your quiz and test scores on Progress Charts 1 through 6. Use the charts to monitor your achievement and set goals for future study.

The left column of each chart shows the percentage correct on quizzes and tests. The bottom row of Progress Charts 1 through 4 refers to relevant units to study for each quiz.

Example of Progress Chart 1 — Reading Quizzes

% Correct	Quiz 1	Quiz 2	Quiz 3	Quiz 4	Quiz 5	Quiz 6	Quiz 7	Quiz 8	Quiz 9	Quiz 10
100%	10	25	10	25	10	25	10	25	10	25
		24		24		24		24		24
		23		23		23		23		23
90%	9	22	9	22	9	22	9	22	9	22
		21		21		21		21		21
80%	8	20	8	20	8	20	8	20	(8)	(20)
		19		19		19		(19)		19
70%	7	18	(7)	18	(7)	(18)	(7)	18	7	18
		(17)		17		17		17		17
		16		(16)		16		16		16
60%	(6)	15	6	15	6	15	6	15	6	15
		14		14		14		14		14
50%	5	13	5	13	5	13	5	13	5	13

Example of Progress Chart 5 — Tests

% Correct	T1 R	T1 L	T1 S	T1 W	T2 R	T2 L	T2 S	T2 W	T3 R	T3 L	T3 S	T3 W	T4 R	T4 L	T4 S	T4 W	T5 R	T5 L	T5 S	T5 W
100%	44	34	24	10	44	34	24	10	44	34	24	10	44	34	24	10	44	51	24	10
	43	33			43	33			43	33			43	33			43	50		
	42		23		42		23		42		23		42		23		42	49	23	
	41	32			41	32			41	32			41	32			41	48		
90%	40	31	22	9	40	31	22	9	40	31	22	9	40	31	22	9	40	47	22	9
	39	30	21		39	30	21		39	30	21		39	30	21		39	46	21	
	38	29			38	29			38	29			38	(29)			38	45		
	37		20		37		20		37		20		37		20		37	(43)	20	
	36	28			36	28			36	28			36	28			36	42		
80%	35	27	19	8	35	27	19	8	35	(27)	19	8	35	27	19	(8)	35	41	19	(8)
	34	(26)			34	(26)			34	26			34	26			34	40		
	33		18		33		18		33		18		33	25	18		33	39	18	
	32	25			32	25			32				32				32	38		
70%	31	24	17	(7)	31	24	17	(7)	31	24	17	(7)	31	24	17	7	(31)	37	17	7
	30	23			30	23			30	23			(30)	23			30	36		
	29		(16)		(29)		16		(29)	22	16		29	23	(16)		29	34	(16)	
	28	22			28	22			28				28	22			28	33		
60%	(27)	21	15	6	27	21	(15)	6	27	21	(15)	6	27	21	15	6	27	31	15	6
	26	20	14		26	20	14		26	20	14		26	20	14		26	30	14	
	25	19			25	19			25	19			25	19			25	29		
	24		13		24		13		24		13		24		13		24	28	13	
	23	18			23	18			23	18			23	18			23	27		
50%	22	17	12	5	22	17	12	5	22	17	12	5	22	17	12	5	22	26	12	5
	21	16			21	16			21	16			21	16			21	25		
																		24		

COMPLETE SKILL PRACTICE

PROGRESS CHARTS

PROGRESS CHART 1

Reading Quizzes

Circle the points earned for each quiz. Draw a line to connect the circles.

% Correct	Quiz 1	Quiz 2	Quiz 3	Quiz 4	Quiz 5	Quiz 6	Quiz 7	Quiz 8	Quiz 9	Quiz 10
100%	10	25	10	25	10	25	10	25	10	25
		24		24		24		24		24
90%	9	23	9	23	9	23	9	23	9	23
		22		22		22		22		22
		21		21		21		21		21
80%	8	20	8	20	8	20	8	20	8	20
		19		19		19		19		19
70%	7	18	7	18	7	18	7	18	7	18
		17		17		17		17		17
		16		16		16		16		16
60%	6	15	6	15	6	15	6	15	6	15
		14		14		14		14		14
50%	5	13	5	13	5	13	5	13	5	13
		12		12		12		12		12
		11		11		11		11		11
40%	4	10	4	10	4	10	4	10	4	10
		9		9		9		9		9
30%	3	8	3	8	3	8	3	8	3	8
		7		7		7		7		7
		6		6		6		6		6
20%	1	5	1	5	1	5	1	5	1	5
Units to Study	1.1 thru 1.2	1.1 thru 1.2	1.3	1.1 thru 1.3	1.4 thru 1.5	1.1 thru 1.5	1.6 thru 1.7	1.1 thru 1.7	1.8 thru 1.9	1.1 thru 1.9

PROGRESS CHART 2

Listening Quizzes

Circle the the points earned for each quiz. Draw a line to connect the circles.

% Correct	Quiz 1	Quiz 2	Quiz 3	Quiz 4	Quiz 5	Quiz 6	Quiz 7	Quiz 8
100%	10	10	10	10	10	10	17	17
							16	16
90%	9	9	9	9	9	9	15	15
80%	8	8	8	8	8	8	14	14
							13	13
70%	7	7	7	7	7	7	12	12
							11	11
60%	6	6	6	6	6	6	10	10
							9	9
50%	5	5	5	5	5	5	8	8
							7	7
40%	4	4	4	4	4	4	6	6
30%	3	3	3	3	3	3	5	5
							4	4
20%	2	2	2	2	2	2	3	3
							2	2
10%	1	1	1	1	1	1	1	1
Units to Study	2.1 thru 2.2	2.1 thru 2.3	2.1 thru 2.3	2.1 thru 2.4	2.1 thru 2.4	2.1 thru 2.6	2.1 thru 2.6	2.1 thru 2.6

PROGRESS CHART 3

Speaking Quizzes

Circle the points earned for each quiz. Draw a line to connect the circles.

% Correct	Quiz 1	Quiz 2	Quiz 3	Quiz 4	Quiz 5	Quiz 6	Quiz 7	Quiz 8
100%	8	8	8	16	16	16	24	24
				15	15	15	23	23
90%							22	22
	7	7	7	14	14	14	21	21
80%				13	13	13	20	20
							19	19
	6	6	6	12	12	12	18	18
70%				11	11	11	17	17
							16	16
				10	10	10	15	15
60%	5	5	5	9	9	9	14	14
							13	13
50%				8	8	8	12	12
	4	4	4	7	7	7	11	11
40%				6	6	6	10	10
							9	9
	3	3	3	5	5	5	8	8
30%							7	7
				4	4	4	6	6
20%	2	2	2	3	3	3	5	5
Units to Study	3.1 thru 3.4	3.1 thru 3.4	3.1 thru 3.4	3.5 thru 3.10	3.5 thru 3.10	3.5 thru 3.10	3.1 thru 3.10	3.1 thru 3.10

PROGRESS CHART 4

Writing Quizzes

Circle the points earned for each quiz. Draw a line to connect the circles.

% Correct	Quiz 1	Quiz 2	Quiz 3	Quiz 4	Quiz 5	Quiz 6	Quiz 7	Quiz 8
100%	5	5	5	5	5	5	10	10
90%							9	9
80%	4	4	4	4	4	4	8	8
70%							7	7
60%	3	3	3	3	3	3	6	6
50%							5	5
40%	2	2	2	2	2	2	4	4
30%							3	3
20%	1	1	1	1	1	1	2	2
Units to Study	4.1 thru 4.5	4.1 thru 4.5	4.1 thru 4.5	4.6 thru 4.10	4.6 thru 4.10	4.6 thru 4.10	4.1 thru 4.10	4.1 thru 4.10

PROGRESS CHART 5

Tests

Circle the points earned for each test section. Draw four separate lines to connect the circles for Reading, Listening, Speaking, and Writing. See the example on page 789.

% Correct	Test 1 R	L	S	W	Test 2 R	L	S	W	Test 3 R	L	S	W	Test 4 R	L	S	W	Test 5 R	L	S	W
100%	44	34	24	10	44	34	24	10	44	34	24	10	44	34	24	10	44	51	24	10
	43	33			43	33			43	33			43	33			43	50		
	42		23		42		23		42		23		42		23		42	49	23	
	41	32			41	32			41	32			41	32			41	48		
90%	40	31	22	9	40	31	22	9	40	31	22	9	40	31	22	9	40	47 / 46	22	9
	39	30	21		39	30	21		39	30	21		39	30	21		39	45	21	
	38	29			38	29			38	29			38	29			38	44		
	37		20		37		20		37		20		37		20		37	43	20	
	36	28			36	28			36	28			36	28			36	42		
80%	35	27	19	8	35	27	19	8	35	27	19	8	35	27	19	8	35	41 / 40	19	8
	34	26			34	26			34	26			34	26			34	39		
	33		18		33		18		33		18		33		18		33	38	18	
	32	25			32	25			32	25			32	25			32	37		
70%	31	24	17	7	31	24	17	7	31	24	17	7	31	24	17	7	31	36	17	7
	30	23	16		30	23	16		30	23	16		30	23	16		30	35	16	
	29	22			29	22			29	22			29	22			29	34		
	28				28				28				28				28	33		
	27	21	15		27	21	15		27	21	15		27	21	15		27	32 / 31	15	
60%	26	20	14	6	26	20	14	6	26	20	14	6	26	20	14	6	26	30	14	6
	25	19			25	19			25	19			25	19			25	29		
	24		13		24		13		24		13		24		13		24	28	13	
	23	18			23	18			23	18			23	18			23	27		
50%	22	17	12	5	22	17	12	5	22	17	12	5	22	17	12	5	22	26 / 25	12	5
	21	16	11		21	16	11		21	16	11		21	16	11		21	24	11	
	20	15			20	15			20	15			20	15			20	23		
	19				19				19				19				19	22		
40%	18	14	10	4	18	14	10	4	18	14	10	4	18	14	10	4	18	21 / 20	10	4
	17	13	9		17	13	9		17	13	9		17	13	9		17	19	9	
	16	12			16	12			16	12			16	12			16	18		
	15		8		15		8		15		8		15		8		15	17	8	
	14	11			14	11			14	11			14	11			14	16		
30%	13	10	7	3	13	10	7	3	13	10	7	3	13	10	7	3	13	15 / 14	7	3
	12	9			12	9			12	9			12	9			12	13		
	11		6		11		6		11		6		11		6		11	12	6	
	10	8			10	8			10	8			10	8			10	11		
20%	9	7	5	2	9	7	5	2	9	7	5	2	9	7	5	2	9	10	5	2

DELTA'S KEY TO THE TOEFL IBT®

PROGRESS CHART 6

TOEFL® Scores for Tests

Use the TOEFL Score Conversion Tables on the next page to find your TOEFL scores for each test section. Write each section score below in the correct box for each test. To calculate the total test score, add the four section scores.

Section/Test	Test 1	Test 2	Test 3	Test 4	Test 5
Reading					
Listening					
Speaking					
Writing					
Total Test					

Example

Test 1	Points Earned	TOEFL Section Score
Reading	27	18
Listening	26	19
Speaking	16	20
Writing	7	22

Total test score: 18 + 19 + 20 + 22 = 79

TOEFL® SCORE CONVERSION TABLES

To find your approximate TOEFL scores for Test 1 through Test 5, use the tables below. For each test section, look on the correct line for the number of points you earned, and then find your TOEFL section score on the same line. Record your scores on Progress Chart 6 on page 795.

Reading

Points Earned	TOEFL® Section Score
44	30
43	30
42	29
41	28
40	27
39	27
38	26
37	25
36	24
35	24
34	23
33	22
32	21
31	20
30	20
29	20
28	19
27	18
26	17
25	17
24	16
23	15
22	14
21	13
20	13
19	12
18	11
17	10
16	9
15	7
13–14	6
12	5
10–11	3
9	2
8	1

Listening

Points Earned Tests 1–4	Points Earned Tests 5	TOEFL® Section Score
34	51	30
33	50	29
	49	28
32	48	27
31	47	26
30	46	25
	45	24
29	44	23
28	43	22
27	42	21
	41	20
26	40	19
25	38–39	18
24	37	17
	36	16
23	35	15
21–22	33–34	14
	32	13
20	31	12
19	29–30	11
18	28	10
17	26–27	9
15–16	23–25	8
14	21–22	7
13	20	6
12	18–19	5
10–11	15–17	4
9	14	3
7–8	11–13	2
5–6	8–10	1

Speaking

Points Earned	TOEFL® Section Score
24	30
23	29
22	28
21	27
20	26
19	24
18	23
17	22
16	20
15	19
14	18
13	17
12	15
11	14
10	13
9	11
8	10
7	9
6	8
5	6
4	5
3	4
2	3
1	1

Writing

Points Earned	TOEFL® Section Score
10	30
9	28
8	25
7	22
6	20
5	17
4	14
3	11
2	8
1	5

Delta's Key to the TOEFL iBT®

COMPLETE SKILL PRACTICE

NOTES